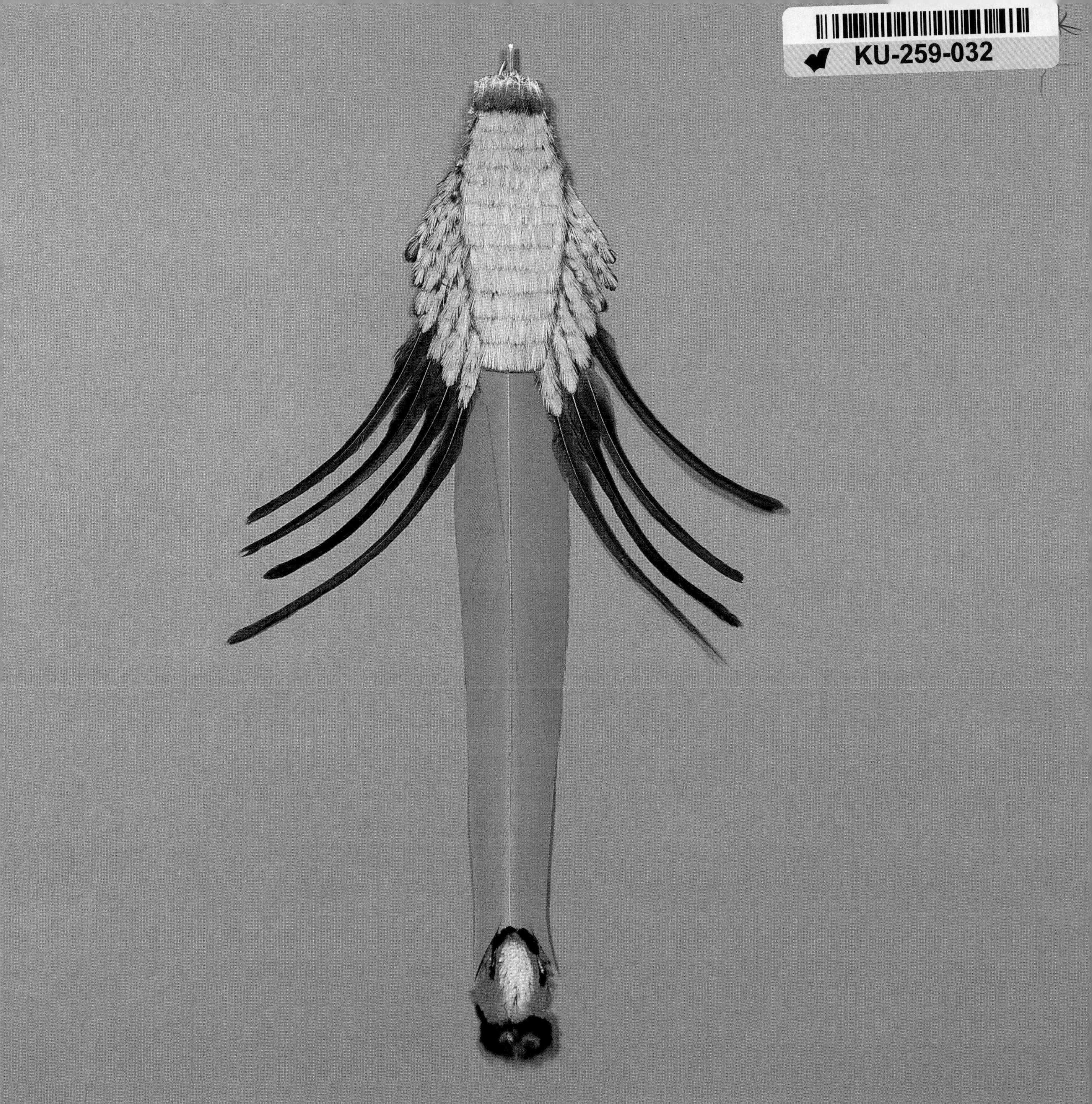

UNKNOWN AMAZON

UNKNOWN

CULTURE IN NATURE IN ANCIENT BRAZIL

AMAZON

EDITED BY COLIN McEWAN, CRISTIANA BARRETO AND EDUARDO NEVES

THE BRITISH MUSEUM PRESS

Published in 2001 by The British Museum Press
A division of The British Museum Company Ltd
46 Bloomsbury Street, London WC1B 3QQ

A catalogue record for this book
is available from the British Library

ISBN 0 7141 2558 X

Chapter 1 was translated from the Spanish by
Benjamin Alberti, and Chapters 5, 6, 8 and 9
were translated from the Portuguese by Izabel Murat Burbridge
and Thomas Nerney.

Designed by Harry Green
Printed in Slovenia

FRONT COVER

Above: A flooded forest (*igapó*)
in the 'blackwater' Curuá river
(photo: Araquém Alcântara).

Below: Anthropomorphic funerary urn lids,
Maracá culture of *c.*14th–17th century AD,
in the Gruta das Caretas near the mouth of the Amazon
(photo: Janduari Simões).

PAGE 1

This feather labret is worn during boys'
name-giving ceremonies among the Urubu-Kaapor
(height 32 cm, width 8 cm; Museu Paraense Emílio Goeldi, Belém, Brazil).
It is made in the form of a fantastic imaginary bird fashioned from the
brilliant plumage of the scarlet macaw and honey-creeper.

PAGES 2–3

Aerial view of a meandering 'whitewater' tributary
that will eventually drain into the Amazon.

RIGHT

The Amazon rainforest from within.

Contents

The Contributors

Cristiana Barreto is an archaeologist currently engaged in the curation of archaeology exhibitions in Brazil and abroad for BrasilConnects. She studied history and anthropology at the University of São Paulo and the University of Pittsburgh, and has conducted most of her archaeological field research in central Brazil. She has published a number of articles on the history and development of Brazilian archaeology and is preparing a book on this subject.

Warwick Bray recently retired as Professor of Latin American Archaeology at the Institute of Archaeology, University College London. He has conducted fieldwork in Colombia (including Colombian Amazonas) and Ecuador, and is a specialist in the study of Precolumbian metalwork. He authored *The Gold of El Dorado* (1977) and co-edited *The Archaeology of Mesoamerica: Mexican and European Perspectives* (1999).

Denise Maria Cavalcante Gomes is a doctoral candidate in archaeology at the Museu de Arqueologia e Etnologia, University of São Paulo, Brazil. Her studies of museum collections from the lower Amazon have been published in several articles and a book entitled *Cerâmica Arqueológica da Amazônia: a Coleção Tapajônica MAE-USP*, now in press.

Vera Lúcia Calandrini Guapindaia is an archaeologist and the curator of the archaeological collections of the Museu Paraense Emílio Goeldi, Belém, Brazil. She has more than fifteen years of experience in both field and laboratory research in Amazonian archaeology, including the study of preceramic sites in the Roraima area, ceramic collections from the Santarém culture, and in the past four years the archaeology of the Maracá river region in the Lower Amazon.

John Hemming, CMG, was Director of the Royal Geographical Society for twenty-one years. He has written many books about the history of the Brazilian Indians including *Red Gold* (1978) and *Amazon Frontier* (1995). He has been on several expeditions to unexplored parts of the Amazon and led the multi-disciplinary Maracá Rainforest Project (1987–8) involving 200 scientists and technicians.

Michael J. Heckenberger, Assistant Professor in the Department of Anthropology at the University of Florida (USA), received his doctorate from the University of Pittsburgh in 1996. He specializes in historical anthropology focusing on the nature and development of late prehistoric social formations and the impact of Euro-American colonialism in Amazonia. He is currently involved in field research in the upper Xingu, southern Amazonia, the central Amazon (Manaus) and Acre in western Amazonia. He is co-editor of the book *Os Povos do Alto Xingu: Cultura e História.*

Colin McEwan is Curator of the Latin American collections at the British Museum, London. He has excavated extensively in South America including Colombian Amazonas. He is the author of *Ancient Mexico in the British Museum* (1994), co-editor of *Patagonia: Natural History, Prehistory and Ethnography at the Uttermost End of the Earth* (1997) and editor of *Pre-Columbian Gold: Technology, Style and Iconography* (2000).

Juliana Salles Machado is reading archaeology and history at the University of São Paulo, Brazil. She is currently engaged in the Central Amazon research project directed by Dr Eduardo Neves since 1998, studying mound formation processes and the Guarita ceramic cultural complex. She has also worked as research assistant on the *Unknown Amazon* book and exhibition.

Eduardo Góes Neves is an archaeologist at the Museu de Arqueologia e Etnologia, Universidade de São Paulo, Brazil. He holds a Ph.D. in anthropology from Indiana University, and his research focuses on the archaeology and oral traditions of the indigenous people of the north-west Amazon. Since 1995 he has been coordinating the Central Amazon Project together with Drs Michael Heckenberger and James Petersen. Results of these and other works have been published in Brazil and abroad.

José R. Oliver is Lecturer in Latin American Archaeology at the Institute of Archaeology, University College London. He has directed excavations in the Virgin Islands, Puerto Rico, Culebra Island and Venezuela. His current research focuses on proto-Taíno settlement patterns and palaeoeconomy in the vicinity of Caguana, Puerto Rico. Recent publications include *El centro ceremonial de Caguana, Puerto Rico* (1998), *The La Hueca Complex in Puerto Rico and the Caribbean* (1999) and 'La región Centro-Occidental' in *Arte Prehispánico de Venezuela* (2000).

Edithe Pereira is an archaeologist based at the Museu Paraense Emílio Goeldi, Belém, Brazil. She has conducted research in the lower Amazon, Xingu and Araguaia river valleys, and directed several archaeological surveys and contract resource management projects in the states of Amapá and Pará. She has published various articles dealing with prehistoric rock art in Amazonia.

James B. Petersen is an Associate Professor of Anthropology and Chair of the Department of Anthropology at the University of Vermont (UVM) in the USA. He holds a Ph.D. in anthropology from the University of Pittsburgh. His interests revolve around ecological anthropology and the analysis of material cultures, and his research includes work in the Caribbean and Amazonia. Among his publications is *A Most Indispensable Art: Native Fiber Industries from Eastern North America*, which he edited.

Gustavo G. Politis is Senior Archaeologist at the Consejo Nacional de Investigaciones Científicas y Tecnicas (CONICET) and Professor at the Universidad del Centro de la Pcia. de Buenos Aires and at the Universidad de La Plata, Argentina. He has conducted archaeological research in the Pampas of Argentina and ethnoarchaeological investigations among the Nukak, hunter-gatherers of the Colombian Amazon. He has written more than seventy articles and three books. He recently edited a book with Ben Alberti about the archaeology of South America.

Denise Pahl Schaan is a Ph.D. candidate in the Department of Anthropology at the University of Pittsburgh (USA). With the support of the Museu Paraense Emílio Goeldi, Brazil, she has conducted archaeological surveys and excavated several archaeological sites in Marajó Island during the past five years. She has also studied museum collections related to Marajoara culture and earlier occupations in the island. Her Master's thesis, *A Linguagem Iconográfica da Cerâmica Marajoara*, was published in 1997, and she has written a number of articles for scientific and electronic journals.

Lucia Hussak van Velthem is an anthropologist and museologist, ex-Director of the Museu de Arte de Belém and Curator of the Ethnographic Collections at the Museu Paraense Emílio Goeldi. She has done extensive work amongst the Wayana, Tukano and Baré Indians of the Brazilian Amazon. She has curated several exhibitions on the indigenous peoples of the Amazon in Brazil. Her studies of the woven universe of the Wayana were recently published as *A pele de Tuluperê: uma etnografia dos trançados Wayana.* Her doctoral dissertation *A bela e a fera: A estética da produção e da predação entre os Wayana* is now in press.

Letter from the President of BrasilConnects

BrasilConnects (formerly Association Brazil+500), in its quest to show Brazilian art and culture abroad, feels privileged to collaborate with the British Museum in supporting the exhibition and this accompanying volume about indigenous Amazonia both past and present.

Amazonia is a region of superlatives, which at the turn of the century has attracted world-wide attention on account of its immense, rich and varied body of natural resources. However, little is known about how native Amazonians have lived in and successfully adapted to this green paradise for thousands of years. This book opens a new window on the Amazon by showing how a range of complex cultural traditions developed within the tropical forest. Few subjects could serve better to illustrate the links between nature and culture than the essays presented here on native Amazonian material culture. And few places could be more appropriate than the British Museum to show these materials to a broad international public.

The exhibition *Unknown Amazon* represents a real turning point in the trajectory of BrasilConnects' plans for celebrating Brazil 500 years through exhibitions of visual arts. By focusing on culture and nature, the exhibition *Unknown Amazon* represents the wider range of activities promoted by BrasilConnects including the support of projects engaged in the preservation of Amazonian flora and fauna. We are pleased that the exhibition and book can bring new light, deepen debates and widen concerns about crucial Amazonian issues.

The project in its entirety represents a true effort of joint enterprise, not only between the two institutions but particularly among the curators. We hope that this collaboration is but the keystone for further partnership in the creation of a permanent gallery at the British Museum.

EDEMAR CID FERREIRA

PRESIDENT OF BRASILCONNECTS

Foreword

JOHN HEMMING

The first Europeans were dazzled by the sight of Brazilian Indians. Pero Vaz de Caminha wrote a famous letter to the King of Portugal about the landing of Pedro Álvares Cabral's flotilla at Porto Seguro in April 1500.[1] In it he told how the first act of barter involved 'a headdress of long feathers with a small tuft of red and grey feathers like those of a parrot … and a large string of very small white beads which looked like seed pearls'. When two naked warriors came aboard a Portuguese ship, they calmly lay down to sleep and took more care to protect their headdresses than to cover their private parts. Caminha's letter noted that the Brazilian Indians were fascinated by their first sight of iron cutting tools, because 'they cut their wood and boards with wedge-shaped stones fixed into pieces of wood and firmly tied between two sticks'. (Metal tools have remained the main lure for contacting isolated tribes, from Cabral's day to the present. Living in a land of forests, indigenous people find the cutting power of axes, machetes and knives irresistible.)

Coming from the circumscribed world of fifteenth-century Europe, the first observers were fascinated by Indian nudity and by the fine physiques of men and women. Vaz de Caminha stressed that there was nothing immoral about this nakedness, and he also noted body paint. He told his King about a group of attractive girls:

> One had her thighs from knee to hip and her buttocks all painted with black dye [genipap], but the rest of her in her own colour. Another had both knees and calves so painted, but her privy parts so naked and exposed with such innocence that there was no shame there.

A body ornament consisting of a string of eight black-necked red cotinga birds (*Phoenicircus nigricollis*) with striking red and black plumage, Tikuna, collected *c.*1880 near the Solimões river (width 65cm; Museum für Völkerkunde, Vienna). A long pendant in the middle is made from a snail shell and an animal bone, which would have resonated in sympathy with the wearer's movements.

Another woman was completely covered in body dye, and some of the men wore quarterings of black and red (anatto) dyes. Amerigo Vespucci, who reached Brazil as a passenger aboard another Portuguese fleet two years later, also waxed lyrical about the naked beauty of the Indians.[2] He and other early chroniclers depicted them as noble savages living in a terrestrial paradise. Vespucci praised the skill and elegance of native architecture. He also noted that the country contained a profusion of plants, fruits, fish, molluscs and game – but absolutely no domestic or farmable animals.

Early French chroniclers described the sophistication of bows and arrows. The Protestant pastor Jean de Léry wrote (*c.*1560): 'Their bows are so much longer and stronger than those we have here [in France] that one of our men could scarcely draw one, far less shoot it.'[3] He also marvelled at their archers' prowess.

> Naked as they are and without any armlet, they can draw and shoot them so fast that, with due respect to the good English bowmen, our savages, holding their supply of arrows in the hand with which they hold the bow, would have fired off a dozen while [the English] would have released six.

Léry noted the 'great wooden swords and clubs' that were wielded with the dexterity and fury of a martial-arts master. His contemporary, the Catholic priest André Thevet, described Tupinambá ornaments – feather headdresses and diadems worn behind the neck and as a fluffy bustle, shell necklaces, lip-plugs of emerald-coloured (jadeite) stones, nut rattles on shamans' calves, and body paint. He also mentioned large pottery vessels in which the Indians brewed their maize beer, and their hammocks, baskets and few domestic appliances.

Fascination with Brazilian and Amazonian Indians was soon eclipsed by the discoveries and conquests of other great civilizations in the Americas, including the Aztec and Inca. With Europe flooded by Mexican and Peruvian precious metals, together with a few Precolumbian masterpieces, there was no interest whatever in the artistic output of lowland Indians. The main legacy of the first views of indigenous people of eastern South America was political and philosophical. The early observers reported that these peoples flourished in their land of plenty, without benefit of kings, written law or organized religion. As hunters, slash-and-burn farmers, fishermen and gatherers, they had no concern about lack of resources, so that they had no personal greed and did not try to accumulate surplus wealth. These observations were not entirely accurate, but they inspired subversive political theories, which verged on an attack on monarchies and the legal and ecclesiastical establishments. Theories based on Americans being noble savages appeared first in the writings of Erasmus and his friend Thomas More but were developed by Rabelais, Ronsard and Michel de Montaigne, by seventeenth-century theorists such as Puffendorf, Spinoza and Locke, and particularly by the eighteenth-century philosophers Jean-Jacques Rousseau, Denis Diderot and Montesquieu, with wry anti-Catholic comment by Voltaire.

These attractive fantasies bore no relation to the reality of what was actually happening in Brazil. The amicable barter of the first decades soon degenerated into slavery and oppression. This was because it was discovered that sugar grew abundantly in north-eastern Brazil, but Indians absolutely refused to perform the backbreaking labour of cutting and milling this very lucrative crop. They were indifferent to the paltry inducements of a market economy, so had to be forced to work as slaves. The few Portuguese who settled in Brazil also made Indians work as their farm labourers, servants, paddlers on river expeditions, gatherers of forest produce, and for the government on public works, buildings and in shipyards. When the supply of indigenous labour dwindled, the settlers turned to Africa as a source of slaves and to enhance their profits.

The Europeans brought two other forces that profoundly affected native populations in Brazil: disease and Christianity. It is impossible to exaggerate the impact of imported epidemics – smallpox, measles, influenza, tuberculosis, pneumonia and (after the eighteenth century) malaria. Chronicles are full of heartbreaking accounts of deaths from diseases against which indigenous peoples had no inherited immunity, with corpses piled unburied and entire communities wiped out. Europeans wanted Indians alive, as labourers, converts in their missions, and subjects of their King. But they were powerless to prevent the catastrophic decline. They had no understanding of the nature of diseases, of their vectors or cures. So the indigenous peoples of the Atlantic seaboard and the Amazon basin were destroyed in one of the greatest demographic tragedies in history. Similar depopulation has continued with every newly contacted tribe, right up to the present day. My estimate of the population of Brazil on the eve of the conquest is

3,250,000, which is in the middle range of other demographers' guesses.[4] The main concentrations of native populations were to be found in the populous settlements along the banks and bluffs of the mainstream Amazon and its principal tributaries. Numbers of Indians maintaining their traditional way of life have fallen ever since 1500. They were down to some 350,000 by the start of the twentieth century and reached a nadir of little more than 100,000 by the 1950s, but are once again rising rapidly.

The most effective of the early missionaries were the Jesuits, who reached Brazil in 1549. Until their expulsion from the Portuguese empire in 1759, Jesuits dominated indigenous affairs. At times they were the Indians' only champions against the excesses of colonists. But they were not disinterested. They were determined to convert Indians and to fill their mission villages. Some tribes responded favourably to the Jesuits' cradle-to-grave paternalism and religious teaching – notably the Guarani of Paraguay and southern Brazil, who were a spiritual people already congregated in large communities. But other groups resented and resisted Jesuit interference with their customs and beliefs. All missionaries were intent on suppressing tribal religion, shamanism, animism and mythology. This involved the destruction of many artefacts, for, as with most human societies, Amazonian peoples created much of their finest output for spiritual purposes. Missionaries also abhorred nudity, and their imposition of clothing meant the loss of body ornaments and the skills that went into their manufacture.

The first Europeans to descend the Amazon river, Francisco de Orellana's expedition of 1542 and the ill-fated Ursúa-Aguirre venture in 1560, marvelled at the pottery – similar to that shown in this exhibition. In the middle Amazon (Solimões) they saw huge jars capable of holding 450 litres, plates, bowls and 'candelabra', all magnificently decorated with incisions and paintings and expertly 'glazed'. They wrote that these were equal to the world's finest porcelain, better than Málaga ware and comparable to Roman. It was 'thin and smooth, glazed and with colours shading off into one another in the style of that made in China'.[5]

The early observers noted many aspects of indigenous art that are constants throughout Brazilian history. They showed that natives are self-sufficient, making all their possessions from the abundant natural products that surround them. Both sexes are highly creative and skilled artisans, even though they work with tools fashioned from a range of natural materials including stone, sharpened bones, shells and woods. Some objects are made of stone or pottery, but most are of wood, bone, fibres and the innumerable vegetable derivatives in the Amazonian ecosystem. Much artistry is devoted to body ornament, particularly skin painting and tattooing. Thus, the majority of indigenous art is temporary and will be washed off skins or consumed by termites and tropical decay. This is important. It is difficult to appreciate the creative skills of people whose production is so ephemeral. Judging by stone and ceramic objects alone gives a much diminished view and only reflects a mere fraction of artistic output. The feather, basketry and wooden objects that appear in museum displays can never capture their natural hues and shimmering iridescence produced by a combination of movement and sunlight: they have lost some of the lustre and beauty they had when in use.

The chroniclers also noticed immediately that there were no domestic animals in the Amazon basin. Surrounded by evergreen tropical forests, indigenous people had to hunt and fish for protein, but they also practised skilful husbandry of forest resources such as the *miriti* palm, and kept turtle populations captive in specially constructed pens to act as a food reserve in times of scarcity. Manioc was the principal staple crop underpinning the tropical forest agricultural system. Amazon Indians are conventionally viewed as being nomadic or semi-nomadic, farming in temporary forest clearings and frequently moving their villages to exploit the surrounding resources. Nevertheless, as this book makes clear, a picture is emerging of permanent settlements and surprisingly elaborate social institutions and art styles that point to an unsuspected level of complexity.

During the second half of the sixteenth and early decades of the seventeenth century, tiny Portugal, with a population of little over a million, successfully fought off two attempts by the French to colonize the coast of Brazil (at Rio de Janeiro between 1555 and 1570, and in Maranhão in 1612–14); then Dutch, English and Irish incursions in the lower Amazon in 1618–30; and lastly Dutch invasions of Bahia (1625) and then Pernambuco and north-eastern Brazil (1630–54). The first Dutch governor of Pernambuco was the admirable liberal Maurice of Nassau, who brought artists and scientists to his

Brazilian colony. The paintings of Frans Post and Albert Eckhout showed some Indian ethnography. But when the last Dutch were expelled, Portugal jealously closed its huge colony to all outsiders. Interest in indigenous art ceased altogether. When Captain Cook visited Rio de Janeiro on his first circumnavigation in 1768, Portuguese paranoia and xenophobia was such that no British officers were allowed ashore, even though England was Portugal's oldest ally. The naturalist Joseph Banks made a brief landing disguised as a sailor, and expostulated: 'No one even tolerably curious has been here since [the Dutch scientists] Marcgrave and Piso, so it is easy to guess the state in which the nat. hist. of such a country must be.'[6]

Interest in indigenous artefacts as an art form started with the Portuguese scientist Alexandre Rodrigues Ferreira, who was sent to Brazil in 1783 as part of the team to survey the enlarged boundaries of Brazil that the Portuguese had negotiated with Spain. Although a botanist and naturalist, Rodrigues Ferreira made ethnographic studies of tribes of the Rio Negro right up to the Içana and Uaupés, and the upper Rio Branco, modern Roraima; and he wrote studies of native pottery, pipes, masks and architecture. The renowned German scientist Alexander von Humboldt could not enter Brazil because of the Napoleonic wars, but nevertheless this period began to see an end to Brazil's intellectual isolation. The Portuguese royal family took refuge in its South American possession, and one, Bragança, remained after 1822 as Emperor of an independent Brazil. European scientists were admitted at that time: French, with the ambassador of their restored King Louis XVIII; Germans, with the bride of the first Brazilian Emperor; and thereafter a stream of English and other naturalists.

Important studies of indigenous peoples – and collections of their artistry – were made in 1815–17 by the German Prince Maximilian zu Wied-Neuwied and in 1818–20 by the Bavarians Carl von Martius and Johann Baptist von Spix, the first foreigners allowed up the Amazon. The Austrian Johann Natterer filled the anthropological museum of Vienna with objects from scores of tribes between 1818 and 1834, but his notes and writings were tragically destroyed in a house fire. Georg Langsdorff led an important expedition to central Brazil and Amazonia in 1825–7, which included the young French artists Hércules Florence and Aimé Adrien Taunay; since Langsdorff worked for the Tsar of Russia, his material is all in St Petersburg. The French travellers Auguste de Saint-Hilaire, Jean-Baptiste Debret and in the 1840s the Comte de Castelnau all wrote about tribes, but they collected few artefacts. Of the English naturalists Alfred Russel Wallace, Henry Walter Bates and Richard Spruce, the last took a special interest in cultural objects and brought back an important collection now housed at Kew Gardens. They visited the Indians of the Solimões and Negro rivers in the 1850s, particularly the Ticuna with their fantastic zoomorphic masks and bark-cloth hoods, but their great collections were of natural history.

In the latter part of the nineteenth century Brazilians such as António Gonçalves Dias, José Couto de Magalhães and João Barbosa Rodrigues supplied the new National Museum in Rio de Janeiro and the Museu Paulista in São Paulo with indigenous artefacts. Archaeologists excavated *sambaqui* shell-middens and the magnificent early ceramics from Marajó Island in the mouth of the Amazon and Santarém on the lower river. Most of their discoveries are in the Goeldi Museum in Belém do Pará, but some masterpieces are seen in Europe for the first time in this *Unknown Amazon* exhibition. Ethnography in Amazonia then came to be dominated by German scholars. Karl von den Steinen led the first scientific team into the upper Xingu in 1884 and was a pioneer of a new style of anthropological writing that treated Indians as individual human beings. His compatriots Theodor Koch-Grünberg, Paul Ehrenreich and others also made important collections for the museums of Berlin and other German cities. The tireless, ubiquitous and scholarly German, Curt Unkel, who formally adopted the Guarani surname Nimuendajú, transformed Brazilian anthropology in the first half of the twentieth century. Nimuendajú was either with a tribe or on an archaeological excavation (often commissioned by American and Swedish institutions) in every single year from 1909 to his death in 1945. His record of fieldwork, knowledge of indigenous societies and collections of artefacts have never been rivalled. His contemporary Colonel (later Marshal) Cândido Rondon transformed attitudes to Indians and in 1908 founded the non-missionary Indian Protection Service (SPI), which started as a world leader in treatment of indigenous minorities. Rondon has been hailed as the greatest explorer of the twentieth century, and his expeditions contacted many tribes and yielded important ethnographic material. During the past sixty years anthropologists have studied every surviving tribe in the Amazon. The majority of these scientists are Brazilian, but Americans and many other nationalities have also contributed. As well as collecting for museums, such as the admirable Museum of the Indian founded in Rio de Janeiro in 1952, these anthropologists have been active in campaigns to help Indians and guarantee their lands.

The ethnography of Amazon Indians is remarkable because it is alive. Unknown tribes are still being contacted in the fastnesses of the Amazon forests. There is a paradox in the output of material culture among contemporary indigenous societies. In one sense it is very similar because the forest, riverine or savannah terrains are comparable throughout the region, and because tribes hunt, fish, forage, live and organize their societies in the same ways. On the other hand, there is remarkable variety within these general parameters. Even the most common objects such as bows, arrows, hammocks, headdresses, baskets, cooking utensils and ceramics differ markedly between ethnic groups. This is the result of human creativity and ingenuity, and adds to the beauty and fascination of *Unknown Amazon* and other exhibitions. Individual tribes are famous for making particular objects. In featherwork the jewel-like creations of the Ka'apor of Maranhão and the flamboyant headdresses of the Bororo of Mato Grosso, the Karajá and Tapirapé of the Araguaia river, various Kayapó of central Brazil and the Wayana of Brazilian Guiana are notable among the profusion of feather ornaments from all parts of Amazonia. The Karajá are also famous for their ceramic figurines (which are being popularized for saleability), the Ticuna for their masks, and the Tucano, Desana and others of the upper Rio Negro for their basketwork. The Indians of the upper Xingu still have tribal specialities in making mollusc-shell necklaces, canoes, bows, and striking utilitarian pottery and wooden stools. The Asurini of the lower Xingu, Kadiwéu of southern Mato Grosso and Shipibo of the Peruvian Ucayali decorate their pots with individualistic designs. Every tribe has its own style of architecture. Outstanding buildings include the great communal *malocas* (longhouses) of tribes of the Javari valley and upper Rio Negro, the conical or open-circular *yano* or *shabono* of the Yanomami, the elegant lozenge-shaped dwellings of the Xinguanos, and the symmetrical circles of huts of the Jê-speaking Kayapó, Xavante and Timbira groups.

The indigenous peoples of Amazonia are entering the third millennium with guarded optimism. After falling to near-extinction in the mid-twentieth century, numbers have tripled. Most tribes are back to their populations of the late nineteenth century. Indians contacted in colonial times are reduced to reserves that are often too small to be sustainable. But groups contacted more recently, particularly the forest tribes, have achieved large protected homelands. Presently numbering around 350,000 people, the 210 tribes of modern Brazil represent only 0.2 per cent of its national population, and yet they occupy 11 per cent of its vast land mass – their areas are as large as all the core countries of western Europe combined. These successes over land have been achieved only by thirty years of determined, sometimes violent struggle. The Indians themselves are now mobilized in regional groupings, which co-operate most effectively to influence the media, politicians and public opinion. They are helped, encouraged and trained by a great coalition of non-government activists, anthropologists, Indianist officials and some missionaries (whose attitudes have improved dramatically since the 1970s). These NGOs are predominantly from Brazil and Spanish-speaking Amazonian countries, but the British charity Survival is outstanding among international supporters. Although indigenous people's land, health and physical survival seem assured, the future of their way of life is more problematical. There is a danger that tribal societies will be swamped by the trend to global uniformity. But most groups do not want this to happen. They cling to their unique social heritage, and there is a determined revival in ethnic cultures. So they will continue to make the beautiful objects seen in this exhibition, for everyday use and not just museum display.

NOTES

1 Vaz de Caminha 1937: 3–33.
2 Vespucci 1894.
3 Léry 1980.
4 Hemming 1995a; Denevan 1992a.
5 Ortigüera 1581.
6 Banks 1963.

Introduction

EDUARDO NEVES, CRISTIANA BARRETO
AND COLIN MCEWAN

The Amazonian rainforest is widely recognized as one of the most significant and largely intact ecosystems left on earth. It has long been characterized as an essentially untouched natural environment inhabited since time immemorial by a thin scattering of indigenous groups. Under the encroaching pressures of modern economic development the immense potential and future of the Amazon basin is now hotly debated. Its wise management is fast becoming a matter of global concern. There are often sharp divisions between those who advocate the need to make preservation of the natural environment and protection of indigenous cultures the highest priority, and governments who share responsibility for Amazonas as a whole and for whom there is a pressing need to address endemic social problems, including poverty, through development and integration.

As archaeologists, we believe that knowledge about the past has a vital role to play in opening up new perspectives on planning and decision-making for the future. This is particularly true for the Amazon where recent archaeological research reveals a very long sequence of human occupation and documents the existence of densely populated societies well before European contact. Archaeologists have much yet to learn about the internal dynamics of indigenous subsistence systems and the full range and complexity of pre-contact social formations. Nevertheless, we can say with confidence that the rainforest should no longer be seen as a pristine, untouched 'paradise'. The skilful management of both riverine and forest resources by indigenous cultures is based on a deep history of human interaction with, and transformation of, the natural world. These skills build on an immense reservoir of knowledge that has accrued in the course of thousands of years of experimentation and learning. What new archaeological data point to are successful and sustainable adaptations grounded in practical expertise and born of an intimate familiarity with both the limitations as well as the possibilities of this environment.

Amazonian indigenous groups can no longer be stereotyped as small, isolated communities living in the depths of the forest or dispersed along rivers. The perception of simple social structures and a low level of cultural achievement is largely the consequence of catastrophic population collapse, displacement and cultural loss that indigenous populations have experienced since their first contacts with Europeans. Contrary to this stereotype we are now able to trace the lineaments of what can be fairly described as a tropical forest civilization that gave rise to diverse, sophisticated art styles. In this volume we have assembled a substantial body of new data and perspectives on these 'unknown' dimensions of Amazonia's past. By focusing on culture in a tropical forest setting, we recognize that the history of the forest is inextricably intertwined with the history of the people who inhabit it.

Archaeological research also reformulates a central question in contemporary Amazonian anthropology concerning the impact of European colonization and evolving nation states in South America on native Amazonian societies. By focusing on patterns of social and political organization among pre-colonial Amazonian societies, archaeology provides information and insights to compare with the rich body of ethnographic data gathered in the course of the last hundred years. To explore the question of how different contemporary Amazonian Indians and *caboclos* (mixed race) are from their pre-colonial ancestors clearly calls for an integration not only of archaeology and ethnography, but also of linguistics and bioanthropology. A more complete anthropological perspective is needed to overcome the strictures imposed by sub-disciplines and academic divisions. By juxtaposing both archaeology and ethnography from the Amazon we wish to contribute towards this more integrated perspective.

FAR LEFT Detail of a spear with a rattle, decorated with a range of brilliant featherwork, Tukano, collected c.1830 (length 265 cm, diameter 7 cm; Museum für Völkerkunde, Vienna).

LEFT Detail of a blowgun with bone or shell latticework inlay, Baniwa, collected c.1882 (length 315 cm, diameter 6 cm; Museum für Völkerkunde, Vienna).

This magnificent Marajoara funerary urn (Marajoara culture AD 500–1500) features a series of superimposed frontal faces on the body, neck and under the rim (height 91cm; Museu Barbier Mueller Art Precolombí, Barcelona). Prominent modelled zoomorphic heads adorn the sides. The range of techniques applied – incision, excision, modelling and bold polychrome painting – combine to make this vessel one of the masterpieces of Amazonian ceramic art.

Here we do not attempt to provide an exhaustive overview of Amazonian archaeology. Most of the contributing essays emphasize the middle and lower Amazon and are essentially case studies that focus on the rise of complex societies during the first 1500 years AD. The volume is selective inasmuch as it concentrates on the focal assemblages of objects loaned in for the exhibition. This tends to reflect regional research biases as well as the greater archaeological visibility and better preservation of cultural remains for the later periods of human occupation than those currently available for the earlier periods. The tropical forest lowlands of the Amazon basin in common with those of the adjacent Orinoco, as well as the Guayas basin of western Ecuador and the lower San Jorge valley in northern Colombia, exercised a continent-wide cultural influence in South America. These riverine settings have given rise to the very earliest settled agrarian economies in the Americas. Seen from this wider perspective, the volume is but one step towards addressing a much wider range of tropical forest visual and material culture past and present. We would like to think that subsequent initiatives will extend and explore beyond what we have attempted here.

In the middle and lower Amazon recent research seems to confirm that a creative explosion of different ceramic styles occurred about two thousand years ago. The most important of these, widely known as the Amazon Polychrome tradition, appears to have its origins on Marajó Island, where the Amazon meets the Atlantic, and later spreads across much of the upper Amazon, the Guianas and beyond. Even if all the reasons for this surge in cultural complexity are still not well understood, we do know that important changes took place in the social and political organization of native Amazonian societies. In this volume we present a sample of recent research by the current generation of archaeologists committed to bringing new empirical evidence to ongoing debates. These essays capture some of the freshness and enthusiasm (as well no doubt as some of the shortcomings) characteristic of pioneer work, and perhaps mirror something of the feeling of being in the very heart of the Amazon forest itself.

Part I of the volume introduces the reader to some of the new approaches to theory and research in contemporary Amazonian archaeology. The essays by Politis and Oliver examine the processes of cultural adaptation to the rainforest among hunter-gatherer and agricultural societies respectively. Petersen, Neves and Heckenberger address the archaeological signatures of these processes in the form of the phenomenon of the anthropogenic black earth soils known as *terra preta*.

Part II presents case studies of three different ceramic styles in the archaeology of the middle and lower Amazon. Archaeological ceramics have attracted widespread attention among scholars since early European chroniclers commented favourably on the sophisticated pottery they encountered in many villages along the river. The arguments about the existence of complex societies invariably revolve around the origins and relationships between different pottery complexes and styles, although serious iconographic study of these has scarcely begun. The essays by Schaan, Gomes and Guapindaia are innovative steps in this direction.

Part III also focuses on the role of ideology and symbolism in visual and material culture. The chapters by McEwan on seats and related ritual paraphernalia, van Velthem on basketry and Pereira on rock art explore some of the meanings embedded in design patterns and symbolism in very different media. They also draw attention to the links and continuities between the archaeological past and contemporary tropical forest cultures.

Part IV demonstrates the need for new historical perspectives in the study of past and present indigenous Amazonian societies. While the historical review by Barreto and Machado focuses on the relativity implied in the way Europeans have looked at the Amazonian past, Bray explores the historiography of a particular category of artefact: war clubs from Guiana. Finally, Neves addresses the relationship between archaeology and oral traditions, reminding us that in order to understand culture change in the Amazon we need to reassess traditional notions of cultural identity.

Acknowledgements

In the first place we wish to record our sincere thanks to Mr Edemar Cid Ferreira, the President of BrasilConnects, for committing the resources and support that enabled us to bring this project to fruition. Edemar quickly understood the spirit and scope of what we thought might be possible and then moved decisively at every step in the development of the project to help make our dreams a reality. Fausto Godoy (Brazilian Foreign Ministry) ably facilitated the initial contact and exchanges. Both he and later Helena Gasparian (also Brazilian Foreign Ministry) helped guide the project to fruition.

In February 2000 we undertook a curatorial trip to review the principal Amazonian collections held in national and regional museums throughout Brazil. We were met with unfailing courtesy and assistance from our curatorial colleagues. We would like to thank the following institutions and individuals for having contributed in innumerable ways toward the realization of both the book and the exhibition: Museu Nacional, Rio de Janeiro – Dr Luiz Fernando Dias Duarte (Director), Dr Fátima Nascimento (Curator of Ethnography), Dr Tânia Andrade Lima (Curator of Archaeology) and Dr Tereza Bauman (Museology department); Museu do Indio, Rio de Janeiro – Dr José Carlos Levinho (Director), Dr Ione Couto and Dr Lucia Bastos (conservator); Museu de Arqueologia e Etnologia, Universidade de São Paulo – Dr Paula Montero (Director), Dr Maria Isabel d´Agostino Fleming (Chair of the Scientific Division), Gedley Braga (Conservator), Celia Maria Cristina de Martini (Keeper), Marilucia Bottallo (Head of Archives) and Wagner Souza e Silva (photographer); Museu Paraense Emílio Goeldi, Belém – Dr Peter Mann de Toledo (Director), Dr Lucia van Velthem (Curator of Ethnography), Dr Vera Lucia Guapindaia (Curator of Archaeology) and Dr Roberto Araújo (Head of Department of Human Sciences); Municipal Museum of Santarém – Mr Elson Amaral de Souza and Mr Renato Sussuarana, Mayor of Santarém; Museu do Homem do Norte, Manaus – Dr Regina Vasconcellos (Director); Museu do Indio de Manaus – Sister Judith (Director); Instituto Histórico e Geográfico do Amazonas, Manaus – Dr Robério dos Santos Pereira Braga (President) and Col. Manoel Roberto Lima Mendonça; Universidade Federal do Pará, Laboratório de Antropologia – Dr Carmen Izabel Rodrigues; Instituto do Patrimônio Histórico e Artístico Nacional, Belém (IPHAN) – Dr Elizabeth Nello Soares and Dr Ana Lucia Nascentes Abrahim (Regional Coordinators).

In March 2000 we embarked on another curatorial trip to view and evaluate Amazonian collections in European museums. Again both museum directors and curatorial colleagues often went to extraordinary lengths to assist us in our quest. We gratefully acknowledge the support and collaboration of Museu Antropológico da Universidade de Coimbra, Portugal – Dr Paulo Gama Mota (Director), Dr Maria do Rosário Martins (Curator) and Dr Manuel Laranjeira; Museu Nacional de Etnologia, Lisboa, Portugal – Dr Joaquim Paes de Brito (Director); Etnografiska Museet I Göteborg, Sweden – Dr Jan Amnehall (Director) and Dr Sven-Erik Isacsson, whose untimely and unexpected passing away earlier this year deprives us of a much valued friend; Ethnologisches Museum, Berlin, Germany – Dr Richard Haas (Curator of the Department of American Ethnology) and Dr Helene Tello (Conservator); Museum für Völkerkunde, Vienna, Austria – Dr Peter Kann (Director) and Mrs Kann; Museu Barbier-Mueller Art Precolombí, Barcelona, Spain – Dr Ana Casas (Director), Mr Pepe Andreu (External Relations Executive), Dr Elisabeth Casellas (Curator) and Katharina Simons. We would like also to express our thanks to Mr Jean-Paul Barbier-Mueller and Mrs Laurence Mattet, Director of Musée Barbier-Mueller, Genève, Switzerland, and to Mr Claudio Angelo from São Paulo, who first told the curators about the Barbier-Mueller Collection.

In Portugal we counted on Dr Luiz Oosterbeck from Instituto Politécnico de Tomar and Dr José Antonio Fernandes Dias for advice and assistance. We also thank Ms Martine Piednoir at the Bibliothèque Sainte-Geneviève in Paris for her gracious and prompt response to our request for photographic material.

In July 2000 a Ceramic Workshop took place in the Museu de Etnologia e Arqueologia da Universidade de São Paulo led by the British Museum conservators Janet Quinton and Barbara Wills. We would like to thank everybody involved in this initiative – the first such gathering of conservators and curators in Brazil – and especially Dr Maria Isabel d'Agostino Fleming and Gedley Braga at MAE for hosting the event and for providing all the practical support that made it such a success.

In São Paulo invaluable backing and administrative expertise from the BrasilConnects office was provided by Prof. Nelson Aguilar, Chief Curator, and Mr Emilio Kalil, Director of Exhibitions, and his team. Paula Amaral, exhibition producer, Juliana Salles Machado, Research Assistant, and Angela Freitas, Conservator, have contributed steady and diligent production work. On both curatorial trips we were accompanied by photographer Fernando Chaves, whose skilled photography of Brazilian and European collections graces this volume. We thank Mirian Almeida for her help in arranging much of our travel, and Dr Denise Studart for assistance in London with the planning and execution of the curatorial trips. The project has also benefited from important advice from Ana Helena Curti. The initial translations of several draft manuscripts were undertaken by Izabel Murat Burbridge, Thomas Nerney and Benjamin Alberti. Caio Vassão and Sérgio Francisco provided excellent object illustrations.

In London we thank the members of the Exhibition Forum at the British Museum for their strong backing and belief in the viability of the project. Geoffrey House (Head of Exhibitions) and Tony Doubleday (Head of Secretariat) assisted with aspects of both the sponsor's and the subsidiary Loan Agreement with Brazil as well as with diplomatic and financial matters. We are particularly grateful to the members of the Exhibition Advisory Board: Sir David Attenborough, Prof. Warwick Bray, Dr John Hemming, Dr Stephen Hugh-Jones, Dr Joanna Overing, Sir Ghillean Prance and Prof. Peter Rivière. We particularly remember Dr Darrell Posey (University of Oxford) who passed away late last year. He was a pioneer in recognizing and researching the wealth of ethnobiological knowledge among living Amazonian traditions, and especially among the Kayapó with whom he worked closely for many years. He was a particularly enthusiastic supporter of this project from its inception and will be sorely missed.

His Excellency Ambassador Sergio Amaral graciously hosted various gatherings at the Brazilian Embassy in London that enabled us to combine business and social exchange in a convivial setting. Secretaries Ademar Seabra da Cruz Jr. and Roberto Abdalla, together with Tassy Barham (BrasilConnects coordinator in London), have helped facilitate contact between the project and the Embassy. We also thank the Board of Trustees of the Royal Botanic Gardens, Kew, as well as Dr Peter R. Crane (Director) and Dr Naomi Rumball (Curator – Economic Botany Collections).

The catalogue and exhibition team in London has borne the burden of editorial support that has played such a vital role in seeing the project through to completion. Jasmin Pinho assumed the role of Project Coordinator in June 2000 and brought a rare blend of

Carved wooden bowl in the form of a double-headed jaguar, lower Amazon (height 10.5 cm, width 21 cm; British Museum). It may have been used as a mortar for preparing hallucinogenic snuff derived from the seeds of *Anadenanthera peregrina.*

organizational skill and enthusiasm to the project. During critical stages in the production of this volume we counted on the unwavering commitment and dedicated work of Cristiane Matsunaga and Maria Magro. We owe a special debt of gratitude to Garth A. Denning who invested great care and patience in rendering so much of the graphic work that enhances the volume. Jude Simmons and Robin Kiang offered valuable assistance in generating some of the digital graphics. We express appreciation to all the contributing authors for their spirit of collaboration and forbearance under the duress of demanding deadlines, and we particularly thank Dr John Hemming for finding the time to prepare the foreword amidst a busy travel schedule.

In the Department of Ethnography, British Museum, Ben Burt, Sarah Posey and Jonathan King kindly read and commented on some of the manuscripts. Thanks also to photographers Mike Row and David Agar; Jim Hamill in the Students Room; library staff, especially Harry Persaud, Carmen Grannum-Symister, Renée Evans and Lucia Navascues; and Dean Baylis, Alison Deeprose and Sue Vacarey of the General Office.

For additional advice, interest and moral support in ways large and small we also extend thanks to Edward Posey (Gaia Foundation); Fiona Watson (Survival International); Fiona Worthington (COAMA – Programme for the Consolidation of the Colombian Amazon); OIBI – Organização Indígena da Bacia do Içana; Carlos Alberto Ricardo and Nicole Freris (COIAB – Coordination of the Indigenous Organizations of the Brazilian Amazon); and Luciene Pohl (FUNAI, Fundação Nacional do Índio, Manaus).

We gratefully acknowledge the patience of the British Museum Press editors Coralie Hepburn and Teresa Francis and the BMP production team. The perseverance and good humour of Colin Grant, volume editor, in the face of daunting odds have been deeply appreciated. Designer Harry Green accomplished a formidable task with customary panache. His wise head and keen eye together with the cartographic skills of his colleagues Bob Travis and David Hoxley were instrumental in ensuring that the volume would finally see the light of day.

Finally, we owe heartfelt thanks to our respective partners, families and friends. They may not always entirely understand our avocation for things unknown, but have nevertheless tolerated our absences and provided the practical and moral support without which the enterprise would surely have foundered.

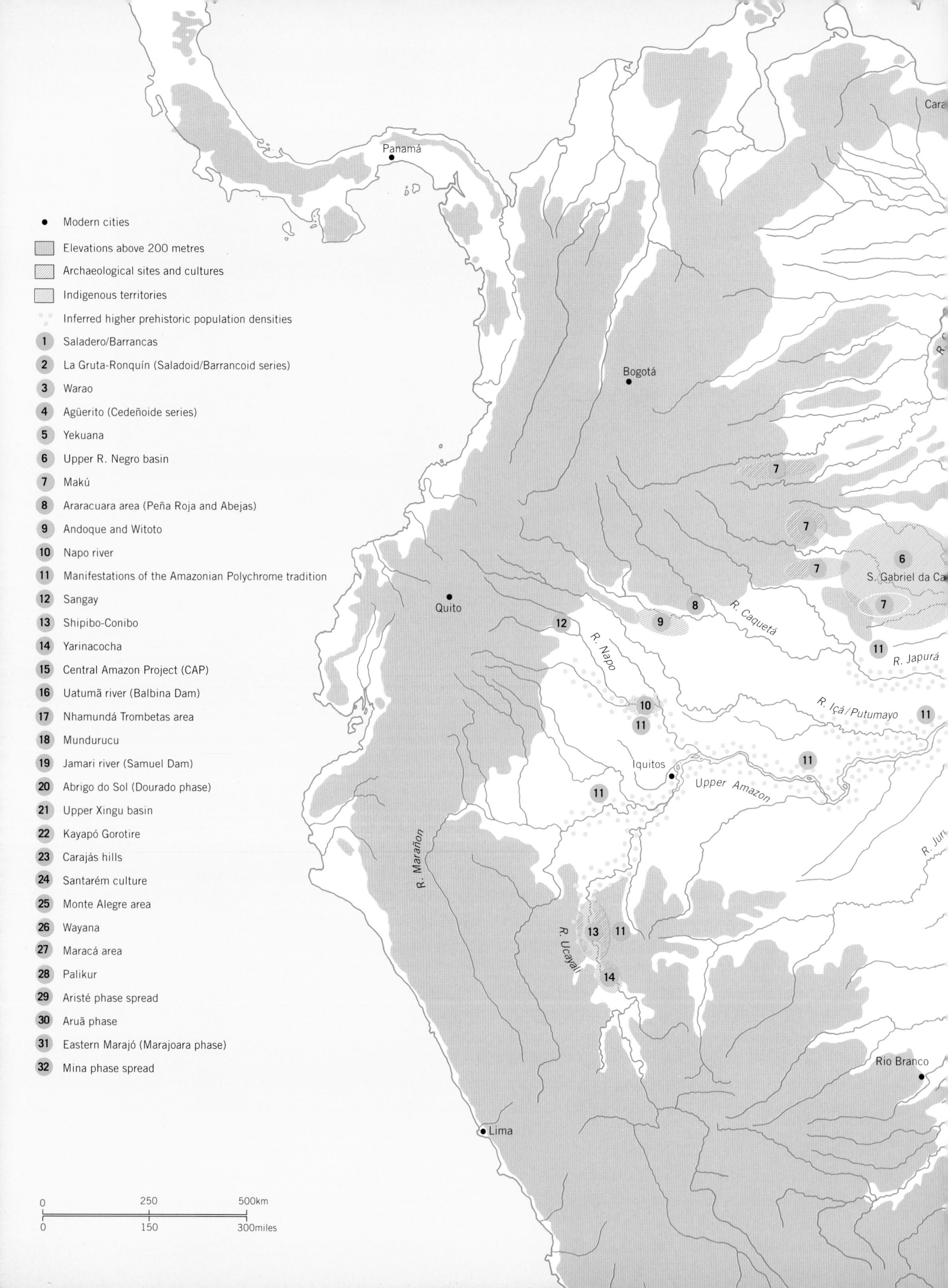
Panamá
Bogotá
Quito
Lima
Iquitos
Rio Branco
S. Gabriel da Ca
Cara
R. Caquetá
R. Japurá
R. Napo
R. Içá/Putumayo
Upper Amazon
R. Marañon
R. Ucayali
R. Juru
Modern cities
Elevations above 200 metres
Archaeological sites and cultures
Indigenous territories
Inferred higher prehistoric population densities
1 Saladero/Barrancas
2 La Gruta-Ronquín (Saladoid/Barrancoid series)
3 Warao
4 Agüerito (Cedeñoide series)
5 Yekuana
6 Upper R. Negro basin
7 Makú
8 Araracuara area (Peña Roja and Abejas)
9 Andoque and Witoto
10 Napo river
11 Manifestations of the Amazonian Polychrome tradition
12 Sangay
13 Shipibo-Conibo
14 Yarinacocha
15 Central Amazon Project (CAP)
16 Uatumã river (Balbina Dam)
17 Nhamundá Trombetas area
18 Mundurucu
19 Jamari river (Samuel Dam)
20 Abrigo do Sol (Dourado phase)
21 Upper Xingu basin
22 Kayapó Gorotire
23 Carajás hills
24 Santarém culture
25 Monte Alegre area
26 Wayana
27 Maracá area
28 Palikur
29 Aristé phase spread
30 Aruã phase
31 Eastern Marajó (Marajoara phase)
32 Mina phase spread
0 250 500km
0 150 300miles

N
EQUATOR
Area shown in detail on next page
Area shown on main map
ATLANTIC OCEAN
Georgetown
Paramaribo
Cayenne
Macapá
Belém
Monte Alegre
Santarém
Manaus
Porto Velho
R. Branco
R. Negro
R. Trombetas
R. Erepecuru
R. Paru de Este
R. Jari
R. Araguari
R. Nhamundá
R. Amazon
R. Solimões (Amazon)
R. Madeira
R. Tapajós
R. Xingu
R. Purus
R. Araguaia
R. Tocantins
R. Gurup
1
3
5
11
15
16
17
18
19
20
21
22
23
24
25
26
27
28
29
30
31
32

Chronology of Archaeological Cultures in the Middle and Lower Amazon

BC 10 000 · 8000 · 6000 · 4000 · 2000

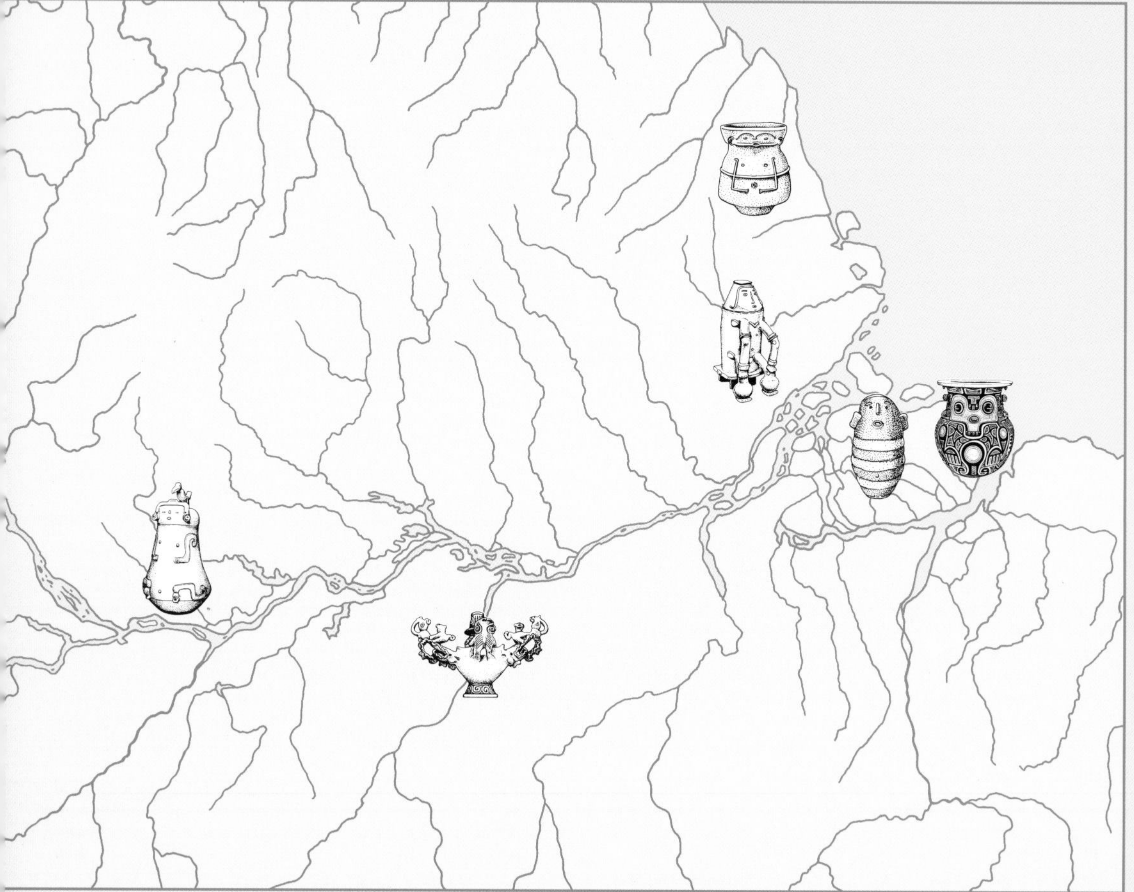

MINA

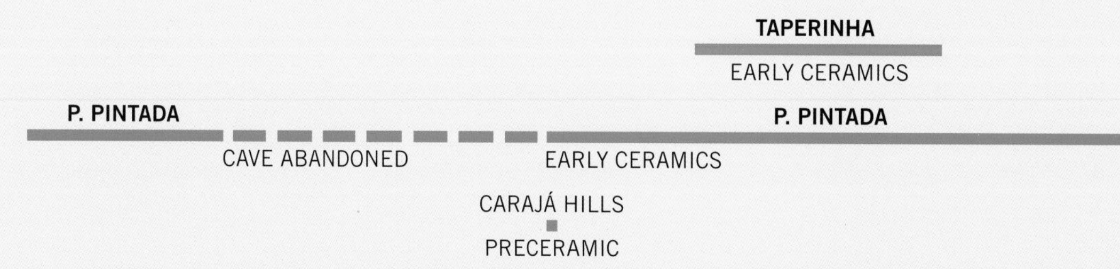

MIDDLE AMAZON

BP 12 000 · 10 000 · 8000 · 6000 · 4000

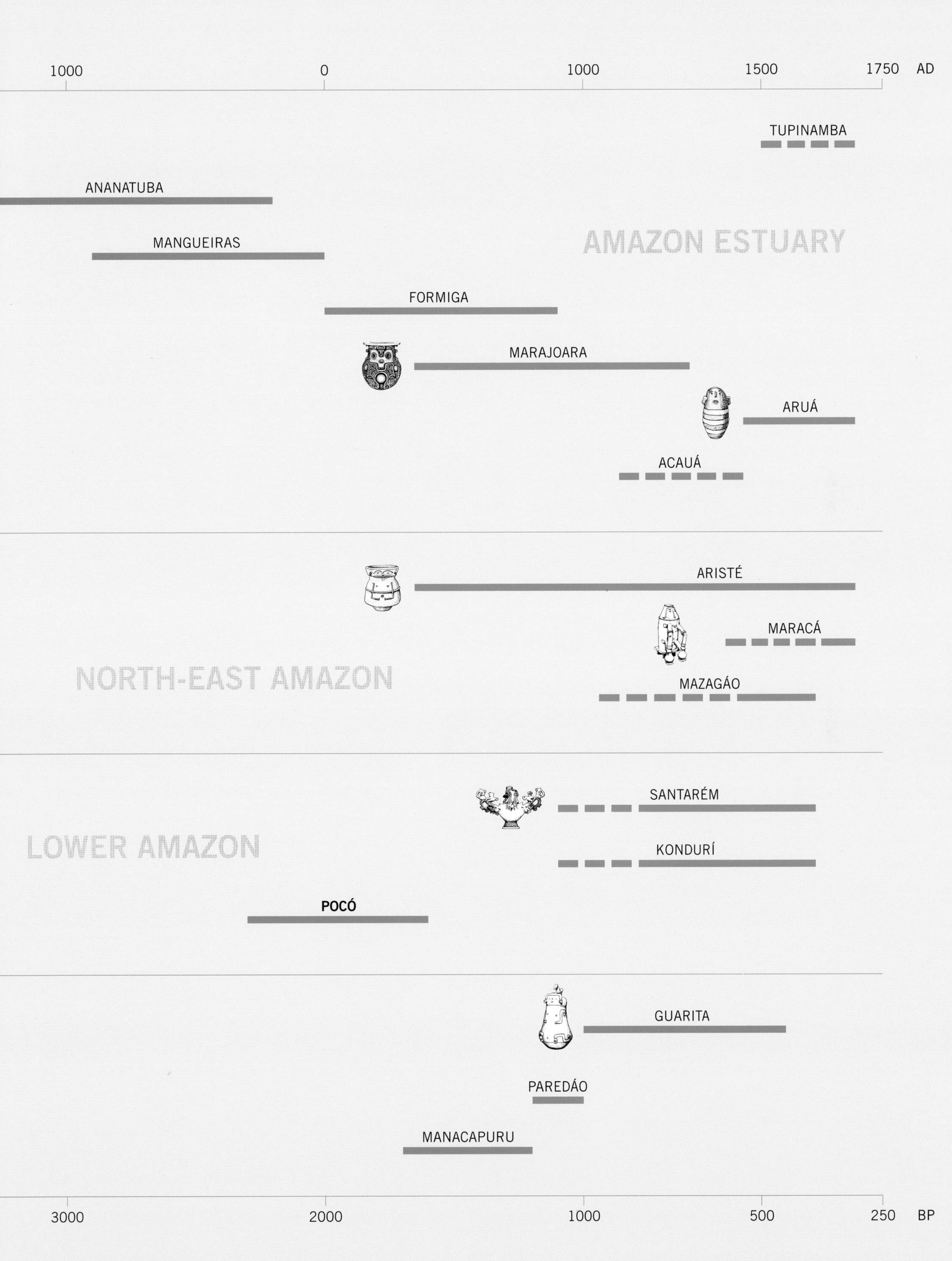

1000
0
1000
1500
1750
AD
TUPINAMBA
ANANATUBA
MANGUEIRAS
AMAZON ESTUARY
FORMIGA
MARAJOARA
ARUÁ
ACAUÁ
ARISTÉ
MARACÁ
NORTH-EAST AMAZON
MAZAGÁO
SANTARÉM
LOWER AMAZON
KONDURÍ
POCÓ
GUARITA
PAREDÁO
MANACAPURU
3000
2000
1000
500
250
BP

PART I

ECONOMY AND

SUBSISTENCE

1

Foragers of the Amazon

The Last Survivors or the First to Succeed?

GUSTAVO POLITIS

Introduction

The first people to inhabit the Amazon basin were foragers or, as they are also called, hunter-gatherers. These groups practised a range of subsistence activities including hunting (fig. 1.1), fishing, collecting wild fruits, tubers and palm nuts and exploiting other products such as honey, insects and fresh water shells. They were characterized by a close-knit egalitarian social organization based on strong kin ties and shared communal patterns.

1.1 Nukak man pursuing a monkey with blowpipe and darts (see also figs 1.15–16).

Human occupation and adaptation to the Amazon is an area of debate in which models from cultural ecology have played a central role.[1] These models have been shaped by two powerful and complementary ideas that have dominated studies of Amazonian foragers. One is that foragers represent the original populations that were progressively displaced to the inter-fluvial areas, or *terra firme* (see Oliver, this volume), during the Holocene period by riverine horticultural peoples, where they have lived a nomadic lifestyle with a precarious resource base ever since. The second idea is that the tropical rainforest in general, and the Amazon in particular, is so hostile and lacking in certain basic nutritional components that human occupation was conditional upon and only occurred after the domestication of some key plant species.[2]

These ideas have strongly influenced much of our thinking about both past and present-day foragers. Typically it is inferred that Amazonian foragers were circumscribed by the advance of other more organized indigenous societies (principally riverine horticulturists) or by Western colonists (at first Europeans, and subsequently *criollos*) towards the interior of the rainforest. They are then supposed to have lived in this apparently hostile environment – one imposed upon them rather than chosen by them – where living conditions are demanding and procuring sufficient daily sustenance is a hazardous enterprise. The idea that the tropical forest environment imposes inherent limitation on the poten-

tial for cultural development of the Amazon dominated agendas between the early 1950s[3] and the late 1980s. These views continue to pervade forager studies. Nonetheless, our survey of present-day foragers can challenge this view if we are prepared to look at them through a wider lens than that provided by ecological functionalism.

An alternative perspective presented here addresses the possibility that Amazonian foragers live in their environment of choice as a result of their historical and evolutionary trajectory. It also recognizes that foragers have played an active part in the construction of the landscapes that they currently occupy and have occupied for many millennia. Throughout their history Amazonian foragers have, of course, continuously interacted with other groups and have been subject to a variety of pressures such as competition for land and resources, slavery, social pressure and warfare. However, there is no reason to assume that these interactions were substantially different to those that took place between other indigenous groups (horticulturists and fisher folk, for example), nor that the result was always unfavourable to the foragers.

In order to understand some aspects of the life of Amazonian foragers in the past and present I will discuss ethnographic and ethno-archaeological information on the Makú of the north-west Amazon, who are generally considered to be 'typical' foragers. My discussion will focus on the Nukak, a Makú group with whom I carried out ethno-archaeological fieldwork for a total of approximately six months over several field seasons between 1990 and 1996.[4] The Nukak currently inhabit the inter-fluvial area between the Guaviare and Inirida rivers in the Colombian Amazon. I will examine how these present-day foragers can help in the study of past foragers, elucidating such aspects as their patterns of use and subtle transformation of the rainforest, as well as how their cosmologies mediate and influence the way they exploit a range of natural resources.

Apart from the environmental models, there is also an essentially European, non-materialist trend in anthropological studies of Amazonian indigenous people, whose leading exponent is Claude Lévi-Strauss.[5] This school emphasizes 'the cognitive and symbolic value of the material dimensions of social life studied by cultural ecologists from an adaptive viewpoint'.[6] Its supporters have endeavoured to understand the cosmology and mythic structures of Amazon societies by employing an analytical approach in which adaptation is not considered to be a priority. According to these studies, Amazonian cultures were not shaped by their environment, since neither the climate nor the natural habitat was the driving force for change.

This integrated approach has been developed by the noted Colombian anthropologist Gerardo Reichel-Dolmatoff. The impact of his thinking on archaeology has been significant,[7] although not especially on the interpretation of Amazonian foragers.[8] Reichel-Dolmatoff focuses on the study of Amazonian cosmology and myth, and proposes that they represent a collection of ecological principles in which a system of social and economic norms with a high adaptive value was codified.[9]

These trends have been reflected in the way the study of taboos or food restrictions among Amazon indigenous peoples has been developed. Such restrictions are central to the analysis of forager populations, both present and past. For some authors[10] the food restrictions found among Amazonian groups are merely the result of a sophisticated management of faunal resources. This view gained greater currency when it was hypothesized that food taboos among neo-tropical groups might indicate – at least partially – an adaptive adjustment to the availability of game, and that in some way this represented 'longer term' planning and foresight and a way of preserving scarce resources.[11] From this perspective the food taboos are merely an expression of the real reason for such restrictions: the appropriate management of game to allow for sustainable exploitation over the longer term.

For other researchers the reasons for the food taboos must be sought in the ideological realm at the heart of Amazonian cosmology, which is based on certain principles that differentiate it in fundamental ways from Western thought.[12] In this view human beings are not placed on a higher scale in the natural order than other creatures, nor do humans represent the absolute pinnacle of a pyramid of complexity; rather, they are intimately linked with all the other components that make up the world: animals, plants, rocks and the diverse natural elements. Human beings and animals are closely related by analogy as well as by ancestral and spiritual essences due to the fact that both belong to a single cosmic society whose interaction is regulated by the same rules that govern relations between human beings.[13] Every animal or plant has a spirit or 'master' who must be addressed and negotiated with by means of ritual complexes in order to be of use. Every Amazonian indigenous person knows a series of formulas or daily rites that allow them to hunt an animal or gather fruit without breaking the natural and supernatural order or confronting the dangerous spirits who control the world. In this context the culture-nature or natural-supernatural dichotomy has no meaning, since human beings are inseparably amalgamated with nature and the supernatural. From this perspective the alimentary prohibitions on some species in the Amazon, especially animals, are seen as a set of coherent cultural practices derived from a body of beliefs in which animals and their spirits are central elements. Consequently, taboos and restrictions are necessary prescriptions that enable the 'negotiation' of daily existence with the 'masters' of animals and plants, so that the approval of these powerful spirits can be secured to use natural resources.

Whatever their origin and cause, food taboos in the Amazon have a significant effect on the manner in which the Amazon indigenous groups utilize forest resources. Such restrictions have impinged upon a wide range of fauna and flora in subtle and varied ways over a long period of time. In the short term this behaviour may not have appeared to have had a significant impact on animal populations, as it would merely have caused temporary changes in the density of certain species. However, its cumulative influence in the long term must have been greater and could, in some fashion, have affected the structure of animal, and especially mammal, populations in the Amazon.

It has been widely accepted for some time that human food procuring behaviour alters local flora.[14] However, whether the floral structure of this biome was significantly altered by foragers and how this process may have operated have yet to be properly assessed. From the perspective of historical ecology,[15] it has been shown how Amazonian societies (principally horticulturists) have significantly modified some components of the rainforest. In the Colombian Amazon, for example, it has been observed that at least 30 per cent of geological samples of late quaternary sediments show traces of 'anthrosoils'.[16] These soils are also known as *terra preta* or *terras pretas de índios* and are the result of significant human modifications of the rainforest, mostly, but not exclusively, due to slash-and-burn horticultural practices (see Petersen *et al.* and Oliver, this volume).[17] Here I will attempt to demonstrate – using the Nukak and other Makú groups as a case study – that mobility within the rainforest and the use that groups make of plant resources modifies, in a subtle yet sustained way, the distribution of particular plants, and especially those used for food. This progressively increases the productivity of an area through the concentration of edible species, in a continuous process known as resource patch generation.

In the following sections I will examine these inadequately discussed aspects of the archaeology of foragers. I will argue that the way in which these groups played a role in constructing important elements in the environment they inhabit is derived from a combination of residential mobility and the gathering of forest fruits. I will also discuss how cosmology, which in its operative dimension manifests itself in food taboos on animals, has influenced the ways in which Amazonian groups have exploited the faunal communities of the rainforest. Of course, these two aspects do not exhaust the many cultural practices employed by Amazon foragers to modify their environment. As our understanding of these societies improves, we will undoubtedly be better able to evaluate their influence on the immense – but not virgin – Amazonian tropical rainforest.

The Makú: the 'typical' Amazonian foragers

There are several present-day groups in the Amazon basin and elsewhere in the lowland tropics who maintain, or until recently maintained, a hunting and gathering way of life. Some are from the Tupi-Guarani language family, such as the Héta,[18] Guajá[19] and Sirionó.[20] It has been proposed that they are the product of a process of 'regression', having had in the past an economy with a greater reliance on horticulture which they subsequently abandoned due to the impact of Western colonization.[21] The 'horticultural past' of these groups does not diminish their potential use for understanding the forager way of life. But it does have a simple yet profound implication: namely that among South American foragers the adoption of horticultural practices is reversible and the incorporation of cultivated plants into their diet is not a linear process that once embarked upon cannot be abandoned. These examples demonstrate that, under specific conditions that make it difficult to subsist with a large horticultural component, indigenous groups can return to a foraging way of life, or significantly increase hunting and gathering to ensure their survival.

The foragers that inhabit the north-west Amazon have been grouped under the generic term Makú, a name that came to have a pejorative meaning.[22] The word spread in the ethnographic literature following the work of Koch-Grünberg (1906, 1909), who recognized the existence of several of these groups between the Negro, Tiquié-Uaupés and Japurá rivers. Later on, Rivet and Tastevin (1920) examined Koch-Grünberg's work and arrived at the conclusion that all the languages of the groups generically denominated Makú had a common origin in a single mother tongue. As such, they proposed the existence of the Makú-Puinave linguistic family, which not only included the groups mentioned, but some riverine horticulturist-fisher folk as well.

There are currently six recognized ethnic/linguistic Makú groups distributed geographically between Brazil and Colombia,[23] principally on the eastern side of the Negro river between the Guaviare and Caquetá-Japurá rivers (fig. 1.2). The six groups are: the Hupdu, Yuhup, Dow, Nadob, Kawka or Bará, and Nukak. Some of them have been relatively well studied, and there are published monographs available on the

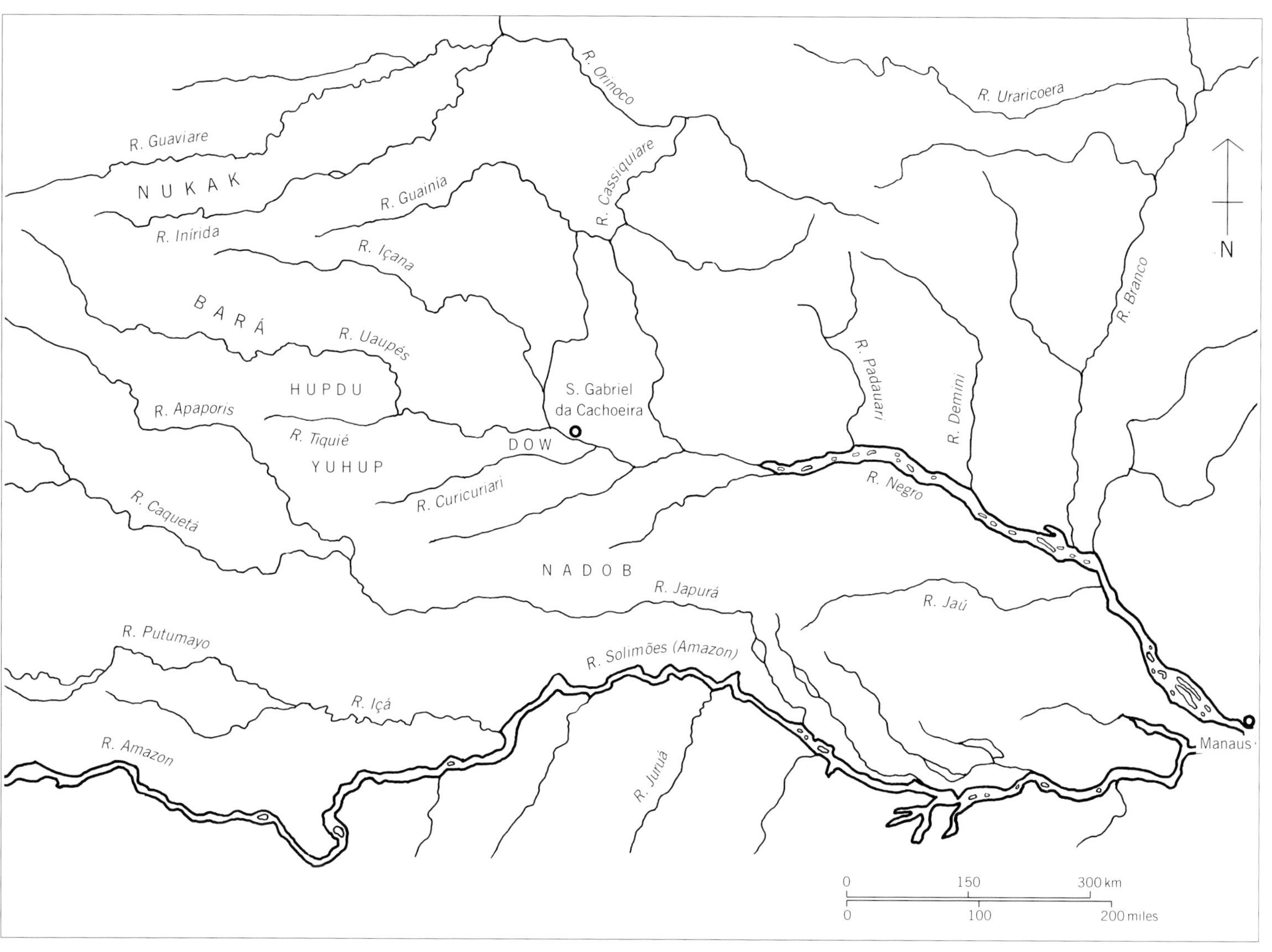

1.2 Distribution of Maku groups in north-west Amazonia.

Hupdu,[24] Yuhup,[25] Bará[26] and Nukak.[27] There are fewer scientific references for the other two, with the Nadob being the least well known.[28] The Dow are probably the least numerous and the most strongly affected by contact, as they live in the vicinity of the city of São Gabriel da Cachoeira. A first point to bear in mind when undertaking an anthropological analysis of any of these groups is that the term 'Makú' is itself vague and imprecise. Despite some affinities in their ways of life and language, the term encompasses distinct human groups who have experienced the impact of Western society in variable and significantly different ways.

In fact, by the time they were studied the six known Makú groups had all adopted some horticultural practice. Nonetheless, in the case of the Nukak (the most traditional) this still represented only a small proportion of their annual diet (less than 5 per cent) at the time my fieldwork was carried out. In other cases, such as among the Hupdu and Bará, horticulture contributes significantly to subsistence, and its impact goes beyond diet, with a notable influence on mobility patterns. The Bará and Hupdu are considered foragers because it is known that up to several generations ago their subsistence was almost exclusively based on the hunting and gathering of wild products, rather than being in this condition at the time they were studied (the Bará in

1968–70 and the Hupdu in 1974–6). Nonetheless, they have been portrayed as 'pure hunter-gatherers' on numerous occasions. For example, Sponsel (referring to the work of Silverwood-Cope) stated that the Makú 'subsist exclusively by foraging without recourse to agriculture',[29] in spite of the fact that a single Bará family consumes on average 100 kilos of manioc weekly, which they harvest from their own gardens where they also cultivate other domesticated species.[30] Similarly, the Hupdu spend some six months in their residential base during which time 'carbohydrate [is the] base of the diet, more than 80% of which is derived from manioc'.[31] The Yuhup were also in a similar state when they were studied by Pozzobon (1992).

The Nukak experienced regular contact with Western society later than the other Makú groups.[32] In the early 1980s the New Tribes missionaries made contact with several bands from the east of the territory. At the end of this decade there was more frequent contact with the colonists who were entering the area, and around this time the anthropological studies also began. During my fieldwork the Nukak occupied a territory of approximately 10,000 sq. km, and the population was estimated at between 400 and 500 people. Nukak are organized in autonomous exogamous bands composed of several families (usually no more than five), with between twelve and forty-four individuals per band. Most co-resident groups consist of between twenty and thirty individuals. Such bands are part of a larger affiliation group (the *munu*) and share adjoining territories within which larger group re-organizations, marriages, social visits and rituals take place.[33] At least six of these large affiliation groups have so far been recognized. Altogether, lack of hierarchical organization, strong solidarity patterns and high residential mobility are among the outstanding characteristics of the Nukak people.

1.3 Nukak summer residential camp.

Mobility and environment

One line of enquiry into how foragers modify the environment is to examine their mobility patterns. The population alters the natural distributions of flora and fauna when they relocate to other parts of their territory. Mobility patterns are substantially different between the various Makú groups. One of the principle causes is probably the different degree of contact and change among each group. Moreover, the incorporation of the various components of agricultural subsistence generally results in prolonged stays near gardens. In this sense the Nukak are the most mobile, and the Dow move their residences least frequently.

As with other forager populations,[34] the mobility of the Nukak revolves around two axes, one residential and the other logistical. We understand 'residential mobility' to mean the relocation from one dwelling site to another, which leads to the construction and occupation of a new camp. 'Logistical mobility', in turn, implies that one or several individuals travel away from the residential site to carry out specific tasks (obtain resources, gather information, conduct ritual activities, etc.), but the residential base camp remains unchanged. Logistical mobility can occur on a daily basis, when individuals leave and return to the residential base within the same day, or it can be more complex and prolonged, in which case it may involve the construction of transitory camps for one or several nights' use.

Analysis of the residential mobility of the Nukak is based on two variables: distance and frequency. I estimate that the average distance between camps is 7.72 km and the duration of occupation of each camp is 3.3 days. However, it is not the same all year

round because there is a difference between the rainy season (from April to the middle of November) and the dry season (fig. 1.3).[35] I have also assessed the daily logistical mobility for both seasons. In general the minimum distance travelled to procure resources is difficult to estimate, as the Nukak also collect both wild and domesticated vegetable products, and hunt, fish and gather insects on the outskirts of the camps. They move a maximum distance of approximately 9 km from the residential camp. The resource procurement parties are generally made up of adult and adolescent men. Among their principal objectives are hunting, the gathering of honey and other honeycomb products, fishing, and the securing of plant materials for the manufacture of tools. Women may occasionally take part in these trips, but generally their contribution to subsistence centres on the collecting of wild fruit and occasionally domesticated plants from gardens in the vicinity of the camps. In short, the average daily logistical mobility (moving further than 1 km from the camp) is 8.41 km[36] and the time spent on the trips is variable, with a ten-hour maximum. They take place almost exclusively during the day and only rarely will the party return to camp after nightfall. No significant differences have been observed between the two seasons with reference to this type of mobility.[37]

The other type of logistical mobility is far less frequent due to the fact that it implies spending one or several nights away from the residential camp (which remains in continuous occupation by part of the band). Within this category are included the visits to the Blowpipe Hills to procure the canes that grow in this rocky formation for use as blowpipes. The parties are made up of several men who bring back canes for themselves and possibly for some relatives. Particular circumstances (for example, illness or fights) may force some of the men to spend the night in a transitory camp, although this happens rarely.

The mobility pattern of the Nukak in the 1990s (and possibly before this as well) was considerably different from the other Makú. During Reid's (1974–6) study of the Hupdu, residential mobility was limited and groups remained in the same camp between two and six years. Two types of logistical mobility were observed. One occurred almost daily: 'they go out from their settlements to distances of up to three hours' walk away, returning from a different route'.[38] In order not to exhaust the hunting areas close to the camp it was important that the Hupdu only returned to the same area after two weeks had passed. The other type of logistical mobility occurred when the hunting areas were more than half a day's distance away, in which case several or all the Hupdu families who lived in the same camp moved into the forest to hunt, fish and gather fruit.[39] On average, the families made this trip once a month, and its duration varied between two and thirty days. During these foraging trips the Hupdu constructed small camps of lean-to shelters (similar to the residential camps of the Nukak) which they occupied for three to five days. These relocations were fairly frequent and allowed the Hupdu to exploit distant and diverse areas. Reid calculated that each family spent around 70 days per year in the rainforest on these foraging trips, and that mature men and adolescents may have spent as many as 100 days engaged in these activities.

The Bará appear to have a similar mobility pattern to that of the Hupdu, although we have fewer details. Silverwood-Cope estimated that the Hupdu in the area of the tributaries of the Macú-Paraná 'live only a few years – sometimes months – in each village'.[40] Furthermore, based on the account of a forty to forty-five-year-old adult, he calculated that this individual had moved semi-permanent residences approximately every five years. Obviously, the Bará spend an indeterminate period of the year away from their camps on foraging trips, during which time they also construct lean-to dwellings similar to the Nukak camps. Silverwood-Cope did not specify the time the Bará spend in the rainforest hunting and gathering.

According to the data recorded for them, the Yuhup and Nadob pattern would appear to be closer to that of the Bará and Hupdu than the Nukak. In other words,

1.4 A woman weaving in a hammock in a winter residential camp.

they spend a large part of their time in residential camps, only entering the forest on logistical trips (which women also participate in) and constructing temporary camps that they live in for a few days at a time.[41]

Transforming the forest

As we have seen, the high residential mobility of the Nukak is one of their most striking characteristics. Their residential mobility values are among the highest in the world. The Hupdu also have a fairly high logistical mobility, creating many camps that are successively abandoned in the forest. The situation is probably the same among the Bará and Yuhup. The combination of movement and the consequent selective exploitation of plant and animal resources undoubtedly has a significant effect on the structure of those parts of the tropical rainforest occupied by hunters and gatherers, especially if we bear in mind that this process, or similar processes, have been occurring continuously over a period of thousands of years. A detailed look at the type of alteration of the forest caused by the Nukak will allow a better understanding of some of the modifications that may have been generated by tropical rainforest foragers in the past.

There are 113 recorded plant species utilized by the Nukak (substantially more than is recorded for the other Makú).[42] The best-represented family are palms (Arecaceae); its 15 species and diverse categories of use (for food, utensils, construction and fuel) confirm its widespread employment and general importance to indigenous Amazonian communities (fig. 1.4).[43] The Moraceae family follows, with 10 species used for food, making it the group with the greatest nutritional potential. Finally,

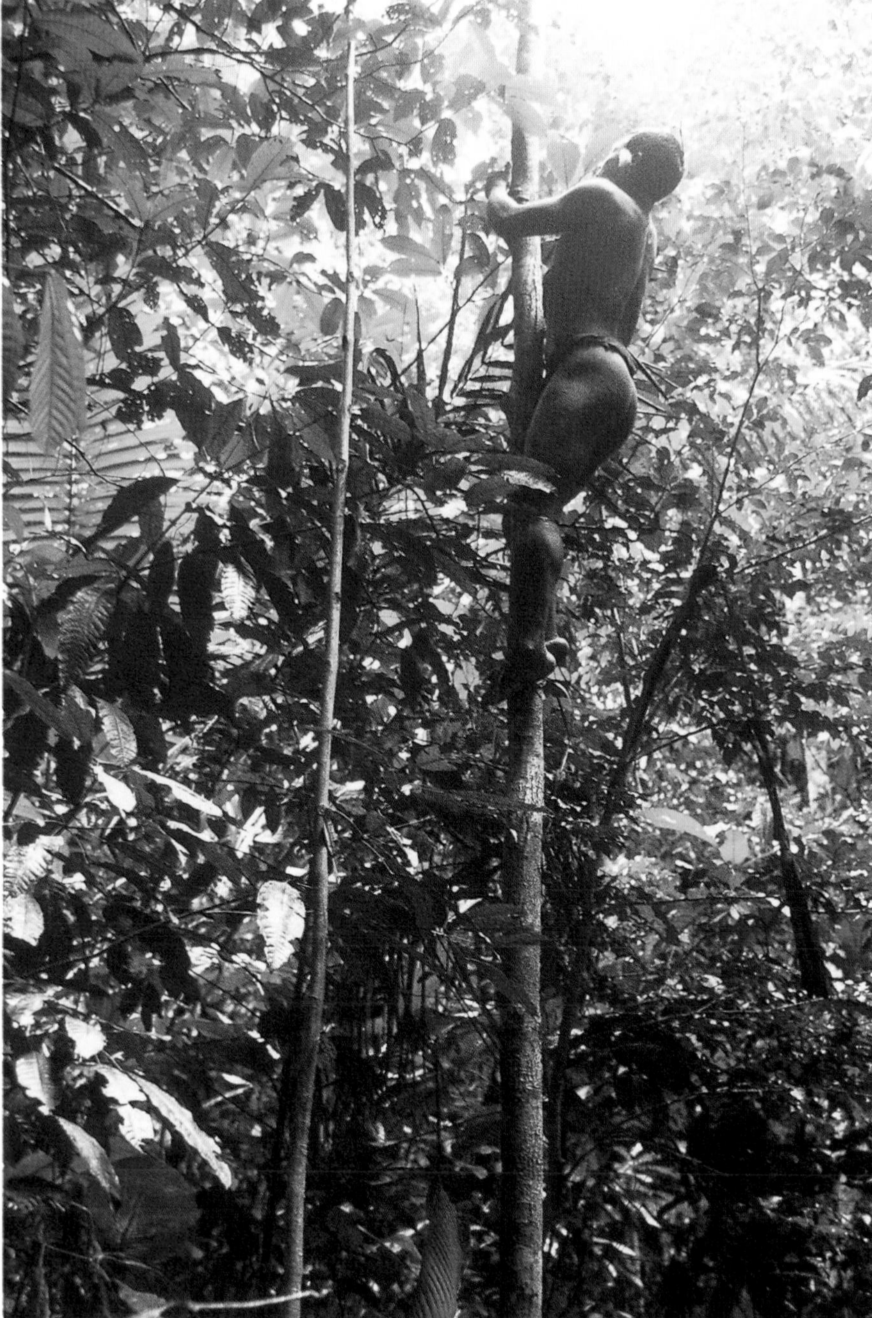

LEFT **1.5 A Nukak man climbing up a palm to gather fruit.**

RIGHT ABOVE **1.6 A Nukak woman processing plantain seeds (*Phenakospermum guyanense*).**

RIGHT BELOW **1.7 A Nukak woman wrapping plantain flour in leaves prior to boiling.**

the Burseraceae family consists of 5 species, the majority used for food (fig. 1.5).[44]

Of the 113 recorded species, 90 are uncultivated rainforest species (figs 1.6–7). Among the 23 species cultivated by the Nukak in their small gardens, the majority correspond to plants recently incorporated into their horticultural practices as a result of their relationship with the missionaries and colonists. The extent of these practices among the Nukak prior to recent contact has yet to be explored in any depth. Some authors suggest that the Nukak possessed small-scale, traditional horticulture that was replaced over time by introduced species.[45]

In several previous works I and other colleagues have argued that the Nukak are active agents in the concentration of useful species, due to the quantity of seeds that

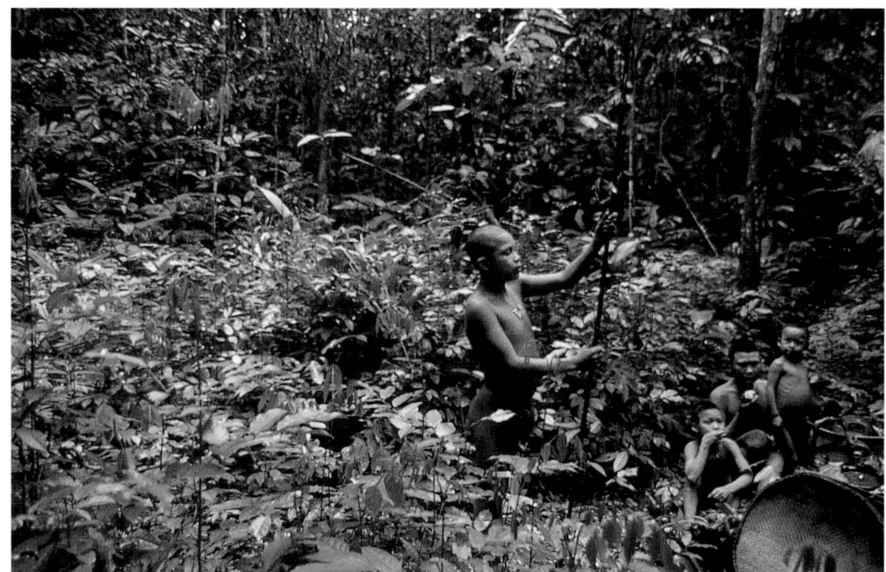

LEFT 1.8 A mass of edible plants growing from the seeds left on the site of an abandoned camp. Although such sites are rarely reoccupied, they may be revisited regularly to gather ripe seeds and fruit in season.

BELOW 1.9 Different stages of processing *seje* (*Oenocarpus bataua*) fruits at a residential camp. The fruit is prepared by a combination of pounding and boiling. Discarded seeds will germinate after a site has been abandoned.

1.10 Winter residential camp just after abandonment. Abundant food debris and some discarded objects can be seen on the ground.

they leave behind on abandoning a residential camp.[46] It has been suggested that the large concentrations of trees such as *seje*, plantain, *guaná*, *juansoco* and *juiú* could be a consequence of the activities of the Nukak. As such, the use of the products of the rainforest and knowledge of their management could result in the formation of patches dominated by species that are intensively used by the Nukak, principally as food.

This process has been interpreted as the unintentional result of the abandonment of camps whose floors were carpeted with the seeds of edible species (fig. 1.8). As camps are almost never reused, many of these seeds germinate and, due to their sheer numbers, have a greater competitive advantage over other seeds. Also, because the canopy remains intact, the area of the abandoned camp is not covered by other strong competitors for sunlight, such as vines, which otherwise would create a tangled forest. At the same time abundant organic waste collects on the camp floors and in the areas of refuse accumulation, thereby contributing to the fertilization of the inhabited spaces. This provides an additional germination advantage for the seeds discarded in these areas. Moreover, in the case of *seje*, which has extremely hard seeds, the processing of the fruit – the removal of the epicarp and the mesocarp – is a mechanical action that facilitates germination (fig. 1.9).[47] The whole process implies that the natural distribution of a particular species is affected and it gradually

1.11 Nukak people eating honey from a beehive on a recently felled palm tree.

becomes even more concentrated in certain sectors of the rainforest.[48] The frequent relocation of the residential camps therefore produces various derived food sources in the form of 'wild orchards', which the Nukak frequent in their mobility cycles. In other words, the Nukak leave a resource patch behind them when they abandon and relocate camp. They are 'creating' a patch after an occupation/abandonment sequence, rather than merely locating the camp in a patch of concentrated, useful trees (fig. 1.10).

The impact of the transformation is difficult to estimate, but on the basis of information from the surface area occupied by the residential camps one can get an approximate idea of the magnitude of the total area affected. Based on the camp surface data,[49] and bearing in mind that a band constructs and occupies around seventy or eighty camps a year, the area altered through this process can be estimated at as much as 6,400 sq. metres annually per band. The zones peripheral to the camp (where seeds are also discarded) must also be taken into account, as well as the multiple modifications that are produced by moving about in the forest.

However, even though the high concentration of some species may be the result of residential and logistical mobility, not all concentrations of trees, especially wild palms, should necessarily be attributed to human agency. For example, there are species that for intrinsic reproductive strategies form dense populations, as is the case with the tacaynut (*Caryodendron orinocense*). Others, such as plantain, develop in areas of unstable soils. These species have been observed in large concentrations crowning the low ridges that characterize a good part of the physiography of Nukak territory. *Muriti* or *moriche* (*Mauritia flexuosa*) is another species that forms clusters and is naturally abundant in poorly drained areas.[50]

A further Nukak forest management strategy is noticeable along the relocation routes the groups take. It is related to clearing during the gathering of the fruit of some palms and fruit trees, such as *seje* and *juansoco*, which stimulates the development of seedlings of these species. The Nukak also fell large branches of various tree species, such as cowtree (*Brosimum utile*) and *guaná*, thereby inducing greater productivity through what could be considered a vigorous pruning (fig. 1.11). Such practices could potentially change a forest originally characterized by a great diversity but low density of species into one with a high density of species utilized by the Nukak, causing the homogenization of flora along relocation routes.[51]

Although there are no other parallel studies yet undertaken in such detail for other groups of Amazonian foragers, we can surmise that similar processes were operative. For example, Reid mentions that during his journeys through Hupdu territory, 'their paths often passed through patches of secondary forest, in various stages of regrowth from old settlement and garden sites'.[52] Furthermore, Reid states that he could identify these patches of secondary forest up to forty years after their creation. For the Bará, who consider more than 54 wild species edible (although they consume far fewer), the easiest way of reaching fruit is to fell the tree. They explain that 'there are so many young trees that will later bear fruit that the natural resources will never be exhausted'.[53] Considering this information on the gathering of fruit by the Hupdu and Bará, as well as their mobility (especially logistical), it is probable that these groups are also creating resource patches and modifying the natural density of plant species in ways similar to those described here for the Nukak.

There are further examples from other areas of the Amazon of the distribution of certain wild species being interpreted as a consequence of human activity, such as the way in which liana vine, bamboo, Brazil nut, *babaçu* and several other palms appear in clusters.[54] In general, the groups involved are horticulturists who also manipulate useful wild species, concentrating them in certain sectors of the landscape and thereby increasing their productivity.[55] Although the archaeological evidence is meagre with reference to this phenomenon, some abnormal concentrations of plants have been noted and attributed to human activity.[56] For example, sites assigned to the Mabaruma and Koriabo phases in coastal Guyana are associated with dense stands of

1.12 Dam made of palm leaves to create a pool of still water for barbasco fishing. Barbasco (*Lonchocarpus* sp.) is a fruit that acts as a powerful fish poison.

large bamboo.[57] Concentrations of the *babaçu* (*Orbignya phalerata*), *pupunha* or *chonta* (*Bactris gasipae*), and *tucumã* (*Astrocaryum aculeatum*) palms occur at archaeological sites along the Jamarí river and the adjacent upper Madeira. The seeds of these species have been found in habitation refuse, which indicates that they have been exploited ever since the beginning of the sites' occupation, *c.*2500 BP.[58]

Here I have demonstrated that the Nukak are able to obtain the basic components of their diet (including carbohydrates and proteins) in adequate quantities from the undomesticated animals and plants of the Amazon.[59] Furthermore, the sequence of occupation and subsequent abandonment described above concentrates wild species of high nutritional value such as *seje* (*Oenocarpus bataua*) and plantain. Finally, it is important to recognize that the Nukak and other Amazonian foragers annually consume significant quantities of many other resources, such as large numbers of fish (figs 1.12–13), honey and other honeycomb products, beetle larvae (*mojojoi*), fresh water crabs, ants, etc., which constitute an important part of their diet.[60] As a consequence, horticultural practices that present-day foragers have adopted are, I would suggest, best understood as the result of opportunities presented by historical processes and population dynamics, and not simply as an indispensable necessity that they are obliged to follow in order to maintain adequate nutritional levels and sustain viable populations in the Amazonian tropical rainforest.

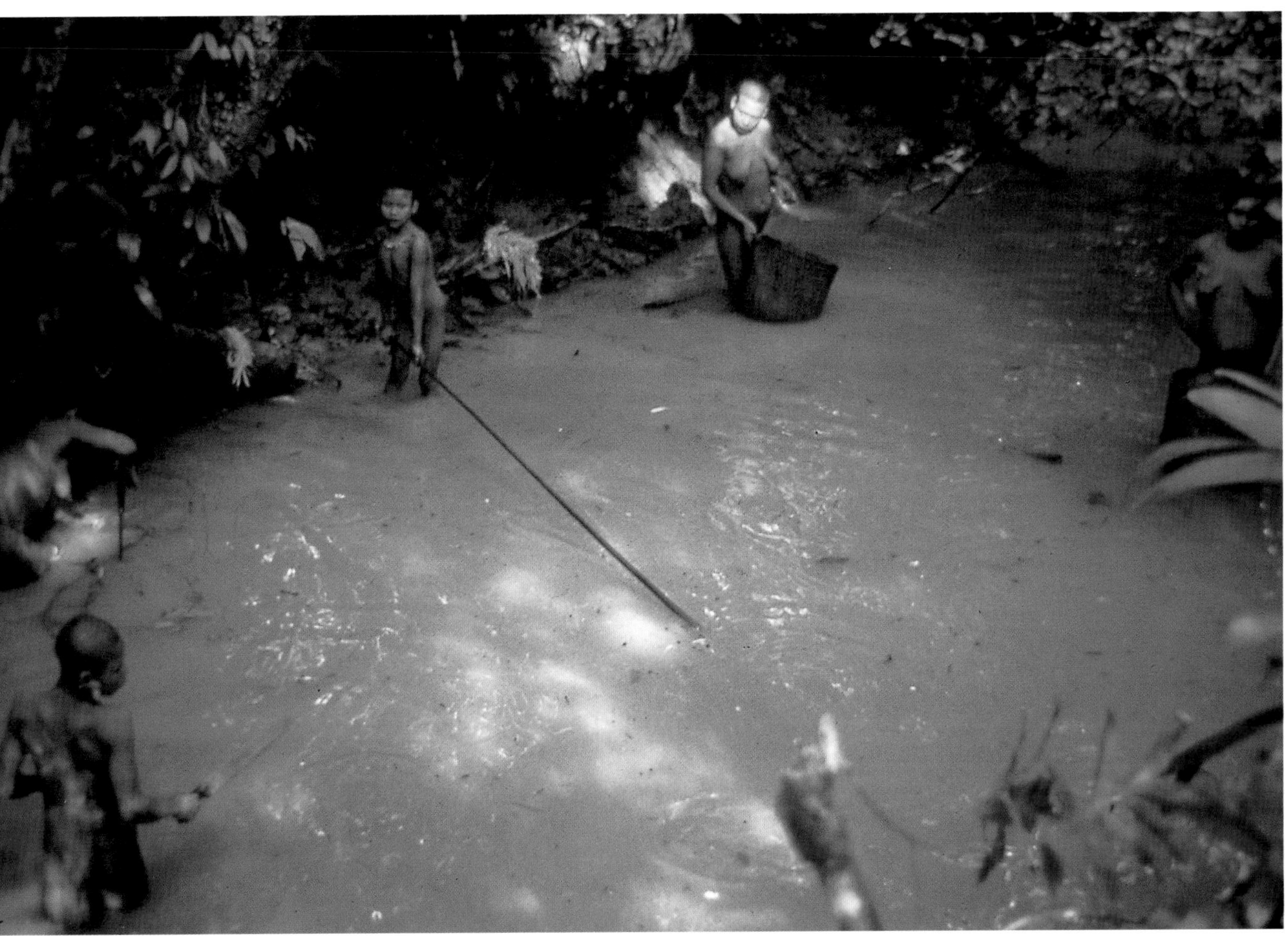

1.13 Nukak women fishing during the dry season in the pond waters of a creek that has been poisoned by immersing a basket of barbasco fruits in the water.

Selective hunting

In Nukak territory there are dozens of edible mammal and bird species, an extremely wide variety of fish and an enormous number of insects that offer nutritional options. However, only some of these are actually consumed by the Nukak. The reasons for this selective usage are related to their cosmology and the way in which they interact with the natural and supernatural worlds.

The hunting of wild animals plays an important role in Nukak life, due to both the economic advantages and the status of hunting as a means of communication and articulation with the supernatural world. The most sought-after game are monkeys (*Cebus apella, Lagothrix lagotricha, Alouatta seniculus*, etc.), which are relatively abundant in the rainforest (figs 1.1 and 1.14–16). Almost daily a Nukak hunter will arrive

1.14 A Nukak man with blowpipe and darts during a hunting trip.

at camp with one or more small monkeys (maximum weight 10 kilos), which are butchered and cooked by his wife. Although parts of the kill are usually shared with the other families in the band, the animal's head always remains in the pot of the hunter's family. However, the hunter never actually consumes the head of his kill, because if he does he will lose his good aim. This is because the power and essence of an animal is concentrated in its head. To eat it, therefore, would be a grave error – a challenge to the dead animal's spirit that would be paid for by the inevitable failure of future hunts.

Other game that the Nukak hunt includes certain species of birds, agouti (*Dasyprocta* sp.), caymans (*Caiman sclerops*) and peccaries (*Tayassu tajacu* and *Tayassu peccari*). The last are relatively important to their diet, especially the white-lipped peccary, a mammal that weighs up to 60 kilos and travels in groups of several dozen individuals. It is hunted with a spear, and to this end trips are organized in which all the men of the band take part (fig. 1.17). As soon as one or more animals are killed they are butchered in a dry place close to the kill site, and only the head and some of the entrails are discarded. The rest of the animal is carried back to the camp, where a grill is set up on the outskirts to smoke the kill. The women and children watch from the camp, as they are prohibited from eating the meat of the peccary. This clearly explains why the head of the peccary is left at the butchering site: it would make little sense to bring it back to the camp, as the hunters may not eat it and it is taboo for the women and children.

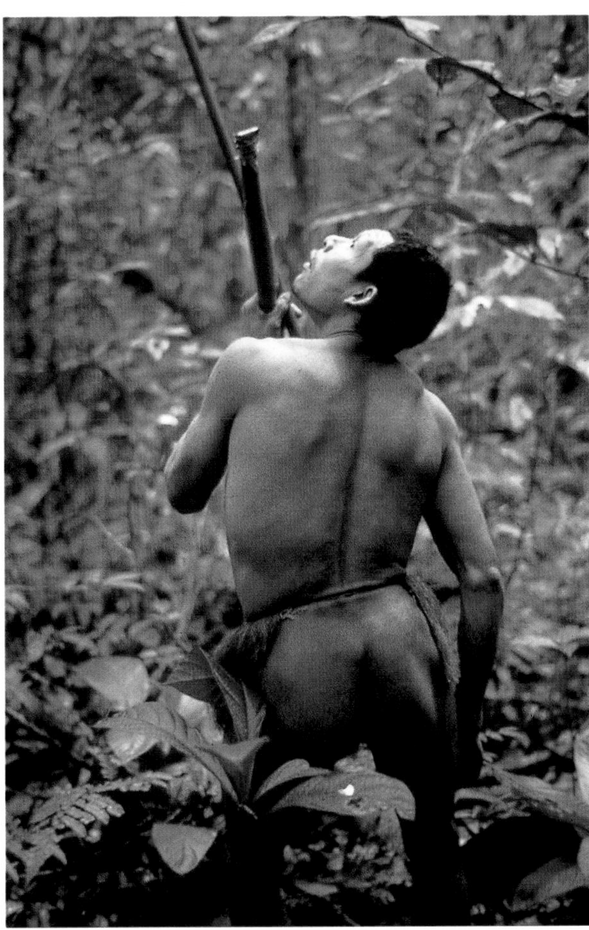

ABOVE 1.15 A Nukak man carefully watching his prey in the trees and loading his blowpipe with a dart.

ABOVE RIGHT 1.16 A Nukak man at the moment of blowing a dart tipped with poison at a monkey.

There are also restrictions on other animals, inasmuch as their flesh is regarded as somehow 'impure'; certain kinds of duck, the red *pava* (*Penelope purpurascens*), capybara (*Hydrochoerus hydrocaeris*) and sloth (*Bradipus tridactilus*) are all edible from a Western perspective, but for Nukak their consumption would cause discomfort, illness or perhaps even death. Some species of fish, duck, *pavas*, coatimundi, etc. appear to have a status as 'anti-food', since they may cause wasting.[61] These animals produce their thinning effect only on the members of certain bands, on particular people or during certain periods of life (for example, during pregnancy or sickness).

There are several animals that the Nukak neither hunt nor eat: the jaguar (*Pantera onça*), deer (*Mazama* sp.) and the tapir (*Tapirus terrestris*). To the Nukak they are not actually animals. Rather, they consider them to be powerful ancestral spirits that don the skins of these animals in order to move about freely in the forest. These beings are not the representation of superior spirits. Rather, they *are* the actual spirits in the guise of animals, and they live out their existence in the forest habitat. The Nukak, in trying to explain the status of these animals in our terms, state that 'they are like people', the same phrase that other indigenous Amazonians use to indicate the status of powerful animal-spirits.[62]

To understand the reverence with which these animals are regarded, it is necessary to comprehend Nukak cosmology with its roots in the Amazonian world. For them the universe is divided into three superimposed planes. The highest level is where the sun and moon live, and where there is also an abundance of all types of food including cultivated plants. All the principal spirits of Nukak who have died live on this level. However, every person has three spirits, and the other two go to different places. The second spirit, *yorehat* (roughly translatable as 'clarity'), travels to an underground place in the middle level where 'the house of the tapir' is found. The tapir occupies a central position on this level. The deer and jaguar live there too; they are in reality the *yorehat* souls of ancestors who have taken this form. This underground place is only a few metres from the surface of the earth and the animals go out at night to the *salados* (pools of salty water that animals visit in order to lap up the salt). Hence, the tracks of deer, jaguar and tapir that abound on the banks of the *salados* are irrefutable proof to the Nukak that these pools are indeed places that are connected to the underground, where the animal-spirits emerge. The third spirit that everyone possesses is the *nemep* (akin to 'darkness', and with a similar meaning among the Bará), and while a person is alive this spirit manifests itself as their shadow. When a Nukak dies, the *nemep* remains on the surface in the middle world where it lives in sacred trees, going out at night to cause mischief. The last world is the 'world of below', a deep and far-off plane where powerful spirits dwell. Only exceptionally strong people are able to 'travel' there in dreams, but they always run the risk that their own soul will remain in this realm, trapped for eternity.

This brief review of Nukak cosmology exemplifies how beliefs about the universe have direct consequences on which animals are hunted and who eats them. It demonstrates the important point that the exploitation of fauna by foragers is strongly mediated by cosmology, in such a way that factors like distribution, density and accessibility to animal populations do not correlate directly with the potential nutritional value of the animals as game. In other words, food taboos operate selectively on human predation and this, in turn, has implications for the long co-evolutionary history of human and animal populations in Amazonia.

1.17 A Nukak man hardening the point of his wooden spear in the hearth of a lean-to shelter.

How long have these processes been going on?

I have described and explained some of the ways in which foragers today are modifying the rainforest. I have also speculated upon the cumulative impact we might expect these practices to have in the long term. But since when might these, or similar processes, have been taking place? Since when have foragers been subtly yet continuously transforming the Amazon rainforest? A rapid look at the archaeological information on foragers will serve both to evaluate the temporal depth of this process and to challenge the hypothesis that it is impossible for foragers to survive in the rainforest without the contribution of cultivated plants.

To begin with, it must be emphasized that the archaeology of Amazonian foragers is still in its infancy and reliable data are extremely scarce. In general, archaeological research has focused on horticultural groups.[63] In one review paper discussing prehistoric Brazilian foragers it was concluded that 'although Amazonia incorporates more than half of Brazil, data on foragers are too sparse and imprecise to warrant discussion'.[64] In the same vein others have argued that in the Amazon 'there is no preceramic horizon; apparently the original colonists practised a mixed subsistence economy of farming and foraging and/or fishing'.[65] Although it is true that forager sites in the Amazon suffer from relatively low visibility, it is equally true that there have been few research projects focused on locating these kinds of sites. Fortunately, the situation has changed in the past decade and currently several sites are yielding the first signs of evidence of the way of life of past Amazonian foragers.

The Monte Alegre area in the north bank region of the lower Amazon has provided some of the strongest evidence with which to refute the model of the non-viability of pure foragers in the rainforest and support a late Pleistocene (about 10,000 years BP) antiquity for the occupation of the Amazon.[66] The name 'Monte Alegre' is used to denominate the finds from the Caverna da Pedra Pintada, located in the high plains 10 km away from the Amazon river. Thousands of flakes and twenty-four formal tools have been found in the earliest levels at this site. In these lower levels there is also burnt wood in hearths, along with thousands of fruit and carbonized seeds from the tropical rainforest deposited during the occupation of the site. The majority of the species represented still thrive in the remnants of tropical rainforest in neighbouring areas, and include many that present-day foragers consume. The faunal remains are badly preserved, but include bone fragments of rodents, tortoises, turtles, snakes, amphibians and large, unidentified land mammals. Freshwater shells are also plentiful. Fifty-six carbon samples were obtained from wood and carbonized seeds excavated from the deepest levels of the site, giving radiocarbon dates of between *c.*11,200 and 10,000 BP. For Roosevelt and colleagues the arrival of humans at the cave is marked by a group of four dates ranging between 11,145±135 and 10,875±295 BP. They argue that the cave was visited periodically by foragers for more than 1,200 years. During these visits fruit, a wide variety of terrestrial game, and both avian and riverine fauna were eaten, artefacts were manufactured and the walls of the caves were painted.

The main criticisms of this work are directed towards the postulated antiquity of the earliest human occupation. Several authors consider an age of *c.*10,500 BP for the initial occupation of the site more probable.[67] Nonetheless, beyond the chronological precision, it seems reasonably clear that the initial occupation of Monte Alegre by foragers can be placed at the end of the Pleistocene period, at which time the site was surrounded by a tropical rainforest similar to that which currently exists (see discussion about the environmental changes during the late Pleistocene period in Oliver, this volume).

Other authors, whose work is generally less well known or insufficiently published, also indicate that further sectors of the Amazon have been occupied by foragers since at least the beginnings of the Holocene period. A variety of artefacts has been reported from the lower and middle courses of the Jamarí river, a south-bank tributary of the Madeira river (Rondonia state, Brazil).[68] These include large flaked bifaces, end and side scrapers and hammerstones made of chalcedony, quartz, crystalline rocks and basalt. These materials were grouped into two 'preceramic' phases: Itapipoca and Pacatuba, assigned chronologically on the basis of eight C14 dates between *c.*9000 and 5000 BP. The initial human occupation of this zone at the beginning of the Holocene period is said to have occurred 'when climate and biota probably were similar to those at present',[69] in other words, when a tropical rainforest existed in the area similar to that found today.

Further strong evidence comes from the Peña Roja site, on the banks of the Caquetá river in the Colombian Amazon (see also Oliver, this volume).[70] A forager occupation level has been identified and dated to around 9000 BP. The macro-botanical remains found in this level include several plant species, with palms representing 68 per cent of the total. Many of these palms are the same as those the Nukak and other Makú currently exploit: *Oenocarpus bacaba*, *Mauritia flexuosa*, etc. The macro-plant and pollen evidence clearly indicates that a tropical rainforest existed in the middle Caquetá when the initial human occupation occurred at the beginning of the Holocene period.

Other examples could be added to the evidence outlined above for an early occupation of the tropical rainforest, such as the sites in the Orinoco valley assigned to the Atures I period dated to between *c.*9200 and 7000 BP.[71] Also of interest is the appearance of particles of charcoal in a lake core near the mouth of the Amazon dated to 12,868–12,682 cal. BP, which could indicate the arrival of humans in the region.[72] These particles suddenly become especially abundant between 10,893–10,412 cal. BP. All this evidence indicates that in the later Pleistocene and early Holocene periods some parts of the Amazon were occupied by foragers who, like the contemporary Nukak, made intensive use of a variety of undomesticated palms and selectively hunted the mammals that inhabited the region. It seems therefore that the above and other evidence[73] does not lend support to the model that proposes that foragers cannot live in the rainforest for considerable periods without the nutritional complements from domesticated plants, nor does it support the existence of environmental limiting factors in the development of Amazonian forager populations.

Conclusions

If past Amazonian foragers had similar behavioural patterns to present-day foragers, one would expect their impact on the biome over the millennia to have been considerable. In other words, the Amazonian tropical rainforest as we know it is the cumulative result of continuous human activity since the late Pleistocene. Archaeology has shown that the Amazon has been occupied by foragers from at least 10,500 BP and by sedentary village horticulturists from 6,000–5,000 BP (see discussion in Oliver and in Petersen *et al.*, this volume). Present-day Amazonian indigenous groups are themselves conscious of past human activity. They believe that every aspect of the current landscape has been transformed in equal measure by their ancestors, other indigenous groups and the forces of nature and the supernatural.[74] For them the tropical rainforest is something created and passed on by ancestors and spirits since the beginning of the world, a legacy that they are responsible for using wisely.

Here I have presented a substantially different panorama to the opposing view outlined at the beginning of the paper, in which Amazonian foragers are supposed to have found themselves cornered in a hostile environment of scarce resources and in a state of precarious equilibrium. The foragers of the past were, without doubt, builders of their environment. They combined their exceptional zoological, botanical and ecological knowledge with a cosmology that bestowed upon nature a hierarchical position similar and sometimes superior to that of humans. The construction of the landscape was not only a strategy to concentrate resources or increase productivity, but rather it was also a way of negotiating their lives with the 'masters' that controlled nature. It was a means of integrating themselves into a cosmos where human beings must survive daily in a universe full of spirits more powerful than themselves.

Acknowledgements

Julian Rodriguez Pabon, Dairon Cardenas and Gustavo Martinez helped me during fieldwork and also analysed the data collected. The research project among the Nukak was funded by the Wenner-Green Foundation for Anthropological Research (two grants) and by the Instituto Amazonico de Investigaciones Cientificas (SINCHI), Colombia.

NOTES

1 Anthropology has provided us with several models for the interpretation of Amazonian archaeology. Among those that have had the greatest impact are the so-called environmental models of Amazonian socio-cultural evolution, which have a long tradition in the anthropological studies of the region (Steward and Faron 1959; Lathrap 1968a). These environmental models, which have been developed within a cultural ecology framework, have generated abundant, especially quantitative, data with which to approach the study of Amazonian indigenous societies and they have also been useful in explaining some aspects of human adaptation to tropical rainforests. However, they have brought with them a degree of ecological functionalism, which has unfortunately transformed some into prime examples of the mechanical projection of a Western pattern of rationality onto indigenous societies, both past and present.

2 This idea was formalized in the Bailey and Headland model, which is supposed to hold not only for the Amazon but also for all tropical rainforests the world over, and has fomented an active debate (Bailey and Peacock 1988; Bailey *et al.* 1989; Bailey *et al.* 1991; Headland and Bailey 1991; Bailey and Headland 1991). The bases for the model were not initially the same for these two authors. In early works Headland proposed that carbohydrates were the limiting factors, while Bailey and his collaborators also took into consideration fat and other nutrients. They also added temporal depth to the argument about the nutritional deficiencies of the tropical rainforest, emphasizing the absence of archaeological sites that corresponded to the period prior to the presence of horticulture in this biome. After discussing several archaeological examples, the authors conclude that resources in 'pre-agricultural rainforest habitats were probably so poor, variable and dispersed that they could not support viable populations of human foragers' (Bailey *et al.* 1989: 62). The hypothesis was later extended to the point that it was proposed that human beings could not have inhabited such environments until they had developed ways of altering the distribution and abundance of edible plants through the processes of plant domestication and tropical rainforest clearance. Hence, it was argued that usable environments for human populations during a large portion of the history of humanity were more restricted than had previously been considered (Bailey *et al.* 1989). This argument was also supported by Sponsel (1989: 45), who has claimed that in the Amazon foraging and farming are not only complementary but are in fact necessary for viable human populations.

3 Steward 1946–50.

4 Politis 1996a & b, 1999.

5 Lévi-Strauss 1969, 1971, 1973.

6 Viveiros de Castro 1996: 181.

7 Reichel-Dolmatoff 1976a, 1986.

8 See discussion in Gnecco 1995.

9 Reichel-Dolmatoff 1976a.

10 E.g. Kaplan and Hill 1992.

11 Ross 1978: 5, 1980.

12 Lévi-Strauss 1969, Viveiros de Castro 1992, Reichel-Dolmatoff 1986 and Århem 1990, among many others.

13 Århem 1990.

14 Rindos 1984, Harris 1989.

15 Balée 1994, 1998.

16 Pedro Botero and Juan Manuel Herrea, pers. comm.

17 Meggers 1971.

18 Kozák *et al.* 1979.

19 Balée 1994.

20 Holmberg 1969.

21 Clastres 1981; Lathrap 1968a.

22 This is not a self-denomination as none of the indigenous groups call themselves by this name.

23 Pozzobon 1992.

24 Reid 1979.

25 Pozzobon 1983, 1992.

26 Silverwood-Cope 1990.

27 Politis 1996b; Cabrera *et al.* 1999; Mondragón 1991.

28 Münzel 1969-74

29 Sponsel 1986: 73.

30 Silverwood-Cope 1990.

31 Reid 1979: 93.

32 Wirpsa and Mondragón 1988; Reina 1990, 1992; Mondragón 1991.

33 Politis 1996b: 59–65; Cabrera *et al.* 1999.

34 Binford 1980; Kelly 1983.

35 In the rainy season the average distance between camps is 3.85 km (based on a sample of 12 camps), while in the dry season it is 8.05 km (based on a sample of 18). The average number of occupation days in the rainy season is 4.8 (based on a sample of 13 camps), while in the dry season it is 2.6 days (based on a sample of 20).

36 Based on a sample of 27 camps.

37 For the rainy season the average is 8.52 km (based on a sample of 14 camps) and for the dry season it is 8.30 km (based on a sample of 13). Our data indicate that the sector exploited around the residential camp does not exceed a radius of 9 km.

38 Reid 1979: 30.

39 Reid 1979.

40 Silverwood-Cope 1990: 74.

41 Pozzobon 1983.

42 These plants are grouped into 44 families of vascular plants according to the phylogenetic scheme proposed by Cronquist (1981). Of these, 34 correspond to Magnoliopsida (dicotiledoneas), 9 to Liliopsida (monocotiledoneas) and 1 to Pteridophyta (Cárdenas and Politis 2000).

43 Prance *et al.* 1976; Palacios 1989; Galeano 1992; Cárdenas *et al.* 1997.

44 The wild species most commonly consumed are seje (*Oenocarpus bataua*), plantain or tarriago (*Phenakospermum guyanense*), bacaba palm (*Oenocarpus bacaba*), popere (*Oenocarpus mapora*), guaná (*Dacryodes peruviana*), patataá (*Helicostylis tormentosa*), juansoco (*Couma macrocarpa*), juiú (*Attalea* sp.), etc. (see complete list of species in Cárdenas and Politis 2000).

45 Mondragón 1991; Cabrera *et al.* 1999.

46 Politis 1992; Politis and Rodríguez 1994; Cabrera *et al.* 1999: 244–62; Cárdenas and Politis 2000: 85–8.

47 Balick 1986: 66; Cabrera *et al.* 1999: 255.

48 Even without modifications in the phenotype or genotype.

49 The average area was 86.1 sq. metres (min. 32.5 sq. metres, max. 178.9 sq. metres), based on a sample of 32 camps.

50 Cárdenas and Politis 2000: 87.

51 Cárdenas and Politis 2000: 88.

52 Reid 1979: 28.

53 Silverwood-Cope 1990: 50.

54 Balée 1989; Moran 1993a.

55 Posey 1982.

56 Meggers 1992.

57 Evans and Meggers 1960: 72–3.

58 Miller 1992a.

59 See Politis 1996b for more detail.

60 E.g. Stearman 1991; Dufour 1987.

61 Politis and Saunders, in press.

62 Reichel-Dolmatoff 1986.

63 See summary in Neves 1999a and other chapters in the present book.

64 Schmitz 1987: 56.

65 Sponsel 1986: 73.

66 Roosevelt *et al.* 1996.

67 Tankersley 1997, Haynes 1997, Reanier 1997, but see the rebuttal in Roosevelt *et al.* 1997.

68 Miller 1992b.

69 Miller 1992b: 42.

70 Cavelier *et al.* 1995; Gnecco and Mora 1997.

71 Barse 1990, 1995.

72 Behling 1996.

73 E.g. Colinvaux and Bush 1991; Stearman 1991.

74 Reichel-Dolmatoff 1990; Rival 1998: 237.

2

The Archaeology of Forest Foraging and Agricultural Production in Amazonia

JOSÉ R. OLIVER

'Agricultural potential' is not something inherent in nature. The concept contains the word 'culture'.[1]

2.1 A mature *chacra* of an Andoque settlement on the banks of the Caquetá river. What appears to be an untidy garden is in effect a highly productive agrosystem that mimics the diversity of the surrounding tropical forest.

Introduction

Agriculture is, *sine qua non,* the underlying economic base of complex societies in the New World.[2] All pre-contact civilizations in the Americas depended upon the development of agriculture, and this is as true for the Amazon basin as it is for the Andean highlands. When, how and in what ways did humans became reliant on agriculture in Amazonia? What led to the shift from food procurement to agricultural-based food production, how did different kinds of agricultural systems develop, and what were the consequences for human societies? One of the most significant shifts in the way we now approach Amazonia's past is to recognize that the tropical 'forest' is not a homogeneous entity, but rather a complex ecological mosaic offering markedly different potentials for its inhabitants.

In this chapter I will discuss what we presently know about the nature and development of agriculture, and the processes of food acquisition, preparation, consumption and/or storage in Amazonia. I will address four main issues. First, I will evaluate the palaeoenvironmental, palaeobotanical and archaeological evidence for the earliest known food procurement systems in the Amazonian tropical forest. Second, I will explain why we know so little about the shift toward and subsequent diversification of ancient agricultural systems in Amazonia. Third, I will describe some of the various agroeconomic systems that developed in different macro-habitats of Amazonia. Finally, I will focus on one of the most important of all native Amazonian cultigens, a veritable 'super-crop', manioc (or *yuca, mandioca* [*Manihot esculenta* 'Crantz']).

As any agroecologist will tell you, an 'agricultural plot' is essentially a modified micro-habitat managed by systematic human intervention. Simultaneously, it is still very much affected by non-human agencies which modify what one might call the 'natural habitat', ranging from climate to creatures and from micro-organisms to soil chemistry. The extent of human-induced disturbance varies considerably with time and place, and ranges from a nearly imperceptible – to western eyes – alteration with respect to the 'undisturbed' biotic conditions, as is the case of palm groves maintained by many groups including Nukak foragers in the Guaviare territory in Colombia (see Politis, this volume), to more significant disturbances of the 'natural' forest, as is the case with the multiple crops found in modern

Amazonian cultivated fields *(chacra* or *chagra)*, such as those of the Andoque or Tukano of the Amazonian forests of Colombia (fig. 2.1).[3] An understanding of the 'natural' habitat as a contrasting unit to the managed and altered agricultural habitat is useful to appreciate how indigenous knowledge of agriculture and agricultural techniques (hereafter 'agrotechnology'), and food production systems developed.

There are many subtle ways in which human agency can and has altered the 'natural' habitat over the millennia, so that the popular image of a 'virgin' Amazonian forest is more an illusion than a reality.[4] In the last thirty years western scientists have begun to recognize that there is a complex and subtly graded range of strategies applied to the exploitation of both wild and managed forest food resources. This culminates in the neat, well-bounded and intensely modified micro-habitat that is a *chacra* field.[5] To understand how agricultural systems in Amazonia evolved and diversified, one must first glance at the modern forest habitats and then go back in time some 11,000 years to a period when the last Ice Age (late Pleistocene) was in transition to modern climatic conditions (early Holocene).

Modern Amazonian forest habitats

At present, all the American neotropical rainforests together account for about half the global total, of which the largest proportion (4–5 million sq. km or 4,545 million hectares) is found in Amazonia.[6] At a very general level, the Amazon basin can be divided into two broad topographic zones. The *várzea,* or floodplain forests, encompass a total area of less than 80,000 sq. km or around 2 per cent of the Amazon basin. The remainder is *terra firme* (or uplands), an area of about 5 million sq. km or about 98 per cent of the Amazon basin. This enormous *terra firme* 'upland forest' has recently been shown to have a diverse array of different habitats, increasing in number as research accumulates.[7]

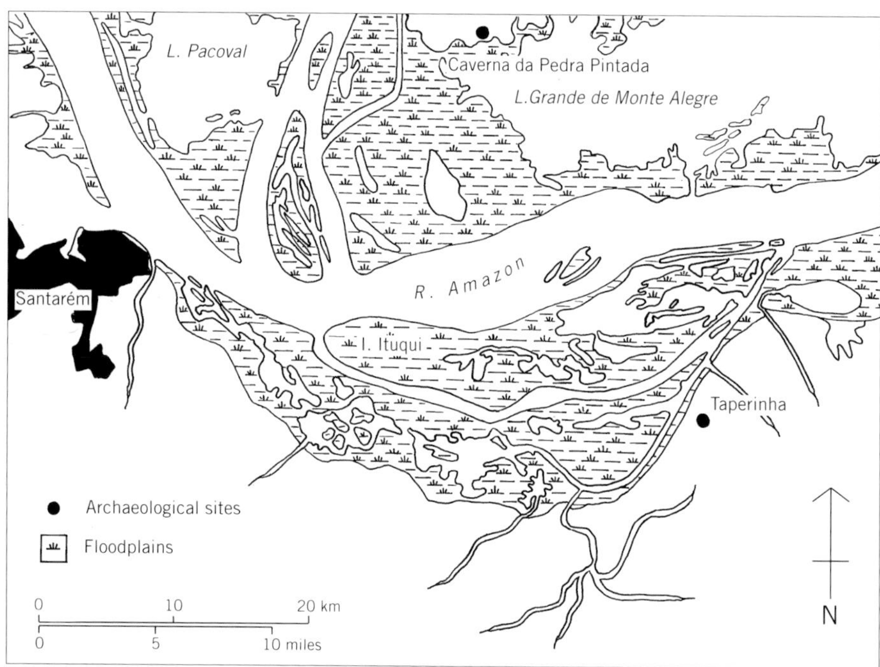

2.2 Map of early sites in the Santarém and Monte Alegre area, lower Amazon. The map shows the sharp boundary between the *várzea* habitat and the older upland sediments where tropical rainforest once stood. Sites related to the Taperinha phase are located along the edge of the upland.

At least four major macro-habitats can be distinguished: (1) the savannahs, or tropical grasslands; (2) 'blackwater', or heath forests; (3) upland forests; and (4) *várzea*, or floodplain forests (fig. 2.2). Moreover, each macro-habitat is composed of a myriad of smaller distinct ecosystems. For example, in the upland areas of northwestern Amazonia human-made palm tree forests have been identified in the last decade and a half. In addition, an immense, dendritic network of major rivers and their tributaries traverse the lowlands. These break down into: (a) the nutrient-rich 'whitewater' rivers, such as the Amazon, Madeira, Purús and Ucayali, (b) the moderately rich 'clearwater' rivers such as Tapajós and Xingú, and (c) the nutrient-poor 'blackwater' rivers, centred in the Río Negro basin. Each forest habitat and hydrochemical regime varies in terms of the terrestrial and aquatic food web it is able to support, and in its agricultural potential.[8]

The rainforest of the late Pleistocene and early Holocene was long believed incapable of attracting or supporting human occupation because of the limiting ecological conditions. Until recently it was thought that Amazonian 'Tropical Forest Culture', as an adaptation and way of life, emerged much later than civilizations that developed in other areas such as the Andean highlands and coast of Peru,[9] and that, in order to have arrived at this set of shared cultural traits, it must have evolved in a homogeneous and unchanging tropical forest environment with severe food resource limitations.[10] The Amazon environment was naïvely portrayed as a 'counterfeit paradise' whose resources could only support simple village farming societies, characterized by a low population density and lacking political authority beyond the village.[11] Likewise, the shifting slash-and-burn based agroeconomy that developed over time was construed as the most optimal and efficient system – if not the only one – for extracting food resources from the tropical forests of Amazonia. It was believed that any other form of intensifying agricultural food production would result in environmental and cultural degradation.[12]

In fact, to speak of a uniform 'tropical forest' culture based on 'swidden agriculture' (see p. 67) is a gross oversimplification. The Amazonian forest habitat is anything but a homogeneous and uninterrupted 'virgin' tropical rainforest. Nor has the forest remained unchanged in the short as well as the long term.[13] To understand how a range of forest and river food resources were exploited, and how food procurement (foraging) changed to food production (agriculture) over time, the environmental history of the Amazon must be addressed.

The Amazonian landscape in the late Pleistocene to early Holocene transition

The late Pleistocene (18,000–12,500 BP) to early Holocene transition (12,500–9000 BP) time periods witnessed dramatic climatic and vegetation changes on a global scale; the tropics were no exception.[14] Until quite recently virtually nothing was known about the character and nature of Amazonian habitats during this critical transition period.[15] It was hypothesized that during the Late Glacial Maximum (*c.*18,000–12,500 BP) the region was cold and very arid, with open vegetation areas (savannahs) having greatly expanded at the expense of closed-canopy moist forests. The Pleistocene moist forests were thought to have been reduced to a patchwork of isolated 'islands' (refugia), where flora and fauna took refuge and where different species subsequently evolved and spread as the climate improved at the beginning of the Holocene, eventually reaching its present configuration. The Pleistocene refuges were like biogenetic 'storehouses' that would guarantee species diversity during warmer and wetter periods (glacial 'interstadia') like the present one.

In the last Ice Age cycle the South American continent was much cooler and drier than it is today. Recent research indicates that temperatures in the Andean highlands were as much as 9° C lower.[16] In the lowlands, including Amazonia, temperatures were lowered by 6° to 9° C and accompanied by an estimated 25–40 per cent reduction in precipitation. The consequences were a 1,500-metre downslope spread of Andean forest species that today are limited to more than 1,500 metres above sea level; the partial replacement and/or reduction of lowland evergreen rainforest by montane or drier forest vegetation types; and the expansion of various types of open vegetation similar but not identical to modern-day savannah types.[17]

Among several climatic variables, two in particular have important implications for evaluating vegetation distribution and its potential for economic exploitation by humans during the late Pleistocene.[18] The first is an estimated 33 per cent reduction in the level of atmospheric carbon dioxide (a 'green-house' gas that was 'trapped' in oceans and glaciers), to which plants react in different ways. Put simply, some groups of plants, such as tubers and most tropical forest trees, thrive under higher concentrations of carbon dioxide than other plant groups, such as cacti, bamboo, sedges and many grasses.[19] The second variable entails the *seasonal* variation of rainfall and temperature, to which also plants respond in particular ways.

Tuberous roots, for example, are specialized organs for the storage of starch (high-energy carbohydrates) that develop in response to marked dry and wet seasons. During the late Pleistocene wild ancestors of the most important modern staple root crops, such as manioc (*Manihot*), sweet potato (*Ipomoea*), yams (*Dioscorea*), arrowroots (*Maranta*) and cocoyams (*Xanthosoma*), were most likely to have occurred naturally in relatively low numbers and densities as a result of a lowered carbon dioxide environment and the reduced contrast between wet and dry seasons.[20] Tuberous plants would be at a competitive disadvantage with plants of a different type of metabolism, such as the wild grasses (e.g. savannah), including the ancestor(s) of maize (*Zea mays*). The low atmospheric carbon dioxide would be an important inhibiting factor in the development of effective cultivation systems (such as those based on tubers) in tropical forests.[21] Wild tuberous plants during the late Pleistocene would have had stunted tubers in climates with more homogeneous mean temperatures and precipitation, and are likely to have been low-ranked, dispersed food sources for late Pleistocene hunters and gatherers/foragers in Amazonia. Modern climatic conditions began to prevail from around 12,000 to 10,000 years ago.[22]

Towards the end of the last Ice Age the deep-water ocean circulation patterns underwent a major reorganization, thus again further increasing the production of carbon dioxide that warmed oceanic and terrestrial surfaces.[23] This change would have increased the adaptive advantage of wild tuberous plants. The transition to a Holocene climatic-vegetation regime was far from being a uniform process and seems to have reached near 'modern' conditions in different times and places, between *c.*12,500 and 9000 BP

The critical question, insofar as Amazonia is concerned, is when the tropical humid forests began to expand once more at the expense of open vegetation types in the lowland Neotropics. Because this climatic change fostered the advance of lowland forests at the close of the Pleistocene, humans were faced with the need to adjust their food-foraging strategies by increasing their investment in searching for and processing food plants.[24]

During the Pleistocene it has been proposed that wetter, elevated areas of tropical South America became habitats for rainforest plant and animal species retreating from the extreme arid, open and expansive lowland vegetation.[25] These postulated 'refuges' are thought to have had a fragmented geographical distribution in Amazonia. Their existence is largely inferred from modern species distribution in which an unusually high number of different species are found to be unique (endemic) to each refuge, such as lizards, passerine birds and *Heliconius* butterflies. Experts are, however, currently divided as to whether such refuges existed or not, and about the extent to which open vegetation expanded geographically at the expense of the rainforest.[26]

Achaeologist Betty J. Meggers, who is one of the leading proponents of the 'refugia' theory, argues that since refuge forests were very limited in geographic extent in glacial times, these 'island' habitats would be too restricted to provide adequate food resources for human habitation.[27] If so, then ancient cultural and subsistence adaptations must have been drawn toward savannah or open-vegetation areas rather than tropical rainforest environments. The assumption that such refuges existed allowed Meggers to argue that the tropical rainforest habitats of Amazonia were not occupied or exploited by humans (hunters/gatherers) until they expanded, well into the Holocene.

Another group of scholars does not accept the idea of a highly reduced and fragmented rainforest, pointing to other causes for the modern 'patches' of high species endemism. They point out that the Amazonian Pleistocene climate was drier, although not arid, and that the scale of forest reduction and the extreme degree of aridity required by the 'refuge theory' are not strongly supported by current palaeobotanical data.[28] Yet others are more cautious, concluding that both scenarios are not necessarily mutually exclusive.[29]

However most experts agree that large tracts of contiguous tropical rainforest were present during the last Ice Age. It is also clear now that the image of vegetation, such as savannah moving across the landscape, retreating or advancing as a single assemblage, is quite false. Rather, every plant and animal species found its own route to survival, and the community of plant and animal species was constantly changing as the environment changed.[30] Understanding these developments is the key to deducing the shift in foraging and food procurement strategies in the early Holocene.

For long it was believed that agriculture was invented rather quickly, leading to the domestication of plants and, in due course, to settled life and civilization.[31] This idea no longer holds much credence anywhere in the world, including Amazonia. Rather, agriculture followed domestication and settled life. Simply put, domestication is the long-term result of predator–prey (human–plant/animal) relationships where both populations stand to benefit, while agriculture in its broadest sense refers to human behaviour that creates a new kind of ecological succession (an agroecology), where the life-cycle of the cultivars are under human control. But before food production based on domesticated crops (agriculture) emerged, there was a long (and still is) and protracted period of mutually beneficial (symbiotic) human–plant interactions.[32] In procuring food and other plant resources by foraging, human beings began to alter the landscape well before any systematic cultivation took place, while creating the necessary opportunities for residential stability (sedentism) and domestication to develop, such as clearing land around camp sites or setting fires in grasslands to hunt animals.

The 'Broad Spectrum Diet Revolution' theory provides a key to the question of why it might be advantageous to shift from a proven foraging system to the untested and therefore potentially risky practice of agricultural production. It is no coincidence that the initial stages of domestication leading to agriculture began at the end of the Pleistocene, when dramatic climatic shifts began to occur. The basic argument is as follows. Food plant resources that form the diet of a foraging group are not those most abundant in a given area, but those that are most efficient to procure in terms of effort expended for calorific return. As the abundance of these high-ranked plant resources in a given area declined at the close of the Pleistocene, efficient foraging would have required investing less time in searching for high-ranked plants and more time in searching for and handling a wider range of lower-ranked resources. As high-ranking plant resources declined, efficient foragers would choose a broader, more diversified diet because they would obtain a higher return rate than could be achieved by searching for the depleted, dispersed high-ranked resources. A reduction in search time would allow foragers to invest time in food processing and storage, adding to the nutritional value and use-life of the food resources. The increased breadth of diet and the decreased search time would lead to a smaller foraging range and thus to increased sedentism.[33]

Such changes in breadth of diet may well result in socio-demographic shifts, depending on the nature and characteristics of the food resources entering the diet. But it is important not to view changes deterministically. If the development of sedentism, domestication and agriculture were inevitable, modern foragers like the Nukak would simply not exist (see Politis, this volume), nor would formerly sedentary agricultural groups, like the Gorotire Kayapó, have 'reverted' to 'nomadic agriculture' in the early twentieth century. One possible direction a given group can take is, of course, toward sedentism, house gardening and eventually agriculture. As the opportunity arises to concentrate an increasing number of high-ranked food plants within the home area, while still foraging for a broad suite of low-ranked food sources, it would be expected that at some point in time the optimal efficiency in terms of effort invested will shift to bringing high-yield plants under human control.

The next section will look at what the archaeological evidence in Amazonia has to 'say' about narrow- and broad-spectrum diet strategies, and whether or not these conform to the assumptions spelled out by the 'Broad Spectrum Diet Revolution'.

The archaeological evidence of the late Pleistocene to early Holocene

The long-held conventional view that the 'First South Americans' exclusively favoured a narrow-spectrum diet and specialized in 'big game hunting' (e.g. mastodon, megatherium, palaeohorses) has recently been demonstrated not to apply everywhere in South America, and most particularly not in the moist forest regions of Amazonia.[34] I shall now examine in some detail the nature of the earliest food-foraging strategies in three specific regions within Amazonia. These case studies illustrate the kinds of processes at work that gradually and almost imperceptibly led to agricultural-based societies.

The Pedra Pintada Palaeoindian Foragers

Some of the earliest evidence for late Pleistocene to early Holocene hunting and gathering adaptations to the tropical rainforest habitat has emerged from archaeological excavations at Caverna da Pedra Pintada, near Monte Alegre (fig. 2.2).[35] Fifty-six radiocarbon dates ranging between 11,700 and 9880 BP are associated with early foraging groups who, in the course of repeated visits, left flaked stone tools, such as knives, gravers, scrapers and stemmed projectile points (fig. 2.3). An elegant pictographic rock art began with the earliest occupants of the cave (see Pereira, this volume). Plant and animal remains at this site unequivocally demonstrate an exploitation of rainforest trees, palm trees, river mussels, fish and turtles, and to a lesser extent terrestrial mammals, all of which point to habitats that are similar, though not necessarily identical, to the modern tropical rainforest, *várzea* (floodplain) forest, in addition to the river's aquatic resources.

Among the plant remains identified are: the leguminous *jutaí* (seeds for flour, medicine, varnish, wood for construction); the edible *castanha do Pará*, or Brazil nut;

the *achu* (edible starchy fruit); the *pitomba* (nutritious seed); and the *tarumã*, a *várzea* (floodplain) tree whose seeds are used today as fish bait. Palm seeds from *sacurí*, *curuá* and *tucumã* were also identified, and are valued today for their nutritious edible fruits and as a source of raw material.[36] All of the palaeobotanical remains are still found in the eastern Amazon and Atlantic rainforests, in the lower Amazon *terra firme* and the sandy *várzea* forests. Most of the trees that have been identified fruit from December to February, the rainy season, while *sacurí* and *curuá* palms fruit throughout the year.[37] The palm trees tend to proliferate in disturbed habitats and in regimes of high rainfall. Although animal bones were poorly preserved, the most important were river fishes, including the giant *pirarucú* and *taíra*, which are today most abundant and easily fished during the dry season. Juvenile land tortoise and aquatic turtle bones were also identified.[38] Aquatic turtles (and eggs) are easily captured at the height of the dry season, when they lay eggs in the sandbars and beaches within the floodplain. Instead of the conventional image of a big-game hunting economy with a narrow-spectrum foraging diet, Palaeoindian subsistence for the nearly two millennia in Pedra Pintada cave appears to have been broad-spectrum tropical forest and river foraging.[39]

2.3 This straight-stemmed triangular projectile point from Tapajós river is one of several isolated finds of hafted spear-points in the lower Amazon region (height 8.5 cm, width 4 cm; Museu Paraense Emílio Goeldi, Belém, Brazil). Similar stemmed projectile points used for hunting game have also been found at Caverna da Pedra Pintada.

The middle Holocene Archaic period occupants at Caverna da Pedra Pintada continued a similar broad-spectrum diet pattern of rainforest, floodplain and river exploitation, even as their tool complexes changed and ceramic technology had come into use around 7580 BP[40] These initial pottery-making (Paituna phase) groups were likely to have been temporary visitors from settlements probably located along or near the edge of the lower Amazon floodplain, and were closely related to the Taperinha phase occupations to be discussed below.

Elsewhere in Brazilian Amazonia, around 11,000–8,000 years ago, there is ample evidence for the presence of other late Pleistocene to early Holocene human occupations encompassing diverse upland forest and savannah habitats. The Itaparica tradition, for example, is characterized by large quartzite scrapers worked on one side and rare stemmed triangular projectile points. Subsistence data indicate a focus on a broad spectrum of river fauna and forest tree fruits. The Dourado tradition, comparable to Itaparica, is represented by the famous Abrigo do Sol rock-shelter site located in the Matto Grosso do Sul region, dating between 11,500 and 6000 BP.[41]

The Peña Roja foragers and itinerant gardeners of the Araracuara region

The site of Peña Roja is located 26 km downstream from the Araracuara and Yarí river confluence, on the north margin of the middle Caquetá river, named Japurá in Brazil (figs 2.4, 2.6).[42] It is the earliest preceramic occupation in the tropical rainforests of the modern Colombia-Brazil border. Three radiocarbon dates bracket the earliest occupation between 9250±140 and 8090±60 BP[43] Based on extensive palaeobotanical research in this area, it is known that a humid, warmer period began around 10,500 BP, marking the transition to the early Holocene. Between 9000 and 8000 BP the climate became somewhat drier, though still warm. *Cecropia*, a pioneering tree, became abundant at this time. Throughout these periods the pollen data are indicative of a tropical rainforest. Between 6500 and 4000 BP the climate changed again to very humid and warm, more so than at present. The Peña Roja preceramic occupation was followed by a hiatus and a much later reoccupation around the Christian Era by ceramic-using groups. Anthropogenic 'black soils' *(terra preta)*

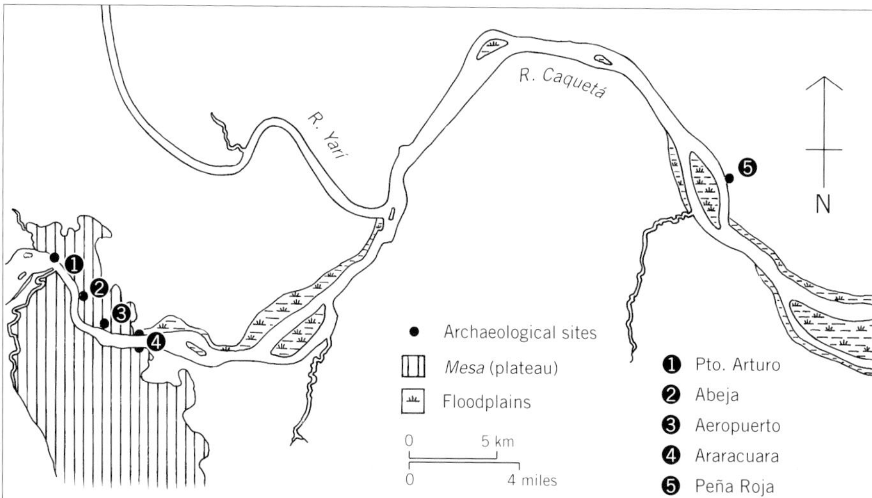

2.4 Map of archaeological sites in the vicinity of Araracuara, middle Caquetá, Colombia.

developed during the late occupation, after 1800 BP, as a result of intensive human activity (see Petersen *et al.*, this volume).[44]

The archaeological excavations recovered an astonishing quantity and range of well-preserved palm seeds and fruits, alongside flaked and ground stone implements, from preceramic levels (9250–8100 BP). Together with soil analyses, these data illustrate the character of the ancient subsistence activities. Abundant charcoal was also recovered, from which fifteen kinds of wood have recently been identified.[45] Among the modern Andoque in the Caquetá these woody species are used as fuel for smoking (meat/fish) and lighting, construction, domestic artefacts, weapons, musical instruments, pottery, canoes, ritual artefacts, ornaments, food, fish/hunt bait, rearing larvae, medicine and poison. In addition to various edible wild fruits, useful plants identified include fish poisons, one of which (*Cayorcar glabrum*) is today also added to *curare,* a poison mixture that paralyzes the respiratory and nervous system, and is used on blowgun darts for hunting terrestrial animals and birds high in the forest canopy (see fig. 1.1).

The great majority of the seeds recovered are of palm trees belonging to the genera *Oneocarpus*, *Mauritia*, *Maximiliana* and *Astrocaryum*. Curiously, the only fully domesticated palm so far known, the *chontaduro* or peach palm, is absent.[46] Nevertheless, palm fruit processing was one of the most important activities carried out at the site, and their nutritional value should not be underestimated. For example, the oil of the *seje* palm seeds has a nutritional value comparable to olive oil; its protein content is said to surpass that of legumes and graminae; the beverage made from seeds has a value comparable with human milk and superior to cow milk. *Seje* seeds predominate in the preceramic phase, becoming rare during the later agricultural-ceramic occupation phase. It does not naturally grow in dense stands, except where human agency is involved. A beverage is produced by boiling the seeds in water or by grinding them, straining the pulp and adding water. In addition the rachis of the palm leaves is used as fibre for basketry. During the fruiting season (March–June) it also attracts spider monkeys, macaws and toucans.

The *moriche* or *burití* palms, whose seeds only occur in the preceramic phase, grow in swamps or permanently flooded areas (fig. 2.8). During the high flood season fish become the major seed consumers; during low flood periods land and semi-aquatic mammals are attracted by the seeds, primarily tapir, peccary and agouti.[47] All of the *moriche* palm is useful. Seed pulp/juice can be fermented to produce an alcoholic drink *(chicha)* or consumed directly. Drink preparation requires heating the seeds in water or roasting them, then grinding them to separate the flesh from the seed nut. The seeds also produce a nutritious, starchy flour, while the leaves, petiole and trunk have uses such as hammock fibre, thatch, basketry and wood for construction. Moreover, the palm's trunk harbours nutrient-rich beetle larvae, much sought after as a delicacy by modern Indians. The *moriche* also fruits from March to June. It is hardly exaggeration to say that these palm trees, by themselves, are veritable convenience stores and delicatessens rolled into one. The main limitation is the three- to four-month peak fruiting season.

The Peña Roja stone artefacts are those that might be required by someone working with a range of tropical woods and fibres. Stone flakes were used for side-scraping. Other stone tools produced by using a different flaking technique (bipolar) resulted in small blades with sharp edges for cutting. Some blades show retouching to sharpen the cutting edges. Stone burins and drills were used for engraving and for puncturing. Cobbles and pebbles show abrasion and wear either on one edge or at the distal ends, suggesting various pounding and grinding activities. Larger cobbles were used as chopping tools. Coarse sandstone slabs were used as abraders, some tinted with a red pigment. Overall this tool kit strongly suggests work on wood and vegetable fibre, not specifically hunting, fishing or butchering animals.[48]

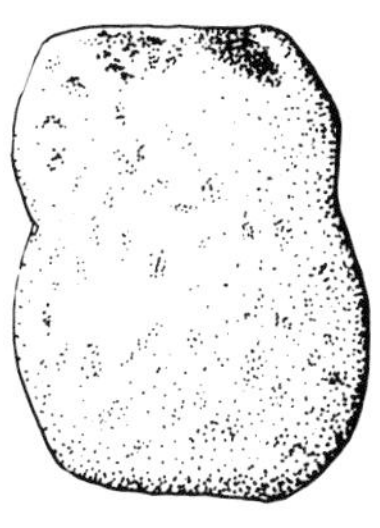

2.5 A stone axe (*c.*9000 BP) used for felling forest trees from the Peña Roja site in the middle Caquetá. Finds of stone axes coupled with palaeobotanical evidence for patches of cleared forest may be indicative of early cultivation practices.

Most important, however, the tool assemblage at Peña Roja also included stone axes with side notches for hafting to a wood handle, and a number of mortar-like stones and pestles *(manos)* for nut-cracking and pounding vegetable matter (fig. 2.5).[49] The presence of notched axes indicates tree-felling, and possibly hoeing for limited soil tillage or digging for roots. Equally significantly, microbotanical analyses revealed the presence of domesticated *lerén* root crop (*Calathea*), bottle gourd and calabash.[50]

The preceramic occupants at Peña Roja are primarily characterized as foragers who practised small-scale domestic gardening. Perhaps one might suggest the descriptive term of 'itinerant gardeners' for the Peña Roja groups, somewhat akin to the 'nomadic agriculture' strategy developed by the post-1900s Gorotire Kayapó of the middle Xingú or perhaps even more like the Nukak foragers who harvest and cultivate wild roots, including some domesticated plants (fig. 2.7), in the Guaviare forest (see Politis, this volume).[51] While the modern Nukak studiously avoid setting up camps directly on older camp sites (so as not to interfere with the palm forest/orchard that developed *in situ* since), the nature of the archaeological deposits at the Peña Roja site seem to suggest continual or more intense refuse accumulation. But whether this is the result of frequent and recurrent return visits to the same camp site after relatively short foraging rounds or of more extended residence periods cannot yet be determined.

One possible scenario, admittedly speculative, is a four- or five-month stay at Peña Roja to coincide with the March through June fruiting season of the various palm trees, which also attract potential game. If the *lerén* root crop was cultivated in domestic gardens, the nine-month maturation period it requires would imply that during the tuber's growth stage the inhabitants would be free to forage away from this camp site (some time after July) and harvest the tubers upon their return around March. For example, in modern agricultural plots, manioc continues to produce and be harvested and continually re-planted in swidden plots for about two years after the

ABOVE 2.6 An Andoque rubber camp site on the banks of the Yarí river in the Araracuara region. Immediately behind the thatched house to the far right a house garden is set close to the forest.

farmer stops weeding.[52] What would have been required to maintain the garden would be, precisely, periodic visits to that camp's domestic garden. If the early inhabitants also maintained small-scale domestic gardens *en route* and around other temporary encampments, they would also have an underground stock/storage of root crops awaiting weeding, harvesting and replanting. Thus, people could be moving from one garden to the next, rather than only shifting *chacras*, and scheduling the 'trekking' to coincide with the fruiting of wild trees and palm groves (orchards). These itinerant gardeners would be actively involved in the dispersion of seeds (such as palms) and other useful plants suitable for the various habitats around the camps. If this were the case, the radius of itinerant foraging and gardening would probably be less than if there were a nearly total reliance on foraging for scattered wild plants and the pursuit of game.

It is only some time before 4700 BP at Abeja site (Tubaboniba phase) and other nearby sites located some 26 km upstream from Peña Roja that there is significant evidence of forest slash and burn, mainly associated with maize pollen. For the Tubaboniba preceramic phase (before 4700 BP) archaeologists have identified a localized expansion of savannah over tropical forest species, associated with abundant charcoal (i.e. fires), along with the cultigens soursop, manioc and maize.[53] The gap in the archaeological record between before 4700 and 8000 BP (fig. 2.9) in the region is unfortunate, as this is when the shift to early agriculture is likely to have occurred.[54] Marked by a stratigraphic discontinuity in the excavation around 4700 BP, the Abeja site was abandoned for the next three millennia, thus producing a second gap in the record.

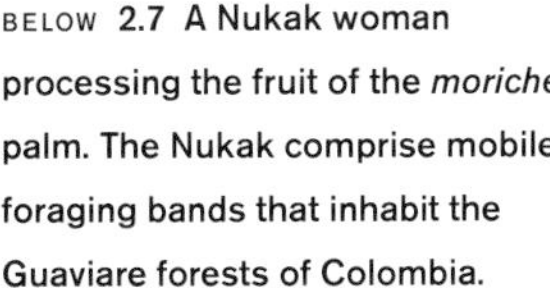

BELOW 2.7 A Nukak woman processing the fruit of the *moriche* palm. The Nukak comprise mobile foraging bands that inhabit the Guaviare forests of Colombia.

RIGHT 2.8 *Moriche* or *buriti/miriti* palm (*Mauritia flexuosa*) trees. Palm groves flourish in swampy or flooded areas along rivers and deltas and are often actively propagated by humans. The mature red seeds are ready for harvesting and served as a highly nutritious food resource among indigenous riverine populations in Amazonia.

The next reoccupation, the Méidote phase, occurred around 1800 BP (*c.* AD 150) and continued until about 800 BP (*c.* AD 1200), after which time Abeja site was abandoned and the forest regenerated in the area.[55] During the Méidote occupation ceramics related to the Camani ceramic complex first appeared in the Caquetá region.[56] Camani/early Méidote ceramic vessels are occasionally decorated with a red slip, but most often are plain. These include large and medium hemispherical vessels, vessels and bowls with a concave-convex profile and flanged or triangular thickened rims, and the ubiquitous *budare* or flat clay griddle most probably used for baking cassava *(casabe, beijú).*[57] Also present are *topias,* or solid hourglass or cylindrical ceramic objects used to rest vessels and griddles over fire hearths, items that still persist today among the Andoque and many other Amazonian groups.

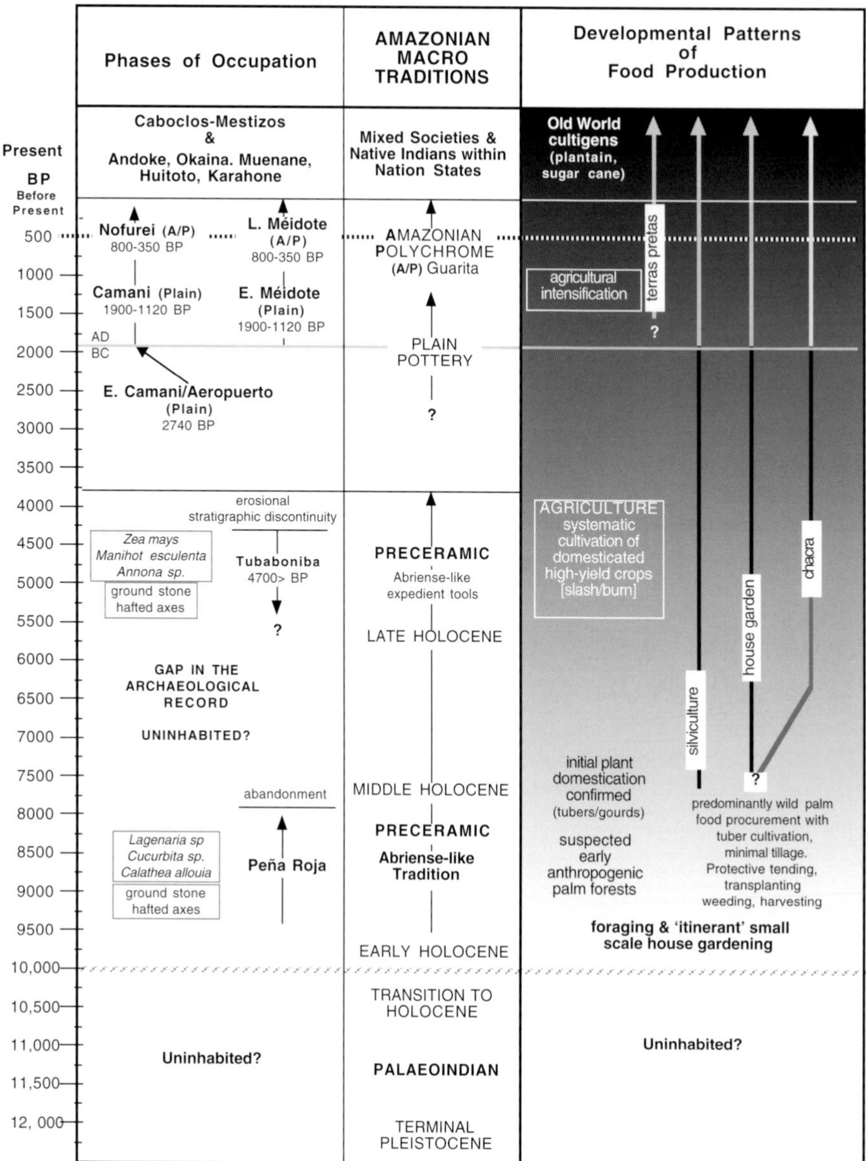

2.9 Cultural chronology for the Araracuara region in Amazonian Colombia, showing the different phases of archaeological occupations and principal Amazonian cultural traditions.

Around 1045–1000 BP a different, more complex set of vessel forms with excised and white/red painted decoration of the Amazonian Polychrome ('Guarita') tradition, locally represented by the Nofurei complex or style, appeared in the region (fig. 2.8). It is unclear whether the ceramic change from Méidote/Camani to Nofurei implies the invasion of new ethnic groups from the Japurá or upper Negro areas – where local variants of Nofurei are reported for various sites – or a local development in ceramics (e.g. Camani adopting new shapes and decorative techniques and designs). This Amazonian Polychrome 'macro-tradition' may have its earliest representatives in Pocó-Bõa Vista sites (Nhamundá-Trombetas rivers) and the Marajoara phase of Marajó Island (see Schaan, this volume).

Excavations at various Camani/Méidote-Nofurei ceramic sites in Araracuara-Caquetá clearly suggest intensive agricultural practices (including slash and burn) and an increasing range of crops being cultivated. By about 1150 BP (AD 800) concentrated human activity is registered at the Aeropuerto site (fig. 2.4) by the devel-

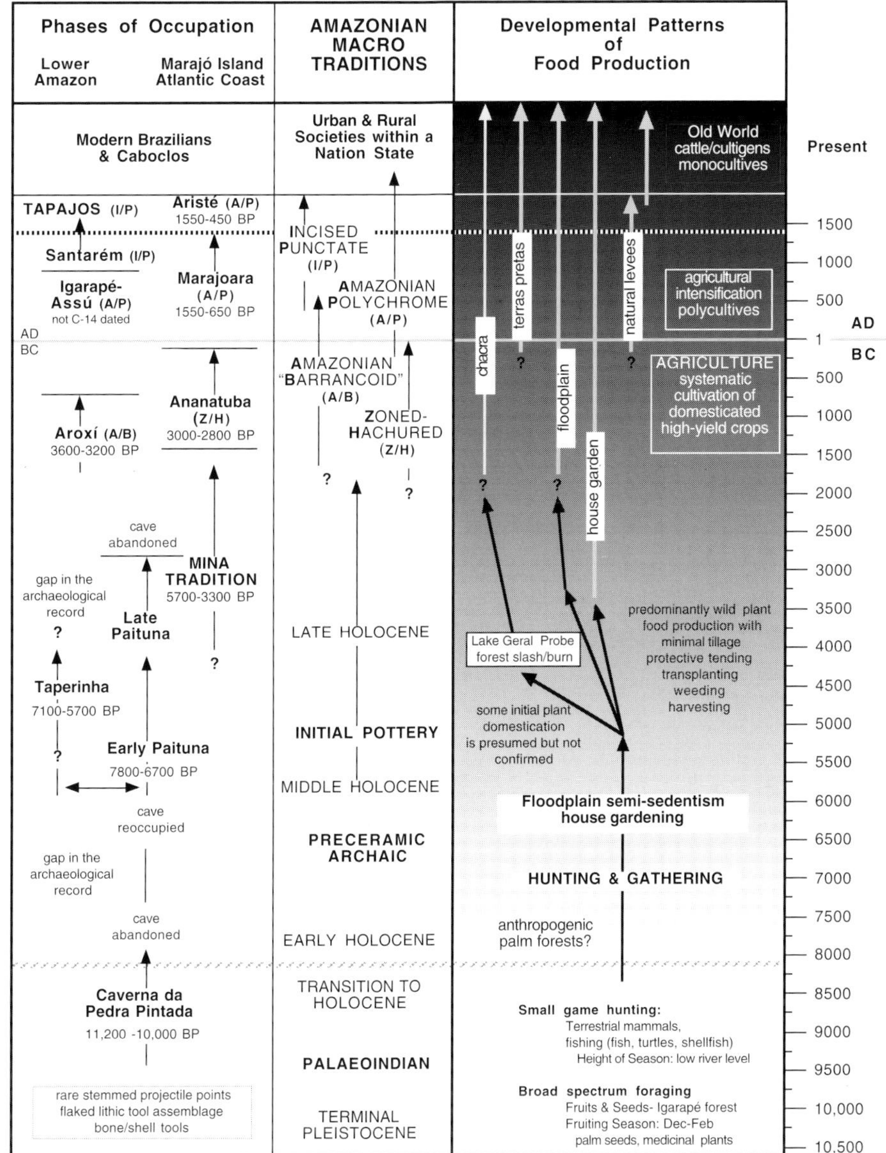

2.10 Cultural chronology for the lower Amazon, Marajó Island and Atlantic coast regions in Brazil highlighting the major developments in food production. Foragers and farmers practised seasonal hunting and food procurement strategies that continue to this day.

opment of rich organic, man-made 'black soils' that are sought today by Andoque and Witoto (or Huitoto) indigenous groups as prime agricultural land (see Petersen *et al.*, this volume). In addition, at the Aeropuerto site palaeobotanical and sediment analyses suggest the transportation of alluvial silt mixed with aquatic algae from the floodplain as a method of soil enrichment. High organic domestic refuse, plus aquatic algae and alluvium makes for excellent bedding (and mulching). It is calculated that 245 tons of silt and algae or 90 tons of mulch would be required to cover one centimetre of topsoil over one hectare, with the implication of high labour investment and social organization.

Pedra Pintada and Peña Roja present differences as well as similarities in adaptive strategies within a pattern of tropical lowland hunting, foraging and, in the latter case, itinerant gardening. While no domesticated food plants have been detected at Pedra Pintada, at least one significant root crop and two technological crops are present at Peña Roja, although some 1,000 to 2,000 years separate these two sites.

Fish and river-mollusc gathering and small-game hunting and processing appeared to be a more prominent activity at Pedra Pintada, yet poor bone preservation at Peña Roja demands caution. Peña Roja's stone tool assemblage included implements to grind vegetable fibre and crack seeds, and axes for tree-felling. It can be predicted that when the archaeological gap between 8000 BP and before 4700 BP in Araracuara-Caquetá is bridged, the new information will reveal a shift from foraging and itinerant farming to agriculture, although all these food procurement and production systems are still present among Amazonian groups today. As discussed, an agricultural system that included forest slash and burn with manioc, maize and papaya cultivars was already in place before 4700 BP. The next gap in knowledge to bridge, between 4700 BP and 2740 BP, is perhaps even more critical, as by this time some sites are well on their way toward intensive agricultural production that includes black soils and mulching techniques.

When one compares the developmental history of the Araracuara region (fig. 2.9) with that of the lower Amazon and Atlanctic coast (fig. 2.10), particularly in terms of the evolving patterns of food procurement and production (right-hand columns), it becomes apparent that there are regional, localized differences in the appearance of particular food systems in each region. These, however, also reflect unevenness and large gaps in the state of our archaeological knowledge.

The semi-sedentary fisherfolk of the initial ceramic period

At the Taperinha site near Santarém (fig. 2.2) archaeologists have partly confirmed a prediction made almost twenty-five years ago that archaeologists would find an early human occupation characterized by relatively sedentary fisherfolk dedicated to the intensive exploitation of fish resources and the tending of what can best be described as house gardens.[58] The original hypothesis also predicted that 'proto-Neolithic' fisher-gatherer sites would yield the earliest ceramics in Amazonia, if not the Americas. It was not until recently that archaeologists empirically demonstrated that such initial ceramics were indeed present by 7080 BP at Taperinha and even earlier, around 7600 BP, at Caverna da Pedra Pintada – a tradition that continued for at least another 2,500 years, until about 4500 BP (fig. 2.10).[59]

The presence of small, gourd-like ceramic vessels in the case of Taperinha may well imply that plant preparation for consumption required controlled heating (cooking/boiling) to make it digestible for humans. In fact, some ceramic fragments reveal traces of the tell-tale carbon residue from cooking. In this instance the sand-tempered ceramic vessels seem to indicate indirect evidence that food plants – not necessarily all domesticated – were being gathered and cooked by boiling, which required the kind of temperature control that, for example, heated rocks dumped in impermeable baskets or gourd vessels could not provide.[60] The other vessel shape is a simple open bowl with a slightly incurved wall, perhaps used for serving food or storage rather than for cooking. A small fraction (3 per cent) of the pottery bears incised or punctated geometric designs on the shoulder or rim.[61] Both the Paituna (at Pedra Pintada cave) and Taperinha ceramic complexes are similar in technology, form and decoration. Sandstone grinding implements, along with a few stone flakes, bone awls, molluscs and turtle-shell scrapers, complete the typical Taperinha (and Paituna) artefact assemblage. Fish and shell-fish molluscs are the dominant animal food remains.

The semi-sedentary fishing and gathering pattern also appears early on along the mouth of the Amazon (eastern Pará State), associated with a long-lasting ceramic tradition known as Mina.[62] Typically Mina (and related Uruá-Tucumã) ceramics are, again, simple globular to hemispherical bowl shapes tempered with shell or sand, occasionally bearing a red (iron oxide) slip, but lacking incision.[63] The earliest Mina sites, such as Ponta das Pedras, Porta da Mina and Sambaquí do Uruá, date between 5700 BP and 3300 BP. There are some forty freshwater shell midden and marine shell-mound *(sambaquí)* sites located on the estuarine and mangrove habitats of the lower Amazon and Atlantic coast (see map, pp. 20–21). Uruá fresh-water shell middens (3900–3500 BP) have also yielded polished stone axes, which may suggest forest clearing and, perhaps, incipient cultivation.[64]

Simultaneously, in the nearby Carajás area (8000–3500 BP), at sites such as Caverna do Gavião, a preceramic tradition focused on unifacial stone technology (flaking on one side or facet only) persisted until 3500 BP. The Carajás preceramic occupations also showed a broad-spectrum dietary adaptation to tropical forest, river and savannah resources. It is probable that Mina-Carajás sites with ceramics of comparable age to the Paituna or Taperinha complexes will eventually be detected.

Despite the presence of ceramics in the Paituna-Taperinha and Mina-Uruá-Tucumã sites, none have as yet yielded hard evidence of domesticated plants, nor can their economy be said to be primarily based on agricultural systems. Also the apparent absence of domesticated plants and other 'technological' plants (i.e. non-food plants), such as gourds, cotton and fish poisons, is likely to be a problem of sampling and/or preservation. It is well worth emphasizing that a lack of hard evidence is not proof of absence. The presence of gourds (for net-floats), cotton (for nets) and fish poisons would have been clear evidence for the intensification of fish and aquatic fauna procurement.[65] As things stand, the evidence does not contradict the hypothesis of semi-sedentary, riparian-estuarine-mangrove oriented fisherfolk characterized by broad-spectrum foraging for plant and aquatic fauna. Whether they already maintained domestic gardens remains to be empirically demonstrated. Even with all the new archaeological data that have accrued, the number of actual excavations in the lower Amazon and coast of Pará pales in comparison to the number of extensive shell-mound sites that have been investigated around Santarém and from the mouth of the Amazon to the east coast of Pará. Many of the early sites may lie deeply buried, obscured by later intensive and extensive occupations. It is expected that, as investigations intensify, questions about the nature and degree of sedentism, house gardening and other subsistence practices will be resolved.

It is, however, a safe bet that sometime between 8000 and 5000 BP the house garden, or experimental plot (as intimated at Peña Roja), had become a widespread, standard feature of riverine settlements, from which successful suites of cultivars were gradually relocated into systematically cleared (e.g. slash-and-burn) agricultural fields. Several important domesticated cultigens, such as manioc, have been recovered in sites far removed from where these cultigens were most probably first domesticated in the Neotropical lowland forests. For example, for manioc to be present in the Zaña Valley, in north-western Peru, between 8400 and 6000 BP implies that its domestication had to have already occurred in Amazonia at a point in time well before 8400 BP. Significant forest clearing by slash and burn occurred around 5300 BP in association with maize at Lake Ayauchi in Amazonian Ecuador. Slash-

and-burning was also detected in Lake Geral in eastern Amazonia around 5760 BP, though not associated with cultigens.[66] In sum, forest slash and burn was in place between 6000 and 5000 BP and we may surmise that some form of systematic farming was being practised (see map, pp. 20–21).

The Formative and post-Formative periods (4000–2000 BP): the unknown Amazonia

The period ranging between *c.*4000 and 2000 BP in Amazonia is referred to by archaeologists as the 'Formative', to indicate the presence of sedentary village farmers and nascent complex polities.[67] Unfortunately, it is precisely during the Formative that the data on palaeoeconomy (especially subsistence) in most parts of Amazonia are very scarce. The lack of knowledge about the critical shift from incipient to intensified agroeconomies is one of the big 'unknowns' in Amazonian prehistory.

There appears to be a marked increase in the number and size of Formative sites dating after about 4000 BP. The known sites reveal enormous quantities of broken sherds from ceramic vessels used for food preparation, cooking (including *budares*, or clay griddles), food presentation, consumption and storage, as well as specialized vessels for ritual activities including burial. This evidence leads us to conclude that agriculture provided the bulk of subsistence in terms of calories, although we may suspect that in a balanced, healthy diet plant foraging as well as fishing and hunting would have remained significant, as they still are today (see Petersen *et al.*, this volume). While this is a reasonable inference, the fact is that during the Formative period the empirical evidence regarding subsistence patterns is often lacking, as much of the excavations and analytical efforts by archaeologists have focused on recovering and analysing ceramic and stone artefacts. Studies of form, decoration and/or technical attributes have nearly always been directed towards establishing regional chronological frameworks. As a result archaeologists interested in palaeoeconomy and subsistence can only offer educated guesses or hypotheses about the precise nature of the food production systems that were in operation.

What is clear is that by 4000–3500 BP (initial Formative period) sites with elaborate ceramic assemblages are found throughout the greater Amazonian lowlands, especially along river bluffs, adjacent to floodplains and relatively close to main-stream channels. The La Gruta-Ronquín, a Saladoid tradition/series complex characterized by white on red painted geometric designs, incised-modelled lugs and a wide range of vessels, including clay griddles (i.e. to bake cassava or *farinha)* appeared 'suddenly' and fully developed along the middle Orinoco (Venezuela) in bluffs, sand bars and back *caños* (creeks) from 4600–3000 BP. Perhaps an even earlier Agüerito-Cedeñoid ceramic tradition (5300–4000 BP), with *budares,* was excavated at a point bar, in a sandy deposit of the Orinoco-Apure confluence.[68] In the middle Ucayali, around the Yarinacocha oxbow lake, the Tutishcainyo tradition with zoned-incised/hachured decoration and a complex set of vessels appeared sometime around 4000–3800 BP.[69] Others could be mentioned, but the palaeobotanical and palaeoeconomic data are simply too scarce to be able to specify the agroeconomic systems that characterized the sites belonging to any of these Formative traditions.[70]

What kinds of agroeconomic systems developed and when? How and why did they develop and how did they diverge, spread and intensify? What were the social consequences in terms of palaeodemography, social organization and economy? The answer to many of these questions is, for the time being, largely hypothetical.[71]

The diversity of agricultural systems in Amazonia

As we have seen, the supporting palaeoeconomic data for the Formative (*c.*4000–2000 BP) and even up to European contact (AD 1540s) period are rather scarce. Drawing upon the available ethnohistoric, ethnological and ethnobotanical information, archaeologists can infer several distinct agricultural systems that have evolved over the last four to five millennia in Amazonia. The most ubiquitous system, known as swidden, shifting or slash-and-burn agriculture is the best known and is still practised today. Space will not allow an examination of all these systems and their variations, but two examples will be discussed here. The first is an intensive agricultural system employed in the rich floodplain habitats of western Amazonia today; the second one is a swidden *(chacra)* system practised today in the nutrient-poor, *terra firme* blackwater forests in the Uaupés interfluves of the upper Negro basin (see map, pp. 20–21).

Intensive agriculture in the western Amazonian floodplains

The Amazon experiences annual floods that overflow its banks, inundating the forest up to 50 km away from the main channel in certain areas such as around Lake Coarí. These floods are also affected by the influence of marine tides that extend some 600 km upriver from the mouth of the Amazon. Periodic and permanent swamp forests growing on the floodplains of the whitewater rivers are known as *várzea* in Brazil. The *igapó* swamp forests and *caatinga amazônica* xeromorphic forests develop only in association with blackwater rivers, and reflect the nutrient-poor (oligotrophic) environment that sustains them, whereas the *várzea* (eutrophic) forest is sustained by moderate to rich, silt-laden rivers. *Várzea* forests are not, however, uniformly the same throughout the Amazon and its tributaries. There are at least four major floodplain zones, each with distinct ecosystems and, hence, with varying potential for plant and animal food resource exploitation and for sustaining larger and denser populations.[72]

One of these major zones is the upper Várzea, whose forests cover an extensive region west of Manaus and can be further divided into several floodplain systems, amongst which are the Ucayali-Acre basins (Peru-Brazil) to the west and the Pastaza-Marañón basin (Peru-Ecuador) to the north-west. Both exhibit a high diversity of biotopes (microhabitats) as a result of the dendritic and meandering river patterns and the renewal of nutrient-rich floodplain sediments derived from the geologically young Andes. In these areas the fluvial landscapes include innumerable river meander cut-offs and oxbow lakes *(cochas)* that provide particularly rich niches for aquatic fauna exploitation during the dry season, and also attract abundant terrestrial game.[73]

When viewed from the air, about 25 per cent of the upper floodplain forests adjacent to the meandering rivers, such as Río Manú (Ucayali basin), show a conspicuous series of parallel vegetation strips or bands populated by different species. Every year, after flooding, the rivers change course and are laterally displaced 50–300 metres on average. New alluvial banks are created, upon which a new primary succession of plants becomes established.[74] Each strip represents a different stage of plant succession. Forests here never climax as the annual flood destroys the developing growth.[75] At Cocha Cashu National Forest, on Río Manú (Peru), a transect from river bank to inland comprises a succession of different tree species – *Tessaria* (50–100 metres inland), *Cecropia* (125–200 metres) and *Ficus-Cedrela* (200–300 metres) – before reaching a late succession forest on the higher levees that are not flooded most years.[76] Further inland one reaches the *terra firme* bluffs, located over 10 metres above mean river level at Cocha Cashu. The bluffs are found at the contact zone between old and recent alluvium, beyond which mature forests predominate. This natural vegetation succession would most certainly not have gone unnoticed by early prehistoric groups in their interactions with actual or potential plant resources. It provides valuable clues to gauge the extent, magnitude and periodicity of the floods in different *várzea* landforms. Some high levees may witness flooding in cycles of 50 years or more; other landforms, lower levees and *playas* (beaches), flood every year. Cultigens, therefore, must be selected to articulate their growth cycles with the expected rhythms of flood maxima and minima, just as different fluvial landforms are selected as agricultural plots to suit crop requirements. These are precisely the practices observed among modern *várzea* farmers *(riberinihos, varzeiros)* and native groups (e.g. Shipibo-Conibo).[77]

The best strategic piece of 'real estate' for settlement location in Amazonia is to be found on stretches of stable river bluffs. Settlements on bluffs, like modern towns today, would have access to the rich floodplain econiches and *terra firme* forests on older alluvial soils and, as a bonus, avoid the problems of periodic high floods.[78]

Archaeologist D.W. Lathrap proposed twenty-five years ago that a non-shifting, intensive agriculture developed in the rich floodplain soils, while in the old alluvium bluffs the agriculture of riverine-oriented societies would be based on a system of twenty-five- to fifty-year crop rotation involving 'a bewildering arsenal of crops'. Lathrap went as far as to predict that in Amazonia such an intensive bluff-and-floodplain agricultural system developed first and earliest out of something like the descendants of Taperinha. He further argued that shifting slash-and-burn agriculture was 'a secondary, derived and *late* phenomenon' in Amazonian prehistory, which developed after the *várzea* had become densely occupied by sedentary agriculturalists, while the occupation of the forested interfluves, away from the rivers, remained sparsely populated until much later.[79]

By way of contrast, cultural geographer William Denevan recently proposed that intensive agriculture-sustaining settlements with dense populations developed in a 'patch pattern' in both the floodplain/bluff zones and in the interior forest. He argues that the floodplain and the forest patches with intensive agriculture and dense populations were separated by large, sparsely populated areas. These circumscribed areas of intense agricultural development are related to one or several of the following features: (a) the complementary rich resources of bluff-*várzea* locations, (b) the uneven access to river channels and floodplains, (c) the inefficiency of stone-axes in constantly creating new agricultural fields from mature forests, and (d) the development of rich black and brown soils from previous, sustained human disturbances.

While Lathrap tended to view most of the bluff-*várzea* zone as having the same potential for intensive agriculture and high population density and *terra firme* interfluvial forest/savannah areas as having low population density, Denevan proposes pockets or patches of high intensity occupation in both *várzea* and *terra firme* environmental mosaics.[80] These two different views and predictions on agricultural potential and palaeodemographic trends are in the process of being tested by ongoing archaeological work.

The succession of cultivation zones, as practised today by Tamshiyaku *ribereños* (river settlers) near Iquitos (Peru), bears out the significance of the complementary relationship between bluff and *várzea* settlements (see map, pp. 20–21). This is a particularly effective strategy for optimizing the exploitation of both riverine and forest resources. Here permanent, annual and short-fallow as well as long-fallow fields are maintained with different suites of crops.[81] Close to the main river channel, on the *playas*, fast-growing crops such as peanuts or Asian rice are grown. On rich alluvial mudflats with silty loam soils, slightly inland from the sandy beach zone, short-season growing crops, such as maize, beans and (nowadays) watermelon, are cultivated. In the same microhabitat the Shipibo Indians of Panaillo would grow the same range of crops plus sweet potato. As the *playa* and mudflat soils are renewed every year, plots do not need to be shifted or left fallow and can potentially be farmed annually, but the area that remains above water level long enough for cropping is comparatively small. When settlements are located in the flood zone (e.g. Panaillo), the houses are built on platforms set on stilts *(palaffites)*. *Palaffites* were also reported for the sixteenth-century Yurimagua-Solimões polity.[82] The lower levee zones, which often surround lakes *(cochas)* and swamps, and are flooded most years, are cultivated with tree orchards (including star apple, hog plum, guava and sapota) and gardens of manioc, maize and other annual crops.

On higher levees, above flood level for most years, tree orchards and gardens of manioc, plantains and other annuals (mainly aroids, arrowroots and sweet potatoes) are cultivated, and house settlements usually with house gardens can be and are established on ground level. Here slash-and-burn and (short fallow) shifting plots are usually required, as silt renewal is infrequent. The swamp forests that develop around shallow lakes are often dominated by the highly nutritious palm tree stands well adapted to wetland conditions.[83] Deeper back-swamp lakes and side channels, also supporting palm trees among other wetland vegetation, are extremely rich (especially during the dry season) in fish and aquatic fauna, and also attract terrestrial fauna. Indeed, superimposed upon this *várzea* landscape is an ecological zonation of fish and game.[84] Finally, on the bluffs situated between young, rich (Holocene) alluvium and the old alluvium of *terra firme*, settlements with house gardens/orchards are established, with a succession of *chacras* stretching beyond into the rainforest. Some parts of the bluff, in addition, contain extensive fertile anthropic black soils *(terra preta)* sought by farmers since they can sustain cultivation for longer periods and accommodate nutrient-demanding crops, like maize, beans or peanuts (see Petersen *et al.*, this volume).

While some archaeologists have described the nature of *várzea* fishing and cultivation productivity in terms of a 'boom and bust' scenario determined by the seasonal rise and fall of river flood levels, the situation, as inferred from the Iquitos data, cannot be reduced to such a simple contrast.[85] One must consider all the different cultivation and food resource niches in the *várzea,* from the sand bars and *playas* to the bluffs and adjacent *terra firme* interfluves, simultaneously as one integrated production system.[86] The relevant question is not whether intensive, year-round agriculture was possible in the Amazonian bluff-floodplain, but when and how these became a single, integrated agrosystem, and in what zones along the major Amazonian river systems was such integration feasible.

Because of the dynamics of fluvial geomorphology it is to be expected that most of the archaeological evidence has been literally washed away from within the floodplain. Not surprisingly, the remaining archaeological sites are to a large extent found on the more stable and older bluffs (or those protected by local geological formations), some now at quite some distance from current active channels.[87] This archaeologically observed pattern, first noted by Lathrap in the middle Ucayali, nevertheless cannot fully account for when and how bluff occupants may have integrated the diverse floodplain and bluff agricultural and food resource ecozones into a comprehensive and intensive agricultural system.[88] But at some point in history it did occur in some regions, as there is supporting evidence from sixteenth- and seventeenth-century ethnohistoric documents describing complex, densely populated societies along some segments of the Amazon river, such as the Tapajós, Yurimagua-Solimões and Aparia-Omagua (see Neves, this volume).[89] In short, the subsistence economy of the societies exploiting the bluff-*várzea* zones today, such as the Tamshiyaku *ribereños* of Iquitos or the Shipibo Indians of Panaillo and San Francisco, are an inadequate measure of the full capability of bluff-*várzea* food production systems that were operative in the past.

The Tukanoan swidden agriculture in the blackwater forest

Blackwater or 'heath' forests are entirely different from the whitewater *várzea* of the Ucayali-Acre basin. Forest types are differentiated into *igapó*, a luxuriant flood-forest, and *caatinga amazônica,* a xeromorphic vegetation assemblage.[90] Precipitation in the heath forest is high, but it does experience short, irregular dry periods. Soils developing in this habitat tend to be of very low fertility so that much of the nutrient web circulates between the forest litter and the atmosphere above. The *caatinga amazônica* is characterized by a 'dwarf' forest (6- to 20-metre high canopy) that grows on a superficial, thin, peat *(mor)* humus layer that overlies the hydromorphic quartzy sands (bleached silica), which in turn overly a hard iron-pan. It is prevalent in most parts of the upper Río Negro and its affluents, such as the Içana and Uaupés rivers. The forest is oligotrophic as it grows in a nutrient-poor environment. Trees show a greater development of fine root layer and of toxic substances (e.g. alkaloids, polyphenols) that inhibit the predation of their leaves, which in turn seems to limit the herbivore populations.[91] The black or dark blue waters of the Negro basin derive from the high levels of tannin that come from the chemical decomposition of the vegetation. Low trophic levels (light energy reaching lower river depths) and available dissolved oxygen levels also result in a lower fish and aquatic biomass. Fish can be up to fifteen times less abundant here than in other Amazonian aquatic environments. A blackwater forest is, indeed, a fragile ecosystem.[92] Within the Negro basin, to which blackwater forests are circumscribed, there is a mosaic of somewhat richer upland soils precisely where the Tukanoans establish their gardens.

2.11 A *chacra* in the middle Amazon area planted with manioc.

Native Amazonians of the upper Negro basin today, mainly Tukanoan and Arawakan speakers, have developed remarkable socio-economic strategies in response to these severe environmental limitations. These include maintaining lower population densities than those achieved elsewhere in Amazonia; relying on swidden agriculture, hunting and specialized fishing techniques to cope with low trophic levels; and maintaining a dispersed settlement pattern and a social organization that is based on degrees of hierarchy and segmentation, and regulates control over (though not 'property ownership' of) the territory and its resources.[93]

Tukanoan *chacras (poé)* are complex ecosystems in their own right, as they intentionally 'mimic' the same basic principles of the rainforest food-web dynamics and ecology (figs 2.1, 2.11).[94] Although the Tukanoan *chacras* are invariably dominated by ten, twenty or more varieties of bitter manioc, they will include at least five or six additional high-ranking crops, mainly yams, arrowroots, cocoyams, maize and the African-originated plantains. Peanuts, sugar cane (also European introduced) and *Solanum* sp. shrubs (used for making refreshments), to name just a few of the minor crops, are also found in smaller numbers. *Yajé* and *epená* hallucinogenic plants, coca shrubs, various medicinal plants and fish poisons are also found in *chacras.* After slash-and-burning, cultivars are planted according to soil types, the colour qualities and odours of the ashes, and the degree of carbonization of trees (described by Tukanoans as manifesting different 'energies', or *bogá).* Manioc, yams, plantains, sugarcane and pineapples are always planted near the ashes of large trees or at the foot of carbonized tree stumps because they need 'black' (charcoal), whereas *guamo* trees and fish poisons, for example, do not because they emit their own 'odours' that attract their particular insect communities, larvae and pollinators. Ashes, charcoals and odours most probably play a major role in controlling bacterial, fungal, viral and plant pathogens, including nematodes. As Reichel-Dolmatoff noted, the Tukano 'woman knows this well [and] calculates in detail where to locate insect-attracting plants to protect staple foods'.[95]

Several *chacras* at different stages of production will be maintained by individual families of a *maloca* (multi-family house or longhouse). A young productive *chacra* (*poé*) will last on average for a maximum of one year, after which the Tukanoans cease tending and weeding; it becomes *poé sarí* ('recuperated garden'), implying that it is in the process of being returned to the forest. The *poé sari* will, however, continue to produce for quite some time, as manioc is constantly harvested and stalks replanted. After weed invasion and other secondary pioneering forest species take over, and after soil nutrient depletion makes even manioc (and tuber) harvesting inefficient, the *chacra* becomes *via'dó,* an 'old garden'. Still these old gardens are periodically visited to dig up manioc and collect firewood, or for other special purposes. They are in effect transformed into fruit orchards: the Tukanoan women plant fruit trees such as *guamo* (*Inga* sp.) and selectively weed to encourage particular tree seedlings to grow, such as *Cecropia sclerophylla*; the older the *via'do,* the more fruiting trees are found. Most of these trees do not occur naturally, they are cultivated. Sweet potato or *batata,* a climbing vine, is also encouraged to expand in *via'do* fields because it can spread about the ground without interfering with other crops, as it would do in *poé* or *poé sarí* fields if left unattended. In other words, the *via'do* functions as a food reserve. Fallow, yet productive *via'dó* fields will remain so for about eight to ten years, after which they may once again become *poé.*[96]

Tukanoans will also maintain domestic gardens in proximity to the *maloca* compound. In contrast to other upland rainforest societies, Tukanoans *appear* to maintain a less diverse stock of house garden plants, but the fact is that a full inventory has yet to be undertaken by ethnobotanists.[97] The domesticated, highly nutritious *burití* or *moriche* palm is a ubiquitous component of the house garden. In addition, a minimal list includes lianas that yield a juice used to dye fishing nets black/brown (makes them invisible to fish); genipap (Rubiacae) bushes whose leaves yield a black pigment used in body decoration; *carayurú,* from which a red pigment used in body decoration is extracted; various fruiting trees like *guamo*; food crops like arrowroots; and stimulants such as tobacco and coca.[98]

Finally there are the ancient, abandoned *chacras* and old house sites, *nëngë via'do,* whose 'ownership' is not within the memory of the present generation of Tukanoans. They know that these were sites once inhabited by humans, 'other people', in particular the 'Tapir People', who, the Tukanoans claim, were the original inhabitants and historically preceded them in the upper Negro basin. These spots are recognized by their distinct vegetation, by the darker soil colours and the presence of 'escaped' cultivars, all of which are conceived as the 'seeds of the ancients' *(ohtéri mëra).* The *nëngë via'do* may contain peach palms, *umarí,* genipap and *guamo* trees, papaya (*Carica papaya*), aroid root crops, and the hallucinogens *yajé* and *epená.* The Tukanoans regard these ancient loci as seed-stocks, genetic store-houses, of the highest quality. According to Reichel-Dolmatoff, the existing food plants and fruits are not eaten, but all the seeds and vegetative parts (in the case of tubers) can be selected for use in their own house gardens or *chacras*.[99] The conservationist practice, if accurately described by Reichel-Dolmatoff, may be recent, as it is likely that in old and ancient fields during the 'neo-lithic era' (no machetes or iron axes) tree felling would be less time consuming and more efficient in secondary forest growth than in climax forests.

In spite of the tremendous importance that the full range of crops and wild food plants have, the Tukanoans extract most of their caloric requirements from manioc. It has been calculated that among the Desana (Tukanoans) of the Yapú settlement some 80 per cent of all caloric intake came from bitter manioc, with another 10 per cent from tree fruits and other cultivars.[100] While the percentage of the total protein intake is dominated by fish (45 per cent) and meat (12 per cent), manioc still commands a 'respectable' 21 per cent.[101] Insect grubs and larvae harvested in both the forest and gardens represent about 4 per cent of all protein sources. In the poor nutrient environment of the blackwater forests manioc has decisive advantages over all other crops in terms of total calories and yield. Manioc's deficiency of essential (as opposed to non-essential) proteins is supplied primarily by fish and secondarily by terrestrial game.

The Tukanoan, like so many other upland rainforest peoples, have a symbiotic (mutually beneficial) relationship with plants, animals and resources that follows sound, sustainable ecological principles. The Tukanoans do not see themselves as occupying a superior place in the natural order of things, but rather as being an integral 'component' of the ecosystem. Their behaviour, attitudes and decisions on resource exploitation and conservation are not just determined or regulated by what western scientists would conceive of as ecological knowledge alone, which they clearly have, but also take place within the framework of a sophisticated native cosmology and ideology. Within this world view 'exploitative' and 'conservationist' behaviour, and different courses of action and options, are mediated and explained by myths and oral lore where spirits and ancestors, with whom Tukanoans are constantly 'negotiating' – often through hallucinogenic *yajé* ceremonies – are the owners and regulators/managers of places, resources and situations.[102] This integrated way of perceiving the relationship between human beings and the natural world is referred to as 'ecosophy'.[103] Precisely because Tukanoan ecosophy was so sophisticated, it was once prematurely assumed that such knowledge systems, along with the outward manifestations – swidden agriculture in particular – were extremely ancient and all of a piece throughout Amazonia.

But how ancient is the Tukanoan swidden agricultural system? By what processes did this efficient agriculture develop in the blackwater forests of the Negro basin? Was there a different agroeconomic system in place *prior* to its development? The archaeology of this region, particularly in the Içana-Uaupés drainage, is largely unknown.[104] The Tukanoans themselves argue that they are relatively recent arrivals in a region once dominated by the 'Tapir People'. Yet, further downstream in the lower Río Negro extensive anthropogenic black soil archaeological sites dating to around the Christian era, perhaps even earlier, seem to suggest higher population densities than could be sustained by current Tukanoan swidden agriculture. These *terra preta* sites are probably not the result of multiple, ephemeral reoccupations, as some archaeologists insist. Archaeological sites such as Açutuba are quite large, complex settlements evincing a high degree of sedentism and, necessarily, of established agricultural fields within a circumscribed radius. These systems were probably maintained for long periods (per-

2.12 'Watu Ticaba, a Wapisiana Village', from Robert Schomburgk's *Twelve Views in the Interior of Guiana*, 1841. This nineteenth-century engraving of a Wapishana settlement depicts some of the steps involved in processing manioc tubers into cassava, from drying the round cassava bread on thatched roofs to baking it in round clay griddles.

haps using multicrop rotation) and were more elaborate than anything practised today (see Petersen *et al.*, this volume).[105] How, when and exactly why hypothesized agrosystems such as these were replaced by the kind of shifting agriculture currently in use remain open to future investigation.

Manioc the 'super-crop' and its importance in Amazonia

By the sixteenth century manioc had long been the staple crop of preference among almost all native populations in the tropical lowlands of South and lower Central America (fig. 2.12). It was the staple crop that astounded Christopher Columbus and his band during their voyages (1492–8) in the Caribbean islands. They commented repeatedly on how manioc was central to the economy of the powerful and densely populated Taíno chiefdoms in the Haiti-Dominican Republic (Hispaniola).[106] In La Vega Real, Hispaniola, the Spanish reported huge agricultural fields planted with manioc using a technique called *montones* (mounds), consisting of rectangular or rounded topsoil mounds, all of a standard dimension. This is clearly a large-scale version of the system described for the modern Kuikurú in the upper Xingú.[107] It is ironic that the Spanish conquest itself was in large part made possible by using manioc-derived products like cassava bread, which served as a storable food reserve on many voyages and over-land expeditions.[108] How could this seemingly humble and toxic tuber have become, in effect, a 'super-crop' central to Amazonian indigenous subsistence and social development?

Manioc the 'super-crop'

Manioc (*Manihot esculenta* 'Crantz') is only surpassed by Asian rice among the top staple crops in the tropics.[109] There are several reasons for this. It can be grown in a wide range of environmental conditions and still provide consistently good yields. It is easy to cultivate by cutting stem stalks and replanting (vegetative propagation). It can be stored 'live' underground for two or more years. It is drought resistant and at the same time tolerates temporary flooding before rotting. Its many cultivated varieties have a range of natural toxicity that provide defences against many potential herbivores and predators, safeguarding it against crop failure. Equally important, of all the tubers, manioc provides the highest source of food energy (calories) that the body needs to replace for work performed.

Measurements taken from the fresh, edible portion of the tuber yield the highest proportion of carbohydrates by weight and calories of any Amazonian root crop.[110] One of the most obvious reasons for the prevalence of manioc cultivation in Amazonia is that it surpasses all other root crops in terms of sheer quantity of calories generated from its carbohydrate content, providing a source of high-yield energy that the human body needs to replace that lost in daily work.[111] The tuber, however, is deficient in essential proteins.[112] Although manioc leaves are not widely processed and consumed as food today, they may have been in the past, even though there are more effective ways of obtaining the high quality fats and proteins (e.g. in fish, turtle and game) that the leaves contain.[113] Protein deficiency is the reason why manioc alone cannot constitute a balanced diet, and why in Amazonia forest plant foraging, aquatic and terrestrial game are critical for a healthy population.

Two varieties tend to be recognized: sweet manioc *(yuca dulce)* with lower toxic levels, and bitter manioc *(yuca brava)* with higher levels, but there is a continuous variation of toxicity between these.[114] As mentioned above, one advantage of this toxicity is to provide a chemical defence against herbivores and pathogens, thus minimizing crop loss and helping to maintain expected crop yields. In addition, cultural mechanisms to avoid crop loss to pathogens and herbivores include shifting agricultural fields, cultivating multiple crops (which deflects predators) and intercropping many different varieties of manioc, as each variety is likely to have varying resistance qualities. The Aguaruna (Jívaroans), for example, maintain up to a hundred or more varieties in all their *chacras* combined, and the Xinguanos recognize more than forty varieties.[115] Modern attempts to focus cultivation on a single manioc variety have resulted in increasingly severe losses to predators.

Generally, the richer the nutrient sources (e.g. soil), the better manioc is able to tolerate predation; the poorer they are, the less able is manioc to cope with predation, and hence the higher the toxic defences are. Thus, the highest concentration and diversity of cultivated bitter manioc is precisely in the oligothropic blackwater forests of Amazonia. Herbivore pressure and nutrient resource availability affect manioc yield and correlate positively or negatively with toxicity. To summarize, manioc can grow in sub-optimal conditions and still yield close to its potential biomass.[116]

Another important advantage of manioc is 'live storage' underground, where it can remain for two to three years without spoiling. Its nine- to eighteen-month maturation allows staggered planting so that there is always ready-to-harvest manioc available year-round. Stored bitter manioc tends to live longer than sweet manioc. Manioc can also be stored for short (days) or for longer periods (years), depending on the product's stage of food processing. Storage techniques vary considerably from group to group. Among the Tukanoans (Uaupés-Içana) processed pure manioc starch is stored to produce later, for example, *mingau,* which has a glutinous texture like porridge, and *sireira,* a pure starch cassava bread, considered a luxury and delicacy and charged with symbolism. *Sireira* is used as a special food for males during their rites of passage to manhood. The pressed, raw starch is stored in pits 60–120 cm deep and 45–60 cm in diameter. The starch is dumped into the pits, whose walls are lined with plantain leaves, over which a 10–15 cm thick protective layer of manioc fibre is laid. The fibre acts as a bait for maggots, the main predator of the starch. The plantain leaf lining is folded at the top, and the pit is sealed by a tightly compacted layer of earth. These stores are laid down a year in advance of use and last for up to two years or more. Indeed, the Tukanoans occasionally dig on sites long abandoned in search of forgotten, but still edible stores. Dry pit storage requires plantain lining replacement (and removal of any maggots) every three to four months. Moreover, a range of tree and palm seeds (like *buriti, umarí*) are also stored in pits using the same technique.[117]

2.13 Manioc grater from the Içana river, upper Amazon (93 x 38.5 cm; Board of Trustees of the Royal Botanic Gardens, Kew). The shape and decorative motifs communicate information about ethnic affiliation as well as myths and legends related to manioc production. Sap (from *Couma dulcis*) is used to secure the sharp granite chips that are inserted into the surface of the grater.

The elaboration of cassava 'bread'

At least twenty-five major categories of manioc foods and beverages have been reported.[118] Their preparation requires a sequence of simple to highly complex techniques and stages, both to obtain the desired taste and texture, and in the case of the bitter varieties to eliminate the toxic prussic acid. One of the most elaborate recipes for the preparation of a food derived from manioc is that for cassava 'bread', or *casabe/beijú* (fig. 2.14: II). Several of the activities during the cooking stages discussed below can be recognized in the Wapishana (or Wapixana, Arawakan speakers of Guiana) scene depicted in fig. 2.12.

Harvesting manioc tubers from the *chacra* is typically made easier by using a wooden digging stick although nowadays the iron machete is the preferred instrument. Tubers are usually carried in vegetable fibre woven baskets to the village. Among some groups, these are temporarily placed in pits below the creek's water line (e.g. by the seventeenth-century Omagua) or left under water in a stream for a day or two to soften and ferment (e.g. by the modern Andoque, Colombia) before reaching the 'cooking' shed.

Fresh tubers are first washed and then skinned or peeled and sliced (see fig. 2.14: II), using convenient scraping and cutting tools traditionally made from wood, shell or stone. Often these scrapers and blades are multifunctional and are employed on other materials besides manioc. Frequently the tubers (or slices) are rinsed again before they are pounded or grated into pulp. Pounding is often done with hollowed, cylindrical wooden trunks *(pilón)* and a heavy mace *(mazo),* larger than the ones depicted for the Nukak (see Politis, this volume).

Other Amazonian groups, instead of pounding, grate the tuber, which may first be cut into a few large pieces with a stone (or nowadays metal) blade/knife. Again, these blades can be used for other activities (e.g. basketry fibre cutting). A board of hardwood is cut and shaped, and grating teeth made of fine wooden splinters (as in Xingú) or of minute triangular stone flakes are then inserted into the board's surface

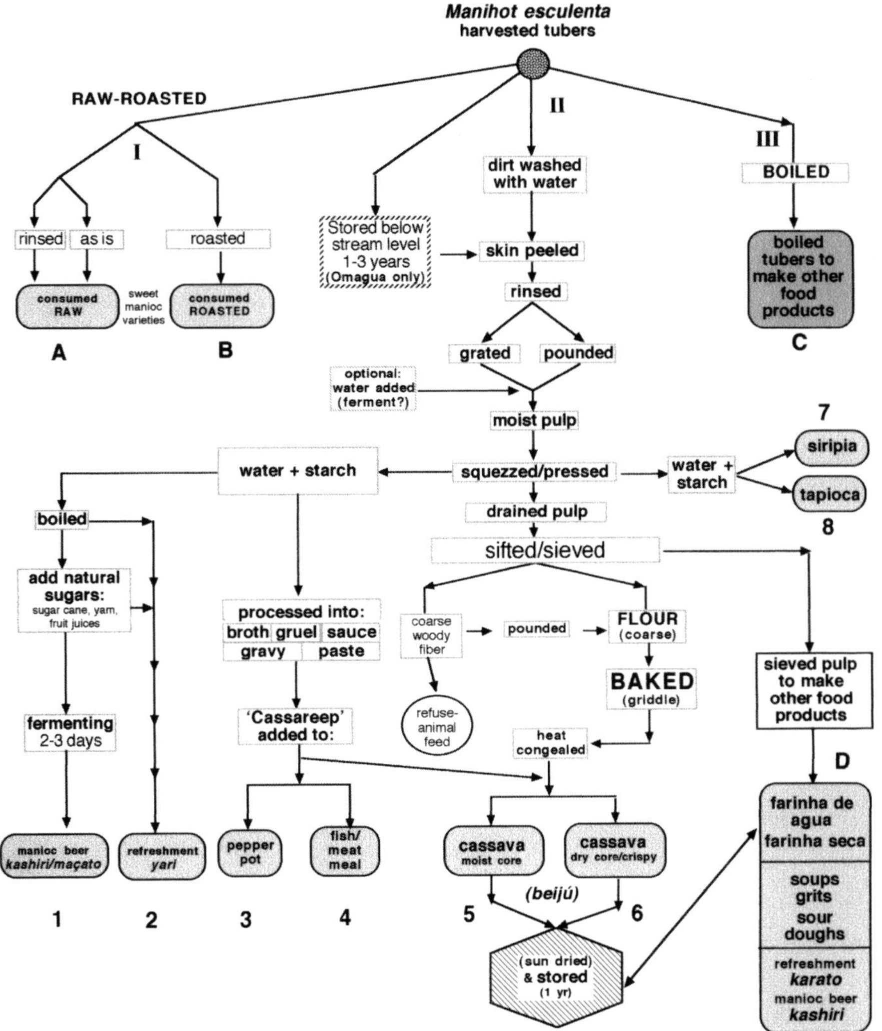

2.14 Stages of manioc production. This diagram shows the sequence of processing activities involved in producing some of the foods derived from manioc tubers. Cassava core, or *beijú*, and alcoholic beverages are shown in greater detail. The steps involved in processing the raw tubers often enhance the nutritional content and chemical composition of the final product.

and affixed with a vegetable resin (fig. 2.13). These graters are often elegantly decorated and come in various shapes (rectangular, hourglass, etc.), depending on the ethnic group. Although grating boards are specialized artefacts, they can also be used to grate a range of other tubers from which pulp is required. As well as being functional, they are also important aesthetic vehicles that convey symbolic information. In modern times, throughout the Guiana-Orinoco regions, neighbouring groups of different ethnic and linguistic affiliation strive to obtain through trade and exchange the grating boards manufactured by the Yekuana Indians (Carib speakers), as these are deemed to be the proper and best ones.[119] The grating board is sometimes placed inside a large open ceramic vessel, leaning against one side. These vessels usually have reinforced rims, as this is where most of the stress is applied. Rims with a triangular or flanged cross-section, for example, probably strengthened a vessel in this way. These kinds of rim sherds are commonly found in large numbers at many Formative and post-Formative Amazonian archaeological sites (see Petersen *et al.*, this volume). The action of grating and pressing through a sifter over a vessel produces use-wear signatures at the point of stress (at the rim), which in some instances have been observed in the archaeological ceramics.

Once grated, the still moist pulp is either squeezed in a long, tubular, collapsible,

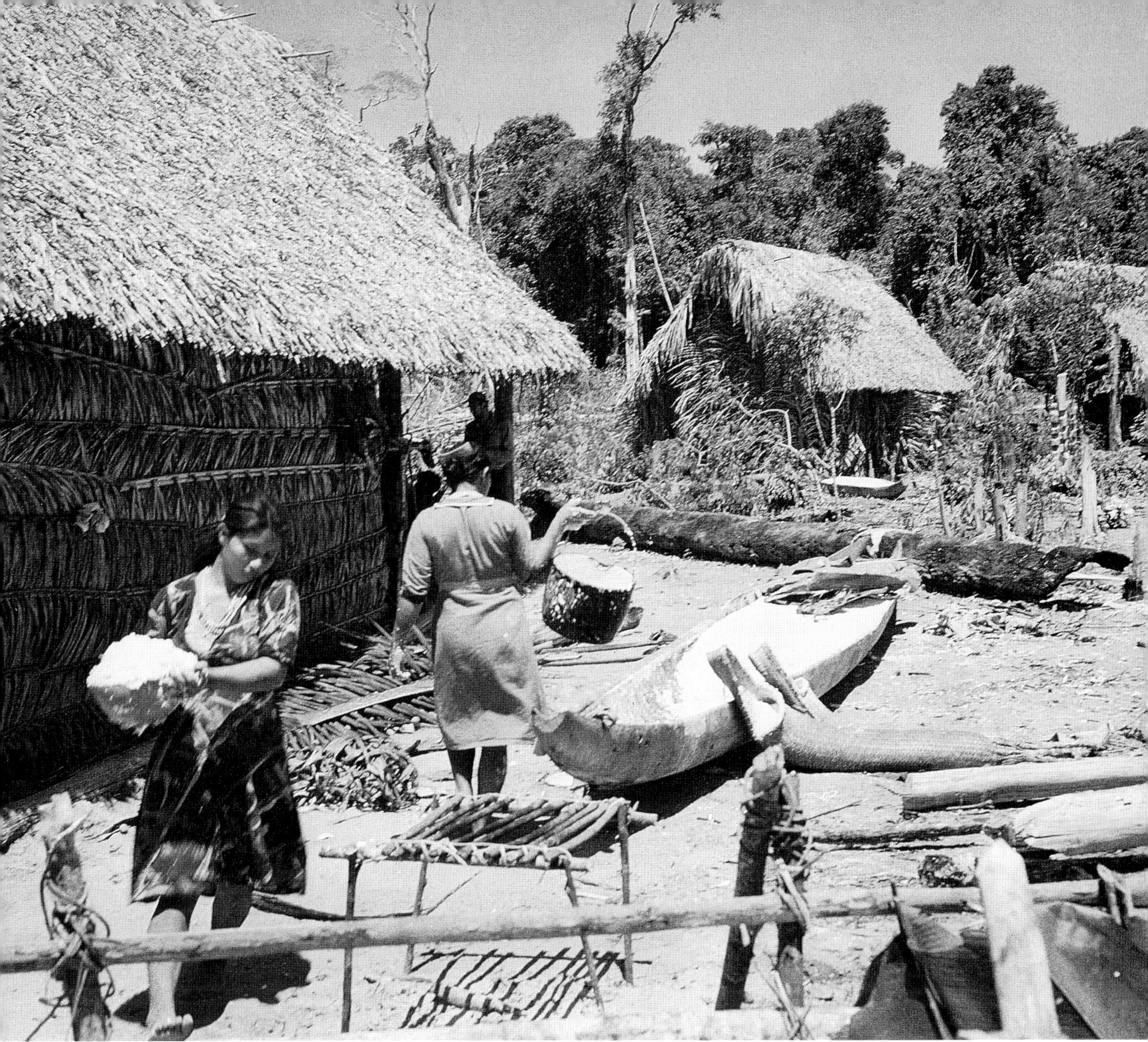

ABOVE 2.16 Manioc processing in a Yabarana settlement in Manapiare, in the Ventuari region of Venezuela. The *tipití* is resting on the side of an old canoe that is full of squeezed manioc. The canoe often functions as a fermenting and storage vat.

LEFT 2.15 A Yekuana Indian squeezing out the poisonous manioc juice with a basketry-woven *tipití*. The juice that is collected (water, starch and cyanuric acid) is not discarded but processed into other products including *kashiri*, or *masato*, and tapioca (see fig. 2.14).

cylindrical basket (or *tipití)* or pressed with a rolled fibre mat-like strainer (e.g. Xinguanos). The *tipití* is usually quite large and is hung vertically from an erected wooden frame (as the Baré and Yekuana do), and at its bottom a wooden pole (lever) serves to compress the *tipití* and apply maximum squeezing force (fig. 2.15). It is rather like wringing a wet towel to squeeze out the water. Some ethnic groups, like the Baré, Yekuana and Yanömanö, hang the *tipití* in pairs (male and female *tipití);* others use a simpler system of a single vertical pole from which the top end is hung, and a single lever pole at the bottom. The water and starch residue is collected in a ceramic pot placed directly below the *tipití*, or in the case of *tipití* pairs the liquids falls into a wooden trough. A third common way of separating water and starch residue from the pulp is by erecting a tripod from which the *tipití* hangs over a basket mesh sitting on a large ceramic vessel. The squeezed or drained pulp is dumped into containers, which may be of several kinds and sizes. It is not uncommon to dump it into a canoe and then cover it with broad leaves, such as plantain (fig. 2.16). The process from harvest

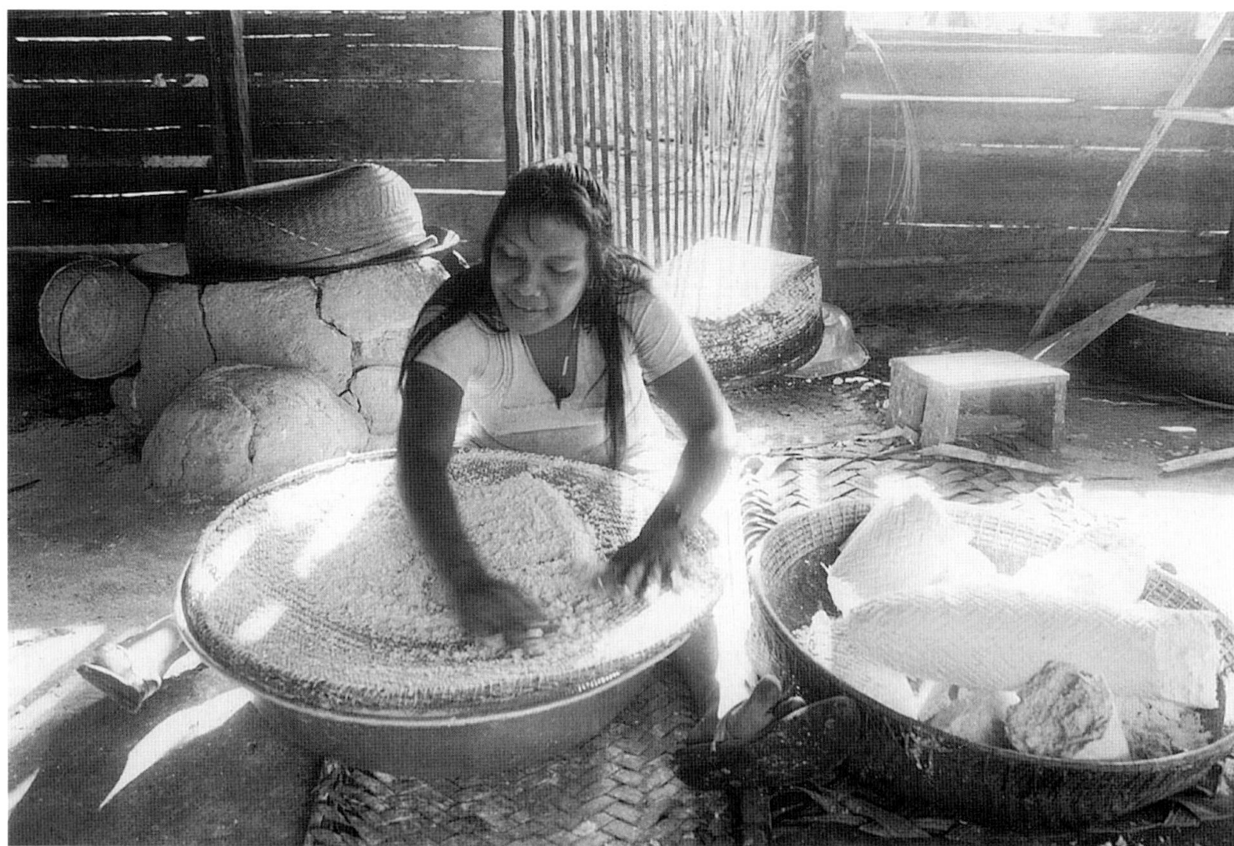

2.17 A Baré woman from the upper Negro region sifting manioc flour. Around her, manioc pulp and flour are seen in various stages of preparation.

up to this point (drained pulp stage in fig. 2.14: II) generally involves a day's work, after which the drained pulp is left to 'sit' or 'rest', which implies a twelve- to sixteen-hour fermentation process before the next preparation stage begins. Less frequently, some groups like the Tukanoan, prefer to perform all the stages, from harvesting to cooking the ordinary cassava bread (and *mingau* beverage) in the same day and for immediate consumption.

The drained starch and water are not wasted but collected for later processing into fermented beer (*kashiri, masato*), a non-alcoholic beverage (*mingau, yarí*) or *cassareep, siripa* or *tapioca.* Ceramic (and now enamel or plastic as well) vessels are used to collect the squeezed starchy water, where it is left to decant in order to separate the heavier, 'pearly starch' from the water. Archaeological ceramics showing chemical erosion resulting from manioc prussic acid and other acids have been detected in the upper Xingú as early as AD 900. Many of the vessel shapes strictly associated with manioc cooking and food-serving are present among modern Xinguanos (e.g. Waurá, Kuikurú) and can also be traced directly back to Ipavú-phase (AD 900–1600) archaeological occupations.[120]

Usually on the next day the drained pulp is sifted through a succession of ever finer-meshed round basket sieves, and then pounded and/or ground again to obtain manioc flour (fig. 2.17). Alternatively the sieved 'dough' is rolled into balls or loaves to eventually obtain *farinha seca* or *farinha de água,* or to be processed as soups, grits and other foods (fig. 2.14: D). The by-products of the sieving process, the coarse and woody fibres extracted from the sieved pulp, are usually discarded, but often constitute food sources for animals (dogs, ants and, nowadays, chickens), or may be pounded and sieved again, and added to the previously sieved flour. Among many groups, a round, shallow basket sieve (*panara* or *guapa*) that comes in varying mesh-sizes is used to sieve the coarser flour, depending on how fine the flour is desired to be. The flour is then baked on a round ceramic (or nowadays metal) griddle, where heat congeals the starchy flour into a round tortilla-like cassava 'bread'. If it is removed before being well baked, it retains a moist core and it does have a pleasant flavour when eaten by itself. If the relatively dry flour is constantly stirred (often using paddles, but convenient tools like canoe oars may be also used), then a thin, crispy cassava is obtained; to our western tastes it lacks flavour. It is the 'crispy' cassava bread that is most often used just as people in the Mediterranean use (wheat) bread, as an adjunct to dip into sauces during a meal. The baked cassava bread with a moist core is frequently left to dry on the roof of cooking sheds, on fibre mats or hanging (folded) on a 'clothes line'. If not immediately consumed, cassava bread can be stored for a year or more.

In the course of manioc food preparation a range of tools, artefacts, receptacles, baskets and other materials are used. With some exceptions, such as the *tipití* press, most of these are not specially manufactured for manioc processing. Almost all these artefacts can also be used to process other tubers and foods. In regions where maize is a staple crop or cultivated along with manioc, maize 'pies' *(arepas)* are also baked in clay griddles, although usually the clay griddle has a slight concavity and is thinner than those that are ethnographically known to be used only for baking manioc flour into cassava. In short, those artefacts that are more likely to be preserved in the archaeological record (stone, shell, ceramic) are multipurpose. Canoes are, indeed, used as receptacles (and fermentation vats) for the temporary storage of drained pulp, although their primary function, of course, is for river transport. Canoe oars can likewise substitute for the wooden paddles that turn over the cassava bread. It is this kind of artefact multifunctionality that in the absence of direct palaeobotanical data makes the correlation of archaeological materials with a specific type of crop or food difficult to establish beyond reasonable doubt.

Conclusion

From an archaeological perspective, there is little direct evidence that manioc and *only* manioc was being prepared for consumption and/or storage.[121] The assemblage of instruments and equipment that remain as a kind of 'signature' of the process of manioc preparation are very nearly invisible in the archaeological record. Faced with such limited evidence, archaeologists can easily underestimate the volume of food procurement and production that Amazonian agricultural systems could have sustained. We archaeologists sometimes ask ourselves what we would expect to find as evidence of food procurement and processing if we were investigating the remains of groups like the Nukak 5,000 years from now. Research such as that described in this volume among the Nukak or Tukanoans helps make the past intelligible to the present. The most important lesson to be learned is that in Amazonian prehistory hunter-gatherers did not evolve in an inevitable, linear direction towards agricultural systems and beyond to intensified agriculture. Once a particular food strategy developed, it remained an option – alongside others – that could be called on when advantageous. Some Kayapó groups found it necessary to shift from a settled to a 'nomadic agricultural' pattern; the very ancient Peña Roja foragers possibly practised 'itinerant gardening'. The settled Tukanoan farmers spend considerable time hunting, fishing and foraging, much like the early Holocene foragers did; the Nukak continue to pursue foraging strategies. Many Ge-speaking groups (e.g. Xavante) alternate between settled farming periods and months of trekking as hunter-gatherers. By assiduously recovering the evidence of particular strands of the complex tapestry of Amazonian history, from the present far back into the past, we will be able to discern ancient patterns and generate explanations for the processes that led to these changing food system configurations.

Acknowledgements

The author wishes to thank Mariano Mejía, Head of Public Services of the Information and Documentation Unit of the Centro de Internacional de Agricultura Tropical in Cali, Colombia, for his invaluable assistance in tracking down specialized references on manioc biogenetics and nutrition research. This chapter could never have come to fruition without the able assistance of the editors and Ben Burt, as my syntax sometimes approached that of 'Portuñol' rather than English. I am also thankful to E. Neves, G. Politis, M. Heckenberger and G. Ardila Calderón for sharing their information as well as for their comments on my paper. I am particularly grateful to Colin McEwan and Stephen Hugh-Jones for their input not just in editorial matters but in the content as well. Warwick Bray most kindly allowed me to reproduce several of his photographs. Finally, I wish to acknowledge here all the archaeologists – Brazilian, Colombian, Venezuelan and international – who got their hands 'dirty' in the field so that this overview could be provided. This chapter is the fruit of their work, although I alone am responsible for its shortcomings and any errors of interpretation.

NOTES

1 Denevan 2001: 302.

2 For a non-specialist discussion of humankind's quest for food, spanning the earliest hominid ancestors to modern times from a global perspective, consult Crowe 2000. From a cultural geographer's point of view Denevan's (2001) most recent publication, 'Cultivated Landscape of Amazonia and the Andes', is strongly recommended. Also for specialized discussion from an archaeological viewpoint consult the volume edited by Gosden and Hather (1999), and for a palaeobotanist's view consult Piperno and Pearsall (1998).

3 Politis 1996b: 172–84; 1999: 109. The Andoque (or Andoke) are found in the Middle Caquetá river of the Colombian Amazonas territory (see Andrade 1993: 63–85). The Tukano are found in the Vaupés region of Colombia (see Reichel-Dolmatoff 1996, C. Hugh-Jones 1979). For a general description of *chacra* systems of the Upper Negro-Orinoco-Ventuari basins, consult Harris 1971.

4 Posey 1994: 271–2, 278; the volume edited by Posey and Balée (1989) provides excellent documentation on this point. On agroforestry and forest resource management consult Balée 1998.

5 Harris 1971; Johnson 1983: 29–63; Carneiro 1983: 111–35; D.L. Dufour 1993a: 47–68; Andrade 1993: 65–85.

6 Whitmore 1990: 10; Moran 1993b: 9.

7 Moran 1993b: 21, 29.

8 Roosevelt 1989; Posey and Balée 1989; Roosevelt *et al.* 1991; Balée 1998.

9 Meggers 1954, 1957.

10 Steward and Faron 1959: 288–91.

11 For an extended critical review, see Neves 1998a, 1999a.

12 Meggers 1954, 1957, 1971, 1996.

13 Whitmore 1990: 81ff.; Campbell and Frailey 1984; Colinvaux *et al.* 1996a & b; Bush *et al.*, 1989; Roosevelt 1994: 6; Bray 1995; Meggers 1982, 1987.

14 Years 'BP' means radiocarbon years before present, where 'present' is arbitrarily defined as AD 1950.

15 A well-written discussion of climatic changes during the Late Glacial Maximum is found in Wilson *et al.* 2000.

16 Hooghiemstra and van der Hammen 1998: 155–9; Hasternath 1981: Appendix IV.

17 Consult Piperno and Pearsall (1998: 90–107) and Wilson *et al.* (2000: 174–81). While palaeobotanical knowledge and the quality of data have dramatically increased, the number of deep sediment probe data points in the Neotropics are too few as yet to establish more accurately the spatial boundaries between major vegetation units. Such vegetation reconstruction maps have misled some people into thinking that they are 'equivalent' to modern vegetation maps. Modern vegetation maps are hardly ever based on pollen, phytoliths or even charred micro-remains; they are based on a different set of data and criteria that allow for much greater and a different kind of resolution and detail. Direct comparisons are, therefore, tenuous at best.

18 Piperno and Pearsall 1998: 102–3; also Wilson *et al.* 2000: 61–5, 108–10.

19 Plants metabolize energy sources using three

photosynthetic pathways, C3 (carbon isotope 3), C4 (carbon isotope 4) or CAM, which stands for 'Crassulacean Acid Metabolism'. CAM is 'a different kind of metabolism that allows CO2 to be absorbed at night when water loss is minimal and to be stored and used next day for photosynthesis' (Whitmore 1990: 212). As palaeobotanists Piperno and Pearsall (1998: 103) explained, 'plants that are better able to compete in a lower CO2 environment are [those] that use the C4 and CAM photosynthetic pathways 'because their leaf anatomy allows them to photosynthesize carbon more efficiently ... Plants that use the C3 photosynthetic pathway include virtually all the tree and understory growth of a tropical forest, including various wild tubers, and may have been at a competitive disadvantage in the late glacial world. C3 annuals experience significantly lowered productivity when grown in a low CO2 environment. Lowered CO2 would have exacerbated drought stress and further promoted the expansion of C4 and CAM open land [grasses] at the expense of some C3 forest species [including tubers]. It may have led to more open forest canopies because of lowered light use efficiencies during photosynthesis.'

20The scientific names are: manioc (*Manihot esculenta*), sweet potato or *batata* (*Ipomoea batatas*), yams or ñame (*Dioscorea* spp.), arrowroots (*Maranta* spp.) and cocoyams (*Xanthosoma* spp.)

21 Sage 1995 cited in Piperno and Pearsall 1998: 103.

22 Marked wet and dry seasons are not only relied upon by tuberous C3 plants like manioc, but also other C4 ancestral relatives of modern domesticates like *teosinte* (*Zea* spp.), from which modern maize (*Zea mays*) descended (Piperno and Pearsall 1998: 110ff.; on maize, see Pearsall 1995).

23 The consequent retreat of glaciers and the warming of the ocean surfaces resulted from the changes in the latitudinal and seasonal solar radiation received by the Earth's surface (part of what is known as the Milankovitch Effect), and became important in regulating global weather, particularly precipitation and temperature (see Piperno and Pearsall 1998: 107; Wilson *et al.* 2000: 109–10).

24 It is critical because 'it is tied to the disappearance of the megafauna and open-land plants, and it necessitated full-time exploitation of forests by human groups'. Moreover 'the late-glacial Neotropical landscape was far more productive per unit of labor effort in terms of both wild animals and plants than were Holocene environments. Changes in the flora and fauna consequent to climatic change at the close of the Pleistocene when lowland tropical forest advanced on the landscape would have necessitated some marked adjustments in foraging strategies and almost certainly involved a higher investment in searching for and processing food items than those of Pleistocene antecedents' (both quotes from Piperno and Pearsall 1998: 102–5).

25 Whitmore 1990; Wilson *et al.* 2000: 175–7; see also Meggers 1982.

26 Following Colinvaux, Piperno and Pearsall have rejected the refugia theory, because 'little of the palaeobotanical information derived from Amazonia can be reconciled with refugial theory' and because 'empirical data from palaeoecology has resulted in a much clearer understanding of the distribution and composition of forests during the Pleistocene'. The observed modern biological endemisms did not occur because of a vast advance of savannah 'engulfing' the rainforest (thus creating 'island' refugia) due to Pleistocene aridity but because of the Ice Age-induced cooling and lower CO2 concentration, whose combined effects on biological species were further compounded by altitude. In this scenario the effects of biological endemism and diversity (technically known as 'vicariance') are due to not to vegetation barriers (savannah over forest habitats) but to these climatic variables and the isolates themselves.

27 Meggers 1957, 1982, 1987.

28 Colinvaux *et al.* 1996a & b.

29 Hooghiemstra and van der Hammen (1998: 158).

30 Colinvaux 1998: 8. One example of this comes from the pollen profiles of the Colombian Araracuara rainforest, which showed some twelve individual species of plants that today only occur in the sub-Andean forest, but which were part of the plant community over 5,000 years ago (Mora *et al.* 1991; Archila Montañéz 1999).

31 For a succinct discussion of the earlier views and how they have changed, see Harris 1989 and 1991.

32 Consult Rindos 1980, 1984, 1989 (on mutualism and co-evolutionary theory), Lathrap 1984 (for a critique of Rindos and the role of human intentionality) and Pearsall 1995: 159–60 (for a summary discussion of this subject).

33 Piperno and Pearsall 1998: 17–18. The 'broad spectrum diet' argument here summarized is in fact a predictive model (known as the 'diet breadth model) based on 'optimal foraging' theory. These models/theories have borrowed heavily from behavioural ecology and micro-economic theories. For further specialized references see Winterhandler 1981, Hill *et al.* 1987, Hawkes and O'Connell 1992, and Kaplan and Hill 1992.

34 For a broad synthesis on this early period in Amazonia, see Roosevelt 1999a: 312–15, 1998: 190ff., and Dillehay *et al.* 1996: 145–204 for a detailed critical review.

35 Roosevelt *et al.* 1996: 373–84; Roosevelt 1998: 195–7.

36 Roosevelt *et al.* 1996: 379. The scientific names are *jutaí* (*Hymenaea parvifolia*), *castanha do Pará*/Brazil nut (*Bertholetia excelsa*), *achuá* (*Sacoglotis guianensis*), *pitomba* (*Talisia esculenta*), *tarumã* (*Vitex*, cf. *V. cymosa*), *sacurí* (*Attalea microcarpia*), *curuá* (*Attalea spectabilis*) and *tucumã* (*Astrocaryum vulgare*).

37 Roosevelt *et al.* 1996: 379.

38 The scientific names of the fish are *pirarucú* (*Arapaima gigas*), *taíra* (*Hoplias malabaricus*); the juvenile tortoises and aquatic turtles are from the genera *Cryptodira*, *Testudinidae* and *Pleurodira*.

39 Roosevelt *et al.* 1996: 380.

40 Roosevelt 1995; Roosevelt *et al.* 1991: 1621–4; Roosevelt *et al.* 1996: 380.

41 Schmitz 1987; Miller 1987; Prous 1991. The site Toqueirão da Pedra Furada, close to São Raimundo Nonato, Piauí, Brazil, has laid a claim for the earliest human occupation in the New World, but it lies outside the Amazonian tropical forests (see details in Meltzer *et al.* 1994, Guidón *et al.* 1996 and Parenti *et al.* 1996; for a very brief summary, see Roosevelt 1998: 312–15).

42 All the data from Peña Roja and Abeja are obtained from Mora *et al.* 1991; Cavelier *et al.* 1995: 27–44; Llanos Chaparro 1997; Archila Montañez 1999.

43 The list of radiocarbon dates on Araracuara-Caquetá can be obtained from Archila Montañez 1999: 72, 80.

44 Herrera 1981. On other Araracuara-Caquetá anthropogenic soil research see also Herrera *et al.* 1980–81, Eden *et al.* 1984, McEwan 1985 and Andrade 1986.

45 About 78 per cent of all the seeds recovered have been identified and 68 per cent are of palm trees. Seed recovery is as follows: 26,708 seeds, of which 16,024 belonged to 11 palm species and 9,080 to various species of wild fruits (of which 1,604 were unidentified). In addition, 424.8 kg of wood charcoal were recovered from preceramic levels, resulting in 12 different tree families and 15 identified taxa. The much later ceramic occupation (associated with Camani and Nofurei ceramics) revealed 11 woody taxa, 10 of which overlapped with those present in the preceramic levels (Archila Montañéz 1999: Table 7.1).

46 The scientific name of *chontaduro*, or peach palm, is *Bactris gasipaes*. Illustrations of the palm species mentioned here can be consulted in Acero Duarte 1982; Cárdenas and Politis 2000; Barbosa Rodrigues 1989.

47 The scientific names of the animals are tapir (*Tapirus terrestris*), peccary (*Tayassu pecari* and *Tayassu tajacu*), agouti (*Agouti paca*). The *moriche* or *burití* palm is *Mauritia flexuosa*.

48 The Peña Roja lithic assemblage just described conforms to the Abriense tradition, best known from several sites in the Sabana de Bogotá (Colombian Andes). This is a widespread lithic tradition covering much of north-western South America, including Panama and Ecuador. As Warwick Bray (1984: 305–58) notes, Abriense lithic tools continued to be produced well into European contact in Colombia, alongside all kinds of innovations and new technologies.

49 See Llanos Chaparro 1997.

50 Piperno, cited in Archila Montañez 1999: 174. The microbotanical materials were 'phytoliths' (literally, 'plant stones'). These are silica bodies carried by various parts of the plant cellular structure that are preserved quite well in most soils long after everything else in the plant decays. The scientific names of the domesticated plants are *lerén* (*Calathea* cf. *allouia*), bottle gourd (*Lagenaria* sp.) and calabash (*Cucurbita* sp.).

51 See Posey 1994: 271–86. For the Nukak see Politis 1996b, 1999 and this volume.

52 Johnson 1983: 56–7 (Machiguenga gardens) or Carneiro 1983: 103–4 (Kuikurú gardens).

53 The scientific names for soursop, manioc and maize are, respectively, *Annona* sp., *Manihot esculenta* and *Zea mays*; see Mora *et al.* 1991.

54 The dates around 4700 BP were obtained at the interface between the Ab and AB soil horizon that marked the end of the Tubaboniba preceramic period. The interface marks a pedological discontinuity and an erosion episode. It is reasonable to assume that the preceramic occupation terminated around 4700 BP and that the occupation is earlier. The evidence of forest slash and burn and the cultivation of maize, manioc and soursop must also date to before 4700 BP, perhaps as early as 5000 to 6000 BP. Given the terminal date of 8500 BP for Peña Roja palm foragers/itinerant farmers, the transition to agriculture would have to have occurred between about 8000 and 5000 BP (see Cavelier *et al.* 1995; Mora *et al.* 1991).

55 Early Méidote ceramics were tempered with 91 per cent *caraipé*, the bark of some tree species, and ash with lesser inclusions of iron oxides and quartz.

Toward the end of the phase kaolin clays were preferred and *caraipé* constituted about 20 per cent of the temper, with larger amounts of ash. The caraipé ash used in ceramic manufacture today by the Muinane group is obtained from *Curatella americana*, *Simmondsia chiensis* or *Eperua purpurae*.
56 Mora *et al.* 1991: 43ff.; see also Herrera *et al.* 1980–81, Eden *et al.* 1984, Andrade 1986.
57 Although the English language has adopted the term 'cassava' to refer to the plant and tuber, in Spanish America this term refers only to baked food products made from manioc flour, namely cassava 'breads'. The term originated from the Taíno (Arawakan/Maipuran speakers) of the Greater Antilles who used the name *casabe* or *casabi* to describe the ordinary round, baked flour cake (known in Brazil as *beijú*). It is unwise to confuse the food product with the tuber or plant, as much as it is to confuse wheat with bread or the vast range of foods produced from wheat.
58 Lathrap 1977: 724–5.
59 Roosevelt *et al.* 1991; Roosevelt 1995: 121–6.
60 The invention of pottery is independent of either the domestication of plants or the establishment of agriculture. For a detailed discussion see Oyuela Caicedo 1995.
61 Roosevelt (1995: 125–6) described the Taperinha gourd-shaped vessel as *tecomate*. *Tecomate* is a term borrowed from Central America and refers to the cucurbit or gourd-like shape of ceramic vessels that lack a defined neck (also often called 'neckless *ollas*'). These neck-less *ollas* are among the earliest shapes found in Colombia (by 6000 BP) and Panamá (by 4500 BP) and in the Mesoamerican tropical lowlands (see Barnet and Hoopes 1995). Could the incised designs that suddenly appear in ceramics simply represent a transfer of bottle-gourd/cucurbit engraved designs into a new medium (ceramic), as demonstrated for the up to 5,500-year-old ceramics of Valdivia, Ecuador (see Lathrap 1974)?
62 Brochado and Lathrap 1982; Brochado 1984.
63 Brochado 1984; Brochado and Lathrap 1982; Simões 1981a; see also discussion in Roosevelt 1995.
64 See Mario Simões' references cited in Lathrap and Brochado 1982 and in Roosevelt 1995, 1997b.
65 See Sauer 1952; Lathrap 1977.
66 Piperno and Pearsall 1998: 244–65, 280–81. See also Bray 1995.
67 Roosevelt 1999a: 319–24 (discussion of the Formative period in greater Amazonia).
68 Cruxent and Rouse 1958–9; Rouse 1978; Roosevelt 1980, 1997a; Vargas 1981; Zucchi and Tarble 1982, 1984; Zucchi *et al.* 1984; Lathrap and Oliver 1987; Zucchi 1987, 1988, 1992, 1999.
69 Early Tutishcainyo lacks any absolute dates (Lathrap 1958, 1970); 4000–3800 BP is estimated on the basis of cross-dating with the Kotosh-wairajirca phase in the Callejón de Huaylas (central Andes) of about 3800 BP.
70 Heckenberger 1996, 1998; Neves 1999a; Petersen *et al.*, this volume; Heckenberger *et al.* 1999; Hilbert 1968; Roosevelt 1980, 1997a; Zucchi 1987.
71 A simple figure will suffice to bring home the depth of challenges awaiting future Amazonian archaeology. Presently, there are probably less than ten archaeologists, national and international, actively carrying out fieldwork projects in the 4,545 million hectares of Amazonia, a rate of 454.5 million hectares per archaeologist to be investigated! Little wonder that vast regions remain essentially unknown.
72 Moran 1993b: 88ff.
73 Denevan 2001: 58–61
74 In such dynamic fluvial environments, the floodplain landscape and adjacent *terra firme* bluffs are constantly, and sometimes abruptly, being re-sculptured. The destruction of archaeological sites is a fact and, of course, a limitation recovering data on prehistoric occupations within the floodplain. Work by Lathrap (1968b) and more recent investigations, such as Salo *et al.* 1986 and Pärssinen *et al.* 1996: 345–59, provide an example of the effects of avulsion and lateral displacement in the middle Ucayali where the river has destroyed archaeological sites and displaced historic groups (see also Denevan 2001: 114).
75 Whitmore 1990: 116–17.
76 Ibid.; Salo *et al.* 1986: 254–8.
77 For Shipibo multiple microhabitat resource exploitation in the *várzea*, see Denevan 2001: 90–97 and Bergman 1980.
78 See Denevan 1996: 654–81. Earlier, Lathrap (1970: 44) noted: 'The tropical forest farmer living on the bluff in the bluff of old alluvium adjacent to the active floodplain could simultaneously farm the limited but excellent recent alluvial soils in an intensive and continuous manner and the poor but essentially unlimited soils of the old alluvial deposits using slash-and-burn agriculture.' P. Hilbert (1957: 2–3) was among the first to note this.
79 Lathrap *et al.* 1985: 55.
80 Compare Lathrap 1970, 1977 with Denevan 1996, 2001: 127–30.
81 Data from Iquitos are summarized from Denevan 1996. Denevan (2001: 112) believes that long-fallow fields were unlikely to have been present in prehistoric times, as stone-axes would have made the clearing of mature forest inefficient. Instead, short-fallow periods would be preferred before tree-cutting and re-planting.
82 Porro 1994.
83 *Mauritia flexuosa* is known as *buriti* in Brazil, *mirití* in the Caquetá and Vaupés-Içana basin, *chonta* or *chontaduro* in Perú, and *moriche* in Venezuela. The generic 'peach palm' is often also used to refer to this species.
84 Denevan 1996, 2001: 58–61, 90–97; Coomes 1992; Hiraoka 1985, 1986, 1989; Meggers 1971: 121–49. For quantitative figures on fish and game capture consult Beckerman 1993, Bergman 1980 and Stocks 1983.
85 For 'boom and bust' interpretation of *várzea* productivity, see Meggers 1971: 146ff.
86 The 'integrated production system' I discuss is similar to what Denevan (2001: 113–14) calls bluff-*várzea* complementarity. In terms of settlement location, Denevan (2001: 114 n. 1) would prefer the contrast to be between riverine and interfluve instead of between *várzea* and *terra firme*.
87 This is one major reason why Lathrap's (1977) model of proto-Neolithic and Initial Neolithic revolution will be very difficult – though not impossible – to test in the field. The floodplain landforms in many relevant parts of Amazonian rivers will have destroyed the sites. See also Denevan 2001: 114.
88 Of course, a bluff site – assuming it to be the main residential locus – can potentially contain subsistence remains that would indicate the range of bluff and floodplain habitats exploited. But it could well be (theoretically possible) that at low flood-level season bluff inhabitants moved to their 'summer' residences within the floodplain, in which case little record will remain at the main bluff residence site of the economic activities in the floodplain.
89 Several excellent studies exist on the ethnohistory of these and other complex Amazon polities (e.g. see Hemming 1995a; Meggers 1971; Myers 1971, 1973, 1992b; Porro 1994: 79–119; and Neves, this volume).
90 For a succinct description of the nature of tropical heath forests world-wide consult Whitmore 1990: 18–23, 144–8.
91 Moran 1993b: 38–41.
92 Whitmore 1990.
93 See Harris 1971 for swidden agricultural systems and the references cited in Reichel-Dolmatoff 1996 on Tukanoan Indians and agriculture.
94 The Tukanoan peoples are well aware of what forest ecologists, such as Whitmore (1990: ch. 5), have underlined as important principles governing the forest food-web dynamics: that flowers develop the same features for particular group pollinators (birds, beetle, bats, etc.); that the particular characteristics of each fruit (colours, odours, shapes) are adapted to particular 'dispersers' (so-called 'mobile-links'); that related plants have similar defensive chemicals, each one fed on by a particular group of insects that have evolved to detoxify particular plant toxins; that several plant webs share the same pollinators or dispersers; that there are some animal food plants that remain critical food resources when all other resources are at a low productive ebb (so-called 'keystone species'); that some animal-plant interactions have developed a one-to-one relationship of interdependence (so called 'close co-evolutionary mutualism'); and that numerous diverse species of plants and animals co-exist in the rainforest by subdividing their food resources. The *chacra*, however, is not a rainforest in miniature but rather involves the application of forest food-web ecology to encourage selected food plants and their protective animal communities to flourish under favourable human-managed conditions.
95 Reichel-Dolmatoff 1996. The scientific names are bitter manioc (*Manihot esculenta*), *yajé* or *ayahuasca* (*Banisteropsis caapi*), epená (*Virola* spp.), coca (*Erythroxylum coca*), *guamo* trees (*Inga edulis* and other *Inga* spp.), plantain (*Musa paradisiaca*). On hallucinogenic plants, see Schultes and Hofmann 1992. Note that *coca*, although usually considered a drug, is also an important source of nutrition among Tukanoan males (Hugh Jones 1993).
96 Sweet potato, or batata (*Ipomoea batatas*). In old, sixteenth-century Spanish *Ipomoea* was referred to as *ajes* (singular *aje* – not to be confused with *ají*, the word for chili pepper).
97 For example, the Machiguenga of the upper Urubamba river (Peruvian Amazon) maintain a minimum of 80 cultivated species, including tree fruits, in gardens and *chacras*, of which 8–18 are staple crops found in high numbers in *chacras*, with sweet manioc and maize as the leading staples. The remaining 62–72 cultivars are maintained in varying quantities and admixtures in the village's house gardens (see Johnson 1983). The Siona-Secoya of the Aguarico basin (Ecuador) are estimated to be able to recognize well over 2,000 different useful plant species, of which ethnobotanists have identified 224 belonging to 166 different genera and 69 different families. Only a small fraction constitute the bulk of plant food energy planted in a *chacra*, with both bitter and

sweet manioc as the leading staple crop, followed closely by plantains and maize (see Vickers and Plowman 1984: 3, 34).

98 The scientific names are peach palm (*Bactris gasipaes*), genipap tree (*Genipa americana*), *carayucú* (*Bignonia chica*), *guamo* (*Inga* sp.), arrowroot (*Xanthosoma* sp.), tobacco (*Nicotiana tabacum*), coca (*Erythroxylum coca*), *yajé* (*Banisteropsis caapi*) and *epená* (*Virola* spp.). For most Amazonian hallucinogenic plants, consult Schultes and Hofmann 1992 (pp. 164–71 for data on virola or *epená*).

99 The scientific names are *epená* or virola (*Virola* spp.) and papaya (*Carica papaya*). This practice of conserving *nëngë via'do* resources was described by Reichel-Dolmatoff (1996). However, S. Hugh-Jones (pers. comm., 2001) reports that in his experience ancient garden sites are actively exploited by the Tukanoans.

100 Dufour 1993a: 58, also 1983, 1985.

101 With regard to the nutritional value of proteins it is important to bear in mind that not all are essential to maintain a healthy diet (see Wing and Brown 1979: 45ff.). Likewise, the percentages mentioned are based on fresh edible tubers, not on processed, cooked foods prepared from the tuber. Often ethnographic or anthropological reports fail to note this datum, and one must revert to specialized agrobotanical research publications. Those interested in investigating the technical literature on manioc/cassava should get in touch with the Centro de Internacional de Agricultura Tropical (CIAT) in Cali, Colombia, or contact their 'Information and Documentation Unit – CIAT' through the web page <www.cgiar.org>.

102 See Reichel-Dolmatoff 1996; Politis 1999: 99–100.

103 Århem 1993: 110–26.

104 See Zucchi's work (1987, 1988 and 1999) in the Atabapo, upper Orinoco, the archaeological investigations closest to the Içana-Vaupés region.

105 Lathrap *et al.* 1985; Heckenberger *et al.* 1999: 353–76.

106 Manioc did not reach the West Indies as a result of a well-documented, pre-Columbian migration of Arawakan-speaking agricultural people who reached some of the islands around 400 BC (Rouse 1992). This migration is linked to the spread of the Saladoid ceramic tradition/series and can ultimately be traced back to about 2600–2300 BC in the Parmana area of the middle Orinoco (Rouse 1978; Roosevelt 1980, 1997a).

107 Carneiro 1983: 76–7.

108 Rouse 1992; on the Taíno (Antilles) subsistence economy see Moscoso 1986 and Oliver 1998.

109 Schwerin 1985: 260; see Schwerin 1971 on nutrition and manioc foods, and Hugh-Jones and Hugh-Jones 1993 on manioc storage.

110 Slightly over 80 per cent of the fresh tuber weight is edible, of which 25–30 grams per 100 (g/100 g) is in assimilable starch (carbohydrates), which comes to 146 calories per 100 grams (cal/100 g) – as compared to, for example, the yam's (*Dioscorea*) 105 cal/100 g or the Andean potato's (*Solanum tuberosum*) 52 cal/100 g. The manioc tuber, however, is deficient in essential proteins and also has relatively low fat value (0.3 g/100g) (Schwerin 1985: Table 3).

111 It is very difficult to estimate and generalize as to what a healthy daily allowance of calories would be for an indigenous Amazonian household, as work practices (energy expended) and general health status must be assessed for each group (see Wing and Brown 1979). Moreover, sex and age differences must also be considered in calculating calorific requirements, as they may vary widely within and between groups. The National Research Council recommends for adult males in the USA a daily allowance of 56 g of proteins and 2,700 calories. This provides a very rough index with which to compare manioc's potential energy contribution (Schwerin 1985: 261–2). The studies I have been able to consult on native Amazonians indicate that manioc is more than able to efficiently supply the calories needed (e.g. Dufour 1983, 1985, 1988, 1989, 1993a & b, 1994; Carneiro 1983).

112 Nutrition is also difficult to assess because what matters is what is actually absorbed by the body, and only individual blood tests after consuming a particular manioc food product (cassava bread, beverages, etc.) will provide an accurate estimate. This requires large-scale blood sampling, a well-equipped laboratory and expert technicians, all of which are costly and difficult to get into the field (Schwerin 1985: 263). Nevertheless, the fresh edible portions of manioc tubers are fairly rich in Vitamin C and reasonably rich in Vitamin B (more or less like Asian rice). Manioc also contains small amounts or traces of phosphorus, iron, thiamine, riboflavin and niacin. Cooking, boiling, straining and a whole range of techniques in food preparation affect the nutritional composition of the food. For example, there is a suspicion that fermentation augments the protein content of manioc beer and other manioc foods, but there are insufficient data to test this hypothesis. Likewise, it may also make a difference whether the food is for immediate or for delayed consumption. Nutrition studies on the different indigenous and traditional foods derived from processed manioc are rare, so that generalizations made for other Amazonian Indians can be misleading (see Schwerin 1971, 1985; McKey and Beckerman 1993; and Aidoo 1986 on the nutrition of fermented manioc products).

113 Manioc leaf consumption would provide additional fat (0.4–1.3 g/100 g), proteins (4–7.5 g/100 g), and carbohydrate energy (55 cal/100 g) (Schwerin 1985: Table 3).

114 The tuber, bark, stems and leaves contain two cyanogenic glucosides that, when they enter into contact with glucosides, release free prussic acid (HCN) in a liquid state. Cyanogens are also released in a gaseous state, and both states are defences against a range of predators. Free prussic acid, even at sub-toxic levels, causes the breakdown of the sheath (myeline) that protects nerve cells, leading to neurological disorders and even death. Most mammals, including humans, are able to detoxify prussic acid, but the rate of detoxification limits the amount of prussic acid an organism can detoxify. To do so, manioc consumers need high amounts of an essential and critical nutrient (the aminoacid methionine) that must be replaced. Fish and other terrestrial game proteins have high levels of methionine, and thus are an essential defence against the cumulative effects of sub-toxic levels of prussic acid consumption (McKey and Beckerman 1993: 83–95; see also Dufour 1988, 1989, 1994).

115 McKey and Beckerman 1993: 83–96; Mejía Gutiérrez 1991, 1987: 15–22; Arguello 1988: 86–96.

116 McKey and Beckerman 1993: 83ff. Also consult Dufour 1988, 1994: 175–82; Nobre 1973: 9–13.

117 Hugh-Jones and Hugh-Jones 1993: 589–94.

118 Schwerin 1971.

119 Butt Colson 1973.

120 Heckenberger 1996: 33, 1998; for acid composition of some manioc varieties, see Silva 1976: 235–6.

121 As Roosevelt (1989: 30–62) has pointed out, human bone analyses (e.g. bone collagen/isotope, osteopathology) can contribute much towards a better understanding of diet, nutrition and health (e.g. see van der Merwe *et al.* 1981: 536–8), and is another independent way to assess subsistence efficiency. But far more bioanthropological analyses need to be carried out, as only a handful of results have been obtained thus far. Even when well-preserved skeletons are recovered, these represent, statistically speaking, only a small fraction of the total population of the settlement they are supposed to typify. Thus, when biological health status indicators are only available from a few individuals, it is simply common sense not to generalize these results to a whole community, much less a population or the entire Amazon basin. As palaeobotanist L. A. Newsom (pers. comm. 2001) has commented in regard to the Caribbean (and presumably elsewhere), phytolith, pollen, macrobotany and palaeonutrition (bone isotope/apatite analyses) studies more often than not seem to yield different results, or are at odds with each other when they should reinforce each other, if based on samples from the same archaeological contexts. In part this is due to different methodological procedures and also to the production of different kinds of evidence. Nevertheless, it is clear that 'consilience of induction' (see Oliver 1991) can best be reached by the 'jumping together' of multiple and independent lines of evidence pointing to one or a few most likely explanations. Explanations about the nature, character and evolution of food production systems and their consequences on Amazonia peoples do indeed require a multidisciplinary effort. The exciting challenge for the future is to create multidisciplinary teams to work together towards this common cause.

3

Gift from the Past

Terra Preta and Prehistoric Amerindian Occupation in Amazonia

JAMES B. PETERSEN, EDUARDO NEVES AND MICHAEL J. HECKENBERGER

[T]he soil of many late prehistoric Amazonian archaeological sites is literally colored black from the abundance of carbonized plant remains, hence the Brazilian term *terra preta do Índio* (black Indian soil).[1]

A mosaic of black earth patches, scattered throughout the Amazon basin, provides evidence that precontact native populations were in many cases large and sedentary.[2]

Permanent and semipermanent production systems were probably characteristic of the bluff zones where there is archaeological and ethnohistoric evidence of relatively dense population concentrations. *Terra preta* soil is indirect evidence of intensive ... cultivation.[3]

The cultural complexity represented in a *terra preta* site cannot be overly stressed. Within the deposit are the physical remains of centuries of overlapping communities with diverse shifting use areas and facilities, each producing a variety of chemical and physical signatures and variable rates of accretion ... Clearly, a *terra preta* more closely approximates a living organism than an inert fossil and it will be far more productive to consider it through dynamic rather than static models.[4]

[I]f these kinds of soils, particularly *terra preta*, are common throughout Amazonia, then the basic assumption made by earlier archaeologists, that Amazonia is an environment that cannot sustain intensive agricultural exploitation or dense human settlement, would seem wide of the mark.[5]

Introduction

Terra preta, or *terra preta de índio*, is a highly significant topic in Amazonian archaeology, since it is the most obvious and to some the most socially relevant vestige of the prehistoric Amerindians who once inhabited Amazonia. These human-modified soils, or 'anthrosols', mark the location of past human habitation and provide very fertile contexts for farming in the region today (fig. 3.1).

Terra preta is very widespread across Amazonia.[6] In Brazil alone, it is found along the Amazon proper, the Aripuanã, Guaporé, Madeira, Mapuere, Negro, Nhamundá, Trombetas, Tapajós, Tocantins and Xingu rivers, among others. It is also known from Colombia, Ecuador, Guyana, Peru and Venezuela. In some parts of greater Amazonia, however, *terra preta* apparently never formed or it was very localized in spite of ancient occupation, as in the lower/middle Uaupés River and parts of the Orinoco drainage.[7]

Archaeologists search out *terra preta* for the clues it provides about the Amazonian past while local farmers have long sought this sometimes deep soil for its richness and 'natural' fertility in a region where soils are often infertile and difficult to cultivate (fig. 3.2). Interest in *terra preta* has a long and venerable pedigree in Amazonia, although its origins, transformations and interpretation are still widely debated.[8]

For the purposes of this essay the most significant questions relating to *terra preta* include the following. Is it, in fact, always a cultural phenomenon? What sort of cultural factors seem to lead to the creation of *terra preta* and which are apparently not so relevant? Can these factors be related to population growth and 'subsistence intensification' (increase in food production and consumption)? What are the implications of *terra preta* in terms of the prehistoric occupation of Amazonia? Various other questions might be asked as well,[9] but we address this topic from an archaeological and anthropological perspective, rather than from a soil science one.

3.1 Modern papaya plantation on *terra preta* soil at the Hatahara site located on a high bluff overlooking the floodplain of the Solimões (Amazon) river, Iranduba, Brazil. These and similar sites are full of archaeological remains, and abundant pottery sherds are visible on the ground.

We believe that the formation of *terra preta* requires intensive and sometimes long-term accumulation of organic waste from human activities not typically found among recent rural occupations in the region, even where *terra preta* was formed prehistorically. Various kinds of human-modified soils, here categorized as *terra preta*, are specifically attributable to habitation refuse and also probably to farming. These soils were formed during the late pre-colonial history of Amazonia, generally dating to at most 1,000–2,000 years before the arrival of Europeans and other newcomers in the region. We suggest that subsistence intensification combined with the growth of Amerindian populations during late prehistory led to the formation of *terra preta*.

3.2 Excavation of a burial at the Hatahara site, with deep *terra preta* and a high density of sherds visible in the sides of the trench. This structure yielded three collective burials with at least ten individuals.

Finally, we believe that the nature and distribution of *terra preta* in Amazonia document intensive occupation of the region by Amerindian societies that have since largely disappeared. Clues about these formerly widespread and hierarchical societies are known only through archaeology and through a few early historic accounts dating to the era of initial European contact in the region in the sixteenth and seventeenth centuries. It is becoming clear that local prehistoric societies once occupied large settlements in many areas where *terra preta* is found today and where local Amerindians are either extinct or reduced to relatively small, autonomous communities at present (fig. 3.3).

Some anthropologists would argue against the position proposed here and suggest instead that indigenous societies in Amazonia have always been small scale, non-integrated and non-hierarchical. Their scepticism about pre-contact social complexity in indigenous Amazonia is due to the appeal of uncritically projecting the present into the past, since contemporary indigenous societies in the region are all effectively small scale and autonomous. Stratified, regionally integrated societies are almost unknown historically, except in some interpretations of the scant details from the early historic record.[10] This ethnographic circumstance is due to the eradication of many Amazonian and other indigenous peoples in South America under the overwhelming impact of colonialism and capitalism. In our view the modern and historically known Amerindian societies in Amazonia do not preserve the full range of socio-political complexity that once existed there. We must look beyond contemporary indigenous societies to model the formation of *terra preta*, and its presence across much of Amazonia says something rather different about the prehistoric societies in these areas (fig. 3.4).

Changing conceptions of *terra preta* and Amazonian adaptations

The close relationship between *terra preta* and prehistoric remains was already recognized by the time archaeology began in Amazonia, that is during the late nineteenth century. In 1879 Herbert Smith, a student and colleague of Charles Hartt (see p. 247),

ABOVE 3.3 Aerial view of intensive farming on *terra preta* at the large Açutuba site, south bank of the Rio Negro, Iranduba, Brazil.

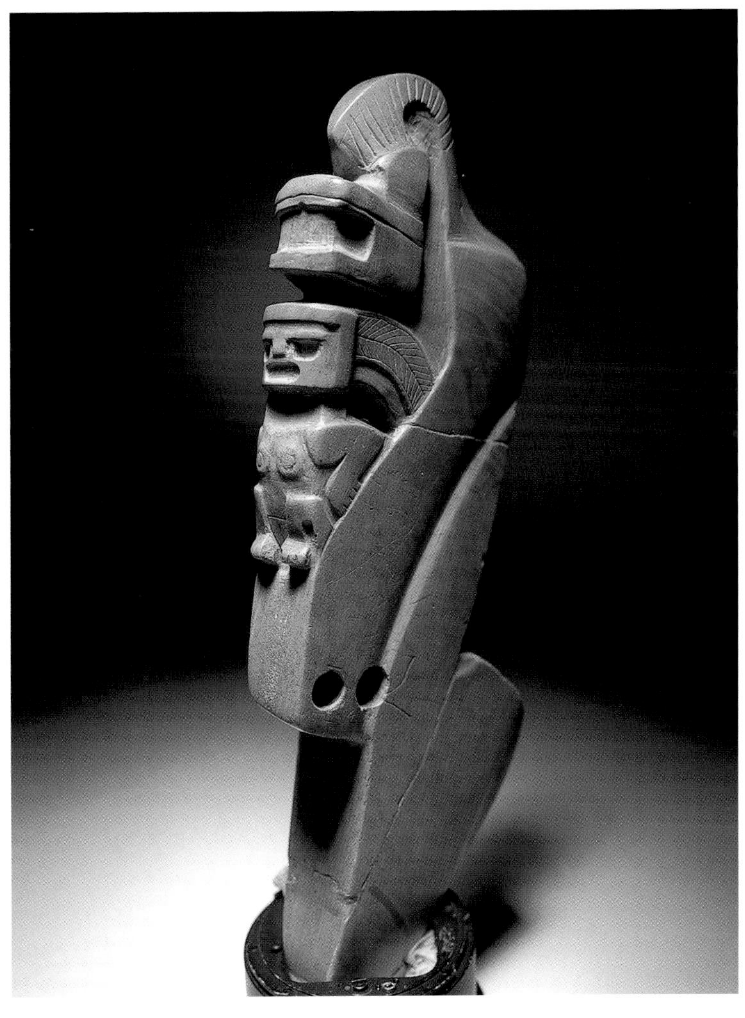

RIGHT 3.4 Lithic stone sculpture from the Nhamundá-Trombetas area (height 28 cm, width 11.3 cm, depth 3.1 cm; Etnografiska Museet I Göteborg). Sculptures such as this are normally found at large sites with *terra preta* in the central and lower Amazon.

commented extensively on *terra preta* in the Brazilian Amazon. He reported on areas in relative proximity to the Tapajós River and the town of Santarém in the lower Amazon: 'This is the rich *terra preta*, "black land," the best on the Amazons. It is fine, dark loam, a foot, and often two feet, thick. Strewn over it everywhere we find fragments of Indian pottery, so abundant in some places that they almost cover the ground' (figs 3.5–6).[11] Smith reported further:

> On the Tapajós the black land occurs at intervals of from one to five miles; but from Panema to Taperinha, and for some distance below, it forms a continuous line; indicating, in fact, a single village, or city, thirty miles long, but extending only a little way in from the edge of the plateau. At intervals there are signs of ancient roads leading down toward the river.[12]

ABOVE AND ABOVE RIGHT 3.5–6 *Muiraquitãs* (polished stone amulets) in the shape of a frog (height 4 cm, width 2.8 cm, depth 1.7 cm) and a fish (height 2.5 cm, width 6 cm, depth 0.4 cm; both Museu de Arqueologia e Etnologia da Universidade de São Paulo). *Muiraquitãs* usually turn up at large sites with *terra preta* in the central and lower Amazon and evidently were traded throughout northern South America and the Caribbean.

Later still, Smith said: 'The bluffs must have been lined with ... villages, for the black land is almost continuous, and at many points pottery and stone implements cover the ground like shells on a surf-washed beach.'[13] Other early accounts cover some of the same issues, but early on Smith had already identified many of the basic characteristics of *terra preta*, most notably its implicit genesis as a result of human activities.

In the early twentieth century explorer-archaeologist William Farabee briefly reported on comparable deposits near Santarém. He noted:

> One of the natives had a few fragments of pottery which he said came from the 'black earth' on the top of the mountains [bluffs], about 10 miles back from the river. Upon investigation, this black earth, as I had supposed, marked the site of an ancient Indian village. The location was on the edge of a high plateau overlooking the Amazon. A number of such sites were located by one of two methods; either by finding the black earth, or by first locating a spring and then, looking for the village site on the plateau top nearby. The black earth marking these sites was found to be from one to two feet deep and covered in some cases, as much as ten acres.[14]

During the 1920s Curt Nimuendajú also correlated *terra preta* with archaeological remains (see fig. 3.1). He said:

> On the south shore of Lago Grande there is scarcely a spur of hills which extends to the edge of the lake that does not have a deposit of black earth on it. Another characteristic of the black earth deposits is the ancient Indian roads which run almost in a straight line from one black earth deposit to another ... The surface of the black earth deposits is usually not flat, but composed of a number of mounds, each several meters in diameter, and each probably representing a home site ... In some places it is almost a meter and a half thick. Potsherds are so abundant that they interfere with the farming.[15]

Soil scientists have also taken up the topic, notably during the later twentieth century, in some cases strongly disagreeing with the cultural attribution for such soils. The cultural versus natural genesis proponents have made their cases for and against these different factors. Proponents of natural genesis have advanced hypotheses for *terra preta* formation related to volcanic ash, volcanic rock weathering and ancient lake or pond sedimentation, among others.[16] In those cases where prehistoric artefacts are associated with *terra preta*, some have even suggested that its fertility would have attracted indigenous settlement.[17] This implies that *terra preta* was formed before human occupation, rather than human activity itself having led to its genesis. Whether or not this is true, the attraction that *terra preta* provides for historic farming and, as we argue here, is likely to have provided for prehistoric farming, is not to be denied regardless of whether it was formed naturally or culturally. In fact, we suggest that once *terra preta* was formed prehistorically, it may have served as an important incentive for continuous occupation or later reoccupation on the basis of its soil fertility alone.

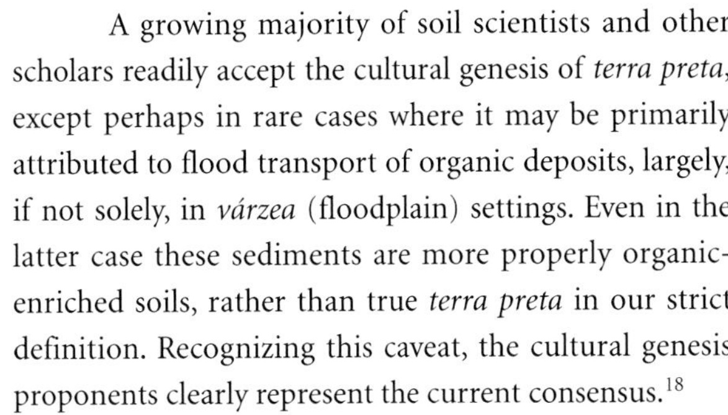

A growing majority of soil scientists and other scholars readily accept the cultural genesis of *terra preta*, except perhaps in rare cases where it may be primarily attributed to flood transport of organic deposits, largely, if not solely, in *várzea* (floodplain) settings. Even in the latter case these sediments are more properly organic-enriched soils, rather than true *terra preta* in our strict definition. Recognizing this caveat, the cultural genesis proponents clearly represent the current consensus.[18]

As noted in one of the opening quotations,[19] the full complexity of factors behind the genesis of *terra preta* is immense and in all likelihood these factors are not yet fully appreciated by most scholars.[20] Recent research by those who assign to it a largely cultural origin has continued to refine our interpretations. For example, most archaeologists and other researchers now attribute such soil to midden deposits, including ash from village fires, the decomposition of organic refuse and the accumulation of waste materials.[21] Others have noted that *terra preta* apparently does not form from the modern agricultural practices of Amerindian and *caboclo* farmers in Amazonia.[22] It can be created in various sediment and soil types, however, with typically high carbon, phosphorus and calcium levels, and less acidity than its unaltered counterparts.[23] Further, a dichotomy has been recognized between *terra preta* found along large rivers and examples found away from rivers: *terra preta* on or near large rivers is significantly larger, deeper and more concentrated in most cases than where it is found elsewhere. This difference seems correlated with more intensive and long-term prehistoric occupation along the larger rivers and less so away from them.[24]

Lighter coloured 'brown soils', termed *terra mulata*, supposedly result from agricultural activities such as forest clearing and burning, rather than refuse disposal, and some differentiate it from darker *terra preta*.[25] All agricultural soils in the tropics, however, are not enhanced as a consequence of farming. In fact, some are degraded.[26] Many argue that this is the case in much of Amazonia where 'short crop, long fallow' cultivation, also known as 'slash and burn' or 'swidden' horticulture, is practised today. In this case farmers will only cultivate a given field for a few years, primarily because of the typical loss of fertility in tropical soils under this farming strategy, although some scholars say that infertility is not the only factor involved.[27] They argue that weed and pest invasion also lead to field abandonment, perhaps as does the ease with which modern trees can be cut down using steel axes. It is possible that prehistoric farmers, who used stone axes for forest clearing, were reluctant to move their fields due to the relative difficulty of clearing trees in the jungle. 'Intensive swiddens' with short-term fallows, if any, may have pertained prehistorically in this scenario, although the use of 'house gardens,' 'patch cultivation' and/or 'agroforestry' might also have provided a way of avoiding regular forest clearing.[28]

Thus, farming in itself does not necessarily lead to the formation of fertile, visibly altered soils like *terra preta* and *terra mulata*. Rather, their formation is dependent on the type and amount of additives, if any, and the nature of the farming practices and other human activities. Following this idea further, apparently only late prehistoric occupations in Amazonia were substantial enough to produce *terra preta*. Available data suggest that farming of some sort dates back as far as 5,000–4,000 years ago, or *c.*3000–2000 BC, in Amazonia, well before *terra preta* deposits have been identified (see Oliver, this volume).[29] Thus, it is unlikely that farming alone was responsible for *terra preta* formation, given its later date of initiation, but rather that sedentism and intensive cultivation were required.

As noted above, contemporary Amazonians, indigenous or not, intentionally seek out *terra preta* for farming and soil extraction for use as fertilizer elsewhere, due to its extraordinary chemical conditions.[30] For example, we have reports of modern intensive agriculture at the Açutuba site where the prehistoric *terra preta* has been intensively farmed without the addition of any fertilizer for nearly forty years (see fig. 3.3). Equally noteworthy is the observation that most contemporary habitations and farm fields in Amazonia do not produce *terra preta* under any circumstances, probably due to the low intensity and short duration of land use,[31] although some have tentatively suggested otherwise.[32] Other scholars have suggested that *terra preta* essentially represents a 'living organism' because of its capacity to regenerate itself under certain management conditions.[33]

In spite of this long history of revealing insights into *terra preta*, a number of twentieth-century researchers working in Amazonia have largely ignored it. They have tended to follow the kind of broad cultural ecological approach championed in the landmark reference and multi-volume publication, the *Handbook of South American Indians* (1948), edited by Julian Steward.[34] With the benefit of hindsight this is perhaps better termed an 'ecologically restrictive' view. Often these scholars emphasize the presence of uniform soil infertility in all non-riverine settings across Amazonia, which is generally the case, except where *terra preta* occurs.

The cultural ecologists and others have continually stressed the apparent dichotomy between generic *várzea* (floodplain) and *terra firme* (non-floodplain) soils in Amazonia. Simply stated, their position is that soil fertility, and thus long-term intensive farming only pertained in floodplain soils of the *várzea* (fig. 3.7). Some treat all floodplains as a single homogenous entity and they do not explicitly recognize variability across regional floodplains.[35] Other researchers implicitly or explicitly use the term *várzea* only for floodplains along the so-called 'whitewater' rivers, or those emanating from the Andes.[36] Still others argue that all floodplains in Amazonia, including those of the two other major river types, 'blackwater' and 'clearwater' rivers, along with 'whitewater' rivers, are technically *várzea* (figs 3.8–9).[37]

This is an important distinction if soil fertility is really a critical factor in determining the nature of indigenous farming. It may be misleading to speak of *várzea* floodplain farming without further qualification because many Amazonian floodplains do

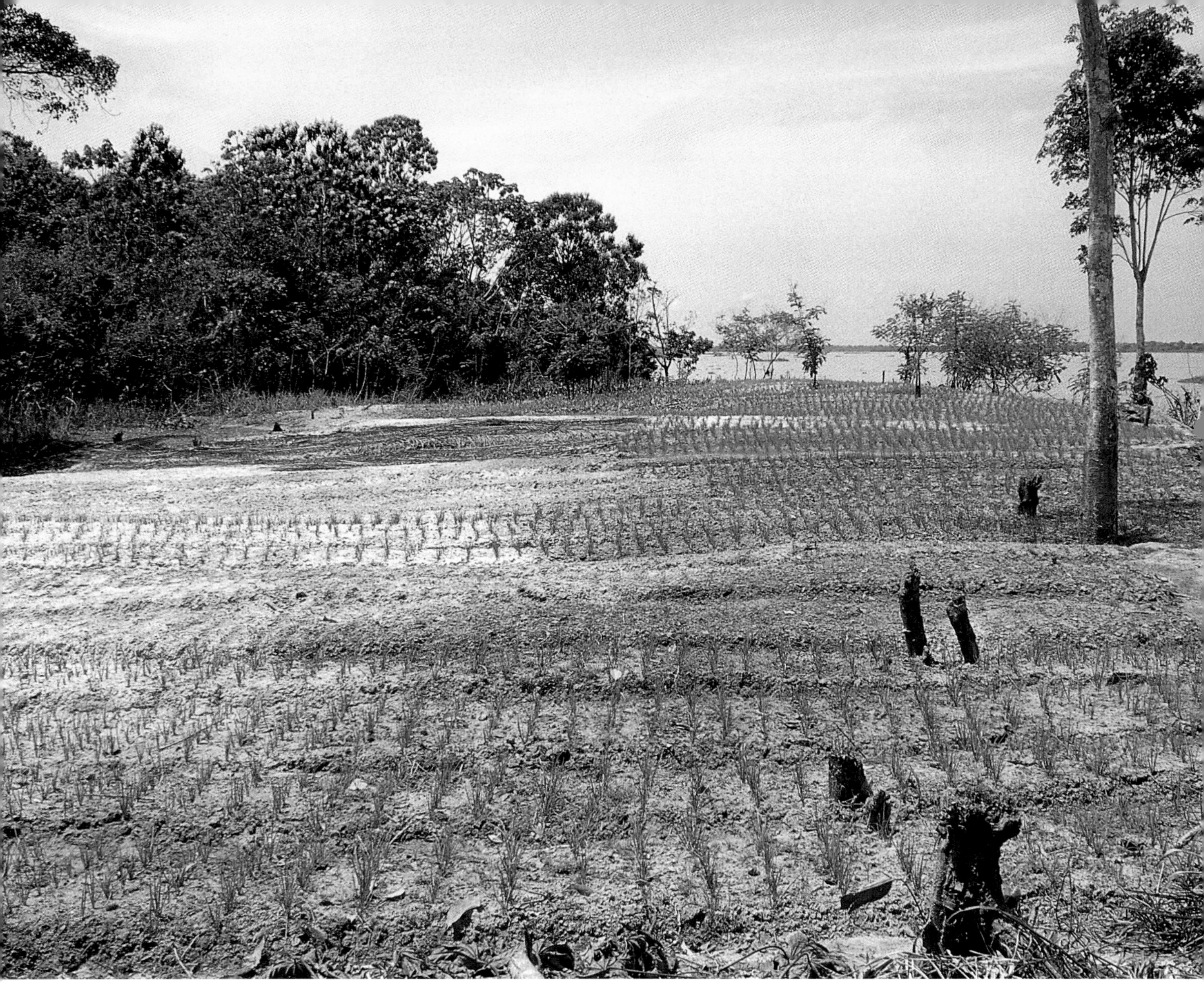

3.7 Contemporary short-term farming in the fertile floodplain (*várzea*) of the Solimões river. Before European contact the floodplains of all the major rivers were intensively farmed for fast growing crops, such as maize and peanuts.

not provide settings that are readily suited to long-term intensive farming. With the exception of the 'whitewater' rivers, Amazonian floodplain soils are often quite infertile, such as those of the Negro and the upper Xingu rivers, for example, presenting limitations similar to the *terra firme*.

Many Amazonianists share the idea that *várzea* farming was essential for the genesis of sedentism and socio-political complexity in the region, but they have offered differing interpretations of the importance of *várzea* farming and the societies that depended on it. Some further believe that *terra firme* adaptations were ecologically restrictive, providing little, if any, basis for the establishment of long-term sedentism across the region. In this view the vast extent of the *terra firme*, representing 90–98 per cent of Amazonia, would be ecologically restrictive.[38] Those settings would consequently dictate the absence or near absence of sedentism, and further support the pattern of social fragmentation among Amerindians who shared and still share 'Tropical Forest Culture'.[39] Other Amerindians once resided along the margin of the *terra firme* and the *várzea*, and thus had greater access to farmland and aquatic resources. Still other indigenous groups, such as the contemporary Pirahã of the lower Madeira or the historic Mura, lived directly within the *várzea* on the basis of historic and ethnographic accounts.[40] In its earliest variants the idea of intensive

ABOVE AND ABOVE RIGHT

3.8–9 Dry and wet season views of the Lago Grande. In the central Amazon, *terra preta* sites are usually located on bluffs that overlook the main rivers or floodplain lakes. In this case the archaeological sites on the north shore of Lago Grande are located more than 5 kilometres away from the Amazon river.

várzea farming was de-emphasized, if noted at all. Likewise, the presence of raised and ridged fields and other extensive earthworks in the Llanos de Mojos of Bolivia, in the *llanos* (grasslands) of Venezuela and along the Guyana-Surinam coast was often overlooked.[41]

Other prominent researchers have generally supported the centrality of this dichotomy between *várzea* and *terra firme* adaptations in Amazonia, sometimes in an attenuated form but nonetheless with a comparable, ecologically restrictive component. Importantly, this camp has generally accepted the likelihood of widespread sedentism and social complexity across the region in different *várzea* and 'bluff' settings on the margin of *terra firme* and the *várzea* floodplain. In this case seed crops, primarily maize, would make variable sedentism and social complexity possible, but only in or near the *várzea*.[42] Perhaps suggestively, little evidence directly documents the importance of *várzea* farming during historic times, beyond scant accounts from the sixteenth and seventeenth centuries (see Gomes, this volume, for further discussion of some of these sources).[43] There can be little doubt, however, about the size and scale of the bluff-dwelling societies, such as the Omágua, who resided along the upper Amazon until the seventeenth century.[44]

Thus it is possible that the centrality of the *várzea* for farming alone has been over-emphasized. Instead, perhaps it was the great wealth of aquatic resources, including fish, manatees and turtles, for example, that attracted people to all riverine settings, rather than just to those on or near whitewater *várzea* floodplains where soil fertility is high (fig. 3.10). In this view floodplain ecology was important, but fertile floodplain farmland was not the sole attraction.[45] It might not have mattered at all in some cases, if upland *terra firme* farming was as productive as it seems to have been.[46] Evidence of substantial archaeological sites and corresponding *terra preta* along 'blackwater' and 'clearwater' rivers discussed below supports the hypothesis that it was some combination of riverine resources and minimally *terra firme* farming that supported large groups over time. Farming in the *várzea* may or may not have been important, depending on local conditions.

RIGHT 3.10 Butter production from turtle eggs, recorded in the colonial period. The large size of many *terra preta* sites indicates progressive intensification in food production along the Amazonian floodplains long before European contact. From Alexandre Rodrigues Ferreira, *Viagem Filosófica* (1783–92).

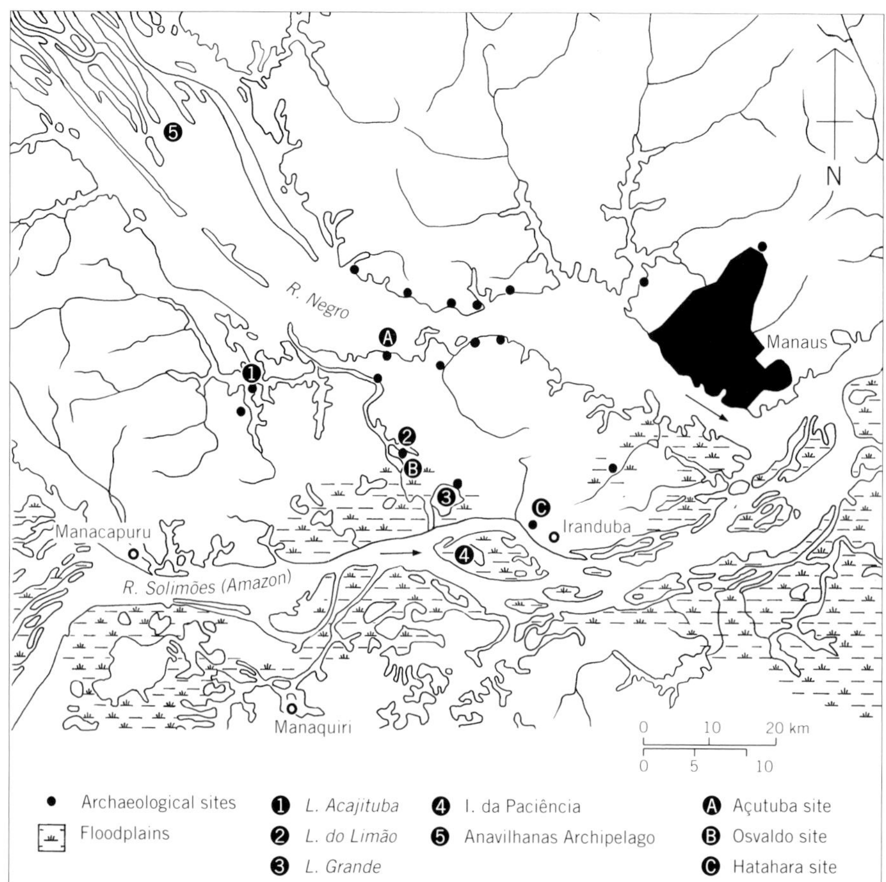

3.11 The Central Amazon Project research area, located at the confluence of the Negro and Solimões rivers, showing the location of archaeological sites mentioned in the text.

Terra preta and intensive human occupation: several examples from Amazonia

We present here a brief summary of our ongoing investigations in several different portions of the Brazilian Amazon, as well as examples from other areas that help illustrate the points advanced above. These examples are based on stratigraphic data from archaeological excavations, radiocarbon dates from these contexts and soil chemistry analyses, including phosphate fractionation.[47]

The first case study is our collective investigation in the research area of the Central Amazon Project (CAP), around the confluence of the Solimões and Negro rivers, which are a 'whitewater' and 'blackwater' river, respectively. The CAP research area includes both *várzea* and non-*várzea* floodplains along those two rivers, as well as *terra firme* settings directly adjacent to and between the rivers and extending to the north, south and west (fig. 3.11).[48]

Intensive excavations at four sites (Açutuba, Hatahara, Lago Grande and Osvaldo) and preliminary data from another fifteen sites in the CAP study area indicate that *terra preta* occurs at nearly all of them, and it is directly correlated with site size and artefact density. It is also clear that *terra preta* is neither completely homogenous nor contemporaneous across at least the larger, more intensively studied of these nineteen sites. The depth of the cultural deposits ranges from one to two metres at the larger sites, and it is sometimes shallower at the smaller sites (fig. 3.2). Other sites have been previously recorded in or near the CAP study area, including *terra preta*, but they remain incompletely reported.[49]

At Açutuba, situated high on the south bank of the Negro River, there are at least

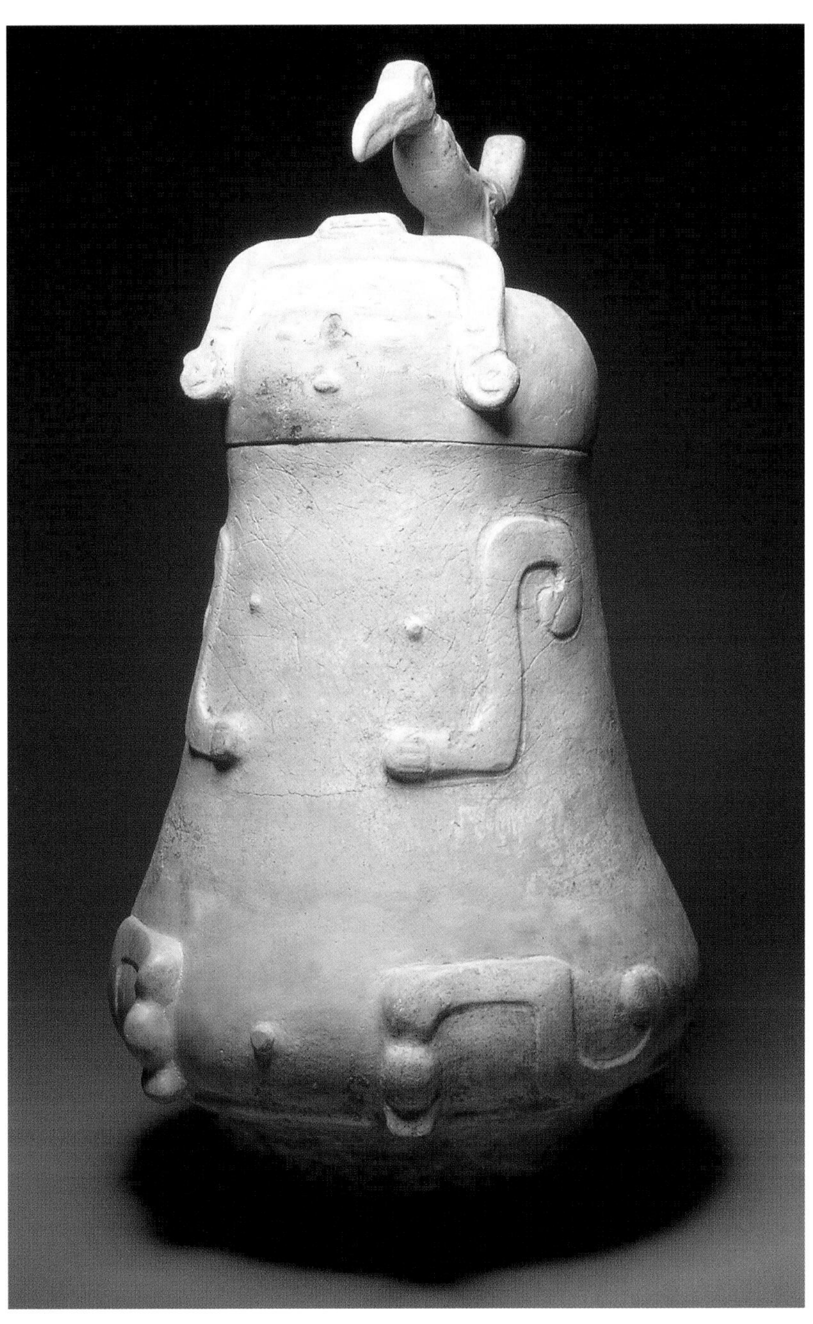

3.12 Anthropomorphic Guarita (*c.* AD 1000–1500) urn with lid, from Silves lake, lower Urubu river, middle Amazon (height 76.5 cm, width 43 cm; Museu Paraense Emílio Goeldi, Belém, Brazil). In the middle Amazon Guarita ceramics are often found at sites with *terra preta* (see also fig. 3.2)

two major occupational episodes, overall minimally spanning the period from about *c.*360 BC to *c.* AD 1400–1500. Tentative evidence of an earlier occupation at 4900 BC is also represented.[50] The formation of *terra preta* began some time before 360 BC in the central area of Açutuba. Elsewhere at the site human habitation and *terra preta* formation apparently began before *c.* AD 150, where dated. The earlier of the two major ceramic complexes in the study area is the Modelled-Incised (or Incised Rim) complex, which is broadly related to the Barrancoid tradition of the lower Orinoco basin and elsewhere.[51] This complex is well represented in all of the site loci directly associated with *terra preta* and it has associated dates as late as AD 850 and AD 920, respectively.

Elsewhere at Açutuba midden deposits show the initiation of *terra preta* development beneath several linear mounds. Intimately associated with Guarita complex ceramics and with broad relationships to the Amazonian Polychrome tradition (fig. 3.12),[52] such deposits began building in the central site area near a tentative plaza by AD 970 and lasted until as late as AD 1440, on the basis of the available radiocarbon dates. However, the uppermost deposits have been disturbed by historic cultivation and thus may not accurately reflect the latest indigenous occupation. Several possible defensive trenches are also documented near the plaza area.

The Guarita deposits are present all across this extensive site, stretching over its entire length of about 3 km (see fig. 3.3). Within the broader suite characteristic of the Guarita ceramic complex, relatively fine polychrome ceramics are largely, if not solely, confined to the central site area near the plaza (figs 3.13–14). In contrast, coarser, finger-punctate decorated ceramics, also related to the Guarita complex, are found all across the site area, suggesting the differential distribution of these two wares. Overall, these data demonstrate the presence of two ceramic wares, with the fine ware probably ceremonial or 'elite' in origin. Phosphate-fractionation values are moderate to very high, indicating intensive activities at Açutuba over a long period.[53]

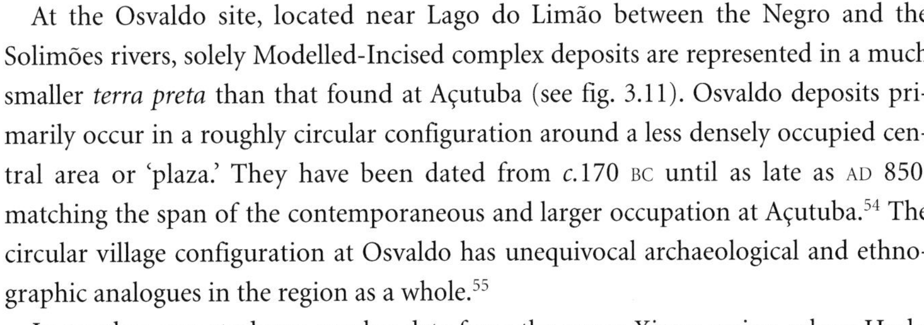

3.13 Polychrome Guarita urn (*c.* AD 1000–1500), provenance unknown (height 60 cm; Instituto Histórico e Geográfico do Amazonas). Guarita ceramics belong to the Amazonian Polychrome tradition, but they differ from their Marajoara phase counterparts in age, location, technology and decorative attributes.

At the Osvaldo site, located near Lago do Limão between the Negro and the Solimões rivers, solely Modelled-Incised complex deposits are represented in a much smaller *terra preta* than that found at Açutuba (see fig. 3.11). Osvaldo deposits primarily occur in a roughly circular configuration around a less densely occupied central area or 'plaza.' They have been dated from *c.*170 BC until as late as AD 850, matching the span of the contemporaneous and larger occupation at Açutuba.[54] The circular village configuration at Osvaldo has unequivocal archaeological and ethnographic analogues in the region as a whole.[55]

In another case study we employ data from the upper Xingu region, where Heckenberger identified more than twenty late prehistoric sites in 1993–4.[56] The upper Xingu study area includes a stretch of the Culuene river and its smaller tributaries and tributary lakes. The Culuene and the Xingu, into which the Culuene flows, are 'clearwater' rivers with non-*várzea* floodplains along them, as well as adjacent *terra firme*. These habitation sites are generally dated after AD 900–1000. Indigenous people have continuously occupied the upper Xingu from at least that time until the present, but the archaeological sites are quite different from the contemporary villages in terms of their size and structural complexity. Prehistoric sites in this area are distinguished by the clear representation of extensive earthworks, including very substantial ditches around some of the larger sites, presumably for protection. In addition, curbed roads, other small mounds and central plazas were represented at the larger sites during late prehistory, *c.* AD 1500–1700.[57] *Terra preta* of varying intensity is found within these sites, in all cases dating after *c.* AD 1000. Phosphate-fractionation data are of low to moderate intensity for the few prehistoric samples tested thus far, showing some correlation with modern Amerindian values in one village.[58]

3.14 Guarita vessel (*c.* AD 1000–1500) with grooved incision and medial flange, from Manacapuru, Solimões river.

Comparable data were also obtained from the Huapula mound site at Sangay in the Selva Alta of Ecuador, near the western margin of the Amazon.[59] Although a longer overall sequence is represented at Sangay, these particular deposits at Huapula are generally dated *c.* AD 740–1180. They can be assigned to the so-called 'Period of Regional Integration', with distant links to the Amazonian Polychrome tradition.[60] A Huapula residential mound produced phosphate-fractionation values reflecting moderately intensive activities undertaken there over the course of 400–500 years.[61] For further comparison and again using directly analogous sediment testing, a circular village in the Caribbean, Trants, situated on the island of Montserrat, produced different fractionation values for residential and non-residential areas, ranging from moderately intensive to very intensive.[62] Well dated at *c.*500 BC to AD 600, Trants is directly contemporaneous with the Modelled-Incised complex to which it is distantly related.[63]

Other phosphate and phosphorous values have been obtained from various portions of Amazonia and elsewhere in northern South America.[64] Although these are not necessarily comparable because of different laboratory methods, they also show that widely represented *terra preta* and related deposits have artificially heightened values and altered characteristics, like those reported here. Intensively modified anthropic soils thus share certain characteristics across much of Amazonia, but much more research needs to be done to refine their comparison.

In sum, phosphate-fractionation data have been obtained from radiocarbon-dated contexts in several different areas of Amazonia and these have been briefly compared to similar data collected elsewhere. These data suggest several things: long-term habitation is certainly recognizable in all three areas; sediment alteration occurred in conjunction with intensive and/or long-term human residence and cultivation there and/or nearby, as confirmed by the sediment analyses and radiocarbon dating; and *terra preta* is primarily the direct manifestation of residential waste, and its most altered examples were unlikely to have been produced solely by farming, whether intensive or long-term in origin. However, *terra mulata* was probably produced by farming. These archaeological sediment data suggest that various non-floodplain settings across Amazonia were the scene of intensive and long-term human occupation during late prehistoric times.

3.15 Anthropomorphic (female) figurine, Marajoara phase, Marajó Island, mouth of the Amazon. The appearance of the Marajoara phase around AD 400 marks the beginning of the Amazonian Polychrome tradition.

Terra preta and Amerindian occupation in Amazonia: a synthesis and interpretation

The dates for the oldest *terra preta* in the CAP study area can be broadly aligned with the other available dates from Amazonia and this may well have very important implications. At Açutuba several different excavations date the inception of *terra preta* formation by at least 360 BC and AD 150.[65] At the Hatahara site on the Solimões river bluffs the oldest and near basal date that seems to be associated with *terra preta* is again *c.*360 BC, a striking parallel to Açutuba, if this date is indeed confirmed. Finally, at the Osvaldo site on Lago do Limão, lying between the Negro and Solimões rivers, the basal date is *c.*170 BC.[66] These dates establish the general contemporaneity of these sites and show that intensive human occupation, leading to the creation of *terra preta*, began essentially around the same time.

At 450 BC *terra preta* at the Paredão site may be slightly older. Paredão is near the modern city of Manaus and thus very close to the CAP study area. However, the date of 450 BC is not necessarily a basal date and some say it may be erroneously old.[67] On the Rio Ucayali in Peru the oldest *terra preta* has been generally dated to *c.*200 BC–AD 100 at Hupa-iya in the Yarinacocha area.[68] Other dates, including 100 BC at Bom Sucesso, 65 BC at Pocó, AD 86 at Itacoatiara and AD 475 at Manacapuru, all in the Brazilian Amazon, minimally date *terra preta* to around the beginning of the Christian era.[69] Elsewhere in Amazonia comparable soils have been dated or estimated to be as old or older than *c.* AD 1 and AD 385 in the Araracuara area on the Rio Caquetá, Colombia, for example.[70] Likewise, further afield from the central Amazon, *terra preta* began to form by *c.* AD 950 in the upper Xingu region.[71]

The available dates for the beginning of *terra preta* across Amazonia generally range between 450 BC and AD 950, a pattern that suggests that its genesis was broadly synchronous over this huge region. The earliest dates seem to cluster around the central and lower Amazon. This broad synchronicity suggests that something rather new began by about 500 BC across much of the region in terms of occupational intensity, and this led to the beginning of *terra preta* formation. If the pattern outlined above is correct, then such changes took part initially in the central and lower Amazon. Not coincidentally, one finds the longest archaeological sequences known in Amazonia there (see papers by Oliver, Schaan and Guapindaia, this volume) and the earliest available dates for the Amazonian Polychrome tradition, at the beginning of the Christian era, are represented by the Marajoara phase on Marajó Island (fig. 3.15).

We suggest that it was the beginning of long-term intensive settlement, or sedentism, that marked the origin of *terra preta* whenever and wherever it appeared. Sedentism, in turn, was correlated with subsistence intensification, most likely some sort of quantum leap in productive activities after population growth. We propose that it was probably a combination of manioc farming and the intensive use of aquatic resources that made sedentism possible. Perhaps the farming included seed crop cultivation such as maize in some or all cases, as noted by various authors,[72] but it is only in the case of *várzea* settings that maize potentially would have been a major crop. This latter assumption is not universally true, however. For instance, among the Tikuna in the large village of Campo Alegre on the upper Solimões with *c.*1300 residents, historic intensification of floodplain agriculture resulted from population growth. This intensification basically involved reproduction of the upland *terra firme* pattern of farming, including continuous reliance on protein-poor plants such as bitter manioc, instead of the adoption of protein-rich plants such as maize, which would supposedly thrive on such fertile soil.[73]

Regardless of the mix or potential mix of crops, Amerindian groups probably responded to human population growth with subsistence intensification of various forms in different areas.[74] This, in turn, wrought additional changes that transformed prehistoric Amerindians societies from egalitarian 'tribes' to stratified 'chiefdoms', on the basis of the available evidence, at least according to some researchers.[75]

The suggestion that agricultural intensification was a potential result of population growth, rather than the other way around, does not establish that this was an inevitable process. Alternative pathways might have included increased aquatic resource harvesting and management, and/or local trade in food resources. In E. Boserup's model population growth is the prime mover, with the consequent corollary that more complex socio-political forms will result from new agricultural systems, as more managerial control emerges by necessity. Although this model has been applied in both Mesoamerica and the Andes,[76] among other settings, it has been criticised, in large part because it relies on a single factor as a prime mover. Ideological and socio-political factors, among others, may have partially instigated sedentism and then regional population growth in the first place, but regardless of this, population growth in itself is a critical factor that should be not overlooked.[77] Population pressure has been previously recognized as a factor in the intensification of prehistoric Amerindian subsistence and in other developments such as warfare in lowland South America. Again, socio-political factors were likely to have been pertinent in one form or another.[78]

A population pressure model may well be useful as a starting place for theories about intensification in Amazonian prehistory. It may be helpful to use it as an initial hypothesis and then try to test it using archaeological data. Carneiro and Lathrap, among others, have previously presented population pressure models to account for cultural evolution in Amazonia.[79] Carneiro posed two alternatives for the emergence of institutionalized stratification, both related to warfare: the conquest of neighbouring polities by dominant leaders and their paramount settlements, or the establishment of alliances between polities against common enemies.[80] For Carneiro it is likely that aquatic resources drew people to the Amazon river before the introduction of agriculture, setting up the conditions for population growth.[81] However, one might quibble a bit with some of the details of his model. For example, why limit the model to the Amazon alone? Since Carneiro speaks of the 'river' as if it were one system, rather than a broad series of different settings and diverse environments, how would the model relate to other significant tributaries such as the Negro, Xingu or Madeira rivers, among many others, which represent distinctive fluvial systems themselves? Just which settings, rivers or otherwise, would suffice to structure the local societies in the fashion called for? What was the demographic threshold for war across time and space?

In the case of Lathrap, reference to population pressure was used to explain prehistoric migrations, which, in turn, accounted for changing ceramic styles, linguistic distributions, and other evidence for cultural traditions and other developments in Amazonia.[82] Ultimately, Lathrap noted that as a consequence of population pressure indigenous Amazonians in some areas also developed intensive agriculture, including the raised or ridged fields that characterize different (but apparently limited) parts of the lowlands of, for example, Bolivia, Colombia, Venezuela and the north-eastern Guyana-Surinam coast. However, Lathrap never fully explored the idea that agricultural intensification may have occurred prehistorically beyond these few limited areas in the broad region and in a portion of the *várzea*. In fact, although he interrelated population growth and resource competition as a mechanism of change, Lathrap did not explore these or any of the other individual components of his model. Nonetheless, the idea that population pressure in Amazonia stimulated cultural development in some fashion should not be dismissed outright without proper testing.

In spite of our reservations, the population pressure factor in Carneiro's and Lathrap's models seems to be suitable for testing in prehistoric Amazonia, at least in some form. We believe that it will be possible soon to demonstrate settlement hierarchies in different parts of the region during late prehistory, including the lower Negro area and perhaps the upper Xingu. However, these inferences are not yet proven, nor has the presence of chiefdoms been conclusively demonstrated in more than a few areas. Even after demonstrating settlement hierarchy and the corresponding existence of chiefdoms in different settings, the matter of coercive versus voluntary ascendancy of a chiefly leader in Carneiro's model will, we suspect, always remain untestable. This is due to the poor resolution typically characteristic of the archaeological record in the region and often elsewhere as well. Moreover, social and ideological variables, including political capital, may have intervened in one or more of these cases and it is possible that warfare was not a determining causal factor at all. Instead, alliance building and trade in exotic goods may have been critical social factors, as the flip side of the social interaction variable. However, the available ethnohistoric information and limited archaeological data do, in fact, suggest that warfare was a relevant factor during late prehistory, at least locally.[83]

Some may find it tenuous or even foolhardy to associate *terra preta*, population growth, subsistence intensification (or more specifically, agricultural intensification) and cultural evolution in Amazonia, but we have no doubt that these variables are somehow interrelated. All who have first-hand experience with extensive, even huge multiple-hectare *terra preta* sites in Amazonia will surely be sympathetic to this view. Between us, we have travelled across a broad representative range of Amazonian landscapes and visited (and sometimes lived among) contemporary Amerindians in different areas. We have never failed to be impressed by the widespread distribution and sheer scale of *terra preta* development in many riverine areas. This is often the most monumental and enduring material testimony to the indigenous polities that once thrived in the Amazon. They are also an invaluable resource for contemporary Amazonian farmers, Amerindians or not. In sum, *terra preta* represents a fine example of how Amazonian culture and nature mix in surprising and unexpected ways.

Even though we cannot fully agree among ourselves about the degree of socio-political complexity in prehistoric Amazonia, we all share the conviction that *terra preta* is quite extraordinary in relation to the archaeological record world-wide and we link it to 'formative' and more complex societies. Disagreement from others will probably arise as a result of the speculative nature of our interpretations and the limited data we have produced thus far. We feel that this disagreement is important, especially if our individual and collective bias stimulates tightly focused research, including both site-specific and regional studies, in the future. We hope that such research will allow us to ultimately answer these and other challenging questions in Amazonian archaeology.

Acknowledgements

Many people have contributed to our individual and collaborative research across Amazonia in many different ways. The various sources of support that have made our research possible are the Museu de Arqueologia e Etnologia, Universidade de São Paulo; the Museu Nacional, Universidade Federal do Rio de Janeiro; the Carnegie Musuem of Natural History; the University of Pittsburgh; the Univeristy of Florida; the University of Maine at Farmington; and the University of Vermont. Funding was provided by these institutions at different times, along with grants from the National Science Foundation, the Social Science Research Council, the Wenner-Gren Foundation, the William T. Hillman Foundation and the Fundação de Amparo à Pesquisa do Estado de São Paulo (FAPESP). Many individuals have also contributed in terms of advice, information and published literature. These people include William Barse, Robert Bartone, Robert Carneiro, William Denevan, Gertrude Dole, Carlos Fausto, Bruna Franchetto, Victor and Mary Catherine Heckenberger, Dirse Kern, Afukaka Kuikuru, Colin McEwan, Emilio Moran, Thomas Myers, Lee Newsom, José Oliver, James B. Richardson, Anna Roosevelt, Stephan Rostain, Aad Versteeg, Eduardo Viveiros de Castro, David Watters, Sandra Wellington, William Woods, Irmhild Wüst, Aritana Yawalipiti and Colin McEwan, among others. The CAP study area map was originally drawn by Marcos Castro and the photographs were produced by Eduardo Neves and Jim Petersen. As is customary, however, we alone are responsible for any errors or omissions herein.

NOTES

1 Roosevelt 1991: 128.

2 Smith 1980: 553.

3 Denevan 1996: 669.

4 Woods 1995: 162.

5 Whitehead 1996: 247.

6 E.g. Denevan 1996; Eden *et al.* 1984; Hilbert 1968; Roosevelt 1989; Simões 1974; Smith 1980; Woods and McCann 1997.

7 Neves 1998b; W. Barse, pers. comm. 1998.

8 E.g. Denevan 1996, 1998; Falesi 1974; Heckenberger *et al.* 1999; Meggers 1971, 1995; Myers 1973, 1992a; Roosevelt 1987, 1989, 1993; Woods 1995.

9 See Woods 1995: 162.

10 See Shorr 1999, for an exception: the Tikuna Amerindians in the large village of Campo Alegre on the Upper Solimões River.

11 Smith 1879: 144–5.

12 Ibid: 169.

13 Ibid: 238.

14 Farabee 1921: 156.

15 Nimuendajú, cited in Palmatary 1960: 18–21; see Nimuendajú 1948.

16 E.g. Falesi 1974: 210–14; Pabst 1991: 14–15; Smith 1980: 554.

17 Soares 1963, cited in Eden *et al.* 1984: 125.

18 E.g. Denevan 1996: 664–6, 1998: 55–6; Eden *et al.* 1984: 125; Herrera *et al.* 1992; Kern 1988; Mora *et al.* 1991: 77; Pabst 1991: 14–15, 1993; Smith 1980: 555–6; Woods 1995; Woods and McCann 1997.

19 Woods 1995: 162: figs 1 and 2.

20 Woods (1995: 165) argues: 'Few individual features of intrahabitation activity areas encompass more than a few meters or tens of meters horizontally or result in a homogenous deposit. In addition, refuse disposal patterns must be considered when attempting to link deposits to activity areas. Complicating the interpretation of this already complex situation are processes of anthropogenic and natural physical disturbance including tillage, feature emplacement, trampling, compaction, tree fall, sheet wash, gullying, slumping, and bioturbation by soil fauna, and diagenetic change oxidation and reduction, volatilization, leaching, and plant uptake.'

21 Herrera *et al.* 1992; Mora *et al.* 1991: 77; Smith 1980: 555.

22 Woods and McCann 1997.

23 These include latosols/oxisols, podzolic soils/ultisols, podzols/spodosols and others. For definitions see Holliday and Goldberg 1992 and Moran 1993a: 11–14.

24 Smith 1980: 557, 563–4; see also Denevan 1996: 664–6, 1998: 55; Eden *et al.* 1984: 125–126.

25 Eden *et al.* 1984; Herrera *et al.* 1992: 102; Mora *et al.* 1991: 76–7. This distinction has been usefully pursued by Woods and McCann (1997; see also Denevan 1998: 55–6), who correlate the term *terra mulata* with this form of 'dark soils' as being attributable to burning and perhaps mulching.

26 Archaeological analysis of the issue of soil degradation is still relatively uncommon, but one comparative analysis shows the difference between soil degradation and soil enhancement. The first example shows that erosion has occurred prehistorically in the south-west United States. In this case the only positive change is that the thickness of upper (A) horizon was increased as result of terracing, while soil fertility decreased. Organic matter, phosphorus, phosphate-fractionation and nitrogen values decreased as well and sediment compaction increased (Sandor 1992: 227–30). Elsewhere in an example from the Andes of Peru, where more stability has been characteristic and fertilization has been typical, agriculture demonstrably increased soil fertility, along with thickening the upper (A) horizon again. Organic matter, phosphorus and nitrogen all increased, and pH was favorably enhanced as well, all as a consequence of careful soil management (Sandor 1992: 240). Similar examples of soil enhancement through intentional and unintentional human activities are known through archaeology. In some cases the resultant 'anthrosols' are greatly enhanced in comparison to their non-altered parent materials (e.g. Eidt 1984; Herrera *et al.* 1992; Mora *et al.* 1991; Petersen 1996).

27 E.g. Meggers 1971: Table 1.

28 Denevan 1992a, 1996: 669–71, 1998: 56–7.

29 E.g. Roosevelt 1980: 61, 1991: 113–15; cf. Meggers and Evans 1983: 302.

30 E.g. Denevan 1996: 665, 1998: 55; Smith 1980: 562; Woods 1995: 159; Woods and McCann 1997.

31 E.g. Denevan 1998: 56.

32 Smith 1980: 55–6.

33 Woods 1995; Woods and McCann 1997.

34 E.g. Lathrap 1970: 36–44; Moran 1993b; Meggers and Evans 1957: 19, 28–32, 1983: 292, 317; Willey 1971; Wilson 1999: 179.

35 E.g. Denevan 1996; Roosevelt 1987, 1993.

36 E.g. Meggers 1971: fig. 17; cf. Lathrap 1970: fig. 2.

37 E.g. Moran 1993b: fig. 13.

38 E.g. Steward 1948; see Lathrap 1970: 45–7.

39 Viveiros de Castro 1996.

40 Métraux 1948a: 704, Gonçalves 1988.

41 E.g. Gillin 1948; Métraux 1948a: 414–15; Steward 1948; cf. Denevan 1966; Denevan and Zucchi 1978; Lathrap 1970: 160–163; Rostain 1991; Spencer and Redmond 1992; Versteeg 1985.

42 E.g. Denevan 1996, 1998; Lathrap 1968a, 1970; Myers 1992a; Roosevelt 1980, 1989, 1991, 1993, 1999b.

43 See Porro 1993, 1996.

44 Denevan 1996: 659, 664; Myers 1992b: 132.

45 See Carneiro 1995, n.d.

46 E.g. Carneiro 1961, 1983; Heckenberger 1998.

47 Phosphate-fractionation data were derived using the techniques and laboratory of Robert Eidt, whose extensive soil analyses provide directly comparable phosphate-fractionation values. Eidt's data were obtained from prehistoric contexts in the lowlands of northern Colombia beyond the Amazon proper and they vary widely (1984, 1985). For example, values from various 'garden and residence' contexts vary from 47 to 615 ppm (parts per million), with most less than 100–150 ppm, except where clearly related to 'residential' contexts in one study area. In another area in northern Colombia 'raised fields', 'platform' and 'tumulo' samples ranged from 77 to 7021 ppm, with most less than 2000–2500 ppm (Eidt 1984: 45–97). The highest of these, generally in excess of 500–1000 ppm, are related to residential deposits, associated generally by Eidt (1984: 95) with 'intensive residential activities of the type found in Middle East tells or in urbanized zones.' Elsewhere, Eidt (1984: 43) reports that phosphate-fractionation values 'above 200 ppm indicate more intensive activities such as dwelling areas, intensive gardening, manufacturing, etc. Extremely high total phosphate readings (above 2000 ppm, for example) represent burials, garbage pits, slaughter areas, urbanized zones, etc.'

48 In the CAP study area our ongoing research since 1995 has included several years of initial site survey and test excavations (1995 and 1997), and one season thus far of intensive testing (1999), with laboratory work concentrated in alternate years. Some of the preliminary results for the initial survey and testing work have been published and reported in other contexts, but much of this work has yet to be finalized (Heckenberger *et al.* 1998, 1999; Neves 1999a, 1999b, 2000; Neves and Bartone 1998; Petersen *et al.* 2000).

49 E.g. Hilbert 1968; Simões 1974.

50 Heckenberger *et al.* 1999: Table 1.

51 Lathrap 1970: 113–27; see Hilbert 1968; Meggers and Evans 1961.

52 Hilbert 1968; Lathrap 1970: 155–6.

53 Soil data from Açutuba provide clear evidence of intensive occupation over a long period of site formation. The highest phosphate-fractionation values include 561, 601 and 1327 ppm from the bottom to the top of the intact *terra preta* in the longest dated sequence in one portion of the central site area. These clearly exceed the phosphate-fractionation values of 285 to 349 ppm for the other comparable (and dated) pre-Guarita sequence at the site. In addition, increased organic matter, or carbon, magnesium, calcium, potassium and diminished acidity, among other values, are all characteristic of the more anthropic sediments relative to others at Açutuba.

54 Neves 2000.

55 E.g. Heckenberger *et al.* 1999; Petersen 1996.

56 Heckenberger 1996.

57 Heckenberger 1996, 1998; Heckenberger *et al.* 1999.

58 Upper Xingu sediment data have been collected at one of the large prehistoric sites with extensive earthworks, Nokugu, and at one historically known village for comparison. These data show values of 299 ppm for the presumed plaza and 556 for a residential area at the prehistoric site of Nokugu. At the historic site of Kuikuru I, occupied by several hundred Kuikuru Indians for 10–11 years, phosphate-fractionation values of 72–7 were obtained for the known plaza. Notably, a higher value of 216 ppm was obtained for a known house location, and two substantial middens produced values of 479–550 ppm. Thus, the ethnographic data from the Kuikuru village confirm the representation of different phosphate values across different activity areas, and roughly match those from Nokugu.

59 Obtained through the cooperation of Stephan Rostain and Robert Bartone.

60 Salazar 1993: 27–8.

61 137–410 ppm.

62 370 ppm to 3245 ppm in residential areas and 78–134 ppm in non-residential areas.

63 Petersen 1996: Table 4.

64 E.g. Eden *et al.* 1984: Tables 2 and 4; Falesi 1974: 211; Herrera *et al.* 1992: Table 2; Kern 1988; Pabst 1991: 14; Smith 1980: Table 1; Versteeg 1985: 675, 712; Tables 9 and 23.

65 Heckenberger *et al.* 1999.

66 The onset of *terra preta* formation at both Osvaldo and Hatahara may have happened a little later, perhaps only during the first millenium AD (Neves 2000), which does not invalidate the argument made here.

67 Denevan 1996: 55; Eden *et al.* 1984: 126; Hilbert 1968.

68 Lathrap 1970: 117–20.

69 Denevan 1998: 55; Eden *et al.* 1984: 126–7; Hilbert 1968; Hilbert and Hilbert 1980.

70 Denevan 1996: 666; Eden *et al.* 1984; Herrera *et al.* 1992; Mora *et al.* 1991.
71 Heckenberger 1996, 1998; Heckenberger *et al.* 1999.
72 E.g. Lathrap 1970: 58–59; Myers 1992a: 91; Roosevelt 1980: 61–7.
73 Shorr 1999: 82.
74 Following the initial lead of Boserup (1965) and Carneiro (1970).
75 Some researchers have changed their mind on the issue of socio-political complexity in Amazonia. The late prehistoric moundbuilders on Marajó Island, for example, are no longer held to represent a 'chiefdom' but rather were a sort of 'graded ranked' society. However, remains from the Santarém-Tapajós area are still accepted as a 'chiefdom' in this perspective (Roosevelt 1998). In the case of Marajó we feel that this may underestimate their complexity and perhaps it is splitting hairs too much to differentiate between 'graded ranked' and 'chiefdom' societies on the basis of available evidence.
76 E.g. Cohen 1977; Sanders 1992; Sanders *et al.* 1979.
77 E.g. Conrad and Demarest 1984: 170–73; Drennan 1987: 315; Earle 1991: 84; Feinman 1991: 260; Feinman and Nicholas 1992: 155; Kirch 1991: 133.
78 E.g. Bray 1995: 111–12; DeBoer 1981: 375–6; Lathrap 1968a, 1970: 19–20; Roosevelt 1980: 67–78, 1987: 156, 163–5, 1993: 259.
79 Carneiro 1961, 1970, 1987, n.d.; Lathrap 1968a, 1970, 1972.
80 To Carneiro environmental circumscription alone seems an unlikely causal factor. He has ultimately suggested that 'resource concentration' and 'social circumscription' were likely to have been significant causal factors in the coercive development of complex societies. 'Resource concentration' was initially viewed as follows: 'While there was no sharp cleavage between productive and unproductive land, as there was in Peru, there was a steep ecological gradient. So much more rewarding was the Amazon River than adjacent areas, and so desired did it become as a habitat, that peoples were drawn to it from surrounding regions. Eventually crowding occurred along many portions of the river, leading to warfare over sections of river front. And losers in war, in order to retain access to the river, often had no choice but to submit to the victors' (Carneiro 1970: 737).

Later, Carneiro modified this theory by removing any last element of voluntarism from it. He suggested that social circumscription occurs 'when population density builds up over a wide area, reaching such a point that people are impeded from moving from their current location because all the surrounding land is already occupied. The military and political consequences of social circumscription are clear. Essentially it acts in much the same way as environmental circumscription. A group defeated in war, having nowhere to flee, is then subject to forced incorporation into the political unit of the victors.' (Carneiro n.d.: 22).
81 In his words, 'introduction of agriculture made possible the use of a new riverine resource which had not been previously tapped – *várzea*. This rich soil, whose fertility was replenished annually by the floodwaters of the Amazon, provided an additional lure. Even more people were attracted to the banks of the river,' which gave rise to social circumscription. 'The degree of crowding ... not only intensified warfare ... but made it difficult if not impossible for those groups defeated in war to move out of range of the stronger groups.' They 'were subject to being incorporated, along with their land, into the political unit of the victors. In this manner the Amazon gave rise to an extensive string of chiefdoms which, in the 16th century, formed so conspicuous a feature of that river' (Carneiro 1987: 249).
82 Building on the *várzea/terra firme* dichotomy, Lathrap (1968a: 28) proposed: 'The pattern of outward migration suggested by all these converging lines of evidence could be best explained by the intense and continuing population pressures of the flood plain of the Central Amazon, the most favorable environment for the support of tropical forest culture. This extreme and continuing competition for territory is understandable, if one realizes the limited amount of flood plain – the only ecological niche really suitable to tropical forest culture – available in the Amazon Basin.' Lathrap (1970: 19–20) also suggests: 'This competition for agricultural land has been going on for a long time, and began several millennia before Orellana's voyage of discovery down the Amazon in 1542. The groups who have lost the battle have been many, and they have been pushed further up-stream and off the major rivers into the intervening expanses of jungle. Earlier the struggle was marked by all-out warfare and a flamboyant development of cannibalism and headhunting ... This fight for the limited supply of productive farm land has been the most important single force in the culture history of the Amazon Basin, and more than any other factor is clearly visible in the archaeological record.' Elsewhere, Lathrap (1970: 75) interrelates these factors: 'relatively continuous population pressures, relatively constant rates of migration, and the search for a single kind of ecological niche, good alluvial soils.'
83 E.g. DeBoer 1981; Heckenberger 1996; Myers 1992a; Porro 1994.

PART II

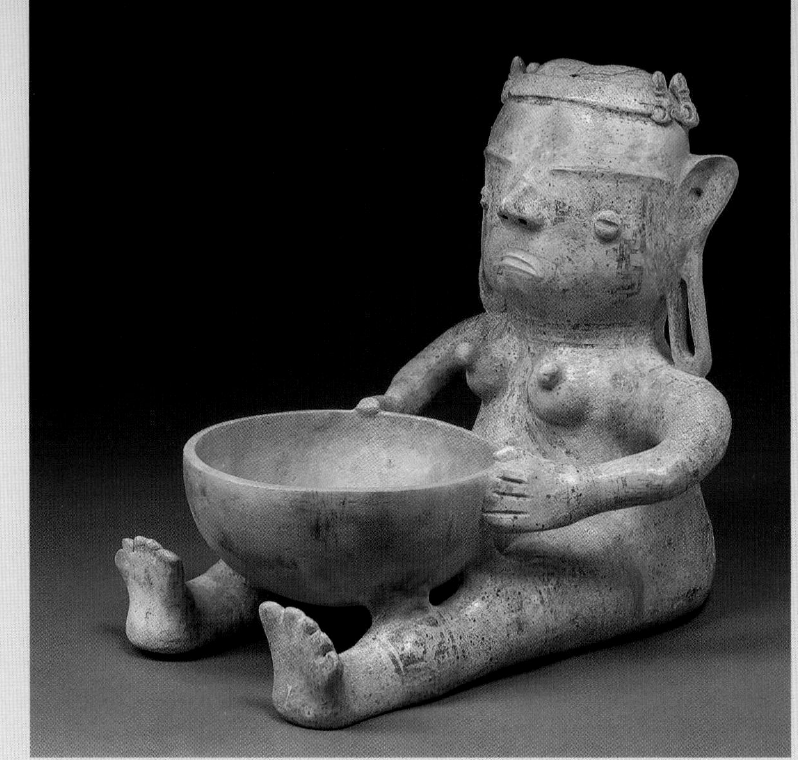

ARCHAEOLOGY

AND SOCIETY

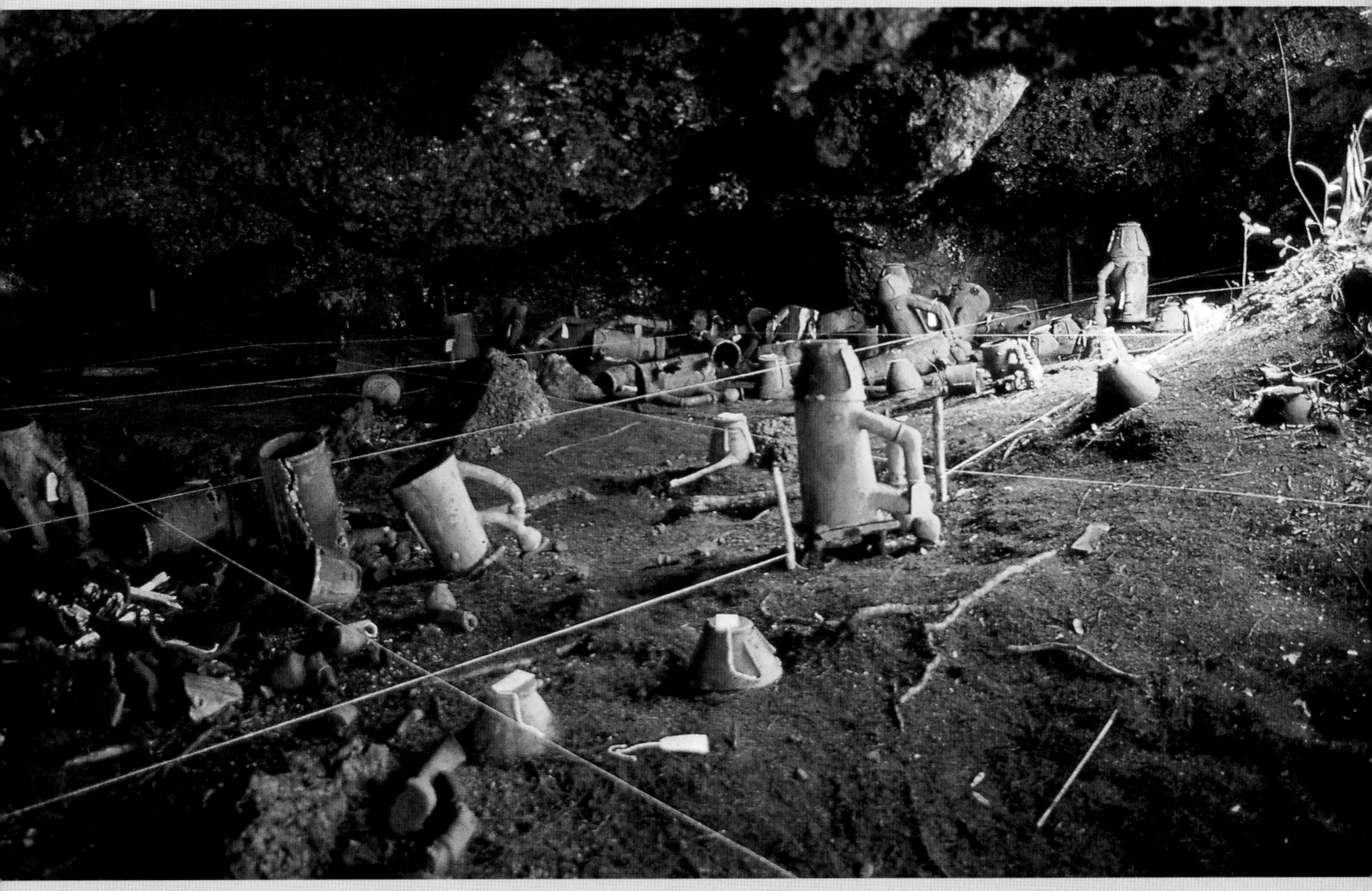

4

Into the Labyrinths of Marajoara Pottery

Status and Cultural Identity in Prehistoric Amazonia

DENISE SCHAAN

A changeable environment

Marajó is the largest island among a maze-like archipelago located at the mouth of the Amazon. Here the main body of the river flows round the north of the island, splitting into a multitude of smaller channels (*furos*) and islands before emptying eastward into the Atlantic Ocean. To the south of the island one channel leads to the Pará river and is then met by the Tocantins before broadening out to form the Marajó bay. With a surface area of some 50,000 sq. km, Marajó Island is larger than Belgium or the Netherlands. Two broad and contrasting ecological zones can be found on the island: the rainforest (*floresta*) covering most of the south-western half and the savannah grasslands (*campos*) in the north-east (figs 4.1 and 4.3). Both are far from flat, having areas of higher and lower topography but never rising much above 10 metres. Other rich and diverse ecological niches are found along the coast and major rivers. These include patches of mangrove swamps, which fringe the eastern edge of the island, and gallery forest, which borders the rivers that traverse the grasslands, and abounds with exuberant flora and fauna .

ABOVE **4.1 Aerial view of south-eastern Marajó Island showing the contrast between the rain forest (*floresta*) and grasslands (*campos*). Heavy seasonal rains result in low-lying areas becoming completely flooded for up to half the year.**

RIGHT **4.2 Marajoara people used large, elaborate ceramic vessels to bury high-ranking individuals, together with their personal items and offerings (height 48 cm, diameter 35 cm; Museu Barbier-Mueller Art Precolombí, Barcelona).**

Life on Marajó Island is governed by a tropical equatorial climatic regime of alternating rainy and dry seasons. These seasonal changes as well as the influence of the annual rise and fall of the Amazon have a dramatic effect on the landscape. For half the year most of the low-lying grasslands are continuously submerged under floodwater, leaving only small, scattered islands of vegetation visible. In contrast, at the peak of the dry season the land dries out and many small watercourses disappear, turning the grasslands into an arid desert.

The alternating seasons also impact directly on the human exploitation of wild resources on the island. During the rainy season as the floods inundate all the low-lying terrain, aquatic life, which was previously restricted to the rivers, can spread over large areas. The dispersal of the fish populations makes them harder to

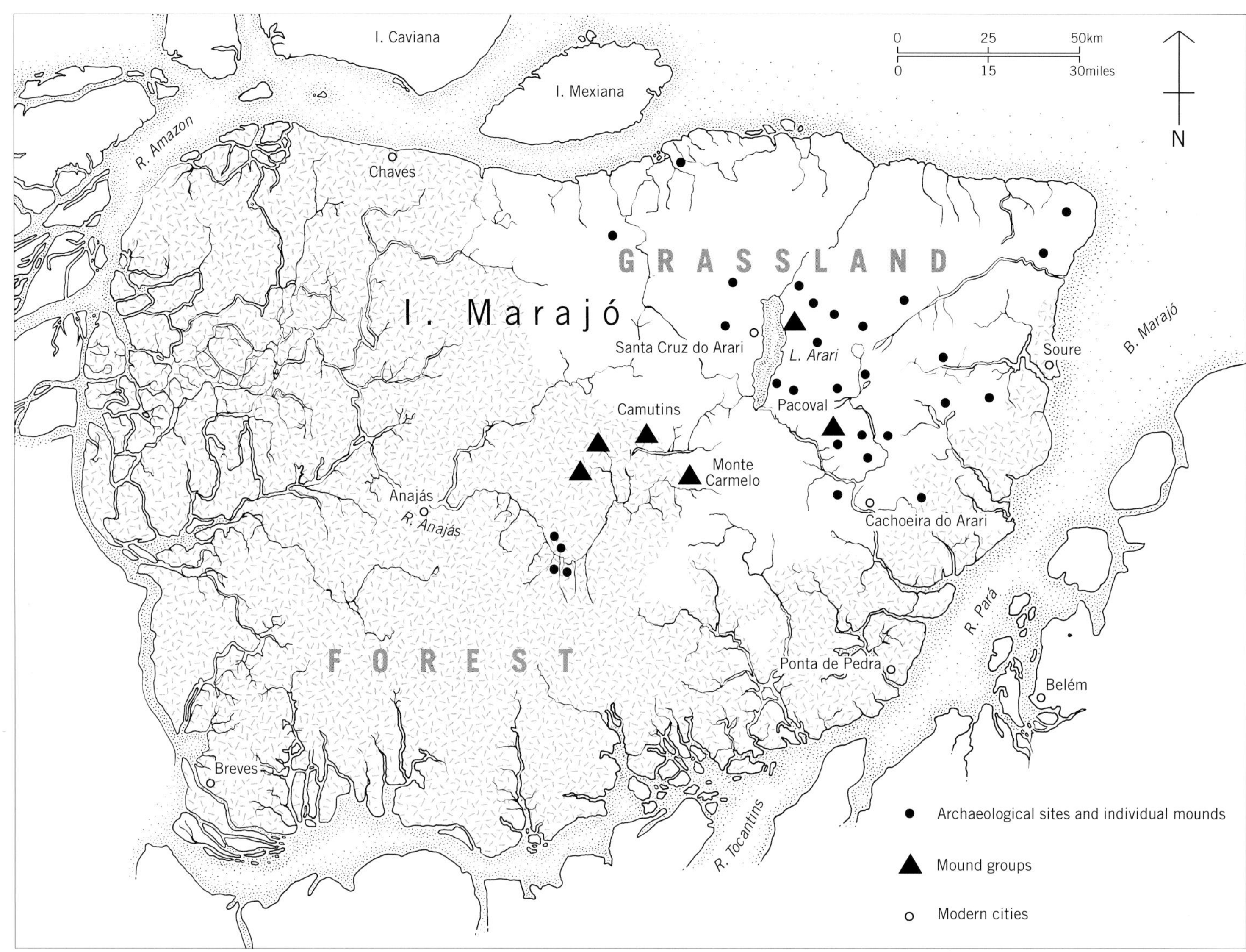

4.3 Distribution map of Marajoara-phase archaeological sites on Marajó Island.

catch causing a shortage of fish resources. At the same time the opposite tends to happen with terrestrial fauna, which clusters on the higher terrain. When the rains stop, the flow of drainage water draws the fish back again into the rivers and seasonal lakes where they can concentrate in huge numbers. In turn, the grasslands and the small watercourses dry out, facilitating the dispersal of terrestrial fauna once more (fig. 4.3).

It is likely that the very first human populations established themselves on the coast in close proximity to the mangroves. They relied mainly on aquatic resources, an adaptation that characterizes early sedentary settlements in the lower Amazon.[1] In Marajó the few known shell middens preserving evidence of this way of life have been largely destroyed by liming operations at the beginning of the twentieth century. However, by extrapolating from similar settings on the nearby mainland, as well as on the Atlantic coast, it is inferred that these shell midden occupations on Marajó Island probably date to at least 5,500 years ago.[2]

From this time onwards the archaeological record shows the spread of small sedentary villages over a large region in the hinterlands of the island. Here people subsisted on wild resources gathered from the forest and the grasslands, and eventually developed incipient forms of agriculture. Some features of their material culture show an early development of techniques that would later flourish during the Marajoara phase around AD 500–1500. For instance, durable and well-finished pottery is already being produced with clear Marajoara traits. These include thick rims, white slip, red painting, brushing and decorative incisions. There are also pottery figurines and pipes, as well as spindle whorls, which indicate that textile production was underway. Furthermore, some of these early settlements show signs of incipient earthworks.[3]

Around AD 500, at the onset of the Marajoara phase proper, the island population seems to increase, both in terms of the number and size of the settlements. Mound clusters begin to appear in the centre of the island, covering an area of more than 20,000 sq. metres around Lake Arari. On the flat grasslands and near the forest, as well as at the headwaters of rivers and small streams, one or two large mounds (8 to 12 metres in height) are found together with a number of smaller ones, forming groups that display a clear hierarchical settlement pattern. The abundance of ceremonial and funerary remains on the higher mounds reinforces the belief that these are political and ceremonial centres to which the smaller mounds were subordinated. The highest mounds were built as a result of the constant accretion of earth laboriously carried in from adjacent areas as well as from the bottom of nearby streams. It is clear that although the mound builders may have initially planned to raise platforms in order to protect themselves from the annual floods, mounds soon became invested with symbolic significance associated with prestige and leadership. This in turn probably stimulated rivalry and competition between regional centres. It is still difficult to specify exactly what kind of political economy integrated these political and ceremonial centres. Nevertheless, we can surmise that they maintained a certain level of regional political autonomy through time, and an ongoing need to articulate and project their cultural identity, as is apparent in the marked differences in mortuary paraphernalia.

During this phase it is clear that Marajó reached a level of social complexity that presents a marked contrast with the egalitarian ethos and small scale of previous settlements and this has stimulated a lively scholarly debate on the nature of Marajoara society. Most authorities now agree that the level of social complexity attained can best be characterized as a chiefdom.[4] This runs contrary to long-standing ideas that the poor soils of tropical forest environments have limited population growth and prevented human groups from organizing into large, dense, permanent settlements.[5] As a consequence scholars are now seeking a comprehensive explanation to account for the emergence of social complexity in the Amazonian tropical lowlands.

In the 1980s Brazilian archaeologist José P. Brochado undertook a study of Marajó Island ecology in order to demonstrate that intensive agriculture could have supported substantial populations.[6] He characterized Marajó as essentially an enlarged floodplain (*várzea*) and suggested that Marajoara populations exploited the island topography as a natural system of raised fields, albeit on a large scale. Following Brochado, Roosevelt has pointed out that the nutrient-rich soils and the seasonal availability of aquatic fauna were indeed factors that must have encouraged populations to concentrate and to build mounds as a basis for more permanent settlements.[7] Although this offers a coherent and appealing explanation, it assumes that population growth and social stratification – with specialization – always entails and necessarily depends upon the development of intensive agriculture.[8] This model has been criticized as a kind of ecological determinism that assigns a passive, adaptive role to indigenous populations.[9]

More field research and excavations are needed to provide a convincing and comprehensive explanation of the cultural processes that led to the emergence of Marajoara culture and its sustained development on Marajó Island in the course of nearly a thousand years. The key to understanding Marajoara social organization, settlement, and subsistence patterns lies in learning more about how indigenous groups played an active role in their interactions with nature and other societies.

This essay explores some aspects of Marajoara beliefs, social organization and ceremonial life by examining motifs and symbols found on some of the most striking objects that survive in the archaeological record. Marajoara pottery comprises spectacular funerary urns, plates, bowls, stools and a range of figurines, as well as the unusual ceramic female pubic covers known as *tangas*, which are decorated with intriguing imagery. Together these formed a complex system of visual communication that endured for many centuries.

Marajoara ceremonial life

Along with a small number of stone tools and adornments, pottery vessels are the principal surviving element of Marajoara material culture. The great majority of these objects come from mortuary contexts and point to the importance of ancestor worship and to the existence of strong beliefs in an after life. Differences in social status are reflected in differential treatment of the dead. High-ranking individuals were accorded funerary rites, which follow a consistent pattern. The treatment of the deceased individual starts with removal of the flesh, probably either by natural decomposition or by boiling of body parts. Red paint was applied to the disarticulated bones, which were meticulously arranged inside ceramic urns, the skulls lying on the bottom.[10] Many Amazonian societies practice flesh removal from the corpse. This relates to the belief that the soul inhabits the bones, and the removal of flesh helps in the transition of the spirit of the deceased into the afterlife.

Sometimes a *tanga* is placed with the skeleton inside the urn and in a few cases under the skull. Miniature vessels, small plates, beads, pendants and stone axes are part of the paraphernalia intended to accompany the dead in his or her journey. The urn is carefully placed in a hole dug inside a house, leaving the vessel rims exposed at ground level. The urn is then covered by a lid, usually an inverted plate or bowl. Figurines, stools and bowls containing offerings, such as food and other objects, are also found around the urn.[11] The presence of the dead inside houses, and possibly temples, reflects a strong link between living people and their ancestors, and indicates the vital role these kind of kinship ties played in reinforcing social identity across the generations.

Differences in social status and related prerogatives held by some individuals certainly determined their burial in larger, more elaborate funerary urns (fig. 4.2). A larger number of better offerings were also allocated to high-status individuals who were likewise buried in the largest mounds. By contrast, in smaller mounds and more distant villages urns were smaller, simpler and associated with fewer objects. But even within the small settlements differential treatment has been documented: elaborate urns containing bones and rare prestigious objects such as basalt axes, and a small accompanying bowl can be found alongside very rustic plain urns. The fact that the funerary urns are generally found in clusters may indicate that members of the same kin group were buried together. A concentration of multiple burials at certain locations may imply that the death of a great chief was accompanied by the sacrifice of slaves and servants, who were buried in smaller, simpler urns around him.[12]

Marajoara ceramics are decorated by employing one or more of four main techniques: excision, incision, modelling and painting. Combinations of these techniques together with the widespread use of white and red slip resulted in remarkably sophisticated patterns.[13] It is generally assumed that groups of skilled artisans were responsible for carefully executing the repertoire of designs following the established conventions.[14] This task would have been very time consuming and probably demanded at least part-time specialists. These specialists were charged with the task of translating creation myths and oral folklore into the visual media offered by textile, wood and pottery. We can imagine that powerful individuals such as heads of lineages and paramount chiefs within Marajoara society would have been responsible for commissioning the most richly decorated elite objects.

It is likely that many ceramic objects were not produced specifically for funerary purposes alone, but would also have been used at feasts and diverse kinds of ritual gatherings and ceremonies. Some of them may also have belonged to the dead during his or her life. Stools, snuffers, figurines, stone axes, and nephrite pendants and beads are likely to have been personal objects. Because these are rare finds in excavated archaeological contexts, appearing only in association with elaborate urns, they can be considered elite prestige items and therefore true symbols of social status and political power. Because workable lithic material is rare or non-existent on Marajó Island, it is clear that the elite obtained objects such as basalt axes and nephrite adornments through trade networks, with possible links to other contemporary and distant complex societies of the Amazon basin and the Caribbean islands.[15]

On the other hand, finely decorated plates, bowls, vases and bottles might have been used during different kinds of communal events such as burials, rites of passage, etc. Many of these objects were broken during use, and the great quantity of broken pottery on the higher and larger mounds indicate that these were places where rituals were most frequently enacted and where great public gatherings took place.

The cultural understanding of nature

Amazonian societies are renowned for incorporating characters and observed behaviour from the natural world in the course of constructing their creation myths and stories to explain how the world came into being. Indigenous myths recorded by missionaries and early ethnographers are peopled by a wealth of both natural and supernatural beings, frequently with no clear division between humans and animals. Animals are often key actors in cultural contexts, sometimes seen as the ancestors of humans and on other occasions as bringing knowledge about how tools and utensils were first acquired and used. They also reveal particular visual attributes that may be taken as cultural markers.[16]

Myths, cosmological order and beliefs about the roles played by animals and people also found visible expression as symbols and motifs. They can therefore be approached through iconographic studies.[17] The range of animal images on Marajoara ceramics leaves no doubt that their imaginative world was inhabited by beings that share many recognizable characteristics with the local fauna but also reveal supernatural attributes. Vessels, urns, plates and bowls display both naturalistic depictions as well as more stylized images of snakes, caymans, lizards, scorpions, owls, king vultures, manatees, turtles, birds, ducks, monkeys, anteaters and jaguars.[18] Composite figures combining elements from more than one animal, as well as from both human and animal beings, are commonly found. Separate body parts such as modelled heads serve as appendages on vessels, making the identification of natural beings on the ceramics a challenging task.

This inventive use of animal elements shows that the different creatures were not simply depicted in a literal, straightforward way. Instead, their physical attributes

4.4–6 Funerary urn (above left: 4.4) with detail of lizard (top: 4.5) on its side (height 100 cm; Musée Barbier-Mueller, Geneva). Reptilians including snakes, lizards (above: 4.6) and caymans are common on Marajó Island. Combinations of human faces and reptilian imagery on large funerary vessels illustrate the close links between human and animal in Marajoara symbolism.

were represented selectively in order to communicate a complex set of ideas. The rest of this essay relates the iconography on ceramic objects to a range of reptiles, animals, invertebrates and birds in the natural world. All were used to express cultural ideas and show the particular way in which Marajoara society represented its reading of nature in visual and material culture.

One animal commonly depicted on the upper bodies of red and excised funerary urns (figs 4.4–5) reminds us of either a cayman (*jacaré-açu*) or a lizard. Although a number of such related species are very common in Marajó, the stylized depiction on the vessels does not permit a specific species identification.[19] The figure is portrayed as if seen from above, showing four limbs with three digits each (fig. 4.5). It is immediately apparent that this is not an accurate rendering of the reptile in question, for the species represented have more digits (fig. 4.6). On the other hand, the pronounced dorsal spine is an important feature of such reptiles as well as being clearly marked in the modelled depictions on the urns. The body seems disproportionately small in comparison to the limbs, and it also lacks the long tail found in lizards and caymans. Paired images of this figure are always placed symmetrically on opposite sides of the vessel (fig. 4.5). Between these, on the other opposing sides, another character is rendered in a very stylized design resembling an inverted face. This particular arrangement of decorative fields – two paired opposing figures – is a recurring pattern found on Marajoara ceramics.

A complex iconographic structure is found on this urn, with different figures and motifs organized in carefully ordered arrangements. This sophisticated symbolic system reveals a coherent way of ordering the world that is replete with meaning. There are five different decorative fields, four of them with human face motifs; human imagery also plays an important role in Marajoara iconography.

The application of paint and slip to enhance the decorative designs on vessels is common (fig. 4.7). First a coat of white slip is applied, followed by a red slip. On the upper body the space between the modelled figures is

4.7–8 Funerary urn (above) with a snake modelled in relief (right; height 60 cm; Museu Nacional do Rio de Janeiro, Brazil). Mythical snakes are recurring images on Marajoara ceramics. Repetitive patterns and recursive design elements seem to have been employed as a kind of mnemonic device for communicating and reinforcing fundamental cosmological beliefs.

modified with incisions and excisions, producing designs in relief. When the very fine layer of red clay is removed, it reveals the white layer, creating a beautiful visual effect.

Double-headed and paired snakes are widely represented in Marajoara iconography and are probably inspired by recurrent Amazonian myths of an ancestral snake. The Marajoara 'mythical' snakes with their triangular-shaped heads show marked similarities to two species of the *Bothrops* genus (*B. atrox* and *B. marajoensis*) popularly known as *jararaca*, both of which are very poisonous.[20] These species are still very common on Marajó, and it is worth noting that during the rainy season animals, including snakes, migrate to the shrinking areas of habitable dry land where they are forced into close proximity with people. It is easy to understand that in the past the way in which people conceived of themselves as human beings and of their place in nature must have been strongly affected by their day to day experiences of, and interactions with, the natural world. It is possible that as a symbol of regeneration and life (e.g. the periodic shedding of their skins), as well as being potentially deadly, snakes in general came to be associated with the world of the dead and therefore with funerary urns.

4.9 This rare solid turtle figurine complements the range of other riverine and forest creatures that feature in Marajoara imagery (length 8.8 cm; Musée Barbier-Mueller, Geneva).

The decoration on the type of cylindrical vessel mentioned above (fig. 4.7), was fashioned using a similar incision/excision technique as described for the upper part of the cayman vessel. The symmetry also follows the same rule, with two paired opposing figures. In combination with naturalistic representations of snakes, in which emphasis is placed on spiral coils representing the coiled body, other fantastic composite faces, also combined with spirals, are found covering the whole external surface of the vessel (fig. 4.8). The roll-out drawing of this vessel allows these figures to be seen in their entirety. The modelled serpent stands out against the incised background design and can be compared with the urn shown in fig. 4.16.

As well as dangerous creatures including poisonous reptiles, there are other animals in Marajoara iconography with which people had a much closer relationship. Some of these, such as turtles, were skilfully managed and provided a vital source of food. Early travellers have reported that Amazonian groups used to keep turtles in pens as a readily available reserve supply of meat, eggs and fat when the need arose (see fig. 3.10).[21] The references to turtles both as mythological creatures and as a food resource seem to contradict Lévi-Strauss's classification of animals in the tropical forest lowlands into two broad groups: those that were good to eat and those that were good 'to think'.[22] The latter category refers to the fact that most mythological histories deal with animals that are not consumed for food. Clearly in the case of turtles they were not only 'good to eat' but also 'good to think' since they feature prominently in myths, stories and oral lore.[23]

The decorative technique on the rare turtle-shaped ceramic object shown in fig. 4.9 was named Pacoval Incised after a mound site located close to Lake Arari, where many objects with a similar decoration were found.[24] This technique involves first applying a layer of white slip, then inscribing the motifs onto the surface and finally emphasizing the incised designs by the application of red pigment. The areas outlined in red create their own decorative field. It is therefore possible to read the motifs in different ways, either by focusing just on the red motifs or by taking into account the whole design.

It is curious that the motifs do not directly replicate the actual patterns of a real turtle carapace as one might expect (fig. 4.10). Nevertheless many other distinctive signifying elements appear as recognizable motifs in Marajoara iconography. For example, turtle-like heads, some of which also have human characteristics, are commonly found as handles on plate rims (figs 4.25–6).

Marajoara iconography is peopled by a host of other birds, reptiles and invertebrates, such as scorpions, and I will now explore some of the ways in which close observation of the natural world may have inspired their appropriation by human beings and how they were used in a cultural context.

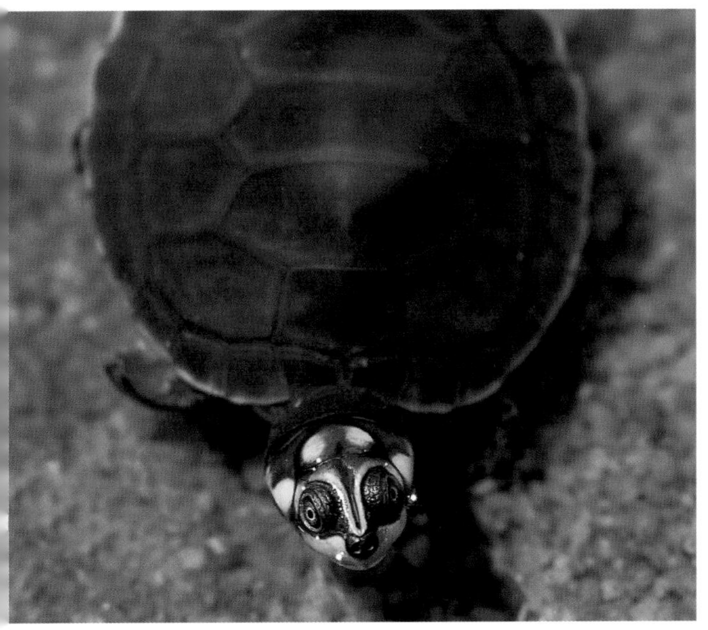

Death and re-birth in a hierarchical society

In the rainy season of 1949 archaeologists Betty Meggers and Clifford Evans excavated a burial group at Guajará mound in north-eastern Marajó.[25] This consisted of superimposed funerary urns, which provided a rare opportunity to consider the significance of such finds in an excavated context (fig. 4.11).[27] The largest urns were found in the lower levels (including urn I, which although from a more recent level follows the same pattern of deposition as described below). This group contained disarticulated bones, found with *tangas*. The bones were marked with red paint and covered by a layer of large sherds, which contributed to their preservation. According to the excavators, urn L (fig. 4.12) contained

ABOVE 4.10 Turtles were an important source of protein for prehistoric Amazonian Indians, and many species are found on Marajó Island (see fig. 3.10).

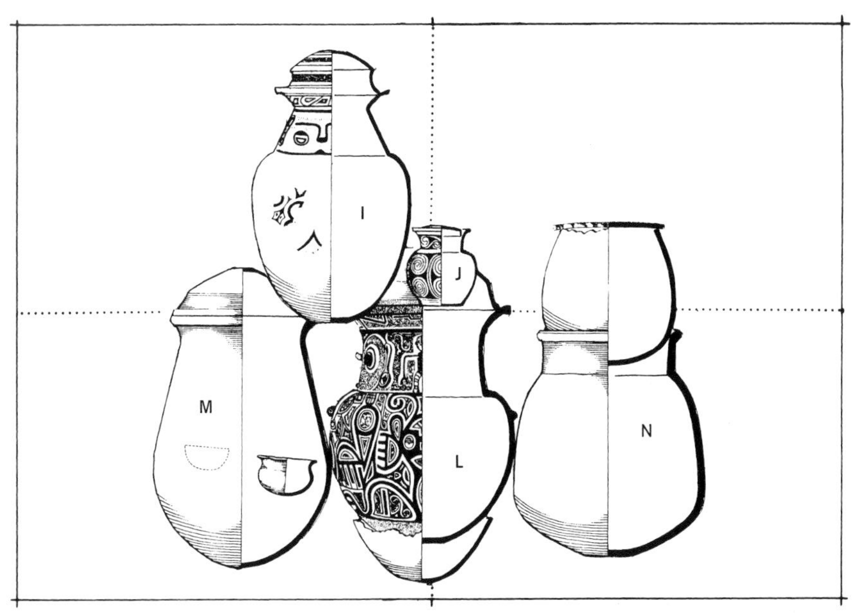

RIGHT 4.11 Profile drawing of a group of Marajoara funerary urns excavated by Meggers and Evans from the Guajará mound (Monte Carmelo group). Such urn groups document important differences in the treatment of the dead, probably based on hierarchical distinctions within Marajoara society.

a

LEFT AND BELOW **4.12–13** This polychrome urn is part of the group illustrated in fig. 4.11 (height 84 cm, width 70 cm; Museu Paraense Emílio Goeldi, Belém, Brazil). The four sides of the urn reveal two opposed pairs of figures, as shown in the drawings (compare a and c, and b and d).

skeletal remains of one individual, possibly a young adult, since the bones were gracile. The femurs were placed in a clear east–west orientation with red paint marks. A plain, orange *tanga* was located on the south-east side.

The interesting fact is that this individual was not buried alone, but together with others. In a bowl below the urn remains of a second burial and a red *tanga* were found. A third burial, composed of bones and also a red *tanga*, was found outside the urn, close to its neck. Two large plain urns flanked urn L. Urn N contained disintegrated bones, and urn M, a two-individual burial. At the bottom of urn M there were bones of an eighteen- to twenty-five-year-old female; over this skeleton lay many animal bones (from small rodents and birds), topped by yet another set of human bones from a male individual probably in his late twenties. The skull from this last burial, also associated with a red *tanga*, shows clear evidence of intentional deformation. All the bones in urn M were covered with red paint, even the smaller ones.

The excavators stress that since the two plain flanking urns (M and N) were located very close to the decorated one, there is no doubt that the three were buried together: 'The elaborateness of the central jar makes it probable that it contained an important personage whose comfort in the next world needed to be assured.'[27]

Urns L, I and J share a similar decorative technique and iconography, belonging to a Marajoara type of urn painted in red and black over white, depicting female attributes. This type is common in sites found west of Lake Arari. The regional distribution of this iconography may reveal that social groups sharing similar interests and descent were living close to each other within the Marajoara domain.

Urn L, a typical example of this type, displays two paired and symmetrically opposite figures (fig. 4.13). There is a horizontal division of decorative fields: an upper band, just below the rim, followed by an upper cylindrical neck; and a lower rounded body. The upper band has geometric motifs and a pair of appendages on opposite sides.

Figs 4.13a and c feature a human-like creature with rounded, protuberant and half-closed eyes, a stylized nose, a 'T' mark on the forehead, and a mouth. A cylindrical adornment hangs below the mouth. The ears have plugs and attached tassels. The rounded body shows stylized arms with four fingers. Roosevelt interprets the geometric motifs inside the arms as stylized bones, in an X-ray form.[28] At the centre a red circle represents the belly or womb (inside which, in many other urns of this type, a human-like figure is depicted). Below the womb a rectangle may represent the biological sex, suggesting that this individual is a female. The geometric motifs covering the body may allude to body painting.

b

c

d

On the neck of the vessel is also found a standing figure with his left arm up and the right arm down (figs 4.13b and d). The hands have just two fingers. The body has some painting on it. Its head is clearly animal-like (maybe a turtle head), since the eyes show bilateral vision. Its legs have stripes, as the Brazilian anteater does. On some urns the figure also displays the body of anteater in a more explicit reference to this animal.[29]

Beneath this on the body of the urn a squatting creature with a human face, round and half-closed eyes (similar to the female figure in figs 4.13a and c), and a geometrical arrangement over the eyes that also resembles the 'T' over the figure in figs 4.13a and c. A stylized nose and mouth complete the face. There are two spirals over the head, two hands with five fingers on the sides (where ears should be placed), suggesting that the figure is compressed or has its face projected over its belly, as is common in some representations.[30] This figure has her legs splayed, and if the oval design between them represents a vagina, it could represent a female figure in a birth-giving position. The legs also recall the shape of frog's legs, recalling the association between frogs and females commonly found in South American Indian mythology.[31]

In some urns variations of this creature appear placed inside the womb of the female figure of figs 4.13a and c, which can be read as indicating pregnancy. Roosevelt suggests that this iconography, in a funerary context, may signify re-birth in the transition of the dead to another world.[32]

Other associations between the iconography found on Marajoara pottery and the social symbolism of death are found, for instance, in the shape of the female figure of figs 4.13a and c. Her arms, eyes and protuberant chest remind us of either an owl or an eagle.[33] The owl is well known for its habit of swallowing whole animals (such as rodents) and regurgitating only their bones or skin (this brings to mind the rodent bones found inside the urn M). It provides a metaphor for the removal of flesh from the bones of the dead individual who is buried and would be reborn (or regurgitated) in the afterlife. The presence of king vultures on other types of funerary vessels could also be an allusion to the Amazonian practice of stripping dead bodies of their flesh, since vultures are known for their habit of eating dead animals.[34]

4.14 Incised snake patterns are used as filler elements to cover the body of this 'female' urn (height 33.5 cm, diameter 20 cm; Museu Paraense Emílio Goeldi, Belém, Brazil). Similar patterns may also have been employed in body painting.

The funerary context revealed by the Meggers and Evans excavation provides vital information about Marajoara mortuary customs. Clear differences in social status are apparent in the way in which the most elaborate urns are flanked by plain urns or by the bones of individuals who were simply buried directly in the ground. It is interesting that two burials without urns close to the L and O urn were associated with *tangas*. The fact that the two individuals buried together in urn M had only one *tanga* with them may indicate that *tangas* are not necessarily assigned to a particular individual, but instead to the multiple burial. In this mortuary context it would not have been a personal item, but rather an offering to be taken to the afterlife.

The fact that the bones were carefully painted red, and that all the *tangas* in this context were also painted red, is significant and can be linked to the use of red colour symbolism in general discussed below.

The material expression of the myth

A range of ethnographic studies have shown that the themes and motifs reproduced on the ceramics and in the material culture of pre-literate societies in general have a rich mythic content.[35] The decorative motifs on ceramics, vessels and other objects were not intended merely as a passive portrayal of a pantheon of mythical creatures. They encapsulate scenes, episodes and stories from oral traditions and leave a vivid and visible record of this animate world. The depiction of these creatures and scenes has an intimate and specific relationship with the way in which the myths themselves are ordered. Lévi-Strauss demonstrated how myths share a similar structure, and that myth narratives are often circular in the sense that episodes are metaphorically related to each other. There are recurrent elements within myths and the end of the story may be connected to the beginning. Likewise, there are often many versions of the same myth, which although differing in detail retain a broadly similar structure. Lévi-Strauss concluded that the structure of a myth or set of myths may be as important as its content. I suggest that the structure and organization of the iconography on the vessels may well reflect fundamental aspects of such myths and stories.

4.15 Detail of fig. 4.14 showing the eye motif surrounded by a scorpion shape.

These ideas offer clues that may help us understand why symmetry and the repetition of patterns are so important in Marajoara iconography. Binary symmetry is a pervasive feature among the main motifs on almost all the objects. Secondary motifs, which usually occupy large areas or bands around the vessels, tend to be repeated in a continuous sequence. If we imagine that these objects were used in social contexts where people would probably have viewed them from various perspectives, it is clear that you would always be able to see the main character and understand the message that the vessels convey. The repetition of patterns, on the other hand, reinforces the visual message in a different way. Moreover, in the same way that myths are not restricted to simple linear narratives, neither is the iconography linear. It demands that the viewer makes the link between images and elements that are displayed in symmetrical as well as circular arrangements. In essence this is a highly visual, metaphorical structure.

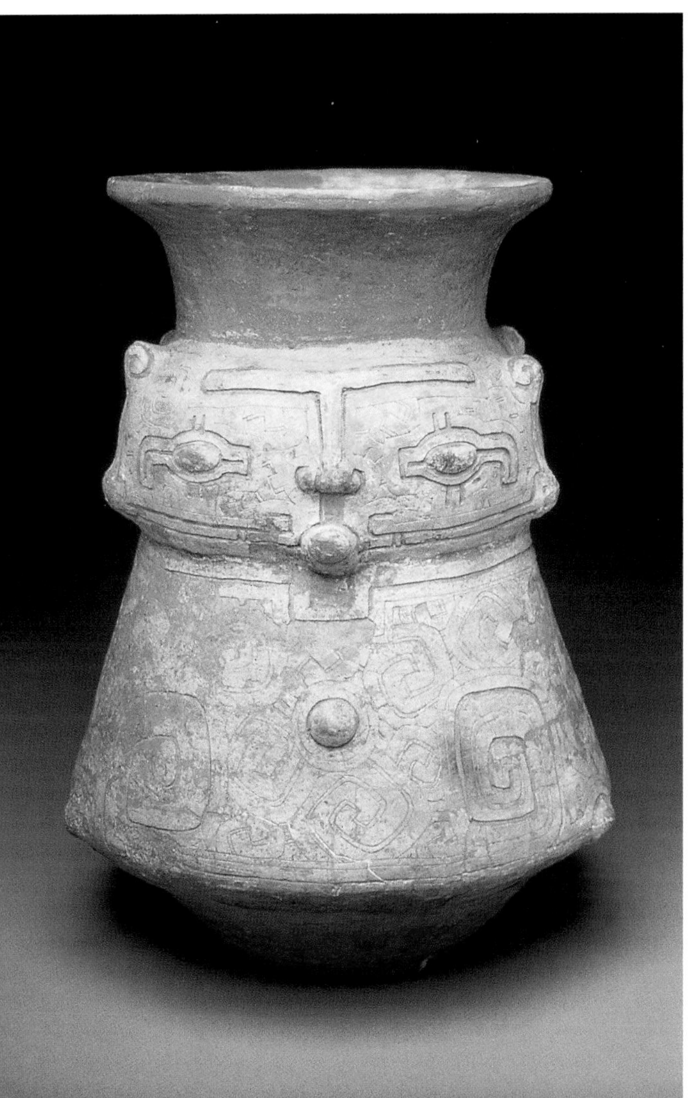

Geometric patterns and meaning

Historically, scholars have referred to a certain category of motifs on Marajoara ceramics as 'abstract' or 'geometric'. These motifs comprise scrolls, spirals, hooks, double lines, steps, circles, etc. A comparison with the use of similar patterns among Amazonian societies today suggests that they might have been used for shamanistic purposes, in curing rites, and in some cases would have represented supernatural animals, mainly their eyes.[36]

Comparisons between the depiction of realistic animals on the ceramics and the geometric patterns have shown that most of these patterns represent parts of an animal's body and can also be related to mythical entities.[37] Most of these motifs are iconic representations of the mythical paired snake, but some are also related to caymans, scorpions and humans. Snakes occupy a prominent place on vessels, often appearing in a repetitive pattern covering their whole body, but also as bands. These patterns are sometimes repetitions of a single element or may appear as two interwoven elements. A careful comparison of the patterns that display a similar structure reveals that they are actually different readings of the same theme.

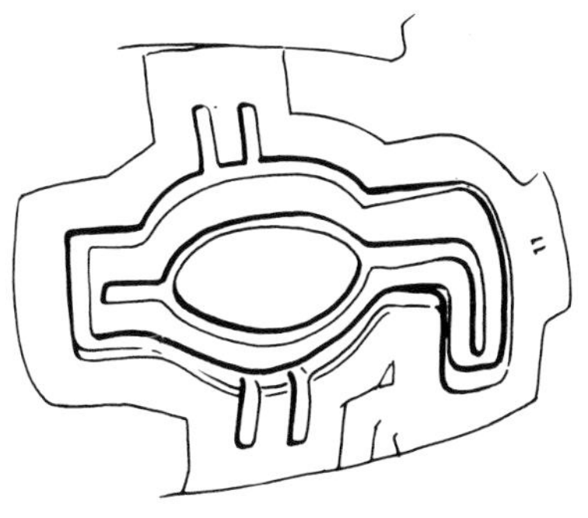

The analysis of another type of funerary urn helps to highlight the relationship between realistic and 'geometric' representations, as well as the different kinds of relations between animals and humans. Female funerary urns decorated with incisions made on white slip are more often found in the mounds located on the eastern side of the island (fig. 4.14).[38] While the painted urns show a paired figure on opposite sides, it is a figure with front and back (figs 4.14 and 4.16). They have oval eyes in relief, framed by a stylized scorpion (fig. 4.15), a small nose, 'V'- or 'T'-shaped eyebrows, and pursed lips. The most common female characteristics are, in general, breasts and

4.16–17 This urn depicts a seated female wearing a *tanga* (height 65 cm, width 33 cm; Ethnologisches Museum, Berlin). It has two small modelled king vulture heads protruding from either shoulder, 'scorpion' eyes and snake-shaped arms (detail below).

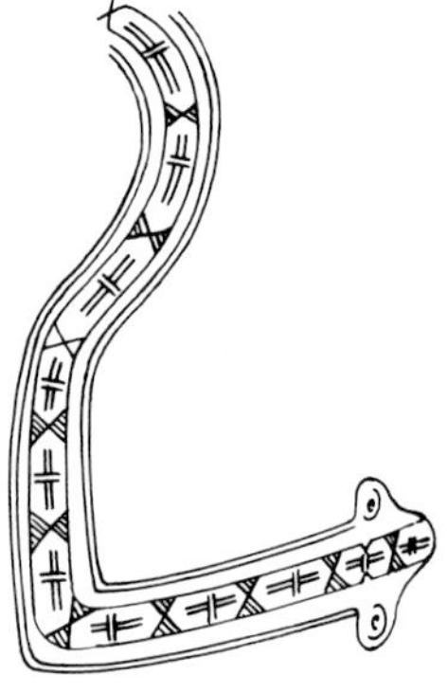

nipples, and a stylized vagina, though these are not all present in every case. A belly button is usually shown retouched in red and recalls the red womb of the painted urn. The bodies of these urns are completely covered with the paired snake motif. Comparisons have been made between these designs and those found in body painting, on the one hand, and with the kinds of images described by shamans in hallucinogenic trance, on the other, where the drugs stimulate the eye retina to see geometric patterns projected onto the objects.[39] Just behind the neck, a 'U'-shaped detail is reminiscent of the horizontal tubular adornment that can be observed as a chest pendant on the painted urns. Parallel lines running from the ears and down the cheeks suggest some kind of ornament or facial painting, and these are also found on certain figurines and human heads on the ceramics. One urn (fig. 4.16) is more anthropomorphic in shape and in its sexual secondary characteristics, which are clearly female. The body is tubular and the head is rounded. She is associated with specific animals: besides the scorpion-shaped eyes, she has snakes as arms (fig. 4.17), and king vultures on her shoulders. It has been suggested that the scorpion might symbolize the sharpening of vision and the magical power of the shaman in his battle against sorcery.[40] It has also been proposed that the figure on this urn might embody shamanic attributes. While performing curing rites in some Amazonian societies, shamans can evoke snakes and scorpions as helpers.[41]

Some of the animals found on these urns are metaphorical (see, for instance, the excised bowl in figs 4.18–19). This bowl is decorated with red slip and a human face modelled on one side, while the whole exterior body is decorated with motifs executed in fine incised lines and excised surfaces. This technique involves removing fine layers of clay from well-defined areas in order to create contrasting patterns of high and low relief. The stylization of scorpions, lizards or caymans, the snakeskin pattern and the paired snakes are highlighted in fig. 4.19. In many cases the animal has a curvilinear tail and is more like a lizard than a cayman.[42] These animal icons merge to form hybrid figures.

The bottom of the vessel has two decorative fields that are apparently symmetrical but close observation reveals that they are not identically symmetrical. Altogether, there are two opposing pairs of lizards, which meet in the centre, blending into a single figure.

4.18–19 Dish with modelled anthropomorphic head flanked by a four-legged creature with a curvilinear 'head' and 'tail' (height 9 cm, diameter 24 cm; Museu Barbier-Mueller Art Precolombí, Barcelona). The roll-out drawing (below) shows the sequence of zoomorphic motifs around the vessel. The base (top right) has two opposed pairs of similar zoomorphs, which merge to form hybrid figures.

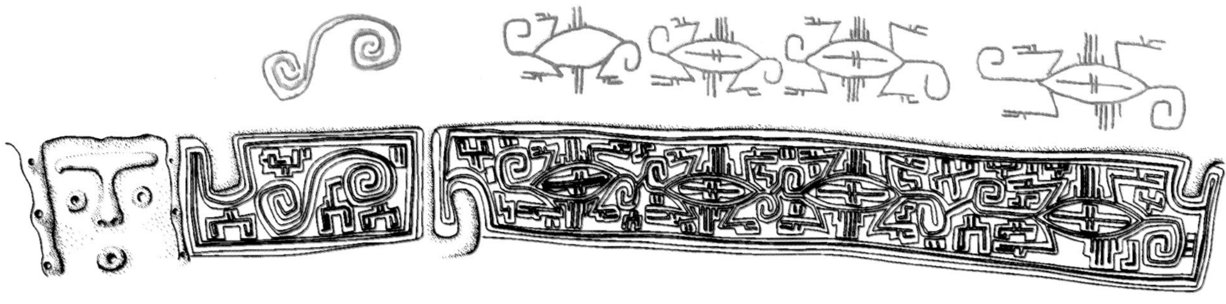

The social meaning of the *tangas*

The triangular pubic covers known as *tangas* comprise the most distinctive kinds of objects in the Marajoara pottery assemblage. Although many contemporary Indians wear *tangas*, they are made of fibre materials, and the only modern correlate in pottery is found among the Panoan tribes of the upper Ucayali river, where they are worn by girls during puberty rites.[43]

Marajoara *tangas* are decorated with either a red or white slip and many are left plain without further decoration. The finest examples, however, are beautifully painted with an array of geometric motifs. Each *tanga* is perforated with small holes at its extremities, which served to suspend it on cotton waist cord. Visible wear marks suggest that they were actually worn before being left as burial offerings. A large number of *tanga* fragments are found on Marajoara sites. There is a wide range of variation in terms of size and shape within a given *tanga* assemblage which implies that *tangas* were specifically made for their owner rather than being a standardized uniform shape.[44]

The design field of painted *tangas* is organized into three superimposed horizontal bands.[45] The motif on the upper band is quite consistent and varies little. The designs are painted in a fine zigzag line traced in black or brown on a white background (fig. 4.20). They may be single or parallel lines combined with solid blocks of colour. For instance, figs 4.20a and d are similar, and 4.20b and c are similar. The intermediate and lower bands reveal considerable variation.[46] The designs had a symbolic significance of a social or religious character, perhaps signalling the social identity and affiliation or membership of the users.

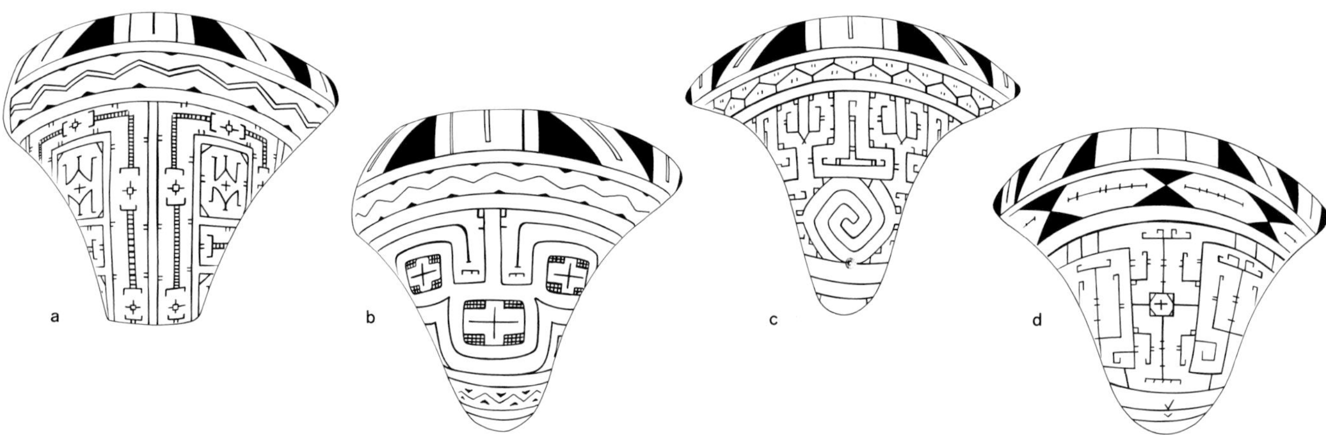

4.20 A range of women's ceramic *tangas* (pubic covers), painted with well-ordered designs. The *tangas* were probably worn during specific communal rituals and ceremonies, and it has been suggested that the designs may have communicated information about the wearer's group affiliation and social status.

The motif on the middle band can, by comparison with similar designs on Marajoara vessels, be identified as the snakeskin pattern. For instance, compare the second band on *tanga* 4.20d with the snakeskin pattern on the arms of the funerary urn (fig. 4.17). While some *tangas* have very similar patterns on this second band, others show more formal variations. Such minor variations may or may not have been significant but I tend to think that they did not affect the fundamental meaning.[47]

Tangas seem to be highly personalized objects and each one is likely to have been the sole property of her owner. They were probably used in rituals in which the designs conveyed visual meanings related to the individual and her position in the society, and perhaps also to the particular rite of passage she was engaged in.

The consistency of the three decorative fields or bands (upper, middle and lower) invites discussion. The almost identical pattern on the upper band is shared by all *tangas*, making all the users in some sense equal. It is possible to suggest that this might express a general group affiliation, not directly tied to an individual. As a female concern, it could conceivably represent a broad social category, such as, for example, young females, married females, widows, etc. The middle band may also be related to a supra-individual level, but differing a little from the first one, because it does not make all the users equal but places them in a specific social category. This category appears to be defined by individuals who are allowed to hold the snake motifs. Subtle differences within this category are defined by the meaningful patterns found in the snake motif assemblage.

While the upper band is characterized by a design found only on *tangas*, and the middle band shows the snake motifs found elsewhere, the lower field exhibits much more variation. The patterns on the lower field could have been individual and family group markers, since they were not restricted only to *tangas* but can be found on a range of other pottery objects.

The red *tangas* found inside Guajará burials underlines their significance in mortuary rites. Although we do not at present have sufficient data to explain the differential occurrence of red and painted *tangas* within and between sites, the red colour was surely also invested with a symbolic meaning related to group membership and social roles.

The construction of the human body in Marajoara iconography

In Amazonian societies an individual's social identity is constructed in the course of the life cycle as she or he matures and passes through different age classes assuming new social roles and responsibilities at each stage. These stages in an individual's life are symbolically and visually signalled by the application of body decoration and the wearing of appropriate ornaments such as ear spools, pendants and necklaces to indicate newly achieved status (see Gomes, this volume). In this sense body and facial painting, the use of ear and lip plugs, scarification, tattooing and the shaving of head hair are physical modifications that accompanied changes in social status, rights and responsibilities.[48] It is possible to find many of these characteristics in the figures also represented on the ceramics. Even if the humans portrayed on the ceramics are supernatural beings, they reflect many elements found in the way Marajoarans conceived themselves.

Many tropical forest societies use the human body as a basis for defining and marking social identity within the framework of a broader cosmological view. Tukano Indians of the upper Negro river, for instance, think of their relationship with the ecosystem as a flow of sexual energy. Their lineages are 'conceptualised in terms of transmission of the physical and spiritual substance, in a dialectic of the exogamy and of the blood (feminine), of the lineage continuity, and of the semen (patrilinear); both sexes contribute with spiritual and physical aspects in the construction of the self'.[49]

The human body is portrayed on a range of Marajoara ceramic objects. In common with agrarian societies around the world anthropomorphic figurines feature prominently. The majority of extant Marajoara figurines are female. Many are phallic in shape and seem to have functioned as rattles with pebbles inside. Some

LEFT 4.21 Many Marajoara figurines have phallic shapes and appear to have had their heads intentionally broken off (height 15.5 cm, width 9.3 cm; Museu de Arqueologia e Etnologia da Universidade de São Paulo, Brazil).

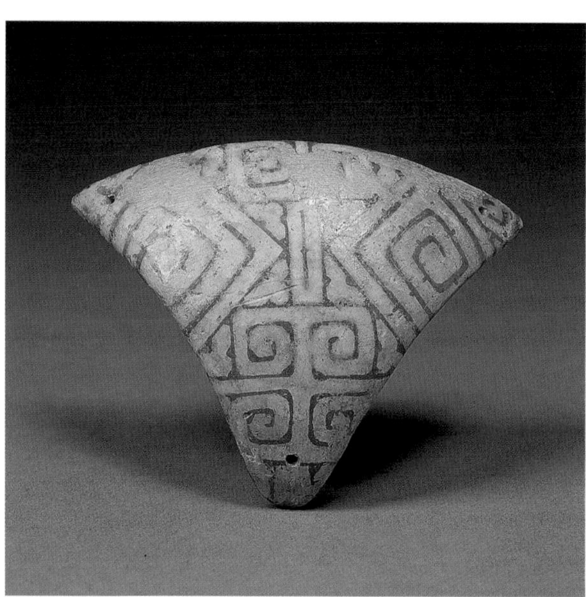

BELOW LEFT 4.22 There are clear similarities between the motifs found on *tangas* and those on other objects such as figurines. Ceramic *tangas* were also left as offerings in burials (height 8.2 cm, width 11 cm; Museu de Arqueologia e Etnologia da Universidade de São Paulo, Brazil).

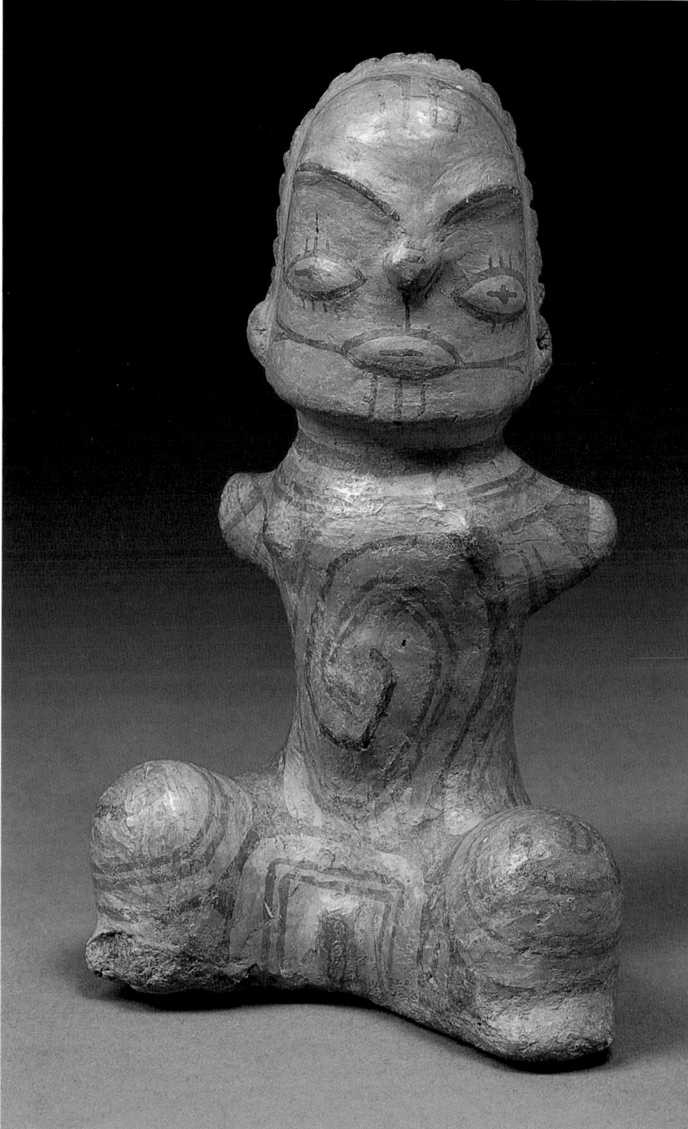

ABOVE 4.23 Female figurines come in a variety of shapes, sizes and decorations that may signal differing social roles and identities (height 22 cm, width 12.5 cm; Museu Paraense Emílio Goeldi, Belém, Brazil).

have holes for hanging. Figurines are often found in funerary contexts as offerings. Most consist of a human head and a stylized body and there is considerable variability in terms of decoration (plain, white or red-slipped, painted, incised, excised), shape and size. Sometimes the shape of the head indicates that skull deformation was practised, and evidence to support this is found in human remains in Marajó.[50]

The arms of the figurine are either absent or truncated. Sexual features, when depicted, are always female: breasts, nipples and pubis. The decoration on the body displays more variability than on the urns, and is suggestive of body painting. Occasionally there are very good examples of a close correlation between the designs on a figurine and those of other ceramic objects including *tangas* (see, for instance, the figurine in fig. 4.21 and the *tanga* in fig. 4.22). In general, the designs emphasize a central point on the belly (figs 4.21 and 4.23). The range of motifs varies, but a common one is that of paired snakes. The lower limbs are, like the arms, often abbreviated and may mean that the figure is in a sitting or kneeling position.

One figurine (fig. 4.23) has a pattern of facial painting that may accurately replicate the designs used in face-painting ceremonies. The scorpion-shaped eyes, just as in the urns, may have been an attribute reserved for use by a particular segment of society. The long forehead suggests hair shaving, and on the top of the head carefully arranged hair is shown. The lines around the mouth, and on the cheeks and chin also correspond to the kind of facial painting found in many other human representations in Marajoara ceramics. All these characteristics suggest that the figurines express ideas about the construction of social identity as part of the process of integrating each individual into the social body as whole.

The fact that many figurines have a phallic shape and also display female sexual characteristics should not be read too literally. Among the Desana Indians of the north-west Amazon, for instance, although phallic objects were used in important ceremonies, some are defined as men and others as women.[51] Observing that female characteristics are displayed on phallic objects is just as intriguing as the fact that male skeletons were associated with *tangas*. Future excavations of burials and study of skeletons will no doubt provide more information on the relation of iconography and biological sexes.

A great number of figurines seem to have been intentionally broken at the neck, a pattern that suggests that they could have been discarded after ritual use. Possible insights into the kinds of contexts in which they were used may be found in descriptions of curing rites carried out by Cuna and Chocó shamans in Colombia. Among these groups, figurines were used as spirit helpers in curing rites, and were either handled by the shaman, standing next to the patient, or were hung around him or her.[52]

The paired order of things

Marajoara iconography is based on ordered pairs of representations using principles of symmetry, opposition and alternation. Moreover, double heads and double bodies abound. Symmetry is a formal concept used to describe a specific arrangement of elements on an object and, since much of Marajoara art is governed by these principles, they surely express fundamental ways in which Amazonian societies perceived and ordered their observations and experiences of the world about them. However, from a formal point of view careful examination of the apparent symmetrical opposition in Marajoara iconography shows that very often the rules are not applied uniformly to the whole decorative field. They may be applied selectively to different design elements, sometimes in unexpected and surprising combinations. This is the case, for instance, with the urn illustrated in figs 4.2 and 4.24. The base is solid red and above it a continuous, spiral-like motif encircles the main body of the vessel evoking the spiralling eddies of flowing water (figs 24a–d). Two painted effigy faces stand in complementary opposition on either side of the neck. Both these, as well as the abstract elements on the underside of the rim, show alternating patterns in the application of red and black pigment (note the treatment of the eyelids for example). The inner rim on the other hand, reveals an even more complex pattern. A straightforward binary symmetry is apparent in the principal two opposing abstract motifs. These are flanked by a tripartite arrangement also composed of opposing nested eliptical motifs, each one of which however differs from all the others (fig. 4.24e).

To discuss the paired order of things in Marajoara visual and material culture, I will now refer to another important category of artefacts: plates. Here I argue that they do not so much represent an abstract theoretical opposition but a set of relation-

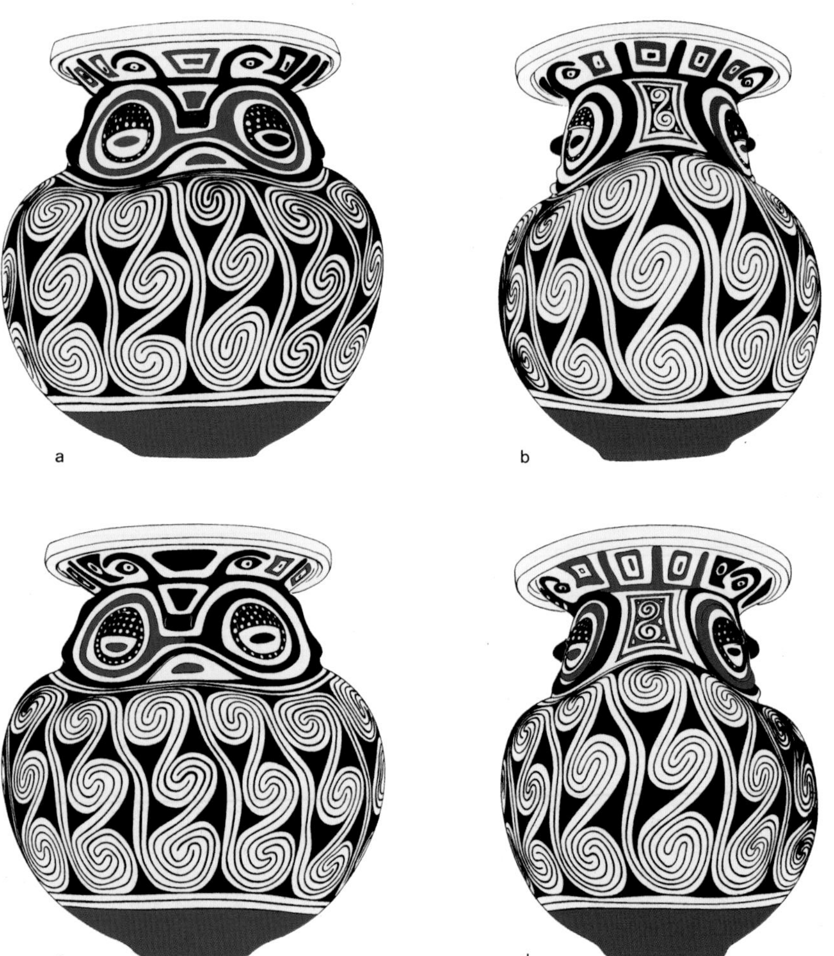

ships that emerges from observing the actual nature of things.[53] One shallow plate with hollow rims (sometimes containing pellets that rattle) has two modelled appendages in the form of heads placed on opposite sides (fig. 4.25). The rim is decorated with deep incised lines over a white slip that covers the whole piece. The bottom surface and the rim interior are decorated with red painted lines forming an intricate design. The two heads have human characteristics with lines of facial painting common to other human representations on Marajoara ceramics. Animal-like features are also present that can be compared to a turtle (fig. 4.26b). The two incisions with painted lines between the back of the heads may suggest a special adornment or

ABOVE **4.24 Front, back and lateral views of a funerary urn, and the design on its inner rim (Museu Barbier-Mueller Art Precolombí, Barcelona). The sequence of curvilinear, spiral motifs running round the body of the vessel recall the eddies and swirls of flowing water. The anthropomorphic face on the neck is similar to images on other large polychrome urns (cf. fig. 4.12).**

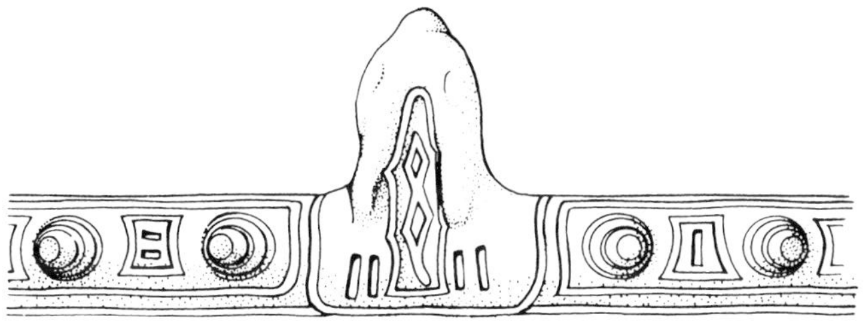

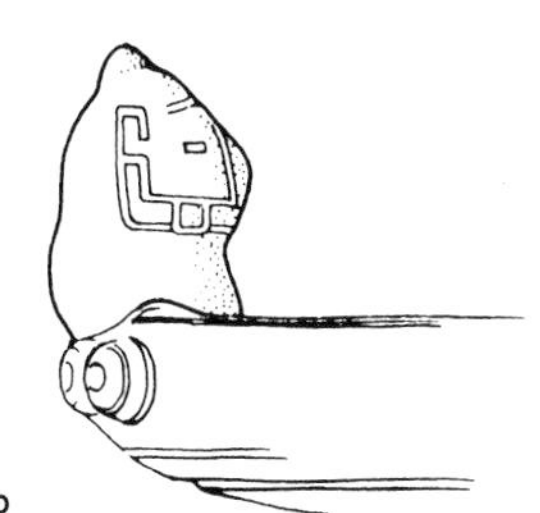

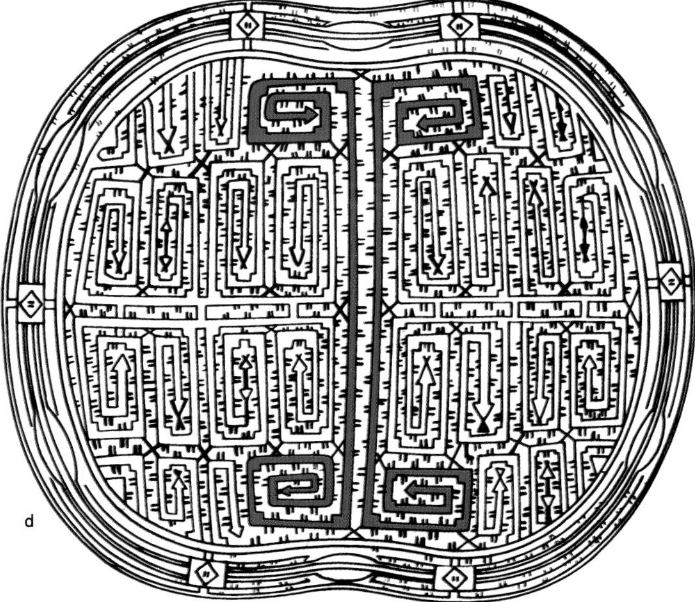

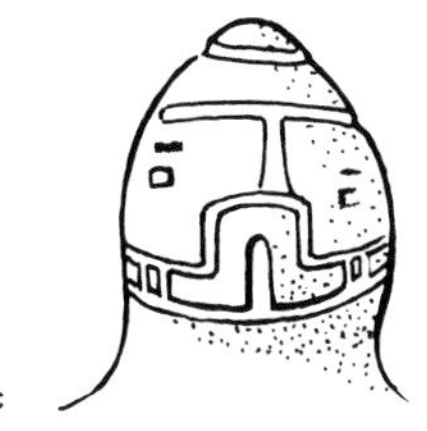

4.25–6 Some of the masterpieces of Marajoara ceramics include shallow bowls like this with recursive, labyrinthine designs painted on their interior surfaces – shown in drawing fig. 4.26d with the central motif emphasized (height 9 cm, width 27 cm; Museu Barbier-Mueller Art Precolombí, Barcelona). The pair of modelled turtle heads on the rim – figs 4.26a–c show the back, side and front of one of them – invest this vessel with animate qualities and suggest that its overall shape may imitate a turtle carapace.

ABOVE **4.27** Two pairs of opposed zoomorphic motifs (possibly reptilians or insects) form the central elements painted on the interior surface of this vessel. Originally there were a pair of modelled heads on the rim (height 8 cm, width 43 cm; Museu Paraense Emílio Goeldi, Belém, Brazil).

LEFT **4.28** The carefully structured design on this plate reflects the fundamental sense of cultural order underlying Marajoara cosmology. These finely decorated plates are often found in association with funerary urns, and food was probably placed on them as offerings to the spirits.

RIGHT **4.29** The ordered symmetry of the design field on this small dish incorporates curvilinear motifs found on other media as well as modelled zoomorphic heads. The heads can be seen either as a turtle or as a snake depending on the viewer's perspective.

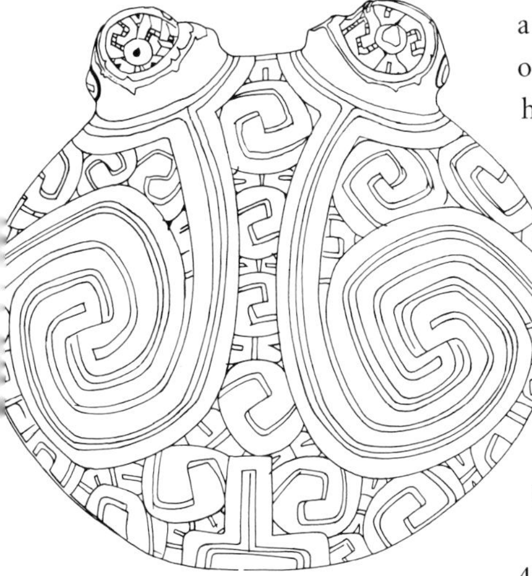

a distinctive hairstyle. The internal motifs form a recursive labyrinthic design. Previously, I have suggested that similar motifs represent mythical snakes with triangular heads.[54] The associations that can be made with these recursive patterns are endless. The two central elements that have been highlighted in fig. 4.26d (compare with figs 4.21 and 4.22) can be separated from the others (notice they are not completely symmetrical) but can also be associated with combinations of any two, three or four elements, thus composing a real labyrinth.

The plates in figs 4.27 and 4.28 have similar characteristics to the one just described. They are shallow and have hollow rims with opposing elements. In fig. 4.27 the creature is similar to the one found on the plate illustrated in fig. 4.25, except for the position of the hands over the mouth. It has been suggested that this could be an analogy for funerary endo-cannibalism.[55]

In the interior of the plate the main figures recall the cayman (compare with fig. 4.19), some patterns are similar to those on the plate in fig. 4.26d, and pairs of small squares between 'V'-shaped lines may indicate small human faces. The plate in fig. 4.28 has two abbreviated heads (compare with the turtle in figs 4.27 and 4.29), and the element below the heads can be compared with that on the neck of funerary urns. It may represent an adornment, but it is also very similar to the central pattern on the upper bands of the *tangas*. From this element issue two long opposed snake arms. If my reading of the two opposite figures is plausible (represented by the abbreviated heads, neck adornment and arms), the central figure is a metaphor for the pregnant belly (compare with the figure on the urn in figs 4.13a and d). From the neck a straight hachured line leads into spirals on the opposite side of the plate. This termination of the snake's tail is frequent, and might mark a special characteristic of the animal (compare with fig. 4.8).

These analyses show that a basic set of quite simple elements is used to systematically build up very complex designs. The intimate symbiotic nature of the relationship between humans and animals, elsewhere shown in myths, shows that there is no clear-cut distinction between nature and culture. Differences between humans and animals are not of an ontological nature, but one of perspective.[56] In this way of viewing the world animals are as social as humans are, humans and animals being relatives, with humans turning into animals while they dream. Sometimes humans and animals can be powerful enemies that respect each other, with humans being both hunters as well as hunted.

To explain this cosmology from a Western perspective and using Western intellectual concepts presents as much of a challenge as trying to ascribe meaning to the motifs and elements observed in the designs. The material order of Amazonian iconography is as complex as their cosmological world. The references I have made to representations of animals on the ceramics are an attempt to demonstrate the role of animals in the Marajoara beliefs and symbolism. Far from being literal naturalistic representations, they are appropriated and incorporated into human culture.

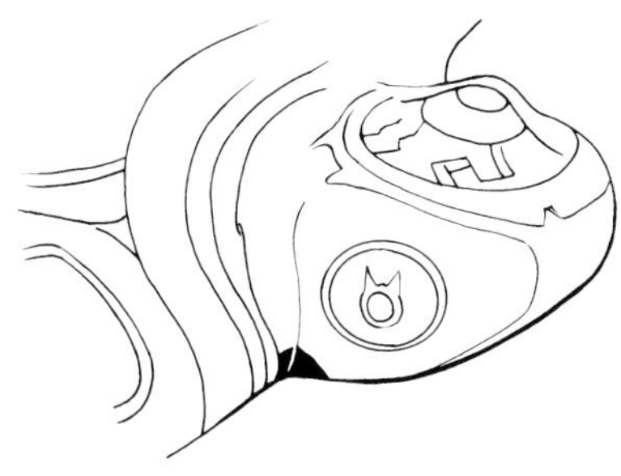

I suggest that to speak of the paired order of things may mean that any given element in the cosmos has its double, which is not necessarily its opposite. The pairs are not merely opposed, but can also be conceived as being complementary. They are part of the same order of things but offer different perspectives on dimensions of the same reality. The hunting of wild pigs by the Juruna is an example of this kind of indigenous perspective.[57] The Juruna say pigs consider themselves as humans, and see hunting as a war where humans (the pigs) are attacked by their enemies (the men). This dual perspective may explain the fact that indigenous Amazonian peoples accept enslavement and cannibalism as natural. For instance, among the Tupinambá war captives are incorporated into the social body of their captors as slaves or even members of families, where they lived in complete harmony until being eaten. Why didn't they escape? We can surmise that perhaps it was because they respected this dual perspective, within which an understanding of the other is an indispensable way of seeing the world – a way that is profoundly different from Western intellectual constructs.

The demise of Marajoara culture

The Marajoara phase is now known as the earliest phase of the Amazonian Polychrome tradition, a pottery style characterized by highly elaborate ceremonial ceramics used in secondary burials. While stylistic characteristics common to the cultures of the Amazonian Polychrome tradition suggest intensive cultural contact, there is no good reason to believe that these peoples were any more closely related than other nearby populations. Cultures are dynamic and change through time. We might ask what kind of contact there may have been between the societies that produced Marajoara, Santarém and Maracá pottery. Many of the similarities that we can identify in their material culture may be a consequence of the flow of ideas that followed the exchange of goods through far-reaching trade networks that linked Amazonian societies shortly before the conquest.

Iconographic studies have much to contribute to our understanding of ancient cultures, but the study and interpretation of Amazonian symbolic systems has scarcely begun. Some promising avenues of research include the study of myths recorded during the contact period, which may, as I have tried to show here, offer insights into Marajoara iconography. The ways in which the body is portrayed on ceramic artefacts can also be used to illustrate aspects of the construction of social identity through body ornament. Shaved heads, ear plugs, lip plugs, hair style and body painting are all potential markers of individual and collective social identity. I have argued that iconographic differences within categories of objects can help us to understand how visual elements may have served to define the relationship between social groups in a given community.

It is now thought that Marajoara society collapsed around AD 1350, when some of the settlements seem to have been abandoned. This does not seem to have resulted in the disappearance of the population, but rather to have been a historical process of change involving the dispersal of the previous strongly hierarchical settlement system, a process not yet fully understood. More recent burials consist of cremations, which also attest to a change in cultural patterns.[58] Although the late period is not well studied, it seems that by the proto-historic period the population was as dispersed as in the long period preceding the Marajoara phase. Marajoara ceramics were, however, still being produced by the time the Portuguese established the first settlement on Marajó Island. Even without the co-ordination and centralization of the ceremonial centres, Marajoara people were still performing some of their rituals and ceremonies until the latter half of the seventeenth century.

Acknowledgements

I wish to thank the editors and Marcia Arcuri for their assistance. I am greatly indebted to Colin McEwan, whose help and stimulating comments were critical in shaping the final version of this text. His passionate dedication to the *Unknown Amazon* project is certainly deeply printed on this book. My special thanks to Norma Russo for her great hospitality in London. I am also grateful to the CNPq (National Research Council/Brazil), Museu Paraense Emílio Goeldi, and the Heinz Foundation for supporting my research and study at the University of Pittsburgh.

NOTES

1 Such adaptations may date back as far as 7,000 BP, following the dates of the Taperinha shell mound, located near the city of Santarém in the lower Amazon (Roosevelt *et al.* 1991).
2 See Simões 1981a for a brief presentation of the shell mounds of the Atlantic shore east of the mouth of the Amazon.
3 The archaeological phases that preceded the Marajoara Phase were called by Meggers and Evans (1957) Ananatuba, Mangueiras and Formiga Phases. The authors (ibid: 223) propose that some Formiga Phase sites were once higher due to artificial construction.
4 Roosevelt 1991 has referred to Marajoara society as a chiefdom.
5 The so-called standard model (Viveiros de Castro 1996).
6 Brochado 1980a.
7 Roosevelt 1991.
8 Viveiros de Castro 1996.
9 Ibid.
10 Although this pattern has been reported repeatedly, there is also some variation, such as the burial of the ashes of cremated bodies. These are found more frequently in the later pre-contact period and usually in smaller urns. This leads us to believe that some important cultural changes were taking place towards the end of the cultural sequence (Farabee 1921, Palmatary 1950).
11 The description of burial patterns in this section was possible thanks to information obtained from various sources (Farabee 1921, Palmatary 1950, Meggers and Evans 1957), including interviews with looters and my own excavations in Marajoara sites.
12 This was a practice common in the pre-Columbian Andes and Mesoamerica (Townsend 1998) as well as in the central Amazon area upstream from Marajó (Neves 2000).
13 Palmatary (1950), and Meggers and Evans (1957) present a comprehensive description of decoration techniques.
14 Roosevelt 1991.
15 See Porro (1987) about trade routes along the Amazon basin, and Boomert (1987) about the green-pendant exchange networks between the Amazon basin and Caribbean islands.
16 Brochado 1980b, Bertrand-Rosseau 1983, Illius 1988, Van Velthem 1992a.
17 Lévi-Strauss 1978, Ribeiro 1987, Vidal 1992, Vidal e Silva 1995.
18 Many authors have contributed to the identification of animal species on Marajoara ceramics, as Netto 1885, Meggers 1947, Palmatary 1950, Roosevelt 1991, Schaan 1997.
19 This section presents an understanding of the relationship between culture and nature as these two categories meet in the production of material culture. However, Viveiros de Castro (1998), in a very timely paper, argues that Amazonian Indians do not conceive of culture and nature as different categories, which helps to explain the blend of human and animal characteristics in the iconography.
20 Observations about the relation between the depiction on the ceramics and the real snakes in Marajoara fauna appear in Roosevelt (1991: 87) and Schaan (1997: 154).
21 Acuña 1946.
22 Lévi-Strauss 1962.
23 See, for instance, Hartt (1885) for an early ethnographic collection of tortoise myths.
24 According to Meggers and Evans (1957) terminology, the use of this technique defines the Pacoval Incised type. Although Pacoval Incised ceramics are more abundant in the mounds located east of the Lake Arari, they do also occur elsewhere.
25 Guajará, Monte Carmelo and Bacatal together form the Monte Carmelo site, located near the Anajás river headwaters. Later to become major figures in Amazonian archaeology, Meggers and Evans were at that time graduate students at Columbia University, New York.
26 See Meggers and Evans (1957: 259–79) for a detailed presentation of the excavation data, including drawings and profiles.
27 Meggers and Evans 1957: 273.
28 Roosevelt 1991: 80.
29 Schaan 1997: 140.
30 For instance in Roosevelt 1991: 60.
31 Wassen 1934a.
32 Roosevelt 1991: 81.
33 Schaan 1997: 142–4.
34 See, for instance, Becher 1959.
35 For an overview of the material culture of different Amazonian societies and its relation to the mythical world see Vidal 1992.
36 Roosevelt 1991: 79.
37 Schaan 1997.
38 General differences between ceramics dug up from the Camutins site (centre-west) and Pacoval site (east) were recognized early on (Hartt 1871, Ferreira Penna 1877a, Steere 1927).
39 Illius 1988.
40 Roosevelt 1991: 82.
41 Roosevelt 1991: 88.
42 S. Carvalho 1975.
43 Meggers and Evans 1957: 416.
44 Meggers and Evans 1957: 382–4.
45 I have carried out a study of thirty-eight specimens of red-on-white *tangas*, which shows that the three decorative fields appear on 63 per cent of the specimens. In the remaining 37 per cent only one or two decorative fields occur. The upper decorative field, however, was present in 77 per cent of the specimens, showing that this pattern was most common.
46 Mordini 1929, 1934b; Meggers and Evans 1957.
47 This statement can be proved either by comparison with differences of speech among individuals who speak the same language and can understand each other (so called free variation in structural linguistics) or through studies of aesthetic anthropology. See Müller 1990.
48 Turner 1980, Viveiros de Castro 1987, Heckenberger 1999.
49 Seeger *et al.* 1987: 22.
50 In common with other Amerindian societies, Netto (1885) first recognized skull deformation on a ceramic head. Roosevelt (1991: 390 and 393) reports that a study of a sample of skeletons from Marajó reveals skull deformation on some adult males and she compares this pattern with the practice among the Omágua of the upper and central Amazon and the Shipibo of the upper Ucayali. According to historic sources, the child's head was intentionally deformed soon after birth, through the placement of the head between two flat wooden plates. The result was an upward elongated forehead that would be a permanent physical mark of high status. The excavation in Guajará, discussed earlier in this essay, also revealed one deformed skull.
51 Reichel-Dolmatoff, cited in Alland 1988: 30.
52 Reichel-Dolmatoff 1961.
53 For the structural anthropologists Lévi-Strauss (1975) and Leach (1976) categories are defined in people's minds in terms of sets of binary oppositions: white is not black, tall is not short, man is not woman, etc.
54 Schaan 1996, 1997.
55 Roosevelt 1991: 81. Endo-cannibalism means the consumption of the flesh of individuals from one's own group or community.
56 Humans and animals share the same nature, and maybe this explains part of the logic of cannibalism in Amazonian societies that shocked Europeans so much during the contact period. For Amazonian groups, eating human flesh is not much different to eating any other animal flesh. See Viveiros de Castro 1996, Lima 1996, Descola 1998.
57 Lima 1996.
58 Farabee 1921, Meggers and Evans 1957.

5

Santarém

Symbolism and Power in the Tropical Forest

DENISE GOMES

Introduction

Santarém pottery, with its rich repertoire of anthropomorphic figurines (fig. 5.2) and elaborate vessels bearing a bewildering menagerie of mammals, reptiles and birds (fig. 5.13), is at first sight quite unlike any other known style from the Amazon. This poses a number of intriguing questions: when was this pottery made? Was it influenced by more complex cultures from outside the Amazon? What kind of society produced it? What is the significance of the unusual shapes and exuberant imagery on certain kinds of vessels? Why were they created, what did they mean and how might they have been used?

Santarém ceramics are named after the homonymous river port located at the junction of the Tapajós and Amazon rivers (see fig. 5.3). A southern tributary of the Amazon, the Tapajós is a clear-water river fed by headwaters that drain the central Brazilian plateau. As with many other rivers in the Amazon basin, a very wide lake formed at the mouth of the Tapajós due to the rise in sea level from the beginning of the Holocene around 10,000 years ago (fig. 5.1). It is around this wide body of water that most of the archaeological sites with Santarém ceramics have been identified.

Early information on the Tapajó[1] Indians that inhabited the Santarém area until the eighteenth century can be gathered from historical sources dating back to the sixteenth century. Indeed, the earliest historical reference to them can be found in Friar Carvajal's chronicle of the Orellana expedition in 1542,[2] the first to traverse the full length of the Amazon river from the Andean cordillera to the Atlantic Ocean in the east (see also Barreto, this volume). The location of the expedition's encounter with the Tapajó can be deduced from the geographical description of the area. Carvajal wrote that Orellana's group remained for one and a half days 'at the mouth of a river [the Tapajós] that flowed in from the right of the one we were sailing [the Amazon], and it was one-league

ABOVE **5.1 Aerial view, Lago Grande de Vila Franca (Santarém, Brazil). Archaeological sites that seem to be the precursors of Santarém culture are located in this area.**

RIGHT **5.2 Seated male figure wearing prominent earspools and a headband (height 32 cm, width 24 cm, depth 22 cm; Museu de Arqueologia e Etnologia da Universidade de São Paulo, Brazil). He is sitting on a low stool, a valued possession of male elders and shamans.**

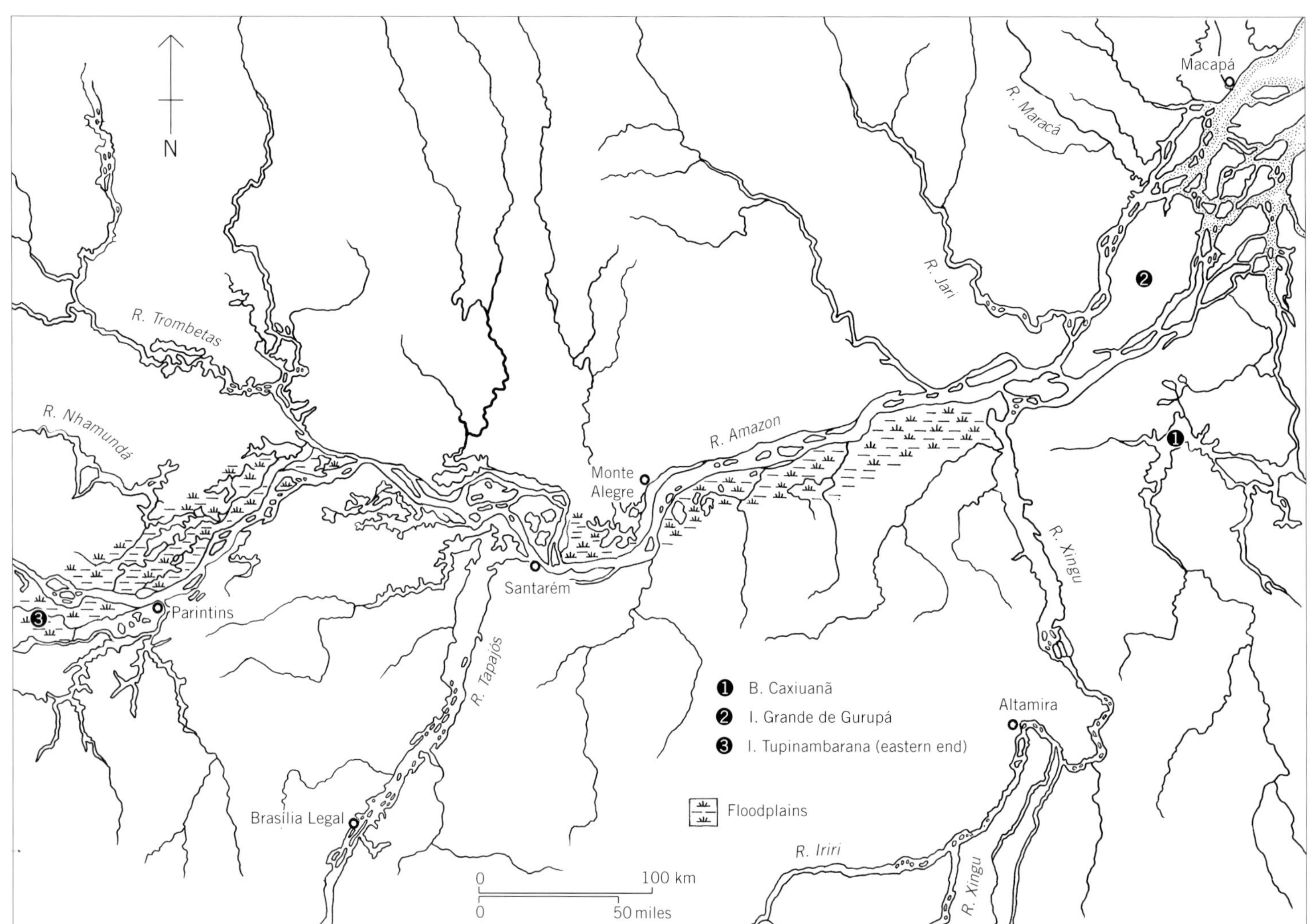

5.3 Map of the distribution of Santarém style according to the archaeological surveys of Curt Nimuendajú, 1949.

wide'.[3] There, although they made no direct face-to-face contact with the Indians, they apparently saw a great number of canoes.

This episode marked the first-known contact between Europeans and the Tapajó and was followed by other exploratory and slaving expeditions[4] before the Portuguese settled in Santarém in the seventeenth century and founded their first religious mission.[5] The missionaries' reports give us an intriguing glimpse of Tapajó social organization, rituals and funerary practices.[6] A careful reading of the historical documents also helps to open up insights into the iconography of Santarém pottery, which is otherwise not directly accessible.

A little more than a century later, in 1637, Pedro Teixeira organized an expedition departing from Pará at the mouth of the Amazon westward to Quito. Alonso de Rojas,[7] the chronicler of the expedition, described the Tapajó as a warm and friendly people who could also become fearsome warriors and cannibals that relished eating their captives. One of the reasons they made war, so it was said, was to seize land from other groups. On his return from Quito to Pará, in 1639, Pedro Teixeira was accompanied by Father Cristobal de Acuña, who reported in his chronicle of the journey that the expedition traded with the Tapajó, obtaining plenty of food: 'ducks, chicken, nets, fish, flour, fruit'.[8] Acuña also points to the warlike demeanour of the Tapajó. He could not hide his surprise at witnessing the submission and lack of resistance of the Tapajó upon being enslaved by the Portuguese. The context of this episode indicates the onset of a process that eventually led to the dissolution of the Tapajó as a distinctive ethnic group by the end of the eighteenth century.

A brief overview of archaeological research

Scientific archaeological research in the area began in the early 1870s with the testing – by the Canadian geologist Charles F. Hartt[9] – of a shell mound at the site of Taperinha located 40 km east of the mouth of the Tapajós.[10] Among the archaeological pottery recovered there were sherds with vestiges of red slip, others unpainted but bearing geometrical incisions, vessel rims with zoomorphic appendages, and basal fragments with palm-leaf imprints, all typical of the Santarém style. Around the same time Brazilian naturalist João Barbosa Rodrigues[11] identified sherds with this style along the banks of the Tapajós river as much as 370 km upstream from its mouth.[12]

In the 1920s the German-Brazilian anthropologist Curt Nimuendajú carried out extensive archaeological surveys in the lower Amazon for the Göteborg Museum of Sweden, identifying a total of sixty-five sites in the Santarém area.[13] Nimuendajú's research extended the known distribution of Santarém pottery westward to Tupinambarana Island and eastward to Grande de Gurupá Island and Caxiuanã bay (fig. 5.3).[14] Although his archaeological reports remain poorly published (with the exception of a posthumous article[15]), they provided grounds for other anthropologists to acknowledge Santarém pottery as evidence of 'an extremely developed indigenous civilisation'.[16] Nimuendajú was not only familiar with the historical data. His fieldwork demonstrated unequivocally that this newly discovered pottery style is found distributed across a considerable area. He noted the existence of a potential site hierarchy around Santarém, the presence of connecting trail networks and the building of wells in areas far distant from the large rivers. Taken together, this new information presented a picture of populous riverine societies that confounded notions of a simplified 'Tropical Forest Pattern' of adaptation usually thought to be more typical of indigenous Amazonian cultural development.

Nimuendajú's research provided the data for one of the first attempts at a thoughtful synthesis of Amazonian archaeology: Erland Nordenskiöld's beautifully illustrated *L'Archaeologie du Bassin de l'Amazone* (1930). In this book he called attention to the stylistic similarities between Santarém ceramics and pottery from the Antilles and Central America, and explained these as deriving from the shared ethnic origin of far-flung Arawak-speaking groups.[17]

After Nimuendajú's research there began in the late 1930s a phase of museum collections studies initiated by Helen Palmatary who worked on several collections first in North American museums, then in Brazilian institutions. Palmatary developed a classification of Santarém ceramics based on vessel size, basal shape and decoration.[18] Following ideas about the spread of culture traits by diffusion which were fashionable at the time, Palmatary surmised that there might be direct connections between the ceramics from Santarém and those of Central America and even as far afield as the Mississippi valley. Although these ideas seem wrong today, Palmatary's and Nordenskiöld's work at around the same time helped to bring Santarém pottery to the attention of a much wider public and helped to place the Tapajó in a historical context, as well as setting parameters for further research.[19]

A similar 'diffusionist' perspective is reflected in Corrêa's 1965 catalogue of Santarém figurines from the Museu Emílio Goeldi.[20] This catalogue follows a model of four major horizon styles for the Amazon advanced by the North American archaeologists Betty Meggers and Clifford Evans of the Smithsonian Institution in the early 1960s.[21] Meggers and Evans also championed the idea that the Amazon had always played a marginal role in the cultural development of continental South America.[22] In the case of Santarém pottery, Correa placed particular emphasis on the idea of cultural contacts and migrations originating in Venezuela and reaching the Tapajós via the many tributaries feeding from the north into the mainstream Amazon.[23]

A contrasting approach to collection studies can be found in the work of Frederico Barata,[24] whose stylistic analyses focused exclusively on the artistic elements without establishing a comparative or historical framework.[25] Barata was the first investigator to make a revealing observation about the dual perspective of modelled zoomorphic elements on the so-called 'caryatid vessels' which are discussed below.[26]

Some decades later Macdonald (1972) made an initial attempt at interpreting the meaning of Santarém iconography. Macdonald examined historical textual descriptions and accounts of indigenous social organization and religion to explore how Santarém iconography might reflect some of the fundamental ways in which the Tapajó ordered their universe.[27] Based on these ethnohistorical accounts, she assigned a mythological significance to both animal and human elements depicted in the pottery.

More recent collection-based studies include Guapindaia's technological assessment of Santarém ceramics concentrating on use-patterns in raw materials, tools and manufacturing techniques,[28] and my own catalogue of the Santarém collection of the Museu de Arqueologia e Etnologia of the Universidade de São Paulo.[29] Thermoluminescence assays of sherd samples from this collection provide some of the few dates for Santarém ceramics currently available and more securely place their date of production from at least AD 900 to 1200.[30]

In the 1980s Anna Roosevelt initiated an ambitious long-term research programme in the Santarém area.[31] This work has provided important data on the beginnings of ceramic production in the Amazon, with implications for the whole American continent (see Oliver, this volume).[32] Roosevelt and her colleagues have not yet published the full results of their work on the Santarém sites. Nevertheless, in her overview of cultural developments Roosevelt characterizes Santarém as the centre of a great chiefdom in the heart of the Amazon, whose apogee lasted from the tenth to the sixteenth century AD. This model envisages several chiefs unifying and controlling an area of some 23,000 sq. km, with densely populated settlements comprising a total population of many thousands of people. It is inferred that chiefs were ranked according to their power and influence, and that they would have collected tribute and deployed the labour pool at their disposal to co-ordinate tasks such as building dwellings and developing transport and defence. Early historical accounts report religious practices focused on the worship of images and mummies of chiefs and ancestors, which probably served to strengthen and affirm the status of chiefs, priests and heads of lineages. The exchange of ideas and trade goods along networks linking these riverine chiefdoms may help to account for the stylistic similarities found between Santarém pottery and other types from distant areas of northern South America.[33]

This brief review underlines the fact that an overview of Santarém archaeology must at present draw as much upon studies of museum collections as information gathered from fieldwork. Nevertheless, even working with the relatively small body of intact Santarém figurines and vessels can – when informed by archaeological, historical and ethnographic information – provide valuable insights into the social, religious and political life of a cultural florescence that was rapidly eclipsed by the impact of European newcomers.

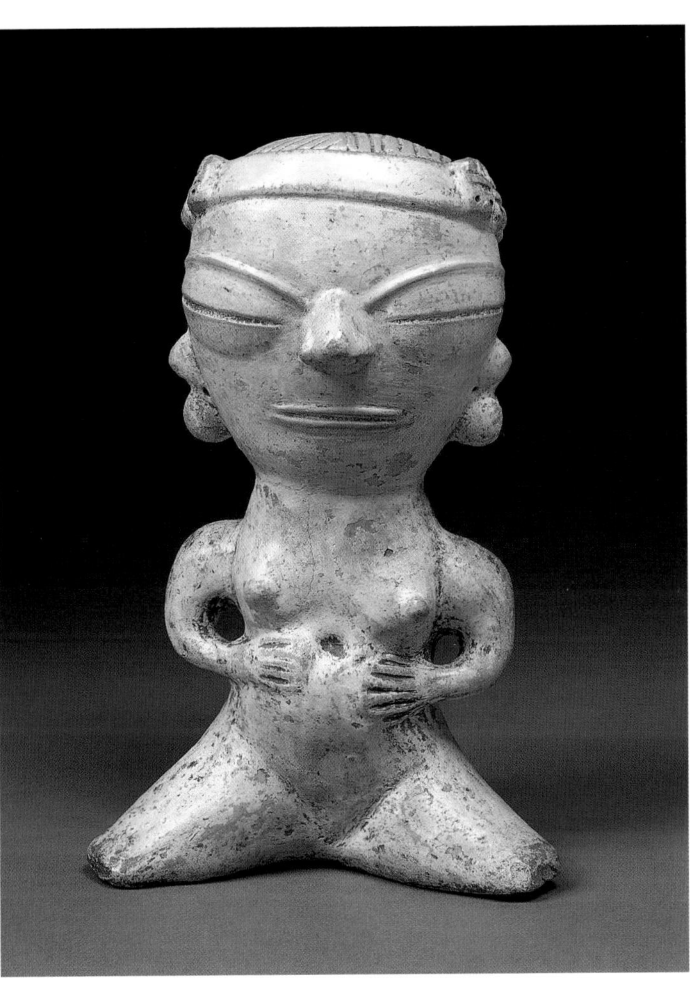

5.4 Figurine of a pregnant woman with her hands clasped to her abdomen. These kinds of figurines may have been linked to domestic fertility cults (height 26.5 cm, width 17.5 cm, depth 11 cm; Museu de Arqueologia e Etnologia da Universidade de São Paulo, Brazil).

Nature and culture in Santarém pottery

The Santarém pottery inventory comprises several distinct kinds of artefacts which can occasionally be surprising. One significant group consists of naturalistic anthropomorphic objects. Within this group there are a range of smaller figurines, usually female (figs 5.4–5 and 5.7), and larger figurines, as well as hollow vessels in the form of seated males (fig. 5.2), probably used for storing beverages or possibly also as funerary urns (figs 5.11–12).[34] The smaller figurines tend to be more stylized than the larger male anthropomorphic vessels. While the female figurines are quite common in museum collections, the male anthropomorphic figures are rarer.[35] Another group of objects includes caryatid vessels (figs 5.13–14), necked vessels (figs 5.20–21), globular vessels (fig. 5.25), plates and bowls, and other rarer items, all of which share in common the application of modelled zoomorphic appliqué figures and the presence of a ring base. While the study of figurines in the former group opens windows into understanding the role of gender and status in Tapajó social organization, it is the complex compositions among the latter group that offers some of the most fascinating insights into the cultural appropriation of nature by an Amazonian society.

The figurines and anthropomorphic hollow vessels

The smaller human figurines range in height from approximately 10 to 30 cm and are nearly all female, although males are occasionally represented as well (figs 5.6). It has been suggested that these artefacts could be related to domestic cults dedicated to female fertility, and to increasing the birth rate among competing agricultural societies.[36]

Typically the females have a semi-circular base instead of legs and feet (fig. 5.4).[37] These figures generally have a stylized, standardized appearance although there are one or two which adopt rather odd positions, such as an individual holding her foot to her mouth (fig. 5.5). Historical accounts give glimpses of the role that women could play in Tapajó society, possibly indicating a matrilineal organization.[38] A case in point is the famous 'Maria Moaçara', reported by Father Betendorf to be a woman of high status and a 'princess by descent',[39] who towards the end of the seventeenth century was sought for consultation as an oracle.[40]

A wide range of body ornamentation is seen in both male and female figurines.

These include ear lobe perforation and ear plugs; wrist and ankle bands (figs 5.5 and 6); and feather headdresses and head bands, which all find parallels in contemporary tropical forest societies. Such ornaments may identify an individual's social role, as is the case today among the Bororo of central Brazil, where it has been shown how differences of feather colour and size in a group of headdresses – the 'paríko' – mark clan affiliation.[41] It has also been suggested that body ornament can be interpreted as part of a strategy of female display to ensure reproductive success in the context of demographic growth.[42]

BELOW LEFT **5.5 Seated woman holding her foot to her mouth. She wears leg bands and her body is richly adorned with body paint (height 14 cm, width 10 cm; Museu Paraense Emílio Goeldi, Belém, Brazil).**

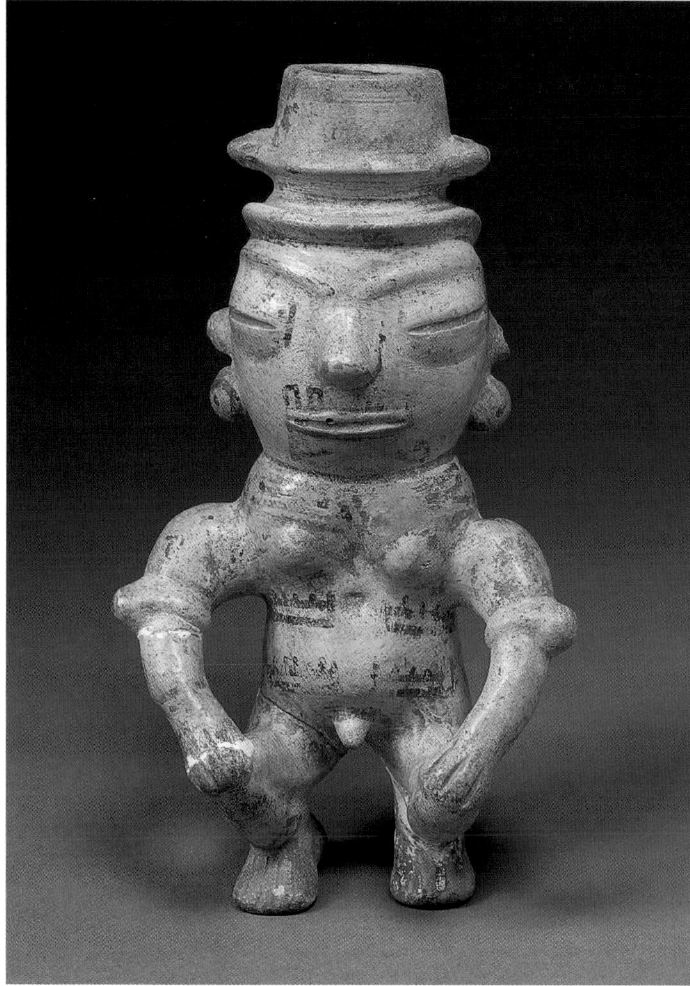

ABOVE **5.6 Male figure with body paint and with his hands on his knees. This is one of a comparatively small corpus of male representations (height 21.5 cm, width 12 cm; Museu Paraense Emílio Goeldi, Belém, Brazil).**

Another figurine portrays a female seated on the ground grasping a large open bowl resting on outstretched legs before her (fig. 5.7). She appears to be an adolescent female whose elegant, elongated, pierced ear lobes perhaps indicate her status in the community as a member of a prestigious lineage. Close examination reveals a wealth of unexpected detail, for the vestiges of black pigment trace an application of body paint that once covered almost her entire body. The designs are best preserved on the face, back, upper arms and lower legs bearing a range of geometric motifs that can be recognized in other media (fig. 5.9).

Moreover, in common with many of the other figurines illustrated here, she wears a band around her head which binds a carefully braided coiffure that is seen to best effect from the rear. Affixed to the head band are two groups of three modelled zoomorphic appendages (fig. 5.8). Careful inspection of these appendages points to marked similarities with a special category of small objects fashioned in semi-precious stones for which Santarém culture is renowned. Known as *muiraquitãs*, these exquisite miniature masterpieces were treasured objects, the raw material for which probably originated far afield in the Guyana highlands.[43] Many *muiraquitãs* are fashioned in translucent gemstones of greenish hue and a great number mimic the form of a frog (fig. 5.10).

BELOW **5.7** Seated woman with a large serving bowl resting on her outstretched legs (height 28.5 cm, width 23 cm; Museu Paraense Emílio Goeldi, Belém, Brazil). Her elaborate body paint, pierced ear lobes and head band with zoomorphic ornaments indicate a special social role and status in the community.

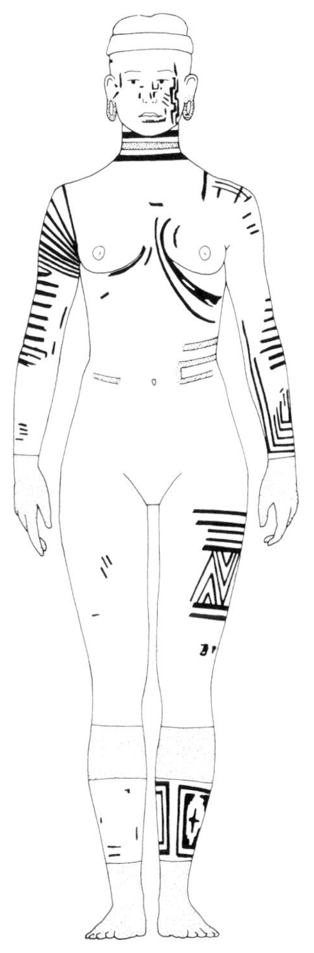

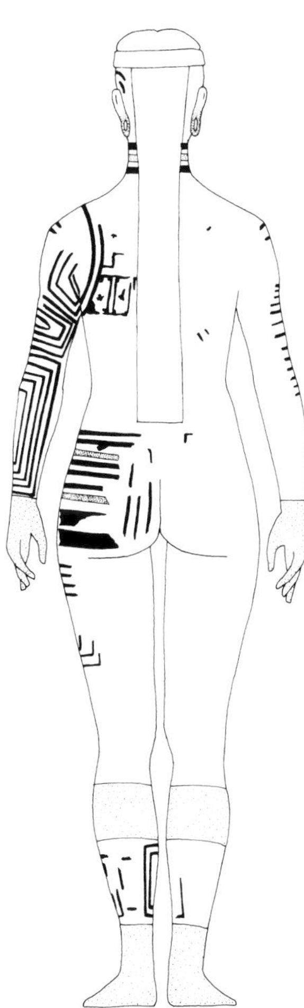

ABOVE **5.9** Drawings of the painted geometric designs and patterns still visible on the front and back of fig. 5.7.

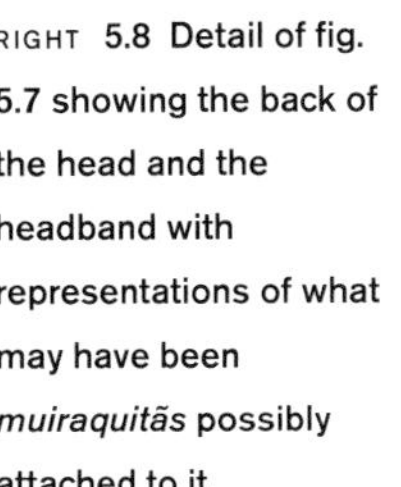

RIGHT **5.8** Detail of fig. 5.7 showing the back of the head and the headband with representations of what may have been *muiraquitãs* possibly attached to it.

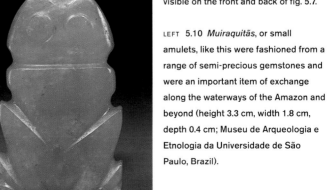

LEFT **5.10** *Muiraquitãs*, or small amulets, like this were fashioned from a range of semi-precious gemstones and were an important item of exchange along the waterways of the Amazon and beyond (height 3.3 cm, width 1.8 cm, depth 0.4 cm; Museu de Arqueologia e Etnologia da Universidade de São Paulo, Brazil).

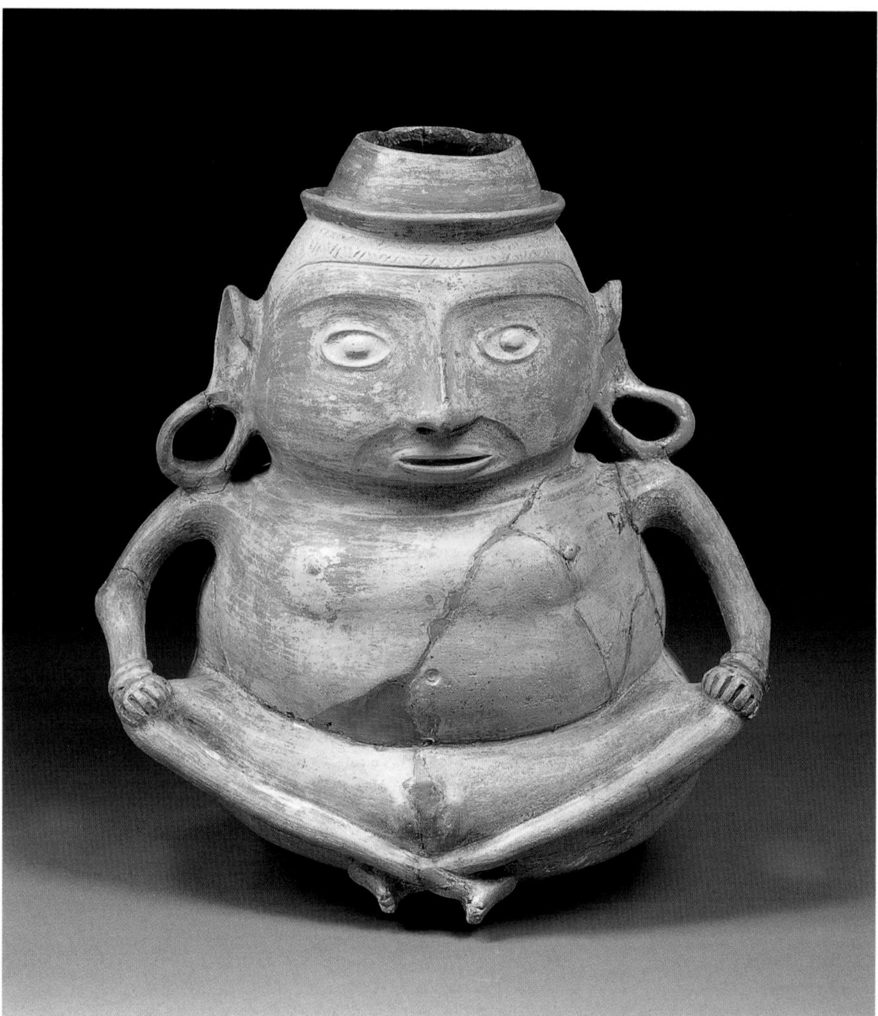

5.11 Anthropomorphic vessel in the form of a seated male with perforated ear lobes. Vessels like these may have been used for storing fermented beverages and also perhaps as funerary urns (height 34 cm, width 93 cm; Museu Nacional do Rio de Janeiro, Brazil).

What might explain this constellation of body ornament and body paint on the seated female figure? Lacking written texts, we must resort to reading the visual vocabulary of motifs and seek analogies in what is recorded of the rituals enacted at key moments in an individual's life cycle, especially the critical transition to full adulthood.

In lowland South America the body can be seen as a 'canvas' upon which an individual's social identity can be transformed and constructed.[44] The deployment of body paint to effect these changes in identity and social role often works in tandem with ceremonies involving masks.[45] This might explain how a young female who is becoming a fully fledged member of adult society would be adorned. We might envisage in this case how her elaborate body paint and other adornments signal her change of status as she assumes a new social identity. This would have entailed her leaving her natal household and the protection of her kin and making the dangerous passage to a new place in society with her prospective husband's family. As such she is charged with the responsibility of conception and child bearing – a procreative role upon which the future life and well-being of the community as a whole depends.

A second group of human-shaped vessels consists of large, hollow, rotund seated males, more than 35 cm high (figs 5.11 and 12).[46] Their form suggests that they could

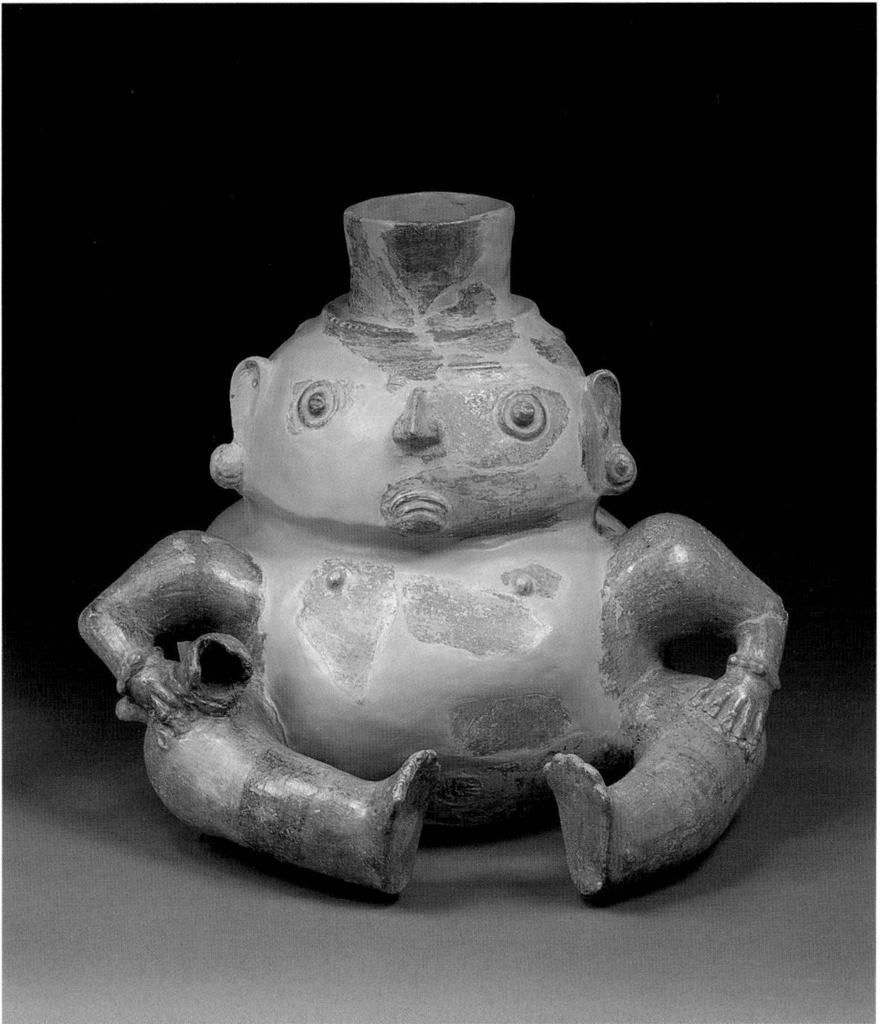

5.12 Anthropomorphic vessel depicting a seated man holding a rattle in his right hand (height 34 cm, width 39 cm; Museu de Arqueologia e Etnologia da Universidade de São Paulo, Brazil). Rattles were frequently used in shamanic curing ceremonies and other rituals.

have been used to hold and serve liquids, probably fermented beverages. These male figures are usually depicted holding a rattle and seated on low stools, which correspond to the wooden stools that are the privileged possession of elder males and shamans among contemporary Amazonian societies (see McEwan, this volume). One seated individual holds a rattle in his right hand (fig. 5.12). These vessels also remind us of the anthropomorphic funerary urns with seated figures that are characteristic of the Maracá phase at the mouth of the Amazon (see Guapindaia, this volume). A number of the figures wear head bands like those on the smaller figurines already described. Likewise these seated males feature perforated ear lobes with prominent ear spools inserted as symbols of their status.

The large dimensions and imposing globular shape of some of these vessels underline the importance of these particular individuals. Historical reports often make reference to ranking and hierarchy in Tapajó society. Writing on Tapajó government in the early seventeenth century, Heriarte,[47] a lay member of the Teixeira expedition noted how 'these Indians are governed by principals, one in each hut of twenty or thirty couples, and all are governed by a great Principal over all of them, who they very much obey'.[48] Clearly this reflects a specific tier of authority in a chiefly hierarchy, the full extent of which we can only guess at.[49]

Tapajó settlements were still very sizeable and densely populated as late as the beginning of the seventeenth century. Describing the place where the contemporary city of Santarém nowadays lies, Heriarte relates that 'this is the largest village and settlement that we have discovered so far in this district. It raises 60,000 bowmen, when war is afoot and since there are so many Tapajó they are feared by the other Indians and nations and thus became the sovereign power in this district.'[50] If a figure of 60,000 may be something of an exaggeration, recent archaeological work in other areas in Amazonia, several hundred miles upstream from Santarém, certainly corroborate the existence of very large settlements throughout the region (see Petersen *et al.*, this volume).[51] In fact there is little doubt that, at the onset of European colonization, the indigenous population of the Amazon was very much greater than today, and it is entirely possible that the figures provided by Heriarte are not too much off the mark.[52]

Together with ranking, it is also likely that some form of institutional division of labour existed among the Tapajó. Betendorf, writing towards the end of the seventeenth century at what was a time of profound change, reports how

> having seen no living person there before, I found in a corner a small boy reduced to bones, lying on the ground, with a piece of manioc bread in his hand ... I gathered him up and took him home ... believing he was still a pagan, I asked why he had not been baptized and an Indian replied it was because he was a slave.[53]

The term 'slave' carries many connotations not all of which may have been strictly applicable in this particular case, nevertheless peonage relationships are not uncommon in lowland South America. In the upper Rio Negro basin, of the north-west Amazon, riverine Tukanoan and Baniwa Indians engage in asymmetric trade and labour negotiations involving peonage with their neighboring Maku groups, who are mostly hunters and gatherers settled in hinterland areas (see Politis and Neves, this volume).[54]

Some mortuary practices also seem to indicate differentiation of individual status or rank. We know that endo-cannibalism was practised among the great chiefdoms of the Middle and Lower Amazon.[55] Heriarte notes, for example, that in the case of the Tapajó:

> Upon the death of one of these Indians, they lay his corpse in a hammock and place all his worldly goods at his feet, and at his head the figure of the Devil, done in their fashion, with needlework, and then put him in especially built huts, where they shrink and eat the meat; and the crushed bones are soaked in wine that their relatives and others drink.[56]

Although endo-cannibalism has been recorded among contemporary Amazonian groups such as the Yanomami[57] and the Desana[58], and historically among the 'Mujaraguanos' (*sic*) and 'Rombos' (*sic*), the Tapajó differ in their treatment of the dead, for some reports hint at the practice of mummification. Betendorf writes:

> There was Father Antonio Pereira, then a missionary at Gurupatyba and Tapajós, where he took action worthy of his great zealousness viz: the Tapajó Indians kept the shrunken corpse of one of their ancestors they called Monhangarypy, meaning first father, whom they honoured with offerings and dances for many years, the corpse hung from the ridgepole of a hut, like a coffin in a tomb ... One night he had the hut where it was kept set on fire, and it was burnt to ashes.[59]

The eighteenth-century chronicle by Father João Daniel confirms the practice of preserving or mummifying dead bodies:

> The Indians answered that they worshipped some bodies and creatures, which they kept well hidden in a hut in the midst of the bush, known only to elders and adults. The priest warned them that they should bring in all these bodies and indeed they brought seven shrunken bodies of their ancestors; and some five stones that they also worshipped. In the face of the Indians' lack of religion and the sight of so much idolatry, the missionary had these idols burnt in public, and he ordered the ashes of the seven dried bodies and the stones to be put in the middle of the river so that along with them would be drowned their blindness, and blind idolatry.[60]

The display of the dead and access to them by their living descendants finds an archaeological parallel in the Maracá area, where anthropomorphic funerary urns were not buried but left visible to the community (see Guapindaia, this volume).[61] The kind of treatment of the dead outlined above, intercession with the ancestors and access to the spirit world are all integral aspects of tropical forest cosmology, and more fascinating glimpses of these distinct ways of perceiving and ordering the world are found in the kinds of vessels that I will now turn to.

The 'caryatid' vessels

Caryatid vessels – so-called because the small crouching modelled figures supporting the bowl recall the elements in classic Greek architecture – comprise the most distinctive, and in many ways the most surprising, vessel forms in the entire Santarém ceramic inventory.

These vessels are shaped by coiling and modelling the clay into three superimposed components: a hollow base; a middle level composed of three modelled anthropomorphic 'caryatid' supports; and a bowl around which are arranged combinations of modelled zoomorphic and anthropomorphic appendages (fig. 5.13). These sophisti-

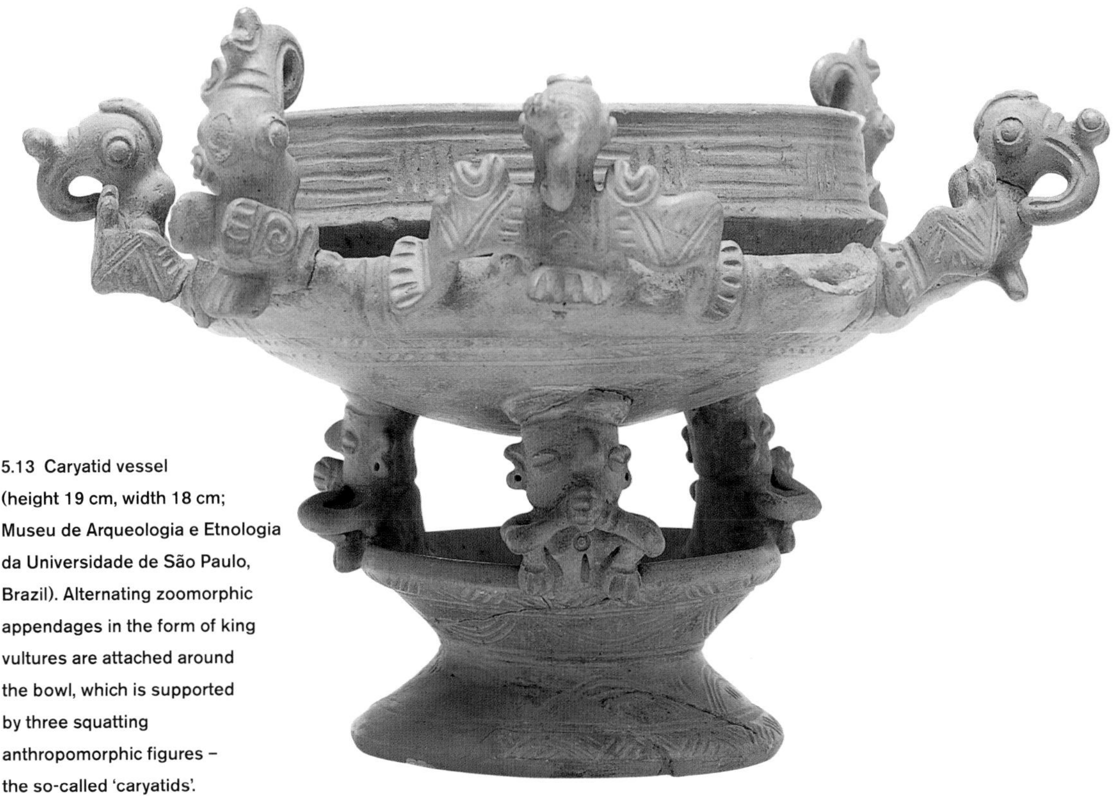

5.13 Caryatid vessel (height 19 cm, width 18 cm; Museu de Arqueologia e Etnologia da Universidade de São Paulo, Brazil). Alternating zoomorphic appendages in the form of king vultures are attached around the bowl, which is supported by three squatting anthropomorphic figures – the so-called 'caryatids'.

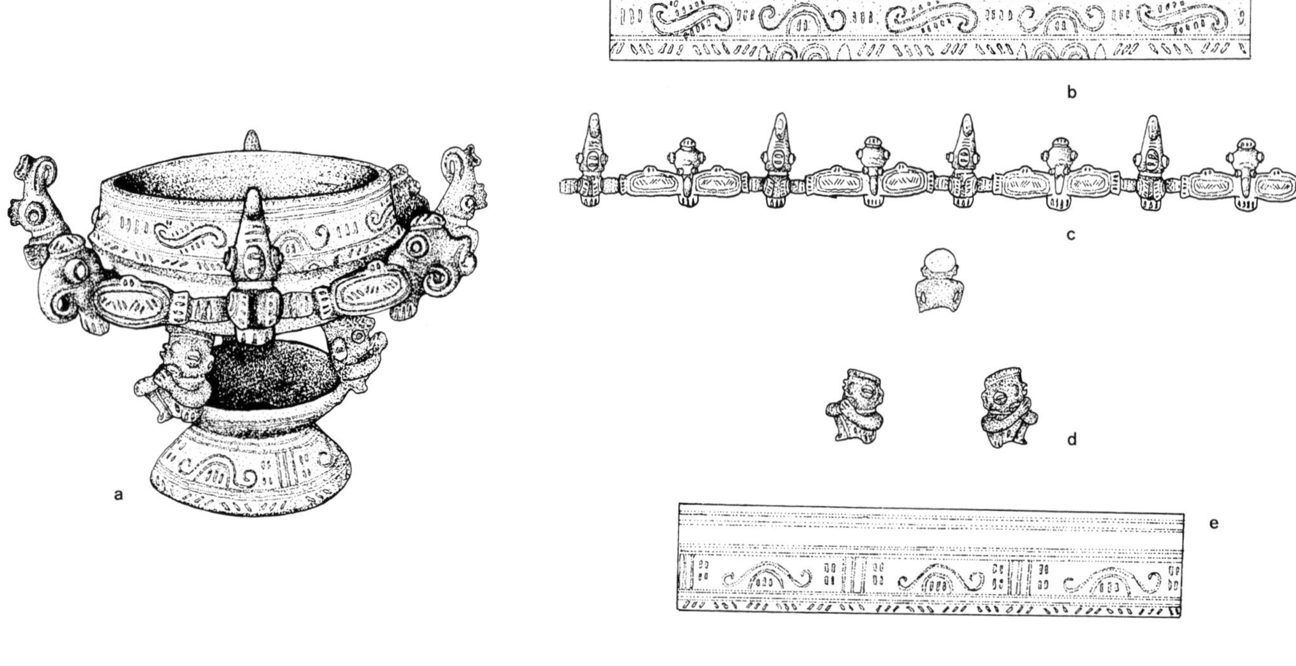

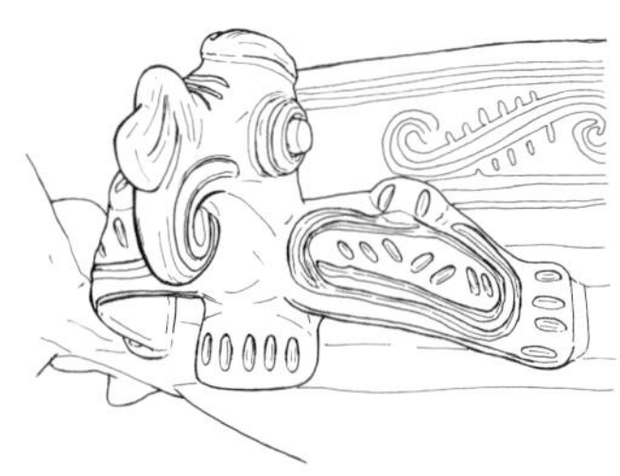

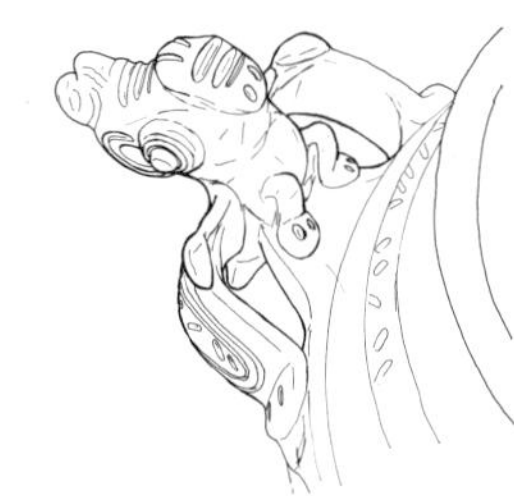

TOP 5.14 Caryatid vessel and its constituent elements: (a) whole vessel, (b) incised patterns around the rim, (c) king vultures arranged at regular intervals, (d) three caryatid figures and (e) incised patterns on the base.

ABOVE 5.15 Different visual perspectives of modelled king vulture appendages on caryatid vessels.

LEFT 5.16 A king vulture – one of the creatures most frequently depicted in Santarém ceramics cated creations reveal surprising subtleties and nuances in the organization of the component elements and their attention to detail.

Caryatid vessels usually have four distinct kinds of decorative elements (fig. 5.14a): first, patterned bands running around the circumference of the rim (fig. 5.14b); second, modelled appendages representing king vultures arranged at regular intervals around the vessel (fig. 5.14c); third, the caryatid figures (fig. 5.14d); and fourth, incised patterns on the base (fig. 5.14e).

The incised decoration on the band around the rim is composed mainly of bilateral motifs but there are also asymmetric elements, combining rotational and bilateral symmetry (fig. 5.14b). The modelled king vultures follow this same translational movement in which the figures alternate between front and back views of the bird also with outstretched wings (fig. 5.14c). Beneath, the small modelled human figures supporting the bowl are arranged in an outward facing radial pattern (fig. 5.14d). Finally, a further application of the principle of bilateral symmetry is also evident in the organization of the motifs on the basal band (fig. 5.14e).

Depending on the angle from which some of the small modelled figures are viewed the animal representation differs. As the viewers perspective changes, so the creature in question appears to metamorphose, assuming a different form, e.g. a king vulture (fig. 5.16) becomes an anthropomorphic figure and vice-versa (fig 5.15).[62]

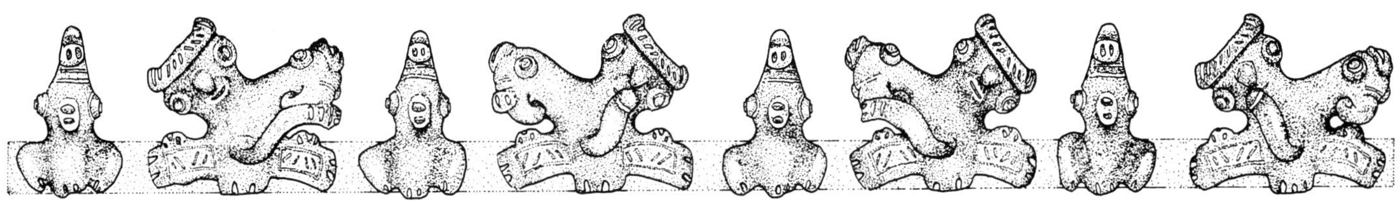

5.17 Various bicephalous king vulture appendages in which two heads share the same body. They recall the kinds of metamorphoses and transformations that occur in the course of shamanic trance.

Bicephalous human-like zoomorphic figures on caryatid vessels call to mind the kind of transformations experienced in shamanic trance (fig. 5.17). Under the effect of hallucinogenic drugs the human themselves shift and metamorphose.[63] This is a world-view where the culture-nature opposition becomes blurred and where, indeed, nature ceases to exist as an external realm.[64]

How then can one conceive of the kinds of social and ritual contexts in which the vessels were created and used? The iconography on caryatid vessels was perhaps bound up with the transmission of oral traditions during collective ceremonies.[65] The caryatids proper, i.e. the female appendages supporting the vessels, are suggestive of these kinds of collective rituals (fig. 5.18). They are usually displayed seated, squatting, eyes or mouth covered by their hands, and in a body posture that finds possible parallels with that of women banned from attending male religious ceremonies, which was widely observed among Amazonian societies (fig. 5.19).[66] Again, in the words of Betendorf:

> The Tapajó had an open area dedicated to the Devil where they gathered for drinking and dancing, telling their women to bring them much wine, *after which they squatted and covered their eyes with their hands so as not to see* [my emphasis], the talk of the sorcerers [shamans] in a thick and hoarse voice persuading them that this was the voice of the Devil, and they put into their minds whatever they wanted.[67]

The link between the textual description and the iconography on the vessels is of

5.18 Roll-out drawing of caryatid vessel showing alternating king vulture appendages and squatting 'caryatid' figures.

course tenuous but nevertheless suggestive. They also lead us to ask why and when such collective community rituals might have taken place and why they might have been so important.

Once more, Heriarte's account offers some intriguing clues when he reported that:

> When the sowing lands are ripe, to each a tenth is allotted, and altogether they store it in the house of the idols, saying that it is destined for *potaba de Aura*, which is the name of the devil in their language; and from this corn they make wine every week, and on Thursday night they carry it in large vessels to a very clean and tidy threshing area beyond the village, where all of the nation gather, and with the sounds of horns and sad and fateful drumming, begin to play for the time of one hour, until there comes an enormous earthquake, that seems to be knocking down trees and mountains; and with it comes the Devil that goes into a house the Indians have made for him, and then with the coming of the Devil all begin to dance and sing in their language, and to drink the wine to the end, and thus they are misled by the Devil.[68]

Among contemporary Amazonian societies, important collective rituals take place at specific times of the year. The ancient use of what Heriarte calls horns probably refers to the long wooden trumpets still played in these rituals. The memory of the great collective rituals among the chiefdoms of the lower Amazon may be preserved in the very toponym 'trombetas', as applied, for example, to the Trombetas river, not far away from the Tapajós. The Portuguese named it after the instruments the indigenous peoples used for their feasts and drinking bouts, to which they were highly disposed.[69] In Heriarte's narrative the devil figure preceded by the sound of the great earthquake might refer to the narrator's vivid impressions of a cacophony of trumpets and of a masked shaman in ritual trance. This passage suggests that such rituals are closely connected with the seasonal agricultural cycle and may be accompanied by the collective redistribution of food and drink. In the north-west Amazon flutes and trumpets are played in the context of ceremonies associated with the 'Jurupari complex',[70] a group of tales on the social and cosmological order transmitted through initiation rituals that emphasize exogamy.[71]

5.19 A squatting female 'caryatid' covering her eyes recalls ethno-historical accounts of collective ceremonies in Amazonia that women were forbidden to watch .

Necked vessels

The so-called 'necked vessels' are composed of three parts: a neck on the top; an oval middle part with six protuberances to which a combination of modelled zoomorphic and anthropomorphic appendages are attached; and a truncated conic hollow

5.20 Necked vessel with zoomorphic appendages comprising cayman, frogs, monkeys and birds (height 18.9 cm, width 31 cm; Museu Paraense Emílio Goeldi, Belém, Brazil). The profusion of animal imagery probably reflects Amazonian notions of cosmological order.

base (fig. 5.20). Four kinds of decorative design are applied with some variation (fig. 5.21a): first, repetitive incised patterns on the neck rim (fig. 5.21b); second, an anthropomorphic face appendage on the middle part (fig. 5.21c); third, also on the middle part, two three-dimensional appendages in the shape of alligator heads, with other animals superimposed (king vulture, bush dog, curassow, etc.), in addition to two toads (fig. 5.21d); and fourth, an incised pattern on the base (fig. 5.21e). On both rim and base one finds bilateral symmetry, while in the centre the zoomorphic appendages follow radial symmetry.

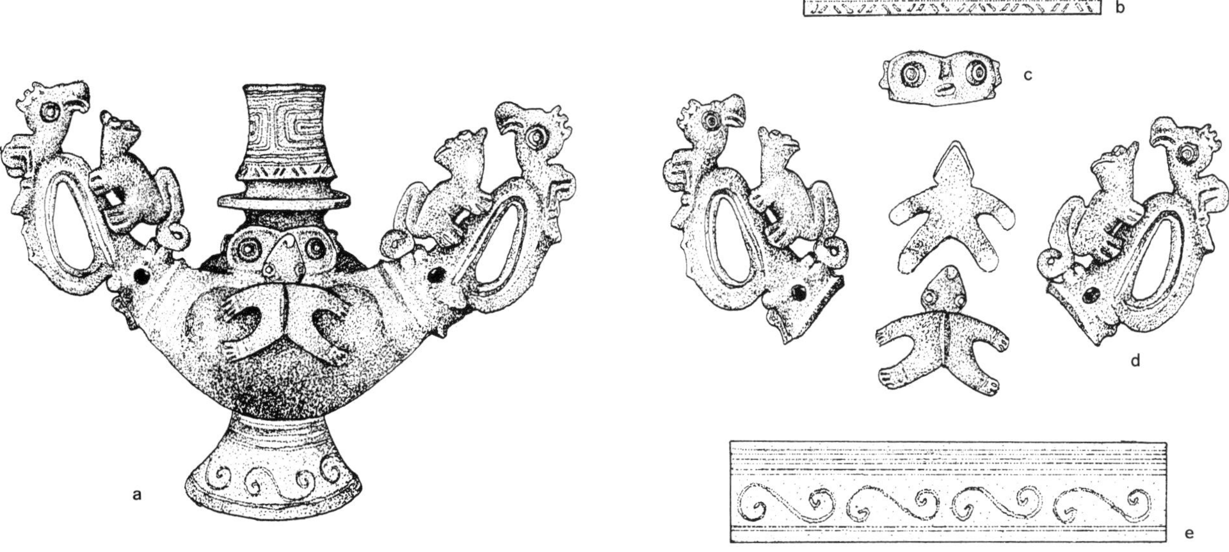

5.21 Necked vessel and its constituent elements: (a) whole vessel, (b) incised patterns around the neck rim, (c) anthropomorphic face appendage, (d) alligator head appendages with superimposed animals and two frogs, and (e) incised patterns around the base.

5.22 Caymans and alligators are powerful riverine predators and often feature on Santarém vessels as fundamental elements supporting different kinds of animals.

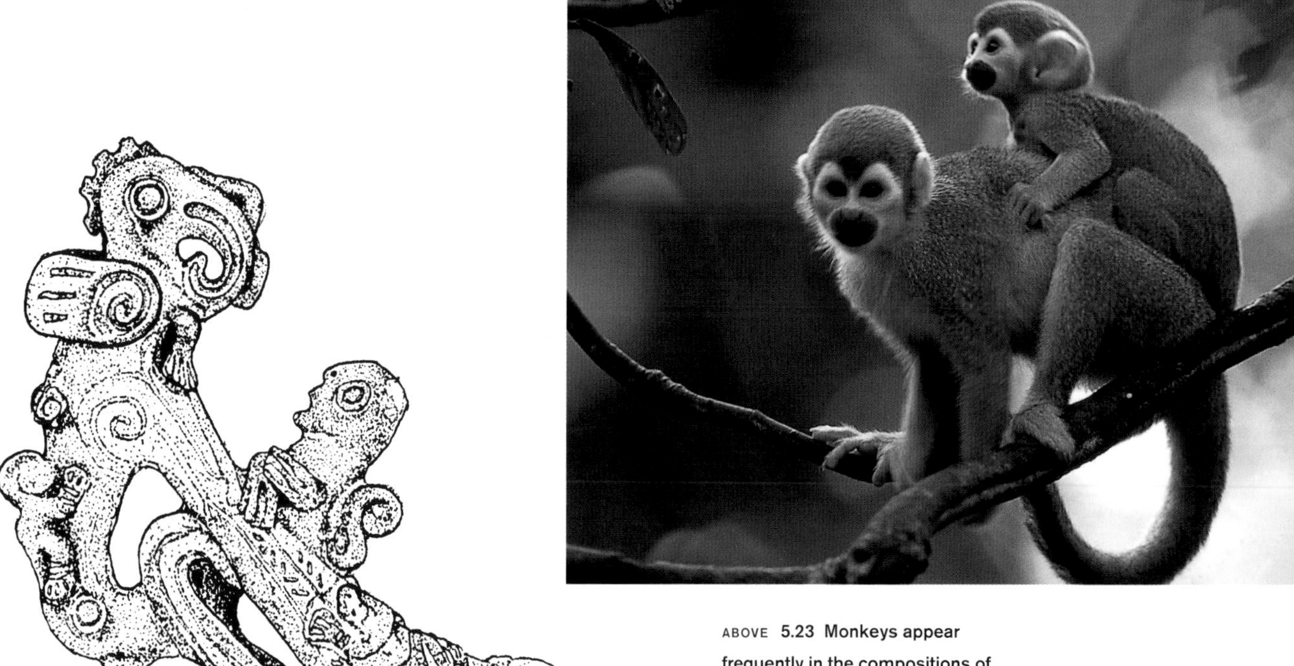

ABOVE 5.23 Monkeys appear frequently in the compositions of tropical animals represented on Santarém vessels.

LEFT 5.24 Detail of the appendage on a necked vessel in the shape of a cayman snout with attached animals including an anthropomorphic figure with a tail.

From the formal point of view anthropomorphic elements occupy their central parts with a cornucopia of tropical animals – caymans, frogs, monkeys, macaws and other creatures – arrayed around them at different levels (figs 5.22–3). This profusion of animal imagery plausibly evokes a kind of creation tale in which the principal actors engage with each other, reinforcing the social order and cosmology during collective ceremonies. Finally, hybrid creatures (anthropomorphic figures with tails) decorate the necked vessels (fig. 5.24).

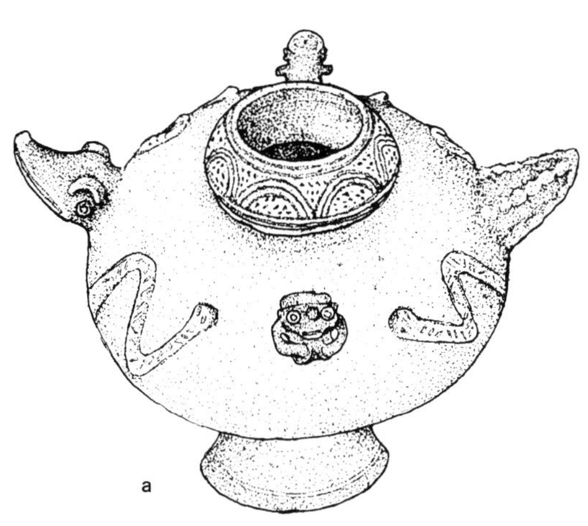

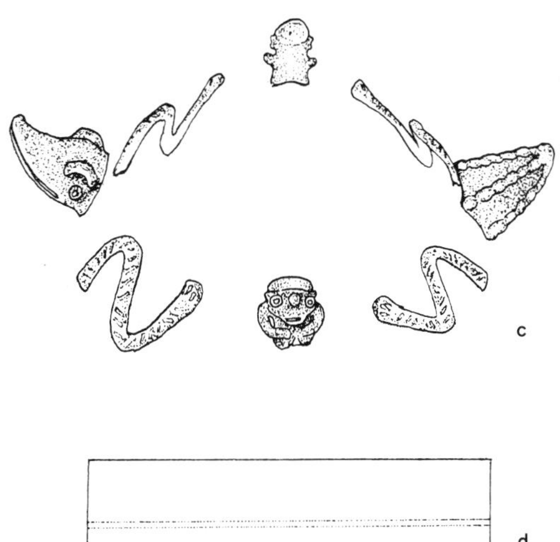

5.25 Globular vessel and details of appliqué appendages: (a) whole vessel, (b) incised patterns on the neck rim, (c) anthropomorphic and zoomorphic appendages (cayman with head and tail and two snakes), and (d) incised line on the base.

The globular vessels and plates

Globular vessels have a much simpler structure, formed by coiling and modelling. They too are divided into three parts: a neck somewhat wider than the ones found on necked vessels; the large globular body to which are attached two appendages representing either an animal's head and tail or human features; and the same truncated conic base as the above types (fig. 5.25a).

They usually have two kinds of decorative design: the neck with incised motifs in which bilaterally symmetrical patterns are clearly recognizable (fig. 5.25b); and appendages that include jaguars, agoutis, alligators and anthropomorphic figures arranged in bilateral fashion. In some cases other iconographic representations (snakes and seated anthropomorphic figures) are added to the basic scheme, resulting in more elaborate compositions and radial arrangements (fig. 5.25c). The base, however, is always plain, bearing no incised bands like those on the rims (fig. 5.25d).

Yet another distinctive kind of vessel comprises shallow plates with appliqué elements on the inner surface as well as around the rim. One such vessel has snake motifs arranged within a quadripartite division of the plate's inner rim (fig. 5.26).

5.26 Bowl with appliqué appendages in the form of serpents in the inner part of the rim and bats and bush dogs in the outside (height 13 cm, width 30.5 cm; Museu de Arqueologia e Etnologia da Universidade de São Paulo, Brazil).

Conclusion: a structured cosmos – order and symmetry in Santarém iconography

The meagre archaeological data combined with a careful study of the historical resources point to Santarém, like Marajó Island (see Schaan, this volume),[72] being an important Amazonian population epicentre.[73] Over time, demographic expansion must have led to keen rivalry among sizeable villages and settlements. Slowly some of the more powerful polities are likely to have controlled a hierarchy of subordinate settlements and perhaps imposed their identity though different media.[74] The stylistic variations in the pottery, both in terms of decoration and technology, provide strong evidence of the existence of a regional style.

The range of Santarém pottery perhaps reflects some aspects of craft specialization and standardized production. Santarém pottery draws on a repertoire of basic elements that are inventively combined. The way in which this was achieved reflects a coherent, highly structured symbolic system.[75]

In asking what might have inspired some of the most sophisticated creations such as the caryatid vessels, I have explored suggestive elements including the metamorphosing animal imagery featuring king vulture iconography and the squatting female figures with their hands over their mouths. The vessels embody fundamental aspects of the way in which order is expressed in material culture. The application of symmetry and the way in which the design patterns form recursive and well-structured sets of relationships communicate organizing principles that also apply to other areas of social life.[76] The carefully ordered iconographic assemblages may also have incorporated elements of mythological significance. Although our archaeological knowledge of Santarém pottery is scant, it can give surprising insights into a hidden world. In this context larger male figurines and urns, sometimes naturalistically depicted, are clearly indicative of social prestige in a tropical forest society. Judging by attributes such as rattles and stools, they represent shamans as leaders of rituals and guardians of cosmological knowledge.

Finally, I have suggested that contemporary Amazonian practices – such as the so-called Jurupari complex – might shed light on the kinds of collective rites and rituals that find expression in the sophisticated compositions embodied in Santarém pottery. The shared cultural elements that I have pointed to indicate that among tropical forest societies there was a pan-Amazonian pattern of social and religious customs that embraced collective feasting, marriage, trade and warfare and that was widely practised by multi-ethnic local groups in pre-colonial Amazonia.[77] The extensive distribution of such a ceremonial complex is confirmed by the ethnohistorical references,[78] and indicates that selected myths and social practices persisted over time because of their adaptive advantages from a biological point of view in selecting for exogamy.

In this sense, I would like to stress the potential of these objects for providing information that extends far beyond an appreciation of their aesthetic qualities. They symbolize a vital connection with one of the last frontiers of the human imagination, how the world was viewed and ordered in the unknown Amazon.

Acknowlegements

I am indebted to Eduardo Góes Neves for his comments and encouragement. Special thanks are due to Marcia Arcuri for all her support.

NOTES

1 In this text, the term 'Tapajós' is used to designate the southern tributary of the Amazon and 'Tapajó' to designate the archaeological culture and people who lived in this area.

2 This is a remarkable report for the multiple references to many densely populated settlements governed by lords or principals, and for the fight against warrior women, the legendary Amazons, on the Nhamundá river. It is in this area that Konduri ceramics are also found.

3 Carvajal 1941: 70.

4 Acuña 1941; Heriarte 1874; Rojas 1941.

5 Betendorf 1910.

6 Betendorf 1910; Daniel 1976.

7 Carvajal 1941: 114.

8 Acuña 1941: 271.

9 Hartt was one of the scientists who followed Harvard professor Louis Agassiz in his Amazonian expedition during the 1870s. Being one of the last major creationist scientists of the nineteenth century, Agassiz wanted to find evidence of former glaciations in the Amazon in order to prove his catastrophist hypotheses.

10 Hartt 1885. A century later, Roosevelt (1995) dated samples from Taperinha to 7500 BP, making it some of the oldest-known pottery in the Americas. If the early dates for this pottery are acceptable this leaves a huge hiatus of several millennia before later pottery complexes including Santarém appear.

11 A botanist by training, Barbosa Rodrigues has also made important contributions to nineteenth-century Amazonian archaeology such as the excavation of the famous, but now destroyed, site of Miracanguera, located around the modern town of Itacoatiara, close to the junction of the Madeira and the Amazon.

12 Barbosa Rodrigues 1875a.

13 Born in Germany in 1883, Nimuendajú died in 1945 among the Tikuna of the upper Solimões, having spent most of his life in Brazil, where he became a major figure in early twentieth-century anthropology. Although Nimuendajú was better known for his ethnographic work, his contributions to Amazonian archaeology were also outstanding. His archaeological research sprang directly from his contacts with Swedish anthropologist Erland Nordenskiöld, who commissioned him to form collections for the Göteborg Museum.

14 Nimuendajú undertook his fieldwork in 1923–6 but the results were not published until more than twenty years later. See Nimuendajú 1949, 1952. Following Nimuendajú's work, only two other research projects have been carried out in the region. These are the Universidade de São Paulo project by Bezerra de Menezes (1972), Prous (1991), and Roosevelt's ongoing research in the area (Roosevelt 1993, etc.).

15 Nimuendajú 1949.

16 See, for instance, Linné 1928, Métraux 1930, Nordenskiöld 1930.

17 Nordenskiöld 1930.

18 Palmatary 1939, 1960. In the USA she studied collections from the University of Pennsylvania Museum of Archaeology and Anthropology, the Museum of the American Indian in New York, the Catholic University of America in Washington DC, and the Göteborg Museum in Sweden. The Brazilian collections studied include those from the Museu Paraense Emílio Goeldi (MPEG), the Museu do Estado de Pernambuco in Recife, the Museu Nacional in Rio de Janeiro, Fundação Brasil Central and several private collections.

19 See, for instance, the later work by Easby 1952, Collier 1989, Corrêa 1965, Guapindaia 1993, Macdonald 1972, Gomes 1999, which all draw upon Palmataray's pioneering efforts.

20 Corrêa 1965.

21 Meggers and Evans (1961). This forty-year-old model still provides the basic chronological framework for Amazonian archaeology.

22 See, for instance, Meggers and Evans 1983.

23 Corrêa 1965.

24 Not an archaeologist by training, Barata was a newspaper man turned antiquities collector who developed a strong interest in Santarém ceramics later in his life.

25 Barata 1950, 1951, 1953a, 1953b, 1954.

26 He based his approach on the anthropological classic *Primitive Art* by Franz Boas (1955).

27 Macdonald 1972.

28 Guapindaia 1993. This research enabled her to divide Santarém ceramics into two main groups, before and after European contact.

29 Gomes 1999. Here I present a revised pottery typology and propose a tentative chronological framework within which the sequence of ceramic complexes might be placed. This is, of course, likely to be modified and refined as new information and dates from stratified archaeological contexts become available.

30 AD 800 $\pm$ 160 to 1150 $\pm$ 210 (Gomes 1999). These dates are based on thermoluminescence testing of sherds from the MAE (USP) collection, run at the Instituto de Fisica, Universidade de São Paulo. This study partially confirms the hypothesis that Santarém pottery ought to date to around AD 1000 to 1500 (Meggers and Evans 1961, 1983; Brochado and Lathrap 1982).

31 Roosevelt 1993, 1995, 1996. Detailed excavation reports of this work have not yet been published.

32 The sites of Taperinha and Pedra Pintada, both located a few dozen kilometres downstream from Santarém, have provided the earliest dates for the beginning of ceramic production in the Americas (Roosevelt *et al.* 1991, 1996).

33 Roosevelt 1992: 80. In addition to relations among communities belonging to the same polity, interaction between larger centres is likely to have taken place, which would help explain the adoption of technological innovations or parts of the symbolic repertoire. Therefore the stylistic traits of Santarém pottery related to the Amazonian Polychrome tradition – such as mesial flanges, 'tear eyes' (Magalis 1975), arched eyebrows and polychrome painting (Gomes 1999) – may be explained through the existence of a network of contacts connecting societies of the middle and lower Amazon river. Although each of the main pottery styles in the period prior to contact (Santarém, Marajó, Maracá, Guarita, etc.) may be viewed as unique, the presence of shared elements identified in the analysis of the pottery indicates the dynamics of a 'tropical forest cultural tradition'.

34 Of course these two functions are not mutually exclusive.

35 Gomes 1999; Guapindaia 1993; Palmatary 1939, 1960.

36 Roosevelt 1988, 1992, 1997a.

37 This kind of base is also called 'semi-lunar'.

38 Roosevelt 1988: 11.

39 Betendorf (1910: 171–3). Betendof was sent to the Tapajó by Father Antonio Vieira, a Portuguese-Brazilian Jesuit priest and humanist, who, like a sort of seventeenth-century Las Casas, fought to protect Indians against enslavement and was persecuted by the Inquisition. Chronicles of religious missionaries, such as Betendorf, who were more interested in indigenous religion than the early explorers, provide an important source on Tapajó culture. Their reports coincide with the final stage of the cultural disintegration of the Tapajó, with the imposition of Christianity and the practice of mass conversion, when individuals from different groups were relocated to Christian villages for indoctrination (Menéndez 1981/2; Porro 1993). From these sources, the earliest available document was written by Betendorf (1910), in the second half of the seventeenth century. Next, one hundred years after the establishment of a mission in Santarém, there is the report of Father João Daniel (1976).

40 Nimuendajú 1949: 98.

41 Dorta 1981.

42 Roosevelt 1988.

43 Boomert 1987.

44 Seeger *et al.* 1979.

45 Baer 1993: 305.

46 Gomes 1999; Guapindaia 1993; Palmatary 1939, 1960.

47 Unlike previous chroniclers, Heriarte (1874) provided specific references on the size of Tapajó villages, their form of government, religion and funeral rites. More than any other, Heriarte's account contributed to the construction of the hypothesis of social complexity in Santarém.

48 Heriarte 1874: 38.

49 The pottery inventory and the historical data provide elements that fit into a chiefdom model for the political organization of the Tapajó as recorded in anthropological literature: Carneiro 1981; Earle 1987. Carneiro (1981), and Flannery and Marcus (2000: 31–2) suggest that chiefdoms do not have a monolithic character but may take on different forms. These authors stress interaction, usually of a competitive nature, as a trait common to chiefdoms, which are never found alone in a given area. Based on these observations, the Tapajó can be viewed as a polity that shared underlying economic and religious practices with other Amazonian societies. Progressive demographic expansion led in particular historical situations to the emergence of social complexity (Drennan 1995, Flannery and Marcus 2000: 31–32).

50 Heriarte 1874: 35.

51 Heckenberger *et al.* 1999; see also Myers 1973.

52 Denevan 1992a.

53 Betendorf 1910: 168–9.

54 Ramos *et al.* 1980. Although parallelisms between contemporary north-west Amazon and historical Tapajó are germane, the scale of labour mobilization between these societies is probably very different. Hence, while the size of ethnographic and archaeological villages in the Uaupés river, upper Rio Negro basin, had not changed significantly during the five hundred years of European colonization, the same did not happen among the Tapajó (see Neves 1998b).

55 See p. 131, n. 55.

56 Heriarte 1874: 36–7.

57 Chagnon 1983.

58 Reichel-Dolmatoff 1971.

59 Betendorf 1910: 353–4.

60 João Daniel 1976: 237–8.

61 In contrast, Amazonian ethnography is full of references to restrictions on even mentioning a deceased person's name.

62 Macdonald (1972) addresses Santarém iconography, linking it with certain features of Tapajó cosmology. Her hypothesis, yet to be confirmed, of a possible Carib origin for the group, resulted in her use of Carib myths and consequent correlation of some pottery decoration with the Warrau mythological narrative. In turn, Roosevelt (1987, 1992, 1996) suggests that the portrayals of king vultures, alligators, snakes, jaguars and toads may be related to warrior symbols, in an implicit allusion to prior studies on the iconography of Panamanian chiefdoms. See also Linares 1977 in Flannery and Marcus 1996.
63 Among Tukanoans, drawings on the walls of the longhouses portraying narratives of the creation of the universe turn into the actual process of creation unfolding before people's eyes while ingesting powerful hallucinogenic substances: Reichel-Dolmatoff 1975, S. Hugh-Jones 1979. See also Reichel-Dolmatoff 1971, Hugh-Jones 1985 and Béksta 1984 for discussions of the symbolic wealth of the decoration and form of Tukanoan *malocas* (communal longhouses).
64 Such operations are characteristic of the so-called 'perspectivist Amerindian thinking' (Viveiros de Castro 1998)
65 Barata 1953a and b; Macdonald 1972; Roosevelt 1997a.
66 Nimuendajú 1949, 1952.
67 Betendorf 1910: 170.
68 Heriarte 1874: 36.
69 According to Heriarte (1874: 39), 'the lands of this Trombetas River (the Portuguese named it after the instruments the indigenous peoples used for their feasts and drinking bouts) bear more manioc than the Tapajó lands and there is much hunting'.
70 S. Hugh-Jones 1979, 1988; Reichel-Dolmatoff 1989; Wright 1992a & b.
71 Reichel-Dolamtoff 1989.
72 Roosevelt 1991.
73 Shennan 2000.
74 Flannery and Marcus 2000; Renfrew 1986.
75 Hays 1995.
76 My observations here are based on my study of the symmetry on the composition of one- and two-dimensional, incised and painted patterns found on the rims, as well as the relative position of the tridimensional appendages, in a sample of seventy-one vessels and large fragments from the Tapajós Collection of the Museu de Arqueologia e Etnologia, Universidade de São Paulo (Gomes 1999).
77 Reichel-Dolmatoff (1989) suggested that the widespread distribution of this ceremonial complex over time and place in the Amazon indicates that selected myths persisted over time because of their adaptive advantages from the biological point of view, i.e. selecting for exogamy.
78 Porro 1993: 22–3.

6

Encountering the Ancestors

The Maracá Urns

VERA GUAPINDAIA

Introduction

Towards the end of the nineteenth century reports began to appear about the discovery of an entirely new style of large funerary urns near the Maracá river in the lower Amazon. Sporadic finds of these intriguing objects continued to be made over the years, but it is only recently that they have begun to attract the scientific attention they deserve and to be understood in their proper cultural and chronological context. The urns are usually found in caves and rock shelters and represent one facet of life and death in a hitherto 'unknown' prehistoric society. Archaeologists are now beginning to gain new insights into these funerary practices although we still know very little about other aspects of the lives of the people who practised them. This essay seeks to place the Maracá material amid the great mosaic of cultural diversity that flourished in the lower Amazon in the centuries before the arrival of Europeans.

Maracá archaeology: a brief history

The archaeological sites in the region of the Maracá river, located in the southern part of the state of Amapá, were first discovered and explored by the naturalist Domingos Soares Ferreira Penna in 1872 (fig. 6.2).[1] In the same year the American geologist Charles Hartt published a note in the magazine *The American Naturalist* about an anthropomorphic funerary urn that Ferreira Penna had shown him.[2]

In 1896 Col. Aureliano Lima Guedes, who was then serving as assistant to the Swiss-Brazilian zoologist Emílio Goeldi, undertook a more general survey of the Maracá region, venturing up both the Maracá and Anauerapucu rivers and their smaller tributaries. Near the Igarapé do Lago, an affluent of the Maracá, Guedes located three archaeological sites that he called 'indigenous moorgues [cemeteries]' on account of the urns that he stumbled upon.[3] He also found blue and white glass beads glued with resin to one of the urn handles as if it were a bracelet, and he concluded that the combination of sculpted objects and glass beads indicated contact with early European explorers.

Nearly twenty years later, in early 1915, Curt Nimuendajú travelled overland to the Maracá river. On this journey he recorded five sites located on *terra firme* (dry land) in an area of *terra preta* (black earth) containing abundant lithic and ceramic materials. Nimuendajú surmised that these sites were recently abandoned, since there was still much secondary forest growth in the vicinity.[4] In the course of his travels Nimuendajú made both archaeological and ethnographic collections for museums in Europe and Brazil.[5]

Around this time William Farabee, an anthropologist from the University of Philadelphia, conducted research on the islands of Porcos and Pará close to the mouth of the Maracá river, a northern tributary of the Amazon.[6] He found anthropomorphic and zoomorphic urns in caves similar to those recorded by Ferreira Penna and Lima Guedes. Farabee believed that the anthropomorphic urns were too small to contain bones, and therefore assumed that they had been used to hold ashes. Again, due to the presence of glass beads, he inferred that the burials were not very old and probably dated to the early colonial period.[7]

By the early twentieth century most of what was known about Amazonian archaeology derived from col-

6.1 Maracá funerary urn representing a female seated on a zoomorphic stool (height 65.8 cm, width 42 cm, depth 43 cm; Museu Paraense Emílio Goeldi, Belém, Brazil)

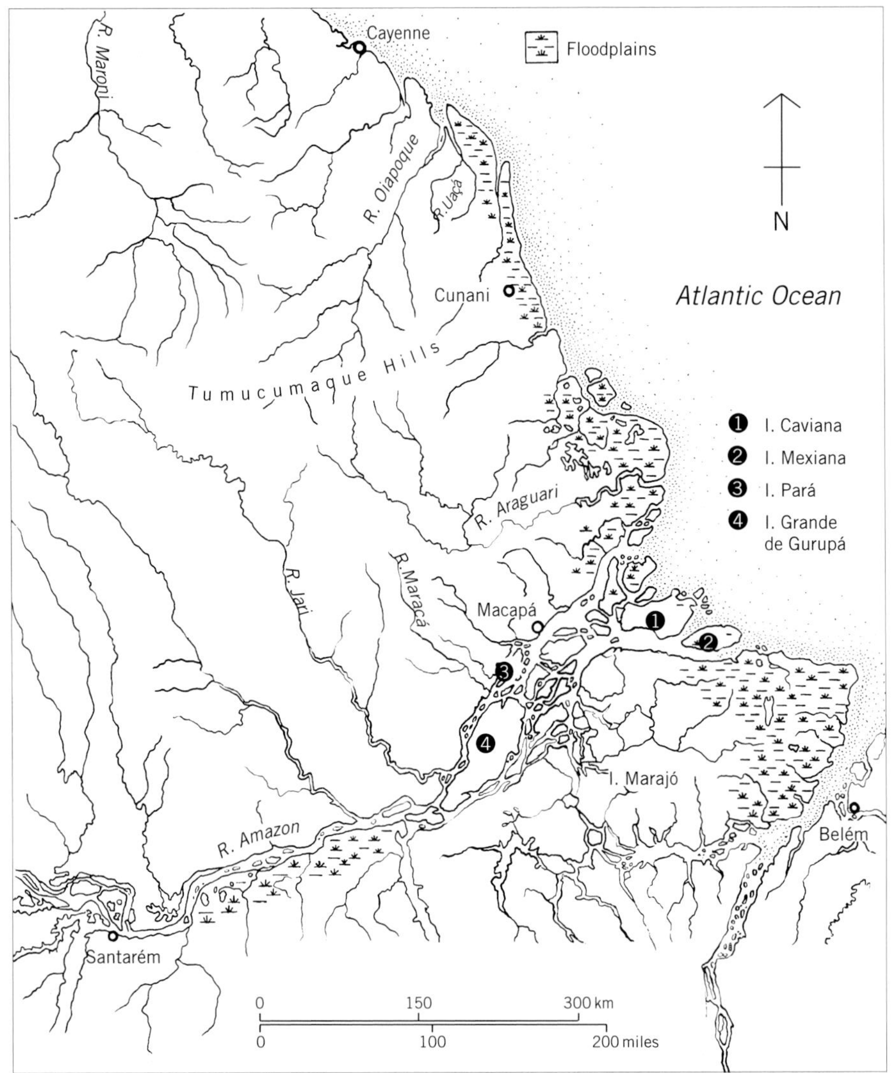

ABOVE LEFT **6.2 Map of the mouth of the Amazon and the state of Amapá to the north.**

lections gathered in the latter part of the nineteenth century by naturalists and, somewhat later, by anthropologists. The existence of these collections stimulated initial attempts at explaining the origins and distribution of the different pottery styles including the Maracá urns.[8]

Following the Second World War investigations began anew with the arrival of Smithsonian Institution archaeologists Betty Meggers and Clifford Evans. They initiated an ambitious research project that set out to survey the mouth of the Amazon river.[9] They did not visit the Igarapé do Lago region but instead opted to study the museum collections of material from that region previously collected by Guedes and Farabee.[10] Meggers and Evans concluded that the pottery-making cultures they identified in what is today called Amapá State – Mazagão, Aristé and Aruã – were derived from elsewhere, were relatively recent and dated to just before European contact. They assumed that the Maracá occupation was geographically concentrated in the Igarapé do Lago region, extending towards Pará Island (see fig. 6.2).[11]

Around 1953 the ethnographer Peter Hilbert is known to have visited the Maracá river region, where he found a site with cave paintings.[12] Later, in 1972, Mário Simões from the Goeldi Museum classified the urns collected by Ferreira Penna and Lima

ABOVE **6.3** Natural environment in the vicinity of the Igarapé do Lago.

Guedes as part of the Maracá phase.[13] More recently Klaus Hilbert undertook a survey in search of pre-ceramic sites and made a stratigraphic cut at the site known as Buracão do Laranjal in a rock shelter near one of the Igarapé do Lago tributaries. There he found lithic artefacts and the remains of hearths,[14] as well as paintings executed in red pigment on the shelter's walls. Besides this pre-ceramic site, Hilbert recorded eight other sites with traces of pottery on the banks of the Maracá river and the Igarapé do Lago, and made surface collections.[15] More recently I have been developing a project designed to investigate the prehistory of the Igarapé do Lago region,[16] and much of the material presented in this chapter derives from this work.

Maracá territory

The main river in the region is the Maracá, a relatively small tributary by Amazonian standards, which flows in from the north to meet the main river. Some 50 km up the Maracá one meets the dark waters of the Igarapé do Lago. From December to May (the rainy season) the creek overflows, forming a large lake. This is also the season when travelling by boat is possible (fig. 6.3). The extended plains are criss-crossed by a maze of channels, creeks and lakes, all of which are subject to inundation during the annual rainy season floods. With the onset of the dry season rainfall decreases and the river level falls, but it does not dry up entirely. There are areas of higher land located north and south of Igarapé do Lago that are dissected by ravines and valleys. To the west old surfaces with rocky sedimentary outcroppings are commonly found, and the geological formation has favoured the development of dens, caves and rock shelters.[17]

The vegetation around Igarapé do Lago is lush and extremely diverse. In the extensive low-lying areas, wild rice (*Oriza sp.*) thrives along with numerous other plant species native to swampy areas, buriti palms (*Mauritia flexuosa*) and other small aquatic plants. On higher and drier ground, stands of large trees such as the Brazil-nut tree (*Bertholletia excelsa*) are found, and extraction of the nuts is the basis of the local economy.[18] Besides manioc or cassava (*Manihot esculenta*), the local staple food, bananas (*Musa paradisiaca*), oranges (*Citrus sinensis*) and lemons (*Citrus limon*) are also cultivated by local farmers. In the rocky, lateritic plateau the plant life changes, giving way to the so-called *canga* vegetation, composed of trees with thin, thorny trunks.

There is an astonishing variety of terrestrial and aquatic fauna, and many species are hunted by the local population for food. Among mammals can be counted jaguars (*Panthera onca*), deer (*Mazama americana*), peccaries (*Tayassu tajacu*), spotted cavies (*Cunilus paca*), coatis (*Nasua nasua*), agouties (*Dsyprocta III*), tapirs (*Tapyrus terrestris*) and many species of monkey (*Cebus erxeben, Saimiri sciurens, Midas ursulus*). A great variety of reptiles are also found, including the black cayman and different kinds of turtles. Birds abound and include spotted egrets (*Leucophyx thula*), hawks (*Ruporis magnirostris*), toucans (*Ramphatos itellinus*), red macaws (*Ara macao*) and flocks of parakeets (*Tiririca chiriri*).

Maracá habitation sites and cemeteries

In the course of archaeological surveys undertaken in the Serra do Laranjal mountains and the Igarapé do Lago headwaters I have located three open-air sites[19] and thirteen cave cemetery sites (fig. 6.4).[20] The fact that sixteen sites have so far been found near the Igarapé do Lago creek in a 32 sq. km survey area gives an indication of the density of prehistoric settlement.

The dwelling sites are found near the margins of the Igarapé do Lago, on higher ground (*terra firme*) but below the level of the caves and some 0.5 km–3km distant from them. The ratio of thirteen cemetery sites to three dwelling sites may be due in part to differences in the survey methods used in the two areas, and an ongoing survey of the Igarapé do Lago and Maracá river margins will certainly increase the proportion of dwelling sites.

The dwelling sites[21] – situated between 20 and 500 metres from the banks of the Igarapé do Lago margins – are all open-air sites with *terra preta* in evidence. They occur along both banks of the Igarapé do Lago, spaced between 2 to 6 km apart. The local population currently makes use of these areas to plant cassava, lemon and papaya, or to raise cattle. The sites typically run parallel to the river and range from 60 metres to 200 metres in length. The dark surface soils containing archaeological materials are no deeper than 60 cm and yield abundant sherds and many polished stone tools.[22]

The vast majority of the pottery sherds clearly belong to a range of domestic utilitarian vessels including cooking pots and receptacles for preparing, carrying, serving and storing a range of food and liquids.[23] One very distinctive ceramic form specific

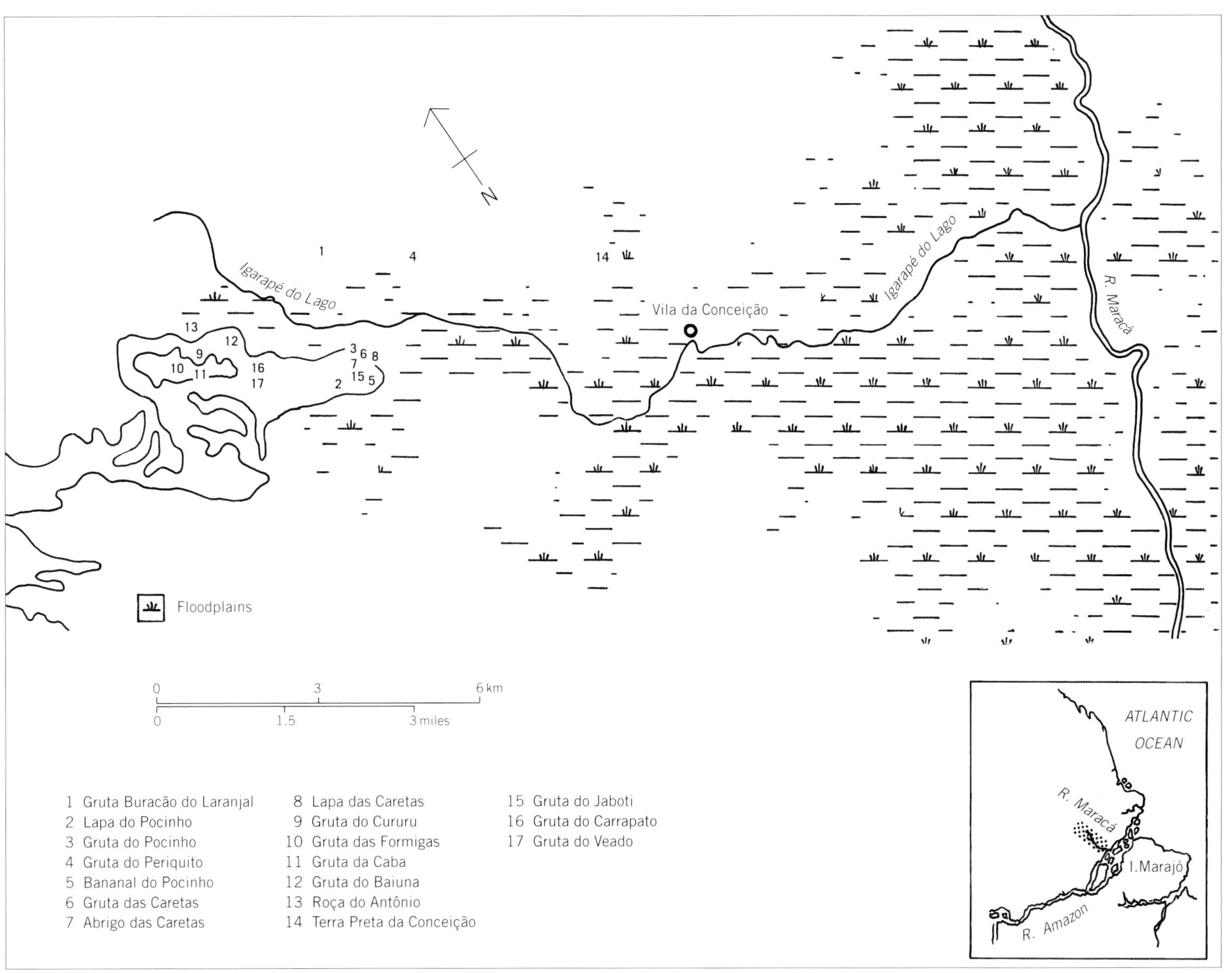

6.4 Map of research area in southern Amapá showing the location of archaeological sites.

to tropical forest culture is the manioc bread (*beiju*) roaster measuring between 25 and 40 cm in diameter. This pottery is made of clay tempered with ground rock, sometimes mixed with a siliceous tree bark (*cariapé*), charcoal or ceramic fragments. Coiling and modelling techniques were used for fashioning vessels and shaping handles and decorative appendages. Vessels are decorated with both painting (white and red) and several plastic techniques (incised, engraved, punctate, finger punctate and scraped decorations). Among the most common motifs are parallel lines or triangular incisions usually located on or near the rims.

Cemetery sites

All the cemetery sites presently known are found in the hills of Serra do Laranjal, distributed across an area of approximately 21 sq. km, with an estimated density of one site per 1.2 sq. km. Caves and shelters of all shapes and sizes were used as cemeteries.[24] Dimensions of caves or shelters vary, many are humid inside due to water leaking from cracked walls, and the rainwater saturates the ground, which is clayey, dark

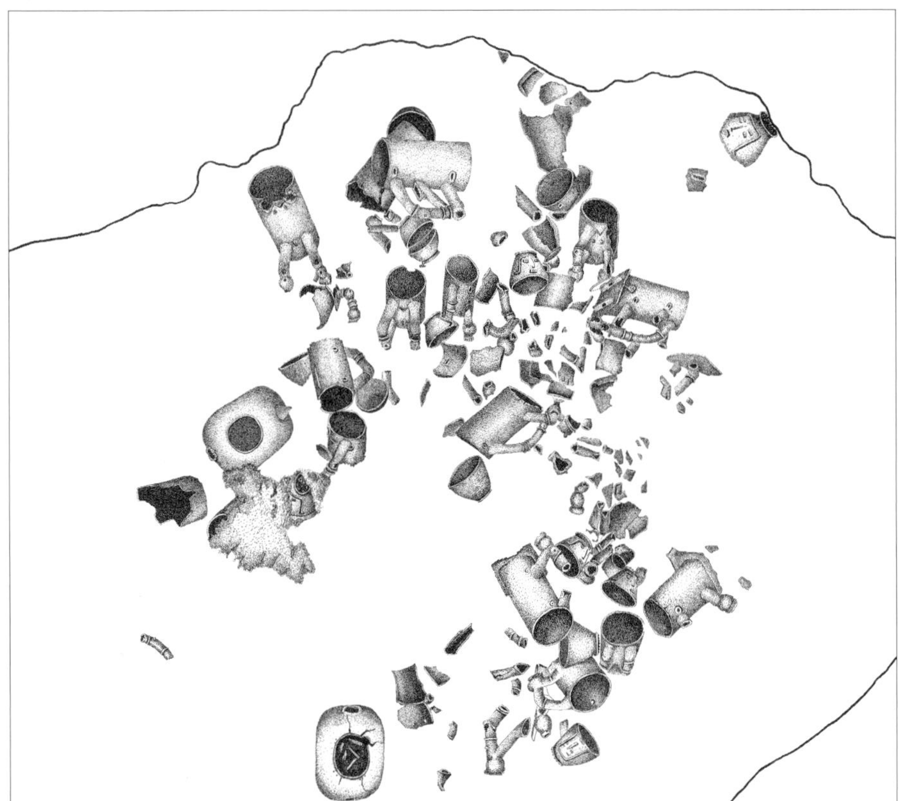

ABOVE **6.5 General view of the spatial distribution of urns found on the surface of Gruta das Caretas (Caretas cave).**

LEFT **6.6 Floor plan of Gruta da Jaboti showing the arrangement of anthropomorphic urns found on the cave floor.**

and moist. In some caves vegetal matter falls through cracks in the roof to accumulate on the cave floor. Signs of mammal, bird and reptile activity are often found. There are also a great variety of insects, whose remains may be found on the ground, on the walls and on the funerary urns themselves. Termite nests are frequently found inside the urns, enveloping and destroying the human bones.

Cemeteries in the Maracá region typically consist of caves or rock shelters containing urns that represent imposing human figures sitting on stools or on small four-legged animals. These urns contain secondary burials and were not buried but left standing on the surface (figs 6.5–6).

There is a differential distribution between habitation sites and the cave sites used as cemeteries. Habitation sites are found in open areas close to sources of water, while the cemeteries are found in more protected, hidden locations. The relatively close proximity of cemeteries and habitation sites, together with the fact that the urns were intentionally placed on the ground surface to assure their visibility, points to the active links that were probably maintained between the world of the living and the world of the dead.

The Maracá urns

There are two basic types of funerary urns: anthropomorphic urns, consisting of a seated human figure on a stool (fig. 6.1), and zoomorphic urns in the form of a standing four-legged animal (fig. 6.7). The urns that Guedes collected in 1896 include yet a third category of cylindrical urns with disc-shaped lids (fig. 6.8). The cylindrical shape and the way in which these were produced is broadly similar to the anthropomorphic urns, while the lids are similar to those found on the zoomorphic urns.

ABOVE **6.7 Zoomorphic urn found at Gruta do Pocinho.**

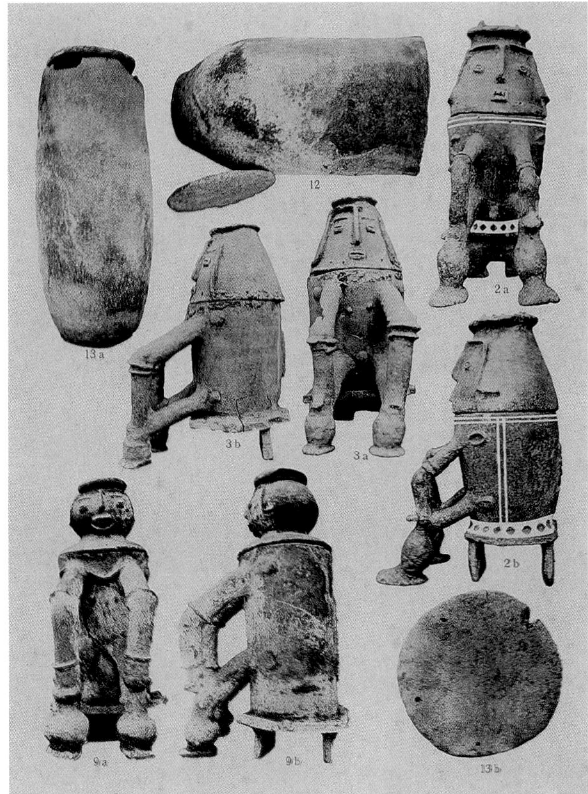

RIGHT **6.8 Plate published by E. Goeldi in 1900 showing the urns found by L. Guedes. Numbers 12 and 13a are the cylindrical or so-called 'tubular' urns.**

According to Guedes's description (1897), the cylindrical urns were not discovered in association with either anthropomorphic or zoomorphic urns.

The anthropomorphic urns are found in larger numbers and vary greatly in size, ranging in height from 20 to 85 cm. They consist of three distinct parts: head, body and seat (fig. 6.9). The head is composed of a removable lid, which is cone shaped with the narrow side facing upwards. The upper part of the head is closed with a disc-shaped cover and decorated with a combination of incisions and modelled relief motifs with, in some cases, small holes. In addition, some lids have a modelled 'T'-shaped appendage on the back of the cover. The height of the heads or lids ranges from 9 to 22 cm, the diameter of the disc-shaped covers ranges from 6 to 16 cm, and the diameter of the lower part of the lid ranges from 9 to 27 cm.

The modelled faces are well defined, featuring eyebrows, eyes, mouth and nose, as well as a framing contour consisting of an attached, shaped coil that demarcates the division between the face and the back of the head (fig. 6.10). The contour coil is usually joined to the coil that forms the nose. Eyebrows, eyes and mouths are also modelled with coils. The mouth has incisions separating the lower and upper lips. In some lids teeth are also represented by vertical incisions. By and large, eyes are rectangular, more rarely they may be circular. There are no explicit representations of ears although two lids display holes on both sides of the face at ear height, on the coil used for the face contour. Chins or adornments are also suggested by appendages in the lower, frontal section. The lower part of the lid has small holes separated by regular gaps around which resin residues are often found. The holes and resin probably served to seal the urn and tie the lid to the main body, since similar holes are also found on the urn's rim, where the lid rests. In addition to the plastic treatment of the surface, some lids were decorated with yellow, white and black paint.

The cylindrical bodies are attached to the upper part of the seat and may be up to half a metre in height.[25] Their lower sections show clearly modelled nipples, navel and genitalia. Male and female figures are represented in equal numbers. The rear part invariably has a modelled vertical element clearly representing the vertebrae of the spinal column (fig. 6.9). There are also small coils appended to the sides of the body, close to the arms and legs. Some pieces also have a coil encircling the body at waist level and applied in the form of a 'U' shape on the chest. The upper limbs are bent in an unusual position, with the elbows turned forward. The limbs are connected to the body immediately below the rim. Each hand

6.9 Drawing of an anthropomorphic urn showing the modelled and painted body ornament. The drawing is based on Goeldi's 1900 plate.

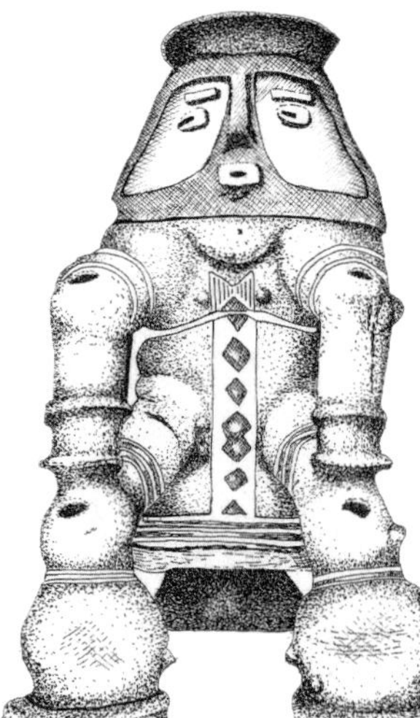

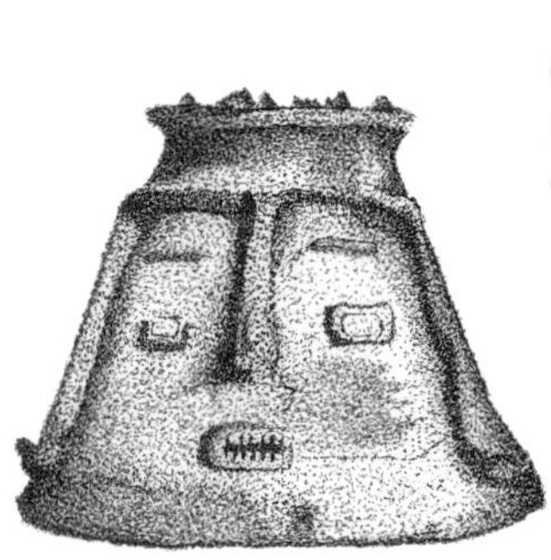

6.10 Lids of anthropomorphic urns representing heads. Note the detailing of the facial elements.

rests on a knee, and the fingers are fashioned by a combination of modelling and/or incisions. Coils represent adornments worn on the forearms and wrists along with other small appendages, and some have traces of paint. The number of fingers and toes varies: in some cases there are up to seven fingers on a hand. Some urns have holes near the elbows and knees. The lower limbs are bent and connected to the body near the seat. The legs are thick, in comparison to the thighs, and some have coils encircling them below the knee, perhaps representing ligatures like those still used by indigenous groups. Round appendages are also found on the sides of the knees and ankles. The feet are flat and rest on the ground.

The modelled stools are low and rectangular in form, ranging from 7 to 10.5 cm in height. The lower parts of the stools are not smoothed, often presenting circular marks probably left by objects used for support during urn construction. In most cases, the legs consist of two ceramic plates (whole or hollow) attached perpendicularly under the seat. Most stools are zoomorphic, and there are clear similarities with the wooden zoomorphic stools widely used by elders and shamans in contemporary Amazonian societies, notably the Xinguano (see figs 7.5–6). A head and tail are represented by appendages on either end of the seat. Viewed from the front, most have the animal's head to the right and the tail to the left. The tails are all alike: a coil 4 to 5 cm long, thicker where it connects to the seat, and the tip is always turned upwards. The zoomorphic heads can be circular, triangular or square in shape. One seat features two heads, side by side. Eyes, nose, eyebrows and mouth are always present. Some of the faces have a human appearance, while others are animal-like, including a bird head.

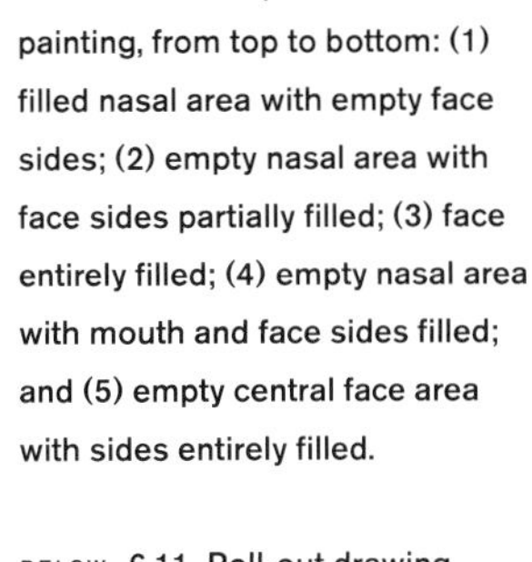

RIGHT 6.12 Urn heads showing variations in the patterns of facial painting, from top to bottom: (1) filled nasal area with empty face sides; (2) empty nasal area with face sides partially filled; (3) face entirely filled; (4) empty nasal area with mouth and face sides filled; and (5) empty central face area with sides entirely filled.

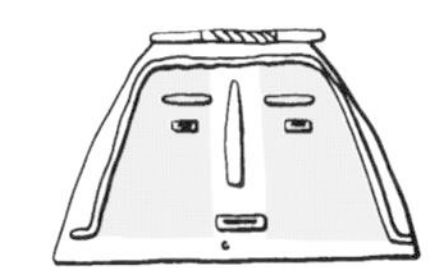

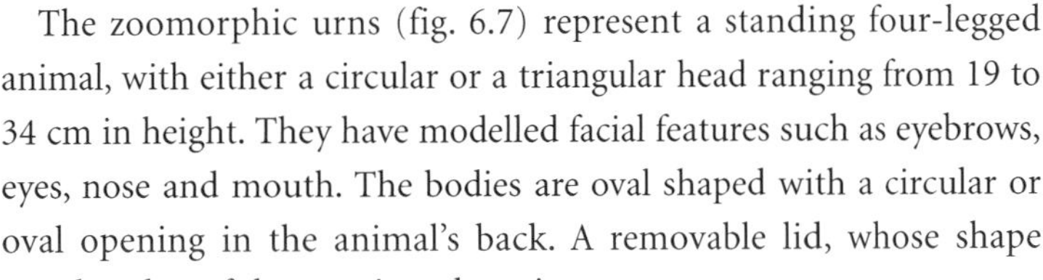

The zoomorphic urns (fig. 6.7) represent a standing four-legged animal, with either a circular or a triangular head ranging from 19 to 34 cm in height. They have modelled facial features such as eyebrows, eyes, nose and mouth. The bodies are oval shaped with a circular or oval opening in the animal's back. A removable lid, whose shape matches that of the opening, closes it.

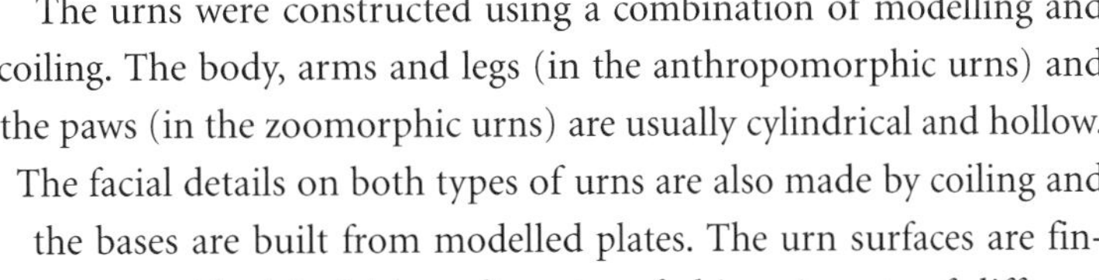

The urns were constructed using a combination of modelling and coiling. The body, arms and legs (in the anthropomorphic urns) and the paws (in the zoomorphic urns) are usually cylindrical and hollow. The facial details on both types of urns are also made by coiling and the bases are built from modelled plates. The urn surfaces are finished in fairly rudimentary fashion. A paste of different texture was used to restore occasional cracks. The same type of resin that was apparently used to seal the urn was also used to fix some appendages to the main body.

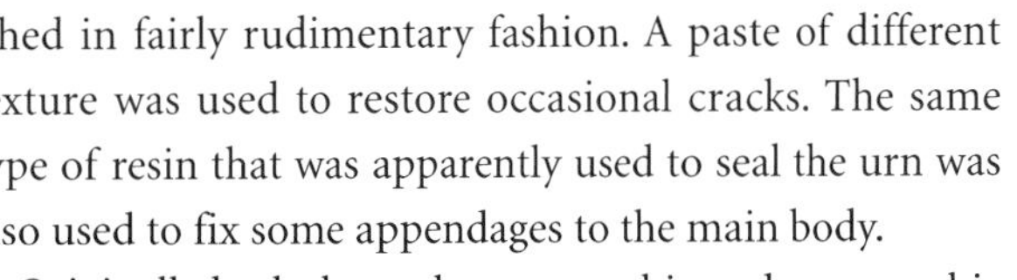

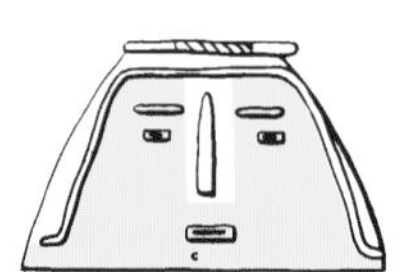

Originally both the anthropomorphic and zoomorphic urns were painted with decorative motifs, the vestiges of which are still visible (fig. 6.11). White, black, yellow and red pigments are all found in different combinations. Some decorative motifs in black and white were drawn in fine lines, approximately 3 to 4 mm wide, suggesting the use of a malleable instrument with a fine tip. A different technique was used to cover large areas with yellow paint.

BELOW 6.11 Roll-out drawing reproducing the body of an urn without the arms, from Gruta das Caretas. Note the arrangement of decorative motifs in horizontal and vertical bands.

The yellow paint may have been applied with a wide-tipped instrument or with fingers, or perhaps splashed haphazardly on the urn.

The urn heads and bodies are all painted. Decorative motifs consist of a combination of four basic elements: diamonds, horizontal lines, vertical lines and sinuous lines. In addition, large areas are filled in with yellow and, more rarely, black. Painting is found on both the faces and the back of the heads. The use of yellow to fill in spaces occurs exclusively on the face, never going beyond the appended coil that marks its limits. Five types of facial painting so far identified are illustrated in fig. 6.12. The combination of these basic elements forms sixteen decorative motifs organized in horizontal and vertical stripes along the length of the body. Horizontal stripes are found around the rim and the base while vertical stripes appear in the middle of the back and on the chest, resulting in two large areas filled with sinuous lines.

The orderly distribution of the drawings and the nature of the decorative patterns suggest that the 'body paintings' embody a deeper meaning than the simple desire to decorate an object. The decorative motifs on the Maracá urns can be compared to the practice of body painting in other archaeological traditions in the Amazon (see Schaan and Gomes this volume), as well as among indigenous groups today in both everyday and ritual contexts.[26] As a number of studies in aesthetic anthropology have already demonstrated,[27] among indigenous groups the drawings, patterns, colours, and even raw materials used in painting both the body and objects for everyday and ritual use are part of a communication system whose rules are shared by all.

Funerary practices

The archaeological evidence of Amazonian mortuary rituals comprises the single most important source of insights into the social organization and beliefs of Amazonian people prior to European contact. In the Maracá area in particular cemeteries enable us to pursue both biological and cultural approaches to studying the dead.[28] The fact that hidden, sheltered locations, such as caves, were used for housing the dead reveals the concern with their preservation and with the funerary rituals themselves. The distribution of urns inside the caves does not seem to privilege a specific area; at times the material is easy accessible, near the entrance, while in others places it is somewhat removed, towards the back. In most caves urns are found near the entrance.[29] Gruta da Caba (Caba cave) has a peculiar characteristic with two distinct areas. The first is a rock shelter almost 2 metres deep. Further inside, along the same wall as the shelter, there is a second area, comprising an 8-metre deep indentation in the rock. There, the urns were deposited in such a way that, upon arriving at the location, one immediately sees them, while in the second area, which is not immediately visible, one finds only pieces of small vessels and quartz fragments.

In two caves where good natural light reaches far into the interior,[30] urns could be spotted upon entering. In Gruta do Cururu, however, the urns could only be seen after venturing 8 metres in and crawling through a passage 80 cm high and 70 cm wide. The chamber is completely dark, so its interior has to be explored by torchlight. At yet another cave, Carrapato, the funerary urns were again not placed in the main chamber but in a smaller and darker inner recess.

Funerary practices in Maracá followed two main stages: the primary funeral,[31] when the soft parts of the body were discarded, and the secondary funeral, in which the disjointed bones were deposited in an orderly fashion inside the ceramic urns.

The lack of cut marks on the bones suggests that they were not scraped to remove the flesh. A practice similar to that observed among the Yanomami may have been used.[32] They place the corpse on a tree and wait for the rotten flesh to detach itself from the bones, while the Bororo pour water on the corpse to speed up the decay process.[33]

As for the secondary funeral, Roth (1924) noted that prior to European contact indigenous groups practised exhumation and disposed of bones in a variety of ways: by burning, grinding into powder to add to beverages, distribution among relatives, deposition in urns or use in other secondary rituals. Secondary burial in Maracá is always of single individuals. A consistent correspondence is found between the gender of the individual and the gender represented on the urn. There is a specific pattern of arrangement of bones inside the urns, as noted by Ferreira Penna, where the 'flat' bones (such as the hipbones) are placed 'in the centre and the bottom, the small bones [including the ribs, hands and feet] on top of these, the long bones [from the legs and arms] leaning on the vessel's walls, and on top of them all the skull, resting in part on the heads of the femur and the humerus'.[34]

The arrangement of the urns in the caves and rock shelters indicates that there was a deliberate attempt to keep them exposed and visible. This was probably linked to a special relationship between cemeteries and villages, including frequent visits, observance of funerals and other rituals, and forms of worship or consultation.[35]

Seating and the dead

It is a very moving experience to come face to face with the funerary urns in a Maracá cemetery, even in cases where most of them are broken and destroyed. The sight of the painted funerary urns standing untouched in their original locations for centuries must have aroused a sense of fear and respect in all who viewed them.

The existence of two types of anthropomorphic and zoomorphic urns suggests that special treatment was reserved for certain people. The distribution of urns in the caves is as follows: in two caves there were only zoomorphic urns; in four caves there were zoomorphic and anthropomorphic urns together, with the former in the minority; in four other caves, anthropomorphic urns with funerary objects were found (a ceramic bead necklace and small vessels); and in two caves, only anthropomorphic receptacles have been discovered (fig. 6.13). Most of the funerary urns are anthropomorphic effigies, leading one to believe that the zoomorphic ones may have been used for restricted purposes – possibly for the burial of persons with special status.

The most striking characteristics of Maracá anthropomorphic urns are the posture of the figures, sitting erect on stools with their hands resting on knees. Their gender is clearly marked. Careful scrutiny reveals the presence of ornaments and body painting on all the urns. If we look to contemporary tropical forest societies we find that adornment use is not necessarily restricted to rituals, but is also part of everyday life. Body painting and ornaments, for instance, are used daily by the Xerente, Xikrin and Kadiweu in order to be integrated with nature and, at the same time, to differentiate themselves from other animals, underlining their human qualities.[36] Among the Xerente, different motifs painted on the body represent clans or 'parties'.[37] Analysis of the paintings in Maracá urns reveals that decorative patterns were distributed across the vessels' surfaces in an orderly fashion, probably signalling the social role, clan affiliation and/or status of a particular individual. The paintings could have served to identify the individual in the world of the living as well as in that of the dead.

	Urns					
	Quant. Anthro.	%	Quant. Zoo.	%	Total	%
Caves						
Lapa do Pocinho	1	0.67	00	0.00	1	0.67
Gruta do Pocinho	19	12.66	7	4.66	26	17.32
Gruta do Periquito	4	2.66	00	0.00	4	2.66
Gruta das Caretas	48	32.00	00	0.00	48	32.00
Abrigo das Caretas	00	0.00	1	0.67	1	0.67
Lapa das Caretas	1	0.67	00	0.00	1	0.67
Gruta do Cururu	12	8.00	00	0.00	12	8.00
Gruta das Formigas	2	1.34	00	0.00	2	1.34
Gruta da Caba	14	9.33	00	0.00	14	9.33
Gruta da Jaboti	18	12.00	3	2.00	21	14.00
Gruta do Carrapato	2	1.34	1	0.67	3	2.01
Gruta do Veado	17	11.33	00	0.00	17	11.33
Total	**138**	**92.00**	**12**	**8.00**	**150**	**100.00**

6.13 Table giving a breakdown of anthropomorphic and zoomorphic urns and their distribution in the different caves.

In addition to body ornamentation, stools are an integral element of the Maracá funerary urns. As with the zoomorphic urns, the stools have a head and tail and the zoomorphic attributes reflected the power and status of its owner. Stools are intended for the leaders, shamans and visitors; they are a male privilege.[38] In his study of sexual and religious symbolism among the Tukano Reichel-Dolmatoff (1971) claims that all objects in material culture, and not simply those intended for shamanic purposes, convey deep symbolic significance. Among others, he cites the example of the stools, objects whose function is not only to provide rest for the body, but also to permit mental concentration. The Tukanoans express this aspect when they use the expression 'he does not have a stool' to indicate that someone is incapable of exercising sound judgement. Shamans also use stools in male puberty rituals. Berta Ribeiro (1995) suggests that the Tukano view stools as signs of elevated status of certain kin groups or individuals occupying a higher position within the social hierarchy. Among the Wanano the act of sitting implies eternity.[39] Connection with the ancestors – that is, a relationship between the living and the dead – can also be established when one is in this position (see McEwan, this volume).

In Maracá one intriguing aspect of seated figures is the fact that females are represented. Since sitting on stools is a male privilege in most indigenous groups, and since the act may have had symbolic significance in Maracá society, we might infer that, at least when facing death, women played a socially significant role, as Roosevelt (1988) has already suggested for the Marajoara phase.

The questions addressed here are far from being conclusively answered. For instance, did the funerary practices apply to everyone in Maracá society or were they restricted to an elite? Did children receive differential treatment? Until now, children's bones have not been identified. Were they simply not preserved because of their fragility? What was the use of the rare small urns that are always found empty? By and large, rituals mark important community occasions, and confirm and reassert group identity. Funerary rituals can be seen as a way of confronting the perplexity that death brings and the desire to promote a connection with the ancestors.

Maracá in the wider archaeological context of the lower Amazon

Because of the seemingly unique characteristics of the funerary urns and their fairly limited regional distribution, the archaeology of Maracá may appear, at first sight, as a localized development in the late pre-colonial occupation of the lower Amazon. If one looks, however, at the wider framework, a different picture emerges. Maracá is just one among a series of different cultural traditions that flourished in the lower Amazon from around the beginning of the second millenium AD onwards. Most of these cultural traditions are very poorly known, with, at best, scanty chronological and geographical information available. Some of them are in every sense unknown, as in the case of the two striking anthropomorphic urns illustrated in figs 7.1–2.[40] These urns combine stylistic elements from different archaeological cultures.[41] The formal seated pose of the male figures on the stools immediately reminds us of the Maracá urns, but a closer look shows major differences. Whereas the head in Maracá has a roughly trapezoidal shape, the head on these urns has a semi-circular shape.[42] Patterns of painting also differ: in Maracá the painting is mostly post-fired with a combination of black, white and yellow, while one of the urns displays the classic black and red on white painting characteristic of the Amazonian Polychrome tradition. Urns such as these boast a wealth of abstract imagery that is matched by few other vessels from the lower Amazon, and hint at what is yet to be discovered.

6.14 Anthropomorphic urn from the Aristé archaeological tradition, northern Amapá state (height 45 cm, width 39 cm; Museu Paraense Emílio Goeldi, Belém, Brazil). Collected by E. Goeldi inside an artificial well in the Cunani river valley, northern Amapá state.

Poor as it is, distribution data reveals what looks like an interesting pattern that deserves to be sketched in the remainder of this text. The people who made the Maracá urns and deposited them in the Igarapé do Lago caves appear to have had their own distinct historical connections and patterns of social interaction when compared with other ceramic traditions: the Mazagão, Aristé and Aruã phases (fig. 6.14).[43] Radiocarbon dates are few, but chronologically these phases all appear to be contemporary and often somewhat geographically contiguous. To the east of the Maracá area, all the way to the mouth of the Araguari river into the Atlantic Ocean (fig. 6.2), one finds sites bearing pottery from the Mazagão phase. On the islands west and north of Marajó Island, such as Caviana and Mexiana (fig. 6.2), at the very mouth of the Amazon, but also on some sites on the mainland in Amapá state, post-Marajoara phase sites bear ceramics belonging to the Aruã phase, named after the Arawak-speaking indigenous population that occupied these areas by the seventeenth century. Finally, Aristé sites are found from the mouth of the Araguari in the south all the way to French Guyana, across the Oiapoque river, in the north (fig. 6.2).

6.15 Quadrangular dish from the Aristé archaeological tradition, collected with the urn in fig. 6.14 (height 20 cm, width 50 cm, depth 41 cm; Museu Paraense Emílio Goeldi, Belém, Brazil). Note the decorative painting inside the vase reproducing a jaguar pelt motif.

Aristé is the best known of these phases, thanks to early archaeological fieldwork by Goeldi in the well-known Cunani artificial wells,[44] and by the ubiquitous Nimuendajú[45] in the Uaçá river.[46] Aristé ceramics are coil made and tempered with a combination of crushed rocks and tree bark. Decoration consists of painting and modelling, producing zoomorphic and anthropomorphic motifs, as can be seen in figs 6.15 and 6.16. Fig. 6.15 shows a dish collected by Goeldi in Cunani bearing an exquisite combination of red paint, imitating the patterns on a jaguar skin (fig. 6.17), and modelled bird-like appendages in each of its corners. The same jaguar skin pattern, this time associated with plastic decoration resembling human features, can be seen in sherds collected by Nimuendajú and reproduced in Nordenskiöld's *Ars Americana* (fig. 6.16).

Part of the area where Aristé sites are found was, in Goeldi's and Nimuendajú's time, occupied by three different indigenous groups: the Arawak-speaking Palikur and the Creole-speaking Galibi and Karipuna.[47] Recent archaeological and ethnographic research in the Uaçá Indigenous Park[48] has shown that there is a very strong association between Palikur oral tradition and the location of Aristé sites.[49] That there should be such an association is not a surprise, since there is historical information that the

ABOVE 6.16 Plate from Nordenskiöld's classic 1930 monograph *Ars Americana*. The uppermost fragment represents a jaguar skin pattern.

ABOVE RIGHT 6.17 Jaguar in the flooded forest.

Palikur have been settling this area since the sixteenth century.[50] What is surprising is the fact that the Palikur survived at all, positioned halfway between Belém and Cayenne, two major colonial settlements (fig. 6.18).[51]

Aristé sites can be divided into two broad categories: open air villages with different visible signs of earthworks, such as well-defined large paths and enclosed walls; and cemeteries located in both granite and laterite rock shelters where funerary urns with secondary burials were deposited in much the same fashion, though in smaller numbers, than in the Maracá caves. Although the association between these sites and Palikur history will need further study, it is tempting to suggest that pre-colonial Aristé sites were occupied by populations speaking a language from the Arawakan family. It is known, for instance, that this was the case with the Aruã from the mouth of the Amazon and other groups along the shore of the Guyanas , such as the Lokono.[52]

In any event these later ceramic phases of the lower Amazon seem to be associated with a general decline in Marajoara culture. In this sense they can be seen as the final points in the very long archaeological sequence of the lower Amazon (see Schaan, this

6.18 Palikur hat collected by Curt Nimuendajú in the 1910s for the Ethnografiska Museet I Göteborg, Sweden (height 67 cm, width 50 cm). Since the sixteenth century the Palikur have been settling in the area where Aristé sites are now being found.

volume), a sequence whose dates seem to cover the entire Holocene period, from the early ceramics of Pedra Pintada, Taperinha and the Mina Phase[53] all the way to the Tapajó, Aruã, Mazagão, Aristé and Maracá. The understanding of the historical processes underlying the patterns in this long sequence holds the key to a better understanding of the archaeology of the whole Amazon basin.

Acknowledgements

I would like to thank my institution, the Museu Parense Emílio Goeldi, in particular Peter Mann de Toledo, Roberto Araújo, Edithe Pereira, Marcos Magalhães, Regina Farias, Raimundo Santos, Jorge Mardock, Daniel Lopes and Carlos Palheta. I am also grateful to the Fundação de Cultura do Estado do Amapá, the Museu Histórico Joaquim Caetano da Silva in Amapá, Sheila Mendonça (Escola Nacional de Saúde Pública/FIOCRUZ), Claudia Rodrigues-Carvalho (Anthropology Department at Museu Nacional), Michael Heckenberger (Department of Anthropology, University of Florida), Colin McEwan, Eduardo Neves and Cristiana Barreto.

NOTES

1 Ferreira Penna 1877a.
2 Hartt 1872.
3 Lima Guedes 1897.
4 Nimuendajú 1927, cited in Meggers and Evans 1957.
5 In Europe these include the Ethnographic Museums in Göteborg (Sweden) and Oslo. An urn conserved in Oslo's museum and illustrated by Nordenskiöld (1930) was surely obtained by Nimuendajú in the course of his explorations in Amapá in 1915. In Brazil the collections made by Nimendajú are now held by Museu Paraense Emílio Goeldi.
6 Farabee 1921.
7 Ibid.
8 Hartt 1885; Netto 1885; Nordenskiöld 1930; Costa 1934. See Neves 1999-2000 for a review and discussion of the literature.
9 This survey included the Marajó, Mexicana and Caviana Islands and part of what was then the federal territory of Amapá. Meggers and Evans 1957.
10 These are housed in the Museu Paraense Emílio Goeldi in Belém and at the University Museum of Philadelphia respectively.
11 They considered their hypotheses to be inconclusive, as they did not examine finds from open sites. Nevertheless Meggers and Evans thought the Maracá period might have been contemporaneous with the last period of the Mazagão phase based on stylistic influences apparent in the urns (Meggers and Evans 1957).
12 The results of his research, however, were not published (Barreto 1992).
13 Simões 1972.
14 One C14 date 3750±110 BP (Beta 30746) places this site in the second millenium BC.
15 Hilbert and Barreto 1988; Barreto 1992.
16 In 1994 Ana Lúcia Machado of the Museu Paraense Emílio Goeldi initiated a research project in the region.
17 Projeto Radam Brasil 1974.
18 Other vegetation includes the following trees: itauba (*Mezilaurus itauba*), wacapou or *acapu* (*Vouacapoua americana*), *sapucaia* (*Lecythes psionis*), laurel (*Laurus mobilis*), and nargusta or *mulateiro* (*Calycophyllum spruceanum*).
19 The dwelling sites are Bananal do Pocinho, Roça do Antônio and Terra Preta da Conceição.
20 The cemetery sites are Lapa do Pocinho, Gruta do Pocinho, Gruta do Periquito, Gruta das Caretas, Abrigo das Caretas, Lapa das Caretas, Gruta do Cururu, Gruta das Formigas, Gruta da Caba, Gruta do Baiuna, Gruta da Jaboti, Gruta da Carrapato and Gruta do Veado.
21 In addition to the three sites recorded by the current Maracá project, there are six others that feature similar characteristics and were recorded by Hilbert and Barreto (1988) throughout the Lago Bayou, below the area where the research is now concentrated.
22 A single radiocarbon date from a seed found between 30 and 35 cm deep indicates the occupation of the area at 360± 40 BP (beta-142117; AD 1445–1645, 2 sigma range).
23 The diameter of the vessel mouths ranges from 8 to 32 cm, while their height ranges from 3 to 20 cm.
24 They range from around 1 to 2.5 metres high, 5 to 16 metres deep and 3 to 21 metres wide.
25 They actually range from 11 to 54 cm in height and from 12 to 26 cm in diameter.
26 Vidal 1992; Silva and Farias 1992; Müller 1992.
27 Silva and Farias 1992, Andrade 1992, Müller 1992, Vidal 1992, Gallois 1992.
28 Guapindaia, Mendonça de Souza, and Ribeiro, unpublished.
29 As in Gruta do Pocinho, Lapa do Pocinho, Gruta do Periquito, Abrigo das Caretas, Gruta das Formigas, Gruta do Baiuna, Gruta da Caba, Gruta da Jaboti and Gruta do Veado.
30 Gruta das Caretas and Lapa das Caretas.
31 The primary funerary practices parallel those recorded by Humboldt (1807), Crevaux (1883) and Roth (1924) among the indigenous peoples of South America.
32 Becher 1959, cited in Montardo 1995.
33 Viertler 1991.
34 Ferreira Penna 1877a.
35 Roth 1924; Malhano 1986; Carneiro da Cunha 1978; Guapindaia, Mendonça de Souza, and Ribeiro, unpublished manuscript.
36 Ribeiro 1987.
37 Silva and Farias 1992.
38 B.G. Ribeiro 1988.
39 Chernela 1993.
40 These urns belong to the Barbier-Müller Museum of Pre-Colombian Art in Barcelona.
41 There is no chronological or geographical information about these urns except that their provenance is the 'lower Amazon'.
42 See Nordenskiöld 1930 (plate XX) for the illustration of a similar head collected by Nimuendajú in the lower Amazon.
43 Meggers and Evans 1957
44 Goeldi 1900.
45 Nimuendajú 1926.
46 While the Cunani flows direct into the Atlantic, the Uaçá flown into Oiapoque bay and from there into the Atlantic.
47 Although they currently speak French Creole, the Galibi and Karipuna are former speakers of Carib languages. Nowadays they are spread over both Brazil and French Guyana.
48 On the Brazilian side they are settled in different villages along the Uaçá and Urucauá rivers, very close to the Atlantic Ocean and the border with French Guyana.
49 Fordred, Neves and Green 2000.
50 Grennand and Grennand 1987.
51 The colonial history of the Palikur is fascinating for it contrasts greatly with other Amazonian areas, such as the upper Rio Negro and upper Xingu basins, where historical continuity between pre-colonial times and the present was only maintained because of the marginal geographic and economic location of these areas. In the case of the Palikur continuity was maintained in spite of all the pressures brought about by contact.
52 Dreyfus 1993.
53 Roosevelt *et al.* 1991, 1996; Simões 1981a.

PART III

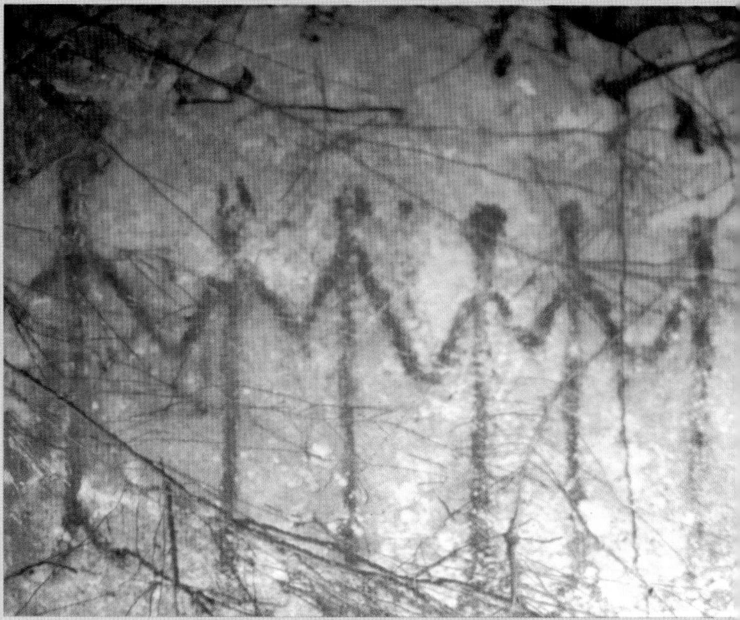

IDEOLOGY – VISUAL AND

MATERIAL CULTURE

7

Seats of Power

Axiality and Access to Invisible Worlds

COLIN MCEWAN

Introduction

Large modelled pottery figurines of imposing seated figures feature prominently in the major archaeological traditions of the middle and lower Amazon. They invariably portray an individual sitting erect in a commanding, formal pose on a small stool.[1] Why were these compelling and accomplished objects so significant? Are they idealized images of shamanic power and rulership? Do they commemorate deceased leaders and ancestors? In what kinds of ritual contexts were they deployed and how might we approach an understanding of the meanings invested in them by their makers?

Each corpus of seated figurines illustrated in this volume provides a different perspective on these questions. The Santarém vessels show naturalistic 'flesh and blood' figures with rotund torsos and pierced, elongated earlobes (see fig. 5.2). Some may perhaps have served as drinking vessels (see figs 5.11–12). The Maracá figures from the lower Amazon were clearly intended as funerary urns and placed together to form communities of seated ancestors in caves especially reserved for this purpose (see figs 6.1 and 6.5). Similar impressive hollow figurines in other styles are also said to come from the lower Amazon, although their exact provenance is not yet known (figs 7.1–2). Like the Maracá urns the heads are separately fashioned as removable lids, suggesting that these too were containers designed to hold the bones of the dead.[2]

The modelled representations of low stools is an integral element common to many of the seated figurines in these archaeological traditions and finds parallels in the wooden seats and stools still used by tropical forest groups today. Nowadays they are popularly referred to as shamans' stools, and the beliefs and practices involved in their use have been studied by anthropologists in a variety of settings.[3] However, in the tropical forest environment all organic objects, including the wooden stools, are eventually devoured or dissolved and disappear with-

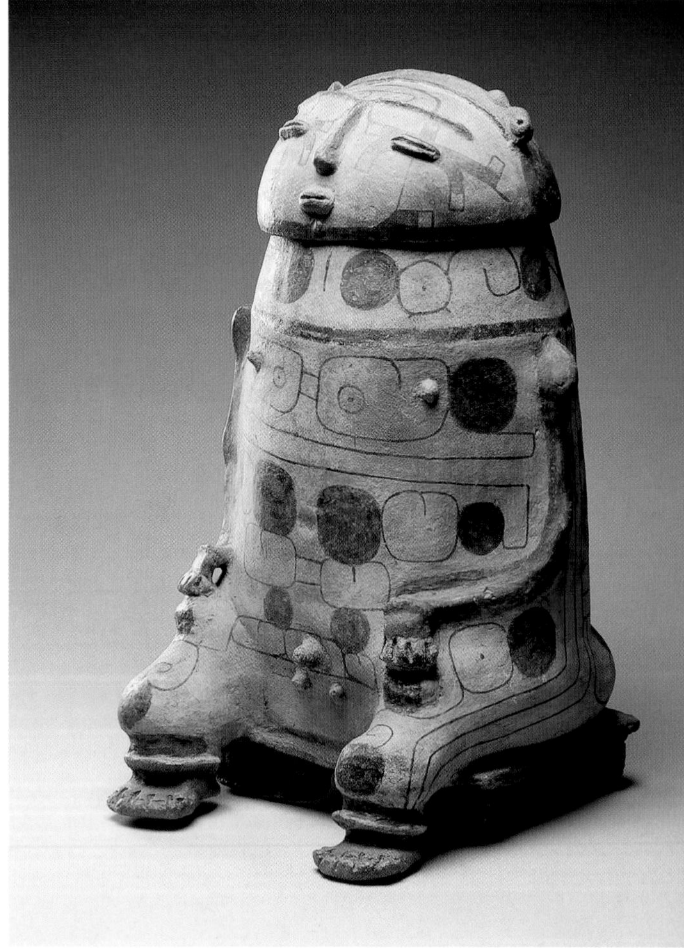

ABOVE AND RIGHT **7.1–2 Modelled representations of imposing male figures seated on low stools (above: height 63 cm, width 43 cm, depth 36 cm; right: height 39 cm, width 19 cm, depth 23 cm; Museu Barbier-Mueller Art Precolombí, Barcelona). These hollow figurines served as funerary urns to hold the bones of dead ancestors. It was considered essential to be seated in order to effect communication with the spirit world. The distinctive painted motifs suggest a possible provenance from as yet unknown archaeological cultures of the lower Amazon.**

out trace. The archaeological figurines depicting seated figures form part of the small inventory of ancient objects fashioned in pottery and stone that survive the vicissitudes of climate and time. In this essay I address the role that seats play in tropical forest cosmology, and especially their links with concepts of vertical axial connections between different levels of the universe. I will show that seats, in common with other sacred objects, bear motifs and symbols that offer a visible thread of continuity between the beliefs and practices of the present inhabitants of the Amazon basin and their precursors.

The origins of seats in the South American lowlands

The distribution of seats and stools in South America embraces a complex mosaic of regional archaeological and ethnographic traditions. These span an enormous area of the tropical forest lowlands that includes much of the Amazon basin and extends into adjacent areas of lower Central America and the Caribbean.[4] Anthropologists have long recognized that wooden stools are one of the key diagnostic traits of these lowland societies, but it is only relatively recently that the great antiquity and unexpected complexity of tropical forest culture have become apparent.[5] As we have seen elsewhere in this volume, the bluffs, floodplains and even the 'deep forest' of the middle and lower Amazon and its principal affluents once supported powerful chiefdoms engaged in continuous competition for territory, resources and prestige. The arrival of Europeans inflicted successive epidemics and disruption on indigenous societies with devastating consequences. As the vast network of competing polities disintegrated, so too did their regional systems of social organization, ranking and rulership. At least some contemporary tropical forest societies appear to represent the marginalized and relatively impoverished remnants of what were once much more complex social structures (see Neves, this volume).[6]

7.3 This is a rare example of a modelled ceramic stool or headrest decorated by a combination of incision and excision that places it within the Marajoara tradition (height 9 cm, width 22.5 cm). The designs encircling the base and on the sitting surface include curvilinear, scroll-like patterns and zoomorphic motifs that show affinities with other styles of the lower Amazon.

An idea of the role that formal seating rituals may have played must therefore be pieced together from disparate sources: the corpus of archaeological figurines, ethnohistoric descriptions given by European travellers from the seventeenth century onwards, and later, more methodical nineteenth- and twentieth-century ethnographic studies. Although the vestiges of ranking in a much truncated form have been documented by anthropologists,[7] the rapid dissolution of the more elaborate forms of ritual practice means that the full range of social and political contexts in which seats were used was never well recorded.[8] It seems likely that wooden seats and benches would have served to mark rank and status in ways at which we can now only guess. The ruptures in the social fabric were paralleled by a reduction in the range and diversity of artistic output. The corpus of wooden stools in ethnographic collections, as well as those still being made today, may not represent the full range of forms originally employed.[9]

No examples of wooden seats have yet been recovered from excavated archaeological contexts in the Amazon basin,[10] but occasional small modelled ceramic seats or headrests have turned up in museum collections. One example has designs executed in a combination of incision and excision that parallel some of the motifs and symbols found on vessels from the Marajoara and lower Amazon traditions (fig. 7.3; cf. figs 7.2 and 4.29). A distinctive kind of small circular ceramic stool or headrest with carefully structured designs incised on the upper surface and around the pedestal base is also known for Marajoara culture (fig. 7.4).[11] The organization of these

7.4 Small modelled ceramic stool or headrest. The carefully structured design on the upper surface serves as a miniature 'cosmogram' dividing the world into four quarters, at the centre of which the person seated becomes an *axis mundi* (height 17.8 cm, width 14.2 cm; Museu Nacional do Rio de Janeiro, Brazil).

designs will be discussed further ahead. Miniature modelled ceramic stools have been recovered from archaeological contexts elsewhere in the tropical forest lowlands dating as far back as the third millennium BC.[12] The fact that the archaeological distribution of seats throughout the riverine lowlands of South America corresponds closely to their ethnographic distribution implies that they have a long history of use among tropical forest groups. The seats arguably form a single related macro-tradition which has undergone divergent evolution.[13] Inevitably we must turn to ethnography to gain the kinds of insights into tropical forest cosmology that are vital to a fuller understanding of the social contexts in which seats are used.

Seats, seating and axiality in tropical forest culture

The notion of being seated embodies core precepts and beliefs and carries profound connotations among tropical forest peoples. A myth told by the Desana of the northwest Amazon tells how 'the Sun ... had his stool and his rattle staff. He had the gourd rattle and carried the hoe on his left shoulder ... everything that the shamans (*payés*) now have, the Sun had.' The Sun referred to here is the Sun Father or Primal Sun (*avé pagë*), which is the true source of all cosmic energy and is invisible to human eyes.[14] The Day Sun (*ëmë abé*), on the other hand, is the visible sun that forms part of our earthbound experience, radiates heat and light and disappears at dusk. Shamans who ascend to the upper cosmos find perpetual light from the feather crown of the Primal Sun who has remained invisible in this realm from the very beginning of creation.[15] The close relationship between seating and the Sun Father in his role as ultimate progenitor is a recurring theme in tropical forest cosmology. Other key actors in creation myths are the culture heroes of ancestral time. In order to think the world into being, they are said to have been seated on their stools like shamans, with head in hands and elbows on knees.[16] A carved wooden stool is therefore a powerful, not to say indispensable, possession for shamans, chiefs and warriors alike.

The first shaman's stool is said to have been carved out of rock.[17] While rock is the hardest and most enduring substance in the visible world, it is merely the material representation for the most enduring thing of all, which is non-substantial essence or soul matter. The cosmologies of tropical forest groups are infused with ideas of this parallel invisible world. Among the Yekuana of the upper Orinoco, for example, each village is referred to as a house *(atta)* and is not only conceived of as a self-contained universe but is actually constructed as a replica of the cosmos. Each Yekuana house is modelled on a pyramidal mountain in the centre of Yekuana-land, although it is short-lived compared to this mountain abode of the culture hero. In turn, the mountain itself is only an ephemeral representation of an invisible, spiritual house essence which is everlasting.[18] A similar set of ideas is found among the Barasana of the north-west Amazon where a mystical house, visible only to shamans, is held to be located in Jaguar Seat Mountain, near the River Pira-Paraná.[19] Likewise the supreme gods of the Warao in the Orinoco delta are said to reside on world-mountains situated at the four cardinal points.[20] Anthropologist Stephen Hugh-Jones describes how the *He*-house initiation rites among the Barasana imply a state of being prior to, and now parallel with, human existence:[21]

> All living creatures have their *He* or spirit counterparts which live in stone houses, the rapids in the rivers and the mountains and outcrops of rock. Human beings too have their *He* counterparts that live in stone-houses (*masa yuhiri wi*). The souls of new-born babies come from these houses and the souls of the dead return to them.

The power of creation is set in the distant past but it is also an ever-changeless present that encapsulates human society.[22]

Wooden stools form part of a core suite of objects that accompany the creation of human beings from spiritual origins. These same cultural objects are an essential means of access to the hidden sources of life. A range of sculpted and painted seats from regional Amazonian traditions feature caymans, turtles, jaguars (fig. 7.5) and raptorial birds of prey (fig. 7.6). Many are powerful natural predators of river, earth and sky on which men model themselves.[23] The seats are traditionally made from very dense tropical hardwoods prized for their durability. Jet black wood such as *guayacán* is often favoured for its colour and lustrous qualities when polished, and even the medicinal properties of the wood can be an important factor in its selection.[24] They are carved from a single block of wood and have either a single pedestal, bilateral feet or four legs supporting the sitting surface. The seats are portable, usually ranging between 30 and 60 cm high and between 50 and 100 cm wide, and are mostly used in and around the communal longhouse (*maloca*). The sitting surface may be a simple horizontal flat slab or a carefully sculpted shallow depression designed to accommodate the sitter's buttocks. A few larger seats and benches show twin arrangements, or extended surfaces that could have supported several individuals.[25] Many plain seats are unadorned, while others are embellished with dense abstract patterns painted in pigments of different colours. Double-headed seats are known, some with the heads of different animals on either side creating a hybrid creature which finds counterparts elsewhere in tropical forest art.

LEFT AND ABOVE **7.5–6 Sculpted wooden shamans' stools are found among a wide range of regional Amazonian traditions (left: height 20 cm, width 19 cm, length 64 cm, Museum für Völkerkunde, Vienna; above: height 27.5 cm, width 32 cm, length 61 cm, Ethnologisches Museum, Berlin). These Xinguano stools are modelled on powerful predators such as jaguars and raptorial birds, which act as mediators between the human and spirit worlds.**

Modern ethnographies of Tukanoan speakers, including the Barasana and Desana of the Uaupés drainage in the north-west Amazon basin, give us some of the best insights into the significance and use of seats in specific social contexts.[26] In these societies stools are reserved almost exclusively for use by males and are the one item above everything else that a shaman must acquire before he can practise his art. Stools are called shamans' things (*kumuno*)[27] and are identified with mountains, the abodes of spirits and the houses of spirit humans and animals that are referred to as people's waking-up houses (*masa yuhiri wi*). The word for canoe (*kumua*) shares the same root, and while canoes are used to travel on water, stools are what shamans use on land to embark on their soul journeys through the different levels of the universe.[28] The stools of ordinary men have four legs, while the shaman's stool has two legs which are said to resemble the forked tail of the swallow-tailed kite, regarded as a shamanic bird.[29] Talismanic birds, caymans, jaguars and turtles are all held to act as mediators between the human and spirit worlds in tropical forest mythology.[30]

Access to this spirit world was actively sought by exploiting a profound knowledge of the special properties of certain tropical forest plants accumulated in the course of countless centuries of experimentation and use. These were carefully prepared and ingested in a variety of ways in order to induce altered states of consciousness. The principal plants were, and still are, tobacco (*Nicotiana* spp.), the jungle vines of the genus *Banisteriopsis*, yopo (*Anadenanthera peregrina*), vihó (*Virola* sp.), coca (*Erthroxylon coca*) and several species of *Datura*.[31] Anthropologists have documented the widespread use of these powerful stimulants and hallucinogenic drugs, especially in connection with shamanistic practices.[32] The shaman must be seated in order to begin contact with the spirit world, hence activities such as smoking tobacco, consumption of *Banisteriopsis* infusions and inhaling snuff are all associated with seats.[33] Sitting on a stool is to sit 'high up' and is considered an essential element in the shaman's quest for visionary powers because it symbolizes a central, axial point of reference from which the shaman mediates, divines, chants or performs his rites and healings under carefully prescribed conditions and at the appropriate times.[34]

BELOW **7.7 Tukanoan elder sitting on a low wooden stool using an elegant sculpted and polished cigar holder to smoke a large cigar. The photograph was taken between 1903 and 1905 by Theodor Koch-Grünberg.**

Other objects are also closely associated with the preparation and consumption of certain of the hallucinogenic substances described above, and the symbols and motifs inscribed and painted on these objects express key aspects of the ideas, beliefs and experiences involved in their use. The accounts of the ways in which seats and stools are used by contemporary Amazonian groups help bring alive a sense for the role that they play in ritual practice and especially at important stages in the human life cycle, such as when young boys are to be initiated into adulthood.[35] While the upper and lower layers of the mythical cosmos are not directly accessible to ordinary experience, it is especially during initiation that they are brought within reach.[36] When seated, an individual, whether he be shaman, elder or novitiate, occupies a liminal space – on the earth but not of it.

Seats, cigars and cigar holders, and the vertical connection with invisible worlds

In the north-west Amazon the distribution of a particular kind of small wooden stool coincides with the use of giant cigars and cigar holders (see figs 7.7–9).[37] Tobacco may be among the oldest cultigens in the Americas and it is inhaled and ingested in many forms.[38] Shamanic powers are said to derive from the Sun's tobacco snuff and involve crossing the vertical layers of the universe. Together the stool, cigar and cigar holder form a complementary set of objects whose primary purpose is to facilitate access to these supernatural realms.[39] The forked cigar holder is an elegant object finely carved in a tropical hardwood and up to half a metre or more in length. It is comprised of three parts: the base, consisting of a long, tapering point to be inserted into the ground; two superimposed flat, 'hourglass'-shaped elements in the centre; and a pair of thin bifurcating prongs at the top between which the cigar is placed.[40]

OPPOSITE TOP **7.8 Detail (a) of a cigar holder showing the two central, superimposed 'hourglass'-shaped elements. The upper element has a continuous zigzag motif running around the inside border, and the lower element is inscribed with a pair of seat symbols turned sideways. The everted cigar holder (b) is interpreted by the Barasana as a man with a large penis (the cigar) protruding from between his legs.**

What might explain the distinctive form of the holder beyond the functional requirements of positioning the cigar and inserting the object in the ground, and why

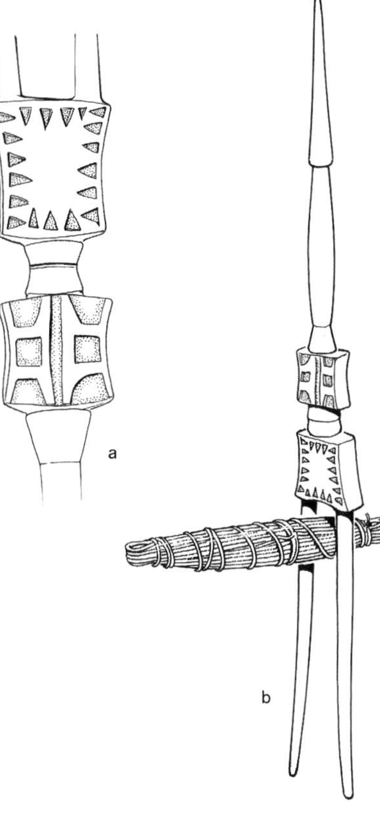

are particular symbols and motifs applied to them?[41] The two superimposed 'hourglass' elements in the central part of the holders are interpolated between the base below and the two prongs above. This distinctive dual arrangement, each with its own particular motifs, is something that we will return to below.[42] The elongated form of the cigar holder itself underlines an awareness of the vertical axial connections between superimposed realms. During its ceremonial use

> the instrument goes from hand to hand among exogamic phratries to reaffirm their alliance. The common name of the cigar holder is *murún-ge*,[43] but it is also designated as *k'ranyeá doári*.[44] This latter term expresses an act of affirmation captured in the way that the forked cigar holder is said to penetrate *Ahpikon-diá*, the paradisiacal 'river of milk' that flows under the earth mirroring the Milky Way in the night sky above. *When the lower end is firmly embedded in the ground the interpenetration is likened to that of a cosmic axis, and when contact is made, children are born and thus communication is established. The forked cigar holder is both man, and the originator of mankind* [emphasis is mine throughout the quotes in this chapter].[45]

These kinds of ritual contexts and beliefs speak of archetypal, creative acts in which human beings are materialized.[46] The use of seats is an integral part of this ritual complex and many cigar holders bear symbols on the central hourglass elements that have been identified as representing stools. A detailed view of one holder reveals that the lower element has just such a pair of seat symbols turned sideways (fig. 7.8a).[47] Pursuing the analogy of the cigar holder as 'man', Stephen Hugh-Jones notes that the Barasana word for hips is *isi kumuro* and that the pelvic bones of a human being have a slight stool-like indentation on the sides. Placed where they are on the cigar holder, the two flanking stools effectively represent the hips. When a large cigar is inserted into the cigar-holder and the object is turned upside down, the base becomes the top part of the body. Beneath this are the two stools as hips and the cigar becomes a very large penis protruding between the bifurcating prongs or 'legs' (fig. 7.8b).[48] As it is normally held with prongs uppermost, the cigar holder thus becomes an inverted male figure with his legs in the air (fig. 7.7). The act of grasping the holder to smoke the cigar therefore signals a symbolic inversion – the world turned upside down.

The upper hourglass form has a continuous zigzag motif running around the inside border (see fig. 7.8a).[49] This zigzag design is found applied in a similar fashion as a border element on other sacred objects, including ritual ceramic vessels, ceramic trumpets, signal gongs and snuff trays (see figs 7.11, 7.13 and 7.14). Likewise the two prongs of the holder terminate in spiral volutes that recall similar design elements on these sacred objects and were also painted on the facades of Desana longhouses (see fig. 12.5).

BELOW 7.9 The four corners of this Desana stool are described as being analogous to the four mountains at the edges of the known world (height 17.5 cm, width 20.5 cm, length 43 cm, Museu Nacional do Rio de Janeiro, Brazil). The upper surface of the seat is decorated with a design resembling that of a woven textile and is divided by a bisecting axial line (see fig. 7.10c).

Seating and the origins of social life: axiality and seating order in the longhouse

The Desana regard the seat as a symbol of stability and wisdom, and when someone is seated, he is said to be protected by benevolent powers. The upper surface of the seat is usually painted with a tightly organized design in black and red resembling that of woven textile held to represent this world and everything created by man (figs 7.9, 7.10a–c).[50] There is a world of meaning invested in this apparently mundane design. Far from being an incidental and repetitive 'filler' element it alludes to weaving as a defining cultural activity that informs many domains of life.[51] Woven seating mats are the quintessential cultural artefact that separate human beings from the bare earth. This weaving pattern is also found on the modelled representations of zoomorphic stools incorporated into the Maracá urns (see fig. 6.1). On some of these the seating surface exposed on either side of the seated figure is methodically scored with a similar criss-cross pattern reminiscent of a woven textile or mat. The two cultural contexts, one ethnographic and the other archaeological, are far removed in space and time, but details like these help to reinforce a sense of underlying coherence in tropical forest culture and cosmology.

The centre of the painted weaving pattern on some stools is deliberately emphasized by the insertion of a diamond-shaped element (fig. 7.10b). Others are bisected by an axial line running from back to front and therefore aligned with the orientation of the person seated (fig. 7.10c, d).[52] Notions of axiality are inextricably bound up with seats and seating in tropical forest cosmology and much of the discussion that follows will revolve around how these ideas find visible material expression in cultural objects. The concept of finding or centering an object is generally related to creative acts and plays an important role in myth and ritual. Among the Tukano the centre is associated with a female principle and is also the spot where an *axis mundi* can be placed, a connecting link between the earth and other cosmic levels that may lie above or below it.[53] Any object that serves as a symbolic *axis mundi* – be it a baton or staff, a cigar holder, a house beam as centrepost, a tree or a vine serving as a ladder – itself becomes a means of communication and, as we shall see, in another sense a phallic axis of fertilization.[54]

In the north-west Amazon selected landmarks are singled out as the origin places of mankind. Each group has its own creation story, based on dim memories of migrations or on vague traditions of its members having come from a certain direction. These favoured places are often large waterfalls surrounded by huge rocks and boulders, many of which are covered with ancient petroglyphs (see Pereira, this volume). Two such spots are of special importance to the Uaupés river Indians: the rocks of Ipanoré on the lower Uaupés, in Brazilian territory, and the Rock of Nyí, near the Meyú Falls on the Pira-paraná in Colombia (see fig. 9.9). Here the Sun Father's search for an appropriate place to bring human beings into existence culminates.[55] These sites lie almost exactly on the equatorial line and it is precisely on the equator that the sun's rays fall vertically upon the earth twice annually and where the Sun's phallic stick rattle was said to have stood upright and would have cast no shadow. The Sun Father was 'measuring the centre of the day' (*ëmë dehko*). When you stand on the equatorial line and look eastward or westward, all the star constellations appear to rise or set vertically, while seen from a few degrees to the north or south, they appear to rise and set obliquely. The equator, then, is a zone of verticality in which a direct connection is established between the celestial sphere and the earth, which is why the Creator chose this place.

Just as the sun rays falling vertically fertilize the earth, so too there is a vertical axial relationship between the sun and seating.[56] As we have already seen, seats and stools are an indispensable accessory that express a man's status as a fully fledged adult

a

b

c

d

7.10 The weaving pattern on the upper surface of many Tukanoan stools emphasizes that its male owner is seated 'high-up' in contrast to women who are usually seated on the ground. The centre of the pattern may be emphasized by a diamond (b), a bisecting axial line (c) or, as in the case of one example from the upper Xingu, a quadripartite design (d).

member of society. The stools figure prominently in initiation rites – a time when the elders confront young boys with the new social roles and responsibilities that they are about to assume and guide them through ritual trials and ordeals toward adulthood. During the *He*-house initiation rite among the Barasana the shamans and elders sit on stools while the young men about to be initiated sit on mats on the floor.[57] Special old stools are reserved for use during this rite. When seats are used by groups of elders they follow a carefully prescribed arrangement within the *maloca*. Among the Desana, for example, Reichel-Dolmatoff describes how

> the longhouse (*maloca*) is the uterus of the sib [community] and as such its structure corresponds to that of the Cosmos. The most important part of the structure is formed by the 'three red jaguars', represented by three pairs of large forked posts and their respective beams, located at the two extremes and in the centre of the building. These three 'jaguars', which are sometimes painted red and adorned with black spots, are interpreted as the guardians and the most important fecundating forces of the dwelling; they 'cover' the occupants. Another important structural unit is formed by a large longitudinal beam that links the three jaguars horizontally and in turn is connected by vertical supports to another large beam that forms the ridge of the roof. This central beam is called *gumu* and is thought to be the representation of the Sun priest (*kumu*). Although it is laid horizontally, it has the meaning of a 'ladder' that penetrates the cosmic levels and forms an axis[58] … The central dividing line in a transverse direction is thought to be indicated by the 'second jaguar',[59] which in its mythical journey travelled from east to west. At the centre of this line, which is the true centre of the longhouse, a wooden seat is placed from which the shaman officiates and recites on the occasion of reunions. It is also the place where the dancers adorn themselves before a feast. It is the most important sacred spot in the maloca: it was the Sun who put this power there.[60]

An analogous set of concepts is embedded in the Yekuana house, as described by Guss:

> Emphasising the four corners of the world, the crossbeams are arranged on an exact North-South axis, with two doors positioned directly below them and two more precisely along the East-West axis. The ten additional beams that form the roof's infrastructure are called 'sky trees' (*hiononoi*), paralleling similar structures said to hold up Heaven itself. All twelve of these roof beams stand just like *kahuna* on the 'star supports', which in the case of the *atta* are the twelve *sidityadi* posts encircling the entire structure. Passing through the middle of the roof to the outside is a long post (*nunudu*),[61] made from one of several species of hardwoods, which extends to the very centre of the house floor. This post is the clearest expression of each village's distinctive place at the centre of the world.[62] It represents the centerpost of the universe, the *axis mundi* by which the two worlds, the visible and invisible, are connected and through which they maintain contact. Here the men gather daily to confer, share food, and do craftwork. It is also where shamans perform their cures and elders discuss their dreams.

In these kinds of social contexts it is worth recalling the small circular ceramic stool or headrest referred to earlier and comparing it with a contemporary wooden jaguar stool. Both have variants of a quadripartite division of the seating surface centred on the middle of the stool (compare figs 7.4 and 7.10d).[63] An analogous arrangement featuring a quadripartite design at the centre of a circular stool is found among the Cashinahua of the upper Amazon.[64] Thus placed, each design functions as a miniature 'cosmogram' organized around a central point of reference. The seated owner is implicitly identified as an individual *axis mundi*; and in turn, on ritual occasions, an assembly of seated individuals would have been housed within the body of the longhouse, the centre post(s) of which served as a 'collective' *axis mundi* for the community, connecting it to the invisible cosmos.

Banisteriopsis and access to invisible worlds

In 1852 the British botanist and explorer Richard Spruce first described the effects of the hallucinogenic vine *Banisteriopsis* when travelling among the Tukano Indians of the north-west Amazon.[65] He observed the bark of the vine being used to prepare an infusion in a special ritual vessel, and also noted that the ground-up bark was occasionally ingested as a finely powdered snuff. The form of these vessels sets them apart from all other domestic wares used for preparing and cooking food (see fig. 7.11a). They stand on a cylindrical pedestal that elevates the body of the vessel (and its potent contents) literally and metaphorically 'off the ground'. These vessels bear distinctive designs and motifs painted in different combinations of bold yellow, white and black pigments.[66] The design applied to the vessel illustrated here is painted in an intense yellow. A continuous zigzag motif runs around the mouth and is repeated around the base of the globular portion of the vessel just above the top of the pedestal. Effectively the hallucinogenic infusion is 'framed' between these bordering zigzag motifs that delimit the top and bottom of the body of the vessel. An opposed pair of vertically aligned bifurcating volutes flanking a central vertical element occupies the medial space: one pair projects downwards from the vessel rim, and the other pair emanates upwards from the base of the vessel. Between the upper and lower volutes lies a horizontal hourglass shape similar in form to the superimposed medial elements found on the cigar holders (see fig. 12.11 for an analogous arrangement).

Preparation and consumption of the *Banisteriopsis* infusion is intimately linked to night-long collective ceremonies, celebrated with the purpose of entering a mythical dimension in which the participants become witnesses to creation.[67] The potion may also be consumed on the occasion of ritual meetings between allies when there is gift exchange accompanied by drinking bouts, dances and songs. Likewise it is shared at important stages in the life cycle such as initiation rituals, and during certain hunting or harvesting rituals. Sometimes only the shamans drink the infusion, or perhaps just a shaman and a patient whose illness he is trying to diagnose and cure.

Reichel-Dolmatoff describes how during such communal convocations *Banisteriopsis* is consumed only by adult men. They sit in a semi-circle facing the interior of the longhouse, while the women are gathered in the dark rear of the building. In the course of the night some eight or ten small cups of the potion are distributed, while the men dance, sing and play different musical instruments such as flutes, pan-pipes and horns, accompanied by the sounds of seed and gourd rattles.[68] Among these instruments is a ceramic trumpet from the north-west Amazon bearing bifurcating volutes similar to those on the ritual *Banisteriopsis* vessel (see fig.

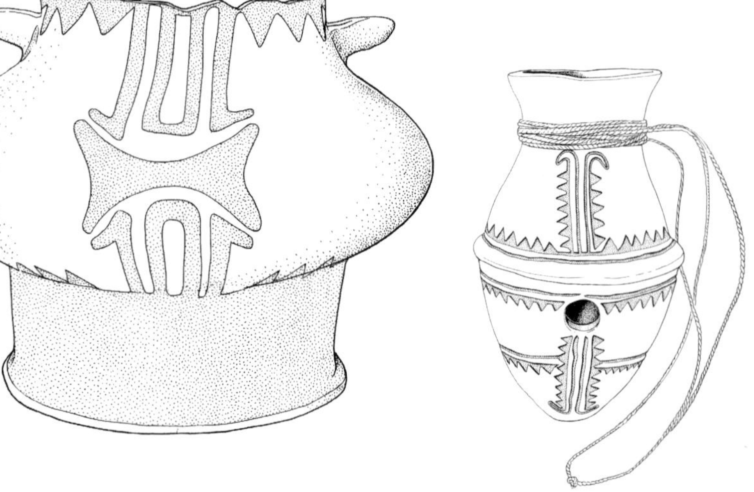

7.11 A special vessel for preparing an infusion of the hallucinogenic *Banisteriopsis caapi* (left: a) and a ceramic trumpet (right: b; height 24 cm). Both feature zigzag motifs as liminal elements placed around the lip and the circumference respectively. Each also has a variation of the distinctive bifurcating 'curling volute' motif.

7.11b). The trumpet is formed by two cones joined at the base with a small aperture close to the medial flange and an opening at one end. The pair of volutes emanates vertically upwards and downwards respectively from the union of the two halves. A continuous zigzag band runs around the circumference of the instrument and also as a fringing element along the volutes. The trumpet is called *gahpi soro* and it symbolizes the vagina of the Daughter of the Sun.[69] It is played while touching the opening rhythmically with the palm of the hand and blowing across the circular orifice located on the upper surface.

Reichel-Dolmatoff goes on to describe how from time to time the women will emerge from the darkness and take part in the dance, only to disappear again after a while. The entire scene is extremely formalized and solemn. The rhythm of the dance becomes more and more coordinated, and dance steps and gestures reach a precision that makes the group appear to be one single organism moving in a highly controlled and precise way. Song and dance become completely fused.[70] The following description is based on Reichel-Dolmatoff's own personal experience of imbibing a *Banisteriopsis* infusion and then recording the kinds of visual effects and perceptual transformations that it produces (emphasis is mine throughout the quotes in this chapter):

> *Banisteriopsis* visions are very colourful. After the first few cups, and after an initial tremor and the sensation of rushing winds, the drug produces a state of drowsiness during which the person concentrates with half-closed eyes on the luminous flashes and streaks which appear in his visual field. This first stage is characterised by the appearance of small, star-shaped or flower-shaped elements which flicker and float brilliantly against a dark background, in kaleidoscopic patterns. There is a marked bilateral symmetry to these luminous perceptions, which sometimes appear as clusters of fruits or feathery leaves. *Grid patterns, hexagons, zigzag lines and undulating lines, rapidly vibrating lines, eye-shaped motifs, many-coloured concentric circles or chains of dots slowly float by, combining and recombining in ever new patterns and changing colours*. The visions appear in horizontal bands or stripes, slightly vibrating and approaching or receding. After a while, the symmetry and the overall geometrical aspect of these perceptions disappears and a second stage sets in … Now large blots of colour will be seen moving like thunder-clouds, and from them emerge diffuse shapes looking like people or animals, or unknown creatures. The Indians interpret these shapes as mythological scenes peopled by ancestors and spirit beings; visions which, to them, bear proof of the essential truth of their cosmogonic and religious beliefs. This is a highly emotion-charged stage, and people gesticulate while talking and singing, but generally look at the floor before them. Eventually all these images disappear; there will be soft music and shapes like wandering clouds, and the men sit silently in a state of blissful serenity.[71]

He observes that the second stage is marked by the onset of true hallucinations. During a *Banisteriopsis* ceremony shamans ask individual participants about aspects of their hallucinations, and explain the range of shapes, colours and motions in terms of mythological scenes or forest spirits, ancestral beings, Tree People, game animals, spirits and others. The mythical scenes seen by the Tukanoans during this second stage of the drug experience can be seen by members of their society alone.

The function of *Banisteriopsis*, then, is to transport people into an ancestral state – to connect past and present.[72] The more sacred the ritual, the stronger the

Banisteriopsis required and the closer the participant comes into contact with the original ancestors. Indians say that the river system of the earth is a *Banisteriopsis* vine connecting longhouse communities to the ancestral east in the same way as an umbilical cord, and that when the vine is cut for use, the scar this leaves is a navel. *Banisteriopsis* is also identified with the fearsome anaconda – a great water snake that is the supreme self-propelling water vehicle.[73] Christine Hugh-Jones describes how:

> Besides creating the ritual in the sense of making the participants perform in the appropriate way, the *banisteriopsis* also creates an alternative experience of time and space to the everyday one. Those who drink it see and hear things beyond everyday reality. Although their souls remain within their bodies it is, as one informant put it, 'as if we were so large that the universe is small by comparison and we can see everything'. Indians also say that the house becomes the universe during the ritual so that the men's door becomes the eastern entrance to the earth we inhabit. Much of the chanting 'shown by *banisteriopsis*' is about the mythical associations of the landmarks on the journey upriver from the eastern entrance made by the group of ancestors. The chanters actually identify themselves with these ancestors, saying, 'We, Fish Anaconda Son (or some other group ancestors) came up river and...', demonstrating that, *although they do not move from their stools, they are travelling in time and space.* The accounts of *banisteriopsis* visions which are filled with anacondas, jaguars, ancestral houses and distant geographical settings fit with this 'ritual frame' achieved by *banisteriopsis*. Indians say that the hallucinations are produced by *banisteriopsis* in the form of an anaconda which, having entered the body, thrashes around inside and slides out as a stream of vomit. Thus, the anaconda form of the ancestors within the universe is united with the anaconda form of the *banisteriopsis* within the bodies of the participants.[74]

Consumption of *Banisteriopsis* facilitates access to an invisible world of creative energy that animates the natural world. The invisible Primal Sun is said to emit a beneficial energy known as *bogá*. Energy flows (*bogá*) and circuits (*dari, dariri*) regulate the reproductive and productive cycles in the forest, river, garden and village, as well as between animals and people.[75] Again we have recourse to Reichel-Dolmatoff's description of how this concentrated energy is composed of three distinct aspects:

> In the first place, *bogá* combines male and female principles in which the concept of 'force' (*turári*) is clearly distinguished from that of 'energy' (*bogá*), the former providing motion and intensity to the latter. *Another spectrum of chromatic energies is called* dári, *meaning 'rays' or 'threads'* (abé dári/*sun threads), a term that can also be applied to a string, a thread, or a vine. The so-called* dári *threads are said to flow in space in a straight line or in a broken line, and appear in a multitude of yellow, orange, and red hues which represent an energy range from male insemination to female fecundity. Dári* threads contain energies not only in a biological sense, but also transmit cultural norms referring to the traditional knowledge of environmental adaptation. A group of wavy threads called *daríri* has a colour range from green and blue to violet. It transmits energies to women relating to their menstrual cycle, and also to plants in which it determines their growth cycles. A third group of threads is called *~náriri*; in trying to explain this sensation, shamans mention phenomena such as heat waves, a slight tremor of the hands, or a scintillating, glimmering sensation on water or wet leaves.

These are *closely serrated lines* which appear in all colours of the spectrum. Another group of *bogá* energies is related to intra-uterine developments and consists of *dot-shaped elements* called *~marári*, *noméri*, and *dobéri*.[76]

Bogá contains another pair of energies that serve quite specific ends. They are called *savéri-da* and *yëbëri-da*, and relate to different stages of plant growth. Reichel-Dolmatoff continues:

> *The term* savéri *refers to incipient growth, to dormant and axillary buds, while* **yëbëri** *indicates ripeness. These two categories of 'threads'* (dári) *energize all plant-life, from the smallest herbs to the tall canopy trees of the dense rainforest.* ~Marári *refers to tiny luminous spots or particles people are said to perceive during drug-induced hallucinations, or in a variety of states of high emotional involvement.* The appearance of *~marári* spots in hallucinations or similar states is technically known as phosphenes. In the literature they are described as very small, many-coloured glowing points, dancing and moving, which the Indians compare with pollen, sand, smoke, sperm, very small seeds, the Milky Way, and fish spawn in a river. All these and similar phenomena in nature or in imagination are said to have a seminal character and, according to the Indians, to perceive *~marári* dots is to become aware of a seminal element, of insemination, of potential biogenesis.[77]

The energy that permeates and enlivens all forms of organic growth therefore consists of two complementary generative forces – one coming from the sun above and the other from below within budding and sprouting plant forms. These creative energies drive the spiralling, unfolding processes of growth that characterize organic life. All these energies emanating from the invisible sun – the seminal threads, embryogenic dots and budding sprouts – are associated with a complete colour spectrum, range of odours, flavours, sounds, shapes, textures, temperatures and other properties, which, in turn, are subdivided into categories indicating hues and intensities. A shaman's power (*turári*) consists in his ability to arrange and harmonize this multitude of energies, to interpret them, and balance them in case he should become aware of any disequilibrium.[78] This world, which is ordinarily invisible, is rendered accessible under the influence of hallucinogens. The perceptual threshold between ordinary reality and this hidden world is marked by powerful impressions of zigzag, serrated and undulating lines as well as geometric forms and glowing points of light. These seem to be precisely the visual elements that inspire many of the motifs and designs in north-west Amazonian art.

At the boundary between the visible and invisible: liminal imagery on sacred objects

Large signal drums once played an integral part in the life of the towns and settlements along all the main waterways of the Amazon (fig. 7.12). They were played at dawn on the day of significant community gatherings, and in the past they were also used to call warriors to arms on occasions of intertribal war.[79] In ritual practice their use was linked to both seats as well as to other sacred instruments.

The drums were carved in the form of a thick, hollow cylinder from a single tree trunk, usually using the same wood as for making canoes. They had a longitudinal opening at the top in the form of a straight slit punctuated at intervals by two or more circular perforations. The instrument was suspended horizontally from liana ropes held up by a frame of four thick stakes and placed in front of the longhouse near the main door. It seems that when the drum was positioned to be played it

7.12 Group of Tukano indians from the north-west Amazon posed before a *maloca*, in front of which a signal drum is suspended from four posts. The photograph was taken between 1903 and 1905 by Theodor Koch-Grünberg.

would have been rotated slightly so that the longitudinal slit was angled toward the drummer.[80] The designs on the body of the drum illustrated here are arranged horizontally in three superimposed bands (fig. 7.13b). The uppermost band consists of two pairs of nested concentric semi-circles which would have faced skyward. Below this a medial band is filled with a repeated diamond pattern. The lower edge of the medial band is marked by a continuous line of zigzag motifs beneath which lies the undecorated base of the drum. The diamonds and stripes of the medial band are said to represent *pamurí-gahsíru*, the Snake-Canoe. In fact the drum was considered to be a replica of the Snake-Canoe in which humanity arrived, and signal drums are described by Tukanoan groups as ancestral anacondas who vomited up the first people from their insides.[81] When people drink beer they also vomit. The ancestral anacondas are referred to in Tukano as 'fermentation anaconda', which makes the anaconda itself into a kind of beer trough.[82] People are quite often buried in beer troughs or canoes to travel through the underworld. The body is usually cremated before burial and the ashes placed in these troughs and sometimes drunk with beer.

Each end of the drum is painted with bold designs in vivid yellow and white pigment (see fig. 7.13a and c).[83] The designs have structural similarities but differ in important details. Both ends of the drum have a continuous bordering zigzag motif running round the outside edge.[84] Both also have a pair of aligned vertical elements terminating in divergent volutes or scrolls that emanate from the edge of the top and bottom of the drum respectively. Surviving drawings and photographs show that the drum was positioned so that these elements did indeed stand vertically in relation to the ground.[85] The aligned vertical elements at either end do not actually meet at the centre of the drum, but are separated by a third element. At one end (fig. 7.13a) the vertical element emanating from the top is flanked by two serrated volutes or scrolls. Beneath it a simplified vertical motif has a single row of dots running up the middle.

Between the two vertical elements lie a pair of semi-circular crescent motifs lying back to back with the vertical element nested in the concavity of each. Each crescent has a row of dots running along the middle, similar to that on the vertical element beneath.[86] The design is completed by a pair of flanking circular symbols with serrated edges positioned in the space between the arms of the crescent and another smaller pair on either side of the vertical element beneath. On the other end of the drum both the vertical elements in the design are again filled with dots and are flanked by the serrated volutes or scrolls already described (compare figs 7.13c and 7.13a). At this end between the two vertical elements lies the distinctive hourglass shape. It is flanked by just one pair of semi-lunar crescents with serrated margins.

7.13 The diamond pattern painted on the body of a signal drum (b) identifies it as the Snake Canoe from which the first human beings emerged (Museu de Arqueologia e Etnologia da Universidad de São Paulo). The opposed vertical 'curling volute' motifs at either end of the drum (a and c) represent the complementary generative forces responsible for all organic growth.

The way in which the volutes extend from above and below towards the centre of the drum, where the distinctive hourglass shape occupies the medial space, replicates the symbolic inversion along a vertical axis described earlier for the cigar holders.

The placement of the zigzag band around the perimeter of both ends of the drum and along the lower border of the design on the body underlines its function as a liminal motif. It is consistently placed at the edges and boundary planes of physical objects and therefore marks the threshold between the visible material world and the invisible spirit world. Reichel-Dolmatoff's comparative study of phosphene-derived images and geometrical patterns suggests that these acquire a practical function in that they have become graphic symbols, or signs, which express the major tenets of Tukanoan society. Certain motifs stood for specific concepts: a bifid or bifurcating form of divergent volutes or scrolls is said to represent the male genitals, while a U-shaped element symbolizes a vagina, a 'door' or a labyrinth (cf. the juxtaposition of these motifs in fig. 7.13a). The opposed vertical elements with their divergent volutes or scrolls that project from above and below can therefore be seen as analogous to the opposing but complementary generative principles described earlier. The vertical axis penetrating from above can be likened to the Sun's generative power. As the Sun Father's representative, the visible sun pervades the universe with a fertilizing life force. It regulates the seasons and, therefore, controls all plant and animal life.[87] Conversely the vertical axis projecting upwards from below corresponds to the forces of growth, budding and sprouting emanating from within the earth.

The union of procreative forces is potentially at its strongest and most effective when the celestial and chthonic forces are aligned in a direct relationship along a vertical axis. This is precisely when the invisible procreative energies erupt into and impregnate ordinary material existence. This union is consummated in the centre or earthly plane marked by the medial crescents at one end (fig. 7.13a) and the hourglass motif at the other (7.13c). The contrast between these two motifs on this particular drum is intriguing. The hourglass motif may represent the material world moulded rather than penetrated by the energies impinging upon it from above and below.

The principal elements and motifs on the drum parallel those already described for the cigar holder, the *Banisteriopsis* vessel and the ceramic trumpet. Similar imagery is found on other sacred objects and instruments including hollow 'thumping tubes', used in ritual chants and songs, as well as on longhouse facades.[88] A complex set of metaphoric associations therefore links the stools, signal gongs, canoes, cigar holders, gourd rattles and trumpets. The fact that the motifs I have described are so consistently applied confers a sense of underlying coherence and relatedness to this body of sacred objects. It suggests that each functioned in particular ritual settings to open access to the invisible, generative sources of life.

7.14 Indian holding a snuff tray from which he is about to ingest snuff through a special bifurcating inhaler. Note the zigzag motif that frames the central depression used to place the snuff. From Alexandre Rodrigues Ferreira, *Viagem Filosófica* (1783–92).

In considering the processes by which all cultural artefacts are extracted and formed from natural materials, David Guss describes how the Yekuana recognize that

> in order to create culture, as represented by the material forms that constitute it such as canoes and drums, one must be able to integrate into it the wild and untamed. This demands much more than simple technical expertise. With every object possessing an invisible double of incalculable power, humans must be able to control the unseen as well as the seen when negotiating the conversion of wild objects into domestic ones. The ritual performance that accompanies every technical activity guarantees that the incorporation of this potentially dangerous new and foreign [element] will not be disruptive. The material transformation of any object – such as a tree to a drum, or an animal to food – must be accompanied as well by a spiritual transformation realigning its symbolic structure with that of the human world into which it is being integrated. It is this humanisation process so fundamental to every material activity, that is the real subject of myths of origin. By recounting how each object was retrieved from the forces of darkness beyond the ordered world of the *atta*, they become models for the process of transformation by which culture itself is created.[89]

This process of transformation from wild to domesticated can, under certain conditions, be reversed. This is made explicit in the last set of objects that I now turn to.

Snuff and shaman-jaguar transformation

Throughout the lowland tropics the hallucinogens described here play an instrumental role in widespread ideas concerning shaman-jaguar transformation.[90] One of the best-known tropical lowland hallucinogens is *yopo* or *cohoba* made from the seeds of *Anandenanthera peregina*, which are ground, roasted, mixed with lime and snuffed (see fig. 7.14).[91] Some of the most expressive and telling imagery connected with altered states of being is to be found on the ritual paraphernalia associated with the preparation and consumption of this powerful snuff.

The imagery carved on the snuff trays from which the powder is ingested reveals the kind of experience that the user is about to embark upon.[92] The handles often assume the form of an anaconda and the object was held in such a way that the user would be faced with the recurved head of the serpent (see fig. 7.14). The outline of a human figure that has been swallowed by the snake is often clearly visible in the body. Just as large constrictors, whether in water or on land, first crush then swallow their prey including, occasionally, unwary humans, so too the shaman who ingests the snuff is said to journey back into the body of the ancestral anaconda. The tray always has a carefully delineated central space onto which the snuff was

7.15 Snuff tray with recurved head in the form of a snake, probably an anaconda (height 4 cm, width 12 cm, length 35 cm; British Museum). The circular central depression for holding the snuff is enclosed by serpentine designs.

placed (fig. 7.15); it is set lower than the surrounding surface and may be square, rectangular or circular. In the example illustrated here (fig. 7.14) the stepped depression in the centre is demarcated by the kind of bordering serrated motif observed on other objects. Once again this motif serves to mark the threshold between the everyday world and a different order of reality.

We have already seen how, in addition to being inhaled by smoking, tobacco can be ingested in the form of snuff. Anthropologist Johannes Wilbert has examined the combination of nicotine-associated physiological, neuropsychological and cultural factors that constitute what he describes as the essential ingredients of 'were-jaguar' shamanism. Shamans assume aggressive postures in their battle against the powers of disintegration such as evil spirits, sorcerers, sterility, sickness and death.[93] Wilbert notes that there are several tobacco-related characteristics of the tobacco shaman that must have likened him to the jaguar, including acuteness of vision, night vision, wakefulness, a raspy voice, a furred or rough tongue and a pungent body odour. The shamanic neophyte, who through ingestion of tobacco receives acute near-vision

7.16 Stone mortar sculpted in the form of a supernatural jaguar possessing a crouching human figure (height 17.8 cm, width 12.3 cm, length 5.8 cm; Etnografiska Museet I Göteborg). The object has a depression in its back (visible in profile) that was probably used to grind the seeds of *Anadenanthera peregrina* to produce a hallucinogenic snuff.

during the day, and the mature shaman, who as a result of advanced nicotine intoxication obtains night vision, need little convincing to consider themselves related to such keen-eyed animals as felines.[94]

A stone mortar is a key artefact used to prepare snuffs (fig. 7.16). This object has a recess at the top in which the seeds were ground into powder using a suitable pestle. Some mortars are powerful miniature masterpieces with a palpable sense of monumentality that belies their small size. The compelling imagery – in this case a powerful supernatural feline, presumably a jaguar, in the act of possessing a crouching human figure – graphically captures the so-called were-jaguar in action.

Conclusion

I began this essay by asking why large figurines of seated figures are apparently so important among the archaeological cultures of the Amazon basin. The individual objects are often far removed in time and space from one another. What binds them together? By exploring the beliefs and activities that are associated with shamans' seats and other ritual paraphernalia among ethnographic cultures (especially those of the north-west Amazon), I have tried to provide a context for understanding the significance these figures may have had for their makers. Their erect posture echoes a concern with vertical, axial connections that is a central tenet of tropical forest cosmologies to this day. The archaeological figures are material embodiments of meanings and beliefs that are intimately bound up with the invisible sources of life. The boundary between the visible and invisible worlds is, I suggest, signalled on material objects in consistent ways that can be recognized and understood. Living shamans and leaders mediate between human communities and these invisible sources of life. Death entails the disintegration of the physical body and the reversion to immaterial existence. As funerary urns containing the bones of the dead, the seated figures preserve the memory of corporeality in visible form. They stand guardian-like at the threshold between visible materiality and the invisible but ever-present spirit world.

Acknowledgements

I am grateful to Peter Rivière, Stephen Hugh-Jones, Warwick Bray, José Oliver and Edward de Bock for valued suggestions and comments, and to Cristiana Barreto and Eduardo Neves for sharing the memorable journeys that made it possible to piece together key pieces in this puzzle. My debt to anthropologists past and present who have worked with Amazonian tropical forest groups is evident at every turn.

NOTES

1. From the time of their initial contact with lowland societies, European travellers describe carved wooden seats and stools of many different kinds. See e.g. Acuña 1941; Wallace 1889: 193, 342.
2. Seated figures in the form of funerary urns (or on the lids of funerary urns) are found throughout the tropical lowlands and in many neighbouring Andean cultures. The torso is formed by the body of the vessel that contains the bones or ashes of the dead. These vessels establish a visible and unequivocal link between seated figures and dead ancestors.
3. Although they have collectively come to be known as 'shamans' stools', ownership was not the prerogative of shamans alone. Stools were used in a range of other ritual as well as secular contexts and many were recognized as being the special privilege of chiefs.
4. Marshall Saville was the first investigator to compile an illustrated list of archaeological and ethnographic examples of seats and stools from South and Central America (see Saville 1910: pls I–III). At the turn of the century he culled the documentary sources for descriptions of seats to complement his field studies, and sought to demonstrate an evolution in the form of the wooden seats towards what he characterized as the 'classic', high-armed Manteño (AD 1000–1500) seats from coastal Ecuador sculpted in stone (Saville 1910: 104–23). Roth also published a table of illustrations intended to 'show the evolution of the bench in regard to symmetry, shape and animal representation'. (Roth 1924: fig. 81). More recently, Zerries has traced the ethnographic distribution of wooden stools in the tropical lowlands (Zerries 1970, 1985). Stahl (1988) lists archaeological representations of zoomorphic stools. The distribution of archaeological representations of seated figures in the form of pottery figurines and funerary urns offers indirect evidence for the prehistoric use of seats. In addition to the Manteño corpus, stone seats are

also known in Panama, Costa Rica and the Greater Antilles. Rare examples of wooden seats have also been found on the north coast of Peru (Chimú) and in the Andean highlands (Inca), the form and iconography of which points to tropical forest antecedents. For a recent survey of seats in the Caribbean area see Ostapkowicz 1998.

5. See e.g. Lathrap 1970, Roosevelt *et al.* 1991, 1996 and Roosevelt 1999b.

6. Lathrap 1968a. See also Politis, this volume, for discussion of this issue.

7. See discussion in S. Hugh-Jones 1979 and C. Hugh-Jones 1979; see also Hartmann 1974.

8. A handful of early written accounts offers a glimpse of formal seating rituals. See e.g. Pineda 1994 for a review of ethnohistoric descriptions of seats in the northern Andes.

9. There is in fact almost no substantial evidence in terms of surviving wooden seats to back this assertion up over the period that we are concerned with. However, in terms of ceramic production, stylistic devolution involving a reduction in the range of vessel forms and simplification of the design repertoire is well documented.

10. Elsewhere in South America wooden seats that probably pre-date European contact occasionally survive as in the case of the Chimú and Inca examples already referred to and Taíno stools from the Caribbean.

11. Similar circular ceramic stools are also found in the Guangala tradition of the coastal lowlands of Ecuador, west of the Andes. The parallels are striking although no direct historical links are inferred.

12. In an unpublished paper Lathrap, Zerries and Norton (n.d.) discuss the range of small clay models of shamans' stools that have been excavated at archaeological sites in the tropical forest lowlands in diverse early formative contexts such as Momil (northern Colombia) and at Valdivia sites on the coast of Ecuador. See e.g. Lathrap *et al.* 1977: figs 117–20, Reichel-Dolmatoff and Dussan de Reichel (1956: 11, 216–17, pl. XX), Meggers and Evans 1961.

13. A comparable macro-tradition also developed independently in equatorial Africa (see e.g. McLeod 1981).

14. Reichel-Dolmatoff 1996a: 59; C. Hugh-Jones 1979: 264.

15. The sun we know in present existence is merely his shadow or remnant (C. Hugh-Jones 1979: 263–4). Hugh-Jones goes on to note that the Pleiades are a present-day manifestation of Romi Komu, only visible at night and during part of the year, whereas Romi Komu as an ancestral figure is permanently in the sky. Present natural weather phenomena and heavenly bodies are representatives of the ancestral ones, which in certain ritual and shamanic contexts – for instance, when shamans travel into the sky – become the ancestral ones.

16. Roe 1995: 52.

17. Peter Rivière (pers. comm.) has pointed out that hardness is an important quality of an individual's condition. A healthy adult is hard in the sense that the whole body, i.e. its different components, are firmly joined together. The tight binding of forearms and calves to make them bulge is expressive of this. Hardness is enduring: the harder something is, the longer it survives. In the human body the opposition is between bones and flesh – after death the former survives much longer. But what endures even longer than either is 'soul stuff'.

18. It is said that Wanadi (the culture hero) himself came down to Earth to reveal the structure of this sacred house to the Yekuana by building the first one in Kushamakari. Today this house can be seen in the form of a mountain located in the centre of the Yekuana homeland. The *atta* that Wanadi built and on which all Yekuana houses have subsequently been modelled was based on his own house – the entire world of Kahuna or heaven. Each of the *atta's* components therefore represents and takes the name of a part of the landscape of this invisible world. Guss 1989: 21.

19. See front jacket illustration of *Under the Milk River* (C. Hugh-Jones 1979) drawn by a Barasana shaman. See also Reichel-Dolmatoff 1975: 192 for a description of Tukanoan concepts of a parallel, invisible spirit world matching our world of empirical reality.

20. See Wilbert 1987: 178. Other deities are located at the intercardinal and solstitial points along the *aitona*, the horizon, the end of the world, as well as at the nadir and the zenith (see discussion of axiality ahead).

21. S. Hugh-Jones 1979: 9.

22. Ibid: 9, 139.

23. See e.g. Roe 1995: 54–5 for a range of zoomorphic stools. Just as both plain stools and zoomorphic stools are found among contemporary groups, so too both are represented in archaeological figurines. Some of the stools in the Maracá funerary urns are clearly zoomorphic (feline?) with diminutive modelled head and tail (see Guapandaia, this volume).

24. See e.g. Lovén 1935: 540; Helms 1986: 25–44; in the Caribbean *guayacán* (*Gúaicacum officuiale*) is the wood of choice, its blackness carrying connotations of night and sacred time representing an inversion of diurnal ordinary time.

25. Zerries 1970: figs 1 and 2.

26. See especially Reichel-Dolmatoff 1975, S. Hugh-Jones 1979. The modern Tukanoan groups of the north-west Amazon basin are of course far distant in time and space from the archaeological cultures of the Lower Amazon that produced the most striking seated figurines. Precisely because of their relative isolation a greater range of material culture has been recorded and collected by travellers and anthropologists from the late nineteenth century on up to the present day. This offers perhaps the best chance therefore of exploring the questions addressed here.

27. *Yai-kumuno/payé*'s stool or *gahpi kumono/yaje* stool (*yaje* is the term commonly used in Colombia for *Banisteriopsis*); Reichel-Dolmatoff 1975: 81.

28. I am grateful to Stephen Hugh-Jones for sharing this observation. See also Reichel-Dolmatoff 1975: 154 who also describes the zigzag designs found on some stools as associated with the Anaconda-Canoe.

29. Reichel-Dolmatoff 1986: 59, 138–9; 1988: 55.

30. See e.g. Roe 1995: 52–5.

31. Reichel-Dolmatoff 1997: 243.

32. The preparation and consumption of these plants usually involve complex ritual paraphernalia. Much of the special equipment and devices such as bowls, snuffing tubes, cigar holders, plates and trays are fashioned from perishable materials including wood and bone, and bound with natural fibres and resins, very little or none of which is likely to survive, save in the most fortuitous circumstances. Those made of pottery (see fig. 7.11 of a *caapi* vessel) or fashioned from stone on the other hand can potentially be recovered archaeologically (see fig. 7.15 of a lithic sculpture in the form of a mortar for grinding snuff).

33. Zerries 1970, 1985. In the Caribbean the *duho* is used for the consumption of *cohoba*.

34. S. Hugh-Jones (1979: 121) and Reichel-Dolmatoff (1988: 55); seated on a bench one 'thinks hard' with concentration, Reichel-Dolmatoff 1971: 110–11.

35. Reichel-Dolmatoff 1978a: 23; cf. Hartmann 1974; Zerries 1970.

36. C. Hugh-Jones 1979: 262.

37. Koch-Grünberg 1909; Wilbert 1972, 1975a, 1987: 91–5.

38. Wilbert 1987: xvii. Wilbert's *Tobacco and Shamanism in South America* is a thorough and authoritative treatment of the subject. In the preface he notes that ritual tobacco is certainly much older than the available archaeological evidence suggests. 'Reaching back to the beginnings of lowland South American agriculture some eight thousand years ago, and possibly even antedating the domestication of food plants, the parent species of the hybrids *Nicotiana rustica* and *N. tabacum* may be the oldest cultigens in the Americas'; Reichel-Dolmatoff 1986: 13; Furst 1976: 27; see also Oliver, this volume.

39. In the drawing by a Barasana shaman referred to earlier on the front jacket illustration for *From the Milk River* (C. Hugh-Jones 1979), the idea of vertical communication between the different levels of the earth is indicated by a vertically aligned smoking cigar. This is described in the caption as 'mist rising through a pipe to the earth's surface', but seems more likely to be a typical large cigar.

40. Reichel-Dolmatoff 1971: 118.

41. This forms past of a broader enquiry into the kinds of questions that can be asked of a visual aesthetic system, the sorts of meanings such systems generate, and how they do so. See e.g. Gow 1999: 229–46.

42. C. Hugh-Jones 1979: 269.

43. From *murú*, 'tobacco'; *ge*, male suffix.

44. From *k'rapíri*, 'to step'; suffix: *nyári*, 'to seize, to assure'; and *doári*, 'to sit down'.

45. Reichel-Dolmatoff 1971: 118; drawing in Koch-Grünberg 1909: 282.

46. A graphic illustration of new beings being conjured out of a cloud of cigar smoke is reproduced in Pineda 1994: 36.

47. See e.g. Zerries 1970, Hartmann 1974. In some examples the upper and lower 'hourglass' forms both have a pair of lateral seat symbols.

48. Again, my thanks to Stephen Hugh-Jones for sharing his observations on the symbolism of the cigar holders. In similar vein Reichel-Dolmatoff suggests that the 'central part of the holder with its two superimposed "hourglass" elements represents the male and female (principles) in our world, and the bifurcating prongs continue this sexual symbolism representing a pair of legs between which the cigar is enclosed' (Reichel-Dolmatoff 1971: 118).

49. The hourglass form itself is said to derive from the imagery experienced as the result of the ritual consumption of hallucinogenic brews such as *yaje* (Reichel-Dolmatoff 1997: 255). It is also conceivable that the significance of the hourglass form is in some sense related to the hourglass-shaped clay pot-stands that support the large circular plates or griddles (*budares*) used for toasting manioc over hearth; cf. Reichel-Dolmatoff 1971: 108.

50. 'The flat surface of the bench is our world and

is decorated with the black and red designs that represent *pamurí-gahsíru* – the ancestral anaconda Snake-Canoe. Sitting on a bench is a protecting posture that, at the same time, forms a yellow-red-blue cosmic axis with the last element, that of comunication, being expressed by the seated and thinking person' (Reichel-Dolmatoff 1971: 110–11).

51. See e.g. Reichel-Dolmatoff's (1978b) analysis of weaving among the Kogi and more recently Guss 1989 on the Yekuana.

52. See also Reichel-Dolmatoff 1975: figs 21 and 62, for drawings of two stools with a bisecting axis incorporated into the seat design. They differ in the kind of seat support. The discussion here of axiality focused on seats and seating is necessarily partial and selective. The reader is referred to ch. 7 in C. Hugh-Jones 1979 for a superb treatment of the full set of ideas and relationships encapsulated in lowland systems of organizing space and time, including horizontal and vertical axiality.

53. Reichel-Dolmatoff 1975: 141; see also Reichel-Dolmatoff 1971: 126.

54. Reichel-Dolmatoff 1975: 141.

55. Ibid: 140–1.

56. See e.g. Roberto Pineda's illustration of Antonio Guzman's (1994: 33) drawing of a 'stool fertilized by the sun'.

57. S. Hugh-Jones, 1979: 119. In general, a distinction is made between women who sit on mats on the floor and men who sit on mats (painted) on stools.

58. Reichel-Dolmatoff (1971: 106). Interestingly, an arrangement of feline sculptures supporting an elaborately decorated central vertical post was observed by Carvajal in a Tapajos or Machiparo village in the middle Amazon. See also Heaton 1988: 205–6. Christine Hugh-Jones notes that midday is called *hasari bota*, 'meeting-up vertical post', which, she suggests, implies that at midday the sun's rays make a direct vertical connection with the earth. 'The sun's post, a small vertical post (projecting upwards) from the centre of the roof spine, represents this vertical connection within the house, and the horizontal east-west beam under the roof is called the Sun's path' (1979: 265–6) .

59. It is called the 'road of *pamuri-gashiru*', the ancestral Snake-Canoe that travelled from east to west on its mythical journey (Reichel-Dolmatoff 1971).

60. Reichel-Dolmatoff 1971: 108.

61. Guss notes that: 'derived from the same root as the Yekuana words for "tongue" (*nudu*), "navel" (*yenadu*), "waja drawing" (*ñenudu*), and "tiger spot" (*ichahe hato ñenudu*), the term is most closely related to the nearly indistinguishable word for "eye" *yenudu*. This synonymity is more than linguistic; the eye is where the most important of each person's six "doubles" or *akato* is located. Identical to the centerpost of the village, it is the location of the celestial spirit dispatched by Wanadi from Kahuña to animate each individual' (Guss 1989: 22).

62. 'Surrounding the centerpost at its base are two concentric circles, mirroring the same division found in the roof above. The inner one, known as the *annaka*, "in the center", corresponds to the dimensions of the *wahu* palm and, like this sacred cap, represents Heaven's inner circle. It is the *annak*, therefore, which is reserved for all ceremonial and rituals occasions. Like Lake Ajuena, with its restorative waters imbued with kaahi, it is the site of initiation and rebirth' (Guss 1989: 22).

63. The head of the jaguar is bisected by a longitudinal axial line, and the image of a reptilian is painted on the underside of the seat (cf. similar images found on Marajoara funerary vessels and in rock art). The seated person occupies the upper human world superimposed on an underworld beneath, metaphorically signalled by a primordial reptilian.

64. Circular Cashinahua stools with a central quadripartite design are illustrated in Kensinger *et al.* 1975: figs 132 and 144.

65. Spruce called the species he discovered *Banisteriopsis caapi*, taking this word from a Tukanoan language, as understood by him. Banisteriopsis is called *gahpí* (D), *kahpí* (T PT U), *kahí* (TT TB BA BS) (Reichel-Dolmatoff 1996a: 62). The botanical species used by Indians are mainly *B. caapi*, *B. inebrians* and *B. rusbayana*. The vine (and the drug prepared from it) is known under a number of vernacular names. In Brazil it is usually referred to as *caapi*; in Colombia, *yaje*; and in Peru and in Ecuador by the word *ayahuasca*, a Quechua term (Reichel-Dolmatoff 1997: 243). For the sake of convenience and consistency I will refer to it by its genus, *Banisteriopsis*.

66. See Reichel-Dolmatoff 1975: 155 for an account given by a Desana shaman of how and why the Sun Father gave *yaje* to humans.

67. Reichel- Dolmatoff, 1996a: 161.

68. Ibid: 162.

69. Reichel-Dolmatoff (1971: 115), citing Koch-Grünberg 1909, vol. 1: 259, notes that these kinds of ceramic trumpets were once characteristic of the Desana but have now largely disappeared.

70. Reichel-Dolmatoff 1996a: 162.

71. Ibid: 162–4.

72. C. Hugh-Jones, 1979: 209–30.

73. Ibid: 230.

74. Ibid: 209–10.

75. See Reichel-Dolmatoff 1996: 32–8 for an introduction to the different categories of energies.

76. Reichel-Dolmatoff 1996a: 32.

77. Ibid: 37.

78. Ibid.

79. Reichel-Dolmatoff 1971: 114.

80. When the drum was not in use, it was kept in the centre of the *maloca*. The drum was called *toá-toré* (from *toá*, onomatopoeic; *toré*, 'cavity, hollow trunk') and represents the uterus of the sib or phratry. The drumstick (*toá-toré padígë*) was called the 'penis of the sun', and the slit represented a vagina. Reichel-Dolmatoff 1971: 113–14; Koch-Grünberg 1909, vol. 1: 276.

81. Reichel-Dolmatoff 1971: 114; C. Hugh-Jones 1979; see also Reichel-Dolmatoff 1996b: pl. 11, showing a Barasana girl decorating her arms with the design of the mythical anaconda.

82. Signal drums connect in turn to the *chicha* troughs which are used throughout Amazonia and which, although apparently of only mundane significance, are in fact of great ritual importance. They, too, used to be painted and decorated rather in the same manner as the signal drums, and young Barasana men pound these troughs as if they were signal drums. Stephen Hugh-Jones, pers. comm.

83. Reichel-Dolmatoff (1975: 176) observes that the colours yellow and white tend to represent a seminal principle associated with the male sex or with solar fertilization.

84. The zigzag bordering motif has also been noted on shaman's stools: 'Otra categoría de tallas mágico-religiosas consiste en los pequenos banquitos que sirven al chamán de asiento durante sus cantos magicos o curaciones. Tienen la misma forma como los banquitos comúnmente usados para sentarse, pero siempre están talhados de incisiones que forman linea en zig-zag en sus bordes. Sólo puede el chamán sentarse en ellos y cuando no está en uso se guardan en un lugar protegido' (Reichel-Dolmatoff 1960: 129).

85. See e.g. Spruce 1908, vol. II: fig. 15, p. 417.

86. Reichel-Dolmatoff describes how 'Every act of coitus is believed to fertilize the woman's blood which, eventually, develops in one of two directions: the birth of a child, or menstruation. In the first case, the process is believed to be as follows: the woman's "vital blood" is imagined as a mass of small red dots that are thought to be "very hot". At their contact with male emission, these dots first become "heated", a stage during which the yellow male element predominates. This process is visualized as a bright yellow background upon which a number of moving luminous dots are projected. This visual image is designated as *noméri*, lit. "to paint with fine dots", and is said to be a fleeting sensation perceived by both partners during the intercourse. It is also said to be a frequent visual sensation at the onset of drug-induced hallucinations' (Reichel-Dolmatoff 1997: 62).

87. Reichel-Dolmatoff 1996a: 32.

88. Cf. for example Reichel-Dolmatoff 1975: figs 42–3,49–53 and figs 58, 64 and 65.

89. Guss 1989: 95.

90. Reichel-Dolmatoff 1975 and Wilbert 1987: 192–6.

91. For an introduction to the use of narcotic snuffs see Reichell-Dolmatoff 1975: 3–24 and 1997: 121–30. In the middle Amazon and the Negro basin the dominant hallucinogenic snuff, known as *epena*, *parica* or *nyakwana*, is prepared from the resin extracted from the inner bark of several species of virola, a slender 7–23 metre tall tree. Virola has a wide distribution extending into the Peruvian Amazon and lowland Bolivia. A second species known as *vilca*, *huilca* or *sebil* (*Anadenanthera colubrina*) is limited to northern Argentina and southern Peru. For example, *cohoba* or *yopo* (*Anadenathera peregrina*) was transported from the Orinoco valley by prehistoric agricultural groups (associated with the Saladoid tradition, *c.*5300–3000 BP) and transplanted into the West Indies, reaching Puerto Rico by 2300–2000 BP. Along with the *cohoba*, specialized ceramic bowls for snuffing were added to the bifurcated tubular snuffing devices that are still used in the Orinoco and Venezuelan/Brazilian Guyana. See also Reichel-Dolmatoff 1997: 124–30 for an account of snuff use among the Desana.

92. Snuff trays or tablets preserve a range of imagery in different pre-contact art styles and traditions. Examples from as far afield as Atacama in northern Chile with Tiahuanaco iconography suggest that this highland culture was instrumental in the adoption and diffusion of the snuff complex across the Andes. See e.g. Wassén 1972, Torres 1987, Torres and Conklin 1995.

93. Wilbert 1987: 192.

94. Wilbert 1987: 195. Wilbert notes links to other talismanic creatures such as the swallow-tailed kite (*Elanoides forficatus*) of the Acawaio and Warao, the *urubu* vulture (*Sarcoramphus papa*) of the Munku and other night hunters such as the bat of the Sanema or the kinkajou (*Potos flavus*) of the Bacairi.

8
The Woven Universe
Carib Basketry

LUCIA VAN VELTHEM

The striking imagery woven into the range of basketry made by indigenous peoples of the northern Amazon excites interest and is an invitation to penetrate their mystery. Baskets are destined for both everyday and ritual use: they fulfil many commonplace functions such as storing small personal objects and holding food; they are used to mediate a variety of social interactions in both initiation and funeral rites; and above all they serve to define social roles and relations, and to reinforce basic social values.[1]

The production of material objects among indigenous peoples can be analysed in various ways. In this essay I will look at some of these, including raw material, form, weaving techniques and decorative elements, with particular reference to the Wayana, a Carib-speaking indigenous people settled on the Paru de Leste river in the northern part of the state of Pará (figs 8.1–2). In turn, this opens up various interpretative approaches, especially how we can try to understand the ways in which different meanings are ordered and transmitted.[2] It is crucial to address the creators' intentions concerning the structure, meaning and importance of these works. This demands a contextualized analysis of indigenous woven artefacts that, besides examining elements such as the graphics, techniques and formal constituents, also addresses the narrative and functional components of this type of craftwork.

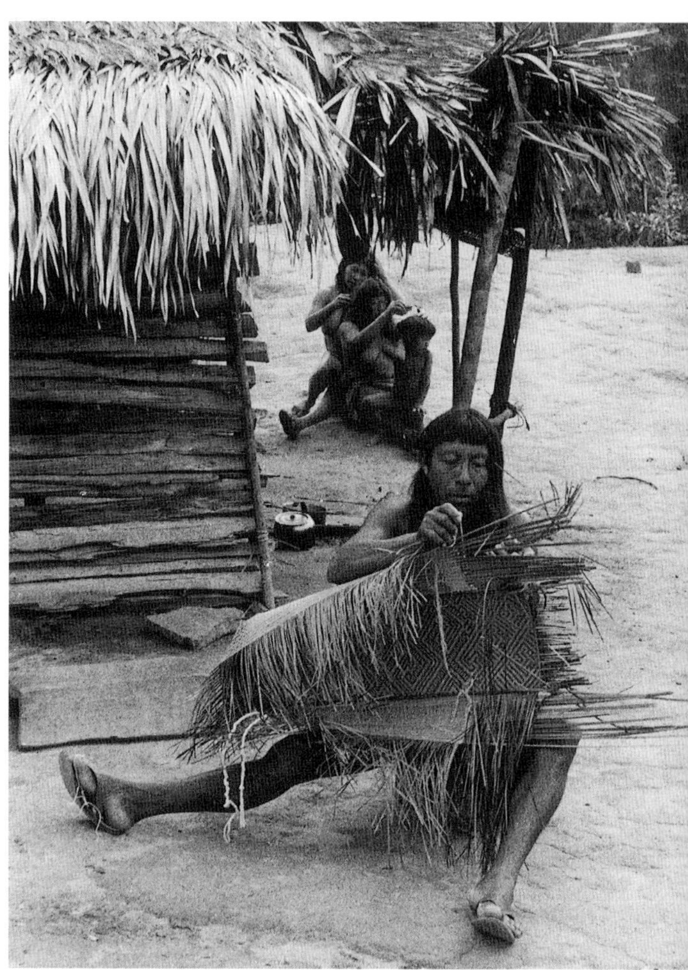

ABOVE **8.1 A Wayana man weaving a decorated carrier basket in a domestic context.**

RIGHT **8.2 Wayana carrying basket (*katari timiriké*), collected by the author, 1978 (height 95 cm, width 45cm, depth 24cm; Museu Paraense Emílio Goeldi, Belém, Brazil).**

The Wayana identify different categories of basketry in a way that takes into account the raw material used, the process by which a piece is made, its decoration and its function.[3] The raw materials and skills used to create the form, decorative patterns and functionality of these objects make up the guiding threads leading into this woven world, unfolding its fabrics and discovering some of its hidden symbolism.[4] Some of the earliest extensive references to indigenous woven goods were made by Walter Roth, who travelled in the area in 1916–17. Before that explorers and scientists in the

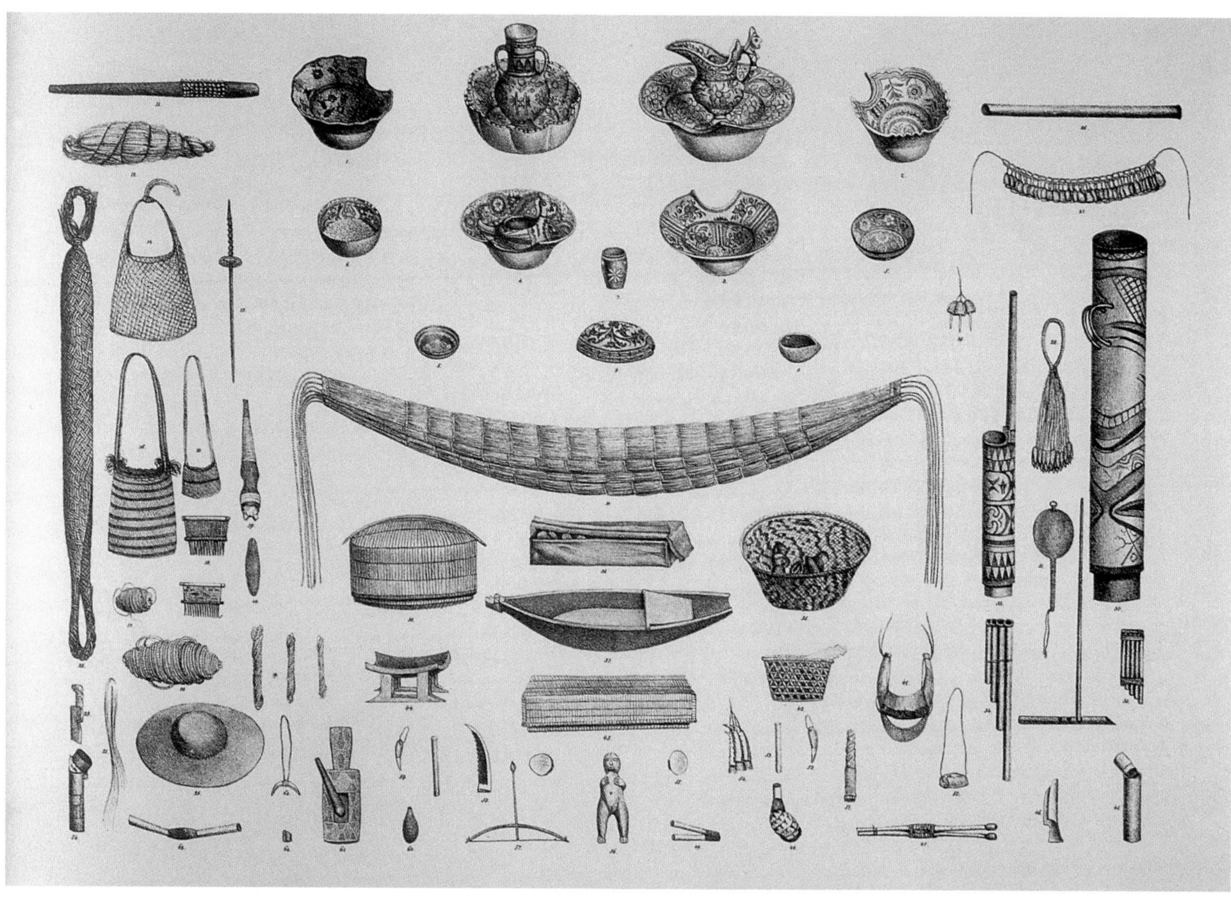

8.3 Indigenous artefacts, including basketry, depicted in Spix and Martius's atlas, *Travels in Brazil in the Years 1817–1820.*

northern Amazon region collected woven objects from peoples they visited but usually only made brief mention of these objects in their work (figs 8.3–4).[5]

Among Carib-, Tukano- and Aruak-speaking indigenous peoples the preparation of the raw material and weaving of plant fibres are male tasks (fig. 8.5). On the other hand, for the Yanomami of Roraima and the Amazon, as for the Maku peoples of the different river basin regions of the north-eastern Amazon region, the weaving and decoration of different types of baskets are characteristically female tasks. This differentiation points to a rigid division of gender roles and subsistence activities that is also found in handicraft techniques. Nevertheless, the process of making artefacts in many cases requires cooperation between men and women to produce the raw materials and implements required to ensure the excellence of the end result. Among the Wayana,[6] for example, the men need cotton thread for various types of fastenings used in their basketry, and the women depend on spindles for spinning cotton into threads.

Forest decorations: the raw materials

The indigenous peoples of the northern Amazon region use a variety of raw materials in making woven goods: open leaves, folioles and petioles of the young leaves of different palm species,[7] several types of lianas and particularly strips of *arumã* (*Ischnosiphon* spp.). The latter is a plant of the Marantaceae family found on humid ground in secondary forests around the headwaters of the region's rivers and streams, and it grows even after being collected and hardly withers. Brazilian ethnologist Berta Ribeiro (1985, 1992) inferred that the raw materials used in indigenous basketry may

8.4 Depiction of a drinking festival in a Carib village. Prior preparations involved processing large quantities of manioc using a range of basketry, as illustrated in fig. 2.12. From *Twelve Views in the Interior of Guiana* by Robert Schomburgk, 1841.

be divided into two main styles: one that uses the more malleable palm fronds, and the other that uses the more rigid liana and *arumã* straws. Basketry from the northern Amazon region is usually of the second type.

The Wayana use three species of *arumã*, known in the Carib language as *wama, karanari* and *kaptehé*, while the Tukano and the Baniwa, from the upper Negro River, in the state of Amazonas, label five species in the latter's Aruak language as: *halépana, póapoa kántsa, oni-póapoani, attíne híorhi* and *tolípa*.[8] In their criteria for classifying woven artefacts the Baniwa include the greater or lesser malleability and durability of the different species. When weaving baskets to sell, neither the Wayana nor the Baniwa use genuine *arumã* (respectively *wama* and *poápoa kántsa*), which is reserved for the production of sturdy utilitarian artefacts for their own use.

The durability of *arumã* is also seen as vital among the Tukano-speaking Arapasso from the Uaupés river basin in the state of Amazonas. Their hierarchical classification of the different *arumã* species is based on this feature, with the two most durable species known as the older brothers and the rest as the younger ones. These descriptions are also passed on to the objects made from each species. Accordingly, a sieve, *siowa*, is made from genuine *arumã* and is part of the class of artefacts considered to be among the 'first-born'.

8.5 Circular sieve for straining cassava dough (*beiju*), collected by Adélia de Oliveira, 1971 (diameter 81 cm; Museu Paraense Emílio Goeldi, Belém, Brazil). This basket is woven by men and used by women among the Tukano from the Içana river, upper Rio Negro basin.

Among the Wayana and Baniwa, collecting *arumã* is exclusively a male task undertaken by the village men either individually or in small groups of close kin. The *arumã* is cut down at the stand, its leaves removed, and its stalks bundled and fastened (fig. 8.6). Then they are carried away in bundles or in disposable baskets purpose-made from palm fronds. When the stalks are to be processed the following day, the basket containing them may be left in the shade beside the basket maker's home. Otherwise, it is left in a damp place at the edge of the village for four days at most, after which the *arumã* begins to rot.

8.6 Baniwa men collecting *arumã*.

The several raw materials used in basketry have to be properly prepared so that the fibres can be worked. Indigenous peoples use *arumã* in two ways, as the raw material needs more complex preparation. In the first the outer layer is not scraped from the stalk and so it will not take paint; it is scored and cut with a knife or fingernail in eight or sixteen strips used to make open-weft baskets or the more robust load-carrying baskets. The other method entails skinning the *arumã* stalk before it is scored, painted and cut in the same number of strips; it is then used for all types of baskets decorated with alternating light- and dark-coloured motifs.

One of the dyes most frequently used by the Wayana, Tukano and Baniwa is obtained from the scraped bark of the ingá (*Inga paraensis*). The resulting pieces of bark are crushed by hand to extract an acid, and then impregnated with the fine soot from a kerosene lamp collected in a clay pan. This dye is spread by hand on the bark-stripped stalk and levelled with the finger to become indelible when dry.

The *arumã* plant has the most symbolic associations of any of the raw materials used by the Wayana, Baniwa, Yekuana and Aparai.[9] Among the Wayana, the symbolism attached to the *arumã* derives from its utility in making both monochrome and light-and-dark baskets. The two uses relate to the Wayana view that these different species of *arumã* possess features of a human-like covering material. So, like human skin, the plant's 'skin' has both a surface layer and a secondary layer. In making woven goods, the 'epidermis' of the *arumã* may be kept intact, resulting in single-colour artefacts, or it may be skinned to take black or red vegetable dye and make artefacts with chiaroscuro inlays.

This property of the material enables it to reproduce 'skins', either the overall skin colour of primordial humans or, with linework, that of the basic supernatural beings, thus permitting their expression in material form. The central point in this

8.7 Cylindrical manioc strainer (*tipiti*) made of unscraped *arumã* and collected by the author, 1995, from the Baniwa of the Içana river, upper Rio Negro basin (height 164 cm, width 22 cm; Museu Paraense Emílio Goeldi, Belém, Brazil).

process is that weaving techniques facilitate the reproduction of the decorated skins of these beings and not just the paintings applied to their skins. The meaning perceived here is that of the intrinsic and the permanent, rather than the superficial and transient. In basketry the base and the decorative motif are one and the same thing, unlike ceramics, in which decoration is applied. It is this sense of everlastingness that links decorative basketry with primordial and supernatural beings, since they too are everlasting.

To clarify the correlations between the *arumã* and the skins of primordial humans and supernatural beings, we have first to recall that, ultimately, procreation is a 'making of skin' through which humans reveal their workmanship. In this view the skin covering a newly born baby is symbolically understood as plumage, as woven feathers. However, on the same basis the skin of a socially integrated adult corresponds more to woven *arumã*, because the perpetuation of the human species particularly seeks to reproduce an ideal form originally conceived by the gods, who in chaotic and creative primordial times created a woman from this material. Confirming this point, the Wayana call themselves *wama ïhem,* 'possessors of *arumã*', because *arumã* is part of their essence.

In 'making' the primordial woman – *Arumana* – the creator god used *arumã* stalks with bark, or 'epidermis'. This was specifically painted with *urucum* (annatto tree) dye, since *arumã* that has not been scraped takes on a red-nut colouring on drying that is known as *tamarê* and corresponds to the tones of body painting using aged annatto. This coincidence shows that the first woman was socialized, since her skin was painted with the aged annatto used by a person who often decorates the body and so is in full use of social prerogatives as an adult capable of creative and procreative actions (fig. 8.7).

The symbolic associations here are the reason for monochrome and red identifying and supporting humans and all humanity in general,[10] and they also underlie the rationale for human body painting. The *arumã* with its 'epidermis' facilitates the production of uniformly woven work, defined as 'skin-painted-in-annatto', which is that of the primordial woman. It is 'scraped' or skinned and painted to render it suitable for the reproduction of an inlaid fabric weave with alternating light and dark hues, which brings out different graphic patterns, characteristic of a 'skin-painted-with-genipap-fruit'. Here it is not a question of reproducing the skin of another ancestral Wayana, but rather that of another being, equally primordial but non-human, a supernatural being. This being is referred to as *Tuluperê* and looks like an eel or serpent. Its paintings are reproduced on Wayana skins, which are symbolically scorched during rituals by applying wasps or stinging black ants attached to a piece of woven straw representing a supernatural being. Another, more profound level of the symbolic association between woven *arumã* and the skins of primordial beings is that both (wovens and skins) represent aesthetic ideals through which artistic sense and human meaning are actualized.

Weaving skins: basketry techniques

In the celestial, aquatic and subterranean domains the production of objects is not effected in a human sense but is of another order. Human production belongs to the earthly domain, the environment where indigenous peoples live, circulate, collect raw materials they need, and develop skills that must be learned and executed according to social rules. The artefacts have to do with living humans, who have bodies that can produce them. The dead belong in another dimension, with different bodily features, and for this reason are incapable of technological action.

Making woven artefacts is an ongoing activity in the indigenous calendar, especially as the artefacts are an important source of income for the Tukano, Baniwa, Yekuana, Wayana, Aparai, and Waiãpi who make and sell baskets in regional markets or through aid organizations. For the Wayana, however, the most appropriate period for this work is between the slashing and burning of bush or forest, or while cleared land is cooling after a fire. During passages, such as the birth of a first-born child, basketry work is suspended, and particularly the use of *arumã*. The powers that emanate from *arumã* weaving affect the newborn, causing illnesses.

Among the Wayana, the space for the production of woven artefacts is well defined. Young bachelors preferably work inside or around the ceremonial house, where they also live. Married men work sitting on stools outside their abodes, on the terrace around them or near one of the entrances. Bachelors and married men, however, prefer to sit around a warming fire in the middle of the village, an eminently male space, and weave. They sit around the fire at dawn and dusk, the two times considered especially appropriate for making woven artefacts. After being exposed to the fall of nightly dew, the raw materials become more flexible and are easier to weave.

The difficulty in weaving an artefact is measured by both the time involved in preparing raw material and the number of stages required to see a basket to completion. Therefore, the more work there is involved not just in weaving but also in applying fastenings, support laths, handles and finishing, the more difficult the craftwork. Pre-pubescent boys readily master the techniques involved in weaving open-weft hampers or panniers, mats and fans – seen as the easiest artefacts to weave. The most difficult is a painted carrying basket, known as *katari timiriké* (fig. 8.2). The making of such an artefact validates the artisan's skill and worth as a Wayana when his wife carries it on a visit to another village.

Indigenous woven artefacts use several techniques that involve the use of hands and fingers but not necessarily in an even manner. Hand and finger movements are not always the same because the number of stems required for baskets and their different parts varies. For the Wayana, the making of each object corresponds to a pattern of gestures that supplies the vocabulary for the different techniques. Basketry, pottery and fine weaving are handicrafts that share the same term *tïkaphé*, 'coming-from-making'. This shared term of reference is based only on the fact that in each of them the hands make similar movements, not because they consider weaving to be the same as making pots or skirts. The nomenclature is derived from the fact that, for most of the time, each hand carries out the same movements and they complement each other to create the artefact. These double gestures indicate a technique in which one works intensely and there is much to be done, unlike activities that require only the fingertips, such as gluing feathers, or techniques where only one hand is needed to work while the other holds the material, such as smoothing bows.

The Wayana classify weaving techniques in two broad categories: close-woven, *warumë*, and spaced-woven, *kararaimë*. The first includes eleven different techniques, which are named according to their function, decorative motifs and design. The name of the basket is also distinguished from that of decorative motif, but there is no differentiation between the latter and the technique used: both have the same desig-

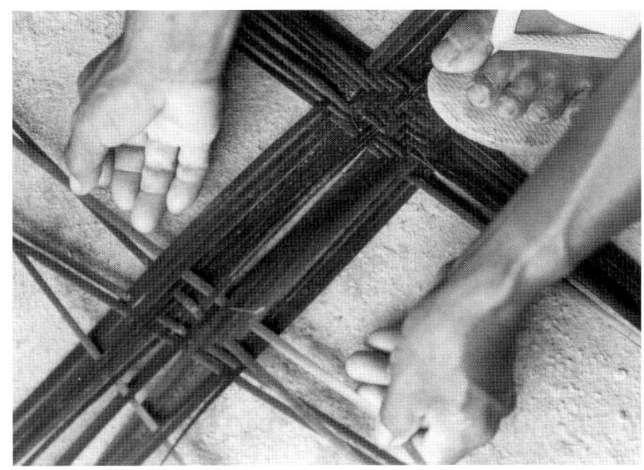

8.8 Sequence showing the weaving of a decorated Baniwa basket, 1999.

nation. The second category includes eight techniques of spaced weave, which are referred to as *mirikut ewú*, 'pattern-of-eyes', and do not have specific names to identify technique, object or decorative pattern.

It is practically impossible to distinguish the beginnings of indigenous woven artefacts, since they fuse with the body of the object itself, particularly in woven recipients. However, there are many different ways of finishing and they are directly related to the morphology of the object being made. From a technical point of view, finishing may be stitched, tied or woven. In the first two cases additional elements may be introduced into the work; in the third case the fibres themselves are bent (fig. 8.8).

Making woven artefacts is not a spontaneous activity: certain rules and mastering techniques must be followed. The know-how derived from gradual learning during the socialization process represents the end result of sexually differentiated social transmission, and this is a key point in distinguishing things created by the gods from those created by humans. Technical knowledge of making objects is referred to as *tuwaré*, i.e. 'to know', 'to be familiar with'; therefore, a skilled basket maker is *wama tuwaron*.

Knowledge is located in the eyes where the *wayanaman* dwell, the 'people-like beings' in other words, the inverted figures seen in the pupils that 'inhabit' the eyes and represent the true source of artisanship. Retaining basket-weaving knowledge means that the figure dwells in the eyes of the basket maker and is an intermediary in the eminently gestural process that leads to the materialization of woven artefacts. The 'vision' referred to here should not be understood as merely the sensory field of the eyes, one through which reality is perceived, but also as knowledge and 'sight', or the understanding of the social prescriptions that bind the Wayana. These prescriptions refer to the appropriate usage of the artefacts as well as to the correct way of making them.

In order to retain his craft knowledge, the artisan has to protect the dweller in his eyes; therefore, he can only work by day, in good light. What is more, in so doing he shows other villagers that he is weaving a basket rather than engaging in sortilege, since both require the same materials. Making woven artefacts at twilight or near a fire may lead to loss of visual acuity, since in these circumstances predatory powers associated with a small rodent can stalk and charge against the dweller in the artisan's eyes, putting an end to it.

These prescriptions are aimed at warding off potentially hostile influences that include diseases caused by social disorders derived from excess or from individual obsession while engaged in craftwork, which are referred to as *tarentekë*. Any man who is constantly making baskets, without attending to subsistence tasks or to the production of other kinds of artefacts, is considered as 'obsessed with *arumã*'; this gives rise to disorders that affect both him and his next of kin, who begin to suffer from bouts of fever. Obsession is not properly a form of human behaviour but rather has to do with the technology of the primordial beings, and this is only desirable during rituals because it leads to metamorphosis. According to the Wayana, the means by which people and objects are made is intimately bound up with an activity based on models created in primeval times by supernatural beings.

Non-human bodies: the shapes of objects

Contemporary human beings and their products are also understood as constituting 'imitations' of the original technological actions of primeval supernatural beings. In other words, making woven objects is meaningful in that it has to do with the idea of continuous imitation and updating of primordial models. It features a kind of creativity that is constructive but not arbitrary; it involves primordial beings as creators par excellence, and the Wayana themselves as their most faithful interpreters.

Wayana-woven objects, whether intended for everyday use or for ceremonies and rituals, have formal features copied from their primeval archetypes and are hence described as *ukuktop*, or 'made-according-to-image', to stress the fact that they are based on a model, preferably in terms of their bodily features but also their aesthetic aspect, functional use or other element of identity. Hence, a sleeve-like basket used to process cassava represents a hanging serpent, and a sieve represents a beehive. Woven objects, therefore, are characterized as the result of an experience and as reproductions of volumes and structures of beings and elements with morphological parameters established in primeval times.

8.9 Baniwa basket woven in a loose mesh used for carrying sweet potatoes.

Among the Wayana, physical representations of archetypal entities may be reproduced in whole or in part. A circular sieve for cassava dough is shaped like the loops of a coiled anaconda, and a loosely woven basket (fig. 8.9) used to carry sweet potatoes personifies the crop of the king vulture (fig. 8.10). Woven objects are perceived and named as if they were whole bodies or parts of bodies (also among the Warao and Yekuana),[11] and are duly assigned heads, limbs, breasts, trunks, genitals, buttocks, ribs, etc., which may be anthropomorphic, zoomorphic or strictly supernatural. Seen from this perspective, material objects are viewed as effigies, as plastic representations or portrayals of primordial beings or of their features – and at some point may even be taken for the originals. Since the meaning of an effigy is connected, preferably, to a representation, artefacts for everyday and ritual use are themselves, ultimately, 'bodies' of beings created in primeval times and may appear in the present time as parts of bodies or as whole bodies.

Everyday artefacts are conceived as being 'transformed bodies'. Several myths describe them as having undergone a process that amounts to their being dismembered, with the resulting suppression of their original, chaotic and uncontrolled characteristics. If everyday tasks are to be undertaken, primeval beings must be dismembered and transformed into objects that humans can master. Thus, the indigenous women may use a woven object (sieve) for processing cassava without fear of being devoured by the serpent it relates to.

Objects for ceremonial and ritual use are another possible materialization of primeval bodies. These objects are characterized by detail and finishing that include non-visual elements such as movements, sounds and fragrances. In these cases the creative experience is so profound and perfect that it generates a metamorphosis, which, in a certain sense, constitutes the divine technology itself. Objects are thus transformed into their original models; they usher themselves and their reality into the midst of Wayana society. These artefacts themselves effect transformations insofar as they affect spatial-temporal reality – and, consequently, human reality. An example of this is a plaque woven from palm frond: from being the representation of a *pacu* (type of fish), it becomes the actual fish and is applied to the skin of an affected young person to (symbolically) 'bite away' the skin. Ritual artefacts must be handled with extreme care, and this sphere of activity is kept under close surveillance through restrictive and controlling practices.

8.10 King vulture depicted in Alexandre Rodrigues Ferreira, *Viagem Filosófica* (1783–92).

Other conceptions involve finished objects that the Wayana call *tiranmai*, 'hung from the central beam', a metaphor to indicate that objects are no longer loose in space, but finally set in their proper place. The action of hanging something up is paradigmatic for the ordering of all woven and other artefacts; furthermore, all that is not placed on the ground or in non-appropriate places is considered as being left to rot. It is fundamentally important that the place of storage be known. Knowledge of this fact confers attributes of visibility on woven objects that go beyond the concrete action of 'seeing'. Thus, the Wayana never touch a shaman's paraphernalia; rather, they pretend to ignore the storage place of these objects that, symbolically, are invisible to their eyes. A traveller's belongings fall in this same category and nobody will interfere with them. Travel takes place in time that elapses without social activity, both for the men and their belongings.

A recently finished woven object is given a positive connotation with the adjective *ijan*, a term that indicates that it is new and not worn. A woven object of this type is highly esteemed because prominent amongst its aesthetic attributes is its 'original' colour that gives it specificity and identity. The colour is derived from the raw material, such as white from *cunanã* (*Astrocaryum paramaca*) or red from unpeeled *arumã* stalks.

The aesthetic ideal asserts that woven objects should retain their original colour throughout their existence, but they are modified by wear, and various dark hues emerge indicating wear and tear of objects. A deteriorated woven object is chromatically perceived as 'black' and considered repulsive, meaning that it has irretrievably lost its most valued attributes. On showing visible signs of deterioration, woven objects become *xitpurimé*, 'truly useless', or *timatai*, 'rotten', in opposition to the description *patukú*, 'useful', an adjective not normally applied to objects, since being useful is such an obvious, intrinsic feature – indeed making useless or unworthy artefacts would be inconceivable.

A damaged woven object definitively loses its aesthetic excellence, but not necessarily its utilitarian function; everyday needs and other factors determine whether it can be reused, and this is predominantly women's activity. Consequently, certain woven objects are not repaired but may be used for a function other than the original one – a handle-less fan may be turned into a child's seat. Other woven objects are repaired and their original form recovered, as in the case of the cassava press, since new stays may be added to broken meshes. Damaged artefacts may be taken apart or modified for other use such as a base for making pottery. However, recycled or deteriorated objects may not be reincorporated to recover their status as aesthetically valued objects.

Decorated serpents: graphic symbols

In northern Amazon basketry most objects made from *arumã* feature elaborate black curves against a light background. These curves may be found in many forms: ornamental motifs, figuration, ornamentation, decoration, design, pattern and graphic symbols. The multiple meaning of a graphic symbol is never self-enclosing but progressively reveals different conceptions, presupposing several levels of interpretation.

Due to the very nature of woven objects, ornamental motifs in basketry have few curved lines and appear to be geometric and stylized. However, on closer observation, another feature stands out, as seen in Tukano, Baniwa, Panare, Yekuana, Tiriyó, Wayana, and Aparai artefacts: the existence of figurative or iconic elements (figs 8.11 and 8.13).[12] The iconic meaning is characterized by the fact that some aspect of likeness brings out the relationship between the visual form and its meanings, and this aspect is intrinsic to the operation of the graphic system. Wayana and Yekuana basketry motifs, for instance, encompass visual referents to a given subject, such as characteristic lines that define an animal or vegetable object as well as supernatural beings, all of which are key elements in the indigenous cosmos.

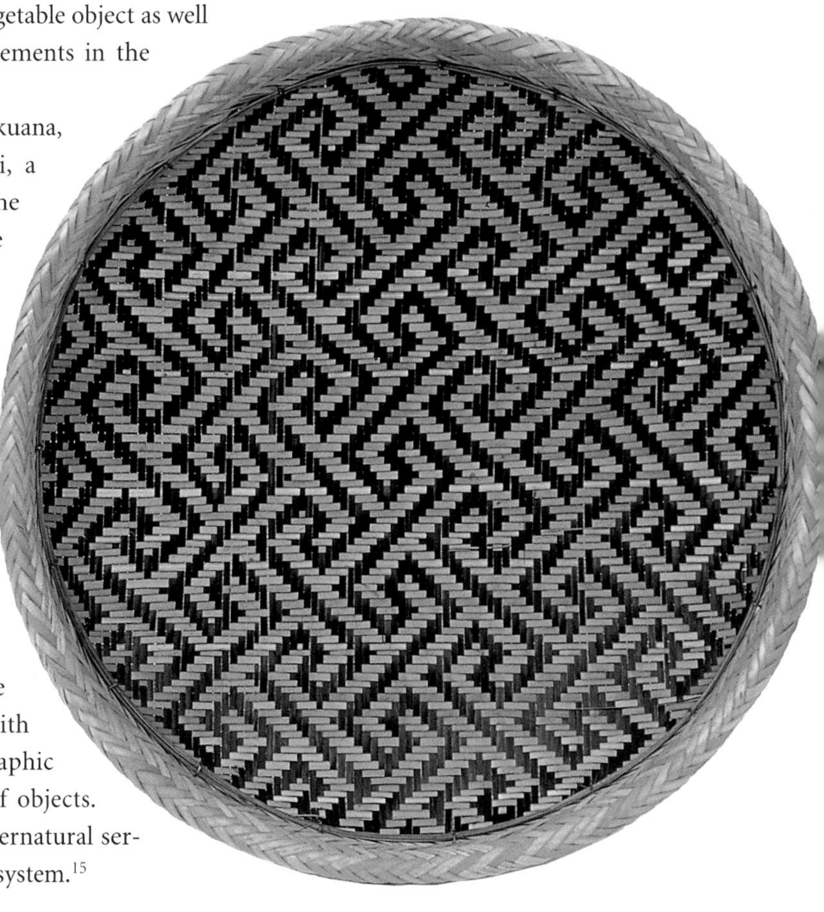

8.11 Circular sieve for serving the cassava dough (*beijú*) from the Werekena, Xié river, upper Rio Negro, collected by Marcio Meira, 1993 (diameter 51 cm; Museu Paraense Emílio Goeldi, Belém, Brazil).

Among the Carib-speaking peoples like the Yekuana, Tiriyó, Waiwai, Kachuyana, Wayana or Aparai, a supernatural serpent is the central figure in the myth of the origin of basketry and decorative motifs (fig. 8.12). The Wayana call it *Tuluperê*; the Waiwai, *Uruperi*;[13] and the Kachuyana, *Marmaruimó*.[14] In the myth it was killed by two gods, who peeled off its skin to discover its colours and apply them to designs and decorations for their sieves, hampers, baskets and other Kachuyana artefacts. The basic features of Wayana in relation to *Tuluperê* indicate that an immense mythical serpent upset travellers' canoes and prevented the Aparai and Wayana from meeting. These peoples then joined to attack and kill this creature. During the struggle they saw that its body was covered with paintings, which they took for their iconographic repertory and applied to different categories of objects. Taking decorative motifs from the skin of a supernatural serpent is also characteristic of the Waiwai graphic system.[15]

The elements in the decorative repertoire form part of Wayana definitions of drawing and also include fundamental notions of graphic symbolism, such as pattern, motif and model, called *mirikut*. This visual language later extended to writing, after contact with other Brazilians. The terms *kusiwa* for the Waiãpi, *menurú* for the Aparai, *menudu* for the Yekuana, *holi* for the Tukano and *goholi* for the Desana mean the same as the Wayana expression, showing the importance of graphic signs as vehicles for many of the basic meanings and principles of indigenous thinking.[16]

The Wayana term for this decoration refers exclusively to an overarching idea of these as inherent and permanent creations of supernatural beings – their 'body painting' – and clearly indicates the non-Wayana nature of the ornamental repertoire. As explained, the main Wayana sources, *Tuluperê imirikut*, 'paintings of the supernatural serpent', were obtained in primeval times from the scales of this snake, which in zoological terms would be an anaconda.[17] This repertoire is used in body painting and both female and male categories of handmade objects, but objects woven from *arumã* show the most varied range of its patterns.[18]

8.12 Anaconda snake (*sucurijú*) with coloured skin patterns. According to Carib mythology, the origin of basketry relates to a supernatural snake whose skin is peeled off by gods in order to reveal its colours and apply them to the woven artefacts.

Woven objects made of *arumã* bring out an important feature in relation to the structuring and distribution of the 'painting' on the bodies of supernatural creatures. Contrasting motifs in light and dark colours are distributed or patterned on faces and abdomens, while motifs on the tail and limbs are not patterned, since strips of *arumã* do not hold paint. The inlaid patterns are differentially laid out, so those that can be seen on only one outer surface are spread along the flanks, but the double-surface markings that are visible from within, too, are concentrated on its belly and indicate, by their location, that this being also has decorated innards – appropriately so, since the belly is where the final act of the 'predatory tragedy' is staged. Used exclusively on decorated carrier baskets, these are seen as the most beautiful and intricate patterns of their kind (fig. 8.13). They are made by the most skilful artists, who, above all, exercise most profoundly the power of visualizing the supernatural world through their creative artistry.

The exegesis of each pattern is based on the fact that iconic characteristics are not univocal: they do not always allude to one single model but may derive from multiple images, with the same graphic signs configuring several models. There are affinities and analogies between them, and they form a representational whole that converges with others in one and the same repertoire, the body painting of the supernatural *Tuluperê*, which, as the representative corollary, constitutes the original concept for all Wayana aesthetics, as it does for a number of Carib-speaking peoples.

The power of the patterns is derived both from their tangible presence and that of the images they work with; they also gain from exegeses that become operative through a cosmocentric reading combining representation and meaning. The former corresponds to the graphic signs in themselves and their multiple meanings. The exegesis, however, goes beyond this and emphasizes animal and supernatural predation and the meanings of the metamorphosis as the central themes of the Wayana cognitive system that directly influence its art and aesthetics. The patterns seek, therefore, to communicate another order that is at the same time representative and conceptual, and each motif, through being different entities at the same time, symbolizes the unity and diversity of indigenous culture.

A pattern is always a documental evocation because it expresses multiple realities. So the ornamental motif of the jaguar represents this animal (figs 8.14–15) and simultaneously a supernatural being of similar appearance but gigantic proportions, as well as a supernatural being identified with the household dog. Finally, all these representations combine to express the painted skin of the supernatural serpent and, therefore, this same serpent too, since the jaguar motif is also one of its decorative elements. Consequently, the understanding of each pattern becomes effective in a more complex figurative sense, since the beings reproduced resemble each other physically but develop in multiple spatial-temporal spheres: both primordial and present day, natural and supernatural. Consequently, patterns have boundaries of signification that are continually changing and bringing out different meanings at different times. In the end all the cognitive and representative experiences come together to express a wider cosmic order embodied in the term *Tuluperê.*

8.13 Decorated round basket used for processing cotton, collected by the author, 1975, from Tuarinké Wayana, Paru de Leste river (height 17 cm, diameter 23 cm; Museu Paraense Emílio Goeldi, Belém, Brazil).

A formal analysis of the patterns shows that representations may be whole or partial – a being may be represented as a whole or just with some aspect or part of its body. In some motifs the very definition of icon has to be expanded because there are patterns whose relationship of similarity to the model is incorporated in the nomenclature. The name of the graphic symbol does not correspond to what is being represented and exegesis is therefore required, so that certain patterns may be classified as 'visual metaphors' for other representations – this is the case of the '(coiled) tail of the capuchin monkey', which, besides representing the monkey, also describes the spiral hair of a certain supernatural being, an anthropomorphous cannibal, and by extension a characteristic of the supernatural animals of this species.

The Wayana see obtaining and using the decorative motifs that are characteristic of supernatural beings as both an opportunity to affirm their own humanity and as a means of opposing this to the domain of the supernatural. In a certain sense this decorative aesthetic represents the visual reinforcement of social life and points to the central position of human beings in the universe that surrounds them.

Moving artefacts: functionality

In the social context basketry and other artefacts constitute one way of expressing artisan specialization, as does the sexual division of labour, which is a feature of the indigenous peoples of the Amazon. Basketry underlines the complementarity between 'making' and 'using' in matrimonial and family life. In this sense, as a principle, men are the makers par excellence of woven objects and women, the users (fig.

8.16). However, this principle is not totally inflexible, since men use some woven objects in certain contexts, whereas certain women are familiar with some elementary basketry techniques.

This complementarity is not restricted to making and using woven objects, but extends to the masculine and feminine notions applied to objects. Wayana men name woven objects according to the raw material used or their ornamental patterns. The women look to the use of baskets, whether as receptacles or as means of carrying things. Each woven object, however, has its proper name, used by both sexes.

Men and women, through differing names for the same woven object, bring out the particular aspects they perceive as being most relevant – the process of making them, their decoration, their use. The first two are appropriate for men and so each woven object indicates the individual's technical and artistic mastery. Women are associated with other aspects of their use, since handling woven objects points to the

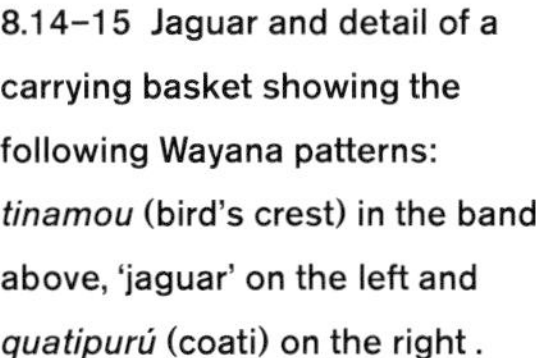

8.14–15 Jaguar and detail of a carrying basket showing the following Wayana patterns: *tinamou* (bird's crest) in the band above, 'jaguar' on the left and *quatipurú* (coati) on the right.

need for processing food and other materials essential for family subsistence and comfort. In village social life woven objects acquire functionality and are the intermediaries in multiple relationships. Women may occupy a prominent position as users of the great majority of the basketwork artefacts, as among the Baniwa and Wayana.

On receiving a woven object, the Wayana woman becomes its owner and uses it in accordance with the requirements of domestic life; or, in the event of pressing need, she may sell it, recycle it or finally discard it when she sees it as old or useless, leading to a new cycle of using and discarding. As a girl grows, she receives a few woven objects from her father or older brother. The ownership and use of woven objects proceeds to grow in terms of variety and size. On reaching adult age, she gets married and receives from the husband and children so many artefacts that she eventually handles practically the whole repertoire. However, with the passage of time and her widowhood, her collection dwindles to just a few objects in old age.

Some woven objects are especially significant in marking the life of a Wayana woman. The first is a tiny liana or *arumã* carrier basket, given to her by her father when she is about five years old. This basket becomes at the same time a toy and a means of learning the tasks assigned to adult women. The girl's relatives may use this small basket, but she is its sole owner and may do whatever she wants with it.

On marrying, the young woman receives the artefacts needed to process cassava, which are made by her husband. They are given to her in a certain sequence, first the sleeve to work the cassava pulp, then a basket to carry the roots, a sieve for straining when making dough, a fan to keep a fire going, and mats to cover the heaped dough balls (cf. Oliver, this volume). These woven objects are considered to be the married woman's property like other kitchen utensils related to domestic life and female attributions that, in this sphere, consist of transforming wild or cultivated products into edible foods.

8.16 Woman carrying manioc in a basket (*atura*).

Newly wed women are given not only the woven objects required for making a range of cassava-derived foods but also artistic pieces woven with thin *arumã* strips and patterned designs used in working cotton or for devices to spin cotton. The processing of wild cassava and cotton comprise two important spheres of married life that are associated with the reproduction of the individual and of society.

The artefact, as the result of creative work, is intimately associated with its maker/owner who must obey rules for making and using it. One restriction prohibits anything that is done with woven objects for the dead – burning, destruction, burial – from being applied to the belongings of the living, because this would cause irreparable physical damage such as precocious ageing or blockage. Objects worn out by use must disappear through the action of time and so are left on the edges of the village. However, when an artist dies, all the woven and other objects that he made must be destroyed. Like their makers, the woven objects are considered to have died and nothing of them should remain as memory. When an Arapasso man is dying, relatives gather all woven objects he executed and used including manufactured ones. The shaman, or *kumú*, places them spiritually in a canoe and ceremonially sends them to the 'house of the returning of life'. After this ceremony living relatives may reuse the objects.

A functional artefact is appreciated among the Wayana because functionality is the ultimate quality of successful creation. With its material, form and decoration, a basket acquires movement through functionality. Furthermore, an object is appreciated because it can be contemplated both in its rightful place in the kitchen or home, statically or dynamically, and executing its appropriate transformative action derived from its functional role.

The functional attributes of an object become highly valued when endowed with specificity and property. In the case of functional specificity this means that the more specialized an object is, the more valuable it becomes, regardless of the context in which it is used, whether in everyday life or in ritual. Woven objects that have a single function, such as the sleeve-basket squeezer or sieve for cassava dough, are more highly appreciated than the loosely woven baskets used to carry fruit.

In relation to their functional properties value derives from the very fact of the woven object being used for its intended function, which is often contained in its name, occasionally attested by a suffix meaning 'containing'. So a basket called *napi-enê*, 'containing sweet potatoes', is only appreciated if it is actually filled with these particular potatoes.

Concluding note

I have endeavoured here to penetrate something of the mysteries that surround indigenous artefacts, particularly those made out of perishable fibre. We have seen how raw materials are processed and how practical aspects of weaving incorporate aesthetically beautiful design elements imbued with deeper significance. These elements are instrumental in myriad ways in mediating daily transactions as well as being an integral part of human engagement with a wider universe of creative action.

Casual viewers and specialists alike can grasp something of the ideas and cultural tensions that resonate in each fibre and motif. The interpretative possibilities do not end here, for if we take a moment to contemplate, it is apparent that the unity and diversity of indigenous cultures is mirrored in the multi-layered meaning invested in every single object.

Acknowledgements

I would like to thank my friends and informants, the Wayana from the Paru river, and the Arapaço from the upper Rio Negro, for their hospitality and patience. I also thank my colleagues from the *Unknown Amazon* team for their care with the manuscript.

NOTES

1 Geertz 1986.

2 Guss 1989: 91.

3 Cf. van Velthem, 1998. A formal typological classification based on shape alone does not adequately represent Wayana technological typology (Ribeiro 1986). Anthropological studies of indigenous basketry in the lowlands of South America have traditionally been preoccupied with the technical aspects involved in the production and use of woven artefacts. The complexity of this technology and the great variety of forms have obliged many researchers to approach it by means of taxonomic studies (O'Neale 1986, Frikel 1973, Ribeiro 1980, 1985, 1986). Another kind of approach focuses on aspects related to form and function (Yde 1965, Wilbert 1975b, Taveira 1982) or to figures associated with marketing these objects (Henley and Muller 1978, Ribeiro 1978, 1981, 1983). The symbolism found in the graphic repertoire of basketry is an important subject and involves a number of other aspects (Reichel-Dolmatoff 1985, Guss 1989, van Velthem 1998).

4 Much of this documentation tends to emphasize the lines or patterns so effectively displayed in indigenous basketry. Several authors (Roth, Frikel, etc.) go so far as to remark that the symbolism used in woven objects has its origin in these patterns. However, it should be stressed that handicraft technique and functionality are equally important. In examining the collection of raw materials and their preparation for the weaving process, the studies show that these aspects of weaving are not merely technical ones, but rather make up a symbolic whole that must be investigated. Further questions arise about the use of basketry work, its function in everyday life and in rituals, and the bans on producing or using it. To a great extent, functionality, of greater or lesser complexity, depends on the form of each object, since a major feature of basketry is precisely its great range of specialized shapes.

5 Richard Schomburgk 1847, Crevaux 1883, Koch-Grünberg 1995, Goeje 1908.

6 Cf. van Velthem 1998.

7 The Wayana use seven different species of closed and open palm leaves.

8 Cf. Ricardo 2000: 19.

9 Cf. Guss 1989, van Velthem 1998, Ricardo 2000.

10 The Wayana conceive the components of the cosmos as beings with body paintings. Thus humans are the only ones who can modify this painting (everyday or ritual); the rest are condemned to wearing the same decoration forever. Furthermore, these body paintings are divided into three types: humans, and specifically the Wayana, are characterized by monochrome designs since their paradigm is the primordial woman; animals are associated with spots or dots, since a surface covered in spots or rounded stains iconically reproduces the skin of the jaguar, a key feature of the fauna of the Amazon; supernatural serpent-like beings are associated with stripes, since a surface with contrasting colours iconically represents the rainbow, which is a physical manifestation of *kamnanaimë*, a supernatural anaconda that emerged during the Creation. The stripe has to do with both this being and other supernatural ones, including anthropomorphic beings, who also had stripes, since as representatives of supernatural beings they shared the same powers.

11 Cf. Wilbert 1975b and Guss 1989.

12 Munn 1973, Pierce 1977.

13 Cf. Fock 1963, Guss 1989.

14 Frikel 1973: 15–20.

15 Cf. Fock 1963.

16 Cf. Ribeiro 1989, Müller 1990 and Gallois 1992 for other references.

17 The anaconda (*Eunectes murinus*), also known in Portuguese as *sucurijú*, *boiuçú*, *boiúna* and *viborão*, is the largest of the American constrictors and is non-poisonous.

18 *Arumã* (*Ischnosiphon* spp.) has a long flexible stalk and is found in waterlogged areas.

9

Testimony in Stone

Rock Art in the Amazon

EDITHE PEREIRA

Introduction

The origins of Amazonian rock art may be as old as the earliest human occupation of the Amazonian basin itself. Paintings at Pedra Pintada cave, Monte Alegre, on the lower Amazon, consist of bold red and yellow symbols and designs, and have been dated to 11,200 BP (fig. 9.1).[1] Other rock paintings at the Pedra Pintada shelter, in Roraima at the edge of the Guyana plateau, date from around 4,000 BP.[2] It appears that marking selected locations in the landscape by rock painting with mineral pigments or by incising and pecking designs into stone (petroglyphs) is a very ancient practice. From earliest times it appears that man has felt the need to leave an enduring trace in the vast geographical expanse of the Amazon. Nevertheless, other areas with evidence of early human occupation, such as the caves on the Carajás ridge in south-eastern Amazon, dating as far back as 8,000 BP, have not yet yielded any signs of rock art.[3] Altogether too few sites have so far been recorded in enough detail to propose any plausible stylistic sequences.

The intermittent history of rock art research can be traced back to missionaries, travellers and explorers in the region (see Barreto and Machado, this volume). Prehistoric rock art in the Amazon basin first came to the attention of European eyes in the seventeenth century. Some observers were curious, others dismissive. They struggled to understand when and why the signs, motifs and representations were created and what they might have meant to their makers. The huge gulf in comprehension between the creators and those who view and record it persists to this day.

The profusion and diversity of rock art bears witness to the integral role it played in tropical forest societies across the millennia. There are tenuous but demonstrable links between the motifs in the art and those found in other media, especially pottery. The inscriptions still exercise a potent hold on the imagination of all who see them, and nowadays this art is assuming renewed significance in defining indigenous identity and affirming long-standing connections with the landscape.

To date, more than 300 rock art sites have been found in the Brazilian Amazon (fig. 9.2). Nevertheless, systematic studies of rock art have only just begun in earnest and this means that there is much basic work to be done. Sites have to be located and logged, markings classified and similarities and differences identified, in order to assemble a graphic corpus for each area. The geographical distribution of known sites reveals certain areas with notable concentrations and others where there appear to be only isolated occurrences, as well as 'empty spaces' where no sites have yet been reported. I have compiled a comprehensive summary of bibliographical data on rock art sites in the whole Brazilian Amazon,[4] with a particular focus on eastern Amazonia. Three main areas of concentration of rock art are apparent: north-western Pará, the lower and middle Xingu and the Araguaia-Tocantins basin.[5] The best-known areas are the collective product of observations made by successive travellers and naturalists, complemented in certain instances by more recent methodical scientific surveys.

To begin with, I will briefly review some of the impressions and speculations gleaned from early accounts. I will then summarize the changing fortunes of rock art studies in Brazilian archaeology and conclude with a case study drawing upon my own efforts to develop a more systematic approach to recording and interpreting rock art.

Historical background

Religious missionaries provide many of the first reports, although they usually mention rock art as a matter of passing curiosity. Probably the earliest record is that of Fr. João de Sotto Mayor in 1656, whose mission was to convert Indians and prospect for gold.[6] His description of the petroglyphs near the Pacajá river in the lower Amazon indicates that their meaning was unknown to

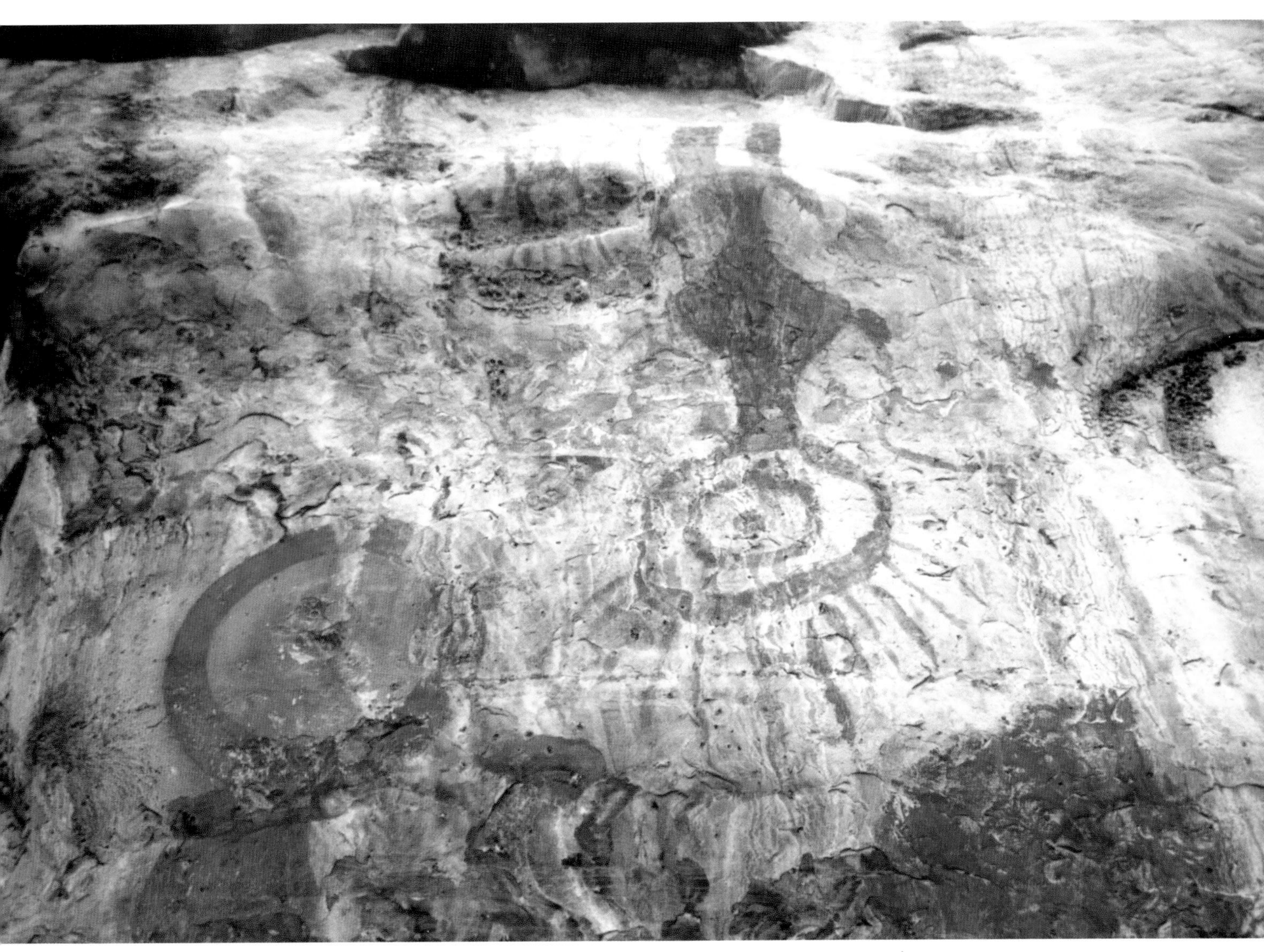

9.1 Rock paintings at the Serra da Lua site, Monte Alegre, lower Amazon, executed in vivid red and yellow pigments. Circles and geometric figures with complex shapes are common in this area.

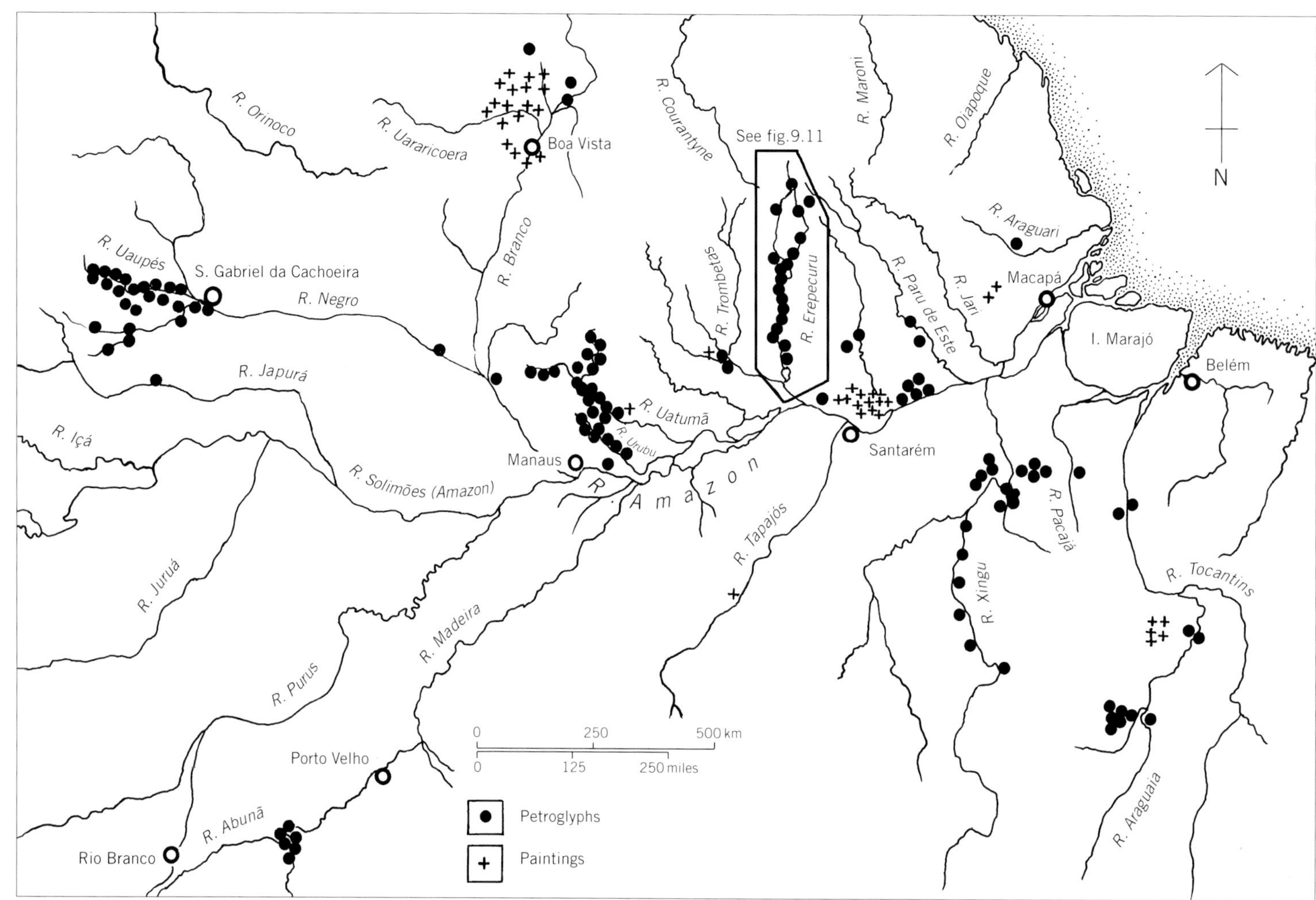

9.2 Map of petroglyph and rock painting sites recorded by early missionaries and travellers throughout the Amazon basin. The sites along the Erepecuru river valley (inset) are shown in detail in fig. 9.11.

the Indians travelling with him, perhaps as a consequence of the changes already brought about by European contact or simply because they themselves were from a different ethnic group:

> Journeying three lengths upstream along this river, I came to a boulder that everyone wanted to see: all along the way we were amongst the Tapejaras Indians, who said that everything was decorated with workings, figures and faces similar to our own saints that they have seen on altars: they said they knew not who was author of that work; some said it was the work of God and others, the devil. All this made us want to see this sight of the stone altar. I found the boulder to be worked by iron tools, and on it were those faces so ugly and misshapen that they might be the work of the devil, which I deduced from the workmanship and by the figure of a crocodile, struck on the other side of the boulder, that was the work of some idle Indians, although so old they did not know who had done it; finally, there is much superstition surrounding the boulder, and it is shown with such lack of reverence that some of the Indians, now Christians, even pleaded for those figures to grant them long lives.[7]

In the eighteenth century Fr. João Daniel described the rock inscriptions at Itamaracá falls on the Xingu river, lower Amazon, and in the town of Itacoatiara, on the middle Amazon, on the banks of the Amazonas river.[8] Bartholomeu Bueno de Campos Leme e Gusmão, a *bandeirante*,[9] mentions petroglyphs on Martírios (Martyrdom) Island, on the lower Araguaia river,[10] so-named because certain symbols among the inscriptions seemed, in their eyes, to represent the implements used in the martyrdom of Christ (such as hammer, nails, ladder, spear and crown of thorns).[11]

An early nineteenth-century account by the German naturalists Spix and Martius refers to petroglyphs along the Japurá river and especially around the Araracuara gorge of the Caquetá river in the north-west Amazon (fig. 9.3).[12] The botanist Richard Spruce in the course of his travels in the region from 1851 to 1853 both recorded and remarked on the petroglyphs he found along these rivers and their tributaries (fig. 9.4). It is worth quoting an excerpt from his account at length to capture something of the way he worked with his guides and informants:

9.3 Petroglyphs recorded by Spix and Martius along the Japurá river reproduced in Jean Baptiste Debret, *Voyage Pittoresque et Historique au Brésil*, 1834.

> As I sketched, I asked the Indians, 'Who had made those figures, and what they represented?' but received the universal reply of the Indian when he cares not to tell or will not take the trouble to recollect, 'Quien sabe, patron?' ('Who knows?'). But I understood enough of Barré to note that in their talk to each other they were saying, 'This is so-and-so, and this is so-and-so.' 'Yes,' I struck in, 'and don't you think this is so-and-so?' Thus led on, I got them to give their opinion of most of the figures. About some they were quite certain; about others they would speculate. Of all the figures the one marked G [fig. 9.4] was that whose origin seemed clearest both to them and to me. It represents a mandiocca-oven (called budári in Barré) – a large circular dish of fireproof pottery, supported on a wall of mud-masonry, which has an opening on one side (rudely figured at *a*), into which fire is put, and another at the opposite (as at *b*), which serves as a flue. Of the articles laid on the budári, *c* is the brush of piassaba tied tightly round at midway, which serves for sweeping the oven before the cassava cake or farinha is spread out to bake; *d* is the palm-leaf fan for blowing the fire; and my Indians would have it that *d´* was another fan, but the hook at the corner (which, whenever it occurs in these figures, indicates a bit of liana-rope by which the utensil is hung up) renders it probable that something else was meant [see Oliver, this volume, for discussion of manioc processing]; *e* is a stage (or shelf) such as may be seen of various sizes hung from the roof of an Indian's hut, but especially over the oven and hearth, the smoke from which acts as an antiseptic to the dried fish and other viands kept on the stages, and also partially keeps off the cockroaches; *f* is either the mandiocca-grater or, more probably, a flat piece of board, sometimes with a hole to insert fingers, which is used to raise the edges of the cassava cake and to aid in turning it over. All these articles are in use to this day throughout a vast extent of the country on the Orinoco and Casiquari.
>
> The figures marked B [fig. 9.5] were declared by my Indians to be dolphins, whereof two species abound in the Amazon and Orinoco.
>
> C they said was plainly the same sort of thing as the big papers (maps) I was

continually poring over. For *a* is the town – often consisting of a single annular house, with a road from it leading down to the caño (or stream leading into the main river, *c*), while *b* is a track leading through the forest to another tributary stream which here and there expands into lakes, while other lakes send their waters to it. There were other figures apparently geographical, but the one I copied was the most complicated and perfect.

D [fig. 9.6] are ray-fishes, which are found of enormous size in the Casiquari and Rio Negro, and sometimes inflict deadly wounds on incautious bathers.

E on Figs. 16 and 18 [figs 9.4 and 6] and perhaps A on Fig. 17 [fig. 9.5] was thought by my companions to be the quiver for holding the darts of the blowing-cane (blow-pipe).

By the time I had covered three sheets with figures, the sun began to beat hot on my head, protected by only a light cap, and although my pilot told me that farther away in the forest there were more granite sheets covered with pictures, I was obliged to content myself with what I had already seen and done; for I had engaged to meet the Comissario of San Fernando at Esmeralda on Christmas Day, and to get there I had still a long voyage before me, going slowly along as I did in my large boat and gathering plants all the way.[13]

9.4 Petroglyphs recorded by Richard Spruce at Laja de Capibara, Casiquiare river, in 1853 (Spruce 1908: 477). According to local Indians G on the diagram represents a manioc oven (*budare*), while E (also in 9.6) could be a quiver holding the darts for the blowgun.

In 1863 naturalist Ferreira Penna recorded petroglyphs at the Itamaracá Falls on the lower Xingu river. Illustrations were sent to Ladislau Netto, then Director of the Museu Nacional in Rio de Janeiro, along with an interpretation of the images:

So, our careful examination of the characters in this very curious cryptography, suggests that they seem to represent nothing more than a great village fortified by a surrounding palisade. On the bottom left of the same image, there are representations of dwellings or rather bunkers, at the entrance to, or path to, the village, as if the local inhabitants had built them for defensive purposes [fig. 9.7]. Three chiefs, whose name or title was connected to the character of the reptiles, by whose figures they were represented, are represented in these bunkers as if in some kind of conference or discussion. One of these lizard-like figures, the one with the longest tail and seemingly representing the people of the fortified village, where he is positioned between the bunkers, receives a message from the other two lizard figures, who seem to be strangers at the village. In addition to these characters, there are curving paths at each end of the village, both of them entrances, if we are to go by the appearance of these unusual curves.[14]

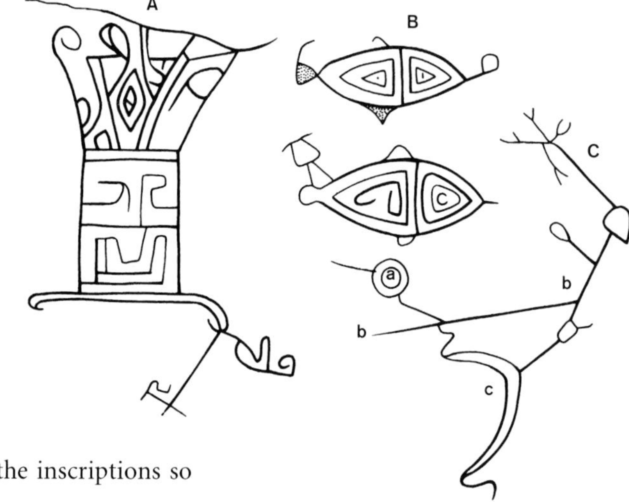

9.5 Petroglyphs recorded by Richard Spruce at Laja de Capibara in 1853 (Spruce 1908: 479). According to his informants motif A is a dart quiver and motif B represents dolphins.

Ferreira Penna also wrote to Tristão de Alencar Araripe, a counsellor at the Brazilian Historical and Geographical Institute, reporting his find and explaining the need to produce a cast of the inscriptions so they could be studied.[15]

It was the geologist, Charles F. Hartt, who undertook the first serious study specifically dedicated to rock art in the Amazon. In 1871 he published an article entitled 'Brazilian Rock Inscriptions', featuring the paintings in the rock shelters of the Serra do Ererê, near the town of Monte Alegre.[16] He describes the colours, shapes and dis-

9.6 Petroglyphs recorded by Richard Spruce at Laja de Capibara in 1853 (Spruce 1908, page 480). According to informants motif D represents ray-fishes.

tribution of the figures and motifs. He also reported petroglyphs on the lower Tocantins river, on the Serra da Escama near the town of Óbidos, and near Serpa (now Itacoatiara) in the middle Amazon, as well as other inscriptions at Mont D'Argent, on the Oiapoque river, in what is now French Guyana.[17]

In a further journey made in 1872 Ferreira Penna noted the existence of rock paintings at Buracão cave.[18] A succession of other travellers also made sporadic references to rock art in disparate locations. Among these are Franz Keller-Leusinger,[19] who described petroglyphs on the upper Madeira river near Bolivia, and João Barbosa Rodrigues, who wrote about the rock inscriptions he found in the Serra da Escama at Óbidos, on the Nhamundá and Urubu rivers, and at Itacoatiara.[20] Barbosa Rodrigues mentions rock inscriptions 'of anthropomorphic, zoomorphic, and fantastic shapes drawn with elaborate curves in combination with straight lines' near the towns of Moura and Airão on the banks of the Rio Negro.[21]

In his study of the Mundurucu Indians Antônio Manoel Gonçalves Tocantins remarks on the paintings he found at a site known as Pedra do Cantagalo, on the left bank of the Tapajós river.[22] On asking about their meaning, he was told by the Mundurucu Indians:

> Mundurucu traditions relate how Caru-Sacaebê, after destroying the Acupary longhouse to punish the ingratitude of the local inhabitants, founded the Necodemos longhouse that became the cradle of humankind. He then inscribed these images between the two villages as a monument to this memorable deed. Caru-Sacaebê made Necodemos strong and wealthy, then followed downstream on the Tapajoz, leaving more markings on its banks so that the Mundurucu would keep alive the memory of his deeds and of his passage among them.

9.7 Petroglyphs recorded by Ferreira Penna at the Itamaracá Falls on the lower Xingu river in 1863.

This same indigenous group referred to the existence of similar paintings in other parts of the Tapajós basin.

In the second half of the nineteenth century and early years of the twentieth century French naturalists Henri and Olga Coudreau explored several rivers in the eastern Amazon. Henri Coudreau reported on rock inscriptions on the Bacajá, Tapajós, Araguaia, Tueré and Xingu rivers. After his death Olga Coudreau continued to explore the Maicuru and Cuminá rivers. On finding rock inscriptions at Cajual Falls, she wrote:

> It is one in the afternoon, we stand before enormous stones covered in indigenous drawings. I do not know if such pictographs could ever be of any use. However I will take every interest in making notes of all the rock drawings I see on the river. Perhaps they will sometime in the future help as evidence of relations in the past between human groups that are often so distant. These pictographs are far removed from the fine inscriptions on the Palauqué, but they show that in the past there were Indians on this river, which is now deserted.[23]

ABOVE **9.9 Petroglyph on a boulder in midstream close to the eastern bank of the Pirá-paraná, one of the major rivers of the Uaupés territory. Known to the Barasana Indians as the Rock of Nyi, this is considered to be the place where the first human beings were created.**

Coudreau's abiding interest in this subject is apparent throughout her work *Voyage au Cuminá* that features several drawings, and her map of the Maicuru river shows a site upstream of Cachoeira Seca where there were 'rocks with drawings'.

The first major compilation of Brazilian rock art was published by Araripe in 1887. In addition to listing a large number of sites, he emphasized the need for more detailed studies of these ancient cultural remains. Subsequent and more synthetic works of the same kind were published and a few interpretations ventured.[24] The first field trips specifically aimed at locating rock art sites also took place around this time. In 1890–91 Stradelli (1900) explored the Uaupés river and noted a large number of rock inscriptions that he viewed at first as little more than a leisure time pursuit of its makers (fig. 9.8). However, after studying the linguistic and mythological aspects of indigenous culture in the region, he came round to thinking that the rock drawings were invested with deeper significance, which he sought to decipher with help from the Indians.

In the early twentieth century German ethnologist Theodor Koch-Grünberg explored the upper Rio Negro and its affluents.[25] His *Südamerikanische Felszeichnungen* (1907) is one of the most important sources of data on rock inscriptions in this region with twenty-nine pages of illustrations and a map, but he concluded that there was no particular meaning in the rock drawings. Koch-Grünberg and Stradelli's diametrically opposed viewpoints created a controversy that was to influence the amateur archaeologists at the time in Brazil. Rock art also came to be seen by some as a form of writing, variously thought to have been made by Greeks, Carthaginians and

LEFT 9.8 Recent photograph of petroglyphs on boulders by the Uaupés river. Early travellers viewed these kinds of rudimentary images as evidence that rock art was essentially a casual and rather meaningless pursuit.

Phoenicians who had explored the region, or as a kind of pre-historic writing from which all other alphabets were derived. There were very few studies exclusively focused on rock art.[26] More often than not it is mentioned incidentally but usually not analysed.[27]

Two of the most significant studies in the 1960s and 1970s are those made by Brajnikov[28] and Reichel-Dolmatoff.[29] The latter examined the use of hallucinatory substances by the Tukanoan Indians of the north-west Amazon who paint the walls of their houses, pottery, gourds, stools and other objects under the influence of the hallucinogen *Banisteriopsis caapi*, commonly known as *caapi*, *yajé* or *Ayahuasca* (see McEwan, this volume). Reichel-Dolmatoff experimented by giving his Tukanoan informants blank pages to draw on while under the influence of yajé. He found that these drawings had motifs similar to phosphenes.[30] Moreover there were clear correspondences with motifs found among the petroglyphs near the rapids in the area, which the Indians interpreted as elements derived from creation myths bound up with the origins of human beings and with human fertility and procreation (fig. 9.9).[31]

In the 1970s and 1980s work began on a number of ambitious archaeological research projects.[32] Rock art sites were reported in only a few cases,[33] including two sites containing paintings and one with petroglyphs in the Trombetas river basin,[34] and three petroglyph sites on the Bacajá river, a right-bank tributary of the lower Xingu.[35] None of these, however, was formally investigated. On the Uatumã river and its tributaries in the central Amazon twenty-one sites with petroglyphs and a cave with paintings were found and two petroglyph styles named Uatumã-Abonari and Pitinga identified.[36] The former style is dominated by geometrical motifs and the presence of masks, whereas the latter comprises mainly zoomorphic figures, no masks, and few geometrical motifs.[37]

On the lower Araguaia river the investigation of threatened sites conducted by local concerned citizens eventually led to the creation of a state park.[38] Here the outstanding site is Martírios Island that I mentioned earlier. Some 2,000 metres long and 700 metres wide, it is liberally covered with over 5,000 petroglyphs.

9.10 Wall of a rock shelter at the Pedra Pintada site, Roraima, with repeated grid motifs painted in red and yellow.

In 1985 a new kind of archaeological conservation project was launched to fight vandalism and implement protective measures at sites in the upper Branco basin.[39] Here two styles were defined: Parimé, in which abstract-linear designs appear most frequently, and Surumu, in which naturalistic signs predominate. A third style is characterized by schematic biomorphic figures with links to other styles in northern South America and the Antilles.[40] Excavations at the Pedra Pintada shelter (fig. 9.10) in Roraima showed that the paintings were made by foragers who occupied the region before 4,000 BP. There is not enough material to offer a chronological sequence for the paintings, but there are suggestive stylistic connections to the north in what is now Venezuela,[41] as well as perhaps Guyana.

As I mentioned briefly in the introduction, investigations at Pedra Pintada cave in the early 1990s revealed paintings dating to 11,200 BP. The dating is based on similarities between the chemical compositions of pigments found in the older excavation strata and those on the cave wall.[42] This date appears to indicate the introduction of cave painting in the region, although it is clearly not possible to prove that all cave paintings are so ancient.[43]

In the upper Madeira basin, near the border with Bolivia, several sites with petroglyphs were found with three distinct styles. Style A was typically executed using a technique of pecking and smoothing the rock surface, and includes motifs such as concentric circles, spirals, undulating lines, straight lines, quadrangular geometrical figures, complex and abstract zoomorphic figures, and stylized masks. Style B is characterized by the same technique but the main motifs are frontal human figures in low relief. Style C was found at just one site on the lower Abunã river, and the technique used involved making fine V-shaped incisions and motifs that are 'straight lines and curves, parallel zigzags forming quadrangular panels, series of dotted lines and curves, triangular masks or anthropomorphic faces (with flattened top and convex sides), and geometrical figures'.[44]

More recently Prous has compiled a comprehensive classification of Amazonian rock art based on travellers' reports, compilations from the first half of the twentieth century, and private photographs.[45] He identifies a Guyanese-Amazonian petroglyph tradition, mainly composed of human figures represented in two ways: a) head only, and b) head and body.[46] It is in general agreement with my own assessment of the petroglyphs from the Ereperucu river basin described below.[47]

9.11 Map of the principal petroglyph groups recorded along the Erepecuru river valley. Many of these groups are found adjacent to rapids and falls. Note that there are variations in scale both within and between groups.

The Erepecuru river region

The Erepecuru river basin in north-west Pará state is one of the most interesting concentrations of rock art, matched only perhaps by those in the Rio Negro basin. Both areas boast an impressive range of sites, many known thanks to the work of nineteenth- and early twentieth-century naturalists and travellers. Nevertheless, it is important to bear in mind that these represent a partial and uneven sample that probably selectively emphasizes the most visible and accessible motifs. Along the Erepecuru and its upper tributaries – the Murapi and Paru de Oeste rivers and the Igarapé Campo Grande – an inventory of twenty-five petroglyph sites has been compiled from such accounts. Nineteen are located along the Erepecuru proper, four at the Paru de Oeste, one at the Murapi and one at the Igarapé Campo Grande. I have systematically compiled all the visual references that are to be found in the historical accounts to create a map showing the spatial distribution of these sites together with a description of the principal techniques and styles (fig. 9.11).[48]

The petroglyph clusters are clearly concentrated at carefully chosen locations along the course of the river and are typically found in three different settings: next to archaeological sites with *terra preta*, in close proximity to large waterfalls and in places where fishing is most productive.[49] Indeed, petroglyphs are first found only upstream from Descanso Island, which is located right above the first set of rapids.

The petroglyphs are visible only during the dry season when the lowering of the

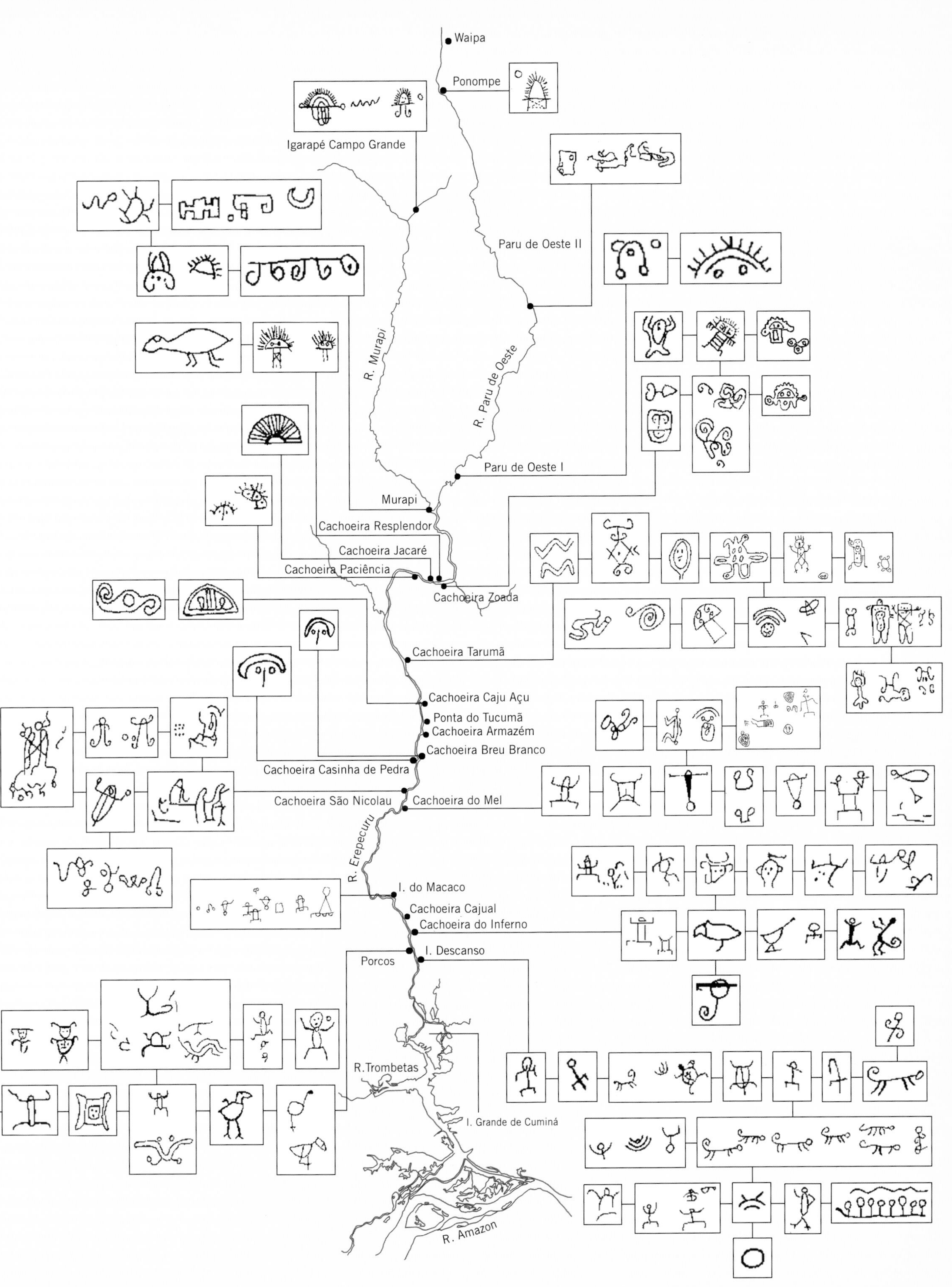

Waipa
Ponompe
Igarapé Campo Grande
Paru de Oeste II
R. Murapi
R. Paru de Oeste
Paru de Oeste I
Murapi
Cachoeira Resplendor
Cachoeira Jacaré
Cachoeira Paciência
Cachoeira Zoada
Cachoeira Tarumã
Cachoeira Caju Açu
Ponta do Tucumã
Cachoeira Armazém
Cachoeira Breu Branco
Cachoeira Casinha de Pedra
Cachoeira São Nicolau
Cachoeira do Mel
R. Erepecuru
I. do Macaco
Cachoeira Cajual
Cachoeira do Inferno
I. Descanso
Porcos
R.Trombetas
I. Grande de Cuminá
R. Amazon

9.12–13 Detail of superimposed rock engravings at the Boa Vista site, Prainha, lower Amazon, including a representation of a human figure with facial adornments and splayed limbs, as shown in the drawing fig. 9.13.

waters changes the landscape. After the flood peak, the river contracts to reveal extensive exposed bedrock surfaces over which narrow streams and rivulets of water flow. The petroglyphs occur either on wide, flat, rocky surfaces or on large boulders.

The typology of motifs is based on analysis of the archive of photographs and drawings from these accounts, as well as on the overlays that I myself have made at Descanso Island. This typology is far from being definitive but it can serve as a point of departure for future research.[50] Out of a total sample of some 218 figures, three principal elements were identified: geometric, anthropomorphic and zoomorphic motifs. The first two are by far the most common, whereas the zoomorphic motifs represent only 10 per cent of the total.

The anthropomorphic glyphs

Humans are represented by both complete figures as well as by representations of disembodied heads. In the full-length figures the heads are often either devoid of any detail or feature geometric motifs that bear little resemblance to actual facial features. In those cases where a face is represented the only recognizable features are the eyes and mouth. The abdomen and limbs can be shown in different ways, commonly as a rectangular form with spindly appendages. In some cases the abdomen has geometric or anthropomorphic filler elements. One such example is found both on the Erepecuru river and also among the petroglyphs of the Prainha area, located about 250 km to the south-east (figs 9.12–13).

Different kinds of body adornments can be observed on the head, face and arms of the whole human figures, as well as on what appear to be items of clothing. The limbs are properly proportioned in relation to the body. Most figures give the impression of being static, although in rare cases the idea of movement seems to be suggested by the position of the arms and legs. These human figures are executed by shallow incisions engraved into the bedrock and range in height from 15 to 100 cm (most being 30 to 50 cm high).[51] Isolated, bodiless heads comprise about a third of all human representations in the Erepecuru assemblages. Semi-circular forms prevail: most have eyes and mouths, fewer have noses or ears, and in only one figure is the face a complete rendering of facial features comprising eyes, eyebrows, nose and mouth.

Both the full-bodied and single heads are invariably depicted frontally in association with geometric motifs or combined with other human figures. The identification of the activities represented in the composite scenes is not easy, for each figure seems to be independently represented from the other.

In the lower Erepecuru the anthropomorphic motifs seem to be much simpler. Faces are absent in most of the figures, the torso is spindly and the arms are raised. Close to the São Nicolau falls there are two whole body figures composed of a combination of volutes. On the Tarumã islands archipelago, anthropomorphs also consist of volute elements but only on the arms, legs and facial outline.

Upstream from the Tarumã islands there are a series of human figures (both complete and isolated heads) drawn in more detail. Some complete figures feature a radial adornment on their heads and faces. The torso is always filled by geometric motifs and many figures also have fingers.

Although subtle differences can be noted in the human representations of the Erepecuru, it is still too early to confidently identify broad stylistic groups in this area. These observations point nevertheless to the range of internal variation found within Amazonian petroglyph tradition.

Zoomorphic glyphs

Among the zoomorphic motifs, monkeys and birds are most common. Monkeys are found at only two sites.[52] They have empty circular heads, spindly trunks, limbs in poses that suggest movement, and a typically long spiral tail. Descanso Island boasts a scene with several monkeys running behind one another in the same direction, the only such scene observed in the Erepecuru. Birds also appear at only two sites and are executed in the same kind of graphic style. Other animals, such as frogs, lizards, fishes and snakes, are represented just once each in the entire region. These are usually rendered in profile. Only one bird is rendered frontally while the snake, frog and lizard are depicted as if seen from above. Zoomorphic motifs range in size from 15 to 100 cm and the head, torso and limbs are shown in proportion.

Geometric glyphs

Geometric motifs account for nearly half the total number of figures. Many comprise symmetrically structured curvilinear elements, and circles and ovals are also common. They range in size from 15 to 50 cm and are executed by incisions of varying depths. Geometric motifs seem to appear in all sites of the region. Following the anthropomorphic figures, they are less elaborated in the lower course of the river and become more complex upstream.

Rock art in the Amazon today

Research and published data on rock art in the Amazon is really quite limited in scope and far from being either fully representative or complete. Nevertheless, some basic patterns in the distribution of styles and motifs throughout the region are apparent.

With regard to rock paintings, there is a range of quite distinct traditions, themes and styles. Four areas stand out: Roraima (fig. 9.10), Alenquer (fig. 9.14), Monte

9.14 Painted scene of a row of human figures holding hands at the Casa da Pedra site, Alenquer, lower Amazon.

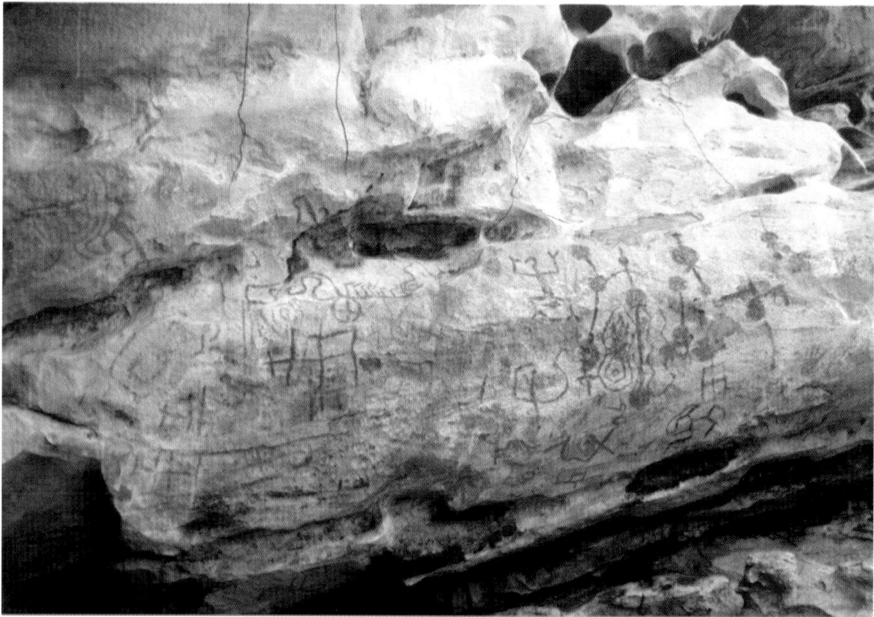

9.15 Painted composition at Pedra do Pilão site, Monte Alegre, lower Amazon, comprising anthropomorphic and zoomorphic representations together with other abstract elements.

Alegre (figs 9.1, 9.15) and Serra das Andorinhas. Petroglyphs, on the other hand, seem to divide into two broad groups lying north and south of the main course of the Amazon proper. Petroglyphs found along the north bank of the Amazon belong to a single, well-defined, Amazonian tradition that extends into neighbouring countries such as Colombia, Venezuela and the Guyanas.[53] This is characterized by frontal anthropomorphic figures with facial features. They may be complete, with head, torso and limbs, or consist of just the head alone. These figures appear either singly or in groups but not in composite scenes. On some of the southern tributaries, such as the lower Araguaia and lower Xingu, zoomorphic motifs predominate (fig. 9.16).

Archaeological context is vital in order to understand more about rock art. In addition to describing the varied motifs, themes and styles, the building of a chronologi-

9.16 Animal figures, human footprints and geometric forms abound at the Pedra das Arraias site, lower Xingu river region.

9.17 Stylized representation of a human face. The correct orientation is uncertain because the boulders may have been displaced. Ponta do Cipó site, Prainha, lower Amazon.

cal framework will help open up new perspectives. Radiocarbon dating offers one way of providing a temporal context. Certain sites in the Prainha region on the lower Amazon feature rock art painted in a combination of black, yellow and red pigments.[54] The black pigment is derived from charcoal which can be dated directly.[55]

Another way of placing rock art in context is to link it directly or indirectly with other elements of material culture that survive in the archaeological record, though studies of this kind are still uncommon in Brazil.[56] On the upper Madeira river, in the state of Rondônia, it has been reported that vessels and potsherds 'bear incised decoration that resembles some stylised masks found in petroglyphs'.[57] Analysis of rock art in Prainha and Monte Alegre as well as Tapajó pottery from the area reveals stylistic similarities with the anthropomorphic motifs on the Monte Alegre pottery and cave paintings, and with the Prainha petroglyphs (fig. 9.17).[58] The parallels are striking and suggestive but require a discriminating study.

The need to explore the possible relations between material culture and rock art has been underlined by recent finds in Amapá. In the Maracá river region, in the south-east of the state of Amapá, a black earth site was excavated, and among the ceramic material collected was a rim sherd with incised decoration featuring a prominent anthropomorphic figure represented in a similar way to those engraved on rock-shelter walls at Prainha.[59] Likewise, at the township of Santana (south of Macapá) an urn sherd was found that is decorated with a face also similar to those on rock inscriptions in Prainha.[60] On the lower Xingu some themes represented in rock inscriptions are also to be found on objects made by indigenous groups living today in the upper Xingu river area.[61]

Archaeological research therefore has a major role to play in the contextualization of rock art and in establishing both cultural continuities and disjunctions. Much remains to be done to explore the relationships between material culture and rock art and the role that these can play together in defining archaeological cultures. These will help to bridge the enormous gaps in our knowledge of the region's history.

Acknowledgements

I would like to thank the Museu Paraense Emílio Goeldi, Dr Peter Mann de Toledo (Director) and Dr Roberto Araújo (Coordinator for the Social Sciences Department), for the steady support of my research activities. I thank also the CNPq (Conselho Nacional de Desenvolvimento Científico e Tecnológico) for providing research resources and a research grant. Thanks to Anne Marie Pessis, who 'opened my eyes' to rock art, and to Gabriela Martin for her constant support of my work. Thanks to Vera Guapindaia and Marcos Magalhães who joined me in my surveys for rock art sites, and to Daniel Lopes, whose lessons, critiques and suggestions have always been helpful. Fieldwork could not have been accomplished without the help of Regina Farias, Raimundo Santos and Raimundo Mardock. I also thank Colin McEwan, Cristiana Barreto and Eduardo Neves for inviting me to participate in this volume, for their careful editing of the manuscript, and for helping to make Amazonian archaeology better known to the general public.

NOTES

1 Roosevelt 1996.

2 Ribeiro *et al.* 1989. 'Pedra pintada' means 'painted rock' in Portuguese. That explains why these sites, which are located several hundred kilometres apart, have the same name.

3 Magalhães 1993.

4 *Amazonia Legal Brasileira* refers to the area as officially defined for planning purposes. According to Section I, Article 2 of Law 5,173 of 27 October 1966, it comprises the states of Pará, Amazonas, Acre and the former Federal Territories of Amapá, Roraima and Rondônia, and portions of the states of Goiás (north of parallel 13), Mato Grosso (north of parallel 16) and Maranhão (west of 44° latitude).

5 Based on analysis of 65 sites: E. Pereira 1990.

6 Sotto Mayor 1914. Although somewhat imprecise, this report provides details of great value for the study of rock art in the Amazon, both for the data it contains and for its old age. This is probably the second oldest such account in Brazil. The oldest is attributed to a commanding officer, Captain Feliciano Coelho de Carvalho, who in 1598 found and copied rock inscriptions on the Araçagipe river, in the state of Paraíba (Brandônio 1943).

7 Sotto Mayor 1914: 167.

8 Daniel 1976: 57, 61–2.

9 Name given to members of the armed expeditions known as *bandeiras* organized from the late sixteenth until the early nineteenth century to explore the backlands of Brazil, seeking for Indians and gold mines.

10 Siqueira 1886: 21.

11 The island and its inscriptions became known as a point of reference for explorers looking for gold. However, as the island remained partly submerged during the rainy season, many travellers failed to find it or the legendary gold mines. The search for gold in the region gave rise to a series of stories about the 'Martyrdom Trail'. Much later, Martírios Island and its petroglyphs were mentioned in several travel logs (Vellard 1931; Couto de Magalhães 1975: 221; M. Ferreira 1974), but the illustrations of the figures were not published until 1948 (Ehrenreich 1948: 91).

12 Spix and Martius 1981: 231, 240–41, 244, 250, 256–7. Like so many Amazonian rivers, the Caquetá river in the Colombian Amazon changes its name when it crosses the border with Brazil, becoming the Japurá.

13 Spruce 1908, II: 476–80.

14 Netto 1885: 541.

15 Araripe 1887.

16 It was translated and published by the *Revista do Instituto Archaeológico e Histórico de Pernambuco* under the title 'Inscripções en rochedos do Brasil' (Hartt 1895). Hartt (1898: 335) again mentions the paintings of the Serra do Ererê in a geological study in the lower Amazonas carried out in 1875–8. Orville Derby, a geologist who accompanied Hartt in the work of the Brazilian Geological Commission preparing studies of the lower Amazonas, mentions cave paintings on the Cachorro hill, on the Cachorro river (a left bank affluent of the Trombetas river), and rock inscriptions on the Serra da Escama mountains in Óbidos (Derby 1898: 379, 371).
17 See also Pereira 1992b for rock inscriptions on Mont D'Argent.
18 Other scholars who subsequently visited this cave include Lima Guedes in 1896 (Lima Guedes 1898), Peter Paul Hilbert in 1954, and Klaus Hilbert in 1988. A travel account by Chmyz and Sganzerla (1991) offers illustrations of many of the paintings found at Buracão.
19 Keller-Leusinger 1874: 50–56.
20 Barbosa Rodrigues 1892.
21 Barbosa Rodrigues 1885: 168–70.
22 Gonçalves Tocantins 1877: 106.
23 Coudreau 1901: 34.
24 Among these publications, those by Carvalho (1909), Brandão (1937), Rouse (1949), J. Pereira (1952, 1967), and Sampaio and Toschauer (1955) deserve special mention.
25 The Içana, Aiary, Cuduiary, Tiquié, Curicuriari and Pira-Paraná rivers.
26 Reports of cave paintings and petroglyphs continued to appear sporadically in different studies, such as the geological and ethnological reports published by the Brazilian Border Demarcation Commission in the first half of the twentieth century (Rauschert 1959, Vellard 1931, Borges 1933).
27 A descriptive summary of the archaeological sites officially registered in the Amazon until the late 1970s included several dozen ceramic sites and only eleven petroglyph sites (Simões and Araújo Costa 1978: 68, 85, 87, 111, 113, 135, 150). In a revised edition, published some years later, the number of listed rock art sites was reduced to eight (Simões 1983: 28–9, 64–5, 67, 72). Likewise a summary of archaeological research carried out by the Museu Goeldi in the Amazon from 1870 to 1981 made a single reference to rock art sites: a photograph of petroglyphs on the middle Urubu river in the central Amazon without providing details of the site (Simões 1981b). Finally, one recent review of the human occupation of the Amazon completely omits any mention of rock art, although the authors were aware of its existence. In 1982 the partial results of the PRONAPABA program, which stands for National Archaeological Research Program in the Amazon Basin, were published without any mention of the region's rock art (Simões and Araujo Costa 1987, Simões and Corrêa 1987, Simões and Kalkmann 1987, Simões and Fróes 1987).
28 Brajnikov (1974) sought to identify similarities between rock art found in Amur-Ussuri, central Australia, and that found in the Amazon and thus confirm A.P. Okladnikov's hypothesis that a culture originating in the lower Amur river (north-east Asia) had been diffused to other regions across the Pacific. The study compared the inscriptions in Marajó pottery, the rock inscriptions on the Japurá river and those found in the Amur-Ussuri region. Okladnikov's hypothesis is highly questionable, and the work itself neither brings any new data on Amazonian rock art nor adds anything to the information that Spix and Martius (1981) collected on the Japurá river. However, it does have the merit of being one of the very few studies in this period to focus on rock art in the Amazon.
29 1967, 1968, 1976b.
30 The bright sensations experienced when the eyes are pressured or stimulated by hallucination.
31 Although Reichel-Dolmatoff's inferences may well have some validity, there is as yet no direct and convincing data to prove that the use of hallucinogens inspired the creation of prehistoric rock art. In the same vein Neves (1998b) has cautioned that all artistic output among Amazonian groups should not be automatically interpreted as stemming from hallucinogenic experiences.
32 These were financed as part of large construction projects such as dams and hydroelectric power plants, and mineral prospecting funded by the federal government to encourage regional industry. In accordance with special Brazilian legislation, such as 'Protection of Archaeological Deposits' (Law No. 3924, 26 July 1961) and, subsequently, Resolution No. 001/86 of Brazil's official environmental body (CONAMA), the contractors commissioned by Great Projects sought research institutes to survey and conserve archaeological sites in the areas covered by the programme.
33 It was not possible to consult reports prepared in the areas around the Balbina and Samuel hydroelectric dams. Data shown for these areas is based only on material published previously. The library of Museu Paraense Emílio Goeldi, where I am a research associate, facilitated access to other reports.
34 Araújo Costa *et al.* 1986.
35 Araújo Costa and Caldarelli 1988.
36 The rock art sites located in this area represent anyway around 70 per cent of the total number of rock art sites recorded in the Brazilian Amazon in the 1980s (Miller 1992b).
37 Corrêa, 1994:145
38 Particularly due to the work of Noé von Atzingen, a naturalist based in the south-eastern Amazon.
39 This work lists twenty sites with cave paintings, eight petroglyph sites, and one with both paintings and petroglyphs (Ribeiro *et al.* 1986, 1987, 1989 and 1996; P. Ribeiro 1999).
40 The denomination of the Aishalton style was also applied to these petroglyphs. Williams (1985)
41 Ribeiro 1986.
42 Based on a new analysis of older work and on results of her own research, Roosevelt assumes that human occupation in the Amazon began long ago and reached the cultural complexity of chiefdoms. This cultural process, she believes, followed a chronological sequence comprising the following periods: Palaeoindian, Archaic, Formative and Chiefdom. Roosevelt sees rock art and lithic artefacts as characteristic of the Palaeoindian (Roosevelt 1992; Roosevelt *et al.* 1996).
43 Differences in style, superimposition, and the existence of thematic and graphic similarity between cave paintings and decorative motifs on the region's pottery raise the need for a certain prudence in the sense of not generalizing this dating to all cave paintings in the Monte Alegre region (Pereira 1996). In 1986 Uruguayan archaeologist Mario Consens also visited some cave painting sites in the Monte Alegre region to assess the archaeological potential of the area. In his report Consens (1988, 1989) offers some general comments on technique, superimposition, conservation and diachronic features of cave paintings, but soon his research in this region was discontinued.
44 Miller 1992a: 227.
45 Particularly noteworthy for summarizing a considerable amount of data on rock art in the Amazon are an annotated bibliography of rock art in Brazil by Colonelli and Magalhães (1975) and yet another, by Albano (1982).
46 Prous 1991, 1994.
47 Pereira 1990, 1994, 1996.
48 For this compilation the works of Coudreau (1901), Aguiar (1943) and Pinto (1930: 257–61, 309–10, 321–2) were particularly important due to their detailed descriptions of the main waterfall and rapids along the Erepecuru, which are also where the petroglyphs abound. Because a detailed map is not yet available, I used the one drawn by Olga Coudreau at the beginning of the twentieth century. This served as an important tool to plot the sites, once all rapids were indicated, and some of the petroglyphs appear as 'drawn rocks'.
49 Frikel 1959: 5.
50 Although there are risks in establishing a typology based on indirect sources, two arguments justify the procedures employed here. First, these are not isolated sites located far away from each other, but rather an aggregate of sites within the same region, with a sample of the glyphs presented in each of them. Second, these are the only sources of information on petroglyphs so far available for the area. This reasoning is strengthened by the fact that it is very difficult to travel through the Erepecuru and that there were no other previous synthetic treatment of its petroglyphs.
51 This can only be observed in the figures from Descanso Island and the Breu waterfall.
52 Descanso Island and Inferno waterfall.
53 Pereira 1996.
54 Pereira 1997.
55 Pers. comm., Conceição Lage, 1999.
56 Ávila 1996, Torres 1996. In other parts of the world the relationship between decorative themes in pottery and rock art has helped to establish a timeline for this prehistoric form of expression. In Spain parallels between decorative motifs in Neolithic Cardeal ceramics and the macro-schematic cave paintings in eastern Spain helped in the chronological determination of the latter (Marti and Hernandez 1988). In Bolivia studies in the Mizque river region (Lewis 1996: 17) and in Quilima (Strecker 1996: 10) also point to possible connections between decorative motifs in pottery and rock art.
57 Miller 1992a: 227.
58 Pereira 1996.
59 Guapindaia 1999.
60 Conserved at the Museu Histórico Joaquim Caetano, Macapá, and donated by an inhabitant of Igarapé do Lago, Santana.
61 Other authors have also noted such similarities. Monod-Becquelin's (1993: 531) study of the body-painting customs of the Trumaí on the upper Xingu points to similarities in abstract motifs on archaeological material dating to the thirteenth century that are still in use to this day.

PART IV

ENCOUNTERS

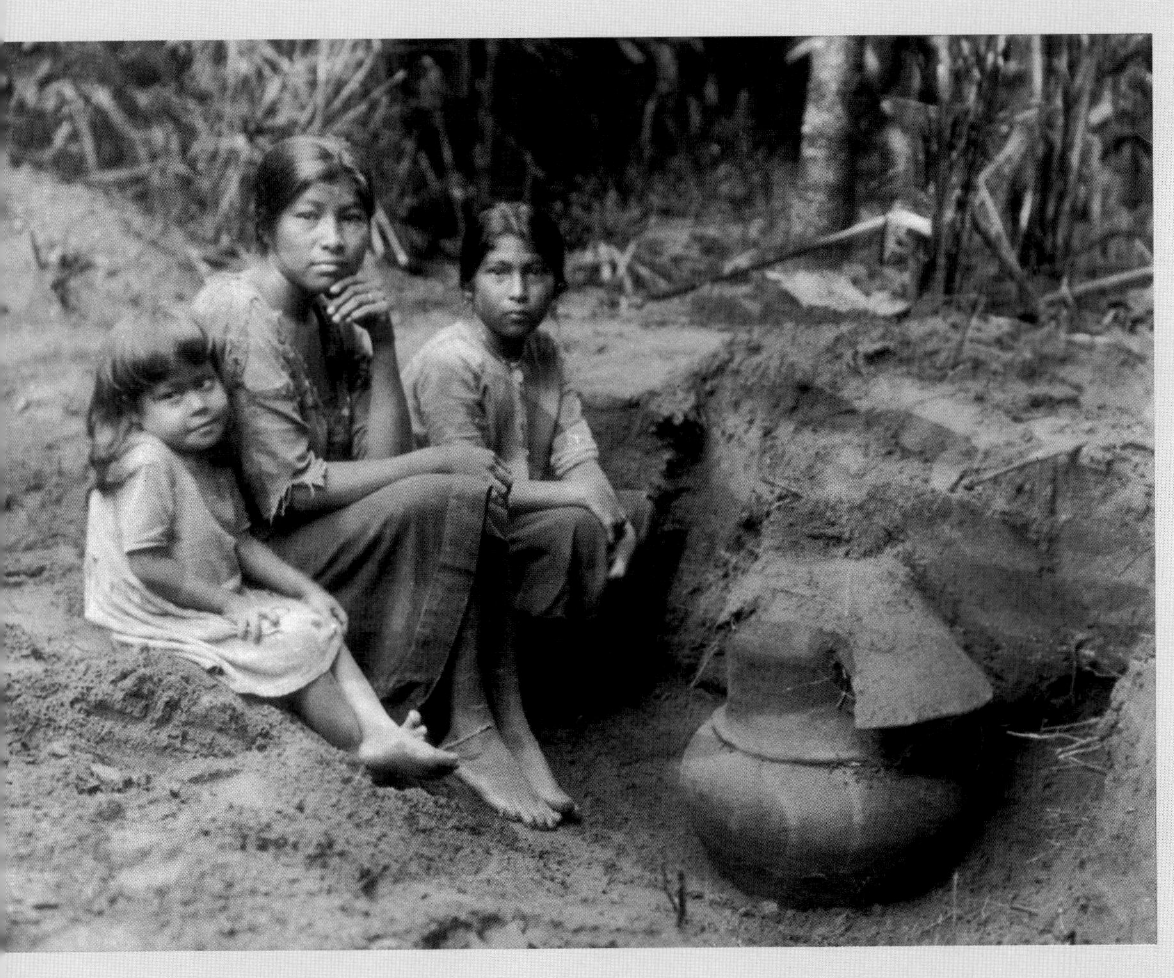

10

Exploring the Amazon, Explaining the Unknown

Views from the Past

CRISTIANA BARRETO AND JULIANA MACHADO

Here, removed by more than a hundred miles from any sign of European culture and surrounded only by the children of the jungle, the travellers felt with greater strength the abyss that isolated them. The total indifference displayed by their fellow red-skinned travellers offered constant motivation for thought about these beings, their present existence, and their past experiences which must have contributed to change them substantially.[1]

Introduction

Since Europeans first travelled down the Amazon in 1542, an extraordinary amount of fascination, mystery and curiosity about past and present Amazonian civilizations has driven explorers to the region. Moved by a variety of ideals, from the search for pure and pristine states of humanity and nature, to the quest for lost civilizations, these travellers have made the Amazon a fertile stage for theories of cultural evolution for over 500 years. Yet, today, considerable gaps in our knowledge keep alive extended controversies about just how ancient, how complex and how different the indigenous societies of native Amazonians were in the past, before European conquest.[2]

While travellers, naturalists and early scientists have proposed a variety of theories to explain human development in the Amazon, most were also aware that they lacked the right tools to prove their theories. Nonetheless, eager to share with the rest of the world their knowledge, understanding and intuitive insights about past and present Amazonia, they wrote travel chronicles, notes, diaries and reports, and reproduced what they saw in a range of graphic imagery in different media (fig. 10.1). Perhaps most importantly, they collected all sorts of objects that they judged might provide clues to understanding indigenous Amazonian societies. In so doing, they documented now extinct ways of life, brought Amazonia past and present into European consciousness, and established the grounds for modern archaeology in the region.

Here we focus on a largely neglected aspect of this long tradition of examining human nature in the Amazon: the theories and ideas advanced by explorers and travellers about the origins and development of indigenous societies, before modern archaeological research. We hope to clarify their influence and effect on current views about past Amazonian societies, and to draw attention to the invaluable research resources left by early travellers in the collections and in written and visual documentation. Despite the cultural distance of these pioneers, their direct interaction with and personal observation of living indigenous societies provided unique and unrepeatable insights into the Amazonian past.

Beyond documents

While today the Amazon is known world-wide for its remarkable cultural and biological diversity, efforts to understand and preserve its resources have yet to draw upon the full range of information to be found in the documentation accumulated over the last 500 years. Most of the indigenous peoples who lived along the Amazon at the time of the arrival of Europeans are now

10.1 Goia savages, lithograph by Jean Baptiste Debret, 1834. 'Indians did not stop offering aid and coming to the captain and bringing to him foodstuffs in abundance, and all with as much orderliness as if all their lives they had been servants' (Carvajal 1970 [1542]: 177). Many of Debret's drawings were inspired by images produced by nineteenth-century travellers such as Prince Maximilian zu Wied-Neuwied and the botanist Carl Philipp von Martius.

extinct, and most who have survived have gone through different processes of territorial displacement, demographic reduction and acculturation. Knowledge about their past depends essentially on what has been registered by explorers, travellers and missionaries, and what can be recovered by archaeological research.

Yet, the popular and scholarly literature on Amazonian explorers is immense. Many primary sources and reprints are available from the early chronicles of contact throughout the sixteenth and seventeenth centuries that relate primal adventures and first voyages through the Amazon.[3] Indeed, the popularity of these early accounts produced an entire genre of adventure or travel literature, where voyages are dramatically retold in the first person. Mass media and film productions such as Herzog's *Aguirre, the Wrath of God* continue to portray travellers in terms of this genre. The ethnographic and aesthetic value of the imagery produced or inspired by such expeditions has also been studied extensively by scholars and admired internationally by consumers.[4] Indeed, the use of images from Amazonian travellers by the academic and art media seems to have boomed with the quincentenary celebrations in 2000 of the first European contact. The written accounts from Amazonian expeditions in the eighteenth and nineteenth centuries have also been explored by scholars since the 1940s, with most research emphasizing their importance for natural history, their rich descriptions of native groups, and the value of extensive compendiums on Amazonian languages and dialects.[5]

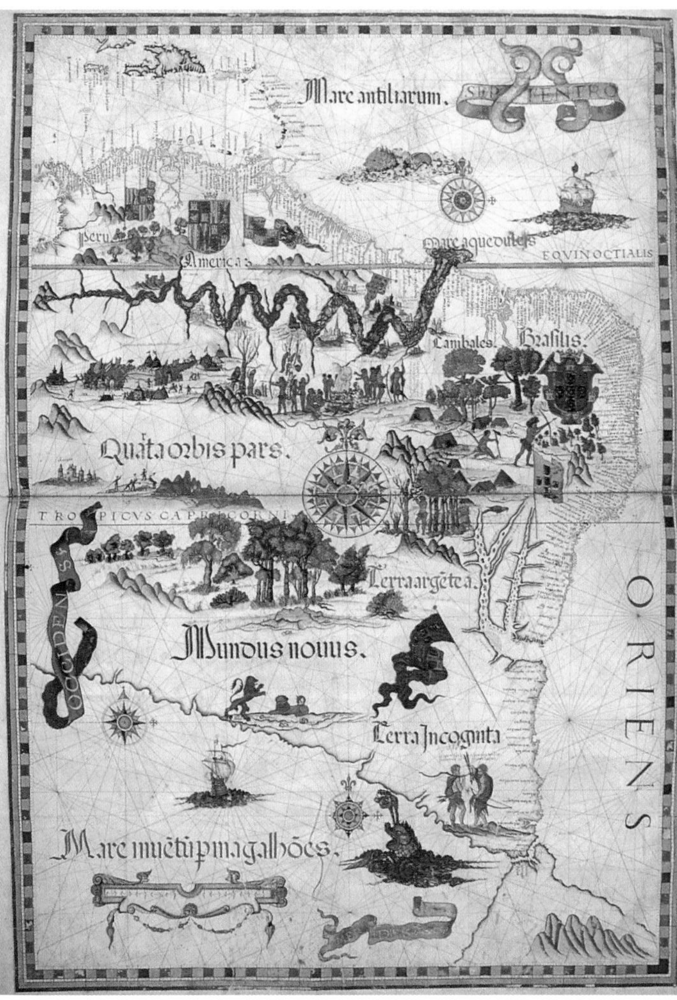

10.2 *Quarta Orbis Pars. Mundus Novus*, 1558. Plate from the atlas of South America by Diogo Homem. Note the depiction of the Amazon river in the shape of a serpent, and the several villages alongside. The name 'Las Amazonas' appears near the mouth of the river.

In contrast to the popularity of travellers' imagery and texts, the ethnographic collections from Amazonia, now spread in museums across the world, have been less explored by specialists, despite efforts made to document them[6] and to display them to museum-going publics.[7] In this respect, the descriptions, imagery and collections of travellers and early scientists are relatively well known as primary sources of research. Major contributions to the knowledge of past Amazonian societies have been achieved by scholars exploring these so-called ethnohistorical sources.[8]

However, this excessive focus on the documentary value of these works and the resultant necessary debates about the reliability of such sources tend to hide a more interpretative and archaeological aspect of this particular historical legacy.[9] Especially in the context of their discussions of ethnographic themes (and according to the cultural and scientific perspective of their times) travellers often recorded their conjectures, hypotheses and theories about the origins and past development of the Amazonian societies they encountered. While some of these interpretations may have absolutely no scientific value for contemporary research, others may fit surprisingly well into modern archaeological debates.[10] However unsuitable or outdated according to current scientific perspectives, as a rich interpretative body of knowledge they cannot be ignored. Analysis of the documentary legacy left by travellers across time, and reflection on their choices of what to collect and how to describe Amazonia in words and images, reveal not only that their perceptions were often determined by theories and interpretations, but also that they experienced amazement and suspended their preconceptions. Documents and collections were often designed to contain selected examples and illustrations of theories. In the natural history field this is certainly the case for nineteenth-century European naturalists such as Louis Agassiz, Alfred Russel Wallace, Henry Walter Bates and Richard Spruce, whose expeditions were influenced in one way or another by the preceding debates on Darwin's theory of evolution. The same considerations should apply for the more cultural or ethnographic content of their legacy.

More recently, and particularly boosted by the re-evaluations engendered by the 500th anniversary of European presence in the Americas, studies of European/Native American encounters have produced new analyses of travel narratives. These indicate that an understanding of the structure of such a genre can not only throw new light on the contexts of these first encounters but also reveal the inherent cultural biases and limitations of such narratives.[11]

Despite the extensive range of readings of this interpretative legacy on the Amazonian indigenous past, a legacy of a perhaps more intuitive nature has been left unexplored. Regardless of their cultural and historical background, sixteenth-century travellers, seventeenth- and eighteenth-century missionaries, nineteenth-century naturalists and twentieth-century ethnographers and scientists (even before the birth of archaeology as a scientific field) all posed very similar questions about the past of the native societies they encountered. Through direct contact with and observation of Indian groups, which in each case occurred with a different degree of intimacy, the individual explorers who discovered particular groups of Amazonian people were inspired to make more generalizing interpretations about their past. Whether or not they were based on observation of subsistence practices, languages, social institutions and systems of belief, this direct contact, and the act of reflecting upon what they had seen, makes their explanations of the unknown past different from pure fiction. This is even more relevant to the extent that we can assume a certain historical continuity between the unknown archaeological past and the observed ethnographic realities.

Although most accounts do not directly address the nature of past human societies in the Amazon (indeed, the past is often of no concern), there is a common pattern of reactions repeated in the records of direct encounters throughout the history of expeditions in the Amazon: travellers are first perplexed and daunted by the extent and the sheer scale of the populous settlements they saw along the banks and bluffs of the Amazon mainstream. Then, after greater interaction with Amazonian societies, travellers note the unexpected order and complexity of Amazonian cultures, so different from anything known or imagined by Europeans. Whether seen through the material culture, the institutions or the language, such complexity could only be explained by longevity, and this in itself demonstrated a certain antiquity in the forms of human life in the Amazon.

The first encounters: conquerors of a river without history

In the year 1500, before the Amazon was discovered from the West by the famous expedition led by Francisco Orellana in 1542, a small fleet commanded by Vicente

Yánes Pinzon, after exploring the recently discovered territories of Cape Verde Islands, encountered a major source of freshwater to the far west. The vast expanse of the mouth of the Amazon (*c.*170 km wide) was crossed by the first Europeans who named it Santa Maria de la Mar Dulce (freshwater sea). It is said that the Spaniards sailed up the river for fifteen or twenty leagues. They reported no evidence of gold, pearls or other riches, just jungle and bellicose natives.

All early voyages by Spaniards to the Amazon were doomed to disappointment. According to much of what we know, these are sad stories about struggles for survival.[12] One could not expect otherwise from expeditions that had set out to find the rich legendary lands of gold (El Dorado) or cinnamon (La Canella).[13] After finding fabulous wealth and empires in both the Mesoamerican and Andean highlands, Spaniards appeared ready to believe in almost any myth about native civilizations. But the Amazon represented a bitter encounter with reality. This unprecedented plunge from high expectations to deep disappointment produced an equally unprecedented variety of mythology. Gheerbrant (1992) reminds us of the range of mythical beings that peopled the first travellers' imaginary realm:

> The first Europeans to set foot in Amazonia let their imaginations run away with them and claimed actually to see and hear everything they had hitherto imagined: from the works of Pliny to Heredotus, from the words of Arabian storytellers to Mogul writers, from tales of knightly derring-do to medieval hagiographies, from cathedral gargoyles to the all-too-lifelike visions of Heronimus Bosch. Seldom have reality and fantasy complemented each other so well.[14]

Perhaps the most famous of these mythological beings were the fierce women warriors, called the Amazons after the Greek myth. First sighted by members of Orellana's expedition up the Amazon, these figures have ever since been inextricably linked to the region by the river's name. Detailed descriptions of Amazons were offered by natives whom the expedition met and by Friar Gaspar de Carvajal (who tells of a memorable encounter with the Amazons on 24 June 1542). Their accounts gave the myth a new life and plausibility at the time. A century later Father Acuña (the chronicler of the next Spanish expedition through the Amazon) wrote about the Amazons in the very first chapter of his book *The New Discovery of the Great Amazon River* (1641), saying that 'the details, on which there is universal agreement, are so precise, it is impossible that a fiction should have entered into so many languages and be met with among so many natives' (figs 10.2–3).[15]

These transpositions of fantastic, imaginary or mythical beings to the Amazonian realm have cast widespread doubt about the reliability of early chronicles. Whatever the reasons for these narrators adopting fantasy and myths (whether to compensate for their disappointment on not finding expected treasures or whether to make their discoveries more interesting, more plausible or even more exotic to their monarchs and the rest of the world), these reasons do not undermine the validity of another very strong sentiment – of amazement with the new world they encounter. Amazement pervades these accounts. And so do subsequent efforts to communicate their perceptions of a certain order and consistency and of a well-established way of life noted by travellers among native Amazonian societies.

Amazement appears in the chronicles of Carvajal, Vasques, Rojas and Acuña in their distinctively emphatic and often exaggerated descriptions of settlements, in particular those of large size. Remarks such as 'villages extend for about eighty leagues', 'very big provinces', 'very numerous and very large settlements', 'we continued to pass by numerous and very large villages ... and the further we went, the more thickly populated', 'a village with a very large public square' pervade the early chronicles.[16]

Besides the large size and number of villages, chroniclers also expressed surprise and admiration for Amazonian political structures, recognizing leaders and chiefs (or 'overlords') for different territorial domains and describing their authority over peoples.[17] Another recurrent surprise was the sophistication of Amazonian material culture (even equating the local pottery with European artefacts), the efficiency of non-metal tools and the extent of indigenous knowledge of natural resources.[18] The practice of warfare, with its rules and strategies, was a further aspect that captured the imagination of early chroniclers. Accounts provide almost flattering descriptions of Indian expertise in warfare which, it should be noted, characterized much of the interaction between early voyagers and Amazonians.

10.3 Engraving of the Amazons by André Thevet, 1557. 'These women are very white and tall, and have their hair very long and braided and wound about the head, and they are very robust and go about naked, with their bows and arrows in their hands, doing as much fighting as ten men' (Carvajal 1970 [1542]: 214).

In sum, throughout these chronicles there emerges a common perception of a well-established people who, although different in many ways from Europeans, yet developed a social order with large settlements, well-organized leadership, strong beliefs and efficient ways of exploiting natural resources that were often compared to European levels of development. There emerges a perception of a people with their own history, which was unexpected, independent from Europe and unrecorded save in myth and oral traditions,[19] but a history nonetheless.

Although no explicit concern with the past of Amazonian Indians can be found in early chronicles,[20] the reported discoveries of classical mythological beings (such as the Amazons) is perhaps an indirect way of attributing to Amazonian Indians a past that was not so unknown and that somehow was already present in their legendary world. Given that the main goal of early expeditions was to conquer and take possession of the newly encountered territories, one apparent mechanism of appropriating this New World was to attribute to it and its peoples a European past.

Missionaries of the jungle: awareness and denial of an indigenous past

The presence of missionaries in the Amazon was a fundamental development in the colonial history of the region after the early 1600s. Missionaries spread rapidly from the mouth of the river to the upper frontiers, trying thereby to control Indian villages against the colonist's private administration and Indian enslavement.[21] Capuchins, Franciscans and, predominantly, Jesuits founded missions in Maranhão and Pará by implanting their own system of village administration. It is estimated that by 1740 approximately 50,000 Amazonian Indians lived in Jesuit and Franciscan missions (fig. 10.4).[22]

By establishing a peaceful (but nonetheless dominating) relationship with Indians, missionaries had the opportunity to interact and live among many of the groups that were soon to be decimated. And because the success of their work depended extensively on their capacity to understand Indian languages and beliefs, the European reli-

10.4 Watercolour of the village of Santa Maria do Rio Branco in Alexandre Rodrigues Ferreira, *Viagem Filosófica* (1783–92).

gious orders were particularly well positioned to grasp the most crucial aspects of indigenous cultural universes. In doing so, they became the very first to compile rich ethnographic and linguistic information, as attested by the chronicles left by missionaries Luiz Figueira (1609), Claude d'Abbeville (1614), Yves d'Evreu (1613, 1615), Antonio Vieira (1660–79), João Felipe Betendorf (1699), Samuel Fritz (1689–1723), João Daniel (1757–76) and others.

However, while missionaries learned how to recognize the belief systems of Amazonian culture, in order to reach the souls of natives, they also had to deny their validity and repress their practice to ensure the success of Christianity. Vieira, in one of his famous sermons, describes Amazonian Indians as 'the most inarticulate people that nature ever created or aborted ... men whose status as men was in doubt, so that the Popes had to define that they were rational and not brutes.'[23] Father Samuel Fritz, who spent nearly thirty years as a missionary in the Amazon and was the author of the first complete map of the river, demonstrates little hope for changing 'his' (*sic*) Indians, almost acknowledging the failure of his Christianizing enterprise:

> they appear of a bad disposition, since all possible means have been tried with them to convert them by kindness, presents, and by sternness of the Spaniards, but no progress has been made, since the wild beasts themselves are more quickly tamed. In their retreats they kill and destroy one another for the iron goods they have received from me, or have carried off by theft from the Omaguas.[24]

From the arrival of the Spaniards and Portuguese in the Amazon until the eviction of Jesuits in 1759 by the Portuguese crown, it had proved almost impossible to turn Indians into devoted Christians. The experienced missionaries seemed to understand the strength of indigenous cultures and the difficulty of transforming these long lasting traditions.

It is not surprising that the close interaction and observation of indigenous cultures led missionaries not only to cultivate a certain respect for the complexity and richness of Amazonian cultures but also generated a genuine curiosity about their past and their origins. Betendorf, for instance, goes to great lengths to describe the indigenous origin myths of villages along the Madeira river, as well as past traditions of the Tapajó.[25] João Daniel provides the most detailed descriptions of the Indians and their customs and is certainly the first to address formally the question of their origins. According to his theory, compatible with the Christian values of the times, Amazonians were the descendants of the lost tribes of Israel, the most striking evidence being the propensity of Indians to adore idols (as among Hebrews), their organization in different 'tribes' and their ignorance of the true God (fig. 10.5).[26] Daniel's chronicles are apparently the earliest attempt to interpret the past of Amazonian Indians based on personal observations of their beliefs and institutions at the time they were encountered. His invaluable descriptions, organized like true ethnographic essays, can be seen as a prelude to the more scientific spirit of eighteenth- and nineteenth-century travellers and naturalists to come.

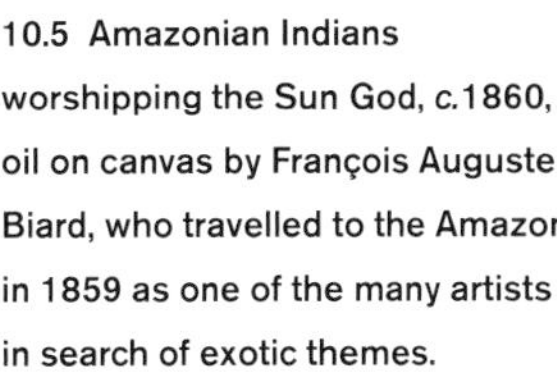

10.5 Amazonian Indians worshipping the Sun God, c.1860, oil on canvas by François Auguste Biard, who travelled to the Amazon in 1859 as one of the many artists in search of exotic themes.

Exploring the Amazon in the age of reason: the search for origins

From the mid-eighteenth century expeditions to the Amazon were driven by a totally new impulse, not defined just by the politics of conquest, the curiosity of discovery and the mission of Christian conversion, but by the study of nature in a rational way, as the new scientific values of the Enlightenment required. Among all remote parts of the world, the Amazon was seen as the one region where nature and humanity could be observed in their most unchanged, pure and pristine forms, an exceptional place for scientific experiments. The voyages of both Humboldt and Darwin to South America, each in its particular context, suggest the new character of motivation among travellers who visited the Amazon.

In addition, according to the new goals of European colonization, the Amazon no longer attracted the attention of travellers for its past potential of yielding legendary cities of gold, but instead for the opportunity to systematically study, document and experiment with the immense unknown natural resources of the Amazon, which could not only be used in Europe but also contribute to the economic development of the new territory. From the beginning of the nineteenth century, and particularly after the transfer of the Portuguese royal court to Brazil (and the official initiatives by the Austrian Grand Duchess and Empress of Brazil, Leopoldina of Habsburg, to bring European naturalists to explore the new country),[27] the Amazon became a true paradise for botanists, zoologists, geologists and other natural scientists.

The first scientific expeditions in Amazonia were conducted by French scientist Charles Marie de La Condamine, who descended the river from 1735 to 1745. The expedition's first goal, as set by the French Academy of Sciences, was to verify questions posed by Newton's theory about the exact shape of the planet. Led by a mathematician (Louis Goudin), these scientist-travellers set out to measure the diameter of the earth at the equator in what is now Peruvian and Ecuadorian territory. Once the official task was completed, La Condamine descended the Amazon in the company of a cartographer, thereby producing the first accurate map of the basin.

Although schooled in the most rigorous rational-scientific tradition, La Condamine admits to being attracted to the region by the 'singularities' of the unknown Amazon such as the mythical village of Manoa d'El Dorado, the golden lake of Parima and the accounts of women warriors.

> So many witnesses in agreement, and each so respectful, that they do not allow us to doubt the veracity of these facts. However, the river, the lake, the gold mine, and even the gold village, attested by the accounts of so many of the witnesses, all of it disappeared like an enchanted castle.[28]

La Condamine's observations of the river, flora and fauna are marked by comments on the great diversity of plants and their possible commercial uses. In trying to understand how the Indians make use of several natural resources, La Condamine not only describes subsistence techniques in details, such as canoe-carving or fishing methods, but also enumerates the virtues of such practices. He observes the way Indians appropriate nature, and the great diversity and complexity of languages spoken by the several groups encountered. He also registers indigenous myths of origin and attempts to explain the genesis of objects such as the *muiraquitãs* (green stone amulets; see Gomes, this volume). He clearly understood that native knowledge about the environment was embedded in a long history of human occupation of the region. He also understood that in the past Amazonian societies must have been much greater in terms of population and diversity. In fact, he appears to be the first to propose that a historical 'tracking' of the different indigenous languages could provide a means to understand how America had been populated.

The next scientific record we have from Amazonian travellers is that of Alexandre Rodrigues Ferreira, a Brazilian who studied natural history in Portugal, and was sent to the region with the difficult administrative task of demarcating the boundaries of the immense Portuguese territory in the Amazon. His journeys in 1783–92, recorded in *Viagem Filosófica*... ('Philosophical Journey through the Captaincy of Pará and Rio Negro'), was the first expedition known to have engaged in the systematic practice of collection of both natural and 'cultural' specimens. Most of Rodrigues Ferreira's diaries deal with the political and administrative questions of representing the Portuguese government

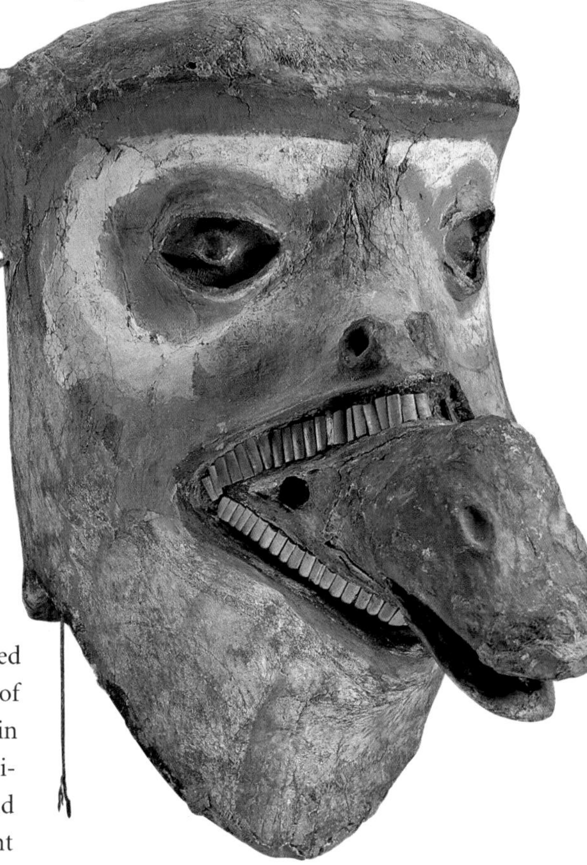

10.6 Jurupixuna mask in bark cloth collected by Alexandre Rodrigues Ferreira, 1783–92 (height 39 cm, diameter of base 21 cm; Museu Antropológico da Universidade de Coimbra).

throughout the already numerous Amazonian fortifications, villages and missions (including the management of Indian slavery and revolts). Nonetheless, he also wrote essays on many of the Indian groups he visited (the Cambeba, the Mura, the Maué, the Karipuna and others), as well as on specific items produced by Indians (such as pottery, pipes, masks, decorated gourds and huts). His companions, José Joaquim Freire and Joaquim José Codina, produced an exceptional collection of illustrations of Amazonian Indians, recording their physical traits, artefacts, houses and villages for a period of nine years along the Negro, Branco, Madeira, Guaporé and Mamoré rivers. Together, Ferreira's descriptions, collected artefacts and illustrations are an invaluable contribution to the ethnography of early historical times in Amazonia (fig. 10.6).[29]

10.7 Indian hunting a jaguar, c.1830/31, oil on canvas by Johan Moritz Rugendas. Rugendas was one of the first travelling artists to be influenced by Humboldt's style of representing tropical nature.

Despite Rodrigues Ferreira's awareness of the cultural diversity along the Amazon, the rapid extinction of many indigenous traditions, and his particular concerns with the documentation of their material culture, he rarely pauses to ask questions about their origins and past. As a natural historian, he contrasts sharply with his colleagues of the times, in that with his obligations to the Portuguese government and his interest in the condition of Indians (he attempted to introduce a more humanizing policy towards Indian labour), he did not allow himself the distance to think about Indians as just another subject of study, such as the flora and fauna of a still very unknown environment.

At the opposite extreme perhaps is the figure of German scientist and explorer Alexander von Humboldt, the most famous naturalist of South America. While he was considered to be a model for creating new aesthetic standards in portraying tropical landscape and making precise scientific observations, his representation of the Amazonian tropics is that of a primal, static and ahistorical state of nature. He is more concerned with vegetation than animal or human life, and the tropical environment is seen as unsuitable for high culture (fig. 10.7).[30]

However, even the absence of human occupation is observed with the careful eyes of a scientist looking for true archaeological records: 'Here no oasis recalls the memory of previous inhabitants; no carvings, no ruins, no fruit tree, once cultivated but now wild, speaks of the work of former generations.'[31] Indeed, in his travels through northern South America (1799–1803),[32] during which he and the French botanist Aimé Bonpland mapped the famous Casiquiare Canal (Casiquiare river) joining the Orinoco and the Amazon systems, Humboldt was to register many archaeological sites (or ruins) and was the first to propose the theory of a one-race origin for Amerindians. They had descended from an Asian race and proliferated through time, undergoing many changes: 'one unique race ... one only organic type, modified by circumstances which will remain for ever unknown'.[33]

This theory inaugurates a long tradition among naturalists and archaeologists of the Amazon, that of placing the origins of Amerindians in a remote (Asian) civilization that had decayed through time. As documentation about contemporary native groups increased, the observed diversity of languages, and of physical and cultural traits, became an even greater challenge to be explained by these early scientists.

Following Humboldt through the same regions some thirty years later, Sir Robert Hermann Schomburgk (sent to South America by the Royal Geographic Society from 1834 to 1839 to explore British Guiana) had a significantly different point of view, which separated the more advanced 'Toltecans' and 'Astecs' from contemporary Amerindians who, he thought, at their origin must have belonged to two different population stocks. Referring to traces of old civilizations in Siberia, he argues (fig. 10.8):

> Similar tumuli, mural defences, hieroglyphs inscriptions, astronomical divisions of time, and zodiacal signs were used by the civilized aboriginal race of America; and as the geographical position of the Bering Strait, and the Alcoustski Islands, admit the possibility of immigration from Asia to America, we are led to believe that the Toltecans, and Astecs arrived that way. They were however expelled by succeeding hordes ... emigrated southward, and became ultimately extinct. The descendants of the later savage tribes, the conquerors of the Ancient Mexicans, constitute at present the aboriginal inhabitants of North and South America, tribes, who though dissimilar in language, possess philological affinities, and are distinguished by the same predilections for a nomadic, or roving and savage life, and are given alike to war and to the chase.[34]

10.8 The first page of *Twelve Views in the Interior of Guiana* by Robert Schomburgk, 1841.

If many travellers had already discovered the material signs of a past with a different type of indigenous occupation of the Amazon,[35] the lack of traits such as monumental architecture, metal work and writing systems disassociated the region from the sorts of ancient civilizations eighteenth- and early nineteenth-century European archaeologists were finding in their excavations, such as in Pompeii or in Egypt. Indeed, scientific interest in studying primitive indigenous populations occurs only later in the history of European ethnology. However, if excavations of these cultures were not yet to be envisaged as a scientific project, the only possibility left was to understand the origins and past of Amerindians through their present. And no other naturalist understood this better than Carl Friedrich Philipp von Martius.

Martius, a young Bavarian botanist among the group of scientists brought by Grand Duchess Leopoldina to Brazil in 1817, spent most of his three-year stay in Brazil travelling in the Amazon in the company of zoologist Johan Baptist von Spix. In fact, Spix and Martius were the first non-Portuguese Europeans to obtain permission to visit the Brazilian Amazon. Martius collected 6,500 species of plants, which formed the basis of his gigantic *Flora Brasiliensis.* Spix and Martius's *Travels in Brazil,* a three-volume account of their scientific observations, complemented by the illustrated 'Atlas', remains a classic work of reference for naturalists and a remarkable artistic document.[36]

Most importantly for the early ethnography of the Amazon, Martius was also responsible for documenting the groups of Indians they encountered in their travels. He did so systematically, by collecting their artefacts – around 740 objects were registered in the Munich collections[37] – and by writing about them in different ways, including formal ethnographies and fiction novels.[38] The most interpretative work, however, is his essay on the 'state of law' among Brazilian Indians where their institutions, customs and laws are examined in order to answer what he believes to be the 'enigmas of Brazilian ethnography':

> What are, then, these red skinned men who inhabit the dense Brazilian forests, from the Amazon till the Prata? Who, in wild bands, wander through the inland Brazilian fields? Do they form one people, are they dispersed parts of one sole primitive people, or are they diverse peoples, neighbours to each other, fragmented tribes, hordes, and families, of several different peoples in their costumes, morals, and languages?[39]

In a systematic examination and comparison of physical traits, rules, institutions, beliefs and languages Martius is the first to attempt to correlate a wide variety of characteristics to classify the different groups. His main ethnographic contribution was the classification of indigenous languages based on their linguistic affinities. Martius not only believed that by understanding the general principles of cultural variation (through classification) he could arrive at the origins and essence of indigenous societies, but he also advanced the idea that the range of variation could only be the product of evolution through time.

> In order to decipher such historical evolutions, the historian is obliged to use the same method as the naturalist; just as the latter investigates the age and succession of geologic formations through the remains of extinct organisms, the former obtains valuable indications about the essence and the previous state of mankind, through the language, and several customs and habits from the remote past, which, in pure or altered states, have been transmitted through the lives of succeeding peoples.[40]

Martius refers to the archaeological records of previous civilizations in the Americas, such as the Inca and Tiahuanaco ruins, as attesting to the great antiquity of the Amerindians. The fact that monumental ruins had not yet been found in the Amazon, according to him, could only be a sign that such cultures had existed in an even more distant past.[41] Here again, although no formal archaeological project was advanced to investigate these past civilizations, Martius, as a good botanist, noted that in the Amazon nature had already been transformed by humans for several millennia. The diversity of languages and other traditions was thus the result of the long-term devolution of such advanced cultures, probably descending from one sole race, as Humboldt had suggested. Martius thereby developed the first consistent theory about the antiquity and complexity of past Amazonian societies. His theory was to influence many, from scholars who defended the idea of Brazilian Indians as being devolved from more advanced cultures, including more popular writings about lost cities of the jungle, to more recent scientific propositions on the external origins of Amazonian peoples, and environmental constraints on human settlement and development of the region.[42]

It is difficult to evaluate the extent to which these pioneering interpretations about past Amazonian societies resulted from direct interaction and personal contact with Amazonian Indians, especially considering that Martius's journey in the region was relatively short, lasting less than three years. Among all naturalists brought by the

Austrian mission, zoologist Johann Natterer was probably the one to have had the longest and closest interaction with native Amazonians. He travelled across Central Brazil and the Amazon from 1822 till 1835, after spending nearly five years in Brazil covering other territories. In 1830 he married a Brazilian woman in Barcelos (Rio Negro) and had a daughter by her. His attraction for the indigenous cultures is well reflected by his compilation of nearly sixty glossaries of native languages and the enormous collection of indigenous artefacts now in Vienna and Dresden (about 1,500 objects from seventy-two different groups) (figs 10.9–10). Unfortunately, his written accounts have been lost.[43]

BELOW LEFT **10.9 Munducucu trumpet collected by Johann Natterer in the Amazon, 1817–36 (height 190 cm, width 14.5 cm; Museum für Völkerkunde, Vienna).**

The Austrian mission set new standards of documentation, description, collection and illustration, bringing an unprecedented rigour to the materials produced by expeditions to the Amazon. Systems of classification used for plants and animals were transposed to cultural items, whether artefacts, languages or physical traits. Illustrations of physical types or objects were juxtaposed so as to enhance comparison of their patterning, variation and similarity, following the Linnaean model for representation of natural specimens (figs 10.11–12).[44]

ABOVE **10.10** ***Le signal de la retraite*****, lithograph by Jean Baptiste Debret (1834) depicting Indians using the same type of trumpet shown in fig. 10.9.**

In Europe, and especially in Britain, a new view on geological history, marked by the favourable reception of Lyell's *Principles of Geology* (1830–33), and the growing interest in evolutionary ideas, also attracted the attention of scientists to the antiquity of humanity. In this context the British naturalists Alfred Wallace and Henry Bates, who travelled across the Amazon in the late 1840s to compile empirical evidence for their theories on biological evolution, were particularly acute in observing and registering the different indigenous groups encountered on their travels. Wallace, for example, dedicated a whole chapter of his *Narrative of Travels on the Amazon and Rio Negro* to the Amazonian 'aborigines'. The work presents detailed lists of names and languages of the many groups encountered along these rivers, as well as descriptions of their physical and other cultural attributes, illustrated by detailed drawings of a few artefacts.[45] Although no comments on their origins are advanced, Wallace does note the great variety of 'tribes and nations', all with their own language and customs, and many of them composed of individuals displaying entirely peculiar physical traits.[46]

Henry Bates, who stayed in Brazil until 1859, also provides detailed descriptions of indigenous groups, especially their rituals, showing a particular familiarity and close interaction with local Indians.[47] Details of his illustrations of Indians show his thorough understanding of such rituals and the importance of particular objects (fig. 10.13). However, it was the British

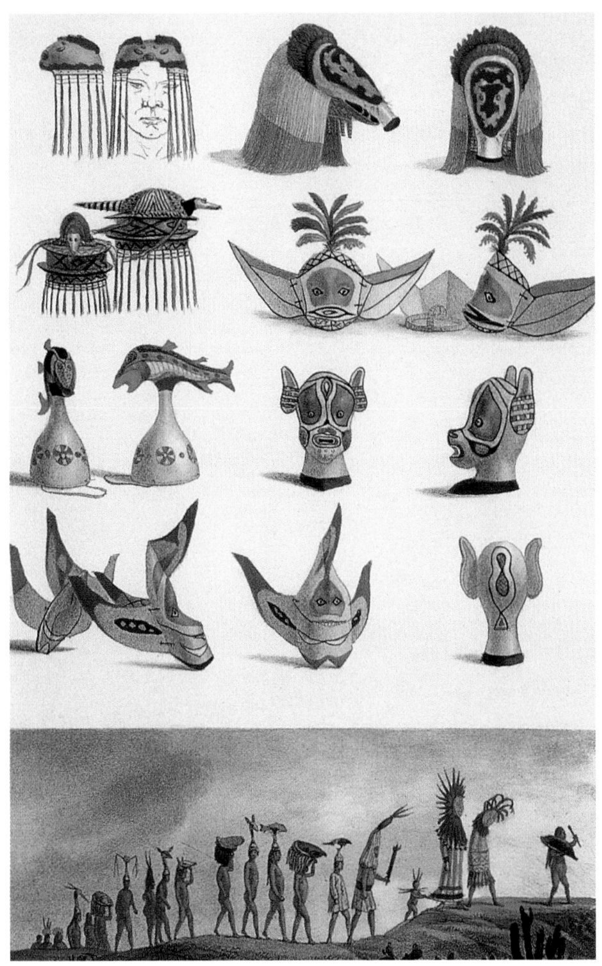

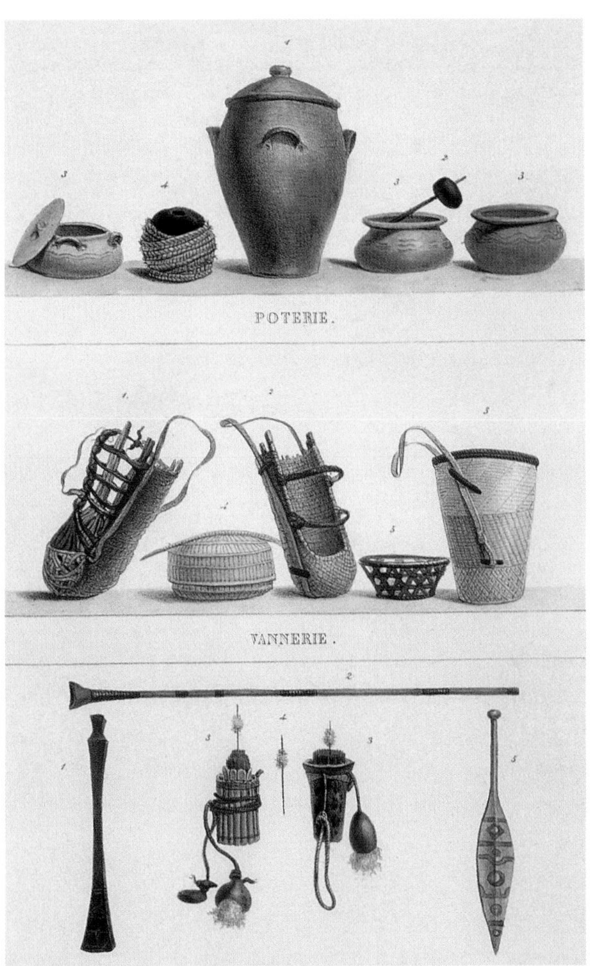

ABOVE 10.11 Tikuna Indians and their masks, by Jean Baptiste Debret, inspired by an engraving in Spix and Martius's atlas, *Travels in Brazil in the Years 1817–1820.*

ABOVE RIGHT 10.12 Pottery, basketry and weapons, lithograph by Jean Baptiste Debret (1816–31).

10.13 Dance with masks during a wedding festivity of the Tikuna Indians, drawing by Henry Walter Bates in *The Naturalist on the River Amazon*, 1863.

botanist Richard Spruce who grasped the intricacies of indigenous Amazonian societies and created the new discipline of economic botany (or ethnobotany).[48] With a culture historian's perspective Spruce was able to reconstruct ancient agricultural systems of Andean communities, based on changes in frequency of botanical remains in the stratigraphy of archaeological deposits. In the Amazon, however, he was more focused on the contemporary uses of plants by the indigenous populations.[49]

Digging up the indigenous past: the origins of Amazonian archaeology

During the second half of the nineteenth century intense debates about the origins of mankind and human evolution not only attracted naturalists to the Amazon but also shaped specific theories about Amerindians' origins. Had they originated in the American continent or had they migrated? Were they all descended from the same people? Had they evolved, or devolved, into diverse peoples? Are contemporary Amerindians at a pristine stage of mankind or are they at an end point of human 'involution', as opposed to evolution? Similar questions posed by Martius at the opening of the century were now being reconsidered, while empirical evidence to answer these questions was being collected.

Brazilian scholars such as Gonçalves Dias and Barbosa Rodrigues were inspired by the indigenist movements and national sentiments associated with republicanism throughout the late nineteenth-century Americas. They also set out to investigate these questions so crucial for the construction of a national past. From 1857 on, Barbosa Rodrigues studied Amazonian pre-history in the valleys of Tapajós, Jamundá, Trombetas, Urubu and other rivers, finding important sites such as the Miracanguera cemetery.[50] His published findings on *muiraquitãs*, lithic statues and rock art advanced a surprisingly modern theory for the peopling of the Brazilian territory. Rodrigues suggested that two different, large migratory waves – an ancient one from Asia and a more recent one, of unknown origin – best explained the characteristics of Amazonian groups.

Another Brazilian scholar, Domingos Soares Ferreira Penna, can be considered the first Amazonian archaeologist in that he not only conceived and founded what later became the Museu Paraense Emílio Goeldi but also wrote many essays on the ethnography and archaeology of the Amazon. His many expeditions along the coast of Pará and islands of the Amazonian mouth led to the discovery of abundant shell and earthen mounds, later excavated by Charles Hartt. Between his expeditions to archaeological sites such as Pacoval, Miracanguera and Maracá, he also lived among different groups, compiling a record of their languages and other ethnographic observations. On the basis of his study of the Aruã vocabulary (a group that inhabited the Marajó Island at the time of the conquest) he was able to propose ideas about how the lower Amazon region had been peopled by succeeding migratory waves from Central America and the Antilles.

The contribution of Ferreira Penna was to inaugurate Amazonian archaeology as an investigation into the ancestors of surviving indigenous groups, a method that maintained close links between the archaeology and the ethnology of the region.[51] In an era when archaeology started to develop its own methods of investigation and in the rest of the country focused on a remote, distant past, this link with the ethnological field was to become an important asset in Amazonian studies, which since then have been kept as one whole body of investigation under the umbrella of the Museu P.E. Goeldi.

10.14 Early archaeological excavations in the lower Amazon, from Curt Nimuendajú's collection of pictures in the archives of the Etnografiska Museet I Göteborg, Sweden.

In 1865 the Swiss geologist Louis Agassiz, Professor of Natural History at Harvard University, organized what was to be known as the Thayer expedition (after his sponsor name). Agassiz's Amazonian expedition focused on fossils, determined to prove the immutability of species and refute Darwin's theory of evolution. Agassiz also believed that Amerindians were autochthonous and that humans had originated simultaneously, or successively, in several parts of the globe. The expedition did not meet its goals, but sent to Brazil Canadian geologist Charles Frederick Hartt, who was to have a great impact on Amazonian archaeology.

Hartt travelled to Brazil four times between 1865 and 1877, conducted geological and archaeological research, and was the first to engage in formal archaeological excavations. First guided by Ferreira Penna, Hartt studied sites on Marajó Island, including both fluvial and coastal shell mounds of the Amazon, and other sites from the Maracá, Aristé and Santarém cultures. His 'Contribution to the Ethnology of the Amazon Valley' published posthumously in 1885 remained a definitive guide for future research in Amazonian archaeology.[52] His work initiated a long tradition of North American scholarship on Amazonian archaeology, one that includes his colleagues O.A. Derby, J.B. Steere (from the University of Michigan) and, later on, W. Farabee, and H. Palmatary (University of Pennsylvania), C. Evans and B. Meggers (Smithsonian Institute), and A. Roosevelt (currently at The Field Museum).

If Ferreira Penna is recognized for putting Amazonian archaeological heritage on the map, Hartt was the first to pursue scientific methods of research archaeology. A third figure, the Brazilian anthropologist Ladislau Netto, was to be remembered as the 'great synthesiser' of the times. He not only published the first synthesis on Brazilian archaeology,[53] but also engaged in considerable field research designed to resolve some of the crucial questions posed by Amazonian finds. Ladislau Netto also con-

10.15 *Maloca* kitchen, Manaus, c.1865, one of the earliest photographs of Amazonian Indians, attributed to Albert Frisch.

ducted excavations with Ferreira Penna for the Museu Nacional (then the Imperial Museum) in the Amazon in 1880. Netto followed the theories proposed by Humboldt and Martius, convinced that Marajó had once been inhabited by foreign peoples. He was the first to recognize Marajó mounds as ceremonial earthworks and to see a possible social hierarchy embedded in the symbolic decoration of funerary urns (see Schaan, this volume).[54]

A common characteristic of these three figures was their eagerness to understand native Amazonia by studying both the archaeological past and the ethnographic present. Even Hartt, despite the bulk of his research activities being more oriented towards geology, developed considerable interest in the ethnography of the region, producing a fine compilation of Mundurucu legends that recognizes the importance of indigenous mythology.

The best example of this perspective on how indigenous cultures should be approached was the selection of forty-eight objects exhibited at the *Exposição Antropológica* organized by Ladislau Netto in 1882, most of which were collected by either Ferreira Penna or Hartt. Objects were grouped either by cultural affiliation (as in the case of the Mundurucu and Mauhé artefacts) or by type of object (such as 'ceramic pots' or 'lithic objects') with no indication of their age apart from those made by 'modern' Indians.[55] The exhibition was a clear statement that indigenous cultures need to be understood as a whole, combining questions about their past with immersion into their present cultural and material expressions.

10.16 Indian women and excavated urns during early archaeological excavations in the lower Amazon, from Curt Nimuendajú's collection of pictures in the archives of the Etnografiska Museet I Göteborg, Sweden.

By the end of the nineteenth century many studies had been published documenting the several digs and findings in the Amazon,[56] and together with the coastal shell mounds of Southern Brazil and the caves of Lagoa Santa (in central Brazil), past Amazonian cultures remained one of the main objects of archaeological research in Brazil for another century (figs 10.14, 10.16).[57]

Personal engagement, commitment and love for the native peoples of the Amazon produced perceptions of this whole, perceptions that transformed documentary research on the Amazonian past and present into profound advances in anthropological understanding. Modern anthropologists of the early twentieth century such as Erland Nordenskiöld and Curt Nimuendajú, who carried out both ethnographic and archaeological research in the Amazon, were able to propose the most compelling theories for human cultural development in the region.[58] This should alert contemporary archaeologists to the importance of ethnoarchaeological research in the region, in as much as Amazonia remains one of the few regions of the globe in which the survival of many indigenous groups allows interpretation of the past to be informed by observations of the present (fig. 10.15).

As the unknown past of native Amazonia starts to be unveiled by modern archaeological research and competing explanations are still open to debate, a look back at the legacies and history of ideas advanced by early conquerors, travellers, missionaries and naturalists should provide a different perspective on both the pace and quality of the acquired knowledge and understanding of its indigenous peoples.

Acknowledgements

We would like to thank the editors Colin McEwan and Eduardo Neves for their careful reading of our text and their helpful suggestions. Dr John Hemming's supportive comments and revisions were greatly appreciated. Our warmest thanks goes to the *Unknown Amazon* team: Marcia Arcuri, Jasmin Pinho, Cristiane Matsunaga, Maria Magro and Paula Amaral have all helped in different ways. We would like to thank especially our friend Eduardo Neves both for involving us in the *Unknown Amazon* project and for sharing in the fun and the challenging exercise of rethinking the Amazonian past.

NOTES

1 From Martius 1992: 91 (author's translation). Quote of Friar Apollonio, a fictional character in von Martius's novel, *Frey Appolonio, Um Romance do Brasil*, written in 1831 by the German botanist but only published in 1992.

2 For the main different perspectives on these matters see Denevan 1992a, 1995; Meggers 1954, 1995; Lathrap 1970; Carneiro 1995; and Roosevelt 1999b.

3 The original texts of the early chronicles of Carvajal, Vasques, Acuña and others have been translated with commentaries in publications such as Markham 1859, Medina 1894, Heaton 1988 and Mello-Leitão 1941a. But see, for instance, Millar 1954 and Gheerbrant 1954 for rewritings of the original narratives.

4 The most complete work on travellers in Brazilian territory is that by Anna Maria de Moraes Beluzzo, *O Brasil dos Viajantes*, 1999, which accompanied the exhibition of the same title in São Paulo in 1994. This three-volume work presents a vast and careful compilation of graphic imagery, and provides fairly complete accounts of expeditions, with biographic notes, lists of available manuscripts and imagery, and other primary sources, as well as a systematic bibliography on the subject. For the presentation of the graphic materials produced by travellers see also Löschner 1978, P. Whitehead 1988, Carelli 1992 and Galard 2000. Harttman's 1975 study remains the main reference for the contribution of European travellers' graphic imagery to Brazilian ethnography.

5 Among these are Baldus 1940; Mello-Leitão 1941a & b; Haskins 1943; Barata 1954; Sampaio 1955, n/d; Palmatary 1965; and more recently Horsh 1980, Oberacker 1968 and Vanzolini 1990.

6 See Dorta 1992 for a compilation of most important Brazilian ethnographic collections, and Ribeiro and van Velthem 1992 for the relevance of studying such collections.

7 There were two recent major exhibitions in Brazil, for instance, entitled *O Brasil dos Viajantes*, 1994, and *Mostra do Redescobrimento*, 2000, the latter with much anthropological content.

8 Textual ethnohistorical sources are the most used for historical reconstructions. Porro (1992, 1993) has explored these sources for the Brazilian Amazon, as did N. Whitehead (1993, 1994, 1995, 1996), whose work is more centred on the Orinoco basin and the Guayanas. For a major historical review of early Amazon based on textual sources see Hemming 1978, 1995a & b, and for the history of Brazil in general see Ribeiro and Neto 1992.

9 See, for instance, Meggers' (1995) objections to the credibility of ethnohistorical accounts and to the use of such sources to interpret archaeological records, and N. Whitehead's (1994: 48) defence of an analytical methodology to explore historical documents and the benefits of coordinating archaeological, ethnographic and historical data for a new understanding of Amerindia.

10 For instance, the theories of von Martius in the 1830s about Amazonian indigenous societies being the descendants of a former highly advanced civilization that has degenerated through time after settling in the Amazonian tropical environment.

11 For examples of travel narrative analysis see Beer 1996 and Raby's (2000) recent work on Victorian scientific travellers, including those who have been in the Amazon such as Wallace and Bates. See also Bray 1993, Pagden 1993 and Todorov 1984 for more general approaches on European/American contact.

12 The following are the most important sources for the early expeditions to the Amazon. For Orellana's expedition (1541–2) there is the narrative of the Dominican Friar Gaspar de Carvajal, the official chronicler of the expedition, entitled *Relacion del nuevo descubrimiento del famoso rio Grande de las Amazonas* (original document in the Academy of History of Madrid). Carvajal's account is known in two forms: the one inserted into Gonzalo Fernandes Oviedo's *Historia General de las Indias* (1864–84) and another first published by Toribio Medina in 1894. Other documents relating to Orellana's expedition were also published by Medina in Heaton 1988. For the expedition of Pedro de Ursua and Lope de Aguirre (1559–61) we have the account by Francisco Vasquez, *Relacion muy herdadera que trata de todo lo que acaeçio en la entrada de pedro de Orsua en el descobriemiento del dorado e omagoa y de larrebelion de don hernando de guzman y del muy cruel tirano lope de aguirre* (original document in the National Library of Madrid). For Pedro de Teixeira's expedition (1639–40) we have the accounts of Alonso de Rojas, *Descubrimiento del Rio de las Amazonas com sus dilatadas provincias* (original document in the Royal Library of Paris), for the travel from Cametá to Quito. The Jesuit Cristobal de Acuña was the official chronicler of the expedition on the way back: *Nuevo Descubrimiento del gran Rio de las Amazonas*, first published in 1641 (see Markham 1859). Mauricio de Heriarte, who joined Teixeira's expedition, also provides a rich account of the Amazon written in 1662 and entitled *Decriçam do Estado do Maranhão, Pará, Corupá e Rio das Amazonas* (see Heriarte 1975).

13 See Hemming 1978 for an extensive study on the importance of gold and the search for El Eldorado among travellers in northern South America.

14 Gheerbrant 1992: 47. Gheerbrant also provides good illustrations of some of the mythical places and beings referred to.

15 Cristobal de Acuña [1641] in Markham 1859.

16 The amazement and surprise this caused are literally expressed in text: some of the inhabited districts 'were so large *they stirred up fear* [in us]', and on reaching a group of large islands (possibly near the mouth of the Tapajós), 'so numerous were the settlements, which came into sight and which we distinguished on the said islands that we were grieved; and they [i.e. their inhabitants] saw us, there came out to meet us on the river over two hundred pirogues, [so large] that each one carries twenty or thirty Indians and some forty, and of these there were many … and they came with so much noise and shouting and in such good order that *we were astonished*' (Carvajal [1542] in Heaton 1988: 218, my emphasis).

17 Porro (1994: 86–7) also stresses this point. See, for instance, Carvajal's references to the main chiefs and territories: 'they all gathered around to look at their overlord', 'we left the territory of the great overlord Machiparo', 'for here was the beginning of the land ruled by Oníguayal' (Carvajal [1542] in Heaton 1988). Referring to the Omagua, Acuña observes that 'they are so much submissive to their principal that [they] do not need more than a word to see their orders instantly obeyed' (Acunã [1641] in Mello-Leitão 1941a: 228). Heriarte writes that the Omagua 'are governed by Principals in the villages; and in the middle of this province, which is very large, there is a Principal, the King, whom they obey with great subjection' (Heriarte 1975: 185).

18 'In this village there was a villa in which there was a great deal of porcelain ware of various makes, both jars and pitchers, very large, with a capacity of more than twenty five arrobas, and other small pieces such as plates and bowls and candelabra of this porcelain of the best ever been seen in the world for that of Malaga is not equal, because it is all glazed and embellished with all colours, and so bright [are these colours] that they astonish, and, more than this, the drawings and paintings which they make on them are so accurately worked out that [one wonders how] with [only] natural skill they manufacture and decorate all these things [making them look just] like Roman [articles]' (Carvajal 1970: 201).

19 See Neves, this volume.

20 Except maybe for Acuña's comments on how

contact with Europeans had produced change among the Indians, having effects that were both negative (such as drunkenness, excessive submission and slaving expeditions) and positive (such as discipline, order and European faith).
21 The famous Jesuit Father Antonio Vieira, in referring to the enslaving practices of conquerors in Maranhão described by his predecessor Capuchin Cristóvão de Lisboa, wrote: 'they razed and burned entire villages, which are generally made of dry palm-leaves, roasting alive in them those who refused to surrender as slaves. They overcame and subjected others peacefully, but by execrable deceit. They would promise them alliance and friendship in the name and good faith of the King. But once they had them off guard and unarmed, they seized and bound them all dividing them among themselves as slaves or selling them with the greatest cruelty' (Vieira 1951). See also Betendorf 1910 for disapproval of the enslavement of Amazonian Indians.
22 Fausto 1994: 91.
23 Vieira 1951.
24 Samuel Fritz in Edmundson 1967.
25 Betendorf 1910.
26 Daniel 1976.
27 The imperial house of Vienna organized a quite considerable group of scientists and experts to accompany the fiancée of the Portuguese prince to Brazil in 1817, with the aim to explore and document her new home country and provide collections of Brazilian specimens for both local and European museums. Among this group were John Emmanuel Pohl (doctor, botanist and geologist from the University of Prague), Johan Natterer (zoologist from Vienna), Johan C. Mikan (botanist and entomologist from Prague) and Thomas Ender (landscape artist). Also part of this group were botanist Carl Friedrich Phillip von Martius and Johan Baptist von Spix, sent by the Archduchess's relative the King of Bavaria, and botanist Giuseppi Raddi from Tuscany, also sent by royal relatives of the Viennese princess. Another central figure in the introduction of naturalists and the organization of expeditions throughout the country was Baron Georg Heinrich von Langsdorff, who was officially sent to Brazil as general consul by the Russian tsar in 1813 and who himself led a famous expedition across central Brazil and the Amazon from 1827 till 1829; see Komissarov 1988, 1994.
28 La Condamine 1992: 75.
29 Rodrigues Ferreira 1786, 1787a–d, 1788, 1933a & b, and 1970, all reproduced in 1974. See also Areia *et al.* 1991a.
30 See Stepan 2000 for a recent study of Humboldt's depiction of the tropics, and Beluzzo 1999 for how Humboldt represents a new model of traveller's imagery.
31 Humboldt (1800) in A. Smith 1990: 232.
32 Because of the rivalries between Spain and Portugal, and the fact that Humboldt had only the Spanish *laissez-passer*, his expedition was not allowed to enter Brazilian territory, reducing his coverage of the Amazon basin only to the upper Rio Negro. See Andra 1964.
33 Humboldt in Mendonça de Souza 1991: 55.
34 Schomburgk 1841: 29–30.
35 See, for instance, the journal of Francisco Xavier Ribeiro Sampaio (1774–5); the account of Franz Keller-Leusinger, *The Amazon and Madeira Rivers, sketches and descriptions* (1874), where petroglyphs along the right banks of the Amazon are described; the descriptions of the rivers Baurus, Branco, da Conceição, de São Joaquim, Itonomas and Maxupo by Francisco José de Almeida e Lacerda (1780–90); and the numerous works by Ricardo Franco de Almeida Serra (1800s), which describe the customs and artefacts of many Amazonian native groups.
36 Spix and Martius 1823–31, 1824.
37 For a description of the ethnographic collection made by Spix and Martius at the Staatlichen Museum für Völkerkunde in Munich see Zerries 1980.
38 See Martius 1867 and 1992.
39 Martius 1982: 12, author's translation of Portuguese version.
40 Martius 1982: 68. Martius's view of human evolution is remarkably well tuned to the evolutionary ideas of the times, as expressed, for instance, in Lyell's *Principles of Geology* (1830–33) and Darwin's *On the Origin of Species* (1859). Although his thoughts are in accordance with the principle of uniformitarianism in geology and biological evolution, his comments on how Americans have devolved are still very much rooted in the popular catastrophism of the times. According to Martius, a series of catastrophes was responsible for the decadence of the earliest superior civilizations that once inhabited the American continent.
41 Martius does mention some archaeological finds in the Amazon, at sites he considers to have been old Indian cemeteries. He refers to ceramic urns where the dead were interred in sites near Manaus, on the Rio Trombetas, and on Marajó Island, in a place called Camutins (Hartt 1871: 17), later investigated by several modern archaeologists.
42 See, for instance, Barbosa Rodrigues's works by the end of the nineteenth century (1875a & b, 1876, 1882, 1889, 1892) or even the theories proposed by Meggers and Evans in 1954, the first modern archaeological research project in the region, which also proposes a similar process of adaptive devolution in the Amazon environment.
43 After a year in Cuiabá Natterer travelled down the Paraguai, Guaporé and Madeira rivers, up the Negro to the Uaupés and Içana rivers, and Casiquiare canal, and down the Branco, Mucajaí, Solimões and Amazon rivers to Belém. Most of Natterer's writings were lost in a fire during the revolution of 1848. The only written records of such materials are Koch-Grünberg's comments on the diaries he has seen. For a history and description of Natterer's ethnographic collection see Kästner 1990, and Becker-Donner n/d.
44 See Beluzzo 1999 for a detailed study of how science and art are integrated in the graphic imagery produced by expeditions of this time.
45An appendix with drawings of petroglyphs he observed on the Uaupés banks comments on the probable antiquity of these records. See also Pereira's essay in this volume about the contribution of these naturalists to the documentation of rock art in the Amazon.
46 Wallace (1853) 1979.
47 Bates (1863) 1979.
48 Spruce travelled through South America from 1849 to 1864 (see Spruce 1908). For comments on his contributions see the volume edited by Seaward and Fitzgerald 1996, in particular the essays by Reichel-Dolmatoff and Nigel Smith about the ethnographic aspects.
49 But see his records of petroglyphs in the Amazon as presented by Edithe Pereira in this volume.
50 Barbosa Rodrigues 1892. This famous site, looted in the nineteenth century, was one of first archaeological sites to be known in the Amazon and to yield the well-known anthropomorphic Guarita urns (see Petersen *et al.*, this volume).
51 See Ferreira Penna 1876, 1877a & b.
52 See Hart 1871, 1885 and 1975.
53 See Netto 1885.
54 See Schaan, this volume, for the contemporary interpretations of decorated Marajoara urns, more than a century after Netto's hypothesis.
55 See catalogue and review of the exhibition, respectively, by Barbosa Rodrigues (1882), and Moraes Filho (1882).
56 See, for instance, the expeditions by Couto Magalhães in 1863, the studies of Amazonian archaeology by Francisco Bernardino de Sousa and Mauricio de Heriarte in 1874, the descriptions of rock art by Antonio Manuel Gonçalves Tocantins, Edward Mathews, and Richard Schomburgk in the 1870s, and most studies published by the Instituto Histórico e Geográfico Brasileiro concerning the Amazonian region.
57 Barreto's history of the Museu Paraense Emílio Goeldi gives a good account of the main archaeological research undertaken in the region in the twentieth century (Barreto 1992). See also Barreto 2000 for a history of Brazilian archaeology and Neves 1999a & b for a synthetic view of modern archaeology and theories of human development in the Amazon.
58 See Nordenskiöld 1930 and n.d., and Nimuendajú n.d.

11

One Blow Scatters the Brains

An Ethnographic History of the Guiana War Club

WARWICK BRAY

This essay concentrates on a single category of artefact, the carved wooden club, variants of which were employed for hand-to-hand combat throughout Amazonia.[1] In Guiana, where European records begin before AD 1600, we can trace the history of these weapons (with changes in shape, decoration and social function) over a period of four centuries, during which Indian culture reacted first to the colonial experience and then to the modern world. This historical approach also provides insights into the formation of Amazonian ethnographic collections in Europe and North America.

Guiana as a cultural subarea

Guiana in its broadest sense includes all the north-eastern part of mainland South America between the Orinoco and the Amazon rivers, extending inland as far as the Rio Negro and the Cassiquiare Canal, and incorporating the former British, Dutch and French colonies, together with the adjacent regions of Brazil and Venezuela.

In terms of its artefact inventories[2] and forms of social organization[3] Guiana is a distinct sub-region within the lowland tropics but was never isolated from the rest of Amazonia. People and trade items moved readily up and down the coast, between the mainland and the Antilles, and along the rivers that link the interior with the Atlantic seaboard. Inland, beyond the headwaters of these rivers, trade routes connected the Amazon and Orinoco drainages by way of the Negro, Branco and Caroni rivers, with a side branch to the upper Essequibo and the interior of Guiana.[4]

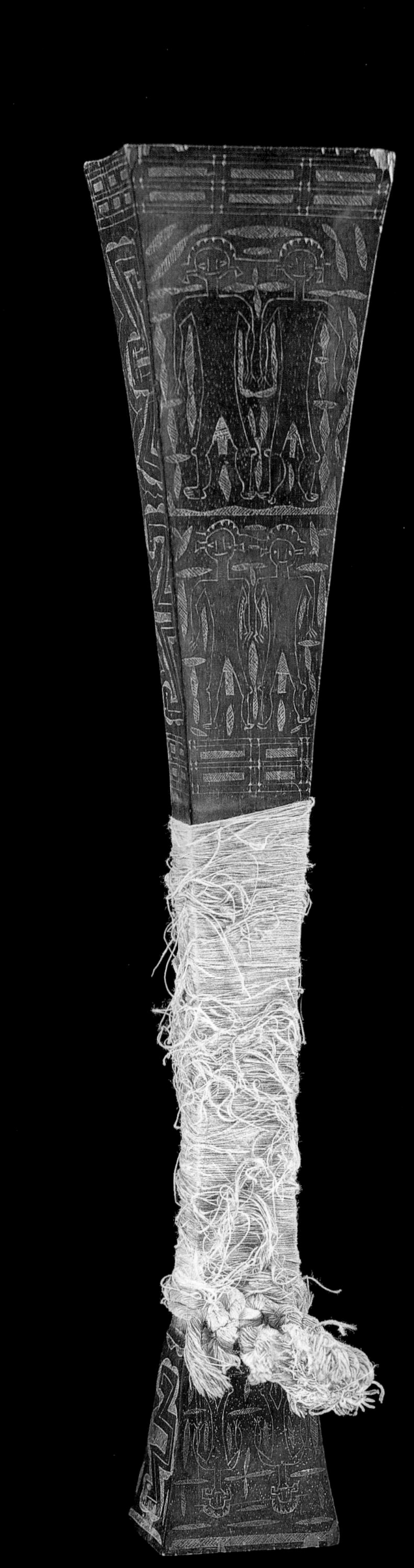

11.1 General view (right) and two details (opposite) of a wooden block-club with a hand grip bound with cotton thread, collected by Alexandre Rodrigues Ferreira between 1783 and 1792, probably on the Rio Branco, Brazil (length 43.6 cm; Museu Antropológico da Universidade de Coimbra).

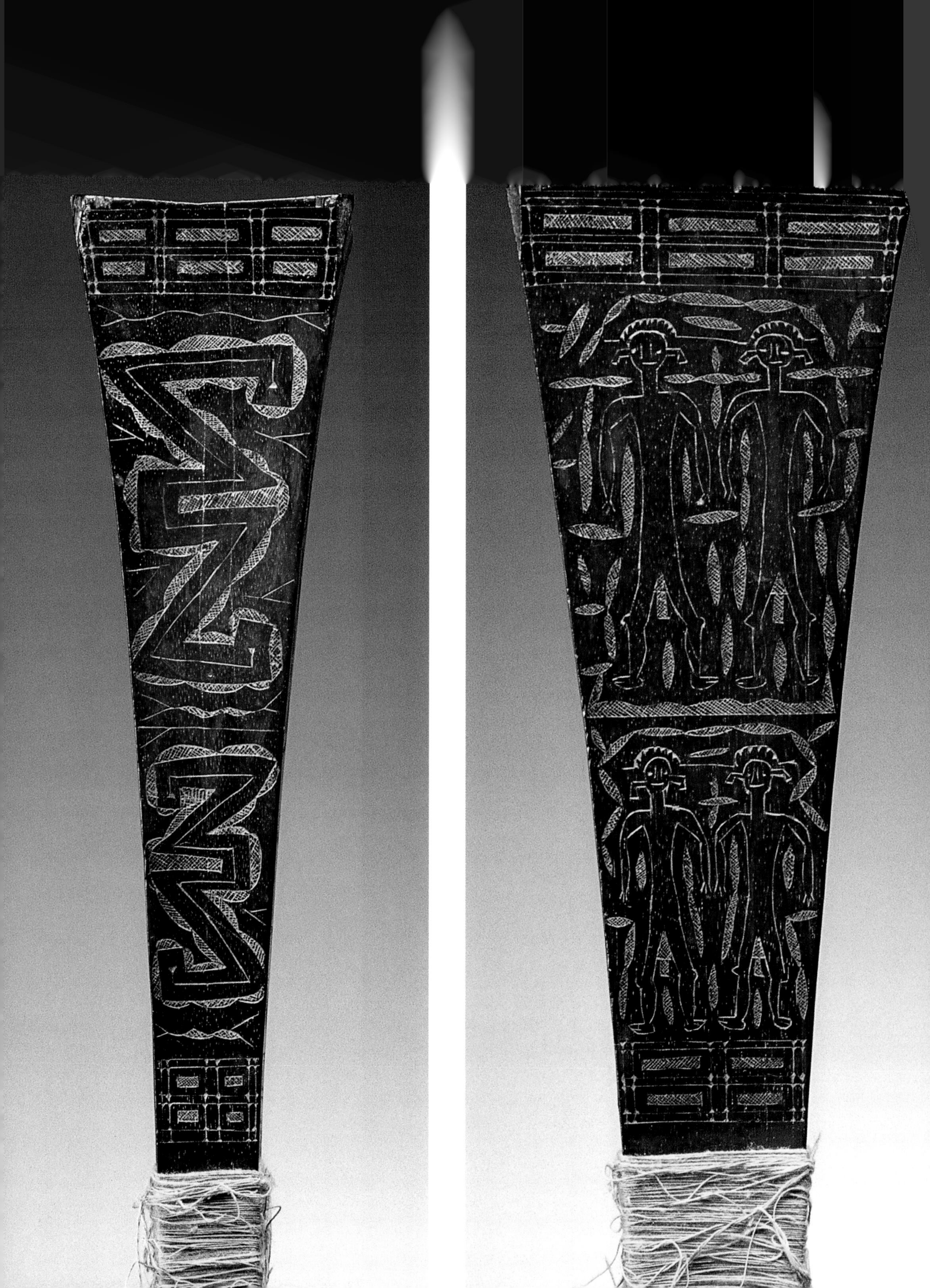

The present study concentrates on the eastern part of this vast territory, from the Rio Branco to the Atlantic. Because the Atlantic seaboard was the first point of contact for the developing maritime connections with Europe, this area and its hinterland provided most of the clubs in early collections. Guiana is also the homeland of one distinctive form that is found nowhere else in Amazonia: the block-club with finely incised decoration (fig. 11.1).

Wooden clubs in the early years of European contact

Wooden objects are rarely preserved on archaeological sites in the humid tropics. Although clubs undoubtedly have a long history in Guiana, the only examples that may be of pre-contact age are a group of items dredged by gold-mining machinery from the rivers of French Guiana (fig. 11.2). One of these clubs (fig. 11.2d) has traces of a diamond-shaped motif incised on one side, which is similar to the 'diamond-and-curl' design found on the earliest clubs in European collections (cf. fig. 11.4).[5] Unfortunately, as accidental finds, these items cannot be accurately dated. All the clubs have flattened, sword-shaped blades. Some are short enough to wield with one hand; others, well over one metre in length, would have required two hands.

A two-handed weapon is shown in one of the earliest European illustrations of wooden clubs in the Caribbean area (fig. 11.3). It comes from the so-called 'Drake Manuscript', written in French during the 1590s, possibly by a Huguenot member of Drake's crew. The caption reads:

> INDIANS OF IHONA. When the Indians have defeated their enemies they make them lie down on the ground, then pound them, and after that give them a blow on the head

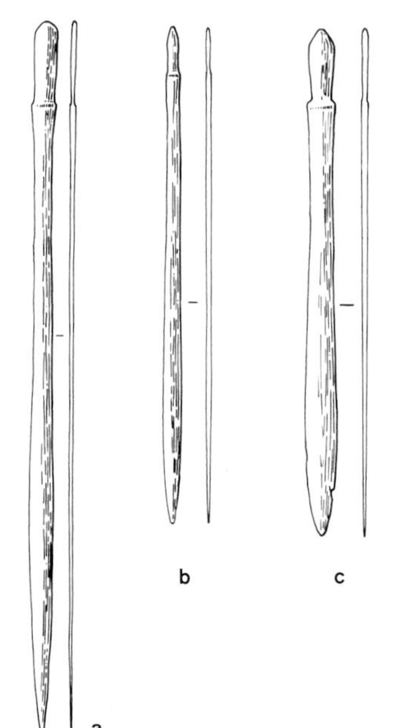

ABOVE 11.2 Wooden sword-clubs, possibly from before the first European contact, found in the rivers of French Guiana. Redrawn from Vacher *et al.* 1998.

LEFT 11.3 Scene from the 'Drake Manuscript' painted in the 1590s, showing a warrior using a long, two-handed club.

> with their sword. When the blood starts flowing, they hold it back promptly, thinking that by this means the body will make a better roast for a solemn feast, calling this a deed of prowess.[6]

The land of Ihona has not been identified and is more likely to be in the West Indian islands or coastal Venezuela than in Guiana, but the shape of the club and the placement of the decoration are matched on the oldest Guiana clubs in European collections. This caption is interesting in other ways, too. It reinforces the European stereotype of the Caribs as cannibals (thereby justifying their conquest and enslavement) and, like many of the early European chronicles, employs the word sword for what is clearly a club. This usage may reflect European perception that, within their respective cultures, the steel sword and the wooden club occupy the same role, as the preferred weapon for close quarter fighting.

Two other illustrations in the Drake Manuscript show wooden clubs in a more domestic context.[7] Both are courtship scenes, in which the prospective bridegroom visits the house of the girl's father, who is seated on a Caribbean-style wooden stool and is holding a club. In these scenes the club is not so much a weapon as an element of formal regalia, a theme I will return to later.

One of the best early accounts from the mainland, written in 1628 or 1629 but based on earlier information, is provided by Antonio Vázquez de Espinosa, who reports on the Carib and Arawak tribes around the mouth of the Orinoco. He mentions clubs of a wood so tough that no axe could cut it,[8] and describes other clubs that are 'stone-edged'.[9] The meaning of this phrase is unclear; it may refer to a club fitted with a stone blade or perhaps to a club with stone chips set along the edges, like those used until recent times by the Apalai and Wayana of southern Guiana.[10]

Vázquez also describes the state of constant warfare between the Arawaks and Caribs, and between the island and mainland Indians. Among the Arawaks, he comments: 'the Indian who is to be made captain has to kill three foes in battle with his war club, which is of a very remarkable striped wood, and he has to make three notches on it, witness to his deeds.'[11] The Garina Caribs had a similar custom, and Vázquez gives a very detailed account of how their war captains were chosen and inducted:

> In order to be commissioned captain among them, one has to kill three of the enemy in battle with a wooden club which is their sword; and when he has succeeded in killing three enemies, he throws his club on the ground and fights no more … [When] the cacique or general who governs them arrives, they retire to their villages or provinces, where they cut off his hair and hang a hammock for him at the highest point of the house where they live; and there they make him fast for a whole year, without his eating or drinking anything but mazato, their drink made from cassava; and 15 days before the end of the year, they go out after big wild ants, almost as large as bees … They throw troops of these into the hammock or bed where he lies, for them to bite and sting him, and he has to endure them with patience and without flinching or showing weakness, for a period of 24 hours; and then they … put on him a feather headdress of many colors; and … they set him between two powerful Indians with two whips such as coachmen use; … [then] they give him many lashes of the whip; and if he shows any weakness or fear, they take him back again for penance, and if he shows valor and fortitude, they all honor and cheer him with much noise.[12]

Since ant-bite ordeals and whipping rituals are documented throughout Guiana until recent times,[13] the whole account can probably be taken as accurate.

At about the same time (1613) Robert Harcourt, on the southern Guiana coast, noted that 'the vsual weapons [of the Arawaks] are Bowes and Arrowes, long staues sharpened at the point, and with fire hardened; wooden Swords and Targets [shields] very artificially made of wood and painted with Beasts and Birds'.[14] These 'swords' must have been one-handed weapons, if the other hand held a shield.

By the time of Harcourt's voyage, coastal Guiana was already coming under European influence. Squeezed between the Spanish settlements of Venezuela and the Orinoco to the north, and the Portuguese territories to the south and west, it was a no man's land, open to trade and colonization from all the mercantile states of Europe.

By 1600 British and Dutch navigators had explored the entire Guiana coast from the Orinoco to the Amazon. In 1595 Sir Robert Dudley sent a boat's crew sixteen days up the Orinoco river, and Sir Walter Ralegh visited the area in 1592, 1595 and 1617.[15] In 1596 Lawrence Keymis, one of Ralegh's former captains, landed at the Amazon delta and surveyed the Guiana coast as far north as the mouth of the Orinoco.[16] He also ascended the river Oyapock (the present border between French Guiana and Brazil) and tried to found colonies there. In 1597 Keymis was followed on the Oyapock by Leonard Berry, and in 1597–8 Adrian Cabeliau visited the area on behalf of the Dutch, whose presence there is attested by both documentary and archaeological evidence from the 1590s onwards.[17]

Exploration was quickly followed by colonization, and in the early seventeenth century the French, Dutch and Danes created companies for trading with the mainland and the Antilles. In the first three decades of the century the focus of North European interest was the Amazon basin and southern Guiana.[18] Later, with the military expansion of the Portuguese from Brazil into the lower Amazon, efforts were concentrated further north. The Dutch colonized the Essequibo river (1616), the Berbice river (1624) and the Corentine (before 1628). By 1633 there was also an English colony on the Surinam. Because of its turbulent politics, and its warlike Indians, Atlantic Guiana became known as the 'Wild Coast', though John Scott, in his *Discription of Guyana* written in about 1669, lists fourteen attempts at colonization by the year 1650.[19] European contact was not limited to the coastal zone, and there is documentary evidence that the Dutch were already trading iron tools and other goods to the Indians of the interior savannah as far west as the Rio Negro.[20] In these early years, before the establishment of stable colonial frontiers, ethnographic items shipped back to Europe could have originated anywhere between the Orinoco and the Amazon.

Among the earliest materials to reach Europe are four wooden clubs and five hammocks that entered the collection of the Tradescant family and are preserved in the Ashmolean Museum, Oxford.[21] All four clubs are two-handed weapons, between 1.14 and 1.40 metres long, rectangular in section, made of dark wood and with expanded ends bearing carved decoration similar in general terms to those of the Drake Manuscript. The wood of two of these clubs has been analysed and proved to be *Brosimum* species, one of the woods still used for clubs and bows in recent times.[22] It is likely that a fifth club of the same type, now in the British Museum, also came originally from the Tradescant collection (figs 11.4–5).[23]

The five clubs are strikingly similar in shape and size, and four of them have carved

designs that are variants of the same pattern, made up of diamond-shaped panels and spiral curlicues. As a convenient shorthand, I have called this the 'diamond and curl' motif.[24] Where these clubs were collected, and by whom, is unknown. They are first recorded in the catalogue of John Tradescant the Younger in 1656, but most of the collection was formed by his father, John Tradescant the Elder, who died in 1637 or early in 1638. In a letter dated 1625 from the Elder Tradescant to Edward Nicholas, Secretary to the Navy, he explains that he was now working for the Duke of Buckingham, who was actively seeking out rare specimens of all kinds. 'It is H Graces Plesure that you should In His Name Deall withe All Marchants from All Places But Espetially the Virgine & Bermewde & Newfound Land … Also to Captain Northe to the New Plantation towards the Amasonians.'[25] If the clubs arrived by the same channels as Tradescant's other specimens, they may already have been in England by the 1620s.

Other clubs in early European collections are surprisingly similar to the ones from Oxford, and share the same 'diamond and curl' ornament. These include five examples, now in Copenhagen, that were recorded in the Danish royal collection in 1689, though one of them probably goes back still further, to the Paludani collection of 1617.[26] A very similar club was in the collection of Ferdinando II de' Medici by 1631, and two more came to the Bibliothèque Sainte-Geneviève, Paris, some time before 1687.[27] This library also has a fine ceremonial baton of the same age (and possibly from the Guiana region) topped by a carved figure holding two trophy heads (figs 11.6–7).[28]

The similarity in shape and decoration between these early clubs is striking and might suggest that all the specimens come from a single region of Guiana. They certainly define an early homogeneous group of Guiana clubs securely datable to the first century of European contact.

While these artefacts have at present no traceable history, we know that explorers, merchants, soldiers and diplomats were all involved in sending curios to Europe. One such gift is recorded in a letter to Charles II of England from Major James Bannister, who was charged with evacu-

LEFT AND ABOVE 11.4–5 General view and detail of a wooden club that probably comes from the Trandescant collection (early seventeenth century) and is now in the British Museum (length 130 cm). It is carved with the diamond-and-curl design characteristic of most seventeenth-century Guiana clubs in European collections.

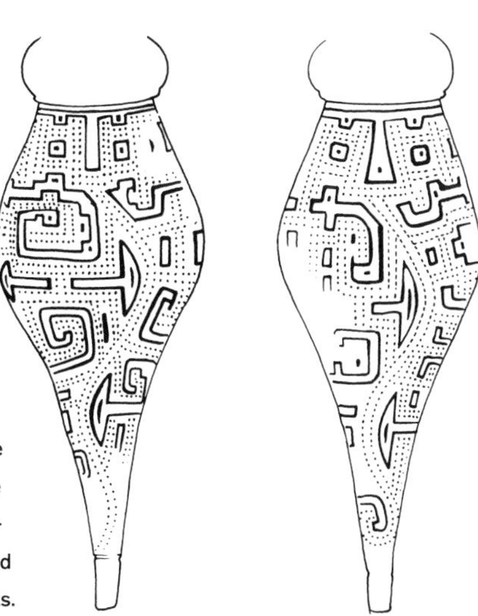

RIGHT 11.6 Two opposite sides of the lower part of the baton illustrated in fig. 11.7. The patterns, painted in black over an orange background, have a generally Amazonian appearance but cannot be matched to any specific regional style. The uppermost motifs appear to represent human faces, and the scrolls are interspersed with axe-like elements.

11.7 Ceremonial baton acquired some time before 1687 and now in the Bibliothèque Sainte-Geneviève, Paris (length 68 cm). The figure at the top holds two trophy heads or perhaps masks (since each head has a face on the reverse as well on the front). The base is painted (see fig. 11.6). The provenance of the baton is unknown but is probably the lower Amazon or Guiana.

ating the British planters from Surinam when the colony was handed back to the Dutch under the Treaty of Breda. In his letter to the king, written from Jamaica on 8 April 1671, the major begs 'his Majesty's acceptance of the small presentment he has presumed to send, viz., two Indian swords, three lances which they mortally poison at their going to war, and one bow made without any iron tool.'[29] Unfortunately, these items cannot be located.

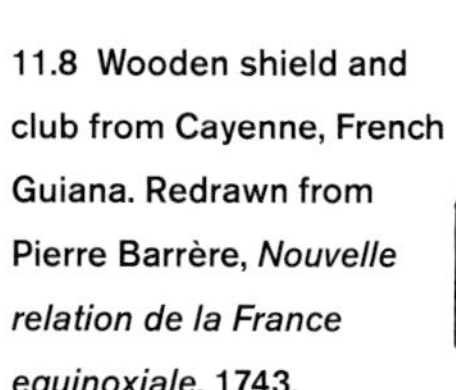

11.8 Wooden shield and club from Cayenne, French Guiana. Redrawn from Pierre Barrère, *Nouvelle relation de la France equinoxiale*, 1743.

The eighteenth century

Europeans had already begun to penetrate the interior of Guiana in the later part of the seventeenth century, but these contacts intensified during the first half of the eighteenth, as traders, gold-prospectors and explorers followed the rivers westwards. By the 1740s the Dutch had reached the Rupununi savannah and linked up with the Portuguese settlements on the Rio Branco, and by 1769 their administration was receiving accurate information about the Macusis and the Wapishanas of the interior.[30] We can no longer assume that items reaching Europe at this time came exclusively from the coastal strip. From the literature of the time it is also clear that the Indian groups were still a political and military force, constantly fighting among themselves and forming alliances with the competing European powers.[31]

Because the colonists were reluctant to give the Indians firearms, most Indian warriors were still using their traditional weapons. A few of these eighteenth-century clubs have survived in European collections. One specimen (a shorter version of fig. 11.4), with the characteristic 'diamond and curl' ornament, was in Dresden by 1721,[32] and a similar one from French Guiana had reached Paris before the revolution of 1789.[33] From the same region of Guiana Pierre Barrère in 1743 described the warriors of Cayenne as 'well armed with their bows, arrows, wooden clubs [*boutous*], stone axes and other instruments of war', and he illustrated these with an engraving (fig. 11.8).[34] This seems to be the first picture to show the distinctive block-club, the short, thick, heavy weapon that dominates all subsequent museum collections from eastern Guiana (cf. figs 11.1, 11.9 and 11.11–12).

A block-club of just this type, with the classic 'diamond and curl' designs, is in the Museo de América, Madrid, and has an interesting history.[35] An old handwritten label reads:

> Mayurucari, a Carib captain, killed with this club the most Illustrious Dr Nicolas Gervasio de La Brid, a native of Leon, France, later consacrated by [Pope] Benedict XIII. His death took place in September 1729. With this same [club] his two chaplains were killed a short time before. With this same was killed V.P. Jr. Andres Lopez, a religious missionary, in Mamo Caño in the Orinoco. The sacriligeous Carib died at the hands of the captain of our escort on the 15th day of August in this year [1]736–7. I confirm the truth of this. Joseph Gumilla [the noted historian of the Orinoco missions] signed it.

The murder of La Brid, in the course of a raid by rebellious Caribs from Guiana, is a well-documented incident and became a popular subject for European engravings.[36] If the museum label is truthful, the Madrid artefact is a rare example of an eighteenth-century club with an exact provenance and date. It is also important because of its transitional or hybrid style. The principal ornament is the diamond-and-curl

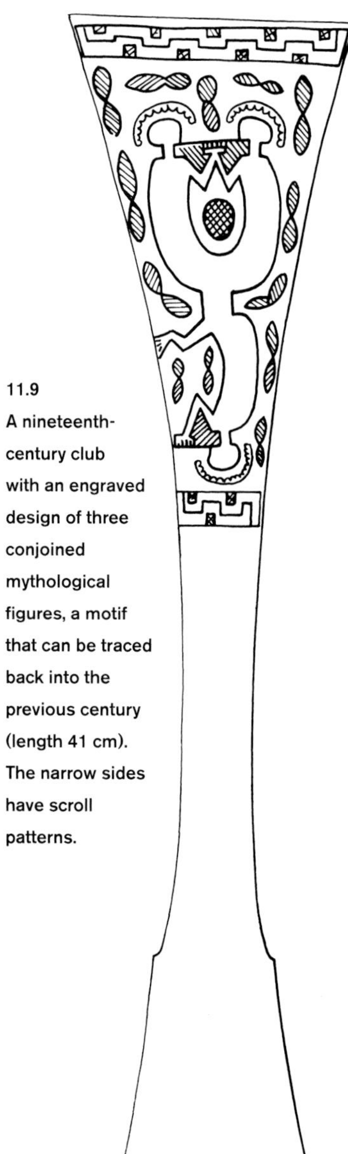

11.9
A nineteenth-century club with an engraved design of three conjoined mythological figures, a motif that can be traced back into the previous century (length 41 cm). The narrow sides have scroll patterns.

motif that looks back to the previous century, but the smaller end of the club has curvilinear ribbon, or arabesque, designs of a kind that become common in later collections (cf. fig. 11.1). For the moment the Madrid club is the earliest documented weapon with this style of engraving.

Some forty-five years later John Gabriel Stedman wrote about his experiences as a soldier in Dutch Surinam:

> I must not forget that every Indian carries a club, which they call apootoo, for their defence. These clubs are made from the heaviest wood in the forest; they are about eighteen inches long, flat at both ends, and square, but heavier at one end than the other. In the middle they are thinner, and wound about with strong cotton threads so as to be grasped, having a loop to secure them round the wrist, as sword-tassels are used by the cavalry. One blow with this club, in which is frequently fixed a sharp stone, scatters the brains ... and on these, besides other hieroglyphic figures, they often carve the number of people they have slain in battle. The manner of fixing the stone in the club is by sticking it in the tree while it is yet growing, where it soon becomes so fast that it cannot be forced out; the wood is then cut and shaped according to fancy.[37]

11.10 Uariquena Indian from Rio Ixié (headwaters of the Rio Negro) with rattle spear and long war club. From Alexandre Rodrigues Ferreira, *Viagem Filosófica* (1783–92).

Stedman's description of how the stone blades were attached does not match my own observations of cut sockets and the use of natural adhesives (and even of wedges).[38] Nor should the carved and incised designs be called 'hieroglyphic', though they do convey symbolic information. In most respects, however, Stedman accurately describes a typical Guiana block-club. In subsequent paragraphs Stedman notes that a dead Indian was buried with his weapons (i.e. old clubs would not remain in circulation), that Indian groups raided each other to capture slaves for the Europeans and that – in an early instance of tourist ethnography – the scalps and bones of dead enemies were sold as curios in Paramaribo.

The closing years of the eighteenth century provide another group of Guiana-style block-clubs, collected by Alexandre Rodrigues Ferreira in the course of his scientific expedition through Brazilian Amazonia in 1783–92. The expedition studied the natural history of the region, made paintings of costumed Indians carrying their weapons (fig. 11.10) and shipped large quantities of Indian artefacts back to Portugal. Ferreira's notes refer to 'small heavy wood maces that I have occasionally sent to the Royal Cabinet, under the name Braçangas, which are the natives' short arms; they bruise and cut like sabres'.[39] Fourteen of these clubs still exist in Coimbra and Lisbon; one of them has an inset stone blade, and seven have finely incised decoration (fig. 11.1).[40] Most of these clubs were probably collected in 1786 along the Rio Branco, where Ferreira encountered Macusi, Wapishana and Waica Indians, though one specimen, with the familiar diamond-and-curl motif, is attributed to the Caripunas of the north bank of the Amazon.[41]

The importance of Ferreira's collection is that it gives some idea of the range of shapes and decorative designs in use at one time and in a relatively restricted area. Combining Ferreira's material with the other eighteenth-century clubs in Madrid and elsewhere, we can show that the old diamond-and-curl style remained in vogue (and is now recorded all over Guiana), but alongside this we find new designs based on delicately incised scroll patterns and human-figure motifs. Exactly where, and when, these designs were invented is still not clear, but their later history is well documented through nineteenth-century museum collections.

The nineteenth century

During the early years of the nineteenth century Guiana began to take on its modern political configuration. In 1814 the Dutch finally ceded to Britain the territory that became British Guiana, and with the establishment of stable administrations the Indians were increasingly drawn into the sphere of European influence.

One consequence of this increased contact was more intensive, though usually unsystematic, collection of souvenirs from the Guiana Indians. Most of the major European museum collections were formed during the nineteenth century, but many items arrived without useful information. Sometimes we have the date and place of collection, or the tribal affiliation, but nineteenth-century missionaries and travellers ignored many of the questions that excite the curiosity of modern anthropologists. In particular, there was a lack of interest in the belief systems of the Indians and in the ways that these were expressed through visual symbols on artefacts of all kinds. We have no direct information, from the Indians themselves, about the significance of the finely engraved human, animal and curvilinear designs on their wooden clubs, and there is now no opportunity to ask.

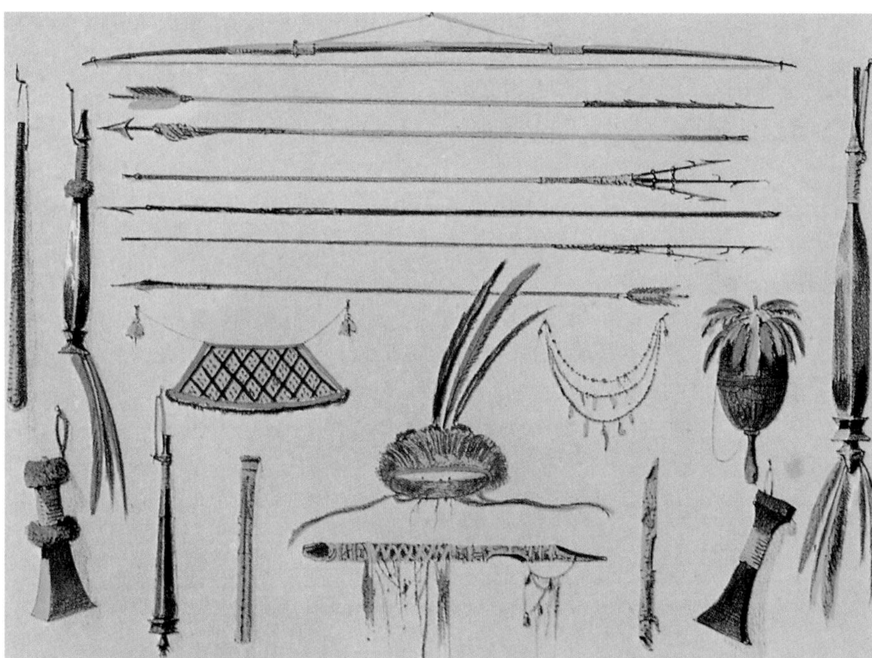

11.11 Weapons and costume items of the Indians of Surinam. The painting shows that several types of club were in use at any one time. From P.J. Benoit, *Voyage à Surinam*, 1839.

This distinctive curvilinear style (fig. 11.1) seems to be the creation of Carib-speaking groups. Richard Schomburgk, in the 1840s, noted that in the British colony the war clubs of the Caribs 'differ from those of other tribes by being decorated with an incised arabesque-like pattern' and that 'these decorations, which are repeated on their flutes, benches, pottery, etc., differ essentially from the designs amongst the remaining tribes'.[42] Similar styles of decoration on pottery and wooden artefacts are also found among the Caribs of Surinam and French Guiana, and reconfirm that the tradition goes back to the eighteenth century.[43]

As well as filling museum cases, the opening up of the interior generated a good deal of scientific writing and travel literature, and some of this is well illustrated. Fig. 11.11, from P. J. Benoit's *Voyage à Surinam*,[44] depicts featherwork and necklaces, a

11.12 Carib Indian from Surinam holding a block-club. From P.J. Benoit, *Voyage à Surinam*, 1839.

woman's bead apron and a set of weapons including several types of club: long ones, block-clubs (fig. 11.12) like those already discussed, and paddle-clubs or sword-clubs with broad, flat, sharp-edged blades. All these forms are well represented in nineteenth-century European museums. As contact with the colonists intensified, the Indian world began to change. Mission stations were established in territories controlled by the Spanish, Portuguese and French as early as the eighteenth century, and in British Guiana from the 1830s onwards.[45] At the same time cutlasses and firearms became more widespread though, as a condition of their friendship, the British insisted that the Indians should stop making war on each other and selling captured slaves.[46] In these new conditions cultural differences between the Indian communities began to break down, and the club as a weapon of war slowly fell into disuse.

The changes were gradual rather than sudden, and inter-tribal wars were still fairly common in the 1840s, when Richard Schomburgk was travelling in British Guiana. On the basis of eyewitness accounts, European as well as Indian, Schomburgk provided a vivid description of traditional warfare:

> The outbreak of hostilities is not preceded by any declaration of war; except that as soon as war is determined by the Palaver, the side taking the offensive tries to get as close as possible to the enemy at night, with a view to making a surprise attack by daybreak … If the contending forces meet in the open, action begins with a war dance wherein the enemy challenge their opponents with a number of contortions and gesticulations, both parties trying in general to influence each other's passions by singing at one another with lampoon and sneer. The combat starts only from a distance with poisoned arrows, of which each warrior takes seven to battle. When these are shot the fight continues with war-clubs and indeed man against man. If one side withdraws, it tries above everything else to rescue its dead, so that these should not fall into the hands of the enemy, a business that is imposed upon the women who accompany the men like pack-animals and constitute the camp-followers. As implicit obedience has to be rendered to the chief in war time, he is distinguished by a brilliant feather-decoration, finer weapons, and a particular kind of body-painting. The warriors are also painted on such occasions differently from what they are during peace: the hair is thickly covered with urucu and feathers stuck in it. Georgetown residents can yet recall the peculiarly gruesome spectacle that presented itself at the last revolt of the Negroes when nude thrillingly painted and fantastically ornamented Warraus, Caribs, Akawais and Arawaks were reviewed on the parade ground prior to the expedition against the blacks, while their women, loaded like beasts of burden with weapons and provisions, formed the rear-guard.[47]

A few years later, William Henry Brett (a missionary writing in 1852) commented that stone-bladed clubs 'were seldom met with' among the Caribs,[48] and includes the following passage on the Arawak-speaking Lokono:

> Their weapons were chiefly bows and arrows and clubs. *One kind of club, which they still make, though now only as specimens of the weapons used by their ancestors* [my emphasis], is of a very formidable description. It is made of the hardest and heaviest wood, and has a broad blade, thick in the middle, and with sharp edges. The handle is covered with cotton, wound tightly round it, to prevent the hand from slipping, and it has also a short loop of the same material which is placed round the wrist. They call it 'Sapakana'. Some of these were of large size, and required both hands to wield them.

They are now well provided with fire-arms and skilled in the use of them.[49]

Brett is clearly describing a paddle-club, or perhaps a sword-club, and his comment makes one wonder how many of the clubs in European collections were made to order, in a deliberately archaic style.

Everard im Thurn, in 1883, illustrates Wapishana or Arecuna paddle-clubs and Macusi block-clubs, and remarks: 'The habit of inter-tribal war having practically disappeared, though only within a few years, such clubs are rarely made.'[50] Specimens with inserted blades of stone or iron were all but unobtainable. 'Of weapons of war the only kind now to be seen is the war-club, called *tiki* by the Carib tribes; and even these are no longer made, and are carried more as ornaments than for use.'[51] After describing the finely incised decoration, he adds: 'Originally, apparently, they differed in shape according to the tribe which made them; but these differences ... seem to be somewhat lost, and most of the various forms of tiki may be seen in the possession of any one of the tribes.' This is a cause of real difficulty to anthropologists trying to attribute undocumented specimens on the basis of style alone.

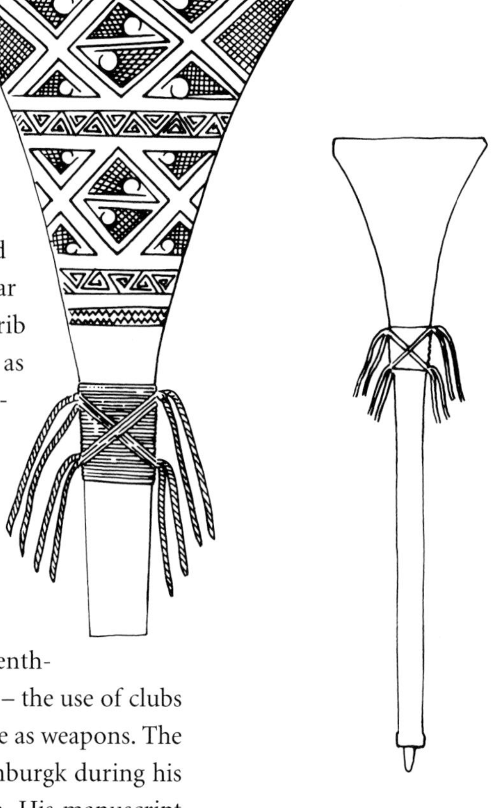

Im Thurn draws attention to something hinted at in the sixteenth-century Drake Manuscript but ignored by most of the early writers – the use of clubs as items of regalia and as costume accessories, in parallel to their role as weapons. The specimen in fig. 11.13, for example, was collected by Robert Schomburgk during his expeditions to British Guiana and donated to the British Museum. His manuscript inventory reads: 'This club, which is peculiar to the Macoosis and Wapishanas, is called Lashpanak [difficult to decipher] and is used by the Chieftain as a badge of office at solemn occasions; he plants it before the place where he takes his seat at Paiwarri feasts.'[52] Schomburgk's use of the word 'plants' suggests that the club was set upright in the ground. This might explain the spike at the end, though his brother Richard Schomburgk comments that the sharp point at the handle-end of many Guiana clubs 'is said to be for the purpose, when the enemy is downed, of sticking it into his ear and driving it into his brain'.[53] Whatever the case, the British Museum club could have served as a functional weapon. Certain other nineteenth-century clubs, which seem too fragile for use in combat, may well have been purely ceremonial, but the documentation is lacking.

In summary, all lines of evidence suggest that by the close of the century war clubs were going out of use among the more acculturated Indian groups, though the artefact maintained its place in rituals and ceremonies.

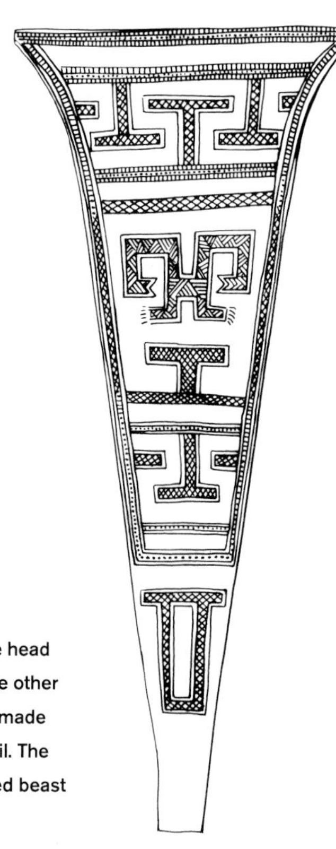

ABOVE RIGHT **11.13 Ceremonial wooden club from British Guiana, donated to the British Museum by Robert Schomburgk in 1836 (length 71.8 cm). The engraved design is a late version of the diamond-and-curl motif (compare figs 11.4–5).**

RIGHT **11.14 Design in the cross-hatched geometric style on the head of a club collected by Jules Crevaux between 1876 and 1881. The other end has a spike (compare fig. 11.13). The club resembles those made by the Apalai and Wayana of southern Guiana and adjacent Brazil. The main design is a stylized representation of a mythical two-headed beast with long claws, similar to the ones on the club in fig. 11.15.**

Epilogue: wooden clubs in the twentieth century

Although the early reports by administrators, missionaries and scientific travellers give useful pieces of information, their observations are sporadic and unsystematic. Serious anthropological fieldwork, often under the patronage of museums, did not begin until the early twentieth century.[54] By that time the Indian groups of the coast, and also the Akawaios, Macusis and Wapishanas of the interior, were already well known to Europeans, but other communities (e.g. the Waiwai, Trio, Wayana and Apalai of southern Guiana) were still relatively unstudied and had very little contact with the colonial world.

11.15 Dance costume of an Apalai war chief, Rio Parù, early twentieth century. He wears a feather headdress and a bast-fibre cape, and carries a dance club with geometric cross-hatched designs representing mythical monsters (see also fig. 11.14).

Anthropologists were, for obvious reasons, attracted to the less acculturated tribes, and twentieth-century collections of clubs have therefore a different geographical orientation from those of the nineteenth. In the interior regions of southern Guiana the fine curvilinear-incised style of decoration was absent or had disappeared by the time of the first ethnographies. There are other differences too. Although wooden clubs were still sometimes used for war,[55] and also for hunting,[56] recent studies give much more attention to their ceremonial use. In this context, as costume items rather than weapons, the hand-grips of clubs become thinner and more fragile; instead of the delicately incised scroll and figure designs, the repertoire is now dominated by simpler, rectilinear, geometric motifs that make a better show from a distance; and paddle-clubs and spatulate forms, which give a larger field for decoration,[57] begin to outnumber block-clubs.

Farabee, in his study of the Central Caribs, observed that the designs on twentieth-century ceremonial clubs are no different from those used in basketry, beadwork, body painting and woodcarving in general, and he suggested that the crosshatched geometrical patterns had basketry origins. Many of the apparently abstract designs represent stylized animals, though he was told that these 'have no relation to a token of the tribe or to a personal protector of the individual'.[58] The Farabee expedition also collected the dance costume of an Apalai war chief (figs 11.14–15)[59] and witnessed a Tcalifona dance in which one of the participant's carried a ceremonial club over his shoulder (while smoking a 15-inch cigar) and two other men 'carried ceremonial clubs as staffs and sang, accentuating the rhythm with a heavy thump of the right foot on the ground'.[60]

Warfare, against European intruders as well as other Indian groups, persisted longest among the Trio and Apalai-Wayana of the Brazil-Surinam border region. Roth described how in the 1920s Trio men carried clubs when they wanted to make themselves 'pretty-pretty' in holiday attire, but insisted that these clubs were also serviceable weapons and not mere ornaments.[61] In a clear reference to the clubbing of animals, the Pemon recognize a star constellation called Tauná (the Master of Lightning and Thunder), depicted as a hunter in the sky, his upraised arm holding a club. By his feet is a cluster of stars representing the roasting frame on which he will barbecue his victims (information provided by Audrey Butt Colson). It is clear, though, that the distinction between war clubs and ceremonial clubs is not absolute. Braun, for example, illustrates a typical Wayana war club, but notes that it was brandished during ant-bite rituals by a costumed shaman dancer.[62]

By the 1970s war clubs had gone out of use, though Frikel[63] and Rauschert[64] were able to collect information on both fighting clubs and dance clubs from people who still remembered the old days. Block-clubs made of hard wood were used in past times, and cylindrical all-purpose clubs were carried for opportunistic hunting, but more characteristic of the Trio and their neighbours was a broad, flat club with a spatula-shaped end, sometimes edged with jaguar teeth or stone chips. One tradition said that after a killing the club was left at the scene; another maintained that warriors adorned their clubs with pieces of scalp taken from their victims. Clubs of the same general form, though smaller and made of lighter wood, were still used in re-enactments of war dances, as well as in purely festive dances. By the 1970s the only clubs being made were for sale to tourists. After four hundred years of European contact the Guiana club has been reduced to a tourist artefact.

In doing so, even in debased form, it has found a new role as a symbol of 'Indianness' (to non-Indians, at least) in a multiracial and multicultural world. Since symbols exist to be manipulated, it is no accident that two block-clubs, one of them painted with traditional Carib designs, were presented to Queen Juliana of the Netherlands on the occasion of her visit to Surinam in 1955.[65]

Acknowledgements

For information, advice and the loan of books I am indebted to Arie Boomert, Simone Breton-Gravereau, Paz Cabello, Audrey Colson, Berete Due, Manuela Fischer, François Gendron, Klaus-Peter Kästner, Arthur MacGregor, José Oliver, Alison Petch, Peter Rivière, Inge Schellerup, Barbara Watanabe, Neil Whitehead and Monica Zavattaro. I also wish to thank the many museum curators who sent information that could not be included in this short essay. I am particularly grateful to Colin McEwan for his editorial suggestions and for providing ideas and information that are not acknowledged individually in the text.

NOTES

1 Apart from its role in warfare, the club was a multipurpose artefact used by hunters (Roth 1929: 10; Frikel 1973: 93), by husbands to chastise errant wives and also as a weapon of execution.
2 Gillin 1948.
3 Rivière 1984: 2–5.
4 Vidal and Zucchi 2000. These routes also figure in the mythology and sacred geography of the Arawak groups. See also Whitehead 1994, Arvelo-Jiménez and Biord 1994.
5 Rostain 1994, II: fig. 200; Vacher *et al.* 1998: fig. 68. Another club was found at low water in the Kukui river (in Akawaio territory in British Guiana) and is now in the Pitt Rivers Museum, Oxford, no. 1954.2.50. My attention was drawn to this item by Audrey Butt Colson.
6 Klinkenberg *et al.* 1996, folio 68.
7 Klinkenberg *et al.* 1996, folios 113 and 124–124v.
8 Vázquez de Espinosa 1942: 86.
9 Vázquez de Espinosa 1942: 69.
10 Rauschert 1981–2: 427.
11 Vázquez de Espinosa 1942: 69.
12 Vázquez de Espinosa 1942: 72–3.
13 Roth 1924: 178, 570–72; Brett 1868: 154.
14 Harcourt 1926: 87. For a shield of this kind, published in 1743, see fig. 11.8. Harcourt's Indian allies were Yaos, recently arrived Arawak-speakers from the Orinoco region.
15 Ralegh 1997.
16 His account is reproduced in Hakluyt 1904: 441–490.
17 Van den Bel 1995: 22–8.
18 Lorimer 1989; Hemming 1978. In 1604 Charles Leigh established a short-lived English plantation on the Oyapock, and this was followed in 1609 by Robert Harcourt's venture (Harcourt 1926). The first French plantation in Guiana dates to 1607.
19 Reproduced in Harlow 1925: 133–48. Scott was Geographer to Charles II.
20 Harlow 1925: lvii, 133; Bos 1998, chap. II
21 Butt Colson in MacGregor 1983: 115–20. Ralegh (1997: 153) reports that the Guiana Indians traded cassava bread, cotton, Brazil wood and hammocks with the Europeans.

22 Richard Schomburgk in the early 1840s commented that the heartwood of the *Brosimum* tree is as hard as iron, and difficult to work, even with steel tools. Im Thurn (1883: 298) describes the process of finishing a club. For the first, rough smoothing, the palate bones of certain fish were used in place of a file, then the final 'sand-paper' polish was given with rough leaves. On Carib clubs the engraved designs were then filled with a white earth to provide a contrast with the dark wood. Making a club was therefore a time-consuming business, though 'the Indian only works when he feels inclined, and spends perhaps several months or longer in the manufacture of a bow or club' (Schomburgk 1922–3, I: 332). In Panama *Brosimum* wood is believed to have supernatural and medicinal qualities, and is used for the manufacture of symbols of office for tribal chiefs.

23 Christy Collection no. 4913. A 1685 catalogue of the Tradescant collection lists 'Quinque instrumenta bellica ex India occidentalis, ex ligno brasiliano confecta' (five [not four] instruments of war from the West Indies, made of Brazilian wood). The British Museum club was obtained by exchange with Oxford in 1868, but there is no further documentation. The Museum has another club of just this type (no. 19781 AM 5.3), which is believed to have been in the collection of Sir Ashton Lever (1729–88). How he came by it is unknown.

24 The design cannot yet be matched in any of the contact-period ceramic styles of Guiana, nor in the rock-engravings of the region.

25 The complete letter is given in MacGregor 1983: 19–20. Roger North had sailed with Ralegh on his 1617 voyage to Cayenne and the Orinoco, and in 1620 founded his own short-lived colony some 100 miles up the River Oyapock were he encountered the Irish and English remnants of Harcourt's settlement living among the Dutch. In 1625 North was back in London organizing a Guiana Company under the patronage of the Duke of Buckingham and in collaboration with that old Guiana hand, Robert Harcourt. In 1928–9 the Company founded two colonies, one on the River Oyapock, the other on the lower Amazon (Lorimer 1989: 85–101). The early collapse of the revived colony brought to an end the English settlement of the Oyapock and the lower Amazon (Harlow 1925: lxxv–lxxvii). North is therefore a possible source for the Tradescant clubs, but the connection cannot be documented.

26 Due 1980: 32 and pers. comm.. Museum nos Hb 16, 18 (Stolpe 1927: pl. III, 6), 19 (ibid. pl. II, 7), 20 (ibid. pl. I, 12) and 21 (ibid. pl. I, 9, wrongly labelled Hb 12). This last is the 'Paludani' club. Another possible connection is the Danish West Indian Trading Company, which operated in Brazil from 1625.

27 The Medici club, illustrated by Stolpe (1927: pl. III, 3), is in the Museo di Storia Naturale, Florence, no. 287 (museological information from Monica Zavattaro). One of the Paris clubs is illustrated by Doggett *et al.* 1992, cat. no. 50. The other is 134 cm long and also has lozenge designs and zigzags (information from Simone Breton-Gravereau).

28 Doggett *et al.* 1992: 101., cat. no. 50; Lehman 1958.

29 Sainsbury 1889: 191, no. 485. I am indebted for this reference to Arie Boomert, who also suggests that these items derive from the Kalina (Caribs) who lived close to the English colony on the Surinam river. Bannister's superior officer, Lord Willoughby (the last British governor of Surinam) was collecting 'vanities ... from Surinam' as early as 1656 (Harlow 1925: 174). A search through the storerooms of European museums might unearth these, and other, early specimens.

30 Van's Gravesande 1911: 61–83.

31 Van's Gravesande 1911; N. Whitehead 1988.

32 Meyer and Uhle 1885, Tafel 10,4.

33 Stolpe 1927: pl. II, 1, and the related specimen in his pl. III, 4, were in the collection of the Botanical Laboratory of the Musée d'Histoire Naturelle before passing to the Musée du Trocadéro (now the Musée de l'Homme; present numbers 81.17.3 and 81.17.2). Another similar club (Dietschy 1939: Taf. IV, 21e) is probably now Musée de l'Homme, no. 34.33.526. It was donated by the Bibliothèque Publique of Versailles, whose collections contained seventeenth- and eighteenth-century pieces. Information from François Gendron.

34 Barrère 1743: 174. See also Saville 1921: 7 and Roth 1924: pl. 14B.

35 No. 1.651, length 47 cm. The Museum has four other clubs that may go back to the second half of the eighteenth century. One of these clubs (1.665) has a design of three conjoined figures, cf. fig. 11.8 (British Museum 11.78/628.1). Another (1.653) has a scroll design resembling those on certain nineteenth-century items. For photographs and information about these items I am indebted to Paz Cabello.

36 N. Whitehead 1988: 111–16, 118.

37 Stedman 1796, vol. 1, ch. xv: 396–7. Quoted also in Saville 1921.

38 The 'sharp stone' is in fact an axe-shaped blade. There are also blades of European iron and, rarely, of hard wood. Stedman's story proved attractive to later writers and is repeated almost verbatim by Brett 1868:134. The club Stedman illustrates has simple geometric decoration; it is not included in the Stedman collection in the Rijksmuseum, Leiden (Whitehead 1986).

39 Areia *et al.* 1991b: 178.

40 The decorated ones are illustrated and discussed by Areia *et al.* 1991b: cat. nos 96–101, 108.

41 Ibid: 183, cat. no. 108. Caripunas were also reported at the mouth of the Rupununi river in 1786 (van's Gravesande 1911: 109).

42 Schomburgk 1922–3, vol. 2: 343; see also vol. 1: 204 on Carib pottery.

43 Merwe 1917; Schmeltz 1897. Stolpe 1927: pl. XVII, 3, illustrates a bamboo flute with this style of decoration, made by the Galibi of French Guiana (Musée de l'Homme no. 78.32.188). It is an eighteenth-century piece once in the Bibliothèque Nationale (information from François Gendron). In general, though not in detail, this ornamentation resembles that on the Aristé pottery in use at the time of European contact just north of the mouth of the Amazon (see e.g. illustrations in Rostain 1994 and Vacher *et al.* 1998).

44 Schriks and de Groot 1980, illus. 74. Clubs also figure in illustrations 86 (a burial scene) and 70/71 (depictions of Carib Indians).

45 Where documentation exists, the majority of fighting clubs in European museums were obtained during the middle years of the nineteenth century. See Stolpe 1927 for an album of illustrations.

46 Van's Gravesande 1911: 110; N. Whitehead 1988: 170.

47 Schomburgk 1922–3, vol. 2: 255–6. Twentieth-century Pemon and Akawaio informants also recall shooting fire-arrows into thatched roofs and clubbing to death the inhabitants as they emerged (information from Audrey Butt Colson).

48 Brett 1868: 134.

49 Brett 1868: 97.

50 Im Thurn 1883: 425.

51 Im Thurn 1883: 298.

52 Robert Schomburgk 1836, item no. 66 [Stolpe 1927: pl. IV, 3].

53 Richard Schomburgk 1922–3, vol. 1: 332.

54 Farabee 1918, 1924; Koch-Grünberg 1923; Roth 1924, 1929.

55 Koch-Grünberg 1923, pls 15, 16, 54. His collection, and Roth's collection in the Smithsonian Institution, Washington, include both fighting clubs and dance clubs.

56 Roth 1929: 10; Frikel 1973: 93

57 In 1845 Robert Schomburgk donated three Waiwai or Taruma clubs to the Ethnographical Museum in Dresden (Meyer and Uhle 1885: pl. 10, 1-3). These are the earliest documented Waiwai clubs. One is shaped like fig. 11.13, and all three are engraved in a geometrical style quite unlike the 'arabesques' of the block-clubs. Farabee 1924: pl. 37, illustrates a group of twentieth-century Waiwai ceremonial clubs with geometrical designs. Some forty years later Yde's (1965) study of Waiwai material culture does not mention clubs at all. See also Roth 1929, pls 1b and 2.

58 Farabee 1924: 116 and figs 7, 8.

59 Reproduced from Farabee 1924: pl. XIX. The photograph is clearly a studio re-creation. The costume is broadly similar to dance costumes used by the Waiwai (Yde 1965: 231–7) and by the Wayana.

60 Farabee 1924: 204.

61 Roth 1929: 10.

62 Braun 1995: fig. 41.

63 Frikel 1973: 92–4.

64 Rauschert 1981–2.

65 They are now housed in The Museon, The Hague (information from Corine Bliek).

12

Indigenous Historical Trajectories in the Upper Rio Negro Basin

EDUARDO NEVES

The nights were beautifully clear. I sat down in the midst of the rapids, on a rock washed by the stream. The water came and went as if it was the river's breathing. The rapids roared and the waves moved constantly among the rocks. The noises resembled the voices of spirits narrating stories from remote times when the ancestors of the current inhabitants engraved in the hard rock the drawings that today are so enigmatic for their descendants.[1]

Introduction

The understanding of the impact of European colonization on native societies is one of the most important tasks of archaeological research in the Amazon. It is known that European colonization caused major ruptures in pre-colonial native Amazonian political, demographic and economic patterns. Although the size of indigenous populations in Brazil has been growing lately and is estimated at around 350,000 people today, this is still very far from the estimates of up to 6,000,000 people in the sixteenth century.[2] With some exceptions, the size of contemporary indigenous settlements is fairly small, seldom reaching more than a few hundred people at most.[3] Archaeological data, on the other hand, indicates that some pre-colonial settlements were very large, being possibly occupied by thousands of individuals.[4]

It would be wrong, however, to assume that the impact of European colonization was an overall monolithic destructive process. Such thinking runs the risk of removing the ability of indigenous people to resist and overcome the pressures exerted by the colonial and national societies over them. This paper challenges this assumption by verifying the antiquity and the transformations of the exogamous multi-ethnic regional network found among the indigenous people of the upper Rio Negro basin at the border of Colombia, Venezuela and Brazil. It works on the premise that the dynamics of social change in the upper Rio Negro were structurally conditioned by indigenous social and cultural categories, both before and after the conquest, a conclusion arrived at through the combined use of ethnographic, linguistic and archaeological evidence.

Past Amazonian societies were politically and economically integrated into multi-ethnic regional networks. The origins and history of those networks have only recently begun to be understood and it is to be expected that they will eventually be traced back well into the pre-colonial period.[5] In fact, historical sources from the seventeenth and eighteenth centuries indicate that networks of the indigenous slave trade linking the Amazonian hinterlands and the different European colonial settlements of the Guiana shore and lower Amazon built on much earlier indigenous pre-colonial trade routes connecting remote areas of northern South America (fig. 12.1).[6] This historical information finds corroboration in the widespread distribution, among archaeological sites of the lower Amazon and parts of the Caribbean, of the miniature green zoomorphic amulet stones known as *muiraquitãs* (see Petersen *et al.* and Gomes, this volume).[7] Equally, contemporary oral traditions of the Wakuénai Indians of the upper Rio Negro basin in Venezuela reveal a sophisticated geographical knowledge of the immense web of rivers composing the Amazon and Orinoco basins, far beyond the upper Rio Negro, as indicated by the places visited by the mythical creator hero Kwái on his ancestral travels.[8]

Amazonian regional systems can be characterized by a number of basic features. First, they are multi-ethnic,

12.1 Feather head-dress, Makuna-ni, upper Rio Negro basin, collected by Johann Natterer, 1823 (height 100 cm, width 55 cm; Museum für Völkerkunde, Vienna). This striking assemblage includes green parrot feathers, scarlet macaw plumes and toucan tail danglers.

with language serving as a major ethnic marker. Second, they are integrated by periodical feasting and also by trade networks, in this case with specialized production of different utilitarian and non-utilitarian goods. Third, as the name implies, these are regional systems where dispersed local populations, settled in villages located sometimes several dozen kilometres apart, interact regularly. Insofar as they can be identified today, regional systems are mostly found around the periphery of the Amazon basin. In Brazil the best known cases are the upper Xingu and upper Rio Negro basins, located respectively on the south-eastern and north-western margins of the Amazon.

The upper Rio Negro and its people

In terms of nutrient levels the upper Rio Negro basin is one of the poorest areas of Amazonia mostly due to the highly acidic sandy soils found there.[9] This has a direct impact both on the vegetation patterns and on the chemical characteristics of the waters of the Negro and its main tributaries.[10] Three basic vegetation types are found: wide stretches of *igapós* (flooded forests), upland forests, and *campinaranas*, whose occurrence is correlated to the increase in sand content in the soils.[11] *Campinarana* plants have thick leaves, thick bark and an abundance of lichens and mosses on the branches as well as on the soil surface.[12] Trees are normally small and thin with most of the biomass at the root layer and not above the surface (fig. 12.2).[13] In some places *campinaranas* are interrupted by stretches of pure sand reaching up to one hectare in extent, a markedly different landscape to what one would normally expect in a rainforest.[14] Upland forests are more common in the region. They include higher species diversity and higher average tree size than

ABOVE RIGHT **12.2** *Campinarana* vegetation on an overland trail between the Uaupés and Aiarí rivers. Stunted trees and specialized mosses grow on the acidic white sandy soils of this area.

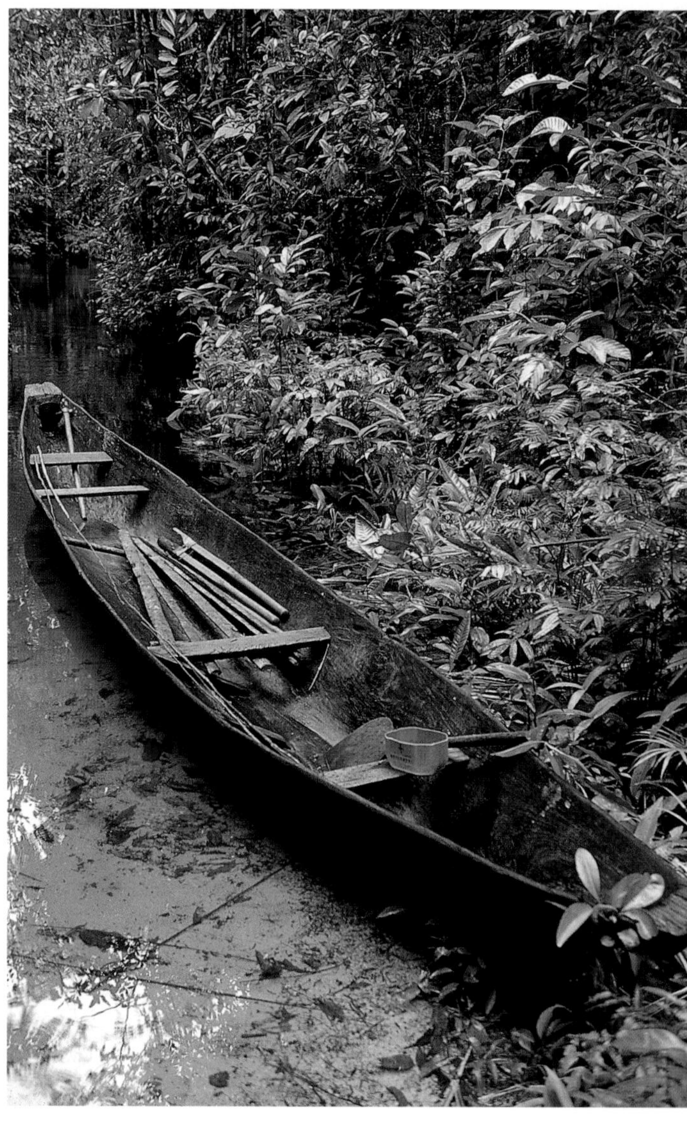

RIGHT **12.3** Dugout canoe, Igarapé Tamanduá, lower Uaupés basin. The blackwater rivers of the upper Rio Negro basin drain the ancient bedrock of the Guiana shield and are consequently almost sediment free.

do the *campinaranas* and are found on hilltops or other places where soils have a higher clay content than in the *campinaranas*. These are the locations where trees are felled for the opening of slash-and-burn manioc gardens.

Every year, in the rainy season, the water level of the rivers rises and extends into the adjacent forests, blocking the drainage of their smaller tributaries and creating a great expanse of flooded forests, or *igapós*.[15] In the Uaupés, as in other parts of the Rio Negro basin, many stretches of *igapó* forests are dominated by stands of the Jauarí palm (*Astrocaryum jauary*), whose fruits, although not consumed by humans, are eaten by several fish species, which makes *igapós* favourite fishing spots in the rainy season.[16]

12.4 Fish traps at the Carurú rapids, middle Uaupés river. In the fragile ecological conditions of the Uaupés traps are used to fish for species that frequent the pools around rocks and boulders.

As its name in Portuguese or Spanish indicates, the Negro and its major tributaries are blackwater rivers (fig. 12.3).[17] In the Amazon basin differences in water colour are related to the conditions of water pH and overall biomass in the headwaters of the rivers.[18] In this sense, the dark colour and acidic pH of the Rio Negro result from the presence of acid compounds dissolved in the water, a process believed to be linked to the soil conditions along the headwaters and drainage areas of the river and its tributaries.[19] Blackwater rivers lack important nutrients necessary for *in situ* primary production and most food sources derive from sources external to the rivers, mainly the surrounding forest.[20] As a consequence, some of the large aquatic mammals and fishes found along the Amazon river and its main tributaries are not found in the upper Rio Negro basin (fig. 12.4).

The upper Rio Negro basin is one of the ethnographically best-known areas in lowland South America thanks to a number of ethnographies, articles and surveys undertaken by trained anthropologists.[21] Besides the ethnographies, there are reports – some of high quality – written intermittently by missionaries, military personnel, bureaucrats and natural scientists from the eighteenth century on (see Foreword, and Barreto and Machado, this volume). From the early reports and ethnographies it had already become clear that the people of the upper Rio Negro share a number of cultural traits that make them appear unique when compared to other known tropical forest societies. Because of this the upper Rio Negro, or the north-west Amazon, has been consistently singled out as a distinct cultural area (or sub-area) in lowland South America.[22]

If the people of the upper Rio Negro appear unique to the casual observer, they nevertheless share many cultural traits with different populations spread over a large area in western Amazonia. Among these traits, one finds things such as the religious use of tree-bark masks; longhouse habitation; the consumption of the hallucinogens *caapí* (*Banisteriopsis caapi*) and *paricá* (*Virola* sp.); secret male initiation rites involving the display and playing of 'Jurupari' flutes; and the use of large signal drums,

12.5 Small Káua longhouse with designs painted on the facade and masked dancers in front, Jurupari rapids, Aiarí river, 1903–5. Just as with other groups in the area, the ancestral language originally spoken by the Káua has been replaced.

known as 'trocanos' among the Tukanoans (see figs 7.12–13). Western Amazonia is an area of great linguistic diversity, composed of a number of apparently independent languages or localized linguistic families, such as Yagua, Tikuna, Bora-Witoto, Jivaroan, Tukanoan, etc.[23] It is likely that this was an area of intense cultural interaction in the pre-colonial past, an interaction achieved in networks encompassing different populations and ecosystems. To this day, extensive overland trails cover large areas in the upper Rio Negro and beyond.[24] It is plausible therefore that interaction in such a network, including trade, warfare and feasting, was effected not only along the riverside network but also through the hinterlands.

The subsequent discussion builds on the Tukanoan groups of the Uaupés basin but it is generally valid for the other indigenous groups of the upper Rio Negro settled along the Negro proper, and the Içana and Xié rivers.

The most striking feature of the social organization of the Tukanoan societies of the Uaupés is that it is regional in nature.[25] This point was already clear to early anthropologists working in the area and is now widely recognized.[26] The regional social organization can be perceived in different realms but most visibly in the exogamy rules that prescribe preferential marriage between cross-cousins.[27] Given that post-marriage rules are patrilocal, young men stay at their fathers' house, whereas young women move to their husbands' fathers' house. As a consequence there is a constant movement of women, in space and time, between local settlements. Since there is a fair amount of linguistic diversity in the area, it is common to find households formed by couples that speak different native languages.

Traditionally, Tukanoan settlements were formed by one or more longhouses with a rectangular plan – sometimes several dozen metres long and several metres wide – such as the ones visited by Alfred Russel Wallace and Richard Spruce in the Uaupés in the nineteenth century (see Foreword, and Barreto and Machado, this volume).[28] In

12.6–7 Contemporary photograph of the settlement at Carvoeiro (above) and early nineteenth-century view of the city of São Gabriel da Cachoeira, Rio Negro (right). Both were indigenous villages that were transformed into colonial settlements as slave traffic grew and the Portuguese crown attempted to assert its control of this area.

the nineteenth century (fig. 12.5) settlements were described as being composed of one or two longhouses, each of them housing different nuclear families with economically distinct households. Nowadays, longhouses are no longer built in the Brazilian side of the Uaupés, having been destroyed by the Salesian missionaries during the twentieth century. They can, however, still be found on the Colombian side.[29]

Overt hierarchical social organization and patrilineal descent rules also distinguish

Uaupés Tukanoans from other tropical forest societies – features that might be seen as a departure from the assumed egalitarianism of these societies. In fact, due to these characteristics, some authors have suggested that Tukanoans of the Uaupés were actually organized into politically complex societies before the European conquest, and that the currently observed hierarchical social organization and patrilineal descent are remains of these past complex social formations.[30] Other hypotheses have also been put forward that attempt to correlate the emergence of hierarchy with the characteristics of ecological scarcity of the area.[31]

The above questions demand historical answers that can be approached through the study of early colonial historical sources, indigenous oral tradition and linguistic analyses, but archaeological research can provide a longer term chronological perspective than the historical sources, which obviously go back only as far as the sixteenth century. Archaeology can also chronologically calibrate those events narrated in oral tradition that left identifiable traces in the archaeological record. Likewise, the ethnographies of the upper Rio Negro basin in general, and the Uaupés in particular, provide general historical hypothetical schemes that can be assessed archaeologically.[32]

Such schemes could be further tested against the hypothesis that the development of those multi-ethnic societies resulted from the pressure exerted by both the Portuguese and Spanish colonizers as they pushed inland and forced native Amerindians into refugee sanctuaries such as the upper Rio Negro basin. It is known that colonial slave trafficking brought about a drastic collapse in indigenous populations in that area. There are reports that around 20,000 Indians were removed from their lands there and taken as slaves in the first decades of the eighteenth century alone.[33] This happened at a time when the Portuguese were pushing up the Rio Negro, creating villages and fortresses on the sites of former indigenous settlements. Among those, there are Barcelos and São Gabriel da Cachoeira (figs 12.6–7). At the end of the nineteenth century and the beginning of the twentieth, local populations suffered a strong setback because of the rubber boom. During this period oral tradition reports that many villages were relocated to places deep in the forest in order to avoid being raided by the Brazilian and Colombian rubber tappers that roamed through the Uaupés. Stories of atrocities committed during the rubber boom era are still heard today, among them those of the infamous Albuquerque brothers, who gained a notoriously gory reputation. It was at the house of one of these 'rubber barons', the apparently more benevolent Germano Garrido y Otero, that German ethnologist Theodor Koch-Grünberg was based while travelling along the upper Rio Negro at the beginning of the twentieth century.

Before attempting to assess those historical hypotheses, it is important to examine the patterns of linguistic distribution in the Uaupés to see how they can illuminate the region's past.

Indigenous languages in the upper Rio Negro: a clue to understanding the past

Four major indigenous language groupings are found today in the Rio Negro basin. In the upper course of the Negro and along some of its tributaries, such as the Içana, people speak different connected Maipuran Arawakan languages. Along the Uaupés and its tributaries, as well as along the upper tributaries of the Apaporis, there are different local groups speaking several related Tukanoan languages.[34] In the broad hinterland area between the Guaviare and the Japurá there are at least six different poorly

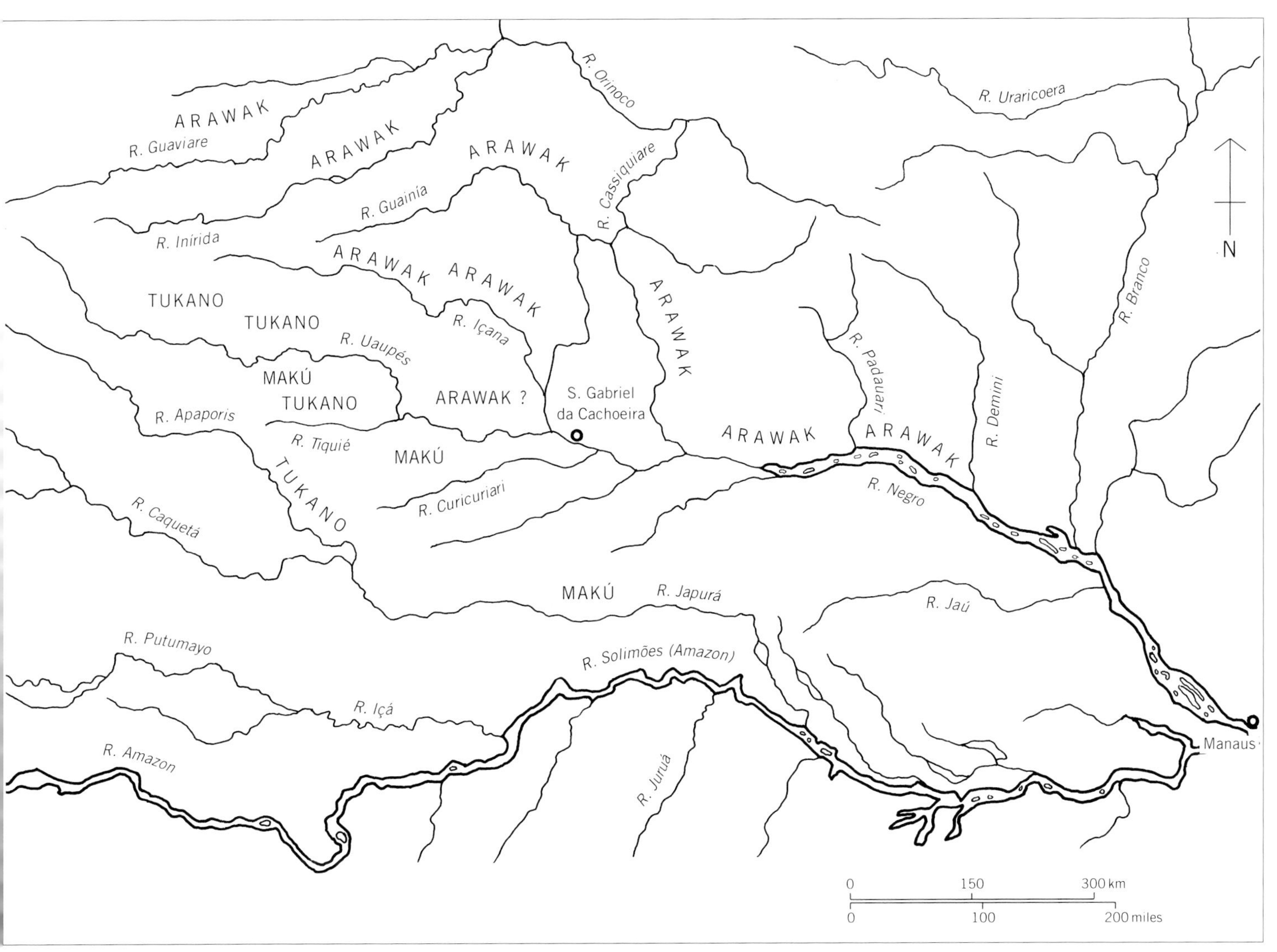

12.8 Map showing distribution of the Arawak, Tukano and Maku languages in the Rio Negro basin. Arawakan is spoken along the Negro and its upper tributaries, except the Uaupés, which is Tukanoan, and the hinterlands, which are Makú.

studied groups of languages spoken by the nomadic Makú (see Politis, this volume). Finally, all the way along the Negro, and also along many of its tributaries, there are speakers of Nheengatú or 'língua geral', a catechism language based on Tupinambá and created by the missionaries in the colonial period.[35] Around the seventeenth century the main course of the Rio Negro was most likely occupied largely by populations speaking Maipuran Arawakan languages.[36] Accordingly, among current Nheengatú speakers, there are indigenous groups such as the Baré and Werekena, who are known to be former speakers of Arawakan languages that switched to Nheengatú due to enslavement, missionary activities and the stress of the rubber boom.[37]

Language replacement seems to be a common process in the upper Rio Negro. What is noteworthy is that it was not always the case that indigenous languages were replaced by colonial or national languages. The Tariana – a group whose history will be discussed further on – provide, for instance, an example of replacement from an Arawakan language to a Tukanoan language.[38] Language replacement notwithstanding, the distribution of languages in the upper Rio Negro indicates a clear pattern. The hinterlands of the west bank are occupied by Makú speakers. In the Uaupés and its main tributaries one finds a block of Tukanoan-speaking groups surrounded by an arch composed of Arawakan-speaking populations settled along the other main rivers (fig. 12.8).

Given the diversity of languages spoken in the whole area (around twenty), it is not surprising that the upper Rio Negro indigenous societies are multilingual. Multilingualism is an integral aspect of the range of economic and social transactions between local populations and it is warranted by exogamic marriage rules. As a consequence of this, many individuals in the area speak on average two or three indigenous languages, besides Portuguese and Spanish.

Against this background of great linguistic diversity, however, one should confront the fact that languages belonging to only three distinct indigenous linguistic families are spoken in the area. This is, therefore, a picture different from other areas of documented multilingualism, such as aboriginal California, the north coast of New Guinea or the upper Xingú in southern Amazonia. In these areas there is or there have been situations of regional multilingualism with a far greater number of languages from unrelated linguistic families being spoken. In the Uaupés, by contrast, all of the spoken languages – with the exception of the Makú – are from the Tukanoan family. The same is true for the Içana, where all of the languages spoken are closely related within the Maipuran Arawakan branch. Thus, the amount of linguistic diversity underlying this multilingual regional system is not so structurally deep as it might seem at first glance, a fact that has important historical implications, meaning that the process of linguistic differentiation happened *in situ* and not elsewhere.[39]

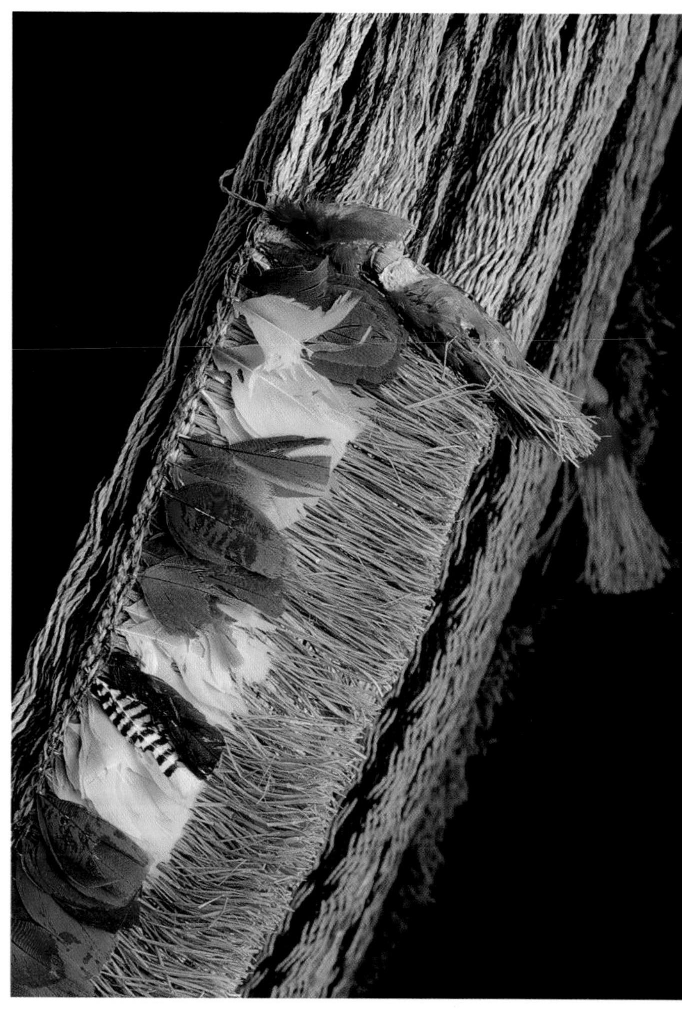

12.9 Detail of a fibre hammock decorated with feathers and collected by Johann Natterer in the 1830s in the Rio Negro basin (Museum für Völkerkunde, Vienna). Organic artefacts do not survive in the archaeological record and this early ethnographic example is testimony to weaving skills that were rapidly lost.

The antiquity of the regional system

As with most of the rest of the world, Amazonian archaeology relies heavily on the use of ceramic analyses and the comparison of ceramic styles over time and space as tools to understand past cultural dynamics. This is not surprising, since the conditions for organic preservation in the Amazonian rainforest are generally poor, leaving ceramic remains as the major source of archaeological knowledge (fig. 12.9).[40]

In the upper Rio Negro basin ceramics are still produced both for local use and for sale (fig. 12.10). Overall there are two general styles of ceramics in the area: along the Içana river – occupied by different Baniwan groups speaking Arawakan languages – one finds *cariapé*-tempered ceramics with both open and closed forms and painted decoration in red over a cream coloured slip.[41] On the Tukanoan-occupied Uaupés, ceramics share the same technology and a set of common forms with those from the Içana, but decoration is different: in this case pots have a general black to dark brown aspect, due to the use of plant resins.[42] In the upper Rio Negro, therefore, ceramic variability does function as an effective marker of linguistic variability,

12.10 Contemporary indigenous ceramics in the Marabitana village, lower Uaupés. The techniques used to produce these vessels do not differ much from those used to create the archaeological ceramics found in excavations in this village.

since it follows the major linguistic divide found in the area, the one between the Tukanoan and Arawakan families (fig. 12.11).

If ceramics are different across language family boundaries, they are very similar within those boundaries, a phenomenon certainly due to exogamy.[43] Ceramic production is traditionally a female activity, a craft learned by girls from their mothers. As young women move, after marriage, from their birth villages to their partner's villages, they bring with them this learned craft. In these new settings they will meet and live with other married women who have also learned to make pottery elsewhere. Such constant movement of women over time and space, and the knowledge they bring, will develop into patterning in ceramic production. In that sense, and given that exogamy is a key feature behind regional interactions in the upper Rio Negro basin, a potential way to assess the chronological origins of such a system could be the identification, in the archaeological record, of the earliest signs of manufacture of ceramics similar to the ones currently produced by both Tukanoans and Baniwans.

Overall, the earliest known dates for ceramics in the Rio Negro basin cluster around the beginning of the Christian era, but it is around the fourth to the sixteenth century AD that a better-defined sequence can be identified.[44] Such a sequence comprises, in the lower Rio Negro, three different cultural units: the Manacapuru and Paredão phases and the Guarita sub-tradition (see Petersen *et al.*, this volume). Guarita ceramics were produced along the Rio Negro basin, from Manaus almost all the way to São Gabriel da Cachoeira, until the sixteenth century, the beginning of European colonization. It is safe to assume a correlation between Guarita ceramics and Arawak populations, since by the sixteenth century most of the main course of the Rio Negro seems to have been occupied by Arawakan groups, such as the T*arumã*, Manao and Baré.[45]

Guarita vessels are decorated by either polychrome painting or plastic decoration such as grooving. They are tempered with *cariapé* in the same way as contemporary Baniwan and Tukanoan vessels, but a real resemblance can be found between the

12.11 Archaeological and contemporary indigenous ceramics from the Solimões and Uaupés rivers respectively: pot and Guarita urn above, and contemporary Desana vessel and *caapí* pot below. Similarities in shape and technology may indicate that wider regional networks existed in the past.

overall shapes of both contemporary Baniwan and Tukanoan vessels and the shapes of some Guarita vessels (fig. 12.11). It is likely that such shared similarities indicate wider social networks in the past, beyond the limits of the upper Rio Negro and down its lower and middle reaches.

To understand indigenous history, information on contemporary and archaeological ceramics can be matched with the oral tradition, so that narratives about the past can be verified archaeologically. Fortunately, there is in the upper Rio Negro a rich body of indigenous oral tradition that is very lively and has also been recorded since the end of the nineteenth century. I will turn now to some of these narratives.

Tariana oral tradition and its archaeological correlates

A defining characteristic of the Uaupés regional system is its flexibility: in other words, outside groups can be incorporated into this system through marriage or the establishment of reciprocal relations. A minimum estimate for the antiquity of this system can, in this sense, be provided through the dating of the arrival of the last indigenous population block in the area. Among the Tukanoans of the lower Uaupés, there is overall agreement that the Tariana were the last indigenous people to settle the area. Such an awareness, expressed in the oral tradition of both the Tukanoans and the Tariana, was recorded by travellers who have been in the Uaupés since around the end of the nineteenth century (fig. 12.12).[46]

In the early 1990s the Tariana were settled in thirteen villages in the lower and middle Uaupés and in the lower Papuri.[47] This is not, however, an area of exclusive Tariana occupation, since one also finds there Arapaço, Pira-Tapuya and Tukano villages. At first glance, the Tariana appear to be similar to the other groups of the Uaupés. They are exogamous and internally divided in hierarchical sibs; they speak the Tukano language; they used to build longhouses; their ceramics were similar to those from other Tukanoan groups; and they inhabit the centre of the Uaupés basin – the area located between the Ipanoré and Iauaretê rapids.[48] The Ipanoré rapids are the place, according to Tukanoan religion, where humankind was created after human beings emerged from a long trip inside an ancestral anaconda. However, the Tariana are a former Maipuran Arawak-speaking population who emigrated from their homeland in the Içana-Aiarí basin to the Uaupés, an event narrated in their oral tradition.

12.12 Uaupés Indian, probably 1785. There are currently no 'Uaupés' Indians in the Rio Negro basin. They probably became extinct or were incorporated into other groups during the nineteenth century.

As with the other Maipuran groups of the upper Rio Negro-upper Orinoco, the Tariana place their origin elsewhere, at the Uaupuí rapids on the Aiarí river (see Pereira, and McEwan, this volume).[49] Instead of seeing themselves coming from inside an ancestral anaconda, the Tariana trace their origin from lightning that struck the Uapuí rapids. The Uapuí rapids are not far from the middle Uaupés. They can be reached by foot through one of the overland tracks that cross the whole region and that connect the Uaupés and the Içana basins.[50]

Currently, the Tariana language has almost disappeared. It is spoken only in two villages – Periquito and Santa Rosa – in the middle Uaupés, both connected to branches of the path that crosses the Aiarí-Uaupés hinterland. The process of replacement of the Tariana language by Tukano was already well advanced by the beginning of the twentieth century, at the time that the German-born ethnologists Theodor Koch-Grünberg and Curt Nimuendajú undertook their travels in the area. Today, with the exception of the above-mentioned villages, Tariana individuals no longer speak their ancestral language.

The Tariana's awareness of their origin is presented in a rich oral tradition that has been recorded by anthropologists, missionaries and Indians since the end of the nineteenth century.[51] The set of narratives collected by Antonio Brandão de Amorim indicate that when the Tariana settled in the lower Uaupés, around the area of Iauareté, distinct Tukanoan groups (the Tukano, Uanano and probably the Pira-Tapuyo) were already living there. Uanano oral tradition indicates that the Tariana had fought and partially displaced Tukanoan groups already in the Uaupés by the time of their migration.[52] However, some authors suggest, contrary to Tariana oral tradition, that the Tariana occupation proceeded upriver, from the lower to the middle Uaupés.[53] The dating of the arrival of the Tariana in the Uaupés is also open to speculation, but there seems to be general agreement that it happened around or before the eighteenth century.[54]

To address this problem, it is useful to examine a body of Tariana oral tradition recorded and published by the Brazilian rubber baron Antonio Brandão de Amorim and by the Italian count Ermano Stradelli. Although without a previous scientific background – since both were lawyers, and Stradelli eventually became a judge in a small upper Amazonian town – Brandão de Amorim and Stradelli shared an interest in Amazonian Indians, and specifically in Indians from the Uaupés. Because of this, they travelled several times up the Rio Negro around the end of the nineteenth century. It is likely that their interest was sparked by the influence of the naturalist and pioneer of Amazonian archaeology João Barbosa Rodrigues, director of the Manaus Botanical Garden at the height of the Amazonian rubber boom of the late 1800s (see Barreto and Machado, this volume). Both men also shared a friendship with Maximiliano José Roberto, a Tariana Indian settled in Manaus, who travelled with them roughly 1,000 km up the Negro and Uaupés to the Iauareté area.

The narratives collected by Brandão de Amorim in the 1880s and 1890s were published posthumously in 1926 in a large, 426-page bilingual piece entitled 'Lendas em Nheengatú e Português' (Legends in Nheengatú and Portuguese).[55] These narratives contain information about places of ancient Tariana occupation in the Uaupés that could be localized and excavated. They are also impressive because they refer to places or toponyms with the same basic details as told by the Tariana more than a hundred years later. Among those narratives, four tell of the events associated with the Tariana occupation of the middle and lower Uaupés, and of the legendary deeds of their chief Buopé.[56] They confirm that when the Tariana settled the area, the Uanano Indians were already settled in this area.[57]

'Buopé's war' is an account of a conflict between the Tariana and both the Uanano and the 'Arara' people.[58] At the time of these events the Tariana, under the leadership of Buopé, were already settled at Iauareté, where they remain today. The conflict started when the Tariana killed their Arara wives, because they insisted on seeing the secret Jurupari rites performed by the men every night in the forest. As a revenge, an Arara party killed Buopé's infant son while he was searching for honey in the forest. The Tariana then launched an attack on the Arara's village, located in the Uaupés several days upstream. This attack resulted in the annihilation of all but one Arara man. This survivor told the Uanano what had happened to the Arara, and that prompted them to launch an attack on the Tariana. To defend themselves, the Tariana built a fortress surrounded by ditches with spiked trenches in a place located inland in the forest, not far away from Iauareté, known as 'serra do Jurupari' ('Jurupari hills').[59] From that place they eventually defeated their enemies. After that the Tariana re-established peaceful relations with the Uanano and other Tukanoan groups and started to intermarry with them. The history of Buopé's war is also narrated, from the Uanano's point of view, in 'Uanano's war'.

Archaeologically, these stories are interesting because they contain references to a number of toponyms in the Uaupés. Thus, the current inhabitants of the area all know about the Jurupari hills, 'maggot's creek' (the place where the Tariana threw the dead bodies of their enemies to rot), 'Caruru rapids' (the ancient homeland of the Uanano) and so forth.

The possibility of identifying and excavating some of the settlements referred to in the narratives of the ancient Tariana wars allows for two important contributions towards the understanding of the history of the Uaupés regional system. First, it establishes the antiquity of the Tariana occupation of the lower Uaupés; and second, it establishes a minimum antiquity for this system itself, since, as stated in the oral tradition, many of the Tukanoan groups now settled in the area – such as the Uanano, Tukano, Cubeo and Arapaço – were already settled there by the time of the arrival of the Tariana. I was able to locate and excavate the ancient fortress on the Jurupari hills thanks to the oral information provided by Tariano men living around Iauareté.

The archaeological testing

The Fortaleza site is located at the top of a hill, roughly 5 km away from the west bank of the Uaupés. This is an anomalous location compared to the predominantly river-oriented settlement pattern of the Tukanoan and Arawakans in the upper Rio Negro basin. The place seems to be an old fallow patch, and in fact a garden had been opened there around ten or fifteen years before I undertook my fieldwork.

The site was located thanks to Sr. Pedro de Jesus Gomes, a Tariana elder. Sr. Pedro knew about the place because he had been taken there by his father, his father by his grandfather, and so on. He said that no ceramics could be seen in the surface of the place but that one could see a defensive ditch in the form of a ring, which had been built a long time ago by the Tariana when they were launching their war against the other groups in the region. This is the place in Tariana oral tradition where the Tariana mythic hero, Buopé, had built his fortress on the Jurupari hill. The similarities between Amorim's transcription, which was collected in the 1880s, and Sr. Pedro's version, told more than a century later were impressive, demanding further fieldwork.

There were no visible signs of archaeological remains on the surface, but what seemed to be the ditch could be seen in some parts. Due to the high vegetation growth in the place it was only later realized that the ditch did not form a continuous ring, but rather that there were two ditches located at the western and eastern edges of the site, in the places were the slope is gentler. Such a configuration, which is obviously defensive, confirms the oral tradition associating this site with past warfare.

After establishing the size and shape of the ditches, the concentration of the subsurface ceramics was mapped in order to define the areas to be excavated. This was done with 144 shovel tests, 5 metres distant from each other, along more than 700 metres of transects opened through the forest. Shovel testing helped identify the frequency of the ceramic remains, all buried from a depth below 20 cm (fig. 12.13). The tests indicated that there was a higher concentration of sherds at the more sloping periphery of the site than at the flat centre of it.[60] Such a structure certainly resulted from the ongoing process of house cleaning and of throwing the garbage outside the residential areas during the occupation span of the village.[61]

The clean central area, which corresponds also to the flat top of the hill, is the place where the ancient Tariana longhouse was located, whereas the peripheral area, with higher densities of ceramic remains, were the discard areas, although no post moulds or other direct indicators of past longhouse construction were identified at the site. Considering that the flat area at the centre of the site measures around 70 by 30 metres at its longest and widest parts, the longhouse built there could not be much bigger than 50 by 15 metres, which gives a figure for the structure of about 750 square metres. Based on the results of the shovel tests, eight areas of the site were chosen for the opening of test pits and trenches.

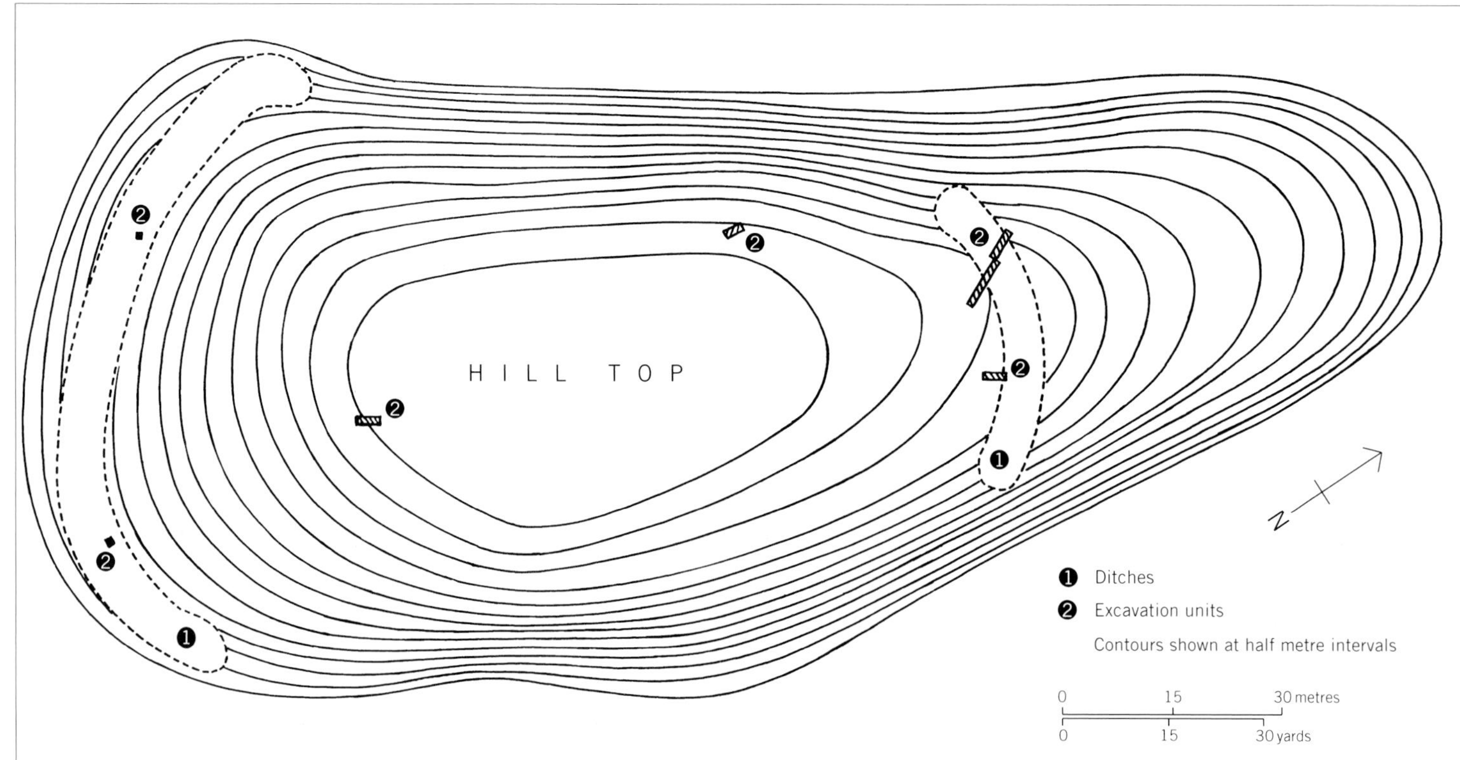

12.13 Site plan of the Fortaleza including the archaeological excavation units. The topographic contour lines and the placement of the two opposing defensive ditches corroborate the defensive function of the site.

The results of the excavation indicate that Fortaleza is a single-occupation site, an assumption warranted by a number of independent variables. First, there is Tariana oral tradition; if it is accurate enough to match the toponyms, the presence of the ditches in the site, and the location of the site, it is also legitimate to assume that the site was occupied only during the time of the skirmishes between the Tariana and the local Tukanoan groups, as is implied in the oral tradition. Second, the atypical position of the site supports this assignment. It is located deep in the forest away from the major streams. From this I infer that it was occupied over what was probably a short time span. Third, there is the homogeneity and low density of the ceramics recovered during excavation. Finally, radiocarbon dating from charcoal samples indicates that Fortaleza was occupied in the late fourteenth to early fifteenth century AD.

The above information allows for the following chronological reconstruction of the history of the indigenous people of the middle and lower Uaupés.

Reconstructing the history of the upper Rio Negro people from AD 1000 to the present

The combination of indigenous oral tradition, archaeological research and linguistic evidence shows that the upper Rio Negro regional system is of pre-colonial origin. Contrary to other areas in the Amazon, the European conquest did not promote the compression of upper Rio Negro populations into refugee areas. Rather, one of the consequences of the European conquest there has been the expansion of some formerly localized Tukanoan-speaking groups into larger areas. Based on that, I suggest that even in the face of the demographic, social and cultural changes brought about by the conquest, the upper Rio Negro regional system is structurally similar to what it was before the sixteenth century. This is because the dynamics of social change in the upper Rio Negro were structurally conditioned by indigenous cultural categories, both before and after the conquest.

At the beginning of the fifteenth century the Papuri and the middle Uaupés were already occupied by Tukanoan-speaking groups for many hundred years, time enough for the branching of Cubeo as a very different language within the Tukanoan family.[62] The middle Uaupés was occupied by the Uanano in its lower course and by the Cubeo in its upper course. At this time Pira-Tapuya and Uanano were not distinct languages. Although it is difficult at this point to provide an estimate for the initial occupation of the middle Uaupés by Tukanoan-speaking groups, linguistic evidence indicates that the earlier Tukanoan populations probably did not migrate from somewhere further down the Rio Negro. If they did, this was long before any local differentiation of the more than fifteen Tukanoan languages had taken place.[63]

The Papuri river is the ancestral occupation area of most of the Tukanoans. In the fifteenth century some of these groups were not linguistically differentiated as they are today. This was probably the case with the Bará and the Tuyuka; with the Desana and the Siriano; and with the Karapanã and Tatuyo. These groups were territorially based along stretches of the Papuri and its tributaries. Thence, the Tukano were based on the Turí *igarapé*, the Desana on the Macucú *igarapé*, etc. They were manioc farmers and fishermen connected among themselves and to other groups of the north-west Amazon by extensive overland tracks. Settlement patterns were similar to the contemporary Uanano: top-ranking sibs occupied downriver areas, whereas low-ranking sibs settled upstream.

The villages at that time were not significantly larger than they are today because of population checks and controls.[64] On the other hand, although manioc was a dependable source of food, the task of opening new gardens with stone axes was far more difficult in some of the upland areas. Hence, plants such as the peach palm (*Bactris gasipae*), which are very high in calories and can be planted in house gardens, were even more reliable as food sources at that time than they are today. The same is valid for other managed, semi-domesticated plants, most of them palms, such as the *japurá* and *bacaba*. The difficulties involved in opening new gardens, the unequal distribution of resources, and the existence of well-defined group territories all stimulated the continuous occupation of the same favoured locations over generations.

Exogamy at that time was not as visible a feature as it is today, since local groups tended to marry within their immediate home range. However, the principle of marriage alliance, as it is expressed today by preferential cross-cousin marriage was already in practice. The abduction of women was a major source of warfare. The periodical intensification in warfare, together with the necessity of protection from the Baniwa of the Içana, led to the construction of villages protected by spiked trenches. Some of these villages were not occupied for extended periods, but only for defensive reasons at times of war.

The hinterlands between the major rivers were already occupied by the Makú, and the pattern of patronage and peonage verified today between riverine Tukanoans and hinterland Makú was already in place. This was a dynamic interaction, and some Makú groups were incorporated as low-ranking sibs among the Tukanoans.

The lower Uaupés and Tiquié were ethnically more heterogeneous, since they were settled by both eastern Tukanoan and Maipuran Arawakan groups.[65] As one moved down the Uaupés towards the Negro, the Maipuran presence increased up to a point, along the Negro itself, where very few or no Tukanoan groups were present. Among

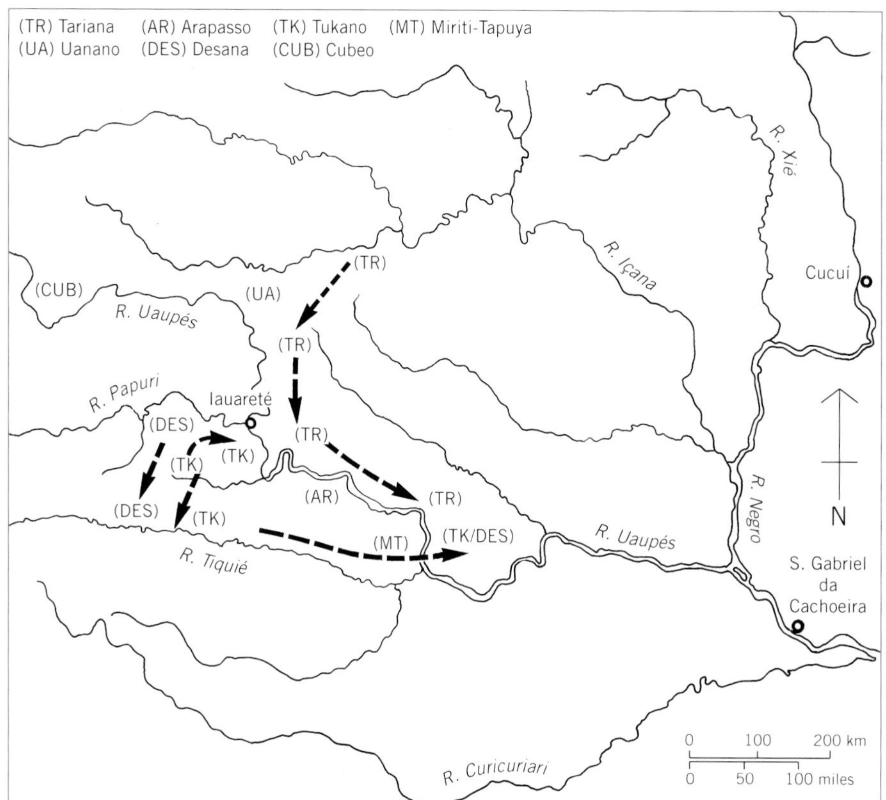

12.14 Map of population movements in the Uaupés basin. The colonial history of Uaupés Indians was dynamic: while some groups remained in their ancient territories, others moved to new areas.

the Tukanoan groups settled in this ethnic frontier, there were the Arapaço and the Mirití-Tapuya, both composed of very small populations today. It is probable that other groups, reported as later disappeared in Tukano oral tradition, such as the top-ranking sib Wauro, were also settled along this dynamic ethnic frontier.[66] By this time the other parts of the upper Rio Negro basin – the Rio Negro proper, the Içana, the Xié and the Guainía – were exclusively occupied by different Maipuran groups for several hundred years. In the lower Uaupés the evidence gathered at the Marabitana I site of ceramics of the Parallel Line tradition dating to *c.*2,500 years ago suggests that the Maipuran occupation of this area may date back to at least this time.[67]

At the beginning of the fifteenth century a group of ancestors of the Tariana moved from the Aiarí river down to the Uaupés (fig. 12.14). The Tariana were not a distinct language group in the Içana/Aiarí but rather a sib, or a number of sibs, within a language group.[68] Eventually they settled around Iauareté and the lower Papuri, an area they have occupied since then.[69] To arrive in the Iauareté area, the Tariana had to cross Uanano territory in the middle Uaupés. This is why there are several references to skirmishes between the Tariana and Uanano in the body of narratives collected by Brandão de Amorim. The Tariana occupation of the Iauareté area generated the conflicts related in Bouapé's war. As described above, the conflict of the Tariana with the Arara and the Uanano was generated because of fights over women (Buopé ordered the killing of Arara women who insisted on seeing the secret, all-male Jurupari rites). These narratives indicate that at the beginning of the fifteenth century, the time that the spiked trench fortress was built on the Jurupari hills at the Fortaleza site, the Tariana were already incorporated into the regional system, since they were intermarrying with Arara women. Eventually, with the cessation of hostilities, the Tariana resettled in Iauareté and began to marry Uanano and Tukano women, among others. At this time the replacement of the Tariana language by the Tukanoan language had not yet taken place.

The Tariana occupation of the Iauareté area remained fairly stable during the initial decades of the European conquest. Towards the end of the seventeenth century, however, the demand for slaves in both the lower Amazon and the Guiana coast promoted an increase in warfare. Tariana oral tradition reports them being engaged at the hinterland end of this network, as they were capturing Makú and Tukanoan Indians to sell as slaves. It is probable that the role of the Tariana in the slave traffic network was enhanced by their strategic control of the Iauareté area that granted them access to both the Papuri and the middle Uaupés.

Among these areas were the lower Uaupés and the Tiquié. The Arapaço and Miriti-Tapuya, who are nowadays reduced to very small populations, are among the groups that occupied this area. In the early 1990s there were only four Arapaço villages in the stretch of the lower Uaupés that ranges from the Urubuquara rapids to the Iauareté rapids.[70] The remaining villages in this area are either Tariana or Pira-Tapuya. Arapaço oral tradition points out, however, that this was their traditional territory before they were almost totally wiped out by an organized collective suicide. This collective suicide took place when the Arapaço threw themselves in a huge hole they dug, with boiling resin inside.[71] The only people who avoided death were two children who thereafter became responsible for the reconstruction of Arapaço society.

It would be out of place to provide an extensive analysis of this myth here, but it can be tentatively correlated with the trauma inflicted upon the Arapaço because of the slave trade. From the eighteenth century certain groups whose original territories were located upstream in the Uaupés and the Papuri started to move down to what had been former Arapaço territory: the area between the Iauareté and Urubuquara rapids. The Tariana made up one of these groups. The lower and middle Tiquié were also emptied of people and a similar process happened there: groups originally settled on the Papuri, such as the Tukano and Desana, started to move across the overland trails and settle along the banks of the Tiquié.

From the end of the eighteenth century the distribution of language groups in the Uaupés has remained basically similar to what it is today. The Maipuran groups from the lower Uaupés were totally exterminated, whereas some Tukanoan-speaking groups such as the Arapaço and Mirití-Tapuya almost suffered the same fate. These emptied areas were further occupied by different Tukanoan-speaking groups whose historical origin is traced back to the Papuri. The major exceptions are the Uanano and Cubeo who have both remained in their traditional territories well above the Iauareté rapids. This may be the reason why the Uanano are one of the few Tukanoan groups who actually follow the ideal of a territorial behavioural pattern through which the settlements of high-ranking sibs are located further downstream.[72] Among the other groups who did not remain in their ancestral territories, but instead moved into the emptied territories in the Tiquié and lower Uaupés, such territorial behaviour is not currently verified.

The Tariana provide a good example of the above assertion. The current distribution of villages in their territory shows a somewhat aberrant pattern, where lower-ranking sibs are located in Urubuquara and Ipanoré, far downstream from the top-ranking sibs settled around Iauareté. However, oral tradition states how these downstream settlements were initially occupied by Tariana populations originating from the Iauareté/lower Papuri area. Mr Laureano Vasconcellos, a chanter (Bayá) and elder of the village of Urubuquara, recounts that eight longhouses have been built by generations of his ancestors since they left the village of Japurá in the lower Papuri until they eventually settled in Urubuquara. Considering that Urubuquara was already settled by the Tariana by the time of Coudreau's travels in the 1880s, and allowing the conservative estimate of one generation (twenty years) for the life span of each longhouse, one arrives at figure of 160 years or a date around 1720 for the time the Tariana started to move down from the lower Papuri towards the lower Uaupés.[73]

Although it has been continuous since then, the occupation of this area by the Tariana and other groups suffered a strong set-back because of the rubber boom at the end of the nineteenth century and beginning of the twentieth century. By the time of Nimuendajú's travels, in the 1920s, the heyday of the rubber boom was already past, but the consequences of its violence could be felt, for instance, in his frequent comments on the Indians' reluctance and fear of establishment contacts with him.[74] Thus, when the Salesian missionaries arrived in the 1920s, they were welcomed by the Indians for the protection they brought against unscrupulous white or mixed-blood rubber barons. In the lower Uaupés one of the missionaries' policies was to bring the hidden Indians back to larger villages along the main river.

12.15 Tukanoan house, middle Uaupés, 1994. Preparation of traditional food using both locally manufactured materials and imported 'industrial' objects: a metaphor for history in the upper Rio Negro.

After Koch-Grünberg and Nimuendajú, upper Rio Negro Indians left 'history' to enter 'ethnography'. Their later fate had already been described by the anthropologists who worked there, but an examination of their history shows that the indigenous people of the upper Rio Negro were able to keep on recreating themselves, worshipping their crystals, drinking their *caxirí*, making their *dabucurís* feasts and raising their children even in the face of the strong disruptive pressure exerted by the conquest (fig. 12.15). In other areas of the Amazon where slaving or rubber tapping was not as intense as in the upper Rio Negro there are very few remaining indigenous societies. How, then, were upper Rio Negro societies able to maintain a strong presence up to the twenty-first century?

Part of the answer to this question can be found in the geographical setting of the upper Rio Negro basin, an area still difficult to access and of little agricultural potential, but geography alone is not a sufficient explanation. Most likely, upper Rio Negro societies were able to survive over the last five hundred years or so because of their capacity for reinventing themselves and their capacity for sometimes forgetting their old languages and picking up new ones along the way, among other examples of flexibility and resilience. Maybe, in the end, they were not crushed because they have been unorthodox and not dogmatic about themselves, following that deep sense of humour so peculiar to Amazonian Indians.

Acknowledgements

This paper benefits from comments by Lesley Fordred-Green. Fieldwork in the Uaupés was in great part funded by a grant from the National Science Foundation of the United States, process DBS/9223763. I would like to thank Senhor Pedro de Jesus, a Tariana elder from the village of Santa Maria, for leading me to the Fortaleza site. Arlindo Maia, Miguel Pena, Ramiro Brandão, Rene and João Falcão, Laureano and Luis Vasconcellos, Floriano Cardoso, Juvêncio Cordeiro, Pedro Ferraz and Eugênio Trindade all shared their houses, boats and good humour during fieldwork. As the Tukanoans jokingly say, we did spend a lot of time laughing 'telling lies to each other' overnight, in long boat trips or during field trips. The help provided during fieldwork by my colleagues and friends Astolfo Araújo, Levy Figuti and Paulo Jacob was very much welcomed. Dr Robin Wright, from the Universidade de Campinas, first brought my attention to the reports of Brandão de Amorim, and I am grateful to him for that. Dr Richard Hass, curator of the South American collections of the Etnographisches Museum, Berlin, has kindly facilitated access to the ceramic collections from Koch-Grünberg for study. It is very fortunate for me that this paper is part of a project that has had the close participation of Colin McEwan and José Oliver. Colin was very helpful in providing advice prior to the fieldwork and José's inspiring doctoral dissertation was a guiding light along the way. The collaboration with Cristiana Barreto has only helped to strengthen our already long-standing friendship.

NOTES

1 Koch-Grünberg 1909 (trans. Eduardo Neves).
2 Denevan 1992a.
3 Exceptions in the Amazon are, for instance, the large Tikuna community of Campo Alegre in the upper Solimões and the multi-ethnic, but mostly Tukanoan, community of Iauareté on the middle Uaupés. Iauareté is formed by several neighbourhoods totalling around 2,000 individuals (Neves 1998b).
4 See, for instance, Heckenberger *et al.* 1999; Myers 1973.
5 Arvello-Jiménez and Biord 1994, Dreyfus 1993, Vidal and Zucchi 2000.
6 Farage 1991, Porro 1987, Sweet 1974, Vidal and Zucchi 2000.
7 Boomert 1987.
8 Jonathan Hill (1993) and Robin Wright (1994) have shown that in the ceremonial chants of the Wakuénai and Hohodene – both groups speaking Maipuran Arawakan languages in the upper Rio Negro Basin – the creator hero Kwai travels through a wide area in the Amazon Basin, going from the Andean foothills to the Orinoco delta, the mouth of the Amazon and beyond (Hill 1993: 45, fig. 2.3; Wright 1994: 139, fig. 1). Although some of the places visited by Kwai, such as Portugal, or the cities of Belém and Rio de Janeiro, can be historically correlated with the European conquest, it is likely that these places have been introduced into a mythical narrative that has origins prior to the sixteenth century. As Hill (1993: 47–8) says, 'in their efforts to understand the colonial period, the Wakuénai have not frozen historical changes into a static mythic order but have actively integrated the arrival of Western peoples into the poetic process of "searching for" and "heaping up" the spirit-names of their mythic ancestors'. Chernela (1988) makes a similar comment about a modified version of the Tukanoan anaconda creation myth she obtained among the Arapaço of the lower Uaupés. The striking feature about the maps of Kwai's mythical travels is that the places he visited roughly correspond to the places where Maipuran Arawakan languages are or have been spoken.
9 Jordan 1985: 90; Moran 1993a: 40.
10 Jordan 1985: 89–90.
11 Pires and Prance 1985: 139; Jordan 1985: 90.
12 Pires and Prance 1985: 141.
13 Moran 1993a: 40.
14 Pires and Prance state that *campinaranas* develop in areas where the climate is suitable for forest, 'but where limiting factors restrict the vegetation cover and the species have adapted to the limiting factors' (Pires and Prance 1985: 140). According to these authors (Pires and Prance 1985: 140), *campinaranas* have a peculiar flora and a generally smaller number of species than upland forests.
15 Jordan 1985: 90.
16 *Igapós* should not be confused with *várzea* ecosystems. While *várzeas* are associated with whitewater rivers, *igapós* occur in areas drained by blackwater, or clearwater rivers (Pires and Prance 1985: 126).
17 The denomination 'blackwater rivers' comes from the well-known taxonomy of Amazonian rivers – blackwater, clearwater and whitewater proposed by Harald Sioli in 1950 (Junk and Furch 1985: 8).
18 Junk and Furch 1985.
19 Goulding, Carvalho and Ferreira 1988: 35.
20 Chernela 1985: 81.
21 Århem 1981; Bidou 1972, 1977; Brüzzi 1962; Buchillet 1990, 1992; Chernela 1993; Correa 1980–81, 1983–4; Galvão 1959, 1964; Goldman 1948, 1963; C. Hugh-Jones 1979; S. Hugh-Jones 1979; Koch-Grünberg 1909–10; Reichel-Dolmatoff 1971; Jackson 1976, 1983; Reid 1979; Ribeiro 1995; Silverwood-Cope 1990, among others.
22 As can be seen in the classifications presented by Steward (1948) and Galvão (1960).
23 Urban 1992.
24 See Neves 1998b: ch. 4, and Vidal 1988.
25 Stephen Hugh-Jones (1993: 96) provides a useful description of the social organization of the Tukanoan societies of the Uaupés basin: 'The Tukanoans are divided into some twenty named exogamic patrilineal groups each having ties to a specific territory and each speaking a different but related language ... Language functions as a badge of identity and is often referred to in the specification of marriage rules: a person should normally marry someone who speaks differently from themselves. Children speak their father's language but also know and understand that of their mother. Repeated marriages between affinally related groups, the outcome of a preference for marriage with a cross-cousin and specifically with the FZD [father's sister's daughter], result in individuals typically marrying people who speak their mother's languages, the basis of a system of widespread multilingualism.'
26 E.g. Goldman 1948.
27 See Jackson 1976: 76, 1983: 132; C. Hugh-Jones 1979; Århem 1981: 152; Chernela 1993: 55.
28 On his first visit to the Uaupés Wallace (1905: 190) described a longhouse thus: 'It was a large, substantial building, near a hundred feet long, by about forty wide and thirty high.'
29 There are several very good descriptions of longhouse architecture, and its complex symbolism and sociological meaning (Bécksta 1984; Brüzzi 1962; S. Hugh-Jones 1979, 1985, 1993; Reichel-

Dolmatoff 1971; and Rodrigues Lamus 1958, among others). S. Hugh-Jones 1985 has shown that the longhouses found in the Uaupés can be seen as a variation of a general pattern of longhouse construction in the greater north-western Amazon, from the north bank of the upper Amazon to the west bank of the Orinoco. The same could be said of the distribution of different forms of tree-bark masks found in this greater area.
30 Århem 1990; S. Hugh-Jones 1993.
31 Chernela 1993; Moran 1990.
32 Nimuendajú 1950; Reichel-Dolmatoff 1989.
33 Wright 1991.
34 The Apaporis does not drain into the Rio Negro basin but is, rather, a major tributary of the Japurá/Caquetá. However, for reasons that should be clear in this chapter, we are considering its upper tributaries, such as the Pirá-paraná, as culturally part of the upper Rio Negro basin.
35 Up to the nineteenth century Nheengatú was widely used as the vernacular language in Amazonia and other hinterland areas all over Brazil. The Rio Negro is one of the few areas of Brazil where this language is still spoken. This fact is interesting because the Rio Negro has never been occupied by aboriginal speakers of Tupian languages.
36 Nimuendajú 1982.
37 Meira 1991, 1993.
38 This process was already well advanced when Nimuendajú visited the upper Rio Negro in the 1920s (unpublished letter to Carlos Estevão de Oliveira). Nowadays, out of the several Tariana languages of the middle and lower Uaupés, the Tariana language is only spoken in the villages of Periquito and Santa Rosa, the ones located more upstream than all others. Curiously, both villages are located close to the entrance of one of the overland tracks that connect the predominantly Tukanoan-speaking Uaupés to the predominantly Arawakan-speaking Içana (Neves 1998b: ch. 4). Koch-Grünberg (1909) noted the same process of language replacement happening among the Cubeo in the early twentieth century.
39 Neves 1999a.
40 These premises have been challenged by recent research. Roosevelt (1991) has demonstrated how the use of adequate field methods allowed for the recovery of micro-organic remains in Marajó Island. Heckenberger (1996) has successfully conducted extensive soil sampling to identify activity areas in archaeological sites of the upper Xingu. Finally, the recovery of skeletal remains of possibly ten individuals associated with plenty of faunal remains in an open-air burial mound adjacent to the Solimões river in the central Amazon (Neves 2000) indicates that conditions of organic preservation can be good even for open air sites.
41 *Cariapé* is a commonly found temper in both contemporary indigenous and archaeological ceramics in tropical lowland South America. It consists of burning, crushing and sieving the siliceous barks of trees of the *Licania* genus.
42 Koch-Grünberg (1909: 225–32) provides rich illustrations of ceramics from the north-west Amazon. Among the extensive ethnographic collections that he made at the beginning of the twentieth century, now stored in the Ethnographic Museum of Berlin, there is a set of more than ninety vessels from both the Içana and Uaupés. Contemporary ceramics from the area have not changed much from these hundred-year-old vessels.
43 Typically, exogamic marriages happen within, and not across, language group boundaries.
44 Heckenberger *et al.* 1999; Hilbert 1968; Simões 1974; Simões and Kalkmann 1987.
45 Nimuendajú 1982.
46 Amorim 1926.
47 Neves 1998b: 199.
48 Brüzzi 1962; Coudreau 1886; Lopes de Sousa 1959; McGovern 1927; Wallace 1905.
49 Vidal and Zucchi 2000.
50 In 1994 I crossed this overland path, hiking from one of its terminal branches at the Uanano (Tukano) village of Carurú in the Uaupés up to the Hohodene (Maipuran) village of Uaupuí on the Aiarí. Such a path was also crossed by Koch-Grünberg and Nimuendajú in the past, several times by Robin Wright in the 1970s, and countless times by previous generations of Tukanoan and Maipuran Indians. It is along this path that Tariana oral tradition indicated that the ancestral migration to the Uaupés took place.
51 Amorim 1926; Chernela 1993; S. Hugh-Jones 1981; Moreira and Moreira 1994; Stradelli 1900.
52 Chernela 1993: 24.
53 Note that the shortest route from the Uapuí rapids area to the Iauareté area goes through the above mentioned paths and then down the Uaupés. The route suggested by Chernela includes a much longer journey all the way down the Aiarí, the Içana, a stretch of the Negro, and then up the Uaupés. Tariana oral tradition is also not totally accepted by S. Hugh-Jones (1981). In his words: 'there seems to be no important reason to believe that in their [Tariana] tradition about the origin in the Uaupuí falls, and least reason to negate Brandão de Amorim Tukanoan tradition on an origin in the Manaus area'.
54 S. Hugh-Jones (1981: 42) places it in the eighteenth century, while Chernela (1993: 24) suggests that it might have happened 'over two hundred years ago'.
55 The narratives of particular interest here have the following names: 'Buopé's war', or 'Guerra de Buopé' (Amorim 1926: 11–22); 'Origin of the Uananos', or 'Origem dos Uananos' (Amorim 1926: 37–46); 'The Uananos', or 'Os Uananos' (Amorim 1926: 47–53); and 'Uanano's war', or 'Guerra dos Uananos' (Amorim 1926: 57–78).
56 Note the similarities in the toponym 'Uaupés', the ethnic designation 'Boaupés' (as in Wright 1992b) and the name of the big man 'Buopé'.
57 Amorim 1926: 47. The Uanano still occupy several villages in the middle Uaupés (Chernela 1993).
58 There is no group in the Uaupés today known as 'Arara'. Amorim (1926: 15) states that the Arara used to be brothers-in-law of the Uanano. He also reports (1926: 17) about the Uanano calling for help among the Arapaço, Desana, Cubeo and Tukano. Could the Arara be a sib of one of these groups? Curiously, the Pira-Tapuya, another group located in the lower Uaupés, are not mentioned by Brandão de Amorim. The Pira-Tapuya today do not marry the Uanano, but their languages are very closely related.
59 Spiked trenches seem to be have been very common in the upper Rio Negro basin in the past. Goldman (1963) says that Cubeo oral tradition refers to them. Chernela (1993: 23) states that: 'as reported by Wanano informants, raiding and warfare were so severe that numerous villages on the Aiarí, affluent of the Içana and the Uaupés rivers, were surrounded by spiked trenches.' Although it is likely that raiding increased in the eighteenth century due to the slave trade, warfare in the upper Rio Negro precedes the European conquest. For further reference on past warfare in the upper Rio Negro basin, see Wright 1990. Elsewhere in Amazonia, there is archaeological evidence of pre-colonial defensive ditches in the upper Xingú (Heckenberger 1996, 1998) and in the area of the confluence of the Negro and Solimões rivers (Neves 2000).
60 This configuration fits the predictions of ethnoarchaeological studies done elsewhere in Amazonia. At a Shipibo village on the central Ucayali, DeBoer and Lathrap (1979) have suggested that the process of archaeological site formation in that setting would form a doughnut-shaped midden at the site.
61 In the Ecuadorian Amazon Stahl and Zeidler (1990) arrived at a similar conclusion, in this case through the analysis of the distribution of microfaunal remains.
62 Waltz and Wheeler 1972.
63 Neves 1999a.
64 Reichel-Dolmatoff 1976a.
65 In the kind of ethnic frontier envisioned by Wright (1992).
66 The identification of the Maipuran group who settled the lower Uaupés is more difficult since there has not been, with the exception of Meira (1991), systematic research among the Maipuran groups settled along the Negro itself in Brazil. Using available linguistic and historical evidence, I suggest that the lower Uaupés was occupied by groups related to either the Baré or the Ueurequena Indians.
67 Neves 1998b: ch. 6; Zucchi 1988.
68 Linguistic data show how the Tariana and the Siusí (a contemporary language group of the Içana/Aiarí) have 77.9% to 83.2% shared cognate pairs, while Tariana and Ipeka have 83.8% to 88.9% shared pairs. Based on these data, Oliver (Oliver 1989: 146, Table 8) has suggested that the branching of Tariana from Siusí happened around 700 years BP, while Tariana branched from Ipeka a little later, around 400 years BP.
69 The village of Iauareté is currently located on the east bank of the Uaupés. This is a consequence of the establishment of the Salesian mission in the late 1920s. Prior to that time, the village of Iauareté was described as being located on the west bank of the Uaupés, adjacent to the mouth of the Papuri, in a place today known as Santa Maria (Lopes de Sousa 1956; McGovern 1927; Wallace 1905). Thus, it is probable that the first Tariana occupations in the Iauareté area were in the place of the current village of Santa Maria. The three archaeological sites I identified in this area date, however, from the turn of the twentieth century.
70 São José, Jebarí, Loiro and Paraná Jucá.
71 Following oral tradition, this place is located around present-day Urubuquara.
72 Chernela 1993.
73 The Tariana downriver movement is also reported by Brandão de Amorim (1926) in 'Buoupé's war'. In this narrative this migration happened after the death of Buoupé, when his two sons fought to succeed him.
74 Nimuendajú 1950.

Bibliography

Acero Duarte, L.E.
1982 *Propiedades, usos y nominación de especies vegetales de la Amazonia colombiana*. Corporación de Araracuara: DAINCO, Convenio Colombiano-Holandés, Bogotá.
Acuña, C. de
1941 Novo descobrimento do grande rio das Amazonas. In *Gaspar de Carvajal, Alonso de Rojas e Cristobal de Acuña: Descobrimentos do Rio das Amazonas*, ed. and trans. C.Melo- Leitão, pp. 126–294. Companhia Editora Nacional, São Paulo.
1946 *Nuevo descubrimiento del gran rio de las Amazonas*. Emece Editores, Buenos Aires.
Aguiar, Brás Dias de
1943 Nas fronteiras da Venezuela e Guianas Britânica e Neerlandeza. In *Separata dos Anais do Congresso Brasileiro de Geografia*, vol. 9, pp. 114–15. Instituto Brasileiro de Geografia e Estatística, Rio de Janeiro.
Aidoo, K.E.
1986 Lesser-known Fermented Plant Foods. Review. *Tropical Science* 26(4): 249–58.
Albano, R.
1982 Bibliografia sobre arte rupestre brasileira. *Arquivos do Museu de História Natural* 4/5: 185–8.
Alland Jr., A.
1988 Phallic symbolism and reproductive expropriation: sexual politics in cross cultural perspective. In *Dialectics and Gender: Anthropological Approaches*, ed. R. Randolph, D. Schneider and M. Diaz, pp. 20–37. Westview Press, London.
Amorim, Antonio Brandão de
1926 Lendas em Nheengatú e Português. *Revista do Instituto Histórico e Geográfico Brasileiro*, Rio de Janeiro 154(100): 9–475. Reproduced by the 'Fundo Editorial da Associação Comercial do Amazonas', Manaus 1984.
Andra, H.
1964 Alexander von Humboldt e as suas relações com o Brasil. *Humboldt*, ano 4, X: 68–74.
Andrade, A.
1986 *Investigaciones de los antrosoles de Araracuara*. Fundación de Investigaciones Arqueológicas Nacionales, Banco de la República, Bogotá.
1993 Sistemas agrícolas tradicionales en el Medio río Caquetá. In *La Selva Humanizada: Ecologia alternativa en el trópico húmedo Colombiano*, ed. F. Corréa, pp. 65–85. Fondo FEN Colombia, Fondo Editorial CEREC, 2nd edn, Bogotá.
Andrade, L.
1992 A Marca dos Tempos: Identidade, Estrutura e Mudança entre os Assurini do Trocará. In *Grafismo Indígena*, ed. L. Vidal, pp. 117–32. Studio Nobel/EDUSP, São Paulo.
Araripe, T. de A.
1887 Cidades petrificadas e inscrições lapidares no Brazil. In *Revista do Instituto Histórico e Geográfico Brasileiro* 50: 228–31.
Araújo Costa, F. and S. Caldarelli
1988 Programa de Estudos Arqueológicos na área do reservatório de Kararaô (PA). Relatório de Viabilidade. 2 vols. Unpublished MS. Museu Paraense Emílio Goeldi, Belém.
Araújo Costa, F., C. do Socorro Fernandes Senna, E. da Silva Pereira and D.C. Kern
1986 Levantamento Arqueológico na Área da Usina Hidrélectrica de Cachoeira Porteira. Relatório de Viabilidade. Unpublished MS. Museu Paraense Emílio Goeldi, Belém.
Archila Montañéz, S.
1999 Characterisation of Charcoal Assemblages from Archaeological Sites in the Colombian Amazon Region: A Model based on Ethnography. Ph.D. thesis, University of London.
Areia, M.L.R., M.A. Miranda and T. Hartmann
1991a *Memória da Amazónia Alexandre Rodrigues Ferreira e a Viagem Philosóphica pelas Capitanias do Grão-Pará, Rio Negro, Mato Grosso e Cuyabá, 1783–1792*. Museu e Laboratório Antropológico da Universidade de Coimbra, Coimbra.
1991b *Memory of Amazonia, Alexandre Rodrigues Ferreira and the Viagem Philosophica in the Captaincies of Grão-Pará, Rio Negro, Mato Grosso and Cuyabá, 1783–1792*. Museu e Laboratório Antropológico da Universidade de Coimbra, Coimbra.
Arguello, A.H.
1988 Prácticas agrícolas y consecuencias genéticas que permitieron una mejor adaptación de los indigenas a la Amazonia colombiana. *Agronomía Colombiana* 5(1–2): 86–96.
Århem, K.
1981 *Makuna Social Organization: A Study in Descent, Alliance and the Formation of Corporate Groups in the North-Western Amazon*. Uppsala Studies in Cultural Anthropology no. 4.
1989 Ecosofía Makuna. In *La Selva Humanizada: Ecologia alternativa en el trópico húmedo Colombiano*, ed. F. Corréa, pp. 105–22. Instituto Colombiano de Antropologia, Fondo Editorial CEREC, Bogotá.
1990 Los makuna en la Historia Cultural del Amazonas. *Informes Antropológicos*, no. 4: 53–9. Bogotá.
1993 Ecosofía Makuna. In *La Selva Humanizada: Ecologia alternativa en el trópico húmedo Colombiano*, 2nd edn, ed. F. Corréa, pp. 110–126. Fondon FEN Colombia, Fondo Ediorial CEREC, Bogotá.
Arvelo-Jiménez, N. and Horacio Biord
1994 The Impact of Conquest on Contemporary Indigenous Peoples of the Guiana Shield. In *Amazonian Indians from Prehistory to the Present: Anthropological Perspectives*, ed. A.C. Roosevelt, pp. 56–78. University of Arizona, Tucson & London.
Ávila, Gabriela Martin
1996 O cemitério pré-histórico 'Pedra do Alexandre' em Carnaúba dos Dantas, RN. *Revista CLIO: Arqueológica* 1 (11): 43–57.
Baer, G.
1993 Para o Melhor Entendimento das Máscaras Sul-Americanas. In *Karl Von Stein; Um Século De Antropologia No Xingu*, ed. Vera Coelho, pp. 289–309. Editora da Universidade de São Paulo, São Paulo.
Bailey, R. and T. Headland
1991 The Tropical Rain Forest: Is it a productive Environment for Human Foragers? *Human Ecology* 19 (2): 261–85.
Bailey, R. and N.R. Peacock
1988 Efe Pigmies of northeast Zaire: Subsistance strategies in the Ituri Forest. In *Coping with Uncertainty in Food Supply*, ed. I. De Garine and G. A. Harrison, pp. 88–117. Clarendon, Oxford.
Bailey, R., M. Janike and R. Rechtman
1991 Reply to Colinvaux and Bush. *American Anthropologist* 93: 60–162.
Bailey, R., G. Head., M. Jenike, B. Owen, R. Rechtman and E. Zechenter
1989 Hunting and Gathering in Tropical Rain Forest: Is it Possible? *American Anthropologist* 91: 261–285.
Baldus, H.
1940 A viagem pelo Brasil de Spix e Martius. *Revista do Arquivo Municipal*, Departamento de Cultura, ano VI, vol. 69, São Paulo.
Balée, W.
1989 The culture of Amazonian forest. In *Resource management in Amazonia: indigenous and folk strategies*, ed. D. Posey and W. Balée. *Advances in Economic Botany* 7: 1–21.
1994 *Footprints of the Forest: Ka'apor Ethnobotany – the Historical Ecology of Plant Utilization by an Amazonian People*. Columbia University Press, New York.
Balée, W. (ed.)
1998 *Advances in Historical Ecology*. Columbia University Press, New York.
Balick, W.
1986 Systematic and Economic Botany of *Oenocarpus Jessenia* (Palmae) Complex. *Advances in Economic Botany* 3: 1–140.
Banks, Joseph
1963 (1771) *The Endeavour Journal of Joseph Banks, 1768–1771*, ed. J.C. Beaglehole. Trustees of the Public Library of New South Wales in association with Angus and Robertson, Sydney.
Barata, F.
1950 A arte oleira do Tapajó I. Considerações sobre a cerâmica e dois tipos de vasos característicos. *Publicações do Instituto de Antropologia e Etnologia do Pará* 2: 1–47.
1951 A arte oleira dos Tapajó II. Os cachimbos de Santarém. *Revista do Museu Paulista* 5: 183–98.
1953a Uma análise estilística da cerâmica de Santarém. *Cultura* 5: 185–205.
1953b A arte oleira dos Tapajó III. Alguns elementos para a tipologia de Santarém. *Publicações do Instituto de Antropologia e Etnologia do Pará* 6: 1–16.
1954 O muiraquitã e as contas dos Tapajó. *Revista do Museu Paulista* 8: 229–59.
Barbosa Rodrigues, J.
1875a *Exploração e Estudo do Valle do Amazonas: Rio Tapajós*. Nacional, Rio de Janeiro.
1875b *Ídolo Amazonico Achado no Rio Amazonas em Commissão Scientifica pelo Governo Imperial*. Typographia de Brown e Evaristo, Rio de Janeiro.
1876 *Antiguidades Amazônicas*. Ensaios de Sciência, 1: 1–82, 92–246.
1882 *Catálogo dos Objetos Expostos na Exposição Antropológica no Rio de Janeiro*. Typographia Nacional, Rio de Janeiro.
1885 *Rio Jauapery. Pacificação dos Crichanás*. Imprensa Nacional, Rio de Janeiro.
1889 *O Muyraquitã Estudo da Origem Asiática, da Civilização do Amazonas nos Tempos Prehistóricos*. Typographia do Amazonas, Manaus.
1892 Antiguidades do Amazonas: Necrópole de Miracanguera. In *Vellosia* 2: 1–40.
1989 (1903) *Sertum Palmarum Brasiliensium* (facsimile of the first edn). Editora Expressão e Cultura, Exped Ltd, Rio de Janeiro.
Barnet, W.K. and J. Hoopes (eds)
1995 *The Emergence of Pottery: Technology and Innovation in Ancient Societies*. Smithsonian Institution Press, Washington DC.

Barrère, Pierre
1743 *Nouvelle relation de la France equinoxiale*. Paris.
Barreto, C.
2000 A Construção de um Passado Pré-colonial: Uma Breve História da Arqueologia no Brasil. *Dossiê antes do Cabral: Arqueologia Brasileira I*, Revista USP, 32–51.
Barreto, M.
1992 Historia da Pesquisa Arqueologica no Museu Emílio Goeldi. *Boletim do Museu Paraense Emílio Goeldi: Antropologia* 8: 203–94.
Barse, W.P.
1990 Preceramic occupations in the Orinoco River valley. *Science* 250: 1388–90.
1995 El periodo arcaico en el Orinoco y su contexto en el norte de Sud América. In *Ambito y ocupaciones tempranas de la America Tropical*, ed. I. Cavelier and S. Mora, pp. 99–114. Fundación ERIGAIE-Instituto Colombiano de Antropologia, Santafé de Bogotá.
Bates, H.W.
1863 *The Naturalist on the River Amazons. A record of adventures, habits of animals, sketches of Brazilian and Indian life, and aspects of nature under the Equator, during eleven years of travel*, 2 vols. John Murray, London.
1979 (1863) *Um Naturalista no Rio Amazonas*, trans. R. R. Junqueira. Editora Universidade de São Paulo, Livraria Itatiaia Editora LTDA, Belo Horizonte.
Becher, H.
1959 Algumas notas sobre a religião e a mitologia dos Surara. *Revista do Museu Paulista*, n.s. XI.
Becker-Donner, Etta
n.d. Die Brasilien Sammlungen. In *Brasiliens Indianer*. Museum für Völkerkunde, Wien.
Beckerman, Stephen
1993 Major patterns in indigenous Amazonian subsistence. In *Tropical Forests, People and Food: Biocultural Interactions and Applications to Development*. Man and Biosphere Series, vol. 13, ed. C. M. Hladik, O. F. Linares, H. Pagezy, A. Semple and M. Hadley, pp.411–24. United Nations Educational, Scientific and Cultural Organization, Paris; Parthenon Publishing Group, New York.
Beer, G.
1996 Travelling the Other Way. In *Culture of Natural History*, ed. N. Jadine. Cambridge University Press.
Behling, H.
1996 First report on the new evidence for the occurrence of *Podocarpus* and possible human presence at the mouth of the Amazon during the Late-glacial. *Vegetation History and Archaeobotany* 5: 241–6.
Béksta, K.
1984 *A Maloca Tukano-Dessana e seu Simbolismo*. SEDUC, Manaus.
Beluzzo, A.M.
1999 *O Brasil dos Viajantes*, 2nd edn. Fundação Odebrecht, São Paulo.
Benoit, P.J.
1839 *Voyage à Surinam: description des possessions néerlandaises dans la Guyane*. Société des Beaux-Arts, Bruxelles.
Bergman, R.W.
1980 *Amazon Economics: The Simplicity of Shipibo Indian Wealth*. University Microfilms International, Ann Arbor.
Bertrand-Rosseau, P.
1983 De como los Shipibo y otras tribos aprendieron a hacer los dibujos (tipicos) y a adornarse. *Amazonia Peruana* V (9): 79–85.
Betendorf, J.
1910 Chronica da missão dos padres da Compahia de Jesus no Estado do Maranhão. *Revista do Instituto Histórico e Geográfico Brasileiro* 72(1). Rio de Janeiro.
Bezerra de Menezes, U.
1972 *Arqueologia Amazônica (Santarém)*. Museu de Arqueologia e Etnologia, São Paulo.
Bidou, Patrice
1972 Represéntations de l'espace dans la mythologie Tatuyo (Indiens Tucano). *Journal de la Société des Américanistes* 61: 45–105.
1977 Naitre et être Tatuyo. *Actes du XLII Congrès International des Américanistes* 2: 105–20.
Binford, L.
1980 Willow smoke and dog tails: hunter gatherers settlement system and archaeological site formation. *American Antiquity* 45(1): 4–20.
Boas, F.
1955 *Primitive Art*. Dover Publications, New York.
Boomert, A.
1987 Gifts of the Amazons: 'Greenstone' pendants and beads as items of ceremonial exchange in Amazonia. *Antropologia* 67: 33–54.
Borges, M.
1933 Inscrições Rupestres no Pará. *Boletim do Museu Nacional* 9: 120–21.
Bos, G.
1998 *Some Recoveries in Guiana Indian Ethnohistory*. VU Uitgeverig, Amsterdam.
Boserup, E.
1965 *The Conditions of Agricultural Growth: The Economics of Agrarian Change under Population Pressure*. Aldine, Chicago.
Brajnikov, E.
1974 De certaines similitudes presentées par les gravures rupestres de l'Amazonie et de la region de l'Amour-Oussouri. *Bollettino del Centro Camuno di Studi Prehistorici* 11: 151–63.
Brandão, A.
1937 *A escrita pré-histórica do Brasil; ensaio de interpretação*. Civilização Brasileira, Rio de Janeiro.
Brandônio (Ambrósio Fernandez Brandão)
1943 (1618) *Diálogos das grandesas do Brasil*. Introdução de Capistrano de Abreu e notas de Rodolfo Garcia. Editora Dois Mundos, Rio de Janeiro.
Braun, Barbara (ed.)
1995 *Arts of the Amazon*. Thames & Hudson, London.
Bray, W.
1984 Across the Darien Gap: A Colombian View of Isthmian Archaeology. In *The Archaeology of Lower Central America*, ed. F. Lange and D. Stone, pp. 305–58. University of New Mexico Press, Albuquerque.
1993 *The Meeting of Two Worlds: Europe and the Americas, 1492–1650*. Proceedings of the British Academy, 81. Oxford University Press, Oxford.
1995 Searching for Environmental Stress: Climatic and Anthropogenic Influences on the Landscape of Colombia. In *Archaeology in the Lowland American Tropics: Current Analytical Methods and Applications*, ed. P.W. Stahl, pp. 96–112. Cambridge University Press, Cambridge.
Brett, W.H.
1868 *Indian Tribes of Guiana; Their Conditions and Habits*. Bell and Daldy, London.
Brochado, J.
1980a *The Social Ecology of the Marajoara Culture*. Master's thesis, University of Illinois.
1980b Religion in Anthropological Perspective. Unpublished MS. Department of Anthropology, University of Illinois at Urbana-Champaign, Illinois.
1984 *An Ecological Model of the Spread of Pottery and Agriculture into Eastern South America*. Ph.D. thesis, Department of Anthropology, University of Illinois at Urbana-Champaign, Illinois.
Brochado, J. and D. Lathrap
1982 *Chronologies in the New World: Amazonia*. Unpublished MS, on file at the Department of Anthropology, University of Illinois at Urbana-Champaign, Illinois.
Brüzzi Alves da Silva, A.
1962 *A Civilização Indígena do Uaupés*. Livraria Salesiana Editora, São Paulo.
Buchillet, Dominique
1990 Los Poderes del Hablar: Terapia y agresión chamánica entre los indios Desana del Vaupes brasileiro. In *Las Culturas Nativas Lationo Americanas A Traves De Su Discurso*, ed. Ellen Basso and Joel Sherzer, pp. 319–354. ABYA-YALA, Quito.
1992 Os Indios da região do alto rio Negro. História, etnografia e situação das terras. Unpublished MS.
Bush, M.B., D.R. Piperno and P.A. Colinvaux
1989 A 6,000 year History of Amazonian Maize Cultivation. *Nature* 340: 303–5.
Butt Colson, A.J
1973 Inter-tribal Trade in the Guiana Highlands. *Antropológica* 34: 1–70. Fundación de Ciencias Naturales La Salle, Caracas.
Cabrera, G., D. Franky and D. Mahecha
1999 *Los nukak: nómadas de la Amazonia colombiana*. Editorial Universidad Nacional, Santafé de Bogotá.
Campbell, K. E. and F. D. Frailey
1984 Holocene Flooding and Species Diversity in Southwestern Amazonia. *Quaternary Research* 21: 369–75.
Cárdenas, D. and G. Politis
2000 *Territorio, movilidad, etnobotánica y manejo del bosque de los Nukak Orientales, Amazonia Colombiana*. SINCHI, Santafé de Bogotá.
Cárdenas, D., D. Giraldo-Canas and C. Arias
1997 Capítulo de Vegetatión. In *Zonificación ambiental para el plan modelo Colombo-Brasilero (Eje Apaporis-Tabatinga, PAT)*, pp. 183–228. IGAC-SINCHI, Santafé de Bogotá.
Carelli, M.
1992 *A La Decouverte de L´Amazonie: Les Carnets du Naturaliste Hercule Florence*. Gallimard, Paris.
Carneiro, R.
n.d. The Ecological Basis of Amazonian Chiefdoms. Unpublished MS, Department of Anthropology, American Museum of Natural History, New York.
1961 Slash-and-Burn Cultivation among the Kuikuru and its Implications for Cultural Development in the Amazon Basin. In *The Evolution of Horticultural Systems in Native South America: Causes and Consequences*, ed. J. Wilbert, pp. 47–67. *Antropologica* supplement publication no. 2. Sociedade de Ciencias Naturales la Salle, Caracas.
1970 A theory of the origin of the state. *Science*, 169: 733–8.
1978 The Knowledge and Use of Rain Forest Trees by the Kuikurú Indians of Central Brazil. In *The Nature and Status of Ethnobotany*, ed. R.I. Ford, pp. 201–16. Anthropological Papers, no. 67. Museum of Anthropology, University of Michigan, Ann Arbor.
1981 Chiefdom: precursor to the state. In *Transition to Statehood in the New World*, ed. G. Jones and R. Kautz, pp. 39–79. Cambridge University Press, Cambridge.
1983 Cultivation of Manioc among the Kuikurú of the Upper Xingú. *Adaptive Responses of Native Amazonians*, ed. R.B. Hames and W.T. Vickers, pp. 65–111. Academic Press, New York.
1987 Further Reflections on Resource Concentration and its Role in the Rise of the State. In *Studies in the Neolithic and Urban Revolutions*, ed. L. Manzanilla, pp. 245–60. BAR International Series 349, Oxford.
1995 The history of ecological interpretations of Amazonia: does Roosevelt have it right? In *Indigenous Peoples and the Future of Amazonia: An Ecological Anthropology of an Endangered World*, ed. L. Sponsel, pp. 45–70. University of Arizona Press, Tucson.
Carneiro da Cunha, M.
1978 *Os Mortos e os Outros*. Editora Hucitec, São Paulo.
Carvajal, G. de
1941 Relação do novo descobrimento do famoso Rio Grande que descobrio por grande ventura o Capitão Francisco de Orellana. In *Gaspar de Carvajal, Alonso de Rojas e Cristobal de Acuña: Descobrimentos do Rio das Amazonas*, ed. and trans. C. Melo-Leitão, pp. 11–79. Companhia Editora Nacional, São Paulo.
1970 Discovery of the Orellana River. In H.C. Heaton (ed.), *The Discovery of the Amazon According to the Accounts of Friar Gaspar de Carvajal and Other Documents*, pp. 167–235, AMS Press Inc., New York.
Carvalho, A.
1909 Prehistória sul-americana; resposta às impugnações dos Srs. Britto e Arminio de Mello Franco. *Revista do Instituto Arqueológico e Geográfico Pernambucano* 14(76): 141–91.
Carvalho, S.
1975 O duplo jacaré (A cerâmica marajoara). *Perspectivas* I(1): 13–34.
1983 A Cerâmica e os Rituais Antropofágicos. *Revista de Antropologia* 26: 39–52.
Cavelier, I.C., C. Rodriguez, L.F. Herrera, G. Morcote and S. Mora
1995 No sola de caza vive el hombre. Ocupación del bosque amazónico, holoceno temprano. In *Ambito y*

ocupaciones tempranas de la América tropical, ed. I. Cavelier and S. Mora, pp. 27–44. Fundación Erigaie-Instituto Colombiano de Antropologia, Santafé de Bogotá.

Chagnon, N.

1983 *Yanomano: The Fierce People*, 3rd edn. Holt, Rhinehart and Winston, New York.

Chernela, J.

1985 Indigenous fishing in the Neotropics: the Tukanoan Uanano of the blackwater Uaupés River Basin in Brazil and Colombia. *INTERCIENCIA*, 10(2): 78–86.

1988 Righting History in the Northwest Amazon: Myth, Structure, and History in an Arapaço Narrative. In *Rethinking History and Myth: Indigenous South American Perpectives on the Past*, ed. Jonathan D. Hill, pp. 35–49. University of Illinois Press, Urbana.

1993 *The Wanano Indians of the Brazilian Amazon: A Sense of Space*. University of Texas Press, Austin.

Chymz, I.

1976 Terminologia arqueológica brasileira para a cerâmica. *Cadernos de Arqueologia* 1(1).

Chmyz, I. and E. Sganzerla

1991 Património Arqueológico da Área da BR 156: Trecho Rio Preto – Laranjal do Jari (Amapá). Unpublished MS. Curitiba.

Clastres, P.

1981 *Investigaciones en Antropologia Politica*. Editorial Gedisa, Barcelona.

Cohen, M.

1977 *The Food Crisis in Prehistory: Overpopulation and the Origins of Agriculture*. Yale University Press, New Haven.

Colinvaux, P.A.

1996 Quaternary Environmental History and Forest Diversity in the Tropical Neoforests. In *Evolution and Environment in Tropical America*, ed. J.B.C. Jackson, A.F. Budd and A.G. Coates. Chicago University Press, Chicago.

1998 Ice-Age Amazon and the Problem of Diversity: New Interpretations of Pleistocene Amazonia. *The Review of Archaeology* 19(1): 1–10.

Colinvaux, P.A. and M. Bush

1991 The rain-forest ecosystem as a resource for hunting and gathering. *American Anthropologist* 91 (1): 153–90.

Colinvaux, P.A., P.E. De Oliveira, P.E. Moreno, J.E. Miller and M.B. Bush

1996a A long pollen record from from Lowland Amazonia: Forest Cooling in Glacial Times. *Science* 274: 85–8.

Colinvaux, P.A., K-b Liu, P.E. de Oliveira, M.B. Bush, J.E. Miller, and M. Steinitz-Kannan

1996b Temperature Depression in the Lowland Tropics in Glacial Times. *Climatic Change* 32: 19–13.

Collier, M.

1989 Tapajós: a summary of their culture at the time of contact. Master's dissertation, George Washington University, Washington.

Colonelli, C. and E. d'Almeida Magalhães

1975 Arte Rupestre no Brasil: uma bibliografia anotada. *Dédalo* 11(21/22): 117–33.

Conrad, G.W. and A.A. Demarest

1984 *Religion and Empire: The Dynamics of Aztec and Inca Expansionism*. Cambridge University Press, Cambridge.

Consens, M.

1988 First rock paintings in Amazon basin. *Rock Art Research* 5 (1): 69–72.

1989 Arte rupestre no Pará: análise de alguns sítios de Monte Alegre. *Dédalo* 1: 265–78.

Coomes, O.T.

1992 Making a Living in the Amazon Rainforest: Peasants, Land and Economy in the Tahuayo River Basin of Northeastern Peru. Ph.D. thesis, Department of Geography, University of Wisconsin-Madison.

Corrêa, C.

1965 Estatuetas de cerâmica na cultura Santarém. *Publicações do Museu Paraense Emílio Goeldi* 4.

Corréa, François

1980–81 Por el camino de la Anaconda Ancestral: Sobre Organización Social entre los Taiwano del Vaupés. *Revista Colombiana de Antropología* XXIII: 39–108.

1983–4 Elementos de Identidad y Organizacion Social entre las Comunidades Indigenas de la Region del Vaupes. *Maguare* (Revista del Departamento de Antropologia, Universidad Nacional de Colombia), no. 2: 97–123.

Corrêa, M.

1994 As gravações e pintura rupestres na área do reservatório da UHE-Balbina – AM. Dissertação (mestrado). Universidade Federal do Rio de Janeiro.

Costa, A.

1934 *Introdução à Arqueologia Brasileira*. Editora Nacional, Rio de Janeiro.

Coudreau, Henri

1886 *La France Équinociale*, vol. II. Challamel Ainé, Paris.

Coudreau, O.

1901 *Voyage au Cuminá; 20 avril 1900 – 7 septembre 1900*. A. Lahure, Paris.

1903 *Voyage au Maicuru; 5 juin 1902 – 12 janvier 1903*. A. Lahure, Paris.

1977 *Viagem ao Tapajós*, trans. Eugênio Amado. Itatiaia, São Paulo.

Couto de Magalhães, J.

1975 *Viagem ao Araguaia*. Coleção Brasiliana 28. Companhia Editora Nacional, São Paulo.

Crevaux, J.

1883 *Voyages dan L'Amerique du Sud, 1878–1881*. Hachette, Paris.

Cronquist, A.

1981 *An Integrated System of Classification of Plants*. Columbia University Press, New York.

Crowe, I.

2000 *The Quest for Food: Its Role in Human Evolution and Migration*. Tempus Publishing, London.

Cruls, G.

1942 *Arqueologia Amazônica*, Revista do Patrimônio Histórico e Artístico Nacional, Rio de Janeiro, 6: 169–220.

Cruxent, J.M. and I. Rouse

1958–9 *An Archaeological Chronology of Venezuela*. Pan American Union Social Science Monographs, no. 6 (2 vols). Pan American Union, Washington DC.

Cunha, O. da

1989 *Talento e atitude: estudos biográficos do Museu Paraense Emílio Goeldi*. Museu Paraense Emílio Goeldi, Belém.

Daniel, J.

1976 Tesouro Descoberto no rio Amazonas. *Separata dos Anais do Museu Nacional* 95, 2 vols.

DeBoer, W.R.

1981 Buffer Zones in the Cultural Ecology of Aboriginal Amazonia: An Ethnohistorical Approach. *American Antiquity* 46 (2): 364–77.

DeBoer, W. and Lathrap, D.

1979 The making and breaking of Shipibo-Conibo ceramics. In *Ethnoarchaeology: Implications of Ethnography for Archaeology*, ed. C. Kramer, pp. 102–38. Columbia University Press, New York .

Debret, J.B.

1834 *Voyage Pittoresque et Historique au Brésil*. Firmin Didot Frères, Imprimeurs de L'Institute de France, Paris.

Denevan, William

1966 *The Aboriginal Cultural Geography of the Llanos de Mojos of Bolivia*. Ibero-Americana, 48. University of California Press, Berkeley.

1992a The Aboriginal Population of Amazonia. In *The Native Population of the Americas in 1492*, 2nd edn, ed. W. Denevan, pp. 205–34. University of Wisconsin Press, Madison.

1992b Stone vs. Metal Axes: The Ambiguity of Shifting Cultivation in Prehistoric Amazonia. *Journal of the Steward Anthropological Society* 20: 153–65.

1995 Native Population of Amazonia in 1492 reconsidered. In *Latin American Geography: Past and Future*, ed. D.R. Stoddart and P.F. Starrs, pp. 19–37. Blackwell, Oxford.

1996 A Bluff Model of Riverine Settlement in Prehistoric Amazonia. *Annals of the Association of American Geographers* 86 (4): 654–81.

1998 Comments on Prehistoric Agriculture in Amazonia. *Culture and Agriculture* 20 (2&3): 54–9.

2001 *Cultivated Landscapes of Native Amazonia and the Andes*. Oxford Environmental and Geographic Studies Series. Oxford University Press.

Denevan, W. and A. Zucchi

1978 Ridged field excavations in the central Orinoco Llanos. In *Advances in Andean Archaeology*, ed. D.L. Browman, pp. 235–46. Mouton, The Hague.

Derby, O.

1898 O rio Trombetas. *Boletim do Museu Paraense de História Natural e Etnographia* 2 (1–4): 371–9.

Descola, P.

1998 Estrutura ou sentimento: a relação com o animal na Amazonia. *Mana* 4 (1): 23–45.

Dietschy, Hans

1939 Die Amerikanischen Keulen und Holzschwerter in ihrer Beziehung zur Kukturgeschichte der Neuen Welt. *Internationales Archiv für Ethnography* XXXVII: 87–205. E.J. Brill, Leiden.

Dillehay, T.G. Ardila Calderón, G. Politis and M. da Conceição de Moraes Coutinho Beltrão

1996 Earliest Hunters and Gatherers of South America. *Journal of World Prehistory* 6 (2): 145–204.

Doggett, Rachel, Monique Hulvey and Julie Ainsworth (eds)

1992 *New World of Wonders: European Images of the Americas 1492–1700*. The Folger Shakespeare Library, Washington.

Dole, G.E.

1960 Techniques of Preparing Manioc Flour as Key to Culture History in Tropical America. In *Men and Cultures*, ed. F.C. Wallace, pp. 241–8. Philadelphia.

1978 The Use of Manioc among the Kuikurú: Some Interpretations. In *The Nature and Status of Ethnobotany*, ed. R. I. Ford, pp. 217–47. Anthropological Papers, no. 67. Museum of Anthropology, University of Michigan, Ann Arbor.

Dorta, S.

1981 Pariko. Etnografia de um artefato plumário. *Coleção Museu Paulista*, Etnologia 4.

1992 Coleções Etnográficas: 1650–1955. In *História dos Índios no Brasil*, ed. M. Carneiro da Cunha, pp. 501–527. Fapesp/SMC, Companhia de Letras, São Paulo.

Drennan, R.

1987 Regional Demography in Chiefdoms. In *Chiefdoms in the Americas*, ed. Robert Drennan and Carlos A. Uribe, pp. 307–23. Lanham, New York and London.

1995 Chiefdoms in northern South America. *Journal of World Prehistory*, 9(3): 301–340.

Dreyfus, S.

1993 Les Reseaux politiques indigènes en Guyane occidentale et leurs transformations aux XXVII et XVIII siècles. *L'Homme* 126/128: 75–97.

Due, Berete

1980 Amerika. In *Etnografiske genstande i Det kongelige danske Kunstkammer 1650–1800/ Ethnographic Objects in The Royal Danish Kunstkammer 1650–1800*, ed. Bente Dam-Mikkelsen and Torben Lundbaek, pp. 17–40. Nationalmuseet, Copenhagen.

Dufour, D.L.

1983 Nutrition in the Nortwest Amazon: Household Dietary Intake and Energy Expenditure. In *Adaptive Responses of Native Amazonians*, ed. R.B. Hames and W.T. Vickers, pp. 329–55. Academic Press, New York.

1985 Manioc as a Dietary Staple: Implications for the Budgeting of Time and Energy in the Northwest Amazon. In *Food Energy in Tropical Ecosystems*, ed. D.J. Cattle and K.H. Schwerin, pp. 1–20. Gordon and Breach, New York.

1987 Insects as food: a case study from the Northwest Amazon. *American Anthropologist* 89 (2): 383–97.

1988 Cyanide content of cassava (*Manihot esculenta*, Euphorbiaceae) cultivars used by Tukanoan Indians in Northwest Amazonia. *Economy Botany* 42 (2): 255–66.

1989 The Effectiveness of Cassava Detoxification Techniques Used by Indigenous Peoples in Northwest Amazonia. *Interciencia* 14: 88–91.

1993a Uso de la selva tropical por los indígenas Tukano. In *La Selva Humanizada: Ecologia alternativa en el*

trópico húmedo Colombiano, 2nd edn, ed. F. Corréa, pp. 65–85. Fondo FEN Colombia, Fondo Editorial CEREC, Bogotá.
1993b The Bitter is Sweet: A Case Study of Bitter Cassava *(Manihot esculenta)* Use in Amazonia. In *Tropical Forests, People and Food: Biocultural Interactions and Applications to Development*. Man and the Biosphere Series, vol. 13, ed. C.M. Hladik, A. Haldik, O.F. Linares, H. Pagezy, A. Semple and M. Hadley, pp. 575–88. United Nations Educational, Scientific and Cultural Organization, Paris; Parthenon Publishing Group, New York.
1994 Cassava in Amazonia: Lessons in Utilization and Safety from Native Peoples. International Workshop on Cassava Safety, Ibadan, Nigeria, March 1–4, Leiden (Netherlands). Working Group on Cassava Safety. In *International Institute of Tropical Agriculture*: 175–182.

EARLE, T.
1987 Chiefdoms in archaeological and ethnohistorical perspectives. *Annual Review of Anthropology* 16: 279–308.
1991 The Evolution of Chiefdoms. In *Chiefdoms: Power, Economy, and Ideology*, ed. T. Earle, pp. 1–15. Cambridge University Press, Cambridge.

EASBY, E.
1952 The pre-conquest art of Santarém, Brazil. Master's dissertation, Faculty of Philosophy, Columbia University.

EDEN, M., W. BRAY, L. HERRERA AND C. MCEWAN
1984 Terra Preta soils and their archaeological context in the Caquetá Basin of Southeast Colombia. *American Antiquity* 49(1); 125–40.

EDMUNDSON, G. (ED.)
1967 *Journal of the Travels and Labours of Father Samuel Fritz in the River of the Amazons*. Kraus Reprint Limited.

EHRENREICH, P.
1948 Os Petróglifos da Ilha dos Martírios. *Contribuições para a Etnologia do Brasil. Revista do Museu Paulista*, n.s. 2: 89–93.

EIDT, R.
1984 *Advances in Abandoned Settlement Analysis: Applications of Prehistoric Anthrosols in Colombia, South America*. The Center for Latin America, University of Wisconsin, Milwaukee.
1985 Theoretical and Practical Considerations in the Analysis of Anthrosols. In *Archaeological Geology*, ed. G. Rapp and J. A. Gifford, pp. 155–90. Yale University Press, New Haven.

EVANS, C.
1955 Filiações das culturas arqueológicas no Território do Amapá. In *Anais do XXXI Congresso International de Americanistas (São Paulo 1954)* II. São Paulo.

EVANS, C. AND B. MEGGERS
1960 Archaeological Investigation in British Guiana. *Bulletin of the Bureau of American Ethnology* 177. Smithsonian Institution, Washington.

FALESI, I.
1974 Soils of the Brazilian Amazon. In *Man in the Amazon*, ed. C. Wagley, pp. 201–29. University Presses of Florida, Gainesville.

FARABEE, WILLIAM CURTIS
1918 *The Central Arawaks*. The University Museum Anthropological Publications, vol. 9. University of Pennsylvania.
1921 Exploration at the mouth of Amazon. *The Museum Journal* 12: 142–161. University of Pennsylvania.
1924 *The Central Caribs*. The University Museum Anthropological Publications, vol. 10. University of Pennsylvania.

FARAGE, N.
1991 *As Muralhas dos Sertões. Os povos indígenas no rio Branco e a colonização*. Paz e Terra, Rio de Janeiro.

FAUSTO, B.
1994 *História do Brasil*. Editora EDUSP, São Paulo.

FEINMAN, G.M.
1991 Demography, Surplus, and Inequality: Early Political Formations in Highland Mesoamerica. In *Chiefdoms: Power, Economy, and Ideology*, ed. T. Earle, pp. 229–62. Cambridge University Press, Cambridge.

FEINMAN, G.M. AND L.M. NICHOLAS
1992 Human-Land Relations from an Archaeological Perspective: The Case of Ancient Oaxaca. In *Understanding Economic Process*, ed. S. Ortiz and S. Lees, pp. 135–178. Monographs in Economic Anthropology 10. University Press of America, Lanham, Maryland.

FERREIRA, M.
1974 *As 17 reproduções em bronze das esculturas rupestres dos Martirios do Rio Araguia*. Prefeitura do Município de São Paulo, São Paulo.

FERREIRA PENNA, D.
1876 Breve Notícia sobre os Sambaquis do Pará. *Arquivos do Museu Nacional* 1: 85–99.
1877a Apontamentos sobre as Cerâmicas do Pará. *Arquivos do Museu Nacional* 2: 47–67.
1877b Urnas de Maracá. *Arquivos do Museu Nacional* 2: 69–71.
1973 *Obras completas*, new edn, vol. II. Conselho Estadual da Cultura, Belém.

FLANNERY, K.V. AND J. MARCUS
1996 Cognitive Archaeology. In *Contemporary Archaeology and Theory*, ed. R. Preucel and I. Hodder, pp. 350–63. Blackwell, Oxford.
2000 Formative Mexican chiefdoms and the myth of the 'mother culture'. In *Journal of Anthropological Archaeology* 19: 1–37.

FOCK, N.
1963 *Waiwai: Religion and Society of an Amazonian Tribe*. The National Museum, Copenhagen.

FORDRED-GREEN, L., E. NEVES AND D. GREEN
2000 Sites and stories investigated in the Reversa Uaçá, May–June 2000. A Preliminary Report on the Initial Investigation Prepared for the Wenner Gren Foundation for Anthropological Research, December 2000. Unpublished MS.

FRIKEL, PROTÁSIO
1959 Relatório de viagem ao rio Erepecuru e a Serra do Tumucumaque. Unpublished MS. Museu Paraense Emílio Goeldi, Belém.
1973 *Os Tiriyó: seu sistema adaptativo*. Kom Munstermann Druck, Hannover.

FURST, PETER T.
1976 *Hallucinogens and Culture*. Series in Cross-Cultural Themes. Chandler & Sharp, San Francisco.

GALARD, J.
2000 The Distant View. In *The Distant View*, pp. 36–63, exh. cat. Associação Brasil 500 Anos Artes Visuais, São Paulo.

GALEANO, G.
1992 *Estudios en la Amazonia columbiana, vol. 1: Las Palmas de la región de Araracuara*, ed. J. Saldarriaga and Th. Van der Hammen. Tropenbos, Santafé de Bogotá.

GALLOIS, D.
1992 Arte iconográfica Waiãpi. In *Grafismo Indigena*, ed. L. Vidal, pp. 209–230. Studio Nobel/EDUSP, São Paulo.

GALVÃO, E.
1959 Aculturação Indígena no Rio Negro. *Boletim do Museu Paraense Emílio Goeldi: Antropologia*, n.s. 7.
1960 Areas culturais indígenas do Brasil: 1900/1959. *Boletim do Museu Paraense Emílio Goeldi: Antropologia*, n.s. 8.
1964 Encontro de sociedades tribal e nacional no rio Negro, Amazonas. In *Actas y Mémorias. 35 Congresso Internacional de Americanistas*, Mexico, 1962, pp. 392–420.
Above three titles also found in Galvão's posthumous book *Encontro de Sociedades: Indios e Brancos no Brasil*. Paz e Terra, Rio de Janeiro, 1979.

GEERTZ, C.
1986 L'art en tant que système culturel. In *Savoir local, savoir global. Les lieux du savoir*, pp. 119–51. PUF, Paris.

GHEERBRANT, A.
1954 *Journey to the Far Amazon*. Simon and Schuster, New York, 1954.
1992 *The Amazon: Past, Present and Future*. Harry N. Abrams Inc., New York.

GILLIN, JOHN
1948 Tribes of the Guianas and the Left Amazon Tributaries. In *Handbook of South American Indians, vol. 3: The Tropical Forest Tribes*, ed. J.H. Steward, pp. 799–860. Bureau of American Ethnology Bulletin 143. Smithsonian Institution, Washington DC.

GNECCO, C.
1995 Praxis cientifica en la periferia: notas para historia social de la arqueologia colombiana. *Revista Española de Antropologia Americana* 25: 9–22.

GNECCO, C. AND S. MORA
1997 Late Pleistocene/early Holocene tropical forest occupations at San Isidro and Pena Roja, Colombia. *Antiquity* 71: 683–90.

GOEJE, C. DE
1908 Verlag der Toemoekoemak-Expeditie. In *Tijdschrift van het Koninklijk Nederlandsch Aardrijkshundig Genootschap* XXV: 945–1169. Leiden.

GOELDI, E.
1900 *Escavações arqueologicas em 1895*. Memorias do Museu Goeldi, Belem.

GOLDMAN, IRVING
1948 Tribes of the Uaupés-Caquetá Region. In *Handbook of South American Indians, vol. 3: The Tropical Forest Tribes*, ed. J.H. Steward. Bureau of American Ethnology Bulletin 143. Smithsonian Institution, Washington DC.
1963 *The Cubeo: Indians of the Northwest Amazon*. University of Illinois Press, Urbana.

GOMES, D.
1999 Reescavando o passado: um estudo do vasilhame cerâmico da Coleção Tapajônica MAE-USP. Master's dissertation, Faculdade de Filosofia, Letras e Ciências Humanas, Universidade de Sao Paulo.

GONÇALVES, M.A.T.
1988 Nomes e cosmos: uma descrição da sociedade e da cosmologia Mura-Praha. Master's dissertation, Programa de Pos-Graduação em Antropologia Social, Museu Nacional, UFRJ.

GOSDEN, C. AND J. HATHER (EDS)
1999 *Prehistory of Food*. Routledge, London.

GOULDING, M., M.L. CARVALHO AND E.G. FERREIRA
1988 *Rio Negro: Rich Life in Poor Water*. SPB Academic Publishing, The Hague.

GOW, PETER
1999 Piro Designs: Paintings and Meaningful Action in an Amazonian Lived World. *Journal of the Royal Anthropological Institute*, n.s. 5: 229–46.

GRENNAND, F. AND P. GRENNAND
1987 La côte d'Amapa, de la bouche de l'Amazone à la baie d'Oyapock, à travers de la tradicion orale Palikur. *Boletim do Museu Paraense Emílio Goeldi: Antropologia* 3: 1–77.

GROSS, D.
1983 Village Movement in Relation to Resources in Amazonia. In *Adaptive Responses of Native Amazonians*, ed. R.B. Hames and W.T. Vickers, pp. 429–49. Academic Press, New York.

GUAPINDAIA, V.
1993 *Fontes históricas e arqueológicas sobre os Tapajó: A coleção Frederico Barata do Museu Paraense Emílio Goeldi*. Master's dissertation, Universidade Federal de Pernambuco.
1999 A Cerâmica Maracá: História e Iconografia. In *Arte da Terra: Resgate da Cultura Material e Iconográfica do Pará*, pp. 43–53. Museu Paraense Emílio Goeldi/SEBRAE, Belém.

GUAPINDAIA, V. AND A. MACHADO
1997 O Potencial Arqueológico da Região do Rio Maracá. Ig. do Lago (AP). In *Boletim do Museu Paraense Emílio Goeldi: Antropologia* 13 (1).

GUAPINDAIA, V., S. MENDONCA AND C. RODRIGUES
2001 A necrópole Maracá e os seus problemas interpretativos em um cemiterio sem enterramentos. *Boletim do Museu Paraense Emílio Goeldi: Antropologia* 17 (1).

GUIDON, N., A-M. PESSIS, F. PARENTI, M. FONTUGUE AND C. GUERIN
1996 Nature and Age of the Deposits in Pedra Furada, Brazil: Reply to Meltzer, Adovasio and Dillehay. *Antiquity* 70: 408–21.

GUSS, D.
1989 *To Weave and Sing: Art, Symbol, and Narrative in the South American Rain Forest*. University of California Press, Berkeley.

Hakluyt, Richard
1904 *The Principal Navigations, Voyages, Traffiques & Discoveries of the English Nation*, vol. 10. Hakluyt Society, London.
Hames, R. and W. Vickers
1983 *Adaptive Responses of Native Amazonians*. Academic Press, New York.
Hammen, T. van der
1981 Appendix IV: The Pleistocene Changes of Vegetation and Climate in the Northern Andes. In S. Hastenrath, *The Glaciation of the Ecuadorian Andes*, pp. 125–45. A.A. Balkema, Rotterdam.
Harcourt, Robert
1926 (1613) *A Relation of a Voyage to Guiana*. Hakluyt Society, London, series II, vol. LX.
Harlow, V.T. (ed.)
1925 *Colonising Expeditions to the West Indies and Guiana, 1623–1667*. Hakluyt Society, London, series II, vol. LVI.
Harris, D.R.
1971 The Ecology of Swidden Cultivation in the Upper Orinoco Rain Forest, Venezuela. *Geographical Review* 61: 475–95.
1989 An Evolutionary Continuum of People-Plant Interaction. In *Foraging and Farming: The Revolution of Plant Explotation*, ed. Harris and G. Hillman, pp. 1–8. One World Archaeology Series. Unwin Hyman, London.
1991 *Settling Down and Breaking Ground: Rethinking The Neolithic Revolution*. Twaalfde Kroon-Voordracht Gehouden Voor De Stitching Nederlands Museum Voor Anthropologie en Praehistorie, University of Amsterdam. Joh. Eschendé en Zonen, Haarlem.
Hartmann, Gunther
1974 Sitzbank und Zigarrenhalter: Zusammenhange mit dem Medizinmannwesen bei einigen Indianergurppe Nordwest-Brasiliens. *Tribunes* 74: 137–56.
Hartt, C.F.
1871 The ancient Indian pottery of Marajó, Brazil. *American Naturalist* 5: 259–71.
1872 On the occurrence of face urns in Brazil. *American Naturalist* 6 (10): 607–10.
1876 Notas sobre algumas tangas de barro cozido dos antigos indígenas da Ilha de Marajó. *Arquivos do Museu Nacional* 1: 21–5.
1885 Contribuição para e ethnologia do valle do Amazonas. *Arquivos do Museu Nacional* VI: 1–174.
1895 Inscripções em rochedos do Brasil. *Revista do Instituto Archeológico e Histórico Pernambucano* 47: 301–29.
1898 Monte Alegre e Ererê. In *Boletim do Museu Paraense de História Natural e Ethnografia* 2 (1–4): 334–5.
1975 *Geology and Physical Geography of Brazil*. Huntington, New York.
Harttman, T.
1975 *A Contribuição da Iconografia para o Conhecimento de Índios Brasileiros do Século XIX*. Coleção Museu Paulista, São Paulo.
Haskins, C.P.
1943 *The Amazon: The Life History of a Great River*. Doubleday Doran, Garden City, New York.
Hastenrath, S.
1981 *The Glaciation of the Ecuadorian Andes*. A.A. Balkema, Rotterdam.
Hawkes, K. and J. O'Connel
1992 Optimal Foraging Models and Subsistence Transitions. *Current Anthropologist* 33: 63–6.
Haynes Jr., C.
1997 Dating a Paleoindian Site in the Amazon in Comparison with Clovis Culture. *Science* 275: 1948.
Hays, K.
1995 When is a symbol archaeologically meaningful? Meaning, function and prehistoric visual arts. In *Archaeological Theory: Who Sets the Agenda?*, ed. N. Yoffe and A. Sherratt, pp. 81–92. Cambridge University Press, Cambridge.
Headland, T.
1987 The Wild Yam Question: How Well Could Independent Hunter-Gatherers Live in a Tropical Rainforest Environment? *Human Ecology* 15 (4): 463–91.
Headland, T. and R. Bailey
1991 Introduction: have hunter-gatherers ever lived in Tropical Rain Forest independently of agriculture? *Human Ecology* 19 (2): 115–22.
Heaton, H.C. (ed.)
1988 (1934) *The Discovery of the Amazon*. AMS Press Inc., New York.
Heckenberger, M.
1996 War and peace in the shadow of empire: sociopolitical change in the Upper Xingu of Southeastern Amazonia, A.D. 1400–2000. Ph.D. thesis, Department of Anthropology, University of Pittsburgh.
1998 Manioc agriculture and Sedentism in Amazonia: The Upper Xigú Example. *Antiquity* 72 (277): 633–48.
1999 The enigma of the great cities: body and state in Amazonia. In *A outra margem do ocidente (Brasil 500 anos: experiência e destino)*, ed. Adauto Novaes. Companhia das letras, São Paulo .
Heckenberger, M., E. Neves and J. Petersen
1998 De onde surgem os modelos? As origens e expansões Tupi na Amazônia Central. *Revista de Antropologia* 41 (1): 69–96.
Heckenberger, M., J. Peterson and E. Neves
1999 Village size and permanence in Amazonia: two archaeological examples from Brasil. *Latin American Antiquity* 10 (4): 535–76.
Helms, Mary W.
1986 Art Styles and Interaction Spheres in Central America and the Caribbean: Polished Black Wood in the Greater Antilles. *Journal of Latin American Lore* 12 (1): 25–44.
Hemming, J.
1978 *The Search for El Dorado*. Michael Joseph Ltd, London.
1995a *Red Gold: The Conquest of the Brazilian Indians*. Papermac, London.
1995b *Amazon Frontier: The Defeat of the Brazilian Indians*. Papermac, London.
Henley, P. and M. Muller
1978 Panare basketry: means of commercial exchange and artistic expression. *Antropológica* 49: 29–130.
Heriarte, M. de
1874 *Descriçam do Estado do Maranham, Pará, Corupa, Rio das Amazonas*. Carlos Gerold, Vienna.
1975 Descrição do Estado do Maranhão, Pará, Corupa e Rio das Amazonas. In *História Geral do Brasil*, ed. F.A. de Varnhagen, 8th edn, Melhoramentos, vol. 3, pp. 171–90. São Paulo.
Herrera, L.
1981 Relaciones entre las ocupaciones prehispánicas y suelos negros en la cuenca del Río Caquetá en Colombia. *Revista CIAF* 6 (1–3): 225–42.
Herrera, L., W. Bray and C. McEwan
1980–81 Datos sobre la arqueología de Araracuara. *Revista Colombiana de Antropología* XXIII: 183–251.
Herrera, L.F., I. Cavelier, C. Rodríguez and S. Mora
1989 Los alfareros de la Amazonia: El caso de Araracuara. In *Memorias del Simposio de Arqueología y Antropología Física. V Congreso Nacional de Antropología, Villa de Leyva*. Serie Memoria y Eventos Cientificos ICFEs, ICAN, Universidad de Los Andes, Bogotá.
1992 The technical transformation of an agricultural system in the Colombian Amazon. *World Archaeology* 24 (1): 98–113.
Hilbert, K. and M. Barreto
1988 *Relatório de viagem do projeto arqueológico de levantamento de sitios pré-cerâmicos no rio Maracá-AP.* Unpublished MS. Museu Paraense Emílio Goeldi, Belém.
Hilbert, P.
1955 A cerâmica arqueológica da região de Oriximiná. *Publicações do Instituto de Antropologica e Etnologia do Pará* 9: 1–76.
1957 Contribução arqueologia do Amapá. *Boletim do Museu Paraense Emílio Goeldi: Antropologia* 1: 1–41. Belém.
1968 *Archäologische Untersuchungen am Mittlern Amazonas*. Dietrich, Berlin.
Hilbert, P.P. and K. Hilbert
1980 Resultados preliminares de pesquisa arqueologica nos rios Nhamunda e Trombetas, Baixo Amazona. *Boletim do Museu Paraense Emílio Goeldi* 75.
Hill, J.
1993 *Keepers of the Sacred Chants: The Poetics of Ritual Power in an Amazonian Society*. University of Arizona Press, Tucson.
Hill, K., H. Kaplan, and M. Hurtado
1987 Foraging Decisions among the Aché Hunter-gatherers: New Data and Implications for Optimal Foraging Models. *Ethnology and Sociobiology* 8: 1–36.
Hiraoka, M.
1985 Floodplain Farming in the Peruvian Amazon. *Geographical Review of Japan* (Ser. B) 1–23.
1986 Zonation of Mestizo Riverine Farming Systems in Northeast Peru. *National Geographic Research* 2: 354–71.
1989 Agricultural Systems of the Floodplains of the Peruvian Amazon. In *Fragile Lands of Latin America: Sustainable Development*, ed. J.O. Browder, pp. 75–101. Westview Press, Boulder, Colorado.
Holliday, V.T. and P. Goldberg
1992 Glossary of Selected Soil Science Terms. In *Soils in Archaeology: Landscape Evolution and Human Occupation*, ed. V.T. Holliday, pp. 247–54. Smithsonian Institution Press, Washington DC.
Holmberg, A.
1969 *Nomads of the Long Bow: The Sirionó of Eastern Bolivia*. The Natural History Press, New York.
Hooghiemstra, H and T. van der Hammen
1998 Neogene and Quaternary Development of the Neotropical Ran Forest: The Forest Refugia Hypothesis, and a Literature Overview. *Earth Science Reviews* 44: 147–83. Elsevier Science Ltd.
Horsh, R.E.
1980 Albuns de Viajantes que estiveram no Brasil na Primeira Metade do Século XIX. *Boletim Bibliográfico Mário de Andrade*, vol.41, III, IV, Jul/Dec. Instituto de Estudos brasileiros, São Paulo.
Hugh-Jones, Christine
1979 *From the Milk River: Spatial and Temporal Processes in Northwest Amazonia*. Cambridge University Press, Cambridge.
Hugh-Jones, S.
1979 *The Palm and the Pleiades: Initiation and Cosmology in Northwest Amazonia*, Cambridge University Press, Cambridge.
1981 Historia del Vaupés. *Maguare* (Revista del Departamento de Antropologia, Universidad Nacional de Colombia) 1: 29–51.
1985 The Maloca: a word in a house. *The Hidden Peoples of the Amazon*, ed. E. Carmichael, S. Hugh-Jones, B. Moses and D. Tayler. British Museum Publications, London.
1993 'Food' and 'Drugs' in Northwest Amazonia. In *Tropical Forests, People and Food: Biocultural Interactions and Applications to Development*. Man and the Biosphere Series, vol. 13, ed. C.M. Hladik, A. Haldik, O.F. Linares, H. Pagezy, A. Semple and M. Hadley, pp. 533–48. United Nations Educational, Scientific and Cultural Organization, Paris; Parthenon Publishing Group, New York.
Hugh-Jones, C. and S. Hugh-Jones
1993 The Storage of Manioc Products and its Symbolic Importance among the Tukanoans. In *Tropical Forests, People and Food: Biocultural Interactions and Applications to Development*. Man and the Biosphere Series Vol. 13, ed. C.M. Hladik, A. Haldik, O.F. Linares, H. Pagezy, A. Semple and M. Hadley, pp. 589–94. United Nations Educational, Scientific and Cultural Organization, Paris; Parthenon Publishing Group, New York.
Humboldt, A. von
1807 *Voyage aux regions equinoxiales du nouveux continent, faits dans le anées 1799 a 1804*. Schoel, Paris.
Illius, B.
1988 Die Grosse Boa. Kunst und Kosmologie der Shipibo-Conibo. In *Die Mythen sehen*, ed. M. Münzel, vol. 2, pp. 705–35. Frankfurt.
Im Thurn, Everard F.
1883 *Among the Indians of Guiana, Being sketches chiefly anthropologic from the interior of British Guiana*. London.
Jackson, Jean
1976 Vaupés Marriage: A Network System in the

Northwest Amazon. In *Regional Systems: vol. II, Social Systems*, ed. C. Smith. Academic Press, New York.
1983 *The Fish People: Linguistic Exogamy and Tukanoan Identity in Northwest Amazonia.* Cambridge University Press, Cambridge.

Johnson, A.
1983 Machiguenga Gardens. In *Adaptive Responses of Native Amazonians*, ed. R.B. Hames and W.T. Vickers, pp. 29–63. Academic Press, New York.

Jordan, Carl
1985 Soils of the Amazon Rainforest. In *Amazonia*, ed. G. Prance and T. Lovejoy, pp. 83–94. Pergamon Press, Oxford.

Junk, Wolfgang and Karin Furch
1985 The Physical and chemical properties of Amazonian waters and their relationships with the biota. In *Amazonia*, ed. G. Prance and T. Lovejoy, pp. 3–17. Pergamon Press, Oxford.

Kaplan, H. and K. Hill
1992 The evolutionary ecology of food acquisition. In *Evolutionary Ecology and Human Behaviour*, ed. E. Smith and B. Winterhalder, pp. 167–202. Aldine de Gruyter, New York.

Kästner, K.
1990 As Coleções Etnográficas do Museu Estatal de Dresden. Unpublished MS.

Katzer, F.
1933 Geologia do Estado do Pará. In *Boletim do Museu Paraense de História Natural e Etnografia* 9.

Kelly, R.
1983 Hunter-Gatherer mobility strategies. *Journal of Anthropological Research* 39 (3): 277–306.

Keller-Leusinger, F.
1874 *The Amazon and Madeira Rivers: Sketches and Description from the Note-Book of an Explorer.* Chapman and Hall, London.

Kensinger, K., Ph. Rabineau, H. Tanner, S. Ferguson and A. Dawson
1975 *The Cashinaua of Eastern Peru*, ed. J.P.Dwyer. Studies in Anthropology and Material Culture 1. The Haffenreffer Museum of Anthropology-Brown University, Rhode Island.

Kern, D.
1988 *Caracterizasão pedólogica de solos com terra preta arqueológica na região de Oriximiná - Para.* M.A. thesis, Universidade Federal do Rio Grande do Sul, Porto Alegre.

Kirch, P.
1991 Chiefship and Competitive Involution: The Marquesas Islands of Eastern Polynesia. In *Chiefdoms: Power, Economy, and Ideology*, ed. T. Earle, pp. 1–15. Cambridge
University Press, Cambridge.

Klinkenberg, Verlyn, Ruth S. Kraemer and Patrick O'Brian
1996 *Histoire Naturelle des Indes: The Drake Manuscript in the Pierpont Morgan Library.* W.W. Norton, New York and London.

Koch-Grünberg, Theodor
1906 Die Makú. *Anthropos* I: 877–906.
1907 *Südamerikanische Felszeichnungen.* Ernst Wasmuth, Berlin.
1909 *Zwei Jahre unter den Indianern: Reisen in Nordwest-Brasilien, 1903/1905.* 2 vols. Wasmuth Verlag, Berlin.
1923 *Vom Roraima zum Orinoco: Ergebnisse einer Reise in Nordbrasilien und Venezuela in der Jahren 1911–1923*, vol. 3. Strecker & Schröder, Stuttgart.
1995 (1909) *Dos años entre los indios. Viajes por el noroeste brasileño*, 2 vols. Universidad Nacional, Santafé de Bogotá.

Komissarov, B.N.
1988 *Expedição Langsdorff ao Brasil, 1821–1829 Iconografia do Arquivo da Academia de Ciências da União Soviética*, vols I, II, III. Alumbramento/Livroarte Editora, Rio de Janeiro.
1994 *Expedição Langsdorff: Acervo e Fontes Históricas*, trans. Marcos Pinto Braga. Editora Unesp, Fundação para o Desenvolvimento da Unesp, DF: Edições Langsdorff, São Paulo, Brasília.

Kozák, V., D. Baxter, L. Williamson and R.L. Carneiro
1979 The Hetá Indians: Fish in a dry pond. *Anthropological Papers of the American Museum of Natural History* 55 (6): 349–434.

Lacerda, J.B.
1881 Crânios de Maracá, Guyana Brasileira. *Achivos do Museu Nacional.* 4: 35–45.

La Condamine, C.M.
1992 *Viagem pelo Amazonas 1735–1745.* Nova Fronteira, Rio de Janeiro, EDUSP, São Paulo.

Lathrap, D., D. Collier and H. Chandra
1977 *Ancient Ecuador: Culture, Clay and Creativity 3000-300 B.C.* Field Museum of Natural History, Chicago.

Lathrap, Donald E., Otto Zerries and Presley Norton
n.d. *Shamans' Stools and the Time Depth of Tropical Forest Culture.*Unpublished MS. University of Illinois at Urbana-Champaign, Illinois.

Lathrap, D.W.
1958 The Cultural Sequence at Yarinacocha. *American Antiquity* 23 (4): 379–88.
1968a The 'Hunting' Economies of the Tropical Forest Zone of South America: an Attempt at Historical Perspective. In *Man the Hunter*, ed. R. Lee and R. DeVore, pp. 23–9. Aldine, Chicago.
1968b Aboriginal Occupation and Changes in River Channel on the Central Ucayali, Peru. *American Antiquity* 33 (1): 62–79.
1970 *The Upper Amazon.* Thames & Hudson, London; Praeger, New York.
1972 Alternative Models of Population Movements in the Tropical Lowlands of South America. *XXXIX Congreso Internacional de Americanistas, Actas y Memorias* 4: 13–23.
1974 The Moist Tropics, the Arid Lands, and the Appearance of Great Art Styles. In *Art and Environment in Native America*, ed. M.E. King and I. Taylor, pp. 115–58. Special Publications, The Museum of Texas Tech University, No. 7. Texas Tech Press, Lubbock.
1976 [1956] Radiation: The Application to Cultural Development of a Model from Biological Evolution. In *The Measures of Man*, ed. E. Giles and E.J. Frielãnder, pp. 494–532. Peabody Museum Press, Cambridge, Massachussets.
1977 Our Father the Cayman, Our Mother the Gourd: Spinden Revisited or a Unitary Model for the Emergence of Agriculture in the New World. In *Origins of Agriculture*, ed. C. A. Reed, pp. 713–51. Mouton Press, The Hague.
1984 Review of 'The Origins of Agriculture: An Evolutionary Perspective'. In *Economic Geography* 60: 339–44.

Lathrap, D.W. and J.R. Oliver
1987 Agüertio: El complejo polícromo más antigüo de América en la confluencia del Apure y Orinoco. *Interciencia* 12 (6): 274–89.

Lathrap, D.W., A. Gebhart-Sayer and A.M. Mester
1985 The Roots of Shipibo Art Style: Three Waves on Imiríacocha, or There Were 'Incas' before the Incas. In *Journal of Latin American Lore* 11 (1): 31–119.

Leach, E.
1976 *Culture and Communication: The Logic by which the Symbols are Connected.* Cambridge University Press, Cambridge.

Lehman, Henry
1958 Un bâton de cerémonie du XVIIe siècle. *Miscellanea Paul Rivet* 2: 297–304.

Léry, Jean de
1980 *Histoire d'un Voyage Faict en la Terre du Brésil* (*c.*1560), ed. Paul Gaffarel, Paris; trans. in Samuel Purchas, *Hakluytus Posthumus*, ed. Hakluyt Society, vol. 16, 518–79.

Lévi-Strauss, C.
1962 *La pensée sauvage.* Paris.
1969 *The Raw and the Cooked.* Jonathan Cape, London.
1971 *L'Homme nu. Mythologiques 4.* Libraire Plon, Paris.
1973 *From Honey to Ashes: Introduction to Science of Mythology 2.* Harper and Row, New York.
1975 *Antropologia Estrutural 2.* Tempo Brasileiro, Rio de Janeiro.
1978 *Mito e significado.* Edições 70, Lisbon.

Lewis, R.
1996 Arte Rupestre de la Cuenca del Rio Mizque. In *Arte Rupestre de los Andes de Bolivia*, pp. 17–21. SIARB (Sociedade de Investigación del Arte Rupestre de Bolivia), La Paz.

Lima Guedes, A.
1897 Relatório sobre uma missão ethnográfica e archeologica nos rios Maracá e Anauera-pucu. *Boletim do Museu Paraense de Historia Natural e Ethnografia* 2: 42–64.
1898 Aureliano Pinto Lima. Relatório sobre uma missão ethnographica e archeológica aos rios Maracá e Anauerá-pucú (Guyana Brazileira), realizada pelo Tenente-Coronel Aureliano Pinto Lima Guedes. Julho a Setembro de 1896. *Boletim do Museu de História Natural e Ethnografia* 2: 46.

Lima, T.S.
1996 O dois e seu múltiplo: reflexões sobre o perspectivismo em uma cosmologia Tupy. *Mana* 2 (2): 21–47.

Linné, S.
1928 Les recherches archéologiques de Nimuendajú au Brésil. *Journal de la Societé des Americanistes de Paris* XX: 71–91.

Llanos Chaparro, J.M.
1997 Artefactos de molienda en la región del medio rio Caquetá en la Amazonia colombiana. *Boletín de Arqueología* 12 (2). Fundación de Investigaciones Arqueológicas Nacionales, Banco de la República, Bogotá.

Lopes de Sousa, Boanerges
1959 *Do Rio Negro ao Orenoco.* Publicação 111. Ministério da Agricultura, Conselho Nacional de Proteção aos Indios, Rio de Janeiro.

Lorimer, Joyce (ed.)
1989 *English and Irish Settlement on the River Amazon 1550–1646.* Hakluyt Society, London.

Loschner, R.
1978 *Deutsche Künstler in Latinamerika. Maler und naturforscher des 19 Jahrunderts illustrieren einen Kontinent.* Exh. cat., Ibero-Amerikanischen Instituts Preussischer Kulturbesitz, Berlin.

Lovén, Sven
1935 *The Origins of the Tainan Culture, West Indies.* Göteborg.

Lowie, R.H.
1948 The Tropical Forests: An Introduction. In *Handbook of South American Indians, vol. 3: The Tropical Forest Tribes*, ed. J.H. Steward, pp. 1–56. Bureau of American Ethnology Bulletin 143. Smithsonian Institution, Washington DC.

Macdonald, R.
1972 The order of things: an analysis of the ceramics from Santarem, Brazil. *Journal of the Steward Anthropological Society* 4(1): 39–55.

McEwan, Colin
1985 Amazonian terra preta soils: Clues to Pre-Columbian population dynamics in the Amazon Basin. *Arqueología Contemporánea* 2 (1): 3–10. Buenos Aires.

McGovern, William Montgomery
1927 *Jungle Paths and Inca Ruins: The Record of an Expedition.* Hutchinson & Co, London.

MacGregor, Arthur
1983 *Tradescant's Rarities: Essays on the Foundation of the Ashmolean Museum, 1683, with a Catalogue of the Surviving Early Collections.* Clarendon Press, Oxford.

MacGregor, Arthur, Melanie Mendonça and Julia White
2000 *Ashmolean Museum Oxford: Manuscript Catalogues of the Early Museum Collections 1683–1886 (Part I).* BAR International Series 907, Oxford.

McKey, D. and S. Beckerman
1993 Chemical Ecology, Plant Evolution and Traditional Manioc Cultivation Systems. In *Tropical Forests, People and Food: Biocultural Interactions and Applications to Development.* Man and the Biosphere Series vol. 13, ed. C.M. Hladik, A. Haldik, O.F. Linares, H. Pagezy, A. Semple and M. Hadley, pp. 83–112. United Nations Educational, Scientific and Cultural Organization, Paris; Parthenon Publishing Group, New York.

McLeod, Malcom
1981 *The Asante*. British Museum Press, London.
Magalhães, M.
1993 *O tempo arqueológico*. Museu Paraense Emílio Goeldi, Belém.
1994 *Arqueologia de Carajás: A presenca Pré-Histórica do Homen na Amazonia*. Companhia Vale do Rio Doce, Rio de Janeiro.
Magalis, J.
1975 *A seriation of some Marajoara painted anthropomorphic urns*. Ph.D. Thesis, University of Illinois at Urbana-Champaign, Illinois.
Malhano, H.
1986 A construção do espaço de morar entre os Karajá do Araguaia: aldeia, casa e cemitério. *Boletim do Museu Nacional* 55.
Markham, C.R. (trans. and ed.)
1859 *Expeditions into the Valley of the Amazons 1539, 1540, 1639*. Burt Franklin Publisher, New York. (Originally published by the Hakluyt Society.)
Marti, B. and M. Hernandez
1988 *El Neolitic Valencià. Art Rupestre i Cultura Material*. Servei d'Investigació Prehistòrica/Diputació de València. València.
Martius, K.C.
1867 *Beiträge zur Ethnographie und Sprachenkunde Amerika's Zumal Brasiliens. Von Dr. Carl Friedrich Phil. v. Martius. I. Zur Ethnographie. Mit ein Kärtchen. (I Zur Sprachenkinde.)* Friedrich Fleisher, Leipzig.
1982 *O Estado do direito entre os Autóctones do Brasil*. Editora Itatiaia, Belo Horizonte; Editora Universidade de São Paulo, São Paulo.
1992 *Frey Apollonio, Um Romance do Brasil*. Editora Brasiliense, São Paulo.
Medina, J.T. (ed.)
1894 *Descubrimiento del Rio de Las Amazonas*. Imprenta de E. Rasco, Bustos Tavera, Núm. I, Sevilla.
Meggers, B.
1947 The Beal-Steere collection of pottery from Marajó Island, Brazil. *Papers of Michigan Academy of Science, Arts and Letters* XXXI: 193–213.
1954 Environmental Limitations on the Development of Culture. *American Anthropologist* 56: 801–24.
1957 Environmental and Culture in the Amazon Basin: An Appraisal of the Theory of Environmental limitations. In *Studies in Human Ecology, Social Science Monograph*, ed. A. Palerm, vol. 3, pp. 71–89. Panamerican Union, Washington DC.
1960 Review of the archaeology of the Lower Tapajós Valley, Brazil. *American Anthropologist* 62: 1104–5.
1971 *Amazonia: Man and Culture in a Counterfeit Paradise*. Aldine, Chicago.
1982 Archaeological and Ethnographic Evidence Compatible with the Model of Forest Fragmentation. In *Biological Diversification in the Tropics*, ed. G.T. Prance, pp. 483–96. Columbia University Press, New York.
1987 The Early History of Man in Amazonia. In *Biogeography and Quaternary History in Tropical America*, ed. T.C. Whitmore and G.T. Prance, pp. 151–212. Clarendon Press, Oxford.
1992a Tropical Forest Environment and Archaeology: A View From Amazonia. In *Environment and Archaeology, New World Conference on Rescue Archaeology, Proceedings*, ed. A.Gus Pantel, K. Schneider and G. Loyala-Black, pp. 208–22. Organization of American States – United States Department of Agriculture – Forest Service Southern Region.
1992b Judging the Future by the Past: The Impact of Environmental Instability on Prehistoric Amazonian Populations In *Indigenous Peoples and the Future of Amazonia: An Ecological Anthropology of an Endangered World*, ed. Leslie Sponsel, pp. 15–43. University of Arizona Press, Tucson.
1995 Amazonia on the Eve of European Contact: Ethnohistorical, Ecological, and Anthropological Perspectives. *Revista de Arqueología Americana* 8: 91–115.
1996 *Amazonia: Man and Culture in a Counterfeit Paradise*. Aldine, Chicago; Smithsonian Institution Press, Washington and London.
Meggers, B. and C. Evans
1954 *Uma Interpretação das Culturas da Ilha de Marajó*. Instituto de Antropologia e Etnologia do Pará, Publ. 7, Belém.
1957 Archaeological investigations at the mouth of the Amazon. *Bureau of American Ethnology Bulletin 167*. Washington DC.
1961 An experimental formulation of horizon styles in the tropical forest of South America. In *Essays in Pre-Columbian Art and Archaeology*, ed. S. Lothrop, pp. 372–88. Harvard University Press, Cambridge, Mass.
1983 Lowland South America and the Antilles. In *Ancient South America*, ed. J. Jennings, pp. 287–335. W.H. Freeman and Company, San Francisco.
Meira, Márcio
1991 Baniwa, Baré, Warekena, Maku, Tukano: os povos indígenas do 'baixo rio Negro' querem ser reconhecidos. *Povos Indígenas no Brasil 1987/88/89/90*, pp. 135–40. CEDI, São Paulo.
Meira, Márcio (ed.)
1993 *Livro das Canoas: documentos para a história indígena da Amazônia*. NHII/USP-FAPESP, São Paulo.
Mejía Gutiérrez, M.
1987 La estrella fluvial del orinoco-Colombia, área de alta diversidad de yuca brava *(Manihot esculenta* Krants). *Colombia Amazónica* 2 (2): 15–22.
1991 *Diversidad de yuca Manihot esculenta Krantz en Colombia: visión geográfico-cultural*. Corporación Colombiana para la Amazonia, Araracuara, Bogotá.
Mello-Leitão, C. (trans.)
1941a *Carvajal, Rojas e Acuña, Decobrimentos do Rio das Amazonas*. Companhia editora Nacional, São Paulo, Rio de Janeiro, Recife, Porto Alegre.
1941b *História das Expedições Científicas no Brasil*. Companhia Editora Nacional, São Paulo.
Meltzer, D.J., J. Adovasio and T. Dillehay
1994 On Pleistocene Human Occupation at Pedra Furada, Brazil. *Antiquity* 68: 694–714.
Mendonça de Souza, A.
1991 *História da Arqueologia Brasileira*. Pesquisas, Antropologia, no. 46. EDUNISUL.
Menéndez, M.
1981/2 Uma contribuição para e etno-história da área Tapajós-Madeira. *Revista do Museu Paulista* 28: 289–388.
Merwe, B. W.
1917 Dutch Guiana Pottery. *The Museum Journal* 8: 180–85. University of Pennsylvania.
Merwe, N. van der, A.C. Roosevelt and J. Vogel
1981 Isotopic Evidence for Prehistoric Subsistence Change at Parmana, Venezuela. *Nature* 292: 536–8.
Métraux, A.
1930 Contribution a l'etude de l'archéologie du cours supérieur et moyen de L'Amazone. *Revista del Museu de La Plata* XXXII: 145–85.
1948a Tribes of eastern Bolivia and the Madeira headwaters. In *Handbook of South American Indians, vol.3: The Tropical Forest Tribes*, ed. J.H. Steward, pp. 381–454. Smithsonian Institution, Washington DC.
1948b Tribes of the Middle and Upper Amazon River. In *Handbook of South American Indians, vol.3: The Tropical Forest Tribes*, ed. J.H. Steward, pp. 687–712. Smithsonian Institution, Washington DC.
Meyer, A.B., and M. Uhle
1885 *Seltene Waffen aus Afrika, Asien und Amerika*. Königliches Ethnographisches Museum zu Dresden 5. Leipzig.
Millar, G.R.
1954 *Orellana Discovers the Amazon*. Heinemann, London.
Miller, E.
1987 Pesquisas arqueológicas paleoindígenas no Brasil occidental. In *Investigaciones Paleoindias al Sur de la Línea Ecuatorial*, ed. L. Núñez and B.J. Meggers, pp. 37–61. Estudios Atacameños no. 8. Universidade del Norte, Instituto de Investigationes Arqueologicas, San Pedro de Atacama
1992a Adapatacao agrícola pre-histórica no alto rio Madeira. In *Prehistoria Sudamericana*, ed. B. Meggers, pp. 219–29. Taraxacum, Washington.
1992b *Arqueologia. Ambiente. Desenvolvimento*. Electronorte/PNUD, Brasilia.
Mondragón, H.
1991 Estudio para el establecimiento de un programa de defensa de la comunidad indigena Nukak. Informe final presentado al programa de Rehabilitación Nacional (PNR) de la Presidencia de la República de Colombia. Unpublished report. Santafé de Bogotá, Colombia.
Monod-Becquelin, A.
1993 O homem apresentado ou as pinturas corporais dos indios Trumais. In *Karl von Steinen: un século de antropologia no Xingu*, ed. V. Coelho, pp. 511–62. FAPESP/EDUSP, São Paulo.
Montardo, D.
1995 Práticas Funerárias das Populações Pré-coloniais e Suas Evidências Arqueológicas – (Reflexões Iniciais). Master's thesis, Pontifícia Universidade Católica do Rio Grande do Sul, Porto Alegre.
Mora, Santiago, Luisa F. Herrera, Inés Cavelier and Camilo Rodríguez
1991 *Cultivars, Anthropic Soils and Stability: a preliminary report of archaeological research in Araracuara, Colombian Amazon*. Latin American Archaeology Reports, no. 2, University of Pittsburgh.
Moraes Filho, M.
1882 *Revista da Exposição Anthropologica Brazileira*. Julho, Rio de Janeiro.
Moran, E.
1990 *A Ecologia Humana das Populações da Amazônia*. Vozes, Petrópolis.
1993a *Ecologia humana de los pueblos de la Amazonia*. Fondo de Cultura Económica, Mexico.
1993b *Through Amazonian Eyes*. University of Iowa Press, Iowa City.
Mordini, A.
1929 I 'courvre sex' precolombiani in argilla dell'isola di Marajo. *Archivio per l'Antropologia e l'Etnologia* 59: 41–53.
1934a Gaetano Osculati e l'archaeologia del medio Rio delle Amazoni. *Archivio per l'Antropologia e l'Etnologia* 64: 185–201.
1934b Les cultures precolombienne du bas Amazone et leur developpement artistique. *Actes du Congres Internationale des Americanistes*, session 24: 61–65. Hamburg.
Moreira, Ismael P. and Angelo B. Moreira
1994 *Mitologia Tariana*. Instituto Brasileiro de Patrimônio Cultural, Manaus.
Moscoso, F.
1986 *Tribu y clases en el Caribe antigüo*. Universidad Central del Este, San Pedro de Macorís, República Dominicana.
Müller, R.
1990 *Os asurini do Xingu. Historia e Arte*. Editora da Unicamp, Campinas.
1992 Mensagens Visuais na Ornamentação Corporal Xavante. In *Grafismo Indígena*, ed. L. Vidal, pp. 133–42. Studio Nobel/EDUSP, São Paulo.
Munn, N.
1973 *Walbiri Iconography: Graphic Representation and Cultural Symbolism in Central Australian Society*. Oxford University Press, London.
Münzel, M.
1969–74 Notas preliminares sobre os Kaboré (Makú entre o rio e negro o Japurá). *Revista de Antropología* 17–20: 137–81.
Myers, T.
1971 Aboriginal Trade Networks in Amazonia. In *Networks of the Past: Regional Intercation in Archaeology*, ed. P.D. Francis, E.J. Kense, and P.G. Duke, pp.19–30. Archaeological Association, University of Calgary.
1973 Toward the Reconstruction of Prehistoric Community Patterns in the Amazon Basin. In *Variation in Anthropology*, ed. D. Lathrap and J. Douglas, pp. 233–52. Urbana Illinois Archaeological Survey.
1992a Agricultural Limitations of the Amazon in Theory and Practice. *World Archaeology*, 24 (1): 82–97.
1992b The Expansion and Collapse of the Omagua. *Journal of the Steward Anthropological Society* 20: 129–52. Department of Anthropology, University of Illinois at Urbana-Champaign, Illinois.

Netto, L.
1885 Investigações sobre a Arqueologia Brasileira. *Archivos do Museu Nacional* 6: 257–554.
Neves, E.
1998a Twenty Years of Amazonian Archaeology in Brazil (1977–1997). *Antiquity* 72 (277): 625–32.
1998b Paths in Dark Waters: Archaeology as Indigenous History in the Upper Rio Negro Basin, Northwest Amazon. Ph.D. Dissertation, Indiana University.
1999a Changing Perspectives in Amazonian Archaeology. *Archaeology in Latin America*, ed. G.G. Politis and B. Alberti, pp. 216–43. Routledge, London.
1999b Complexity or Not in the Amazon? Paper presented at the Fourth World Archaeological Congress, Cape Town.
1999–2000 O Velho e o Novo na Arqueologia Amazônica. *Revista USP, Dossiê antes de Cabral: Arqueologia Brasileira* 44: 86–111.
2000 *Levantamento archaeológico da area de confluência dos rios Negro e Solimões*. Unpublished MS.
Neves, E. and R. Bartone
1998 Preliminary results of an archaeological survey in the central Amazon. Paper presented at the 63rd meeting of the Society for American Archaeology, Seattle.
Nimuendajú, C.
1926 *Die Palikur-Indianer und ihre Nachbarn*. Göteborg.
1927 Streifzug vom Rio Jari zum Maracá. *Petermanns Geographische Mitteillungen* 73: 356–8.
1948 Tribes of the Lower and Middle Xingu. In *Handbook of South American Indians, vol. 3: The Tropical Forest Tribes*, ed. J.H. Steward, pp. 213–43. Bureau of American Ethnology Bulletin 143. Smithsonian Institution, Washington DC.
1949 Os Tapajó. *Boletim do Museu Paraense Emílio Goeldi* 10: 93–106.
1950 Reconhecimento dos rios Içana, Ayarí e Uaupés. *Journal de la Societé des Americanistes*, XXXIX: 125–82.
1952 The Tapajó. In *Kroeber Anthropological Society Papers*, ed. J.H. Rowe, vol. 6, pp. 1–25. Berkeley.
1982 *Mapa Etno-Histórico do Brasil e Regiões Adjacentes*. Instituto Brasileiro de Geografia e Estatísitica, Brasília.
n.d. *A Survey of Amazon Archaeology*, trans. Sig Ryden. Ethnography Museum of Goteborg.
Nobre, A.
1973 Mandioca var. amarela de Amazônia. *Boletim Técnico do Centro de Tecnologia Agricola e Alimentario* (5): 9–13.
Nordenskiöld, E.
1930 *Ars Americana, vol. l: L' Archéologie du Basin de L'Amazone*. Les Éditions G. Van Oest, Paris.
n.d. *The Cultural History of the South American Indians*, ed. C. Lindberg. MAS Press Inc., New York.
Oberacker, C. H.
1968 *Viajantes Naturalistas e Artistas Estrangeiros no Reino e Primeiro Império do Brasil. Revista Humboldt*, vols VIII, XVIII.
Oliver, J.R.
1989 The Archaeological, linguistic and ethnohistorical evidence for the expansion of Arawakan into Northwestern Venezuela and Northeastern Colombia. Unpublished Ph.D. dissertation, University of Illinois at Urbana-Champaign, Illinois.
1991 Donald W. Lathrap: Approaches and Contributions in New World Archaeology. In *Antropológica* (75–6): 5–60. Fundación de Ciencias Naturales La Salle, Caracas.
1998 *El Centro Ceremonial de Caguana, Puerto Rico: Simbolismo iconográfico, cosmovisión y el poderío caciquil taíno de Borínquen*. BAR International Series no. 727. Archaeopress, Oxford England.
O'Neale, L.
1986 (1949) Cestaria. In *Suma Etnológica Brasileira V:2, Tecnologia Indígena*, ed. B. Ribeiro, pp. 323–50.Vozes, Petrópolis.
Ortigüera, Toribio de
1581 *Jornada del Río Marañón*. In various editions including *Biblioteca de Autores Españoles desde la Formación del Lenguaje hasta Nuestros Dias. Continuación*, ed. M. Meléndez Pelayo, vol. 15, Madrid (1905–); and trans. in *Gaspar de Carvajal, The Discovery of the Amazon River*, ed. Bertram T. Lee and H.C. Heaton, New York (1934).
Ostapkowicz, Joanna
1998 Taíno Wooden Sculpture; Rulership and the visual arts in 12-16th century West Indies. Unpublished MS, Sainsbury Research Unit for the the Arts of Africa, Oceania and the Americas.
Oyuela Caicedo, A.
1995 Rocks versus Clay: The Evolution of Pottery Technology in the Case of San Jacinto-1, Colombia. In *The Emergence of Pottery: Technology and Innovation in Ancient Societies*, ed. W.K. Barnet and J. Hoopes, pp. 133–45. Smithsonian Institution Press, Washington DC.
Pabst, Erich
1991 Critérios de distinção entre terra preta e latossolo na região de Belterra e os seus significados para a discussão pedogenética. In *Boletim do Museu Paraense Emílio Goeldi: Antropologia*, n.s. 7 (1): 5–19.
1993 Terra Preta: Ein Beitrag Zur Genese-diskussion auf der Basis von Geländearbeiten bei Tupi-Völkern Amazoniens. Ph.D. Dissertation, Gesämthochschule Universität, Kassel.
Pagden, A.
1993 *European Encounters with the New World: From Renaissance to Romanticism*. Yale University Press, New Haven.
Palacios, P.
1989 Algunos aspectos sobre la utilización del bosque amazónico (notas preliminares). II Simposio Colombiano de Etnobotánica, Popayán.
Palmatary, H.
1939 Tapajó pottery. *Etnologiska Studier* 8: 1–136.
1950 The pottery of Marajo Island, Brazil. *Transactions of the American Philosophical Society* 39 (3): 259–358.
1960 he archaeology of the Lower Tapajós Valley – Brazil. *Transactions of the American Philosophical Society*, n.s. 50: 1–243.
1965 *The River of the Amazons: Its Discovery and Early Exploration 1500–1743*. Carlton Press, New York.
Parenti, F., M. Fontugue and C. Guerin
1996 Pedra Furada in Brazil and Its 'Presumed' Evidence: Limitations and Potential of the Available Data. *Antiquity* 70: 416–21.
Pärssinen, M.H., J.S. Salo, and M.E. Räsänen
1996 River Floodplain Relocations and the Abandonment of Aborigine Settlements in the Upper Amazon Basin: A Historicasl Case Study of San Miguel de Cunibos at the Middle Ucayali River. *Geoarchaeology: An International Journal* 11 (4): 345–59.
Pearsall, D.M.
1995 Domestication and Agriculture in the New World Tropics. In *Last Hunters-First Farmers: New Perspectives on the Prehistoric Transition to Agriculture*, ed. T.D. Price and A.B. Gebauer, pp. 157–92. School of American Research Press, Santa Fé, New Mexico.
Pereira, E.
1990 As gravuras e pinturas rupestres no Pará. Maranhão e Tocantins – Estado atual do conhecimento e perspectivas. Master's thesis, Universidade Federal de Pernambuco.
1992a Análise preliminar das pinturas rupestres de Monte Alegre (PA). *Boletim do Museu Paraense Emílio Goeldi: Antropologia* 8 (1): 5–24.
1992b Arte rupestre na Amazonia – notas sobre um manuscrito. *Revista CLIO: Arqueológica* 1 (8): 183–90.
1994 Registros rupestres do noroeste do Pará. *Revista de Arqueologia* 8 (1): 321–35.
1996 Las pinturas y los grabados rupestres del noroeste de Pará – Amazonia – Brasil. Doctoral thesis, Departamento de Arqueologia e Pré-história, Universidade de Valencia, Valencia.
1997 As pinturas e gravuras rupestres no noroeste do Pará, Amazonia, Brasil. *Revista CLIO* 1 (12): 87–98.
Pereira Jr., J.
1952 O Segredo das Itacoatiaras. *Revista do Instituto Histórico e Geográfico de São Paulo* 48: 189–212.
1967 *Introdução ao Estudo da Arqueologia Brasileira*. Bentivegna, São Paulo.
Pessis, A.M. and Niède Guidon
1992 Registros rupestres e caracterização das etnias pré-históricas. In *Grafismo indígena: Estudos de Antropologia Estética*, ed. L. Vidal, pp. 19–33. Studio Nobel, São Paulo.
Petersen, J.
1996 Archaeology of Trants, Montserrat. Part 3: Chronological and Settlement Data. *Annals of Carnegie Museum* 65(4): 323–61.
Petersen, J.B., M.J. Heckenberger, E.G. Neves, R.N. Bartone and J.G. Crock
2000 Collapse among Amerindian Complex Societies in Amazonia and the Caribbean: Endogenous and/or Exogenous Factors? Paper presented at the 65th annual meeting of the Society for American Archaeology, Philadelphia.
Pierce, C.
1977 *Semiótica*. Editora Perspectiva, São Paulo.
Pimentel, J.
1998 Estudo das representações antropomórficas na cerâmica Marajoara (apliques, apêndices e estatuetas). Relatório final de pesquisa, Programa PIBIC/CNPQ. Belém, MPEG, inédito.
Pineda Camacho, Roberto
1994 Los bancos taumaturgos. *Boletim Museo del Oro* 36: 3–39.
Pinto, Augusto Octaviano
1930 *Hidrografia da Bacia do Amazonas*, vol. 1, pp. 257–61, 309–10, 321–2. Imprensa Nacional, Rio de Janeiro.
Piperno, D.R.
1999 Report on Phytoliths from the Site of Peña Roja, Western Amazon Basin. Unpublished MS submitted to the Eriagie Foundation, Bogotá.
Piperno, D.R. and D.M. Pearsall
1998 *The Origin of Agriculture in the Lowland Neotropics*. Academic Press, New York-London.
Pires, João Murça and Ghillean Prance
1985 The Vegetation Types of the Brazilan Amazon. In: *Amazonia*, ed. Ghillean Prance and Thomas Lovejoy, pp. 109–45. Pergamon Press, Oxford.
Politis, G.
1992 La Arquitectura del Nomadismo en la Amazonia Colombiana. *Proa* 412: 11–20.
1995 *Mundo de los Nukak, Amazonia Colombiana*. Fondo de Promoción de la Cultura, Bogotá.
1996a Moving to produce: Nukak mobility and settlement patterns in Amazonia. *World Archaeology* 27 (3): 492–511.
1996b *Nukak*. Instituto Amazónico de Investigaciones Cientificas SINCHI, Santafé, Bogotá.
1999 Plant exploitation among the Nukak hunter-gatherers of Amazonia: between ecology and ideology. In *The Prehistory of Food*, ed. C. Gosden and J. Hather, pp. 99–126. Routledge, London.
Politis, G. and J. Rodriguez
1994 Algunos aspectos de la subsistencia de los Nukak de la Amazonia colombiana. *Colombia Amazónica* 7 (1–2): 169–207.
Politis, G. and N. Saunders
In press. Archaeological correlates of ideological activity: food taboos and spirit-animals in an Amazonian hunter-gatherer society. In *Consuming Passions, Archaeological Studies of Material Culture*, ed. P. Miracle. McDonald Institute, Cambridge.
Porro, A.
1987 O antigo comércio indígena na Amazônia. *D.O. Leitura* 5 (6): 2–3.
1992 História Indígena do Alto e Médio Amazonas, Séculos XVI a XVIII. In *História dos Índios do Brasil*, ed. Manuela Carneiro da Cunha. Companhia das Letras/FAPESP, São Paulo.
1993 *As Crônicas do Rio Amazonas: notas etnohistóricas sobre as populações indígenas da Amazônia*, Vozes, Petrópolis.
1994 Social organization and political power on the Amazon floodplain: The ethnohistorical sources. In *Amazonian Indians from Prehistory to the Present: Anthropological Perspectives*, ed. A.C. Roosevelt, pp. 79–94. Arizona University Press, Tucson.
1996 *O povo das águas: ensaios de etno-história amazônica*. Vozes/EDUSP, Petrópolis.

Posey, D.
1982 Keepers of the Forest. *Garden* 6 (1): 18–24.
1994 Environmental and Social Implications of Pre- and Postcontact Situations on Brazilian Highlands: The Kayapó and a New Amazonian Synthesis. In *Amazonian Indians from Prehistory to the Present: Anthropological Perspectives*, ed. A.C. Roosevelt, pp. 271–86. Arizona University Press, Tucson.
Posey, D. and W. Balée (eds)
1989 Resource Management in Amazonia: Indigenous and Folk Strategies. In *Advances in Economic Botany*, no. 7. New York Botanical Garden, Bronx, N.Y.
Pozzobon, J.
1983 Isolamento e Endogamia. Observações sobre a organização social dos Indios Makú. Master's thesis, Universidade Federal do Rio Grande do Sul.
1992 Perenté et démographie chez les indiens Maku. Doctoral thesis, Université Paris VII.
Prance, G., W. Rodriguez and M. Freitas da Silva
1976 Inventário Forestal de um hectare de mata de terra firma km 30 da Estrada Manaus-Itacoatiara. *Acta Amazonica* 6 (1): 9–35.
Projeto Radam Brasil
1974 *Folha AS-22-Belém. Levantamento de Recursos Naturais 5*. Departamento Nacional Pesquisas Minerais, Rio de Janeiro.
Prous, A.
1991 *Arqueologia brasileira*. Editora da Universidade de Brasilia, Brasilia.
1994 L'Art rupestre du Brasil. Préhistoire Ariégeoise. *Bulletin de la Société Prehistorique Ariège-Pyrénées* 49: 77–144.
Raby, P.
2000 *Bright Paradise: Victorian Scientific Travellers*. Chatto and Windus, London.
Ralegh, Sir Walter
1997 (1596) *The Discoverie of the Large, Rich and Bewtiful Empyre of Guiana*, ed. Neil L. Whitehead. University of Oklahoma, Norman.
Ramos, A., P. Silverwood-Cope and A. Oliveira
1980 Patrões e clientes: relações intertribais no alto rio Negro. In *Hierarquia e Simbiose*, ed. A. Ramos, pp. 135–82. HUCITEC, São Paulo.
Rauschert, M.
1959 Felszeichnungen am unteren Erepecuru. *Zeitschrift für Ethnologie* 84 (1): 110–23.
Rauschert, Ulrike
Armas de Guerra e Padrões Guerreiros das Tribos Karib. *Revista do Museu Paulista*, n.s. 28: 423–34.
Reanier, R.
1997 Dating a Paleoindian Site in the Amazon in Comparison with Clovis Culture. *Science* 275: 1948–9.
Reichel-Dolmatoff, G.
1960 Notas etnográficas sobre los indios del Chocó. *Revista Colombiana de Antropología* IX: 75–158.
1961 Anthropomorphic figurines from Colombia, their magic and art. In *Essays in Precolumbian Art and Archaeology*, ed. S.K. Lothrop, pp. 229–41. Harvard University Press, Cambridge, Mass..
1967 Rock paintings of the Vuapés: An Essay of interpretation. *Folklore Americas* XXVII (2): 107–13.
1968 *Desana: simbolismo de los Indios del Vuapés*. Universidade de los Andes, Bogotá.
1971 *Amazonian Cosmos: the Sexual and Religious Symbolism of the Tukano Indians*. The University of Chicago Press, Chicago and London.
1975 *The Shaman and the Jaguar: A Study of Narcotic Drugs among the Indians of Colombia*. Temple University Press, Philadelphia.
1976a Cosmology as ecological analysis: A view from the rainforest. *Man*, n.s. II (3): 307–18.
1976b O contexto cultural de um alucinógeno aborígene – *Banisteriopsis Caapi*. In *Os alucinógenos e o Mundo Simbólico: o uso dos alucinógenos entre os índios da América do Sul* pp. 59–103. EPU: Editora da Universidade de São Paulo, São Paulo.
1978a *Beyond the Milky Way: Hallucinatory Imagery of the Tukano Indians*. UCLA Latin American Center Publications, Los Angeles.
1978b The loom of life: Akogi principle of integration. *Journal of Latin American Lore* 4 (1): 5–27.
1985 *Basketry as Metaphor: Arts and Crafts of the Desana Indians of the Northwest Amazon*. Occasional Papers of the Museum of Cultural History 5. University of California, Los Angeles.
1986 A Hunter's Tale from the Colombian Northwest Amazon. *Journal of Latin American Lore* (1): 65–74.
1988 *Orfebrería y chamanismo: Un estudio iconográfico del Museo del Oro*. Medellín.
1989 Biological and social aspects of the Yurupari complex of the Colombian Vaupés territory. *Journal of Latin American Lore* 15 (1): 95–135.
1990 Algunos conceptos de los indios Desana del Vaupés sobre manejo ecológico. In *La Selva Humanizada; Ecología Alternativa en le trópico húmedo Colombiano*, ed. F. Corréa, pp. 35–41. Instituto Colombiano de Antropologia, Fondo Editorial CEREC, Bogotá.
1996a *The Forest Within: The World-View of the Tukano Amazonian Indians*. Themis Books, London.
1996b *Yuruparí: Studies of an Amazonian Foundation Myth*. Harvard University Press, Cambridge, Mass.
1997 *Rainforest Shamans: Essays on the Tukano Indians of the Northwest Amazon*. Themis Books, London.
Reichel-Dolmatoff, G. and A. Dussan de Reichel
1956 Momíl: Excavaciones en el Sinú. *Revista Colombiana de Antropología* V: 109–334.
Reid, H.
1979 Some aspects of movement, growth and change among the Hupdu Makú Indians of Brazil. Ph.D. dissertation, Department of Social Anthropology, Cambridge University, Cambridge.
Reina, L.
1990 Actividades relacionadas con los Nukak. *Mopa-Mopa* 5: 17–25. Instituto Andino de Artes.
1992 Los Nukak: caceria, recolección y nomadismo en la Amazonía. In *Diversidad es riqueza*, pp. 62–4. Instituto Colombiano de Antropología, Bogotá.
Renfrew, C.
1986 Introduction: peer polity interaction and socio-political change. In *Peer-Polity Interaction and Socio-Political Change*, ed. C. Renfrew and J. Cherry, Cambridge University Press, Cambridge.
Ribeiro, B.
1978 O artesanato indigena como bem comerciável. *Ensaios de Opinião* 5: 68–77.
1980 *A civilização da palha. A arte do trançado dos indios do Brasil*. Doctoral thesis, Faculdade de Filosofia, Letras e Ciências Humanas, Universidade de São Paulo.
1981 O artesanato cesteiro como objeto de comércio entre os indios do alto rio Negro, Amazonas. *America Indigena* 61 (2): 289–310.
1983 Artesanato indigena, para que, para quem? In *O artesão tradicional e seu papel na sociedade contemporânea*, pp. 11–48. FUNARTE/INF, Rio de Janeiro.
1985 *A arte do trançado dos indios do Brasil. Um estudo taxonômico*. Museu Paraense Emílio Goeldi, Belém; Instituto Nacional de Folclore, Rio de Janeiro.
1986 A arte de trançar: dois macroestilos, dois modos de vida. In *Suma Etnológica Brasileira V.2: Tecnologia Indígena*, ed. B. Ribeiro, pp. 283–322. Vozes, Petrópolis.
1987 Arte India. In *Suma Etnológica Brasileira, V.3*, ed. B. Ribeiro. Vozes, Petrópolis.
1988 *Dicionário do Artesanato Indígena*. Itatiaia/EDUSP, Belo Horizonte.
1989 *Arte Indígena; linguagem visual*. Itatiaia/EDUSP, Belo Horizonte.
1992 A mitologia pictórica dos Desana. In *Grafismo Indígena*, ed. L. Vidal, pp. 35–52, Studio Nobel/EDUSP, São Paulo.
1995 *Os Índios das Águas Pretas. Modo de produção e equipamento produtivo*. EDUSP/Companhia das Letras, São Paulo.
Ribeiro, B. and L. van Velthem
1992 Coleções etnográficas. Documentos materiais para a história indigena e do indigenismo. In *História dos Indios no Brasil*, ed. M. Carneiro da Cunha, pp. 103–12. FAPESP/SMC/Companhia das Letras, São Paulo.
Ribeiro, D. and C. Neto
1992 *A Fundação do Brasil Testemunhos 1500–1700*. Vozes, Petrópolis.
Ribeiro, P.
1999 Caçadores-coletores de Roraima. In *Pré-História da Terra Brasilis*, ed. C. Tenorio, pp. 135–45. UFRJ, Rio de Janeiro.
Ribeiro, P., V. Calandrini and A. Machado
1987 Projeto Arqueológico de Salvamento na região de Boa Vista, Território Federal de Roraima, Brasil – primera etapa de campo (1985). *Revista do CEPA* 14 (17): 1–81.
Ribeiro, P., C. Ribeiro and F. Pinto
1989 Levantamentos arqueológicos no Território Federal de Roraima – 3ª etapa de campo: 1987. *Revista do CEPA* 16 (19): 5–48.
Ribeiro, P., C. Ribeiro, V. Guapindaia and F.P.L. Félix
1986 Projeto Arqueológico de Salvamento na região de Boa Vista, Território Federal de Roraima, Brasil – segunda etapa de campo (1985) – Nota prévia. *Revista do CEPA* 13 (16): 5–48.
Ribeiro, P., C. Ribeiro, V. Guapindaia and A. Machado
1996 Pitture rupestri nel Territorio di Roraima – Brasile. *Bolletino del Centro Camuno di Studi Preistorici* 2: 151–7.
Ricardo, B.
2000 *Arte Baniwa. Cestaria de arumã*. ISA/FOIRN, São Paulo.
Rindos, D.
1980 Symbiosis, Instability, and the Origins and Spread of Agriculture: A New Model. *Current Anthropology* 21 (6): 751–2.
1984 *The Origins of Agriculture: An Evolutionary Perspective*. Academic Press, New York-London.
1989 Darwinism and its Role in the Explanation of Domstication. In *Foraging and Farming: The Revolution of Plant Explotation*, ed. D.R. Harris and G. Hillman, pp. 27–41. One World Archaeology Series. Unwin Hyman, Lodon.
Rival, L.
1998 Domestication as a historical and symbolic process: wild gardens and cultivated forests in the Ecuadorian Amazon. In Avances in historical ecology, ed. W. Balée, pp.232–250. Columbia University Press, New York.
Rivet, P. and C. Tastevin
1920 Affinités du Makú et du Puinave. *Journal de la Société des Américanistes* 12: 69–82.
Rivière, Peter
1984 *Individual and Society in Guiana: A Comparative Study of Amerindian Social Organization*. Cambridge University Press, Cambridge.
Rodrigues Ferreira, A.
1786 Memória sobre a Louça que as Índias do Estado. Códice Biblioteca Nacional 21.127.
1787a Memória sobre os Gentios Jurupixunas, os Quaes se Distinguem dos Outros em Serem Mascarados. Códice Biblioteca nacional 21.1.40.
1787b Memória sobre as Máscaras e Farças que Fazem para os seus Bailes os Gentios Jurupixunas. Códice Biblioteca Nacional 21.1.1.19.
1787c Memória sobre a Figura que Tem os Gentios Mahuas. Códice Biblioteca Nacional 21.1.42.
1787d Memória sobre o Gentio Mura. Código Biblioteca Nacional 21.11.17.
1788 Memória sobre o Gentio Miranha que Habita á Margem Setentrional do Rio Solimões. Códice Biblioteca Nacional 21.2.4.
1933a Memória sobre as Cuias que Fazem as Índias de Monte Alegre, e de Santarém. *Revista Nacional de Educação* I (6): 58–63.
1933b Memória sobre os Instrumentos de que usa o Gentio Mague para Tomar o Paricá. *Revista nacional de Educação* I (8): 74–6.
1970 *Viagem Filosófica às Capitanias do Grão Pará, Rio Negro, Mato Grosso e Cuiabá*. Gráficos Brunner, São Paulo.
1971 *Viagem Filosófica pelas Capitanias do Grão Pará, Rio Negro, Mato Grosso, e Cuiabá 1783–1792*, 2 vols. Conselho Federal de Cultura. Rio de Janeiro.
1974 *Viagem Filosófica pelas Capitanias do grão Pará, Rio Negro, Mato Grosso, e Cuiabá 1783–1792*. Memórias, Antropologia. Rio de Janeiro.
Rodriguez Lamus, Luis
1958 La Arquitectura de los Tukano. *Revista Colombiana de Antropología* VIII: 251–69.

ROE, PETER G.
1995 *Arts of the Amazon*, ed. Barbara Braun. Thames & Hudson, London.
ROJAS, A. DE
1941 Descobrimento do Rio das Amazonas e suas dilatadas provincias. In *Gaspar de Carvajal, Alonso de Rojas e Cristobal de Acuña: Descobrimentos do Rio das Amazonas*, ed. and trans. C. Melo-Leitão, pp. 81–124. Companhia Editora Nacional, São Paulo.
ROOSEVELT, A.C.
1980 *Parmana: Prehistoric Maize and Manioc Subsistence along the Amazon and the Orinoco*. Academic Press, New York.
1987 Chiefdoms in the Amazon and Orinoco. In *Chiefdoms in the Americas*, ed. R. Drennan and C. Uribe, pp. 153–85. University Presses of America, Lanham.
1988 Interpreting certain female images in prehistoric art. In *The Role of Gender in Precolumbian Art and Architecture*, ed. Virginia E. Miller, pp. 1–34. University Presses of America, Lanham.
1989 Resource management in Amazonia before the Conquest. *Advances in Economic Botany* 7: 30–62.
1991 *Moundbuilder of the Amazon: Geophysical Archaeology on Marajó Island, Brazil*. Academic Press, San Diego, CA.
1992 Arqueologia Amazônica. In *História dos Índios no Brasil*, ed. M. Carneiro da Cunha, pp. 53–86. FAPESP/Companhia das Letras/SMC, São Paulo.
1993 The rise and fall of the Amazonian chiefdoms. *L'Homme*, 126–8, XXXIII (2–4): 255–82.
1994 Amazonian Anthropology: Strategy for a new synthesis. In *Amazonian Indians from Prehistory to the Present: Anthropological Perspectives*, ed. A.C. Roosevelt, pp. 1–29. The University of Arizona Press.
1995 Early pottery in the Amazon: twenty years of scholarly obscurity. In *The Emergence of Pottery: Technology and Innovation in Ancient Societies*, ed. W.K. Barnet and J. Hoopes, pp. 115–131. Smithsonian Institution Press, Washington DC.
1996 The origins of complex societies in Amazonia. In *The Prehistory of the Americas*, ed. T. Hester, L. Laurencich-Minelli and S. Salvatori, pp. 27–31. International Union of Prehistoric and Protohistoric Sciences, A.B.C.O. Edizioni, Forli.
1997a The Excavations at Corozal, Venezuela: Stratigraphy and Ceramic Seriation. In *Yale University Publications in Anthropology*, no. 83. Department of Anthropology and the Peabody Museum, Yale University, New Haven.
1997b The Demise of the Alaka Initial ceramic Phase has been Greatly Exaggerated: A Response to D. Williams. *American Antiquity* 62 (1): 353–64.
1998 Ancient and Modern Hunter-Gatherers of Lowland South America: An Evolutionary Perspective. In *Advances in Historical Ecology*, ed. W. Balé, pp. 191–212. Columbia University Press, New York.
1999a The Maritime, Highland, Forest Dynamic and the Origins of Complex Culture. In *The Cambridge History of the Native Peoples of the Americas, Vol. III: South America, Part 1*, ed. F. Salomon and S.B. Schwartz, pp. 264–349. Cambridge University Press, New York-Cambridge.
1999b The Development of Prehistoric Complex Societies: Amazonia, A Tropical Forest. In *Complex Polities in the Ancient Tropical World*, ed. E.A. Bacus and L.J. Lucero, pp. 13–33. Archeological Papers of the American Anthropological Association 9. Washington DC.
ROOSEVELT, A.C. (ED.)
1994 *Amazonian Indians from Prehistory to the Present: Anthropological Perspectives*. Arizona University Press, Tucson.
ROOSEVELT, A., R.A. HOUSLEY, M. IMAZIO DA SILVEIRA, S. MARANCA AND R. JOHNSON
1991 Eighth Millennium Pottery from a Prehistoric Shell Midden in the Brazilian Amazon. *Science* 254: 1621–4.
ROOSEVELT, A., M. LIMA DA COSTA, L.J. BROWN, J.E. DOUGLAS, M. O'DONNELL, E. QUINN, J. KEMP, C. LOPES MACHADO, M. IMAZIO DA SILVEIRA, J. FEATHERS AND A. HENDERSON
1997 Response, Dating a Paleoindian Site in the Amazon in Comparison with Clovis Culture. *Science* 275: 1950–52.
ROOSEVELT, A., M. LIMA DA COSTA, C. LOPES MACHADO, M. MICHAB, N. MERCIER, H. VALLADAS, J. FEATHERS, W. BARNETT, M. IMAZIO DA SILVEIRA, A. HENDERSON, J. SLIVA, B. CHERNOFF, D.S. REESE, J.A. HOLMAN, N. TOTH AND K. SCHICK
1996 Paleoindian Cave Dwellers in the Amazon: The Peopling of the Americas. *Science*, 272: 373–84.
ROSS, E. B.
1978 Food Taboos, Diet and Hunting Strategy: The Adaptation to Animals in Amazon Cultural Ecology. *Current Anthropology* 19 (1): 1–36.
1980 Reply. *Current Anthropology* 21 (4): 544–6.
ROSTAIN, STEPHEN
1991 *Les Champs Surleves Amerindiens de la Guyane*. Centre ORSTOM de Cayenne, Cayenne.
1994 L'Occupation Amérindienne Ancienne du Littoral de Guyana. Collection 'Travaux et Documents Microédités', ORSTROM, Paris; Doctoral thesis, Université de Paris I/Sorbonne.
ROTH, WALTER E.
1924 An Introduction: Study of Arts, Crafts and Customs of the Guiana Indians. In *Bureau of American Ethnology Thirty-Eighth Annual Report (1916–1917)*. Smithsonian Institution, Washington DC.
1929 *Additional Studies of the Arts, Crafts, and Customs of the Guiana Indians*. Bureau of American Ethnology Bulletin 91. Smithsonian Institution Washington.
ROUSE, I.
1949 Petroglyphs. *Bulletin of Bureau of American Ethnology* 5: 493–502. Washington.
1978 The La Gruta Sequence and Its Implications. In *Unidad y Variedad: Ensayos en Homenaje a José M. Cruxent*, ed. E. Wagner and A. Zucchi, pp. 203–29. Centro de Estudios Avanzados-Instituto Venezolano de Investigaciones Cientificas, Caracas.
1992 *The Taínos: The Rise and Fall of the People Who Greeted Columbus*. Yale University Press, New Haven-London.
SAGE, R.F.
1995 Was Low Atmospheric CO_2 During the Pleistocene a Limiting Factor for the Origin of Agriculture? *Global Change Biology* 1: 93–106.
SAINSBURY, W.N. (ED.)
1889 Calendar of State Papers, Colonial Series, America and West Indies, Vol.7, 1669–1674. London.
SALAZAR, E.
1993 Traces of the Past: Archaeology and Ethnohistory of Ecuador's Amazon Region. In *Amazon Worlds: Peoples and Cultures of Ecuador's Amazon Region*, ed. N. Paymal and C. Sosa, pp. 18–43. Sinchi Sacha Foundation, Quito.
SALO, J., R. KALLIOLA, I. HÄKINEN, Y. MÄKINEN, P. NIEMALÄ, M. PUHAKKA AND P.D. COLEY
1986 River Dynamics and the Diversity of Amazonian Lowland Forest. *Nature* 322: 254–8.
SAMPAIO, T.
1955 *Os Naturalistas Viajantes e a Etnografia Indígena*. Progresso, Salvador.
n.d. Os Naturalistas Viajantes dos séculos XVII e XIX e o Progresso da Ethnographia Indígena no Brasil. *Anais da Revista do Instituto Histórico Geográfico Brasileiro, Fascículo 24 da série publicada com as comunicações ao I Congresso de História Nacional, Rio de Janeiro*, 2: 543–94.
SAMPAIO, T. AND C. TOSCHAUER
1955 *Os naturalistas-viajantes dos séculos XVIII e XIX e a etnografia indigena*. Coleção de Estudos Brasileiros, série Cruzeiro, vol. 8.
SANDERS, W.T.
1992 The Population of the Central Mexican Symbiotic Region, the Basin of Mexico and the Teotihuacan Valley in the Sixteenth Century. In *The Native Population of the Americas in 1492*, 2nd edn, ed. W.M. Denevan, pp. 85–155. University of Wisconsin Press, Madison.
SANDERS, W.T., J.R. PARSONS, AND R.S. SANTLEY
1979 *The Basin of Mexico: Ecological Processes in the Evolution of a Civilization*. Academic Press, New York.
SANDOR, J.A.
1992 Long-term Effects of Prehistoric Agriculture on Soils: Examples from New Mexico and Peru. In *Soils in Archaeology: Landscape Evolution and Human Occupation*, ed. V.T.Holliday, pp. 217–45. Smithsonian Institution Press, Washington DC.
SAUER, C.O.
1952 *Agricultural Origins and Dispersals*. American Geographical Society, New York.
SAVILLE, MARSHALL H.
1910 *The Antiquities of Manabí Ecuador. Final Report*. Heye Foundation Contributions to South American Archaeology, vol. 2. New York.
1921 *Bladed Warclubs from British Guiana. Indian Notes and Monographs*. Museum of the American Indian, Heye Foundation, New York.
SCHAAN, D.P.
1996 *A linguagem iconográfica da cerâmica Marajoara*. Master's thesis, Pontifícia Universidade Católica, Porto Alegre.
1997 *A linguagem icongráfica da cerâmica Marajoara. Um estudo da arte pré-histórica na Ilha de Marajó (400–1300* AD*)*. Edipucrs, Porto Alegre.
1999a Cultura Marajoara: história e iconografia (Marajoara Culture: history and iconography). In *Arte da Terra, vol. I – Arte rupestre e Cerâmica*, pp. 22–33. Sebrae/Museu Paraense Emílio Goeldi, Belém.
1999b *Hidrovia do Marajó. Programa de Salvamento Arqueológico nas Áreas de Rectificação dos Rios Anajás e Atuá*. Unpublished fieldwork reports. Museu Paraense Emílio Goeldi, Belém.
2000a Recent investigations on Marajoara Culture, Marajó Island, Brazil. *Antiquity* 74: 285, 469–70.
2000b Os Dados Inéditos do Projeto Marajó (1962–1965). *Revista do Museu de Arqueologia e Etnologia da USP*. USP, São Paulo.
2000c Anajás Project – July 2000 fieldwork stage. Unpublished fieldwork report. Earthwatch Institute/Museu Paraense Emílio Goeldi, Belém.
SCHMELTZ, J.D.E.
1897 Geräthe der Caraiben von Surinam (Niederländisch Guyana). *Internationales Archiv für Ethnographie* X: 60–68. Leiden.
SCHMITZ, P.
1897 Prehistoric hunters and gatherers of Brazil. *Journal of World Prehistory* 1: 53–126.
SCHOMBURGK, RICHARD
1847 *Reisen in Britisch-Guiana in den jahren 1840–1844*. J.J. Weber, Leipzig.
1922–3 (1847) *Travels in British Guiana, 1840–1844*, trans. and ed. Walter E. Roth. Georgetown.
SCHOMBURGK, ROBERT
1836 Inventory of Mr Schomburgk Collection. List of the Indian Collections presented by Robert Schomburgk to the B.M. August 1836. Manuscript on file in the register cupboard at the Museum of Mankind (Ethnography Department of The British Musem).
1841 *Twelve Views in the Interior of Guiana*. Ackerman and Company, London.
SCHRIKS, CHRIS AND SILVIA DE GROOT (EDS)
1980 *Reis door Surinam/Journey through Suriname* (edited reprint of P.J. Benoit, *Voyage à Surinam*, Brussels, 1839). De Walburg Pers, Amsterdam.
SCHULTES, R.E. AND A. HOFFMAN
1992 *Plants of the Gods: Their Sacred, Healing and Hallucinogenic Powers*. Healing Arts Press, Rochester Vermont.
SCHWERIN, K.H.
1971 *The Bitter and the Sweet: Some Implications of the Traditional Techniques for Preparing Manioc*. Paper read at the Annual Meeting of the American Anthropological Association, New York City. Unpublished MS.
1985 Food Crops in the Tropics. In *Food Energy in Tropical Ecosystems*, ed. D.J. Cattle and K.H. Schwerin, pp. 255–85. Gordon and Breach, New York.
SEAWARD, M., AND S.M.D. FITZGERALD (EDS)
1996 *Richard Spruce (1817–1893): Botanist and Explorer*. Royal Botanic Gardens, Kew.
SEEGER, A., R. DA MATTA AND E. VIVEIROS DE CASTRO
1979 A construção da pessoa nas sociedades indigenas brasileiras. *Boletim do Museu Nacional* 32: 2–19.
1987 A construção da pessoa nas sociedades indigenas

brasileiras. *Sociedades indigenas e indigenismo no Brasil*, ed. Oliveira Filho, pp. 11–29. UFRJ/Marco Zero, Rio de Janeiro.

Service, E.

1962 *Primitive Social Organization: An Evolutionary Perspective*. Random House, New York.

Shennan, S. J.

2000 Population, culture history, and the dynamics of culture change. *Current Anthropology* 41 (5).

Shorr, N.

1999 Agricultural Intensification in a Large Tikuna Community. Ph.D. dissertation, Department of Anthropology, Indiana University, Bloomington.

Silva, A. da and A. Farias

1992 Pintura corporal e sociedade: os 'partidos' Xerente. In *Grafismo Indigena*, ed. L. Vidal, pp. 89–142. Studio Nobel/EDUSP, São Paulo.

Silva, M.L. da

1976 Determinacão de acidos organicos em plantas e alimentos da Amazonia. I. Acidos organicos do Tucupi. *Acta Amazonica* 6 (2): 235–6.

Silverwood-Cope, P.

1990 *Os Makü. Povo caçador do noroeste da Amazonia*. Editorial Universidade de Brasília, Brasília.

Simões, M.

1972 Indice das fases arqueológicas brasileiras 1950–71. In *Publicações Avulsas Museu Paraense Emílio Goeldi* 18.

1974 Contribuição à arqueologia dos arredores do baixo rio Negro. In *Programa Nacional de Pesquisas Arqueológicas 5: Publicações Avulsas do Museu Paraense Emílio Goeldi* 26, pp. 165–200.

1981a Colectores-pescadores ceramistas do litoral do Salgado (Pará). *Boletim do Museu Paraense Emílio Goeldi* 78: 1–32.

1981b As pesquisas arqueológicos do Museu Paraense Emílio Goeldi (1870–1981). *Acta Amazônica* 11 (1).

1983 Pesquisa e cadastro de sitios arqueológicos na Amazonia Legal Brasileira, 1978–1982. In *Publicações Avulsas do Museu Paraense Emílio Goeldi* 38.

Simões, M. and F. Araújo Costa

1978 Áreas da Amazônia Legal brasileira para pesquisa e cadastro de sitios arqueológicos. In *Publicações Avulsas do Museu Paraense Emílio Goeldi* 30.

1987 Pesquisas arqueológicas no baixa rio Tocantins (Pará). *Revista de Arqueologia* 4 (1): 11–27.

Simões, M. and C. Corrêa

1987 Pesquisas arqueológicas no baixo Uatumã-Jatapu (AM). *Revista de Arqueologia* 4 (1): 29–48.

Simões, M. and D. Fróes

1987 Pesquisas arqueológicas no baixo/médio rio Madeira (AM). *Revista de Arqueologia* (1): 117–33.

Simões, M. and A. Kalkmann

1987 Pesquisas arqueológicas no médio rio Negro (AM). *Revista de Arqueologia* 4 (1): 83–116.

Simões, M. and A. Machado

1987 Pesquisas arqueológicas no lago de Silves (AM). *Revista de Arqueologia* 4 (1): 49–82.

Siqueira, J.S.

1886 Memorias a respeito do descobrimento dos Martyrios pelo Rev. José Manoel de Siqueira. *Revista da Sociedade de Geographia do Rio de Janeiro* 2: 21–2.

Smith, A.

1990 *Explorers of the Amazon*. Viking, London.

Smith, H.H.

1879 *Brazil: The Amazons and the Coast*. Charles Scribner's Sons, New York.

Smith, N.

1980 Anthrosols and Human carrying Capacity in Amazonia. *Annals of the Association of American Geographers* 70 (4): 553–66.

Sotto Mayor, J.

1914 Diário da jornada que o Fr. João de Sotto Mayor fez ao Pacajá em 1656. *Revista do Instituto Histórico e Geográfico Brasileiro* 77 (2): 157–79.

Spencer, Charles and Elsa Redmond

1992 Prehispanic chiefdoms of the Western Venezuelan Llanos. *World Archaeology* 24(1): 134–57.

Spix, J. and C. F. Martius

1823–31 *Reise in Brasilien in den Jahren 1817 bis 1820*, 3 vols. M. Lindauer, Munich.

1824 Travels in Brazil in the years 1817–1820, trans. Lloyd, 2 vols. Longman, Hurst & Co., London.

1967 *Reise in Brasilien in den Jahren 1817–1820*. Brochaus, Stuttgart.

1981 *Viagem pelo Brasil: 1817–1820*, 3 vols. Coleção Reconquista do Brasil. Itatiaia/EDUSP, Belo Horizonte.

Sponsel, L.

1986 Amazon Ecology and Adaptation. *Annual Review of Anthropology* 15: 67–97.

1989 Farming and Foraging: A necessary complementary in Amazonia? In *Farmers as Hunters: The Implications of Sedentism*, ed. S. Kent, pp. 37–47. Cambridge University Press, Cambridge.

Spruce, R.

1908 *Notes of a Botanist on the Amazon and Andes*, 2 vols. MacMillan and Co. Ltd, London.

Stahl, Peter W.

1988 Prehistoric Camelids in the Lowlands of Western Ecuador. *Journal of Archaeological Science* 15: 355–65. Academic Press, London.

Stahl, P. and Zeidler J.

1990 Differential bone-refuse accumulation in food preparation and traffic areas on an early Ecuadorian house floor. *Latin American Antiquity* 1 (2): 150–69.

Stearman, A. M.

1991 Making a living in the Tropical Forest: Yuqui Foragers in the Bolivian Amazon. *HumanEcology* 19 (2): 245–60.

Stedman, J. G.

1796 *Narrative of a Five Years Expedition Against the Revolted Negroes of Surinam in Guiana on the Wild Coast of South America from the Year 1772 to 1777*. Johnson and Edwards, London.

Steere, J. B.

1927 The Archaeology of the Amazon. *University of Michigan Official Publication* XXIX (9): 20–26.

Stepan, N.

2000 Constructing Tropical Nature. Paper presented at the 3rd Annual Oxford Conference on Amazonia, Oxford.

Steward, J.

1948 Culture Areas of the Tropical Forests. In *Handbook of South American Indians*, vol. 3, ed. J.H. Steward, pp. 883–99. Bureau of American Ethnology Bulletin 143. Smithsonian Institution, Washington DC.

Steward, J.H. (ed.)

1946–50 *Handbook of South American Indians*, 6 vols. Bureau of American Ethnology, Smithsonian Institution, Washington DC.

Steward, J.H. and L.C. Faron

1959 *Native Peoples of South America*. MacGraw-Hill Book Company Inc., New York.

Stocks, A.

1983 Cocamilla Fishing: Patch Modification and Environmental Buffering in the Amazon. In *Adaptive Responses of Native Amazonians*, ed. R.B. Hames and W.T. Vickers, pp. 239–67. Academic Press, New York.

Stolpe, Hjalmar

1927 (1896) A Contribution to the Biology of Ornament. In *Collected Essays in Ornamental Art*. Stockholm.

Stradelli, E.

1900 Iscrizioni indigene della regione dell'Uapés. *Bolletino della Sociéta Geografica Italiana*, Série 4, 1 (37): 457–83.

Strecker, Matthias

1996 Pinturas rupestres de Quilima. In *Arte Rupestre de los Andes de Bolivia*, pp. 9–10. SIARB (Sociedade de Investigación del Arte Rupestre de Bolivia), La Paz.

Sweet, D.

1974 A rich realm of nature destroyed: the Middle Amazon valley, 1640–1750. Ph.D. Dissertation, University of Wisconsin.

Tankersley, K.B.

1997 Keeping Track of Time: dating Monte Alegre and the Peopling of South America. *Review of Archaeology* 18 (1): 28–34.

Taveira, E.

1982 *Etnografia da cesta Karajá. Coleção teses Universitárias*. Universidade Federal Goiás, Goiania.

Thevet, André

1557 *Les Singularitéz de la France Antarctique*. Paris.

Tocantins, A.

1877 Estudos sobre a tribu Mundurucu. *Revista do Instituto Histórico e Geográfico Brasileiro* 40 (2): 73–161. Rio de Janeiro.

Todorov, T.

1984 *The Conquest of America: The Question of the Other*. Harper & Row, New York.

Torres, A.

1996 Estudo dos pigmentos do sitio pré-histórico Pedra do Alexandre – Carnaúba dos Dantas – RN. *Revista CLIO: Arqueológica* 1 (11): 59–70.

Torres, Constantino Manuel

1987 *The Iconography of South American Snuff-Trays and Related Paraphernalia*. Etnologiska Studier Series, 37. Etnografiska Museum, Göteborg.

Torres, Contantino M. and William J. Conklin

1995 Exploring the San Pedro de Atacama/Tiahuanaco relationship. In *Andean Art – Visual Expression and its relationship with Andean Values and Beliefs*, ed. Penny Dransart, pp. 78–108. WorldWide Archaeology Series, vol.13. Avebury Press.

Townsend, R.

1998 Before gods, Before Kings. In *Ancient West Mexico: Art and Archaeology of the Unknown Past*, ed. R. Townsend, pp. 107–35. Thames and Hudson, London.

Turner, T.

1980 The social skin. In *Not Work Alone*, ed. J. Chefas and R. Lewin, pp. 112–40. Temple Smith, London.

Urban, Greg

1992 A história da cultura brasileira segundo as línguas nativas. In *História dos Indios no Brasil*, ed. M. Carneiro da Cunha, pp. 87–102. Companhia das Letras/FAPESP/SMC, São Paulo.

Vacher, Stéphane, Sylvie Jérémie and Jérome Briand (eds)

1998 *Amérindiens du Sinnamary (Guyane): Archéologie en fôret equatoriale*. Éditions de la Maison des Sciences de l'Homme, Paris.

Van den Bel, Martijn M.

1995 Kamuyune: The Palikur Potters of French Guyana. Doctoral thesis in Archaeology, Section Archaeology and Culture History of Indigenous America, Leiden.

Van 's Gravesande, Storm

1911 *The Rise of British Guiana, Compiled from his Despatches*, ed. C.A. Harris and J.A.J. de Villiers. Hakluyt Society, London.

Van Velthem, L.H.

1986 Equipamento doméstico e de trabalho. In *Suma Etnológica Brasileira v. 2. Tecnologia Indígena*, ed. B. Ribeiro. Vozes, Petrópolis.

1992a Das cobras e lagartas: a iconografia Wayana. In *Grafismo indígena*, ed. L. Vida, pp. 53–66. Studio Nobel/Fapesp, Edusp, São Paulo.

1992b Arte Indígena: referentes sociais e cosmológicos. In *Indios no Brasil*, ed. L. Grupioni, pp. 83–92. Secretaria Municipal de Cultura, São Paulo.

1995 *O belo é a fera: a estética da produção e da predação entre os Wayana*. Doctoral thesis. USP, São Paulo.

1998 *A pele de Tuluperê. Uma etnografia dos trançados Wayana*. Museu Paraense Emílio Goeldi, Belém.

2000a Os primeiros tempos e os tempos atuais: artes e estéticas indigenas. In *Artes Indígenas*, pp. 58–91, exh. cat. São Paulo.

2000b Fazer, fazeres e o mais belo feito. In *Os indios, nós*, pp. 174–79, exh. cat., Museu Nacional de Etnologia, Lisboa.

Vanzolini, P.

1990 As primeiras Expedições Zoológicas no Brasil. *Revista da USP* 160 (Jun/Jul/Aug). SãoPaulo.

Vargas Arenas, I.

1981 Investigaciones arqueológicas en Parmana: Los sitios de La Gruta y Ronquín. In *Serie Estudios, Monografías y Ensayos* 20. Biblioteca de la Academia Nacional de la Historia, Caracas.

Vaz de Caminha, Pero

1937 (1500) Letter to King Manoel from Porto Seguro. In *The Voyage of Pedro Àlvares Cabral to Brazil and India. From Contemporary Documents and Narratives*, trans. William Brooks Greenlee, pp. 3–33. Hakluyt Society, 2nd series, vol. 81. London

Vázquez de Espinosa, Antonio
1942 *Compendium and Description of the West Indies*, trans. Charles Upson Clark. Smithsonian Miscellaneous Collections, vol. 102. Smithsonian Institution, Washington DC.
Vellard, J.
1931 Pétroglyphes de la région de l'Araguaya. *Journal de la Société des Américanistes*, n.s. 23 (50): 139–49.
Versteeg, Aad H.
1985 The prehistory of the Young Coastal Plain of West Suriname. *Berichten van de Rijksdienst voor het Oudheid-kundig Bodemonderzoek* 35: 653–750.
Vespucci, Amerigo
1894 'Mundus Novus' and other letters to Lorenzo di Pier Francesco de' Medici, 1503. In *The Letters of Amerigo Vespucci and other Documents Illustrative of his Career*, trans. Clements Markham. Hakluyt Society, London.
Vickers, W.T. and T. Plowman
1984 *Useful Plants of the Siona-Secoya Indians of Eastern Ecuador*. Fieldana-Botany Series no. 15. Field Museum of Natural History, Chicago.
Vidal, L.
1985 Ornamentação corporal entre grupos indigenas. In *Arte e corpo. Pintura sobre a pele e adornos de povos indigenas brasileiros*, pp. 15–19. FUNARTE, Rio de Janeiro.
1992 *Grafismo indígena: Estudos de Antropologia Estética*. Studio Nobel/FAPESP/Edusp, São Paulo.
Vidal, L. and A. da Silva
1992 Antropologia estética: enfoques teóricos e contribuições metodológicas. In *Grafismo indigena*, pp. 279–93. Studio Nobel/EDUSP, São Paulo.
1995 O sistema de objetos nas sociedades indígenas: arte e cultura material. In *A temática indigena na escola*, ed. A.L. da Silva and L. Grupioni, pp. 369–402. MEC/MARI/UNESCO, Brasilia.
Vidal, Silvia
1988 *El Modelo del Processo Migratorio Pre-hispánico de los Piapoco: Hipótesis y Evidencias*. Master's thesis. CEA-IVIC, Caracas.
Vidal, Silvia M. and Alberta Zucchi
2000 Los caminos de Kúwai: evidencias de conocimiento geopolítico de las expansiones y migraciones de grupos arawakos. In *Caminos Precolombinos: Las vías, los ingenieros y los viajeros*, ed. Leonor Herrera and Marianne Cardale de Schrimpff, pp. 87–113. Instituto Colombiano de Antropología e Historia, Bogotá.
Vieira, A.
1951 *Obras Escolhidas, Vol V – Em Defeza dos Índios*. Livraria Sá da Costa (Obras Várias III), Lisboa.
Viertler, R.
1991 *A refeição das Almas*. Hucitec/EDUSP, São Paulo.
Viveiros de Castro, E.
1987 A fabricação do corpo na sociedade Xinguana. In *Sociedades indígenas e indigenismo no Brasil*, ed. Oliveira Filho, pp. 31–41. UFRJ/Marco Zero, Rio de Janeiro.
1992 *From the Enemy's Point of View: Humanity and Divinity in an Amazonian Society*. University of Chicago Press, Chicago.
1996 Images of nature and society in Amazonian ethnology. *Annual Review of Anthropology* 25: 179–200.
1998 Cosmological Deixis and Amerindian Perspectivism. *Journal of the Royal Anthropological Institute* n.s. 4 (3): 469–88.
Wallace, Alfred Russell
1889 *Travels on the Amazon and Rio Negro*. London.
1905 *Travels on the Amazon and Rio Negro*. Ward, Lock & Co., London.
1979 *Viagens pelo Amazonas e rio Negro*, trans. E. Amado. Editora da Universidade de São Paulo, Livraria Itatiaia LTDA, Belo Horizonte.
Waltz, Nathan and Alva Wheeler
1972 Proto Tucanoan. In *Comparative Studies in Amerindian Languages*, ed. Esther Matteson, pp. 119–49. Mouton, The Hague.
Wassen, H.
1934a The frog-Motive among the South American Indians, Ornamental Studies. *Anthropos* XXIX: 319–70.
1934b The frog in Indian mythology and imaginative world. *Anthropos* XXIX: 613–58.
Wassén, S. Henry
1972 *A Medicine-Man's Implements and Plants in a Tiahuanacoid tomb in Highland Bolivia*. Ethnology Study 32. Etnografiska Museum, Göteborg.
Whitehead, Neil L.
1986 John Gabriel Stedman's collection of Amerindian artifacts. *Nieuwe West-Indische Gids* 60: 203–8.
1988 *Lords of the Tiger Spirit: A History of the Caribs in Colonial Venezuela and Guyana 1498–1820*. Foris, Dordrecht and Providence.
1993 Recent research on the Native History of Amazonia and the Guayana. *L'Homme* 126(8): 499–510.
1994 The Ancient Amerindian Polities of the Amazon, the Orinoco, and the Atlantic Coast: A Preliminary Analysis of Their Passage from Antiquity to Extinction. In *Amazonian Indians from Prehistory to the Present: Anthropical Perspectives*, ed. A.C. Roosevelt. The University of Arizona Press, Tucson and London.
1995 The Historical Anthropology of Text: the interpretation of Ralegh's *Discoverie of Guiana*. *Current Anthropology* 36(1): 53–74.
1996 Amazonian Archaeology: Searching for Paradise? A Review of Recent Literature and Fieldwork. *Journal of Archaeological Research* 4(3): 241–64.
Whitehead, P.J.P.
1988 A Disciplina do Desenho: Quadros Etnográficos Holandeses do Brasil Setencentista. *Revista do Museu Paulista*, n.s. XXXIII. Universidade de São Paulo, 1988.
Whitmore, T. C.
1990 *An Introduction to Tropical Forests*. Clarendon Press, Oxford.
Wilbert, J.
1972 Tobacco and Shamanistic Ecstasy among the Warao Indians of Venezuela. In *Flesh of the Gods: The Ritual Use of Hallucinogens*, ed. Peter T. Furst, pp. 55–83. Praeger, New York.
1975a Magico-Religious Use of Tobacco among South American Indians. In *Cannabis and Culture*, ed. Vera Rubin, pp. 439–61. Mouton, The Hague and Paris.
1975b *Warao basketry. Form and function*. Occasional Papers of the Museum of Cultural History, no. 3. University of California, Los Angeles.
1987 *Tobacco and Shamanism in South America*. Yale University Press, New Haven and London.
Willey, G.R.
1971 *An Introduction to American Archaeology, vol. 1: South America*. Englewood Cliffs, Prentice-Hall, New Jersey.
Williams, D.
1985 Petroglyphs in the prehistory of Northern Amazonia and Antilles. In *Advances in Word Archaeology* 4: 335–87. Academic Press, New York.
Wilson, D. J.
1999 *Indigenous South Americans of the Past and Present: An Ecological Perspective*. Westview Press, Boulder.
Wilson, R.C.L., S.A. Drury and J.L. Chapman
2000 *The Great Ice Age: Climate Change and Life*. Routledge, New York and London.
Wing, E. and A.B. Brown
1979 *Paleonutrition. Method and Theory in Prehistoric Foodways*. Academic Press, New York.
Winterhandler, B.
1981 Optimal Foraging Strategies and Hunter Gatherer Research in Anthropology: Theory and Models. In *Hunter-Gatherer Strategies*, ed. B. Winterhandler and E.A. Smith, pp. 13–35. The University of Chicago Press, Chicago.
Wirpsa, L. and H. Mondragón
1988 Resettlement of Nukak Indians, Colombia. *Cultural Survival Quarterly* 12 (4): 36–40.
Woods, W.I.
1995 Comments on the Black Earths of Amazonia. In *Papers and Proceedings of Applied Geography Conferences* 18: 159–65. Arlington, Virginia.
Woods, W. I. and J. M. McCann
1997 The Living Soils of Amazonia. MS on file, Department of Geography, Southern Illinois University, Edwardsville.
1999 The Anthropogenic Origin and Persistence of Amazonian Dark Earths. *Yearbook, Conference of Latin Americanist Geographers* 25: 7–14.
Wright, R.
1990 Guerras e Alianças nas Histórias dos Baniwa do Alto Rio Negro. In *Ciências Sociais Hoje*, pp. 217–36. ANPOCS, São Paulo.
1991 Indian Slavery in the Northwest Amazon. *Boletim do Museu Paraense Emílio Goeldi: Antropologia* 7 (2): 149–79.
1992a Guardian of the cosmos: Baniwa shamans and prophets. In *History of Religions*, Pt 1, pp. 32–58. University of Chicago.
1992b Histórica indigena do Noroeste da Amazônia: hipóteses, questões e perspectivas. In *História dos Indios no Brasil*, ed. M. Carneiro da Cunha, pp. 251–66. Companhia das Letras, São Paulo.
1994 For Those Unborn: Cosmos, Self and History in Baniwa Religion. Unpublished MS.
Zerries, Otto
1970 'Tierbank und Geistersitz in Südamerika'. *Ethnologische Zeitschrift Zürich* 1: 47–66.
1980 *Unter Indianer brasiliens: Sammlung Spix und Martius 1817–1820*. Pinguin-Verlag, Innsbruck.
1985 'Morteros para *parica*, tabletas para aspirar y bancos zoomorfos'. *Indiana* 10 (2): 421–41.
Zucchi, A.
1987 El Negro-Casiquiare-Alto Orinoco como ruta conectiva entre el Amazonas y el norte de Suramérica. Unpublished MS on file at the Instituto Venezolano de Investigaciones Científicas, Caracas.
1988 Las migraciones Maipures: diversas líneas de evidencias para la interpretación arqeuológica. *America Negra* 1: 113–38.
1992 Linguística, etnografía, arqueología y cambios climáticos: la dispersión de los arawako en el noroeste amazónico. In *Archaeology and Environment in Latin America*, ed. O.R. Ortiz-Troncoso and T. van der Hammen, pp. 223–51. Universiteit van Ansterdam-Instuut voor Pre- en Protohistorische Archeologische, Albert Egges van Giffen, Amsterdam.
1999 El alto Orinoco. In *Arte prehispánico de Venezuela*, ed. M. Arroyo, L. Blanco and E. Wagner, pp. 22–33. Galería de Arte Nacional, Caracas.
Zucchi, A. and K. Tarble
1982 Evolución y antigüedad de la alfarería con esponjilla en Agüerito, un yacimiento del Medio Orinoco. *Indiana* 7: 183–99.
1984 Los Cedeñoides: Un nuevo grupo prehispánico del Orinoco Medio. *Acta Científica Venezolana* 35: 293–309.
Zucchi, A., K. Tarble and J.E. Vaz
1984 The Ceramic Sequence and New TL and C^{14} Dates for the Site of Agüerito in the Middle Orinoco, Venezuela. *Journal of Field Archaeology* 11: 155–80.
Yde, J.
1965 *Material Culture of the Waiwai*. Ethnographic Series 10. National Museum of Denmark.

PICTURE CREDITS
Illustrations are listed by figure number unless indicated otherwise.

p. 1 Museu Paraense Emílio Goeldi, Belém Brazil, no. 10597; photo by Denise Andrade
pp. 2–3 Photo by Araquém Alcântara
pp. 4–5 Photo by Sue Cunningham
pp. 8–9 Museum für Völkerkunde, Vienna, no. 82719
p. 14 Museum für Völkerkunde, Vienna, no. 1626
p. 15 Museum für Völkerkunde, Vienna, no.1456
p. 16 Museu Barbier-Mueller Art Precolombí, Barcelona, no. 534-28; photo by Studio Ferrazini-Bouchet
p. 19 British Museum, no. 7204; photo by David Agar
pp. 20–23 Liz Errington; digital work by David Hoxley

1.1, 1.3–17 Photos by Gustavo Politis, 1996
1.2 Garth Denning; digital work by David Hoxley

2.1 Photo by W. Bray, 1977
2.2 Garth Denning after Roosevelt, 1995; digital work by David Hoxley
2.3 Museu Paraense Emílio Goeldi, Belém, Brazil, no. T-1491; photo by Fernando Chaves
2.4 Garth Denning after Mora *et al.*, 1991; digital work by David Hoxley
2.5 Garth Denning after Llanos Chaparro, 1997
2.6 Photo by W. Bray, 1977
2.7 Photo by Gustavo Politis, 1996
2.8 Photo by D.W. Lathrap, 1977
2.9–10 Diagrams by J. Oliver
2.11 Photo by Eduardo Neves
2.12 Robert Schomburgk 1841
2.13 Board of Trustees of the Royal Botanic Gardens, Kew, no. 38689.
2.14 Diagram by J. Oliver
2.15 Royal Geographic Society, London
2.16 Photo by J.M. Cruxent, 1957
2.17 Photo by Beto Ricardo; Instituto Socioambiental – ISA

3.1–3 Photos by Eduardo Neves
3.4 Etnografiska Museet I Göteborg, Sweden, no. 1925.12.2; photo by Håkan Berg
3.5 Museu de Arqueologia e Etnologia da Universidade de São Paulo, Brazil, no. 453; photo by Fernando Chaves
3.6 Museu de Arqueologia e Etnologia da Universidade de São Paulo, Brazil, no. X 642; photo by Fernando Chaves
3.7–9 Photos by Eduardo Neves
3.10 Rodrigues Ferreira 1971, vol. 2, pl. 57
3.11 Garth Denning after Marcos Castro; digital work by David Hoxley
3.12 Museu Paraense Emílio Goeldi, Belém, Brazil, no. 1501-1505; photo by Rômulo Fialdini
3.13 Instituto Histórico e Geográfico do Amazonas, Brazil; photo by Fernando Chaves
3.14 Museu de Arqueologia e Etnologia da Universidade de São Paulo, Brazil; drawing by Sérgio Francisco Monteiro
3.15 Nordenskiöld 1930, frontispiece

4.1 Photo by Denise Schaan
4.2 Museu Barbier-Mueller Art Precolombí, Barcelona, no. 534-31; photo by Studio Ferrazini-Bouchet
4.3 Garth Denning and Denise Schaan; digital work by David Hoxley
4.4–5 Musée Barbier Mueller, Geneva, no. 534-29; photo by Studio Ferrazini-Bouchet.
4.6 Photo by Araquém Alcântara
4.7 Museu Nacional do Rio de Janeiro, Archaeological Collections, no. 8634; photo by Fernando Chaves.
4.8 Drawing by Caio Vassão.
4.9 Musée Barbier Mueller, Geneva, no. 534-10; photo by Studio Ferrazini-Bouchet
4.10 Photo by Araquém Alcântara
4.11 Garth Denning after Meggers and Evans 1957
4.12 Museu Paraense Emílio Goeldi, Belém, Brazil, no. 1561; photo by Fernando Chaves
4.13 Drawing by Garth Denning, coloured by Jude Simmons
4.14 Museu Paraense Emílio Goeldi, Belém, Brazil, no. T 7; photo by Rômulo Fialdini
4.15 Drawing by Garth Denning
4.16 Ethnologisches Museum, Berlin, no. 1980; photo by Fernando Chaves
4.17 Drawing by Garth Denning
4.18 Museu Barbier-Mueller Art Precolombí, Barcelona, no. 534-14; photo by Fernando Chaves
4.19 Drawing by Garth Denning, coloured by Jude Simmons
4.20 Museu Nacional do Rio de Janeiro, Archaeological Collections; drawing by Garth Denning
4.21 Museu de Arqueologia e Etnologia da Universidade de São Paulo, Brazil, no. 6/81 4992: photo by Fernando Chaves
4.22 Museu de Arqueologia e Etnologia da Universidade de São Paulo, Brazil, no. X629: photo by Fernando Chaves
4.23 Museu Paraense Emílio Goeldi, Belém, Brazil, no. T 220; photo by Fernando Chaves
4.24 Museu Barbier-Mueller Art Precolombí, Barcelona, no. 534-31; drawing by Garth Denning, coloured by Jude Simmons
4.25 Museu Barbier-Mueller Art Precolombí, Barcelona, no. 534-27; photo by Studio Ferrazini-Bouchet.
4.26 Drawing by Garth Denning, (c) coloured by Jude Simmons
4.27 Museu Paraense Emílio Goeldi, Belém, Brazil, no. 2206; photo by Fernando Chaves
4.28 Museu Paraense Emílio Goeldi, Belém, Brazil, no. 2204; drawing by Garth Denning
4.29 Musées Royaux d'Art et d'Historie, Brussels, no. AAM 84-7; drawing by Garth Denning

5.1 Photo by Eduardo Neves
5.2 Museu de Arqueologia e Etnologia da Universidade de São Paulo, Brazil; photo by Fernando Chaves
5.3 Garth Denning; digital work by David Hoxley
5.4 Museu de Arqueologia e Etnologia da Universidade de São Paulo, Brazil, no. 1780; photo by Fernando Chaves
5.5 Museu Paraense Emílio Goeldi, Belém, Brazil, no. 501; photo by R. Fialdini
5.6 Museu Paraense Emílio Goeldi, Belém, Brazil, no. 502; photo by Fernando Chaves
5.7 Museu Paraense Emílio Goeldi, Belém, Brazil, no. 516; photo by Fernando Chaves
5.8 Drawing by Garth Denning
5.9 Drawing by Artur Ramos
5.10 Museu de Arqueologia e Etnologia da Universidade de São Paulo, Brazil, no. X641; photo by Fernando Chaves
5.11 Museu Nacional do Rio de Janeiro, Archaeological Collections; photo by Fernando Chaves
5.12 Museu de Arqueologia e Etnologia da Universidade de São Paulo, Brazil; photo by Fernando Chaves
5.13 Museu de Arqueologia e Etnologia da Universidade de São Paulo, Brazil, no. 7/17 186; photo by Fernando Chaves
5.14 Museu de Arqueologia e Etnologia da Universidade de São Paulo, Brazil, no. 7/17 190; drawing by Sérgio Francisco Monteiro
5.15 Drawing by Caio Vassão
5.16 Photo by Araquém Alcântara
5.17 Drawing by Sérgio Francisco Monteiro
5.18 Drawing by Caio Vassão
5.19 Drawing by Garth Denning
5.20 Museu Paraense Emílio Goeldi, Belém, Brazil, no.T 375; photo by R. Fialdini
5.21 Museu de Arqueologia e Etnologia da Universidade de São Paulo, Brazil, no. 7/17 162; drawing by Sérgio Francisco Monteiro
5.22–3 Photos by Araquém Alcântara
5.24 Museu de Arqueologia e Etnologia da Universidade de São Paulo, Brazil, no. 7/17 163; drawing by Sérgio Francisco Monteiro
5.25 Museu de Arqueologia e Etnologia da Universidade de São Paulo, Brazil, no. 7/17 154; drawing by Sérgio Francisco Monteiro
5.26 Museu de Arqueologia e Etnologia da Universidade de São Paulo, Brazil, no. 7/17 239; photo by Fernando Chaves

6.1 Museu Paraense Emílio Goeldi, Belém, Brazil, no. GC17; photo by Denise Andrade
6.2 Garth Denning; digital work by David Hoxley
6.3 Photo by Januari Simões
6.4 Garth Denning after Jorge Mardock; digital work by David Hoxley
6.5 Photo by Januari Simões
6.6 Drawing by Simone Mesquita
6.7 Museu Paraense Emílio Goeldi, Belém, Brazil, no. T-2777; drawing by Jorge Mardock, 1996
6.8 Archives of Museu Paraense Emílio Goeldi, Belém, Brazil
6.9–10 Drawings by Jorge Mardock after Goeldi 1900
6.11–12 Drawings by Garth Denning after Carlos Palheta, coloured by Jude Simmons
6.13 Table by Vera Guapindaia
6.14 Museu Paraense Emílio Goeldi, Belém, Brazil, no. 243; photo by Wagner Souza e Silva
6.15 Museu Paraense Emílio Goeldi, Belém, Brazil, no. T 229; photo by R. Fialdini
6.16 Nordenskiöld 1930, pl. 23
6.17 Photo by Araquém Alcântara
6.18 Etnografiska Museet I Göteborg, Sweden, no. 1926.3.224; photo by Håkan Berg

7.1 Museu Barbier-Mueller Art Precolombí, Barcelona, no. 534-30; photo by Studio Ferrazini-Bouchet.
7.2 Museu Barbier-Mueller Art Precolombí, Barcelona, no. 534-32; photo by Studio Ferrazini-Bouchet.
7.3 Ethnologisches Museum, Berlin, no. VB 1985; drawing by Garth Denning and Hans Rashbrook
7.4 Museu Nacional do Rio de Janeiro, Archaeological Collections, no. 9451; photo by Fernando Chaves
7.5 Museum für Völkerkunde, Vienna, no.173460
7.6 Ethnologisches Museum, Berlin, no. VB 2835; photo by Martim Framkem
7.7 Photo by Theodor Koch-Grünberg, Staatliches Museum für Völkerkunde, Munich;
7.8 Museu Nacional do Rio de Janeiro, Archaeological Collections, no. 558; drawing by Garth Denning
7.9 Museu Nacional do Rio de Janeiro, Archaeological Collections, no. 37441; photo by Fernando Chaves
7.10–11 Drawings by Garth Denning
7.12 Theodor Koch-Grünberg, Völkerkundliche Sammlung der Philipps-Universität, Marburg
7.13 Museu de Arqueologia e Etnologia da Universidade de São Paulo, Brazil, no. 9.3; drawing by Garth Denning, coloured by Jude Simmons
7.14 Rodrigues Ferreira 1971, vol. 1, pl. 121
7.15 British Museum, no. 1949 AM 22.179; photo by David Agar
7.16 Etnografiska Museet I Göteborg, Sweden, no. 1925.12.1; photo by Håkan Berg

8.1 Photo by Lucia van Velthem, 1978
8.2 Museu Paraense Emílio Goeldi, Belém, Brazil, no. 13361; photo by Fernando Chaves
8.3 Spix and Martius 1967, pl. 29
8.4 Robert Schomburgk 1841
8.5 Museu Paraense Emílio Goeldi, Belém, Brazil; photo by Fernando Chaves
8.6 Photo by Pedro Martinelli; Instituto Socioambiental – ISA
8.7 Museu Paraense Emílio Goeldi, Belém, Brazil, no. 36/95B; photo by Fernando Chaves
8.8–9 Photo by Pedro Martinelli; Instituto Socioambiental – ISA
8.10 Rodrigues Ferreira 1971, vol. 2, pl. 83
8.11 Museu Paraense Emílio Goeldi, Belém, Brazil, no. 4893; photo by Fernando Chaves
8.12 Photo by Araquém Alcântara
8.13 Museu Paraense Emílio Goeldi, Belém, Brazil, no. 12823; photo by Fernando Chaves
8.14 Photo by Araquém Alcântara
8.15 Museu Paraense Emílio Goeldi, Belém, Brazil; photo by Fernando Chaves
8.16 Photo by Pedro Martinelli; Instituto Socioambiental – ISA

9.1 Photo by Edithe Pereira
9.2 Garth Denning after Edithe Pereira; digital work by David Hoxley
9.3 Debret 1834, pl. 30
9.4–6 Drawings by Garth Denning after Spruce 1908, figs 16–18
9.7 Archives of Museu Nacional do Rio de Janeiro, Brazil; drawing by Garth Denning after Ferreira Penna.
9.8 Photo by Eduardo Neves
9.9 Drawing by Garth Denning after Reichel-Dolmatoff 1996
9.10 Photo by Pedro Augusto Mentz Ribeiro
9.11 Edithe Pereira and Luis Barbosa; digital work by Robin Kiang
9.12 Photo by Edithe Pereira
9.13 Drawing by Edithe Pereira
9.14–17 Photos by Edithe Pereira

10.1 Debret 1834, vol. 1, pl. 13
10.2 The British Library, Add 5415A
10.3 Thevet 1557
10.4 Rodrigues Ferreira 1971, vol. 1, pl. 63
10.5 Coleção Brasiliana, Fundação Rank-Packard/Fundação Estudar.
10.6 Museu Antropológico da Universidade de Coimbra, Portugal, no. BR 147; photo by Carlos Barata
10.7 Private Collection
10.8 Robert Schomburgk 1841, frontispiece
10.9 Museum für Völkerkunde, Vienna, no. 1210
10.10 Debret 1834, vol. 1, pl. 12
10.11 Debret 1834, vol. 1, pl. 27
10.12 Debret 1834, vol. 1, pl. 34
10.13 The British Library, 10481.d.14
10.14 Etnografiska Museet I Göteborg, Sweden; photo by Curt Nimuendajú
10.15 Collection Gilberto Ferrez/Acervo Instituto Moreira Salles, Rio de Janeiro; photo attributed to Albert Frisch
10.16 Etnografiska Museet I Göteborg, Sweden; photo by Curt Nimuendajú

11.1 Museu Antropológico da Universidade de Coimbra, no. BR 31; photos by Carlos Barata
11.2 Garth Denning after Vacher *et al.* 1998
11.3 The Pierpont Morgan Library
11.4–5 British Museum, no. 4913; photos by David Agar
11.6 Bibliothèque Sainte-Geneviève, Paris; drawing by Garth Denning
11.7 Bibliothèque Sainte-Geneviève, Paris; photo by Nabil Boutros
11.8 Drawing by Garth Denning after Barrère 1743
11.9 British Museum, no.11.78/6281; drawing by Garth Denning after Stolpe 1927, pl. XI, 6a
11.10 Rodrigues Ferreira 1971, vol. 1, pl. 103
11.11–12 De Walburg Pers, Amsterdam
11.13 British Museum, no. 1836/66; drawing by Garth Denning after Stolpe 1927, pl. IV, 3
11.14 Musée de l'Homme, Paris, no. 81.34.134; drawing by Garth Denning after Stolpe 1927, pl. V, 1b.
11.15 University of Pennsylvania Museum; photo by W.C. Farabee, 1924

12.1 Museum für Völkerkunde, Vienna, no. 1923; photo by Fernando Chaves.
12.2–4 Photos by Eduardo Neves
12.5 Photo by Theodor Koch-Grünberg, Völkerkundliche Sammlung der Philipps-Universität Marburg
12.6 Photo by Eduardo Neves
12.7 Robert Schomburgk 1841
12.8 Garth Denning; digital work by David Hoxley
12.9 Museum für Völkerkunde, Vienna, no. 2337
12.10 Photo by Eduardo Neves
12.11 Museu de Arqueologia e Etnologia da Universidade de São Paulo, Brazil; drawing by Sérgio Francisco Monteiro
12.12 Rodrigues Ferreira 1971, vol. 1, pl. 101
12.13–14 Drawings by Garth Denning; digital work by David Hoxley
12.15 Photo by Eduardo Neves

Index